LAW AND PRACTICE OF EU
EXTERNAL RELATIONS

Expanding European Union activity on the international scene has led to development of the legal concepts, principles and rules that govern it. External relations law and practice have also been affected by events within the EU.

This volume takes stock of the recent developments in the external relations law and practice of the EC/EU and investigates the increasing interaction between these different fields of Union competence. The first part of this book addresses issues that are broadly constitutional or institutional in character. The second part deals with various aspects of substantive external relations considered in a geographical or geo-political perspective. The third part selects two specific substantive law areas – intellectual property law and environment law – as examples that illustrate the specific relationship between domestic policy and external relations.

ALAN DASHWOOD is Professor of European Law at the University of Cambridge and a Fellow of Sidney Sussex College. He is also a Barrister in Henderson Chambers and a Bencher of the Inner Temple, specialising in the law of the European Union and appearing regularly in proceedings before the European Court of Justice.

MARC MARESCEAU teaches European Law and Institutions at Ghent University, where he is also Director of the European Institute and Coordinator of the Jean Monnet Centre of Excellence. He has been teaching as a Visiting Professor at various universities and he also taught a course at The Hague Academy of International Law.

LAW AND PRACTICE OF EU EXTERNAL RELATIONS

SALIENT FEATURES OF A CHANGING LANDSCAPE

Edited by

ALAN DASHWOOD AND
MARC MARESCEAU

CAMBRIDGE
UNIVERSITY PRESS

CAMBRIDGE UNIVERSITY PRESS
Cambridge, New York, Melbourne, Madrid, Cape Town, Singapore,
São Paulo, Delhi, Dubai, Tokyo, Mexico City

Cambridge University Press
The Edinburgh Building, Cambridge CB2 8RU, UK

Published in the United States of America by Cambridge University Press, New York

www.cambridge.org
Information on this title: www.cambridge.org/9780521182553

First published 2008
Reprinted 2009
First paperback edition 2010

A catalogue record for this publication is available from the British Library

Library of Congress Cataloguing in Publication data

Dashwood, Alan.
Law and practice of EU external relations: salient features of a changing landscape/Alan
Dashwood, Marc Maresceau.
p.   cm.
Includes bibliographical references and index.
ISBN 978-0-521-89923-9 (hardback)
1. International and municipal law–European Union countries.   2. European
Union–Foreign relations.   I. Maresceau, Marc.   II. Title.
KJE5057.D37 2008
341.242′2–dc22
2008012850

ISBN 978-0-521-89923-9 Hardback
ISBN 978-0-521-18255-3 Paperback

CONTENTS

ABBREVIATIONS

ACP	African, Caribbean and Pacific Group of States
AELE	Association européenne de libre exchange
AG	Advocate General
AJIL	American Journal of International Law
AMM	Aceh Monitoring Mission
AMU	Arab Maghreb Union
AP	Action Plan
APM	Agreement on Public Procurement Markets
Art.	Article
ASEAN	Association of Southeast Asian Nations
CAP	Common Agricultural Policy
CEPOL	European Police College
CCP	Common Commercial Policy
CDE	Cahiers de droit européen
CEEC	Central and Eastern European Countries
CEES	Common European Economic Space
CES	Common Economic Space
CFI	Court of First Instance
CFSP	Common Foreign and Security Policy
CL	Compulsory Licensing
CLJ	Cambridge Law Journal
CMLRep.	Common Market Law Reports
CMLRev.	Common Market Law Review
COREPER	Permanent Representatives Committee
CR	Country Report
CSCE	Conference of Security and Cooperation in Europe
CSDP	Common Security and Defence Policy
CSES	Common Space on External Security
CSFSJ	Common Space on Freedom, Security and Justice

CSR	Common Strategy on Russia
CSRE	Common Space on Research and Education
CT	Constitutional Treaty
DAC	Development Assistance Committee
DSB	Dispute Settlement Body (WTO)
DSU	Dispute Settlement Understanding (WTO)
EA	Europe Agreement
EC	European Community
ECB	European Central Bank
ECJ	European Court of Justice
ECHR	European Convention on Human Rights
ECMI	Economic Centre for Minority Studies
ECOFIN	Economic and Financial Affairs Council
ECOWAS	Economic Community of West-African States
ECR	European Court Reports
ECSC	European Coal and Steel Community
ECtHR	European Court of Human Rights
ed.	editor
eds.	editors
EEA	European Economic Area
EEAg	European Environment Agency
EEC	European Economic Community
EFARev.	European Foreign Affairs Review
EFTA	European Free Trade Association
EIB	European Investment Bank
EIONET	European Environmental Information and Observation Network
ELRev.	European Law Review
EMP	Euro-Mediterranean Partnership
ENP	European Neighbourhood Policy
ENPI	European Neighbourhood and Partnership Instrument
EPE	Energy Policy for Europe
ETS	Emissions Trading System
EU	European Union
EUFOR	European Union Force
EUPOL	European Union Police Mission
EuroMeSCo	Euro-Mediterranean Study Commission
EUROPOL	European Police Office

FAO	Food and Agriculture Organisation
FJ	Federal Journal
FMP	Free Movement of Persons
FTA	Free Trade Area
FTC	Federal Trade Commission
FYROM	Former Yugoslav Republic of Macedonia
GAERC	General Affairs and External Relations Council
GAM	Free Aceh Movement
GAO	Government Accountability Office
GATS	General Agreement on Trade in Services
GATT	General Agreement on Tariffs and Trade
GCC	Gulf Cooperation Council
GDP	Gross Domestic Product
GLONASS	Global Navigation Satellite System
GMOs	Genetically Modified Organisms
HR	High Representative
ICAO	International Civil Aviation Organisation
ICCPR	International Covenant on Civil and Political Rights
ICJ	International Court of Justice
ILM	International Legal Materials
IP	Intellectual Property
IPA	Instrument for Pre-accession
IPR	Intellectual Property Rights
JAI	Justice Affaires Intérieures
JHA	Justice and Home Affairs
JIEL	Journal of International Economic Law
MBI	Market Based Instrument
MDG	Millennium Development Goals
MEP	Member European Parliament
MFN	Most Favoured Nation
MONUC	United Nations Organisation Mission in the Democratic Republic of the Congo
MoU	Memorandum of Understanding
MRA	Mutual Recognition Agreement
NAFTA	North American Free Trade Association
NATO	North Atlantic Treaty Organisation
ND	Northern Dimension
NGO	Non-Governmental Organisation

n.	note
NT	National Treatment
NTA	New Transatlantic Agenda
nyr	not yet reported
OC	Official Collection
ODA	Official Development Assistance
OECD	Organisation for Economic Cooperation and Development
OJ	Official Journal of the European Union
para.	paragraph
paras.	paragraphs
PCA	Partnership and Cooperation Agreement
PDO	Protected Designation of Origin
PEA	Positive Economic Agenda
PESC	Politique étrangère et de sécurité
PGI	Protected Geographical Indication
PIC	Prior Informed Consent
PJC	Police and Judicial Cooperation
PJCCM	Police and Judicial Cooperation in Criminal Matters
PNR	Passenger Name Records
PPC	Permanent Partnership Council
PSC	Political and Security Committee
REACH	Registration, Evaluation, Authorisation and Restriction of Chemicals
RGDIP	Revue Générale de Droit International Public
RRM	Rapid Reaction Mechanism
RSDIE	Revue Suisse de droit international et européen
SALWs	Small Arms and Light Weapons
SC	Systematic Collection
SCIFA	Strategic Committee on Immigration, Frontiers and Asylum
SCM	Subsidies and Countervailing Measures
SDS	Sustainable Development Strategy
SEER	Strategic European Energy Review
SES	Single Economic Space
SME	Small and Medium-sized Enterprises
SOFA	Status of Forces Agreement
SOMA	Status of Mission Agreement

SPMME	Strategic Partnership with the Mediterranean and the Middle East
TABD	Transatlantic Business Dialogue
TAC	Treaty of Amity and Cooperation
TACIS	Technical Assistance Commonwealth of Independent States
TAD	Transatlantic Declaration
TBR	Technical Barrier Regulations
TBT	Technical Barriers to Trade
TEP	Transatlantic Economic Partnership
TEU	Treaty on European Union
TEU revised	Treaty on European Union, consolidated after the Treaty of Lisbon
TFEU	Treaty on the Functioning of the European Union
TL	Treaty of Lisbon
TLD	Transatlantic Legislators' Dialogue
TRIPS	Agreement on Trade Related Aspects of Intellectual Property Rights
TSCA	Toxic Substances Control Act
UDHR	Universal Declaration of Human Rights
UEM	Union économique et monétaire
UK	United Kingdom
UN	United Nations
UNESCO	United Nations Educational, Scientific and Cultural Organisation
UN IPCC	United Nations Intergovernmental Panel on Climate Change
US	United States
US EPA	United Stated Environment Protection Agency
VAT	Value Added Tax
VCTL	Vienna Convention on the Law of Treaties
WHO	World Health Organisation
WTO	World Trade Organisation
YEL	Yearbook of European Law
ZaöRV	Zeitschrift für ausländisches öffentliches Recht und Völkerrecht

NOTES ON CONTRIBUTORS

JACQUES BOURGEOIS is Senior Counsel of the law firm Wilmer Cutler Pickering Hale & Dorr and a professor at the College of Europe (Bruges) and Ghent University, Faculty of Laws. He studied at Ghent University (J.D., *cum laude* 1959) and the University of Michigan (MCL Program 1960) and had his traineeship at the Bar from 1960 to 1962. He was a civil servant of the Commission of the European Atomic Energy Community (1962–5), a member of the Legal Service and subsequently a legal adviser of the Commission of the European Communities (1965–1983), head of the Trade Policy Instruments Division of the Commission of the European Communities (1983–7) and principal legal adviser of the Commission of the European Communities (1987–91). He returned to the Bar in 1991 and is principally engaged in European law (competition, trade, regulatory) and in international trade law.

GÜNTER BURGHARDT served as Ambassador for the European Union in Washington from early 2000 to late 2004 after a 30-year-long career at the European Commission's headquarters in Brussels. He was the Commission's Director General for External Relations from 1993 to 2000. From 1985 to 1993 he held the posts of Deputy Chef de Cabinet, Diplomatic Adviser and Political Director under Commission President Jacques Delors. He joined the Commission as a member of the Legal Service in 1970. He retired from the Commission in 2005 and joined the international law firm of Mayer Brown International as a Senior Counsel. He teaches at Ghent University, Faculty of Laws and the College of Europe in Bruges. He studied law and economics in Germany, France and the UK and obtained a *summa cum laude* PhD from the University of Hamburg with a thesis on European Community law in 1969.

MARISE CREMONA is Professor of European Law at the European University Institute, Florence. Until December 2005 she was Professor of

European Commercial Law at the Centre for Commercial Law Studies, Queen Mary, University of London. Her research interest is in the external relations law of the European Union, including its foreign policy, trade and development policies. From this perspective she is interested in the interaction between regulatory and policy regimes within and between national, regional and international systems. Her current research projects include the legal and institutional dimensions of the EU's European Neighbourhood Policy, the export of norms in EU external policy, the constitutional basis for EU foreign relations law, the relationship between the EU and the WTO, and the role of the EU in relation to the Fair Trade movement.

ALAN DASHWOOD is Professor of European Law at Cambridge University and a Fellow of Sidney Sussex College. He is also a Barrister in Henderson Chambers and a Bencher of the Inner Temple. Before election to his Chair at Cambridge, he was a director in the Legal Service of the Council of the EU. He was the founding editor of the *European Law Review* and is presently one of the joint editors of the *Common Market Law Review*. He is co-author of *Wyatt and Dashwood's European Union Law*, the fifth edition of which has recently been published. He was appointed CBE in 2004.

PIET EECKHOUT has been Professor of European Law at King's College London since 1998, and directs the Centre of European Law. He is an associate academic member of Matrix Chambers, London. Before joining King's he held academic positions at the Universities of Ghent and Brussels (Belgium) and worked in the Chambers of Advocate General Jacobs, European Court of Justice (1994–8). His academic interests and activities cover many different areas of EU law, including external relations, the internal market, state aid, judicial protection, the constitutionalisation process, and fundamental rights protection. He is also very active in the field of international economic law, in particular WTO law. He is editor of the *Yearbook of European Law* and is the author of *External Relations of the European Union: Legal and Constitutional Foundations* (2004) and of *The European Internal Market and International Trade: A Legal Analysis* (1994).

INGE GOVAERE (Law degree, Ghent University, 1987; PhD, European University Institute, Florence, 1994) is Professor of European Law at Ghent University and Director of the European Legal Studies Department at the College of Europe, Bruges. She was the Fulbright Scholar-in-Residence at Cornell University (US, 1998) and a visiting professor at Pittsburgh University and the College of Europe (Bruges and Warsaw). Recent publications include entries in the second volume of *The Oxford Encyclopaedia of EC Law* (2005) and *European Legal Dynamics/Dynamiques juridiques européennes* (2007).

CHRISTOPHE HILLION is Professor of European Law and co-director of the Europa Institute, Faculty of Law, University of Leiden, the Netherlands. He was educated at the University of Rennes (DEA), the College of Europe (MA) and the University of Leiden (PhD). Prior to moving to Leiden, he held academic posts in the law departments of Cambridge University, University College London (UCL) and at the College of Europe (Bruges/ Natolin). His research focuses on the external relations, enlargement and institutional law of the European Union. His publications include *The European Union and Its East-European Neighbours: A Laboratory for the Organisation of EU External Relations* (2008) and *EU Enlargement: A Legal Approach* (2004). He is a member of the editorial boards of the *European Foreign Affairs Review* and of the *Common Market Law Review*.

KIRSTYN INGLIS has been a researcher with the European Institute at Ghent University since 1998 in the field of external relations. In September 2006, she defended her PhD at Ghent University under the title 'European Union enlargement: a legal analysis of pre-accession and transitional arrangements with case studies on EC agri-food and environment law'. Before her time in Ghent, having studied law at Dundee University, she qualified as a solicitor in 1990 and then practised as a trade lawyer in City law firms. Since 1994 she has pursued her interest in food and environment law with specialist consultancies and international institutions based in Brussels.

FRANCIS G. JACOBS KCMG, QC is Professor of Law at King's College London and Jean Monnet Professor. From October 1988 to January 2006 he was an Advocate General at the Court of Justice of the European Communities. Previously, he was Professor of European Law in the University of London (1974–88) and a barrister specialising in European law. From 2005 to 2006 he held the Marcel Storme Chair at the University of Ghent. His most recent book is *The Sovereignty of Law: The European Way* (Cambridge University Press, 2007), part of the Hamlyn Lectures series, intended for the non-specialist.

CHRISTINE KADDOUS studied at Neuchâtel University, Cambridge University and the Institut d'études européennes of the Université Libre de Bruxelles. She teaches European Union law at Geneva University. She is Director of the Centre d'études juridiques européennes of the same university. Many of her publications concentrate on the external relations of the EU, free movement of persons as well as on relations between the EU and Switzerland. One of her recent publications (with Monique Jametti-Greiner) is *Accords bilatéraux II Suisse-UE et autres Accords récents*, Dossier de droit européen no. 16 (2006).

ERWAN LANNON studied law at the University of Rennes as well as political science and international relations at the Université Libre de Bruxelles. He is Professor at the Faculty of Law of Ghent University and at the College of Europe. He has been a consultant to the United Nations Conference on Trade and Development and has worked at the Delegation of the European Commission to Israel. He is presently Liaison Officer for the Euro-Mediterranean Study Commission of the Euro-Mediterranean Partnership. He recently co-edited with Joël Lebullenger *Les défis de l'adhésion de la Turquie à l'UE* (2006).

ORLA LYNSKEY has been a teaching assistant in the Legal Studies department at the College of Europe, Bruges, since August 2005. She read law at Trinity College, Dublin, where she graduated with first-class honours, and went on to obtain a Master's degree in European legal studies at the College of Europe. She will be called to the Bar of England and Wales in 2008.

MARC MARESCEAU studied at Ghent University, The Johns Hopkins University, Bologna and the Institut universitaire de hautes études internationales, Geneva. He teaches on European law and institutions at Ghent University. He is Director of the European Institute and Coordinator of the Jean Monnet Centre of Excellence at the same university. He has held visiting chairs at King's College, London; the University of Bologna; the University of Brussels; Scuola Sant'Anna, University of Pisa; the University of Georgia (US); the Hebrew University of Jerusalem; Libera Università Mediterranea; the College of Europe; Université Montesquieu, Bordeaux IV; Université de Rennes I; Université Paris II (Panthéon-Assas). Many of his publications concentrate on EU external relations. A recent publication is 'Bilateral agreements concluded by the European Community',

Recueil des cours de l'Academie de droit international, 2006, vol. 309, pp. 125–451.

PETER-CHRISTIAN MÜLLER-GRAFF is Professor for European Law, Economic and Private Law and Comparative Law at Heidelberg University and is Director of the Institute for German and European Economic Law since 1994. He chairs the European Graduate School of the Deutsche Forschungsgemeinschaft 'Systemtransformation und Wirtschaftsintegration im zusammenwachsenden Europa' and the Arbeitskreis Europäische Integration. He is a member of the Comité Directeur of FIDE (General Secretary 1994–1996). He is a visiting professor at the universities of Vienna, Zurich, Cracow and Georgetown, and at the College of Europe; he was formerly a visiting professor at Cornell University, Nihon University, and the universities of Nancy and Bordeaux. He is an honorary professor at ELTE Budapest. He was Dean of the Heidelberg Law Faculty (1999–2004), served as Judge at the Court of Appeals of Cologne (OLG-Richter auf Lebenszeit), counselled in questions of the Constitutional Treaty (Convention, German authorities) and represented the Federal Republic of Germany before the ECJ. He is author and editor of many books on European law, economic law and private law, among them *Die Rolle der erweiterten Europäischen Union in der Welt* (2006), *Die Europäische Gemeinschaft in der Welthandelsorganisation* (2000), *East Central Europe and the European Union: From Europe Agreements to a Member Status* (1997) and *Gemeinsames Privatrecht in der Europäischen Gemeinschaft* (1999, 2nd edn).

ELEANOR SPAVENTA is a reader in Law and Director of the Durham European Law Institute. She previously held positions at Birmingham University, where she was a lecturer, and at the University of Cambridge, where she was a Norton Rose European Law Lecturer and a fellow and Director of Studies at New Hall. Her research interests lie in European law and, in particular, in the fields of European constitutional law, free movement, fundamental rights and cooperation in criminal matters in the EU. She is the author of *Free Movement of Persons in the European Union: Barriers to Movement in their Constitutional Context* (forthcoming), the co-author of *Wyatt and Dashwood's European Union Law* (2006) and the co-editor of *Social Welfare and EU Law* (2005).

PETER VAN ELSUWEGE studied international relations and European law at Ghent University. He has worked as an academic assistant at the

European Institute of Ghent University since 2001. In July 2007, he defended his PhD thesis 'EU enlargement and the Baltic states: a legal and political analysis'. His research activities essentially focus on the legal and political consequences of EU enlargement. He also works on related topics such as the relations between the enlarged EU and its new neighbours. One of his recent publications is 'Promoting democracy in the EU's neighbourhood: lessons from the pre-accession strategy', in A. Kasekamp and H. Pääbo (eds.), *Promoting Democratic Values in the Enlarging Europe: The Changing Role of the Baltic States from Importers to Exporters* (2006), pp. 40–52.

RAMSES A. WESSEL is Professor of the Law of the European Union and other International Organisations and Co-Director of the Centre for European Studies at the University of Twente. He is also a member of the Governmental Advisory Committee on Issues of Public International Law; Editor-in-Chief and founder of the *International Organizations Law Review*; Editor-in-Chief of the Dutch journal and yearbook on peace and security, *Vrede en Veiligheid*; and a member of the editorial boards of the *Netherlands Yearbook of International Law* and *Internationale Spectator*. He is the author of *The European Union's Foreign and Security Policy: A Legal Institutional Perspective* (1999) and of a number of other publications in the field of international and European law. His general research interests lie in the field of international and European institutional law, with a focus on the law of international organisations, peace and security, European foreign, security and defence policy and EU external relations in general.

ACKNOWLEDGEMENTS

The origins of this volume lie in the Ghent/Cambridge Workshop on 'Recent trends in the external relations of the European Union', which took place in Ghent in December 2005. The initiative brought together a number of leading specialists in this sphere of EU law and policy. The very stimulating discussion it generated was a starting point for further reflections, which resulted in a collection of papers finalised in early 2008. The organisers of the Workshop, also being the editors of the present volume, would like to express their deep appreciation to all the contributors for their cooperation, diligence and thorough analysis.

The project was part of a Jean Monnet Centre of Excellence activity of Ghent University. It also benefited greatly from support by the VZW Europees Instituut. The editors' sincere thanks are due to the authorities of the Jean Monnet Programme of the European Commission and to the Board of the VZW Europees Instituut. Mr Willy De Clercq, the Chairman of the VZW, deserves a particular tribute for the unfailing encouragement he gave to the project, without which the publication of this book would simply not have been possible. Finally, a special word of thanks goes to Dr Kirstyn Inglis for her invaluable assistance in the editing of some contributions and to Mr Rien Emmery and Ms Magali Carel for their much appreciated help in the preparation of the text.

INTRODUCTION

ALAN DASHWOOD AND MARC MARESCEAU

Part of the fascination of specialising in the law of the European Union (EU) is the sense of firing at a constantly moving target, and nowhere is this more obviously true than in the external relations field. European Union activity on the international scene is expanding rapidly, and there has been correspondingly rapid development of the legal concepts, principles and rules that are needed to organise it. Moreover, external relations law is bound to be affected by all that has been going on domestically within the EU. During the period of the conception, implementation and finalisation of the present volume, the EU has been involved in a gigantic enlargement operation; a Treaty establishing a Constitution for Europe ('the Constitutional Treaty') has been negotiated and signed, and then failed to secure ratification; and a debate has taken place, culminating in the signature on 13 December 2007 of a reforming Treaty, christened 'Treaty of Lisbon' (TL). This will incorporate most of the institutional and substantive reforms envisaged by the failed instrument, while eschewing its constitution-making pretensions.

There seemed to be a real need, therefore, for a volume taking stock of recent developments in the external relations law of the EC and in the law of the Common Foreign and Security Policy (CFSP) that results from Title V TEU, while also investigating the increasing interaction between these different fields of EU competence. Given the pace of change, fast footwork on the part of both editors and authors has been necessary, with adjustments and reorientations right up to the last minute; and we were always conscious that we might be caught out by some event, such as a surprise ruling by the European Court of Justice. However, should that prove to be the case, we trust our readers will find plenty in this volume that is of continuing relevance and interest.

Even in a collection of essays that are focused on legal issues, the political and economic perspectives of external relations can never be far

1

away. Different authors bring different degrees of interdisciplinarity to their work in this area, as well as strongly contrasting views as to the constitutional nature, and ultimate political destiny, of the EU. There are also aspects of external relations law that remain deeply controversial, both technically and in terms of underlying political values, and our contributors have felt no inhibition about taking a clear stand on such matters. This is as it should be, and it hardly needs saying that, apart from their own contributions, the views expressed in these pages by no means necessarily reflect those of the editors.

The range of topics covered in this volume can only be explained historically. The authors are at the forefront of research on the law and practice of EU external relations, and their chosen themes are the result of expert judgment as to the most significant developments in the field, though others would doubtless have chosen differently. Any attempt to impose an artificial framework on such a collection would have been futile. However, the group of contributions seemed to fall naturally into three sections of unequal extent.

The first, and largest, section comprises papers addressing issues that are broadly constitutional or institutional in character: nuances in the application, within the sphere of external relations law, of organising concepts of the legal order such as direct effect; the scope of the respective external competences of the Community, the Union and the Member States, and the interaction between such competences; how to reconcile the EU's sincere commitment to upholding fundamental rights at home and abroad with the need for an effective response to the threat posed by international terrorism; the internal effect of international agreements and the jurisdiction of the European Courts to interpret and apply them; finally, the reforms and potential problems that the Constitutional Treaty would have brought, and how these have been addressed by the Lisbon Treaty. Those various issues are intricately woven into the themes treated by the different contributors. The order in which papers are presented is designed to highlight parallels and contrasts in the approaches adopted.

Francis Jacobs brings his great authority to bear on the fundamental issues of the direct effect of international agreements concluded by the Community, and of the jurisdiction of the European Court of Justice to interpret such agreements; he describes the latter as 'questionable in terms of law, but arguably desirable in the interest of maintaining the rule of law and in the development of a coherent system of law'. Analysis of the more recent case law leads him to conclude, though with caution, that the ECJ's approach may be evolving: as to direct effect, through less emphasis being placed on the nature of the agreement in which the provision in question is found, the focus being rather on the need for the substantive provision itself to be clear, precise and unconditional; and as to interpretation, through increased readiness to construe the language found in international agreements in a similar sense to that of corresponding language in the EC Treaty.

Marise Cremona revisits issues going to the external relations competence of the EU, seeking to draw lessons from the Treaty of Lisbon (TL), in terms of both a better *definition* of competences, express and implied, and a better *division* of competences between the EU, the EC and the Member States. She points out that the difficulty of determining the appropriate legal basis for external action is liable to be exacerbated by the adoption of a single set of objectives, those specific to the CFSP no longer being identified. She is also critical of various provisions of the TL where attempts by the draftsman to formulate principles derived from existing case law fail to reflect its complexity and subtlety. Her insightful analysis of the virtues and vices of the relevant provisions of the failed Treaty have taken on fresh immediacy, since these are largely to be maintained by the TL.

Alan Dashwood explores the function of the present Article 47 TEU in managing the relationship between the Community's external relations competence under the EC Treaty and the CFSP competence of the Union under Title V TEU – an issue that will remain no less alive under the amended Treaties. It is his contention that the protection afforded by Article 47 to the external Community *acquis* does not go so far as to preclude the adoption of a second pillar measure specifically designed to serve one or more of the objectives of the CFSP, merely because the activity to which it relates might conceivably have been the subject of a measure adopted in furtherance of a different objective, under one of the legal bases in the EC Treaty; and such an interpretation of the new Article 40 TEU, which is to replace Article 47, seems even more readily sustainable. This was an instance where the risk we have referred to, of a surprise ruling by the ECJ, materialised. However, thanks to our publisher's flexibility, it proved possible briefly to comment on the judgment in Case 91/05 in an Epilogue.

Piet Eeckhout offers a critique of the position taken by the Court of First Instance (CFI) in the *Yusuf* and *Kadi* cases (at the time of writing on appeal to the ECJ), that it had no jurisdiction to review the legality of Community legislation on human rights grounds, where this could lead, in effect, to the disapplication of a resolution of the UN Security Council adopted under Chapter VII of the Charter. He argues that the CFI's approach is not required by international law itself, and that it does not fit the existing rules, principles and decisions governing fundamental rights protection in the EU. He proposes, instead, a '*solange*' approach, according to which constitutional review of implementing acts should continue to be undertaken at the municipal level, until a satisfactory system of independent human rights review is established at the level of the United Nations.

Eleanor Spaventa raises concerns about the effectiveness of the judicial protection of fundamental rights in the context of EU counter-terrorism measures. She focuses on Common Position 2001/93, which established a list of individuals and organisations believed to be associated with terrorist activities (unlike the situation in *Yusuf* and *Kadi*, the list of those affected had not been drawn up by the UN). As the author explains, Common Position 2001/931 was adopted using mixed second and third pillar competences, to cover, respectively, persons whose alleged activity was external to the EU, and those whose alleged activity was wholly internal. She goes on to analyse the consequences, in terms of the human rights protection available, of being included in the category of 'foreign' or of 'domestic' terrorists. In neither case is the protection found to be sufficient at EU level (though, curiously perhaps, the situation of the domestic terrorist is worse, owing to the absence of a cross-pillar mechanism equivalent to Article 301 EC, which could provide a basis for a challengeable Community act). That being so, it is strongly argued that responsibility should fall upon the national courts, *as a matter of EU law*, to ensure an appropriate measure of fundamental rights review in such cases.

Ramses Wessel addresses issues of competence and responsibility, as between the EU and its Member States, that arise from the developing practice of concluding international agreements in the name of the EU, under the procedure laid down by Article 24 TEU for the purposes of both the CFSP and police and judicial cooperation in criminal matters (PJCCM). While the Member States are not to be regarded as parties to such agreements, there have been attempts to engage their responsibility, for instance, through explicit language in certain PJCCM agreements establishing a connection with obligations arising under existing bilateral agreements with the third country concerned; oddly, though, the expedient of mixity – familiar in agreements to which the Community is party – has not been resorted to. The author goes on to consider the possible internal effect of EU agreements, in the light of the *Pupino* decision of the ECJ on the existence of a duty of loyal cooperation under the TEU, and of recent CFI authority on the duty of national courts to ensure the protection of fundamental rights in situations arising from the EU activity under the second and third pillars.

Pieter-Christian Muller-Graff asks whether the TL enhances the potential for achieving a legitimate and effective Common Commercial Policy (CCP) within a globalised economy. His answer is organised round three particular issues: the enlarged scope of EU competence pursuant to Article 207(1) and (4) of the TFEU, and the corresponding reduction, as compared with the present Article 133(5) and (6) EC, of limitations on the exclusivity of such competence; new features of the overarching primary law context that would promote consistency between the CCP and other aspects of the EU's external action; and projected changes to the rules governing the exercise of competences, notably the enhanced role of the European Parliament in this field, and greater possibilities for the Council to act by qualified majority voting.

Jacques Bourgeois and **Orla Lynskey** set out to answer the question how seriously substantive WTO obligations are taken by the institutions that collectively exercise the Community's legislative powers. In the light of a group of case studies, they reach the conclusion that increasing attention is being paid to WTO concerns, but that the trend towards compliance is much more evident in the Council than in the European Parliament, where there has been a robust insistence on prioritising Community interests and values. The authors', at first sight, surprising explanation for this is the intergovernmental character of the Council; whereas the Parliament, unlike the Member States, does not have an explicit 'sovereignty shield' to protect Community interests against WTO interference.

The second part of this volume deals with various aspects of substantive external relations considered in a geographical or geo-political perspective. In the EU's bilateral, as well as regional, approaches important evolutions have taken place, illustrating certain new tendencies that are deserving of analysis in depth. It should be stressed that EU enlargement, which might be seen as a very special form of external relations, has been deliberately excluded from the scope of this book. It may seem a pity that no specific contributions deal with relations between the EU and Turkey or between the EU and the Western Balkans, but the inclusion of these topics would have skewed the volume too much towards enlargement, something the editors wished to avoid. Having said that, the decision not to include specific contributions on EU enlargement does not mean that this phenomenon has been, or could have been, swept under the carpet. In various contributions it is a starting point for analytical reflection or it may appear in the background of an analytical comment; and in some cases it is even intrinsically interconnected with the subject examined.

One of the main difficulties with the EU's substantive external relations is that these are often difficult to place in precise and accurate legal frameworks. Such difficulty is particularly true for the relations that have been developed with countries in the EU's proximity. This explains why contributors in this section of the book cover topics such as the EU's relations with its 'old neighbours', in particular Switzerland and the European micro-States; also the EU's European Neighbourhood Policy; EU–Russia relations; and relations between the EU and Mediterranean countries. However, the analysis of the substantive bilateral and regional approaches is not limited to the EU's proximity; already covering the Mediterranean dimension proved difficult, if not impossible, without including 'the Wider Middle East'; and, especially, in a volume like this one, the relations between the EU and the US could not be ignored, even if they are, apart perhaps from the relations falling within the WTO scope, first and foremost policy and security oriented.

Christine Kaddous examines in detail how the bilateral relations EU–Switzerland, after the many ad hoc initiatives and the 1992 Swiss rejection of the EEA, led to the conclusion of the series of cluster-type bilateral agreements known as the *Bilaterals I* and the *Bilaterals II*. These approaches allowed the inclusion of topics that were particularly sensitive for one or both of the parties within the scope of the respective batches of the agreements but which could nevertheless be agreed upon as part of a larger package. Of course, one of the remaining fundamental questions in the sophisticated network of relations EU–Switzerland is how long sectoral bilateralisation between the two parties, coupled with a considerable unilateral alignment of Swiss law with the Internal Market *acquis communautaire* and beyond, can continue to prevail without reactivating the Swiss application for EU membership, which has been frozen since 1992.

Marc Maresceau has devoted a study on the, at first sight, curious and perhaps even exotic topic of the relations between the EU and the micro-States of Andorra, San Marino and Monaco on which very little has been written. All these micro-States constitute *sui generis* cases in their relations with the EU. One of the many reasons for this specificity is the historical relationship of these States with their direct neighbour or neighbours which happen to be EU Member States. A second reason for the complexity is the almost exclusively ad hoc basis on which the relations with the EU have been developed. Lastly, neither the enlarged EU nor the micro-States themselves have a clear and well-defined vision of how their mutual relations should evolve in the future. Occasionally, micro-States have been subjected to a particular EU policy as a group, as was the case concerning certain aspects of fiscal law, although so far this remains very exceptional.

Christophe Hillion concentrates on the ENP as it emerged on the eve of the 2004 enlargement and how it developed afterwards. Generally, ENP can be seen as an expression of (very) late awareness that EU enlargement, having as its main objective the enhancement of peace, security and prosperity on the European continent, could also lead to new and sharp divisions in Europe. If this were indeed to be the case then enlargement would not necessarily be helpful to achieve the mentioned political objectives. Although ENP is now largely in place, and not forgetting that it both complements and implements the Partnership and Cooperation Agreements which have been signed with the countries from the former USSR, it is difficult and perhaps still even too premature to assess the concrete results and added value of this new policy.

Peter Van Elsuwege analyses the prospects of the possible signature of the grand Strategic Partnership Agreement between the EU and Russia, which is due to replace the outdated Partnership and Cooperation Agreement. The current prevailing feeling of discontent, if not of mistrust, is not very propitious for such a move. Back in 2004, a bilateral political agreement had been reached between the EU and Russia on the latter's terms of accession to WTO, while a year later the road maps for the gradual establishment of the four Common Spaces have also been agreed upon (economic space, external security, internal security and justice; and research and development, education and culture), and this constitutes the main focus of Van Elsuwege's contribution. Certainly, a lot of what has been achieved, in particular regarding the four Common Spaces, lacks any solid legal framework. This *soft law* engenders documents that by their very nature set out programmes needing further implementation through legal acts. But at least it has an important reference function. Moreover, and this is perhaps the most important point, Russia's present economic strength is largely dependent on its exports to the EU. In other words, Russia needs the EU, just as the EU needs Russia; both are forced to work together.

Erwan Lannon's contribution goes beyond the classical question of the EU's Mediterranean policy and adds the Middle East dimension, including the so-called 'East of Jordan Track' or 'Wider Middle East', for which, of course, no ENP applies. He has good reason to do so, not only because of the Iraq War but also because EU policies towards the countries concerned cannot easily be disconnected from those included in the EU–Mediterranean relations. The core of Lannon's analysis focuses on the EU's overall *Strategic Partnership with the Mediterranean and the Middle East* and highlights this fact. The creation of the *Strategic Partnership* cannot simply be considered as a mere extension of ENP or of the Euro-Mediterranean Partnership. It is, in the author's approach, a new umbrella framework linking two regions that have been artificially disconnected under previous EU policies. Within this new Strategic Framework the 'East of Jordan Track', that embraces Yemen, the Gulf Cooperation Council, Iran and Iraq, is certainly the most challenging.

Günter Burghardt, the EU Ambassador to the US in Washington for five years, has seen it all: from the election of President George Bush Jr., September 11 to the Iraq War and its aftermath. His contribution provides the reader not only with a first-hand account of how all this was perceived in the context of the EU–US relations, but it also offers a sharp analytical insight by someone who was uniquely placed both to observe events as they unfolded and who, at the same time, played his own special role in the seemingly unfathomable and complex game that is EU–US transatlantic relations. A weakened US, after the evident failures of unilateralism, and a weakened EU, digesting with difficulty its enlargement and coping with an institutional crisis, may perhaps, paradoxically, lead to a renewed and stronger bilateral relationship.

The third part of this book selects two specific substantive law areas – intellectual property law and environment law – as examples where important developments have taken place and which tend to illustrate the specific relationship between domestic policy and external relations.

Inge Govaere's contribution illustrates how the EU has attempted to elaborate an intellectual property enforcement strategy in its relations with third countries. The objectives and means of this strategy are set out in an exhaustive manner. In this regard, the increased use of substantive and institutional arrangements in agreements concluded by the EC deserves special mentioning. The paper examines not only the EC's competence in this respect but also the possible delicate interferences of the EC's strategy with public policy choices. The author explains, among other things, how in the area of trade of certain pharmaceutical products with certain third countries with public health problems this has led the EC to adopt trade measures facilitating or even stimulating intellectual property holders to engage in tiered pricing or compulsory licensing of patents.

Kirstyn Inglis concentrates on the EU's external actions in the field of environmental protection. After a short stocktaking of the success and failures of that policy, the author highlights recent trends. Out of the various aspects examined, two merit special attention. First, the effects of EU enlargement on compliance with the environment *acquis*. While in the long run these are expected to be positive, many questions still remain on how the new Member States in reality will be able to adapt to the *acquis* and the long transitional periods in the accession agreements do remain a worrying factor. Another aspect focuses on the role of the ECJ in balancing environmental concerns with trade. The author, while acknowledging that the ECJ raised the profile of the environment dimension in the context of external trade, also sees in the ECJ's approach the potential for increasing conflicts between environmental standards and CCP.

A series of brief summaries cannot do justice to the rich variety of our contributors' reflections. It is our earnest hope and modest expectation that the collection will advance understanding, and provoke further research and writing, in this important field of EU law.

PART I

Constitutional and institutional questions

Direct effect and interpretation of international agreements in the recent case law of the European Court of Justice

FRANCIS G. JACOBS

1.1 Introduction

The Community has wide treaty-making powers. The authors of the European Economic Community (EEC) Treaty were prudent and cautious on this, as on other major constitutional issues, and used the term 'agreement' rather than 'treaty', for example in the original Articles 113 and 228 of the Treaty, and that terminology is still generally used today.

Moreover, the EEC Treaty nowhere contained a general provision on the Community's treaty-making powers. The provision of Article 210 that 'The Community shall have legal personality', which was relied upon by the European Court of Justice (ECJ) in the *ERTA* case for that purpose, seems, as its very terms suggest, concerned not with the *international* legal personality of the Community, but with more mundane matters of domestic law. That is confirmed by Article 211, which concerns the legal capacity of the Community in the Member States. (Contrast Article 6 of the earlier, now defunct, European Coal and Steel Community (ECSC) Treaty: 'The Community shall have legal personality. In international relations, the Community shall enjoy the legal capacity it requires to perform its functions and attain its objectives.')

Indeed, it would have been uncharacteristically presumptuous of the Treaty to purport to confer international legal personality on the Community. Moreover, the exercise of treaty-making powers depends in part on the attitude of third States.

I am grateful to Anne Thies, of King's College London, for her assistance with the final text of this paper.

Initially, however, the Community was certainly intended to exercise the power to conclude trade agreements: so much is clear from the original Articles 113 and 114 of the Treaty and from subsequent practice. Moreover, Article 238 provided that the Community could conclude, with a third State, a union of States or an international organisation, 'agreements establishing an association involving reciprocal rights and obligations, common action and special procedures'.

As is well known, the case law of the ECJ has taken a broad view of the Community's competence, a view based not only on the powers conferred by the Treaty but also on theories of implied powers; and the Community has concluded a large number of agreements, by now probably in excess of a thousand.

Indeed, the ECJ has also taken a broad view of its own jurisdiction in relation to agreements with third States. First, under Article 228 of the Treaty the ECJ had jurisdiction to give an opinion on whether an agreement envisaged is compatible with the Treaty; but it has interpreted that as conferring upon it jurisdiction also to pronounce on the competence of the Community. Second, under Article 177 (now 234) the ECJ has asserted jurisdiction to interpret treaties to which the Community is a party, including 'mixed agreements', on the questionable ground that they are 'acts of the institutions of the Community' under those provisions of the EEC Treaty. It has also interpreted – and attached much weight to – decisions of Association Councils adopted under such agreements, although those decisions can hardly be regarded as acts of the Community institutions.

The ECJ's extensive interpretation of its jurisdiction is questionable in terms of law, but arguably desirable in the interest of maintaining the rule of law and in the development of a coherent system of law. Certainly, it has made possible a rich body of case law in the field of the Community's external relations.

The aim of the present paper is not to examine the basis of the ECJ's jurisdiction, nor the ECJ's approach to the Community's treaty-making powers. It is concerned rather with the treatment by the ECJ of the agreements themselves, and in particular the ECJ's approach in its more recent case law to the two central aspects of such agreements: direct effect and interpretation.

Accordingly, the discussion that follows is in three unequal parts: 1.2 briefly summarises the main lines of the earlier case law on international agreements; 1.3 looks at the ECJ's more recent approach to the issue of direct effect; 1.4 considers the ECJ's more recent approach to the interpretation of international agreements.

The discussion is not intended to be comprehensive: indeed since the present paper was conceived, an invaluable comprehensive and up-to-date study, based on his 2004 lectures at the Hague Academy of International Law, has been published by Professor Marc Maresceau.[1] However, there may still be scope for a more selective essay which tries to present more of a snapshot of the scene.

1.2 The earlier case law in brief

The earlier case law can be presented briefly.[2] As early as 1972, the ECJ had to consider the direct effect of the General Agreement on Tariffs and Trade (GATT), to which, in its view, the Community must be regarded as a party. In considering that issue, in *International Fruit Company*,[3] it had regard, following its approach to the EEC Treaty in *Van Gend en Loos*, to 'the spirit, the general scheme and the terms of the General Agreement'. It reached a negative conclusion on direct effect, just as, many years later, it reached a negative conclusion on the successor to the GATT, the World Trade Organisation (WTO) Agreement.

The ECJ did not, however, adopt a negative stance in relation to other agreements. In 1982, in *Polydor* v. *Harlequin*, in a case raising the issue of the exhaustion of intellectual property rights, it avoided the need to pronounce on the direct effect of the Free Trade Agreement with Portugal, holding instead that the interpretation of the corresponding provisions of the EEC Treaty (Arts. 30 and 36) could not be transposed to the different context of a Free Trade Agreement, so that the exhaustion of intellectual property rights could not be invoked in trade between the Community and Portugal.[4] Later in the same year, in *Kupferberg*,[5] it ruled in favour of the direct effect of the same Agreement, in a case concerning discriminatory taxation, as it ruled in favour of the direct effect of a similar provision of the Association Agreement with Greece in *Pabst-Richarz*.[6]

---

[1] M. Maresceau, 'Bilateral Agreements concluded by the European Community', *Recueil des cours de l'Académie de droit international. Collected Courses of the Academy of International Law*, 2006, vol. 309, pp. 125–451.

[2] See in more detail ibid., pp. 246 *et seq.*   [3] [1972] ECR 1219.

[4] [1982] ECR 329.   [5] [1982] ECR 3641.   [6] [1982] ECR 1331.

Broadly the ECJ favoured, with the notable exception of the GATT and the WTO Agreement, the direct effect of international agreements to which the Community was a party, but took care to interpret their provisions more restrictively than corresponding provisions of the EEC Treaty where that seemed to be the consequence of the different context of the respective treaties.

The ECJ's approach to direct effect goes somewhat further than might be expected. Its approach to interpretation, however, was broadly in accord with classical international law.

1.3 Recent case law: direct effect

It is not always easy to determine whether, and to what extent, the ECJ has relaxed the conditions for direct effect laid down by its previous case law. But the modern case law does seem to depart in some respects from a previous, more stringent approach.

A first possible example is the line of cases starting with *Demirel*. In 1987, the ECJ had in *Demirel* denied direct effect to some provisions of the Association Agreement with Turkey because they were not 'sufficiently precise and unconditional to be capable of governing directly movement of workers' as long as the Association Council had not yet adopted the necessary specific rules (here, the rules on family reunification).[7] Some years later, the ECJ held in *Sevince* that provisions of decisions adopted by the Association Council were directly effective because they were 'clear, precise and unconditional' and because of the purpose and nature of the decisions, which formed part of the Agreement.[8] Subsequently, the ECJ reiterated in many judgments that provisions of Association and Cooperation agreements, as well as those of Association Council decisions, were directly effective and could thus be invoked in national courts, if the purpose and nature of the agreements did not exclude that effect and the provisions were sufficiently 'clear, precise and unconditional'.[9] The ECJ – apparently departing from its approach in *Demirel* where the need for

---

[7] Case C-12/86 *Demirel* [1987] ECR 3719, para. 23.

[8] Case C-192/89 *Sevince* [1990] ECR 3461, paras. 14 *et seq.*

[9] See P. Eeckhout, *External Relations of the European Union: Legal and Constitutional Foundation* (Oxford: Oxford University Press, 2004), pp. 289 *et seq.*, n. 53 with reference to the case law delivered until the year 2000.

Association Council decisions was identified – has also acknowledged direct effect where the 'recommendations' envisaged by the Agreement had not yet been adopted by the Cooperation Council: for example, for the implementation of the non-discrimination principle laid down in the Partnership and Cooperation Agreement with Russia.[10]

1.3.1 Głoszczuk, Kondova, Malik and Jany

The ECJ implicitly acknowledged the direct effect of provisions of associations agreements (Europe Agreements) in its judgments *Głoszczuk, Kondova, Malik* and *Jany*,[11] which concerned the *right to work and to take up an activity as a self-employed person*. Since the ECJ did not question the direct effect of the relevant provisions, but discussed in more detail the scope of these rights – e.g. whether the right to establishment comprised the right to enter and reside – these cases will be discussed in more detail in the section on interpretation.

1.3.2 Ergün Torun

In the context of bilateral relations with Turkey, the ECJ also acknowledged the direct effect of *Association Council decisions* that provided the *right to access the employment market* – as well as corollary rights – in the host Member State.[12] Recently, the ECJ held in *Ergün Torun* that a son of a Turkish national could rely on a provision of a decision adopted by the Association Council established under the Association Agreement with Turkey.[13] Again, this case will be looked at in more detail in the section on interpretation, since it was not the direct effect as such, but rather the scope of the provision that was assessed by the ECJ.

---

[10] Case C-265/03 *Simutenkov* [2005] ECR I-2579. However, the explanation of this point may be that any such 'recommendations' would be non-binding and that therefore their adoption could not be a condition of the direct effect of the Agreements.

[11] Cases C-63/99 *Głoszczuk* [2001] ECR I-6369; C-235/99 *Kondova* [2001] ECR I-6427; C-257/99 *Barkoci and Malik* [2001] ECR I-6557; C-268/99 *Jany* [2001] ECR I-8615; see for a further comment on these judgments C. Hillion, 40 CMLRev. (2003), pp. 465–91.

[12] E.g. Cases C-192/89 *Sevince* [1990] ECR 3461; C-171/01 *Wählergruppe* [2003] ECR I-4301; see Eeckhout, *External Relations*, pp. 289 *et seq.*, n. 53 with reference to further case law.

[13] Case C-502/04 *Ergün Torun* [2006] ECR I-1563.

1.3.3 Pokrzeptowicz-Meyer

In the *Pokrzeptowicz-Meyer* case the question was raised whether the non-discrimination principle in Article 37(1) of the Association Agreement with Poland (Europe Agreement) had direct effect.[14] Ms Pokrzeptowicz-Meyer, a Polish national, had claimed the incompatibility with this provision of a provision of national (German) law according to which posts for foreign-language assistants may be the subject of employment contracts of limited duration whereas, for other teaching staff performing special duties, recourse to such contracts must be individually justified by an objective reason.

According to the Land Nordrhein-Westfalen, Article 37(1) of the Agreement was incapable of having direct effect because the parties to the Agreement had inserted the phrase '[s]ubject to the conditions and modalities applicable in each Member State' in the wording of its first paragraph. In its submission, that phrase qualified the prohibition on discrimination on the ground of nationality and Article 37(1) could not, therefore, be considered to be unconditional within the meaning of the ECJ's case law on direct effect. That submission did indeed find some support in the ECJ's earlier case law.

In my Opinion in that case, although I agreed that the provision might indeed appear to subject the application of the principle of equal treatment between Community and Polish workers to a certain discretionary power of the Member States, I concluded that the obligation not to discriminate against Polish migrant workers on grounds of nationality as regards working conditions was still perfectly capable of application by the national courts in the absence of any such measures. Furthermore, the Agreement did not explicitly exclude direct effect of its Article 37(1) and the purpose and the context of the Agreement could hardly justify a different conclusion. It was not intended to entitle the Member States to reduce substantially the effect of Article 37(1) or perhaps to render the non-discrimination principle nugatory.

Consequently, I stated that 'the reference in Article 37(1) to the conditions and modalities applicable in each Member State must ... be understood primarily as a reminder that, since the conditions of access to the labour markets of the Member States remain in principle a matter of

---

[14] Case C-162/00 *Land Nordrhein-Westfalen* v. *Beata Pokrzeptowicz-Meyer* [2002] ECR I-1049.

national law, the right to equal treatment in employment applies only to Polish migrant workers who satisfy the procedural and substantive conditions for entry and stay on the territory laid down by the relevant national rules'.[15] My conclusion was that Ms Pokrzeptowicz-Meyer was entitled to rely in a national court against a public authority (acting in its capacity as employer) on Article 37(1) of the Agreement, which precluded the application of the national law in question.

In its judgment in *Pokrzeptowicz-Meyer*, the ECJ did not appear to share my doubts and moved more rapidly to the conclusion that Article 37(1) of the Europe Agreement had direct effect, owing to its wording being clear, precise and unconditional. According to the ECJ, the proviso 'subject to the conditions and modalities applicable in each Member State' was 'not to be interpreted in such a way as to allow the Member States to subject the principle of non-discrimination ... to conditions or discretionary limitations. Such an interpretation would render that provision meaningless and deprive it of any practical effect.'[16] Thus, the applicant could invoke the non-discrimination principle – regarding working conditions, remuneration and dismissal of workers – in order to claim that the fixed-term character of her contract needed justification ('objective reason') as was required by German law for fixed-term contracts. The ECJ concluded that the direct effect of Article 37(1) of the Agreement was not negated by the provision according to which the authorities of the Member States remain competent to 'apply, while respecting the limits laid down by the Europe Agreement, inter alia their own national laws and regulations regarding entry, stay, employment and working conditions of Polish nationals'.[17]

1.3.4 Simutenkov

The ECJ followed a similar line of argument in *Simutenkov* where a provision of the Partnership and Cooperation Agreement with Russia was in question.[18] The applicant, a Russian national legally employed as a professional footballer in Spain, had been issued with a federation licence issued to nationals of a State other than Member States of the Community and of the European Economic Area (EEA). His application for a second

---

[15] *Ibid.*, para. 44.   [16] *Ibid.*, para. 24.   [17] *Ibid.*, para. 28.
[18] Case C-265/03 *Simutenkov* [2005] ECR I-2579.

type of licence issued to nationals of those Member States had been refused on the basis of national sporting rules which provided that such a licence could be issued only to nationals of Member States and restricted the fielding of non-Member State nationals in national games. He challenged that refusal before the Spanish courts on the basis that the distinction made by the sporting rules between nationals of Member States of the Community and of the EEA, on the one hand, and Russian nationals, on the other, was contrary to the non-discrimination principle laid down in Article 23(1) of the Partnership and Cooperation Agreement with Russia.[19]

In its preliminary ruling, the ECJ held that the non-discrimination principle in Article 23(1) had direct effect. Having regard to its wording and to the purpose and nature of the agreement itself, the provision contained a clear and precise obligation which was not subject, in its implementation or effects, to the adoption of any subsequent measure. According to the ECJ, Russian nationals legally employed in a Member State were thus entitled to equal treatment. An individual could rely on that provision in requesting a national court to disapply a discriminatory measure without any further implementing measures to that end being required.

Interpreting that provision as having direct effect, the ECJ said, was not contrary to the purpose of the Agreement which was to establish a partnership between the parties with a view to promoting, inter alia, the development between them of close political relations, trade and harmonious economic relations, political and economic freedoms, and the achievement of gradual integration between the Russian Federation and a wider area of cooperation in Europe.

In addition, the fact that the Partnership and Cooperation Agreement was not made with a view to establishing an association between the parties or accession to the European Union but rather with a view to cooperation did not exclude its provisions from having direct effect. It was clear from the case law that agreements establishing cooperation between

---

[19] Article 23(1) of the Partnership and Cooperation Agreement with Russia provided that, subject to the laws, conditions and procedures applicable in each Member State, the Community and its Member States had to ensure that the treatment accorded to Russian nationals legally employed in the territory of a Member State was free from any discrimination based on nationality, as regards working conditions, remuneration or dismissal, as compared to its own nationals. The Contracting Parties were not prevented from applying their own national rules concerning, amongst other things, working conditions to the extent that in so doing they did not nullify or impair the benefits accruing to any Party under the Agreement.

the parties could contain provisions which directly govern the position of individuals where the conditions for direct effect of provisions of an international agreement were fulfilled.

As mentioned above, in *Demirel* the ECJ had denied direct effect to provisions of the EEC–Turkey Agreement because of the still awaited Association Council decisions. Although the Partnership and Cooperation Agreement with Russia provided that recommendations by the Cooperation Council established thereunder were to be made for implementation of that non-discrimination principle, the ECJ did acknowledge direct effect of the non-discrimination principle here.

1.3.5 Alami

In line with previous judgments delivered with regard to direct effect of provisions of the Cooperation Agreements with Morocco and Algeria,[20] the ECJ recently reiterated in *Alami* that the Agreement's *non-discrimination* clause – which is identical in both agreements and covers working conditions, remuneration as well as social security – had direct effect, despite the lack of any implementing measures adopted by the Cooperation Council.[21] According to the ECJ, the task of the Council consisted merely of 'facilitating compliance with the prohibition of discrimination' and could 'not be regarded as rendering conditional the immediate application of the principle of non-discrimination'.[22]

1.3.6 Gattoussi

Very recently, the ECJ had to decide whether Article 64 of the Association Agreement with Tunisia (the Euro-Mediterranean Agreement)[23] – which

---

[20] Cases C-18/90 *Kziber* [1991] ECR I-199 (unemployment allowance); C-58/93 *Yousfi* [1994] ECR I-1353; C-103/94 *Krid* [1995] ECR I-719; C-126/95 *Hallouzi-Choho* [1996] ECR I-4807; C-113/97 *Babahenini* [1998] ECR I-183; C-416/96 *El Yassini* [1999] ECR I-1209.

[21] Case C-23/02 *Alami* [2003] ECR I-1399.

[22] See already Cases C-18/90 *Kziber* [1991] ECR I-199, at para. 22; C-23/02 *Alami* [2003] ECR I-1399, at paras. 22 *et seq.*

[23] Article 64 of the Euro-Mediterranean Agreement is to be found in Chapter I ('Workers') of Title VI ('Cooperation in Social and Cultural Matters') and is worded as follows:

    1. The treatment accorded by each Member State to workers of Tunisian nationality employed in its territory shall be free from any discrimination based on nationality, as regards working conditions, remuneration and dismissal, relative to its own nationals.

confers a *right to equal treatment* as regards working conditions on Tunisian nationals working in the Member States – could be invoked as a legal basis for a right of residence (*Gattoussi*).[24] Mr Mohamed Gattoussi, a worker of Tunisian nationality, had relied on the non-discrimination principle in order to claim a *right to residence*. Despite his being the holder of a work permit with no fixed term and being employed in Germany, the German authorities had imposed a limitation on the duration of his residence permit and asked Gattoussi to leave Germany without delay, failing which he would be deported to Tunisia.[25] It was reasoned that the original justification for granting a residence permit was now lacking because Mr Gattoussi was no longer living with his (German) wife and 'secondly, that a work permit of indefinite duration does not give rise under German law to any right – independent of and prevailing over the terms of the residence permit – to continue in employment and to remain for a longer period of time in the country'.[26] Under German law Gattoussi had not yet gained an independent right to residence, because his lawful cohabitation with his wife had not lasted long enough nor did his circumstances amount to a situation of particular hardship within the terms of the relevant German provisions. Furthermore, the competent authority was of the view that Gattoussi could not rely on any right deriving from the Euro-Mediterranean Agreement, because the prohibition of discrimination laid down in Article 64(1) thereof did not confer on Tunisian nationals any right to remain.

Referring to its previous case law on the right to establishment, work and the non-discrimination principle laid down in the 'Europe Agreements' (*Głoszczuk*), in Association Council decisions (*Wählergruppe*) and in the Partnership and Cooperation Agreement with Russia (*Simutenkov*), the ECJ applied the 'direct effect test'.[27] The ECJ then compared the provision with that of the EEC–Morocco Agreement, which is framed in almost identical terms and whose direct effect had been acknowledged in *El-Yassini*, and emphasised the 'association character' of the Agreement before coming to the conclusion that the provision had direct effect.[28]

---

2. All Tunisian workers allowed to undertake paid employment in the territory of a Member State on a temporary basis shall be covered by the provisions of paragraph 1 with regard to working conditions and remuneration.
3. Tunisia shall accord the same treatment to workers who are nationals of a Member State and employed in its territory.

[24] Case C-97/05 *Mohamed Gattoussi v. Stadt Rüsselsheim*, judgment of 14 December 2006, nyr.
[25] *Ibid.*, para. 14.   [26] *Ibid.*, para. 15.   [27] *Ibid.*, para. 25.   [28] *Ibid.*, paras. 26 *et seq.*

In its judgment, the ECJ concluded that:

> Article 64(1) of the Euro-Mediterranean Agreement establishing an asso-
> ciation between the European Communities and their Member States, of
> the one part, and the Republic of Tunisia, of the other part, ... may have
> effects on the right of a Tunisian national to remain in the territory of a
> Member State in the case where that person has been duly permitted by that
> Member State to work there for a period extending beyond the period of
> validity of his permission to remain.

We reach the result that, with the sole exception of the GATT and its
successor, the WTO Agreement – an exception for which good reasons
have been adduced by the academic community, although with some
vigorous dissent – the ECJ has never accepted that a treaty by which the
Community is bound is not in principle capable of having direct effect;
moreover, when looking at specific provisions of such treaties, the ECJ has
shown itself increasingly ready to recognise those provisions as having
direct effect.

1.4 Recent case law: interpretation

We now turn from issues of direct effect to issues of interpretation. The
recent cases are of interest as suggesting that, notwithstanding the special
features of the European Community (EC) Treaty which traditionally
justified a special approach to its interpretation, the ECJ may now be more
ready than previously to interpret provisions of treaties with third States
in the same way as corresponding provisions of the EC Treaty itself.

As we have seen, in 1980 in *Polydor* the ECJ considered that 'a mere
similarity in the wording of a provision of one of the Treaties establishing
the Communities and of an international agreement between the Community and a non-member Country [was] not sufficient to give to the
wording of that agreement the same meaning as it has in the Treaties'.[29] In
1993 the ECJ held in *Metalsa* that 'the extension of the interpretation of
provision in the EEC Treaty to a comparably, similarly or even identically
wording provision of an agreement concluded by the Community with a
non-member country depends, inter alia, on the aim pursued by each
provision in its own particular context and that a comparison between the

---

[29] Case 270/80 *Polydor* [1982] ECR 329.

objectives and context of the agreement and those of the Treaty is of considerable importance in that regard'.[30]

However, from as early as 1991, in cases concerning the Cooperation Agreements with Morocco and Algeria, the ECJ had held that the concept of social security had to be understood by analogy with the identical concept in Community law, namely Regulation 1408/71 on the application of social security schemes to employed persons.[31] As a consequence, a migrant worker who falls within the scope of application of one of those Agreements, and who is legally employed in the host Member State, is entitled to claim social benefits to the same extent as nationals of this Member State.

1.4.1 El-Yassini

There are nevertheless limits on the scope of the non-discrimination clause. In *El-Yassini*,[32] for example, the ECJ compared the Agreement with Morocco with the Agreement with Turkey. The ECJ emphasised the potential accession of the latter and the fact that the Agreement with Morocco was not intended progressively to secure the freedom of movement of workers; furthermore, no relevant decision had been adopted by the Cooperation Council.[33] Although that did not hinder the ECJ from acknowledging direct effect, it had an impact on its interpretation of the provision and thus the scope of the rights and benefits claimed under the provision.

1.4.2 From Głoszczuk to Ergün Torun

In *Głoszczuk*, the ECJ gave an interpretation of the Europe Agreement with Poland, according to which the *right to establishment comprised the right of entry and residence as corollaries.*[34] Taking into account, however, the different aims of the EC (internal market) and the Association Agreement with Poland (framework for gradual integration), the ECJ did not (explicitly) extend the interpretation of Article 52 EC, as reflected in its case law, to the relevant Association Agreement provision.[35]

---

[30] Case C-312/91 *Metalsa* [1993] ECR 3751, paras. 11 *et seq.*
[31] Case C-18/90 *Kziber* [1991] ECR I-199, para. 24.
[32] Case C-416/96 *El Yassini* [1999] ECR I-1209.
[33] Case C-416/96 *El Yassini* [1999] ECR I-1209, paras. 54–6.
[34] Case C-63/99 *Głoszczuk* [2001] ECR I-6369.   [35] *Ibid.*, para. 52.

Mr and Mrs Głoszczuk are Polish nationals who entered the United Kingdom in 1989 and 1991 on a tourist visa issued for a period of six months. The visas 'contained an express condition prohibiting them from entering employment or engaging in any business or profession in a self-employed capacity'.[36] After the expiry of their visas, the couple stayed illegally in the UK without seeking permission to work.[37] In 1996, the couple applied for leave to remain in the UK on the basis of Mr Głoszczuk's right of establishment: he claimed to have become a self-employed building contractor in 1995 and wanted to 'regularise' the family's stay.[38] They challenged the refusal of their application.

Although not applying the derogation rules established in its case law in the context of the EC Treaty, the ECJ concluded that the right to establishment, entry and residence was not absolute but could be restricted, so long as the rights under the Association Agreement were not rendered ineffective. Accordingly, the host Member States can exercise control with regard to the conditions 'that he genuinely intends to take up an activity as a self-employed person without at the same time entering into employment or having recourse to public funds, and that he possesses, from the outset, sufficient financial resources and has reasonable chances of success'. The relevant UK Immigration Rules were considered to be appropriate for achieving such a purpose.[39] However, according to the ECJ, the host State is obliged to review the person's situation when a new application through the State of origin is submitted. Accordingly, an application of a person – whose presence is otherwise unlawful – can be rejected only after taking into account 'the substantive requirements established by the Agreement'.[40]

In *Kondova*[41] and *Barkoci and Malik*,[42] the ECJ came to the same conclusions: the Europe Agreement's provision on freedom of establishment had direct effect; but it could be restricted by the host Member State. The applicant could be required to show that he has a 'genuine intention' to 'take up an activity as a self-employed person without at the same time entering into employment or having recourse to public funds, and that he possesses, from the outset, sufficient financial resources and has

[36] *Ibid.*, para. 18.   [37] *Ibid.*, paras. 19 *et seq.*   [38] *Ibid.*, paras. 20 *et seq.*
[39] Case C-63/99 *Głoszczuk* [2001] ECR I-6369.   [40] *Ibid.*, para. 67.
[41] Case C-235/99 *Kondova* [2001] ECR I-6427.
[42] Case C-257/99 *Barkoci and Malik* [2001] ECR I-6557.

reasonable chances of success'. Moreover, even where it was not questioned that the applicants had been illegally resident in the host State, the State was considered to be obliged to review the applicant's situation when a new application was submitted through the applicant's country of origin.

In *Jany*, the ECJ took the somewhat unusual step of invoking the rules on treaty interpretation in the Vienna Convention on the Law of Treaties. The ECJ relied on Article 31 of the Vienna Convention to interpret 'economic activities' in accordance with the 'ordinary meaning', which the ECJ sees as that established in the context of its case law on the EC Treaty. According to the ECJ, the meaning of the concept of 'activities as self-employed persons' of Article 43 EC cannot be different from the one in the Europe Agreement, i.e. 'economic activities as self-employed persons'.[43]

The main proceedings were brought before a national court in the Netherlands by several female Polish and Czech nationals who declared that they had established their residence between May 1993 and October 1996 and worked as 'window prostitutes' in Amsterdam; the six applicants had applied to the national authorities for *residence permits to enable them to work as self-employed* prostitutes for compelling humanitarian reasons. When their application was rejected they initiated a legal action, which was also unsuccessful because the national court denied the direct effect of the agreement provision regarding the right to establishment; the applicants then challenged again the decisions of the Secretary of State that had been issued on the basis of the national judgments. In its ruling, the ECJ referred to *Głoszczuk, Barkoci* and *Malik* and acknowledged the direct effect of the freedom of establishment laid down in the Association Agreements between the Community and Poland, and between the Community and the Czech Republic. Again, however, 'the requirement that Polish and Czech nationals wishing to become established in the host Member State must from the outset have sufficient financial resources to carry on the activity in question in a self-employed capacity' were considered to be 'designed precisely to enable the competent authorities of that State to carry out such checks and are appropriate for ensuring that such an objective is attained'.[44]

The ECJ then dealt with the question whether the activity of prostitution as an economic activity was covered only by the definition given in the case law on Article 43 EC or also by the freedom of establishment

---

[43] Case C-268/99 *Jany and Others* [2001] ECR I-8615, para. 37.   [44] *Ibid.*, para. 31.

under the Association Agreements with Poland and the Czech Republic; interestingly, the ECJ again referred in that connection to Article 31 of the Vienna Convention on the Law of Treaties in reasoning that a provision must be interpreted not only by reference to its terms, but also in the light of its objectives.[45] According to the ECJ, the purpose of the Agreement with Poland was 'to establish an association designed to promote the expansion of trade and harmonious economic relations between the Contracting Parties in order to foster dynamic economic development and prosperity in the Republic of Poland, with a view to facilitating its accession to the Communities', that objective being the same with regard to the Czech Republic.[46] The ECJ then came to the conclusion that there was no reason to give the term 'economic activity' a different meaning in the context of the Association Agreement from the one established under the EC Treaty; as a consequence, the activity of prostitution was covered by the freedom of establishment provided for under the Association Agreement.[47]

In *Pokrzeptowicz-Meyer*,[48] the ECJ referred to its case law on *non-discrimination* in the context of the free movement of workers, i.e. its judgment in *Spotti*,[49] and thus interpreted the pertinent provision of the Association Agreement with Poland in the same way as (now) Article 39(2) EC. According to the ECJ, though the 'similar wording' as such was not sufficient to apply the same interpretation, 'the aim and context' of the provision did not justify any different interpretation from the one given in *Spotti*. As a consequence, the Polish applicant could rely on the non-discrimination principle against Germany to the same extent as applicants relying on Article 39 EC, here with regard to *further employment* in Germany.

A similar approach was taken in *Kolpak*, where the ECJ transposed its ruling in *Bosman*[50] to the interpretation of the *non-discrimination principle* of the Association Agreement with Slovakia.[51] Maros Kolpak was a Slovak national, lawfully resident in Germany and goalkeeper for a German handball team. He applied for an unrestricted handball licence, i.e. one that was not marked with the letter 'A' (*Ausländer*, Foreigner) since only a maximum of two players with an 'A' licence were entitled to be fielded at the same time. Kolpak claimed that the Slovak Republic was

---

[45] *Ibid.*, paras. 32 *et seq.*   [46] *Ibid.*, para. 36.   [47] *Ibid.*, para. 37.
[48] Case C-162/00 *Pokrzeptowicz-Meyer* [2002] ECR I-1049; see for further discussion of this case n. 14.
[49] Case C-272/92 *Spotti* [1993] ECR I-5185.   [50] Case C-117/91 *Bosman* [1991] ECR I-3353.
[51] Case C-438/00 *Kolpak* [2003] ECR I-4135.

a State whose nationals were entitled to participate without restriction in competitions under the same conditions as German and Community players by reason of the prohibition of discrimination resulting from the combined provisions of the EC Treaty and the Association Agreement with Slovakia. The ECJ in its judgment acknowledged that the provision of the Agreement did have direct effect, and could be relied upon by Kolpak against the sports federation. The ECJ concluded that the non-discrimination principle laid down in this provision 'must be construed as precluding the application to a professional sportsman of Slovak nationality, who is lawfully employed by a club established in a Member State, of a rule drawn up by a sports federation in that State under which clubs are authorised to field, during league or cup matches, only a limited number of players from non-member countries that are not parties to the Agreement on the European Economic Area'.

Moreover, the ECJ in *Simutenkov* also interpreted a provision of the Partnership and Cooperation Agreement with Russia in the same way.[52] Although the Agreement was not concluded in order to establish an association with the Community, but rather with a view to cooperation, the ECJ concluded that the difference in context and purpose of the two Agreements could not result in a difference in meaning of the principles of non-discrimination in the two Agreements. It is interesting to observe that the ECJ did not compare the nature and purpose of the Partnership Agreement with those of the EC Treaty.

As before in the *Pokrzeptowicz-Meyer* case, the ECJ held that despite the reference to the provisions of Article 23(1) as being '[s]ubject to the laws, conditions and procedures applicable in each Member State' no interpretation could be given which would render the non-discrimination principle meaningless or deprived of practical effect.

The ECJ considered the scope of the *non-discrimination principle* in Article 23(1). It began by citing the following relevant parts of the judgment in *Kolpak*. A rule that limits the number of professional players, nationals of the non-member country in question, who might be fielded in national competitions did relate to *working conditions* within the meaning of Article 38(1) of the Communities–Slovakia Association Agreement inasmuch as it directly affected participation in league and cup matches of a Slovak professional player who was already lawfully employed in the

---

[52] Case C-265/03 *Simutenkov* [2005] ECR I-2579.

host Member State. The interpretation of Article 48(2) of the EC Treaty (now, after amendment, Article 39(2) EC) which it handed down in its judgment in *Bosman*, to the effect that the prohibition of discrimination on grounds of nationality applies to rules laid down by sporting associations which determine the conditions under which professional sportsmen can engage in gainful employment and precludes a limitation, based on nationality, on the number of players who may be fielded at the same time, could be transposed to Article 38(1) of the Association Agreement with Slovakia.

The ECJ noted the similarity in wording of the non-discrimination principle used in the Partnership and Cooperation Agreement with Russia and that used in the Association Agreement with Slovakia. It stated that the difference in context and purpose of the two Agreements could not result in a difference in meaning of the principles of non-discrimination in the two Agreements. Article 23(1) of the Partnership Agreement therefore produced a right to equal treatment similar to that established in *Kolpak* and in *Bosman*.

It also followed from those rulings that a limitation on participation in matches between clubs based on the nationality of the players could not be justified on sporting grounds. No other justifications for such limitation had been advanced.

With regard to *Association Council decisions* also, the ECJ has shown its willingness to interpret provisions in line with its approach taken in the context of market freedoms as laid down in the EC Treaty. In *Wählergruppe*, the ECJ assessed the scope of the non-discrimination principle regarding remuneration and working conditions as specified in Article 10(1) of the decision.[53] The ECJ held that reference should be made to the interpretation of the Treaty provisions on the free movement of workers (Arts. 39, 40 and 41 EC).[54]

In *Gattoussi*, the ECJ followed the view of Advocate General Ruiz-Jarabo Colomer that Member States can restrict a work permit with no fixed term only if that is justified on grounds of public policy, public security or public health.[55] The ECJ referred again to its ruling in *El-Yassini*, stating

---

[53] Case C-171/01 *Wählergruppe 'Gemeinsam Zajedno/Birlikte Alternative und Grüne GewerkschafterInnen/UG'*, and *Bundesminister für Wirtschaft und Arbeit and Others* [2003] ECR I-4301.

[54] Case C-171/01 *Wählergruppe* [2003] ECR I-4301.

[55] Case C-97/05 *Mohamed Gattoussi v. Stadt Rüsselsheim*, nyr, Opinion of AG Colomer, para. 63.

that 'as Community law stood ... the provision providing the non-discrimination principle had to be interpreted as not precluding in principle a host Member State from refusing to extend the residence permit ... where the initial reason for the grant of his leave to stay no longer exists by the time at which his residence permit expires'.[56] The ECJ continued 'that the situation would be different only if, in the absence of grounds relating to the protection of a legitimate national interest, such as public policy, public security or public health, that refusal were to affect the right actually to engage in employment conferred on the person concerned in that Member State by a work permit duly granted by the competent national authorities for a period exceeding that of his residence permit (see El-Yassini, paragraph 67)'.[57]

In a nutshell, if there are no grounds related to the protection of a legitimate national interest, the ECJ leaves Member States (merely) the discretion to limit the right to residence as long as the 'right actually to engage in employment conferred ... by a work permit ... for a period exceeding that of his residence permit' is not affected.

In *Ergün Torun*,[58] the ECJ had to interpret an Association Council decision. Mr Torun, a Turkish national, was born in Germany in 1976 where he had always resided and where his father was legally employed; since 1992, he had held a residence permit of unlimited duration. After completing a period of vocational training as an industrial mechanic he worked in various companies for periods of two to three months and received allowances when unemployed between those periods. From 1997, he developed a drug addiction; his unemployment support was retro-actively withdrawn from February 1998 because he did not attend an interview with a temporary employment agency that was to have offered him a job as a mechanic. In custody from May 1998, Mr Torun was sentenced in March 1999 to a term of imprisonment for a total of three years and three months for armed robbery and the illegal acquisition of narcotics; on 2 September 1999, the *Stadt Augsburg* ordered his expulsion and threatened to deport him. After having exhausted administrative remedies against that decision, Mr Torun took proceedings which went up to the Federal Administrative Court; that court referred the case to the

---

[56] Case C-97/05 *Mohamed Gattoussi* v. *Stadt Rüsselsheim*, judgment of 14 December 2006, nyr, para. 29.
[57] *Ibid.*   [58] Case C-502/04 *Ergün Torun* [2006] ECR I-1563.

ECJ, asking about the effect of the Association Council Decision No. 1/80 on the application of the national law on expulsion.

The ECJ held that the right of the child of a Turkish worker with regard to access to the employment market and to take up salaried employment would be rendered totally ineffective if that right did not embrace the right of residence for the child. The ECJ, referring to established case law, held that the right to residence of a child of a worker could be restricted only where, by his own conduct, he constituted a genuine and serious threat to public policy, public security or public health, in accordance with Article 14(1) of that decision, or where the person concerned had left the territory of that State for a significant length of time without legitimate reason. The applicant could not therefore be deprived of his right of residence on the ground that he was unemployed by reason of a three-year prison sentence, nor because he had lost his entitlement to a right of residence.[59]

1.5 Conclusions

The ECJ has in recent years been remarkably positive in its approach to agreements concluded by the Community (and even to some agreements to which the Community is not a party, notably the European Convention on Human Rights).

This is true in the first place of asserting jurisdiction to interpret the provisions of agreements, and also of related instruments such as decisions of Association Councils: although here the ECJ's exercise of jurisdiction can be traced back to the earliest cases. It is true of the ECJ's approach to the direct effect of such agreements and to their interpretation.

Whereas in earlier periods the ECJ seemed hesitant about according direct effect, in recent case law the ECJ has consistently, and often rather rapidly, rejected objections to direct effect, with the sole though important exception of the GATT/WTO Agreement.

This tendency can be illustrated both where the ECJ examines the issue of the direct effect of the agreement as a whole, and where it examines the direct effect of a particular provision.

The ECJ's approach might be criticised, however, for not always distinguishing the two issues; moreover, when it does so, it regularly addresses them in what may seem the wrong sequence. The ECJ generally considers

---

[59] *Ibid.*, para. 29.

first the specific provision of the agreement, applying the classic tests of
whether the provision is clear, precise and unconditional; it then considers
the agreement as a whole. It might have seemed more logical to take the
reverse order: it seems that it would make little sense to analyse the provision
and conclude that it is apt to have direct effect, but then to negate that
conclusion on the ground that the agreement as a whole is not apt to have
such effect. In practice, however, in the exceptional case where the ECJ
considers that the agreement is not apt to have direct effect, it does start with
the analysis of the agreement as a whole, as it did with the GATT in the
International Fruit Company case.[60] Once the ECJ had reached the conclusion that that Agreement, taken as a whole, did not lend itself to direct effect,
it was able to refrain from examining the specific provisions in issue.

The ECJ's increasingly positive approach to direct effect in its recent
case law can be illustrated by the *Pokrzeptowicz-Meyer* and *Simutenkov*
cases considered above. In the former, the ECJ had little difficulty in
concluding that the specific provision in issue had direct effect, despite the
presence of terms that under its earlier case law might have been regarded
as precluding direct effect.

In *Simutenkov*, the ECJ considered that the fact that the Agreement
provided merely for cooperation between the parties did not preclude
direct effect. It seems as if the nature of the Agreement is now no longer an
obstacle to direct effect, so long as it contains provisions that, as the ECJ
put it in *Simutenkov*, directly govern the position of individuals; the only
real requirement is now that the substantive provisions themselves satisfy
the requirements of direct effect, i.e. that they are clear, precise and
unconditional – and even the requirement of unconditionality, as we have
seen, has been diluted. Indeed, one could almost envisage that the reference to the nature of the agreement as not precluding direct effect has
become little more than a ritual refrain in which an agreement of almost
any nature could be said nevertheless to be capable of having direct effect.
Is the reference to the nature of the agreement, or its object and purpose,
any longer meaningful on the issue of direct effect?

It is perhaps a relic of an earlier period in which the ECJ was more
cautious, and placed more emphasis on the category of agreement in
question. Thus an Association Agreement designed essentially to confer
benefits on the other party at the Community's expense should be held,

---

[60] See Maresceau, 'Bilateral Agreements', pp. 293–4.

for that very reason, to have direct effect, and so to be enforceable within the Community, even though there was no reciprocity; the ECJ accordingly rejected arguments by Member States that such an Agreement should not be enforceable in the absence of reciprocity. Similarly, agreements designed to facilitate the other party's accession to the Community should be accorded direct effect in view of the intended close relationship with that party. On the other hand, an ordinary arm's-length trade agreement with a commercial partner might not be accorded direct effect.

But such emphasis on the object and purpose of the agreement, and on the relationship between the parties, might be open to question. If the substantive provisions of the agreement purport to impose clear obligations, why should they not be enforceable in the courts of the Community and the Member States?

The recent cases before the ECJ suggest that the ECJ may be going down that route. But it would be wrong to assume too much, if only because recent cases may not be wholly representative. The recent cases have been cases in which the Agreements 'directly govern the position of individuals', and in which the fundamental principle of equal treatment, within a Member State of the EU, is at issue. It may be that material context that has led the ECJ to adopt a more positive approach to direct effect. The position might be different if the ECJ were to be confronted by a very different type of scenario, for example under a traditional trade agreement, where the issue was one of, say, the exhaustion of intellectual property rights. However, it may be that in such a case the ECJ would nonetheless accept the direct effect of the agreement but rule, if that proved appropriate, that in view of the nature of the agreement its terms could not be interpreted in accordance with the interpretation of the terms of the EC Treaty.

And similarly with interpretation. In recent cases, the ECJ's new approach to direct effect is mirrored, as we have seen, by its approach to interpretation: the ECJ is increasingly ready to apply the same interpretation as it has developed for the EC Treaty. And again the same qualification may be necessary: how far are the recent cases truly representative?

It remains to be seen, therefore, how far the new approach of the ECJ to agreements with third countries will extend; but we have certainly witnessed, in recent years, a positive evolution in that approach.

Defining competence in EU external relations: lessons from the Treaty reform process

MARISE CREMONA

2.1 Introduction: the Laeken Declaration

The Treaty establishing a Constitution for Europe signed in October 2004 proposed important substantive and institutional changes to the European Union's system of external relations, and the Treaty of Lisbon (TL) signed in December 2007 largely implements these changes in its amendments of the Treaty on European Union (TEU) and the EC Treaty (re-named the Treaty of the Functioning of the European Union).[1] The process of commenting on the drafting of both the Constitutional Treaty and the TL, discussing their implications and evaluating them has all encouraged scholars to look again at the constitutional basis for external relations law, to address some of the remaining ambiguities in the existing state of the law, and to think about the appropriate legal framework for a policy which is ever more important for the future development of the EU. Furthermore, the revised Treaty text itself reflects recent trends in external relations, in the sense of policy developments (e.g. moving forward on security and defence policy), institutional roles (e.g. the role of the European Council), as well as attempting to reflect current thinking and current case law.

In assessing the results of this reform process, the Laeken Declaration of December 2001, which mandated the Convention on the Future of

---

[1] Parts of the present chapter, in particular those which analyse the provisions of the Constitutional Treaty, are drawn from M. Cremona, 'The Union's External Action: Constitutional Perspectives', in G. Amato, H. Bribosia and B. de Witte (eds.), *Genèse et Destinée de la Constitution Européenne* (Bruxelles, Bruylant, 2007) p. 1173. In this chapter, references are made to the consolidated and re-numbered text of the Treaty of European Union and the Treaty on the Functioning of the European Union respectively. This text is available as CM7310 on http://www.fco.gov.uk/Files/kfile/FCO_PDF_CM7310_ConsolidatedTreaties.pdf. References to this text will appear as (for example) Article 40 TEU (revised); Article 218 TFEU.

Europe, still makes a good starting point.[2] Acknowledging that defining and fulfilling its role in the world is one of the key challenges facing the Union ('how to develop the Union into a stabilising factor and a model in the new, multipolar world'), meeting which will require renewal and reform, the Laeken Declaration offers three parameters which can be used to judge the success of the reform process which culminated in the revised Treaty text.

First is the need for a better division and definition of competence within the European Union (EU). This entails not only a greater transparency as to the different types of competence (exclusive and shared) but also the relationship between EU competence and Member State competence and the level at which competence should be exercised. It also requires an examination of the current organisation of competences, whether they are sufficient for the Union's tasks, and an assessment of the proper balance between the dangers of 'creeping competence' and the need to maintain dynamism.

Second, the Laeken Declaration calls for simplification of the Union's instruments in the first place, but also of the existing Treaties, and an assessment of the need to maintain the Union/Communities distinction and the pillar structure.

Third, the Laeken Declaration calls for more democracy, transparency and efficiency of the EU and its institutions. Apart from general issues concerning the efficiency of the institutions (the role of the Presidency, decision-making procedures, for example), the Laeken Declaration highlights a number of questions relevant to external policy: 'How should the coherence of European foreign policy be enhanced? How is synergy between the High Representative and the competent Commissioner to be reinforced? Should the external representation of the Union in international fora be extended further?'

All three of these Convention objectives would provide a useful angle of analysis of the external relations provisions in the TL, separately or together,[3] but for the purpose of this volume, our analysis and evaluation of the TL must necessarily be selective.[4] Here, then, we will focus on the

---

[2] Laeken Declaration on the Future of the European Union, annexed to the Presidency Conclusions, Laeken, 14 and 15 December 2001.

[3] See, for example, B. de Witte, 'Simplification and Reorganization of the European Treaties', 39 CMLRev. (2002), p. 1255.

[4] For further discussion of these issues, see inter alia M. Cremona, 'The Draft Constitutional Treaty: External Relations and External Action', 40 CMLRev. (2003), p. 1347; A. Dashwood, 'The EU

first of the three ('a better division and definition of competence'), although examining this issue will also shed some light on issues of simplification, transparency and efficiency. The definition and delimitation of competence is an aspect of external relations in which the TL has made a significant attempt to rationalise and codify existing law, including case law. It will thus allow us to reflect on the existing constitutional framework for defining competence, an issue at the heart of the Union's external relations policy, reflecting its character as a complex organisation, or system of actors, as well as the tension between the fundamental principle of attributed powers and the Union's ambition to 'assert its identity on the international scene' (existing Art. 2 TEU) and to 'uphold and promote its values' (Art. 3(5) TEU (revised)).

Laeken called for a re-evaluation of the Union's competences with an emphasis on making the division of competence between Union and Member States clearer and more transparent. It identified three sets of questions. The first refers to the need to define the different types of competence (exclusive Union competence, Member State competence, and competence shared between the Union and Member States) and to consider the basis on which it is decided at what level action should be taken. Second, whether there needs to be any reorganisation, redefinition or extension of competences. Third is the question of 'how to ensure that a redefined division of competence does not lead to a creeping expansion of the competence of the Union or to encroachment upon the exclusive areas of competence of the Member States', together with the need to ensure that the Union can maintain its dynamism and react to new developments; are the general competence provisions in Articles 95 and 308 EC adequate and appropriate for this purpose?

In applying these questions to the field of external relations (they do of course have a much wider application[5]), a number of competence-related

Constitution: What Will Really Change?', 7 *Cambridge Yearbook of European Legal Studies* (2005), p. 33; B. de Witte, 'The Constitutional Law of External Relations', in I. Pernice and M. Poiares Maduro (eds.), *A Constitution for the European Union: First Comments on the 2003 Draft of the European Convention* (Baden-Baden: Nomos, 2004); S. Griller, 'External Relations', in B. de Witte (ed.), *Ten Reflections on the Constitutional Treaty for Europe* (Florence: European University Institute, Robert Schuman Centre for Advanced Studies and Academy of European Law, 2003); M. Cremona, 'A Constitutional Basis for Effective External Action? An Assessment of the Provisions on EU External Action in the Constitutional Treaty', *EUI Working Paper*, LAW 2006/30.

[5] For an excellent discussion of competence in the Constitutional Treaty more generally, see P. Craig, 'Competence: Clarity, Conferral, Containment and Consideration', 29 ELRev. (2004), p. 323.

issues can be identified – gaps, weaknesses or ambiguities in the current state of the law – which the constitutional Convention and drafting process might have been expected to (at least partially) resolve. In what follows we will turn first to issues around the *definition* of competence: its scope, how competences might be redefined or extended, and the attempt to reconcile the principle of attributed powers with the dynamism necessary for a pro-active, policy-making, international actor. Second, we will examine the *division* of competence: the nature of competence as exclusive or shared, the relationship between Union and Member State competence, and the need to ensure coherence in the exercise of those competences whether separately or together.

2.2 A better definition of competence

2.2.1 Capacity, legal personality and competence

The ability of the EC and EU to act externally is dependent not only on the existence of specific competences granted by the Treaties explicitly or impliedly (the principle of conferred or attributed powers), but also on the capacity to act internationally, the attribute of international legal personality. As is well known, the international legal capacity of the EC was deduced by the ECJ from what is now Article 281 EC.[6] A fundamental legal weakness in building the Union's role in the world is the ambiguity surrounding the legal personality of the Union itself,[7] together with the complication of retaining a separate international legal personality for the EC. Although Article 24 TEU and the practice of the Union in concluding international agreements under this provision indicate that the Union possesses treaty-making powers, the absence of a clear statement in the Treaty gives rise to confusion and a number of unanswered questions

---

[6] 'This provision, placed at the head of Part Six of the Treaty, devoted to "general and final provisions", means that in its external relations the Community enjoys the capacity to establish contractual links with third countries over the whole field of objectives defined in Part One of the Treaty, which Part Six supplements.' Case 22–70 *Commission* v. *Council* (European Agreement on Road Transport) [1971] ECR 263, para. 14.

[7] R.A. Wessel, 'The International Legal Status of the EU', 2 EFARev. (1997), p. 109; R.A. Wessel, 'Revisiting the International Legal Status of the EU', 5 EFARev. (2000), p. 507; N. Neuwahl, 'A Partner with a Troubled Personality: EU Treaty-Making in Matters of CFSP and JHA after Amsterdam', 3 EFARev. (1998), p. 177; R. Gosalbo Bono, 'Some Reflections on the CFSP Legal Order', 43 CMLRev. (2006), pp. 354–7.

concerning the international responsibility of the Union, the TEU containing no equivalent to Article 288(2) EC. It is possible to conclude agreements that cover more than one pillar of the Union (so-called 'inter-pillar mixity'), but the limited practice to date indicates a perceived need to conclude such an agreement by way of two separate decisions.[8] Indeed, when the ECJ found that the recent agreement with the US on Passenger Name Records had been wrongly concluded on the basis of the EC Treaty, the agreement had to be renegotiated and re-concluded on the basis of the EU Treaty – requiring the US to accept not only a renegotiation of the agreement but also a change in formal treaty partner.[9]

The TL grants legal personality to the Union in Article 47 TEU revised. The separate legal identity of the EC would disappear, and it is provided that the Union will replace and succeed the EC (Art. 1 TEU revised). Legal capacity in each of the Member States is granted to the Union (Art. 335 TFEU, reflecting Article 282 EC) and there is provision for contractual and non-contractual liability of the Union (Art. 340 TFEU). The Treaty does not specify the international legal capacity of the Union, but there is every reason to suppose that Article 47 TEU revised would be interpreted to this effect by the ECJ, following the reasoning in *AETR*. Not only would this change remove the current legal uncertainties over the extent of the Union's international capacity, the international identity of the Union would be clearer, more transparent and more visible to third countries, as well as its citizens. The current gap between a legally correct adherence to the distinction between EC and EU action, and everyday speech – in which all foreign policy action is 'Union action' – would disappear, enhancing clarity.

2.2.2 The question of legal base

The creation of a legal personality for the Union, or, better, the merger of the Union and Community into one single organisation and legal person,

---

[8] The Agreement between the EU, the EC and Switzerland on the Schengen *acquis*, for example, required two separate Decisions on signature by the EU and EC respectively: one on behalf of the EC Council Decision 2004/860/EC, OJ 2004 L 370/78, and one on behalf of the EU Council Decision 2004/849/EC [sic], OJ 2004 L 368/26.

[9] Joined Cases C-317/04 *European Parliament* v. *Council*; C-318/04 *European Parliament* v. *Commission*, judgment 30 May 2006. The original agreement was based on Article 95 EC; the new agreement is based on Articles 24 and 38 TEU: Council Decision 2006/729/CFSP/JHA, OJ 2006 L 298/27.

would not remove the problems of legal base[10] and those that currently arise in an inter-pillar context from Article 47 TEU.[11] The question of characterisation of an international agreement and the legal base for its conclusion is a fundamental question in a system based on attributed powers where the existence of an appropriate legal base is a necessary basis for the existence of competence. As the ECJ stated in Opinion 2/2000:

> The choice of the appropriate legal basis has constitutional significance. Since the Community has conferred powers only, it must tie the Protocol to a Treaty provision which empowers it to approve such a measure. To proceed on an incorrect legal basis is therefore liable to invalidate the act concluding the agreement and so vitiate the Community's consent to be bound by the agreement it has signed.[12]

In addition, the choice of legal base is relevant in determining procedures to be followed (for example, the role of the European Parliament). As such, it has internal constitutional/institutional implications as well as impacting on the scope of Community competence and its nature (exclusive or shared). All this is well understood, and there is no sign that disputes about legal base are growing less frequent; on the contrary, the introduction of treaty-making power under the second and third pillars has made such debates both more likely and more complex. Further, although in earlier cases the ECJ had taken a clear view that the distribution of competence between the Community and Member States is an internal question,[13] more recently the ECJ has stated that the issue of legal

---

[10] See, for example, Opinion 2/2000 *(re Cartagena Protocol)* [2001] ECR I-9713; Case C-281/01 *Commission* v. *Council (Energy Star Agreement)* [2002] ECR I-12049; Case C-94/03 *Commission* v. *Council*, judgment 10 January 2006, all on the question of the proper use of the CCP and/or the environmental policy legal bases, see P. Koutrakos, 'Legal Basis and Delimitation of Competence', in M. Cremona and B. de Witte (eds.), *EU Foreign Relations Law: Constitutional Fundamental* (Oxford: Hart Publishing, forthcoming).

[11] Case C-176/03 *Commission* v. *Council* [2005] ECR I-7879; Case C-403/05 *European Parliament* v. *Commission*, judgment 23 October 2007; Case C-91/05 *Commission* v. *Council*, judgment 20 May 2008.

[12] Opinion 2/2000 *(re Cartagena Protocol)* [2001] ECR I-9713, para. 5.

[13] See, for example, Opinion 2/2000 *(re Cartagena Protocol)* [2001] ECR I-9713, para. 17 in which the ECJ held that the precise delimitation of powers under an agreement (once it was clear that this was a matter of shared competence) was not a question that required the preliminary Opinion procedure of Article 300(6) EC as it does not affect the issue of Community competence to conclude the agreement: 'That procedure is not intended to solve difficulties associated with implementation of an envisaged agreement which falls within shared Community and Member State competence'; also *Ruling 1/78* [1978] ECR 2151, para. 35 in which the delimitation of competence was said to be 'a domestic question'.

base should not be seen as a purely internal affair; rather, the correct legal base is important as a signal to other Contracting Parties of the extent of Community competence and the division of competence between the Community and the Member States, which, it says, is also relevant to the implementation of the agreement at Community level.[14]

If decisions as to legal base are seen as a signal to third countries, the issue of choice of legal base may become even more politicised than it is already, making it more difficult to base that choice purely on 'objective factors which are amenable to judicial review'.[15] Indeed, it is unclear what exactly these objective factors should be when the issue of legal base arises in the context of the conclusion of an international agreement: how relevant, for example, is the appropriate legal base for implementation of the agreement? It may be that a specific 'external' legal base exists for the conclusion of an agreement (as for the Common Commercial Policy (CCP)) unaffected by the question of the appropriate legal base for implementation,[16] but an 'internal' legal base can of course provide an implied basis for external action and the relationship between such external and internal legal bases is not always clear.[17] The ECJ has decided to carry over into the external relations field the approach it has adopted in relation to internal legislation, viz. that where possible a single legal base should be preferred and a multiple legal base should be seen as exceptional.[18] However, we might question whether this is an appropriate approach to the conclusion of international agreements which frequently (certainly more than most Community legislation) bring together a number of disparate objectives under an overall framework. In some cases, of course, a specific legal base exists which can bring together a number of disparate fields of action, such as that for association (Art. 310 EC) or cooperation (Art. 181a EC) but this does not always provide a solution, and will not deal with agreements that are cross-pillar in their coverage. Indeed in the case just referred to, the ECJ ultimately decided that a joint legal base was necessary for concluding the Rotterdam Convention; should this really be seen as exceptional and needing special justification (which in any event in this particular case was not clear)?

---

[14] Case C-94/03 *Commission* v. *Council*, judgment 10 January 2006, para. 55.
[15] Case C-94/03 *Commission* v. *Council*, judgment 10 January 2006, para. 34.
[16] See, for example, Opinion 1/94, para. 29.
[17] Case C-268/94 *Portugal* v. *Council* [1996] ECR I-6177, paras. 47 and 67.
[18] Case C-94/03 *Commission* v. *Council*, judgment 10 January 2006, para. 36.

The 'objective factors' decisive of legal base include, according to the ECJ, the aim and content of the measure. As far as international agreements are concerned, although strictly we are considering the legal base of the Council decision concluding the agreement, the practice has been to deduce the aim of the measure from the content of the agreement itself and thus the aim is that of the parties jointly, and not only that of the EC/EU. Advocate General Léger in the *Passenger Name Records* case, for example, took the view that the common objectives of the EC and the US as expressed in the agreement should guide the decision as to legal base, rather than any implicit unilateral objectives the EC itself might have had in concluding the agreement.[19] Does this imply that only common objectives should be considered? Would unilateral (EC/EU) objectives – which might be specific to the needs of the internal market, for example – never be relevant? Just how important should third-country objectives be to the adoption of an EC act? There is a greater need than has hitherto been recognised by the ECJ for a consideration of the specific characteristics of international agreements when it comes to establishing the criteria for choice of legal base.

We have seen here just some indication of the uncertainties surrounding legal base questions, not only the inevitable uncertainty that arises from the very existence of alternative legal bases but uncertainty as to the criteria to be applied when choosing between them. Should we have expected the revised Treaty to resolve any of these questions? The TL does not refer to the criteria for choosing legal base at all; this would be left, as now, to the jurisprudence of the ECJ, subject to the principle that both the Union (Art. 5 TEU revised; Art 7. TFEU) and the institutions (Art. 13(2) TEU revised) should act within the limits of their powers. This is surely right. At other points in the Treaty where an attempt has been made to codify case law, the results have not been a model of clarity. The lesson here is that we cannot and should not expect the Treaties to resolve all the constitutional issues; important questions such as this are rightly left open to the possibility of evolution and the important benefits of flexibility valued over a (probably unreal) certainty.

On the other hand, we can also point to perhaps unlooked-for effects of changes elsewhere. At present, as we have seen, the choice of legal base for

---

[19] Joined Cases C-317/04 *European Parliament* v. *Council*; C-318/04 *European Parliament* v. *Commission*, Opinion of Advocate General Léger, paras. 128–39.

a particular instrument is determined in part by examining its objectives.
The adoption in the TL of a single set of objectives for all external action,[20]
designed to assist in the construction of a coherent external policy across
all legal bases (internal and external) is likely to make differentiation
between legal bases more difficult. That said, some of the specific policy
provisions do contain statements of objectives. Article 206 TFEU in
relation to the CCP, for example, emphasises trade liberalisation as an
objective alongside the requirement that the Union's commercial policy
will be conducted 'in the context of' the Union's general external policy
objectives and principles. Article 208 TFEU declares that the 'primary
objective' of development cooperation is the reduction and eventual
eradication of poverty alongside a reference to the 'framework' of principles and objectives of the Union's external action. The Common Foreign
and Security Policy (CFSP) provisions, on the other hand, do not contain
a separate set of specific objectives; the current CFSP objectives have been
incorporated into the general objectives. The implications of this for
deciding whether a CFSP legal base is appropriate will be considered below.
External measures based on internal powers (such as environmental policy
or justice and home affairs) will be designed to achieve the objectives
established by the relevant provision, and at the same time are to 'respect
the principles and pursue the objectives' set out in Article 21 TEU revised.[21]
It is, however, difficult to see how a reference in an instrument to one of
the general external action objectives would assist in a decision as to legal
base, an effect that may perhaps lead to a greater emphasis on the content
of a measure.

2.2.3 The boundaries of CFSP competence

The choice of legal base has a different character where, as opposed to
choosing between different EC Treaty provisions, it is a question of choosing
between the EC Treaty and the TEU. In such cases it is truly a matter of
determining where competence properly lies. Within the EC Treaty there is
no real hierarchy of legal bases (although Art. 308 EC should only be used
where there is no other available provision[22]). As between the EC and EU
Treaties, however, a hierarchy is established by the text of the TEU itself,

---

[20] Article 21 TEU revised.   [21] Article 21(3) TEU revised.
[22] See, for example, Case 45/86 *Commission* v. *Council* [1987] ECR 1493, para. 13.

notably Articles 1, 2, 29 and 47.[23] Article 1 TEU makes it clear that 'the policies and forms of cooperation established by this Treaty' are to be seen as supplementary to the European Community, while Article 2 establishes an obligation on the Union 'to maintain in full the *acquis communautaire* and build on it' and Article 29 sets out the objectives of the third pillar which are to be pursued 'without prejudice to the powers of the European Community'. As far as establishing the boundary between the CFSP and EC external competences is concerned, however, Article 47 TEU is the key and, unlike Articles 1 and 2, is subject to the jurisdiction of the ECJ. Article 47 provides that, apart from the specific amending provisions, 'nothing in this Treaty shall affect the Treaties establishing the European Communities'. The meaning of 'affect' is ambiguous. It could be read as a conflict avoidance rule: the exercise of CFSP powers should not conflict with the EC Treaty; so in exercising their powers within the CFSP the Member States must ensure that they comply with their EC Treaty obligations. Insofar as this is an obligation on the Member States it can also be derived from Article 10 EC and is an extension of the obligation on the Member States to comply with the EC Treaty in exercising their own competences.[24] Further, Article 47 may be said to impose an obligation on the institutions of the Union when exercising their powers under the TEU. In interpreting this provision in the context of the boundary between Community competences and the third pillar, however, the ECJ has gone further; it reads Article 47 as protecting the EC sphere of competence, in a way reminiscent of *AETR*: 'It is therefore the task of the Court to ensure that acts [adopted under the third pillar] do not encroach upon the powers conferred by the EC Treaty on the Community.'[25] In *Environmental Penalties* the ECJ is more explicit in defining encroachment in terms of whether the act could

---

[23] R.A. Wessel, 'The Inside Looking Out: Consistency And Delimitation In EU External Relations', 37 CMLRev. (2000), pp. 1146–8.

[24] See, for example, Case C-124/95 *The Queen, ex parte Centro-Com Srl* v. *HM Treasury and Bank of England* [1997] ECR 81, para. 27: 'while it is for Member States to adopt measures of foreign and security policy in the exercise of their national competence, those measures must nevertheless respect the provisions adopted by the Community in the field of the common commercial policy provided for by Article 113 of the Treaty'. Cf. also Case C-307/97 *Saint-Gobain* v. *Finanzamt Aachen-Innenstadt* [1999] ECR I-6161, paras. 56–7; Case C-55/00 *Gottardo* v. *INPS* [2002] ECR I-413, para. 33.

[25] Case C-170/96 *Commission* v. *Council* [1998] ECR I-2763, para. 16. Note however that, unlike the *AETR* rule, the concept of 'affect' does not depend on the exercise of the Community powers.

have been adopted under Community powers.[26] This view of Article 47, as essentially concerned with delimiting fields of action rather than avoiding conflict, is further underlined by the ECJ's equation of Article 47 with the requirement in Article 29 TEU that third-pillar powers must be exercised 'without prejudice to the powers of the European Community'.[27] Then, in deciding whether the measure in question could have been adopted under Community powers the ECJ, basing itself on Community legal base case law, examines both the aim and the content of the measure. In a recent case on the application of Article 47 to the CFSP the Court applied this approach to the second pillar.[28] It held that the 'effect' on Community powers of a CFSP act depends on its aim and content and rejected the argument that in an area of non-pre-emptive competence such as development cooperation, where Member States can continue to act unilaterally or bilaterally or even collectively,[29] they could also choose to use a CFSP instrument as an alternative to exercising competence under a Community legal base.[30] It is 'unnecessary to examine whether the measure prevents or limits the exercise by the Community of its competences'.[31]

Unfortunately, the merging of the EC and EU in the proposed TL would not turn the issue of the boundary of CFSP competence into just another legal base question, since the Treaty seeks to retain a distinction between CFSP competence and other foreign policy competences that derive from the current EC Treaty. Different decision-making procedures apply, and the jurisdiction of the ECJ is (with exceptions) excluded. CFSP/Common Security and Defence Policy (CSDP) competence is not categorised along with other competences as exclusive, shared or supplementary, but is rather set apart within its own Treaty provisions (Art 24 TEU revised, Art 2(4) TFEU). Article 40 TEU revised is intended to safeguard this separation by providing that neither the CFSP nor other Union foreign policies should 'affect' each other. This provision will ensure that the boundary disputes that are, as we have seen, increasingly a feature of foreign relations

---

[26] Case C-176/03 *Commission* v. *Council* [2005] ECR I-7879, paras. 39–40.

[27] Case C-176/03 *Commission* v. *Council* [2005] ECR I-7879, para. 38; the ECJ here makes no distinction between the two provisions.

[28] Case C-91/05 *Commission* v. *Council*, on small arms and light weapons, judgment 20 May 2008.

[29] Case C-316/91 *European Parliament* v. *Council* (EDF) [1994] ECR I-625. Cf. Article 4(4) TFEU.

[30] See contribution by A. Dashwood in this volume, chapter 3.

[31] Case C-91/05 *Commission* v. *Council*, para. 60. The Court held that 'a measure having legal effects adopted under Title V of the EU Treaty affects the provisions of the EC Treaty within the meaning of Article 47 EU whenever it could have been adopted on the basis of the EC Treaty'.

law and practice will not disappear under the revised Treaty regime. Article 40 TEU revised differs from Article 47 TEU in that it appears to be concerned with procedural differentiation and institutional balance rather than division of competence (the CFSP and other external policies would all be *Union* competences), referring to 'the application of the procedures and the extent of the powers of the institutions ... '.[32] More significantly, the 'Chinese wall' between the CFSP and other Union policies (internal and external) is intended to protect both sides; thus it would be incompatible with Article 40 not only for a CFSP measure to encroach on another Union competence, but also if the exercise of the latter were to encroach on CFSP competences.[33] The two types of competence are given equal weight; there does not appear to be a presumption in favour of using non-CFSP powers where that is possible, whereas Article 47 TEU – as we have seen – appears to indicate that where possible an EC competence should be used. This is borne out by the fact that the revised TEU and the TFEU are to have 'the same legal value' (Art 1 TEU revised; Art 1 TFEU). However, if we look again at the scope of the CFSP as set out in the Treaty, problems arise with this 'equal weight' approach which might imply a 'centre of gravity' test.[34] The CFSP is to cover 'all areas of foreign policy and all questions relating to the Union's security';[35] taken literally, the CFSP legal base *could* be used to act in every field of external Union policy (trade, development, cooperation, humanitarian aid, etc.) and the 'equal weight' approach does not help us to decide how to tilt the balance one way or the other. We have also seen that in the revised TEU the CFSP does not have specific objectives, so the hitherto standard approach to legal base, based on aim as well as content, will have to be modified. The solution must be to treat the

---

[32] Compare Article 47 TEU: 'nothing in this Treaty shall affect the Treaties establishing the European Communities'.

[33] In *Yusuf* the CFI showed itself alert to this danger, particularly in the use of Article 308 EC: Case T-306/01 *Yusuf and Al Barakaat International Foundation*, judgment 21 September 2005, nyr, para. 156.

[34] Cf. Case C-155/91 *Commission* v. *Council* [1993] ECR I-939, paras 19–21; Case C-377/98 *Netherlands* v. *European Parliament and Council* [2001] ECR I-7079, para. 27, distinguishing between 'main object' and 'incidental effect'.

[35] Article 24(1) TEU revised. The wording is taken from the existing Treaty provisions (Art. 11(1) TEU) but the TEU does not contain a provision purporting to protect the CFSP from being 'affected' by Community action, see P. Eeckhout, *External Relations of the European Union. Legal and Constitutional Foundations* (Oxford: Oxford University Press, 2004), p. 151; M. Garbagnati Ketvel, 'The Jurisdiction of the European Court of Justice in Respect of the Common Foreign and Security Policy', 55 ICLQ (2006), pp. 84–91.

CFSP ('all areas of foreign policy') as a general competence alongside the specific competences creating distinct areas of external policy. The logic just outlined suggests that despite the apparently even-handed wording of Article 40, the current position – which prioritises Community powers – should effectively be maintained by applying the *lex generalis/lex specialis* principle: the general competence (legal base) should be used only where action under a more specific provision is not possible. Thus, the meaning attributed to 'all areas of foreign policy' in Article 24 TEU revised should (and was no doubt intended to) take account of the *acquis* relating to its scope developed under the existing TEU, a more limited field of activity than that suggested by the words themselves and linked to the current CFSP objectives set out in Article 11 TEU.[36] Only then can the presumed intention behind Article 40 – the maintenance of 'separate but equal' policy fields – be achieved. Thus, a seemingly innocuous amendment to the current provision (which is itself ambiguous), in the context of a different competence structure, does little to clarify the limits of competence and raises a number of new questions.

2.2.4 Express foreign policy competences

The Laeken Declaration posed the question whether we need more, or better defined, express competences. On one view, the addition of new external competences is scarcely necessary as, in addition to the residual provision (Art. 308 EC) which can be used where the necessary powers have not been expressly provided, the ECJ's development of the principle of implied external powers based on internal competences fills any gaps. However, although rulings that a particular action falls outside the competence of the Community altogether are rare, there are limits to both implied powers and the use of Article 308.[37] In addition, the extensive use of either implied powers or Article 308 EC, apart from lacking in transparency (it is not clear on the face of the EC Treaty exactly how far the

---

[36] A. Dashwood, 'The Law and Practice of CFSP Joint Actions', in M. Cremona and B. de Witte (eds.), *EU Foreign Relations Law: Constitutional Fundamentals* (Oxford: Hart Publishing, forthcoming).

[37] See Opinion 2/94 [1996] ECR I-1759, paras. 29–30; see also Case T-306/01 *Yusuf and Al Barakaat International Foundation*, judgment 21 September 2005, paras. 135–57; Joined Cases C-317/04 *European Parliament* v. *Council*; C-318/04 *European Parliament* v. *Commission*, judgment 30 May 2006.

Community's powers extend) may lead to the kind of 'competence creep' that Laeken pointed to as posing a legitimacy problem for the Community. Certainly, a number of new express external powers have been added to the EC Treaty during previous revisions in fields previously covered by implied powers or by the extensive use of existing express powers (such as the CCP). In this way the Member States could specify that these new competences do not exclude Member State powers.[38] As we have seen, the lack of clarity over the limits of EC external competence together with the potentially very broad treaty-making powers granted under the second and third pillars, have already produced uncertainty over the distribution of competence between the pillars.

How does the TL address these issues? One specific gap resulting from the Court's ruling in Opinion 2/94 would be remedied: under Article 6(2) TEU revised, the Union shall accede to the European Convention on Human Rights and Fundamental Freedoms (ECHR). Two points should be added. First, the Treaty provides that the Union 'shall accede' to the Convention, although it must be remembered that accession will of course depend on the agreement of existing parties, and under Article 218(8) TFEU the concluding decision, which must be adopted unanimously, will only enter into force once it has been approved by the Member States according to their respective constitutional requirements. Second, Article 6(2) provides that such accession shall not affect the Union competences as defined in the Treaties; adherence to the ECHR should not be used as a basis from which to imply an extension of Union competence into new fields.

The TL provides a partial rationalisation of existing external relations provisions which are scattered throughout the existing Treaties and are often over-complex. Most specific external relations provisions (that relating to relations with the Union's neighbours is an exception) are contained in Part V of the TFEU. The revision of the CCP provision in Art 207 TFEU is certainly welcome, especially the increased clarity as to its scope, the extension of its objectives and the greater involvement of the European Parliament in the decision-making process.[39] The provisions on

---

[38] See, for example, Articles 174(4) EC and 181 EC. It should be noted, however, that Declaration 10 attached to the TEU states that these provisions 'do not affect the principles resulting from the judgement handed down by the Court of Justice in the *AETR* case'.

[39] See contribution by P.C. Müller-Graff in this volume, Chapter 7.

a CSDP are extended, providing a basis for developing and strengthening this aspect of the CFSP and indeed defining the CSDP as a common policy for the first time, although it should be remembered that for the foreseeable future the military dimension of the CSDP will always be implemented via Member State resources and thus progress requires the ability to work flexibly through groups of willing Member States, either in specific cases or in the form of permanent structured cooperation. Under Article 214 TFEU, the Union is granted an explicit competence in the field of humanitarian aid, including competence to conclude agreements. At present, action in this area is taken on the basis of Article 308 EC and this explicit provision therefore provides greater transparency as to the Union's powers in this area as well as setting out its objectives and the principles on which it is based.

Despite these additions and revisions, however, the picture is still not complete as the external dimension of sectoral policies (agriculture, transport, environment, etc.) are not included in Part V. More important, the general approach to the TFEU, of making minimal changes to most policy sectors, has meant the retention of a number of differences when it comes to their external dimension without any very clear rationale. In relation to energy policy, for example, and transport policy (the *locus classicus* of implied external competence since *AETR*), no express provision is made for external powers.[40] In fact, transport is expressly excluded from the scope of the CCP, a not entirely logical continuation of the historical position.[41] On the other hand, in relation to environment policy,[42] and research and development,[43] also areas of shared competence, the conclusion of international agreements is expressly mentioned in the context of international cooperation. In contrast again, the provisions dealing with supporting, coordinating or complementary action, while providing for international cooperation, do not specifically mention the conclusion of international agreements.[44] However, we cannot assume

---

[40] The external dimension of energy policy is increasingly important; see for example Council Conclusions of 14 March 2006 on a New Energy Policy for Europe; 'An External Policy to Serve Europe's Energy Interests', Paper from Commission/SG/HR for the European Council, S160/06.

[41] Article 207(5) TFEU; this provision by virtue of its reference to Title VI of Part Three and Article 218 TFEU thus provides a kind of indirect legal base for agreements in the field of transport.

[42] Article 191(4) TFEU.   [43] Article 186 TFEU.

[44] See on public health Article 168(3) TFEU, on culture Article 167(3) TFEU, on education and sport Article 165(3) TFEU, and on vocational training Article 166(3) TFEU.

that the conclusion of international agreements in these areas is not in fact within Union competence: the existing Treaty provisions on which these provisions are based have provided the legal basis for agreements; for example the UNESCO Convention on the Protection and Promotion of the Diversity of Cultural Expression.[45] Such agreements, in common with secondary legislation adopted in these areas generally, would not have a pre-emptive effect and should not be used to harmonise Member States' legislation.[46] It would have been preferable to rationalise these provisions into a general clause on international cooperation within Part V. Or, indeed, they could have been omitted altogether in the light of the general competence provision in Article 216 TFEU, discussed below. The resulting piecemeal approach to these different sectoral policy areas is a consequence of the unwillingness on the part of the drafters of the TL to open up new potentially sensitive issues and the consequent retention of much of the EC Treaty virtually unchanged.

Perhaps more surprising but presumably due to the same reluctance is the absence of a systematic reference to external action in relation to the Area of Freedom, Security and Justice (AFSJ),[47] or, indeed, a separate policy Title on this field within Part V, which might have been expected given its importance. Apart from one specific provision on readmission agreements in the context of immigration policy, there is no explicit external competence granted. This omission again reflects the existing Treaty text, and we are reminded that it by no means implies an absence of competence: in Opinion 1/2003, for example, the ECJ held that the Community was *exclusively* competent to conclude the revised Lugano Convention on mutual recognition and enforcement of judgments, on the basis of Regulation 44/2001/EC and Articles 61(c) and 65 EC. There is no lacuna in the sense that Article 216 TFEU would provide the basis for external agreements in this field (alongside Art. 79(3) TFEU on readmission

---

[45] The proposal for a Decision concluding this agreement is based, inter alia, on Article 151 EC; COM(2005)678.

[46] Article 2(5) TFEU; see also Article 207(6) TFEU. Cf. Opinion 1/03, para. 132: 'If an international agreement contains provisions which presume a harmonisation of legislative or regulatory measures of the Member States in an area for which the Treaty excludes such harmonisation, the Community does not have the necessary competence to conclude that agreement. Those limits of the external competence of the Community concern the very existence of that competence and not whether or not it is exclusive.'

[47] Title V of Part Three.

agreements), but there is no real logic to the different treatment of (say) environmental policy and AFSJ.

A similar fragmentary approach is adopted towards provisions structuring the Union's relationship with different groups of third countries. Against the background of the launching of the European Neighbourhood Policy (ENP), it was decided to create a new type of agreement applicable to a specific group of third countries: the Union's neighbours. The placing of this provision in the TEU,[48] next to the provisions on Union membership, rather than in Part V of the TFEU, implies a separate kind of status for neighbouring States, rather than merely a field of external action, a status that is also separate from accession and is based on a 'special relationship', 'close and peaceful relations', 'prosperity and good-neighbourliness', and the 'values of the Union'. Are agreements with the neighbours seen as part of Union foreign policy or as something different? Other special relationships with the Union include the Associated Countries and Territories (Part IV, Arts. 198–204 TFEU) and more general association (Part V, Art. 217 TFEU). These relationships are distinct from economic, financial and technical cooperation, development cooperation and the CCP, which each has its own provision in Part V. The TL thus perpetuates and even extends a tendency to define new legal bases for different categories of relationship. Although it could be argued that the creation of new forms of agreement and differentiated status enhance the ability of the Union to fine-tune its relationships with key groups of third countries, on balance this is outweighed by the lack of clarity as to what exactly the differences entail, exacerbated by the fact that they are to be found in different places in the Treaties and potential issues of appropriate legal base.

2.2.5 Implied external competences

The existence of implied external competence is of course well established by the case law of the ECJ,[49] although its precise extent, and the extent to which implied competences are exclusive, are still the subject of both academic discussion, institutional debate and new case law. Let us take

---

[48] Article 8 TEU revised.
[49] A. Dashwood and J. Heliskoski, 'The Classic Authorities Revisited', in A. Dashwood and C. Hillion (eds.), *The General Law of EC External Relations* (London: Sweet & Maxwell, 2000).

just two examples raised by recent case law: how exactly are internal Treaty objectives to be translated into the external sphere? And to what extent may general legislative provisions such as Articles 95 and 308 EC provide the (implied) basis for external action?

Opinion 1/2003[50] confirmed the existence (and exclusivity) of Community competence to conclude the Lugano Convention, an agreement within a relatively new field of action for the Community (judicial cooperation in civil matters) about which there are differing views among the Member States on the scope and nature of the Community's external powers.[51] The ECJ starts its Opinion by summarising earlier case law on the existence of implied powers:

> The competence of the Community to conclude international agreements may arise not only from an express conferment by the Treaty but may equally flow implicitly from other provisions of the Treaty and from measures adopted, within the framework of those provisions, by the Community institutions (see *ERTA*, paragraph 16). The Court has also held that whenever Community law created for those institutions powers within its internal system for the purpose of attaining a specific objective, the Community had authority to undertake international commitments necessary for the attainment of that objective even in the absence of an express provision to that effect (Opinion 1/76, paragraph 3, and Opinion 2/91, paragraph 7). That competence of the Community may be exclusive or shared with the Member States.[52]

The ECJ here mentions the two traditional bases for implied powers: first, the existence of Community legislation, 'Community rules' whether or not adopted within the framework of a common policy;[53] and second, the existence of a Community objective for the attainment of which Treaty-based internal powers may be complemented by external powers. The first basis for implied powers is founded on pre-emption, the occupation of the field by existing Community law (hence the equation in *AETR* between the existence of the competence and its exclusive nature); the second is based on the principle of *effet utile*, the implication of powers necessary to achieve an expressly defined objective. In Opinion 1/2003 itself, the ECJ

---

[50] Opinion 1/03 of 7 February 2006 on the competence of the Community to conclude the new Lugano Convention on jurisdiction and the recognition and enforcement of judgments in civil and commercial matters, nyr.

[51] Opinion 1/03, para. 28.   [52] Opinion 1/03, paras. 114–15.

[53] Case 22/70 *Commission* v. *Council (AETR)* [1971] ECR 263; Opinion 2/91 [1993] ECR I-1061.

spends little time on the existence of the implied competence, appearing to base it on the existence of (internal) Community legislation, viz. the Regulations on jurisdiction and the recognition and enforcement of judgments in civil and commercial matters.[54] Questions as to the scope, nature and content (and future development) of those rules are regarded as relevant to the issue of exclusivity not to the existence of competence,[55] with one exception: where the Treaty base for the internal legislation excludes harmonisation (for example, Art. 152(4)(c) EC on public health or Art. 151(5) EC on culture) the Community will lack competence to conclude an international agreement encompassing harmonisation.[56]

In striking contrast, the alternative basis for implied powers, not further discussed in Opinion 1/2003, does, however, require attention to be paid to the nature and content of internal rules, and in particular Treaty provisions, in order to identify the 'specific objective' for which internal powers have been granted but for which external powers may be necessary. The importance of that objective, as well as the mere existence of the internal powers, was underlined in Opinion 1/94. In that ruling the ECJ defined the Treaty provisions on services as being essentially concerned with its internal market objective: the liberalisation of services within the Community, rather than services liberalisation *tout court*. This certainly appears to be consistent with Article 49 EC and explains why it was necessary to include express provision for agreements on services within Article 133 insofar as those agreements seek (for example) to promote liberalisation of services outside the internal market. In some cases (intellectual property rights, taxation, establishment of companies, air transport services) a similar link to the completion or functioning of the internal market will be necessary. In other cases (capital movements, for example) the EC Treaty includes external as well as internal objectives; or (social policy, for example) the extent of the Treaty objective is not so clear; or (energy policy, for example) the link between pursuing an external policy and its impact on the internal Community regime is so close that it is difficult to disentangle the two.

The emphasis on Treaty objectives is certainly a logical consequence of applying an *effet utile* principle; as we have seen, Opinion 1/2003 suggests

---

[54] Opinion 1/03, para. 134.   [55] Opinion 1/03, paras. 126–7.
[56] Opinion 1/03, para. 132, see n. 46.

that it does not play a central role where the basis for external competence is simply the existence of internal rules. The fact that Article 65 EC, the legal base for the internal rules in that instance, requires measures to be 'necessary for the proper functioning of the internal market' was held to be irrelevant to determining implied external powers in the field.[57] The two alternative bases for implied powers thus may attach very different significance to the objectives of the relevant Treaty provisions, something which is implicit in the case law but not explicitly explained or justified. A justification may be found in the fact that where the external power is based on internal legislation, that legislation itself will reflect the objectives of its legal base. The result, in either case, is that implied external powers are inherently (and properly) limited and cannot provide the basis for developing an external policy independent of the needs and functioning of the internal regime. For that, under the current Treaty system, explicit powers are needed (such as are granted in fields such as trade, development cooperation or environmental policy). This is coherent in terms of the balance between the necessary flexibility of an implied powers doctrine and the need to ensure compliance with the principle of conferred powers. It does, however, make it difficult to establish a coherent external dimension to the internal market regime as a whole.

Internal market objectives also provide the basis for the more general internal legislative competences, Articles 95 and 308 EC. The limits to Article 308 as a basis for implied external powers were illustrated in both Opinion 1/94 and Opinion 2/94. In the latter ruling in particular, the ECJ held that Article 308:

> being an integral part of an institutional system based on the principle of conferred powers, cannot serve as a basis for widening the scope of Community powers beyond the general framework created by the provisions of the Treaty as a whole and, in particular, by those that define the tasks and the activities of the Community. On any view, Article 235 [now 308] cannot be used as a basis for the adoption of provisions whose effect would, in substance, be to amend the Treaty without following the procedure which it provides for that purpose.[58]

---

[57] Opinion 1/03, para. 131. The Court here is referring to the exclusive nature of those powers, rather than their existence; however, it had already found external competence to be validly based on the internal rules and thus indirectly on Article 65 EC.

[58] Opinion 2/94, para. 30.

In *Yusuf*, the Court of First Instance (CFI) refused to allow Article 308 to stand alone as a Treaty basis for action designed to achieve foreign policy objectives which were essentially those of the Union (CFSP) rather than the Community (at least as expressed in the EC Treaty).[59] The Court considered, but was not convinced by, arguments seeking to show that the functioning of the internal market required action at Community level. Arguments based on internal market needs were put forward, and considered by the Advocate General in the *PNR* case,[60] but were not touched on by the ECJ. The ECJ appears to have regarded the annulment of the Commission's 'adequacy decision' based on the Data Protection Directive, which allegedly formed a prior condition for the agreement between the EC and the US, as fatal to the Council decision concluding the agreement itself. The ECJ's reasoning is brief and ambiguous:

> Article 95 EC, read in conjunction with Article 25 of the Directive, cannot justify Community competence to conclude the Agreement. The Agreement relates to the same transfer of data as the decision on adequacy and therefore to data processing operations which, as has been stated above, are excluded from the scope of the Directive. Consequently, [Council] Decision 2004/496 cannot have been validly adopted on the basis of Article 95 EC.[61]

The adequacy decision was linked to the Data Protection Directive and so a finding that the data transfer covered by the decision fell outside the scope of the Directive was fatal to the adequacy decision. However, it could have been argued that the agreement itself, once it was held to fall outside the scope of the Directive, did not require a prior adequacy decision and could have been based on Article 95 in its own right independently of the Data Protection Directive, on the grounds that it was necessary to achieve a Community objective.[62] The ECJ does not consider

---

[59] Case T-306/01 *Yusuf and Al Barakaat International Foundation*, judgment 21 September 2005, paras. 135–57. The objections disappeared when Article 308 was considered in conjunction with the express provisions on economic sanctions (Articles 60(1) and 301 EC), which did not, however, in themselves cover the case at issue.

[60] Joined Cases C-317/04 and C-318/04 *European Parliament* v. *Council, European Parliament* v. *Commission* (PNR), Opinion of Advocate General Léger 22 November 2005, judgment 30 May 2006.

[61] *Ibid.*, paras. 67–9.

[62] The Council's Decision concluding the agreement refers only to Article 95 and mentions neither the Data Protection Directive nor the adequacy decision in its Preamble: Council Decision 2004/496/EC OJ 2004 L 183/83.

this option (it was not the basis of the Council's submissions) but appears to assume that the agreement could only have been based on Article 95 via the Directive. In other words, the judgment seems to imply that Article 95 can only be used as the basis for implied powers in a case where there is existing Community legislation. It is not clear whether this more general conclusion should in fact be drawn from the judgment or whether the ECJ merely took the view that Article 95 as an 'autonomous' legal base could not be argued in this particular case. Were it to have considered this possibility it might well have concluded that the agreement's security and criminal law enforcement objectives took it outside the scope of Article 95 EC, but it would have been interesting to explore the use of Article 95 in a case where internal market objectives exist side by side with objectives that seem to take the agreement not only outside the scope of Article 95 but outside the EC Treaty altogether.[63] Aspects of this issue have already been touched on above.[64]

We have here only illustrated some of the ambiguities that we meet when attempting to define the scope of implied external competence, even (or especially) in the light of recent case law. Would the TL clarify the position? We have already considered some of the implications of the introduction of general external objectives in the context of choice of legal base and it has emerged from the discussion of implied powers that Treaty objectives are central to identifying their scope. Despite the addition of a few new express external powers, implied powers will remain important under the Treaty of Lisbon. Indeed, they may be said to have been 'constitutionalised' by the addition of a non-specific treaty-making competence for the Union:

> The Union may conclude an agreement with one or more third countries or international organisations where the Treaties so provide or where the conclusion of an agreement is necessary in order to achieve, within the framework of the Union's policies, one of the objectives referred to in the Treaties, or is provided for in a legally binding act of the Union or is likely to affect common rules or alter their scope.[65]

---

[63] Cf. Joined Cases C-317/04 and C-318/04 *European Parliament* v. *Council*; *European Parliament* v. *Commission* (PNR), judgment 30 May 2006, para. 54. In the event, the decision concluding the new agreement is based on Articles 24 and 38 TEU: Council Decision 2006/729/CFSP/JHA OJ 2006 L 298/27.

[64] See text n. 19.   [65] Article 216 (1) TFEU.

The aim of this provision – inserting an unequivocal statement of the existence of treaty-making competence even in cases where the Treaty does not expressly confer such powers – is to increase certainty, and – by setting out the conditions under which such powers arise – to achieve a clearer definition of competence. Difficulties emerge however in the attempt to reflect the case law on this issue – case law which is, as we have seen, complex and sometimes obscure. Three alternative conditions are included, alongside the express provision of competence. According to the first of these, external powers exist 'where the conclusion of an agreement is necessary in order to achieve, within the framework of the Union's policies, one of the objectives referred to in the Treaties'. Now this seems on its face to establish a potentially wider basis for implied powers than hitherto. No longer is there a need for the agreement to be necessary to achieve an objective for which internal powers have been provided (and which is therefore likely, though not inevitably, to be internal in orientation); all that is needed is for the objective to be referred to in the Treaties (which would include the very widely-drawn general external objectives of Article 21 TEU revised), and for the action to take place 'within the framework of the Union's policies'. Thus, external action in the context of the Area of Freedom, Security and Justice, including immigration policy, could be deemed necessary not only for internal market objectives but also in order to safeguard the security of the Union (Article 21(2)(a) TEU revised) or to 'assist populations, countries and regions confronting natural or man-made disasters' (Article 21(2)(g) TEU revised). Article 216(1) might be interpreted more restrictively, to require a closer link between the objective and the policy field, but this is not required by the text. It is also worth noting in this context that the residual powers provision (Article 352 TFEU) also reflects this choice of wording, having removed the requirement of a connection with the common market currently in Article 308 EC.[66] Although Article 352(4) excludes the use of this provision 'for attaining objectives pertaining to the common foreign and security policy', it is not clear which of these general external objectives are CFSP-specific, nor whether the phrase 'within the framework of the policies defined by the Treaties' in Article 352 could be said to

---

[66] Article 216 TFEU provides that action may be taken 'If action by the Union should prove necessary, within the framework of the policies defined by the Treaties, to attain one of the objectives set out in the Treaties, and the Treaties have not provided the necessary powers.'

refer to external policy generally or whether it would be necessary to argue that action was being taken within one of the more specific (non-CFSP) external or internal policy fields.[67] Given the breadth of the objectives defined in Articles 3(5) and 21(2) TEU revised, the former approach would give the Union potentially very wide-ranging external powers. Despite, therefore, the Laeken aim of delimiting the Union's powers more closely, and despite the strengthening of the principle of conferred powers by an express provision that 'competences not conferred upon the Union in the Treaties remain with the Member States' (Article 4(1) TEU revised), the TL has extended the possibilities for the use of implied and residual powers by loosening the link between 'internal' objectives and external action.

Second, it clearly makes sense for the Article on general treaty-making competence to provide that a legally binding Union act may provide for the conclusion of an international agreement. This provision is intended to reflect ECJ case law[68] and, although it does not give any guidance as to the limits of the competence potentially conferred by a legally binding act, commentators argue, surely correctly, that this provision cannot be seen as granting the legislature *carte blanche* to authorise external competence.[69] The principle of conferred powers would require that the agreement facilitates a Union objective as well as the existence of a link between the legal base of the competence-conferring act of secondary legislation and the scope of the envisaged agreement. The existence of an internal act will ensure that the international agreement has an appropriate legal base in the Treaties.

---

[67] Article 308 EC requires action to be 'necessary to attain, in the course of the operation of the common market, one of the objectives of the Community'. The sometimes strained link between external action and the operation of the common market will be less in evidence under Article 352 TFEU, containing as it does a reference to all substantive policy areas, including external action in Part V TFEU. It should be mentioned here, however, that in Opinion 2/94 the Court itself seems to abandon the link to the common market: 'Article 235 is designed to fill the gap where no specific provisions of the Treaty confer on the Community institutions express or implied powers to act, if such powers appear none the less to be necessary to enable the Community to carry out its functions with a view to attaining one of the objectives laid down by the Treaty' (para. 29).

[68] See Opinion 1/94.

[69] A. Hable, 'The European Constitution: Changes in the Reform of Competences with a Particular Focus on the External Dimension', *Europa-Institut Wirtschaftsuniversität Wien Working Paper* No. 67, 2005; S. Griller, 'External Action: Towards More Efficiency, Coherence and Clarity?', lecture at University of London, 10 February 2005.

However, the third possible basis for action is more problematic. Article 216(1) goes on to provide for competence to conclude an international agreement 'where the conclusion of an agreement ... is likely to affect common rules or alter their scope'. The purpose of this provision is not clear. It is clearly derived from the *AETR* line of jurisprudence, which relates to exclusive implied competence, although it omits the reference to exclusivity found in the context of similar wording in Article 3(2) TFEU. It is likely that this phrase is in fact intended to reflect case law derived from *AETR*, which bases implied external competence on the existence of a body of (internal) Community legislation in the field, but without any reference to 'effects'. This approach, already discussed above, is expressed by the ECJ in Opinion 1/2003:

> The competence of the Community to conclude international agreements ... may equally flow implicitly ... from measures adopted, within the framework of those provisions, by the Community institutions (see *ERTA*, paragraph 16).[70]

In fact, I would argue, this basis for competence to conclude an agreement is unnecessary: it is difficult to conceive of a situation where an agreement should be concluded *by the Union* because it is 'likely to affect common rules or alter their scope', but on the other hand that agreement is not 'necessary in order to achieve, within the framework of the Union's policies, one of the objectives referred to in the Treaties'. Why, then, the need for this reference to effects? Worse, it introduces confusion between the existence of competence and exclusivity, between the scope and the nature (exclusive or shared) of Union competence although elsewhere in the Treaties this distinction is carefully drawn. In Opinion 1/2003, as we have seen, the ECJ makes a point of distinguishing between the existence of implied competence and its exclusive or shared character.[71] The effects-based case law is discussed in the context of exclusivity, not in the context of (implied) competence per se which, as the ECJ says, may be shared or exclusive.[72] Thus, the 'effects' condition is essentially concerned with exclusivity – and exclusivity, as its name suggests, is about excluding the power of the Member States to act in a field. Article 216(1) cannot be read

---

[70] Opinion 1/2003, para. 114.　　　[71] Opinion 1 2003, paras. 114–15.

[72] For another recent example of the Court's insistence on the difference between the existence or attribution of competence and its nature (shared or exclusive), see C-459/03 *Commission* v. *Ireland*, judgment 30 May 2006, nyr, para. 93.

as conferring an exclusive competence whenever it applies. In the following section we will see that the confusion between the conditions for the existence of competence and the conditions under which it may become exclusive is exacerbated by the close similarity between the wording of Article 216 and that of Article 3(2) TFEU.

2.3 A better division of competence

2.3.1 Exclusive and shared competence

The Laeken Declaration asks a number of questions about making the division of competence more transparent: 'Can we thus make a clearer distinction between three types of competence: the exclusive competence of the Union, the competence of the Member States and the shared competence of the Union and the Member States?' The Treaties at present have no general statement categorising competences in this way, and the characteristics of exclusive Community competence have been developed by the ECJ. Certainly, since the Single European Act, many new competences have been specifically stated to be 'without prejudice to the Member States' competence' to conclude international agreements,[73] but no Treaty article at present declares any competence to be exclusive except by implication.[74] Within the field of external relations, the conditions under which exclusive competence arises, especially within implied powers, and the implications of exercising shared competence, are the subject of ongoing debate and continuing litigation. Recent case law has emphasised a rationale for exclusivity based on the need 'to ensure a uniform and consistent application of the Community rules and the proper functioning of the system which they establish in order to preserve the full effectiveness of Community law'.[75] Such a rationale founded on the unity of the Community legal order and the uniform application of Community law is behind the exclusivity of CCP powers,[76] as well as

---

[73] See, for example, Article 174(4) EC on environmental policy and Article 181 EC on development cooperation.

[74] For example, Articles 23 and 26 EC on the common customs tariff.

[75] Opinion 1/03, para. 128.

[76] Opinion 1/75/EEC (OECD agreement on a local cost standard) [1975] ECR 1355, see M. Cremona, 'The External Dimension of the Single Market: Building (on) the Foundations' in C. Barnard and J. Scott (eds.), *The Law of the Single European Market: Unpacking the Premises* (Oxford: Hart Publishing, 2002).

forming the basis of implied exclusive competence. In the latter context this is expressed in terms of the possibility that an external agreement, if concluded by the Member State(s), would 'affect' Community rules. For this effect to take place, an actual conflict between rules is not necessary.[77] Rather, it must be shown that the agreement covers a field that is within the scope of common Community rules, or within an area that is already largely covered by such rules; its effect must then be judged by examining the nature and content of both the terms of the agreement and of the Community measures.[78]

The TL attempts to codify these rules and its text is interesting for precisely that purpose – as a restatement of what was perceived by the drafters to be the current state of the law, with some specificities such as the treatment of the CFSP. First, it establishes different categories of competence: exclusive, shared and complementary or supporting (Art. 2 TFEU). Certain competences are allocated to the exclusive and to the complementary categories; all others are declared to be shared.[79] The list of complementary competences does not include any specifically external relations fields of activity but of course the external dimensions of health, culture, tourism and education may well be important. Exclusive competences include the customs union and the CCP,[80] and other fields that

---

[77] C-476/98 *Commission* v. *Germany (open skies)* [2002] ECR I-9855, para. 108; Opinion 1/03, para. 129.

[78] In some cases, the nature of the Community rules is such that any agreement will have an 'effect' on them: such is the case where they expressly provide for the treatment of third-country nationals: Opinion 1/94, para. 95; Opinion 2/92, para. 33; C-476/98 *Commission* v. *Germany*, para. 109; or where a particular issue is completely harmonised: Opinion 1/94, para. 96; Opinion 2/92, para. 33; C-476/98, *Commission* v. *Germany*, para. 110. In other cases, no such effect will be found, such as where both agreement and Community rules provide for minimum harmonisation: Opinion 2/91, para. 18; or where any distortions caused by bilateral Member State agreement could be rectified by autonomous Community action: C-476/98 *Commission* v. *Germany*, paras. 111–12. In any case, a close examination of the agreement and its potential effects will be necessary: 'the Community enjoys only conferred powers and that, accordingly, any competence, especially where it is exclusive and not expressly conferred by the Treaty, must have its basis in conclusions drawn from a specific analysis of the relationship between the agreement envisaged and the Community law in force and from which it is clear that the conclusion of such an agreement is capable of affecting the Community rules', Opinion 1/2003, para. 124.

[79] For the status of CFSP competence, see Section 2.3.2.

[80] The Treaty thus simplifies the current position with respect to the CCP, which is partially exclusive competence but with exceptions in relation to services and intellectual property, in respect of which it is not clear to what extent pre-emption might apply: see, for example, M. Cremona, 'A Policy of Bits and Pieces? The Common Commercial Policy After Nice', 4

have an actual or potential external dimension, such as conservation of marine biological resources and competition policy.

This *a priori* or constitutional exclusivity, where the Member States are as such precluded from acting, is different from pre-emption which applies in the case of shared competence: 'Member States shall exercise their competence to the extent that the Union has not exercised its competence, [or has] decided to cease exercising its competence' (Art. 2(2) TFEU). The distinction is a useful one which is not always brought out clearly in the case law.[81] As the passage just quoted demonstrates, pre-emption depends on Community action, and although the exercise of shared competence may pre-empt Member States' action, the right to exercise their competence may also be 'returned' to the Member States, at least in theory. However, the Treaty then unfortunately muddies this distinction by including, in the category of exclusive competence, following the list of a priori exclusive competences, an attempted synthesis of the case law of the ECJ on exclusive implied external competence, which, as we have seen, is based essentially on the existence of Community rules, that is pre-emption. Article 3(2) provides:

> The Union shall also have exclusive competence for the conclusion of an international agreement when its conclusion is provided for in a legislative act of the Union or is necessary to enable the Union to exercise its internal competence, or insofar as its conclusion may affect common rules or alter their scope.

Not only does this provision fail to distinguish between *a priori* exclusivity and pre-emptive exclusivity (or pre-emption), it also conflates the two separate questions of the existence of implied external competence and the exclusivity of that competence. Dashwood has argued convincingly that this provision is unnecessary as the pre-emptive exclusivity described here is already implicit in the principle of loyal cooperation found in Article 4(3) TEU revised – and indeed in the definition of shared competence in

Cambridge Yearbook of European Legal Studies (2001), p. 61; H. G. Krenzler and C. Pitschas, 'Progress or Stagnation? The Common Commercial Policy after Nice', 6 EFARev. (2001), p. 291; C. Herrmann, 'Common Commercial Policy after Nice: Sisyphus would have done a better job', 39 CMLRev. (2002), p. 7.

[81] See R. Schütze, 'Dual Federalism constitutionalised: the emergence of exclusive competences in the EC legal order', 32 ELRev. (2007), p. 3.

Article 2(2) TFEU.[82] Schütze takes the view that 'from a constitutional perspective, the "self-entitlement clause" of Article 3(2) TFEU is anathema to the very purpose of searching for a "better division and definition of competence in the European Union"'.[83] Article 3(2) does not make any reference to Article 216(1) TFEU (which constitutionalises the idea of implied powers) and yet they are clearly connected. In fact, the almost identical wording of the phrases in Article 3(2) and Article 216(1) TFEU suggests that implied *shared* competence would disappear, that all 'implied' competence, as defined in Article 216(1), would be exclusive, as defined in Article 3(2).[84] Such a reading is hard to defend in terms of outcome. It would entail a potentially large expansion of exclusive competence if it were no longer possible for the Union to exercise non-exclusive competence in fields where there is otherwise no express treaty-making power, including many areas of shared and complementary competence such as justice and home affairs, culture and public health. Given the ECJ's clear affirmation that implied powers may be either shared or exclusive, it is a wholly undesirable departure from that case law to insist that, except where the Treaty expressly provides for shared competence (for example, environmental policy or development cooperation), the Union must have either no competence at all or exclusive competence. Although exclusive competence is necessary in some external policy situations, it does not need to be the norm.

This is not the place to rehearse the legal implications of the exercise of shared competence through mixed agreements, both within the Community legal order and with respect to international responsibility of the Community and the Member States.[85] There is no doubt that in terms of the division of competence between Community and Member States, these are areas of law that still raise many questions.[86] From the perspective

---

[82] A. Dashwood, 'The Relationship between the Member States and the European Union/ European Community', 41 CMLRev. (2004), pp. 372–3.

[83] R. Schütze, 'Dual Federalism'.

[84] In fact, despite the similarity in wording between Article 3(2) and Article 216(1), they nevertheless contain several significant differences; for a discussion of these differences and their significance, see M. Cremona, 'The Union's External Action: Constitutional Perspectives'.

[85] A. Rosas, 'The European Union and Mixed Agreements', in A. Dashwood and C. Hillion (eds.), *The General Law of EC External Relations* (London: Sweet & Maxwell, 2000); J. Heliskoski, *Mixed Agreements as a Technique for Organizing the International Relations of the European Community and its Member States* (The Hague: Kluwer, 2001).

[86] See further the reports of both P. Eeckhout, General Rapporteur, and M. Cremona, Community Rapporteur: in *External Relations of the EU and the Member States: Competence,*

of the TL, the absence of any mention of mixed agreements, either in the provision dealing with the negotiation and conclusion of agreements (Art. 217 TFEU), or in any other provision, is noticeable. The fact that a high proportion of the most important external agreements are mixed is simply ignored. Certainly, the principles underlying the Community/Union law obligations of the Member States and the institutions in the context of mixed agreements are derived from general principles which appear in the Treaty, in particular the 'loyalty clause' or principle of sincere cooperation (Art. 4(3) TEU revised). The clearer articulation of the Union's policy goals, principles and objectives in the TL also establishes normative parameters within which both Union and Member States should exercise shared competence and would thus provide a better basis for coherent policy-making. It might also be argued that the Treaties are not there to provide certainty and legal security to third countries. Nevertheless, some recognition of the phenomenon, especially at the procedural level, would have assisted transparency.

2.3.2 CFSP competence and Members States' powers

In considering the division of competence between Union and Member States as regards the CFSP, the Constitutional Treaty created obscurity rather than clarity. Elsewhere, problems may arise from a perhaps over-zealous attempt to codify case law. Here, there is no case law, and fundamental questions about the nature of competence were left unanswered, to be guessed at by reading between the lines, extrapolating from the current position and taking political reality into account. The TL, by maintaining the separation between the TEU and the EC Treaty/TFEU and by allocating the CFSP to the TEU, has clarified the position to some extent. Of course it is true that the existing TEU does not specify the nature of CFSP competence either, and some commentators have even drawn the conclusion that there is no 'CFSP competence' as such belonging to the Union but only the exercise, within a Union framework, of their own competence by the Member States.[87] Others emphasise the

---

Mixed Agreements, International Responsibility and the Effects of International Law, Proceedings of the 22nd FIDE Congress, 2006.

[87] See authors and case law cited by C. Herrmann, 'Much Ado About Pluto? The Unity of the Legal Order of the European Union Revisited', in M. Cremona and B. de Witte, *EU Foreign Relations Law – Constitutional Fundamentals* (Oxford: Hart Publishing, forthcoming).

unity of the Union (Union/Community) legal system, the autonomy of the Union with respect to its Member States and its international capacity and competences.[88] Denza has pointed out that 'as the intergovernmental pillars have evolved they have developed in some ways into law-making bodies having the advantages of both the European Community and the international legal orders'.[89] The Union is certainly an organisation with its own law-making and treaty-making competences which may be said to be becoming 'a new legal order of international law'[90] although without all the characteristics of the Community legal order, in particular the characteristics of pre-emption, direct effect and primacy within the domestic legal orders of the Member States.[91] The Union and its lawyers have lived with this ambiguity about the nature of Union competence without it resulting in real problems. Why then did the silence of the Constitutional Treaty create new difficulties? The difference here is that CFSP competence was put alongside the old Community competences, certain characteristics of those competences were made more explicit (in particular primacy) and we were told that the Union 'shall exercise on a Community basis the competences [the Member States] confer on it'[92] with no word about whether the CFSP competence should be differentiated and, if so, how.

The TL, in contrast to the Constitutional Treaty, emphasises the distinctive nature of the CFSP in a number of ways: it is dealt with in Title V of the TEU (as revised), and thus set apart from other fields of external competence which are found in Part V of the TFEU; according to Article 24(1) TEU revised, the CFSP 'is subject to specific rules and procedures', including the role of the European Council and the High Representative of the Union for Foreign Affairs and Security Policy, the exclusion of

---

[88] A. von Bogdandy, 'The legal case for unity: The European Union as a single organization with a single legal system', 36 CMLRev. (1999), pp. 894–5; R.A. Wessel, 'The Inside Looking Out: Consistency and Delimitation in EU External Relations', 37 CMLRev. (2000), pp. 1138–45.

[89] E. Denza, *The Intergovernmental Pillars of the European Union* (Oxford: Oxford University Press, 2002), p. 20.

[90] Cf. Case 26/62 *NV Algemene Transport en Expeditie Onderneming van Gend & Loos* v. *Netherlands Inland Revenue Administration*; R. Gosalbo Bono, 'Some Reflections on the CFSP Legal Order', 43 CMLRev. (2006), p. 337.

[91] Although Case C-105/03 *Pupino* [2005] ECR I-5285 illustrates that some at least of the principles developed within the Community legal order may also apply within the Union legal order (in this case, the third pillar).

[92] Article I-1 CT.

legislative acts, and the exclusion (with important exceptions) of the jurisdiction of the ECJ; the flexibility clause (Article 352) does not apply to the CFSP. The role of the Member States is emphasised: they are to 'put into effect' the CFSP, alongside the High Representative (Article 24(1) TEU revised). However the revised Treaties leave unspecified how the exercise of CFSP competence affects Member States' powers: CFSP competence is separated from the three general categories of competence (exclusive, shared and supporting or complementary) in Article 2 TFEU without including any indication as to what form of competence this might be. Supporting, coordinating and supplementing competences are exhaustively listed in Article 6 TFEU and do not include the CFSP; in any event this type of competence is not really apt to describe what is intended to be a distinctive Union policy field. Article 4(1) TFEU states 'The Union shall share competence with the Member States where the Treaties confer on it a competence which does not relate to the areas referred to in Articles 3 [exclusive] and 6 [complementary].' Shared competence is thus the residual category, and nothing is said to exclude the CFSP: on the face of it therefore the CFSP might be said to fall within shared competence. However, shared competence is subject to pre-emption, with certain exceptions (including development, cooperation and humanitarian aid,[93] but with no mention of the CFSP) and it is clear that the drafters did not intend to extend pre-emption to the CFSP. Declarations 30 and 31 to the TL both affirm that the CFSP will not affect the responsibilities of the Member States for the formulation and conduct of their foreign policy, a statement which is intended to reinforce the presumption that pre-emption will not apply to the CFSP (especially since the ECJ would not have jurisdiction to determine the precise extent of that pre-emption in a specific case). Although, therefore, it is logically difficult to imagine a type of competence that is neither exclusive, nor shared nor complementary, the CFSP appears to be a type of *sui generis* competence that shares characteristics of both shared and complementary competences.

In considering the definition of CFSP competence and the division of competence between the Union and the Member States, it is not only pre-emption that is at issue, but also the effect that CFSP measures have within Member States' domestic legal orders, and to what extent they may take priority over conflicting national law. The Constitutional Treaty expressly

---

[93] Article 4(4) TFEU.

included the principle of primacy (Article I-6 CT) although it did not specify exactly what was meant by primacy,[94] and it was not clear whether Article I-6 was intended to apply to the CFSP.[95] The removal of this explicit Treaty provision was one of changes stipulated in the mandate given to the IGC prior to the negotiation of the TL in order to emphasise the non-'constitutional character' of the two revised Treaties.[96] Instead, we have a Declaration (No. 17) re-affirming 'well settled case law' of the ECJ on primacy, but of course existing case law has nothing to say about primacy in relation to the CFSP. Primacy and direct effect are closely linked in that primacy, in the *Simmenthal* sense, operates to require national courts to give effect to directly effective Community law; it is thus hard to see how primacy might be applied in the absence of direct effect. The Treaties being silent on direct effect it is, as now, an attribute conferred by interpretation by the ECJ. However the Court has no jurisdiction over the CFSP, and so prima facie there is no context in which the Court would have the opportunity to declare a CFSP act directly effective and thus (potentially) having primacy over conflicting domestic legislation.

In the absence of enforceable primacy, and direct application of CFSP acts within domestic legal orders, the binding nature of those acts on the Member States becomes critically important. It should be remembered that in excluding the Court's jurisdiction (with some exceptions) from the CFSP, not only is the possibility of preliminary rulings from Member State courts excluded but also the possibility of Commission enforcement actions. In addition to the general statement in Article 4(3) TEU revised,

---

[94] 'The more I think about that provision, the harder I find it to give a precise meaning to the principle of primacy, taken out of its context in the case law', A. Dashwood, 'The Relationship between the Member States and the European Union/European Community', 41 CMLRev. (2004), p. 379. Within the Community legal order, primacy has developed a strong meaning requiring national courts to disapply conflicting national law: Case 106/77 *Simmenthal* [1978] ECR 629; C-213/89 *R* v *Secretary of State for Transport ex parte Factortame* [1990] ECR I-2433. This may be distinguished from the status of international law generally, which, although it regards itself as hierarchically superior to domestic law, does not impose on the domestic legal order the means by which compliance is achieved: E. Denza, 'Lines in the Sand: Between Common Foreign Policy and Single Foreign Policy', in T. Tridimas and P. Nebbia (eds.), *European Union Law for the Twenty-first Century* (Oxford: Hart Publishing, 2004), p. 268.

[95] For contrasting views see E. Denza, previous note, pp. 267–8; Editorial comment, 42 CMLRev. (2005), p. 327; A. Dashwood, 'The EU Constitution: What Will Really Change?', 8 *Cambridge Yearbook of European Legal Studies* (2005), pp. 37–38.

[96] Conclusions of the European Council, Brussels, 21-22 June 2007, Annex 1, para. 3.

Article 24(3) TEU revised reinforces the principle of loyal cooperation and makes the binding character of CFSP acts clear:

> The Member States shall support the Union's external and security policy actively and unreservedly in a spirit of loyalty and mutual solidarity and shall comply with the Union's action in this area. . . . They shall refrain from action which is contrary to the interests of the Union or likely to impair its effectiveness as a cohesive force in international relations.

The wording is based on existing Article 11(2) TEU, although the phrase 'and shall comply with the Union's action in this area' is an addition. Thus, the emphasis is on giving effect to CFSP measures and implementation by the Member States themselves rather than enforcement through courts.

2.4 Conclusion

What, then, can we conclude from this attempt to assess the Laeken Declaration's claim that 'the important thing is to clarify, simplify and adjust the division of competence between the Union and the Member States in the light of the new challenges facing the Union'? Was there a real need to define Union external competences more clearly, to establish more transparently the conditions under which competences may be acquired and to attempt to categorise different types of competence and systematise the differing effects that they have on the exercise of Member State competence? In this analysis we have inevitably focused on areas of difficulty in the current state of the law, in part since those are the areas where we might have hoped for some clarification in the revised Treaties, but even taking this into account there are clearly a number of problematic issues relating to external competence, some of which have been with us since the *AETR* case, and some of which are relatively new. On what criteria should the legal base for external acts be chosen, and should the criteria be the same for international agreements as for autonomous measures? On what basis should we seek to delimit the different competence fields currently represented by the pillars? Is there still a need to keep CFSP competence separate and, if so, what type of competence should it be? On what basis can external powers be implied? Will implied powers generally be exclusive, and to the extent that they may not, on what basis should exclusivity be determined? How is the division of competence between Union/Community and Member States to be reflected in the context of mixed agreements, as a matter of responsibility under both Union/Community law and international law, and should competence be the determining factor here at all?

These questions, and others, are a natural consequence of the nature of the Union as a system of external relations, incorporating different legal orders and institutions each with their own conferred powers and oper-ating alongside the Member States, and at the same time a Union that seeks to 'assert its identity on the international scene'[97] and aspires to 'shoulder its responsibilities in the governance of globalisation'.[98] In *AETR*, the ECJ dealt creatively and constructively with the dilemma of reconciling the principle of conferred powers with the need to provide a dynamic organisation with the tools it needed to match its internal development with a growing international presence.[99] The dilemma still remains, presenting itself in different ways.[100]

The process of drafting and analysing the Constitutional Treaty and the TL has given us an opportunity to reflect on these questions again, but the revised Treaties are more than merely a 'restatement' carried out as a quasi-academic exercise. Among all their other material and symbolic functions[101] they seek to entrench not so much the competences them-selves as the principles on the basis of which competences are allocated. How successful has this process been, at least in terms of the criteria set by the European Council at Laeken? As far as express powers are concerned, the verdict must be largely positive: a greater clarity in defining the common commercial policy, some gaps filled (humanitarian aid, accession to the ECHR), a rationalisation of explicitly external powers into a single Part of the Treaty. The inclusion of a provision on general treaty-making com-petence linked to Union policies and objectives also assists transparency and clarity in defining implied external competences, although the drafting of this provision is unfortunate. Similarly, an explicit classification of

---

[97] Article 2 TEU.   [98] Laeken Declaration.
[99] Dashwood and Heliskoski, 'The Classic Authorities Revisited', in Dashwood and Hillion (eds.), n. 49, p. 6.
[100] As one commentator has expressed it, 'If one takes a closer look at the present allocation of competences, doubts arise, however, as to whether a clear delimitation of competences is possible at all', U. Di Fabbio ('Some Remarks on the Allocation of Competences Between the EU and its Member States'), 39 CMLRev. (2002), p. 1296.
[101] N. Walker, 'After *finalité*? The Future of the European Constitutional Idea', in G. Amato, H. Bribosia and B. de Witte (eds.), *Genèse et Destinée de la Constitution européenne* (Brussels: Bruylant, 2007).

competences into exclusive, shared and complementary is helpful, in spite of some difficulty in attempting to identify when exclusive external competence arises. Also conducive to clarity is the provision confirming that shared competence is the 'default' option, and the specification of what each type of competence implies as far as division of competence between Union and Member States is concerned. The inclusion of general, but specifically external, objectives should help the Union to define an external policy that might reflect internal interests but is not tied to the pursuit of internal objectives. Issues surrounding the choice of competence or legal base would not disappear and in fact the questions currently surrounding the inter-pillar choice of legal base would become more rather than less complex in view of the separation that the Treaty attempts to maintain between the CFSP and other external policy fields.

As far as competence is concerned, the major difficulties and obscurities in the Treaties seem to arise from two causes. First, from an attempt 'to say too much': to try to encapsulate or codify the case law of the ECJ, especially the case law on exclusivity. This would have been best left alone; the case law is still evolving and some aspects of that case law (for example, the continued reference to Opinion 1/76 as a basis for exclusive competence) should have been allowed to fade away rather than be preserved as Treaty principles. The general statement on pre-emption in relation to shared competence – together with the principle of loyal cooperation – would provide a sufficiently clear basis for delimiting competence. Second, obscurity arises from saying too little: the failure to specify in what ways the CFSP does and in what ways it does not share the characteristics of other Union competences. The lesson to be drawn, then, is that a Constitutional Treaty, or a Reform Treaty revising the current founding Treaties, should not shy away from setting out unambiguously the categories of competence and the principles (such as primacy or pre-emption) that underlie the relationship between Union and Member State competence, but that it should not try to provide a snapshot of the current case law establishing how those principles work out in practice. In the same way, if the Treaty provides alongside the principle of conferred powers a necessary level of flexibility through providing for a form of residual competence, such as through the 'flexibility clause' and the non-specific treaty-making power, it should be recognised that the balance between the two will need to be worked out over time by the institutions of the Union, including the ECJ, and will necessarily evolve.

Article 47 TEU and the relationship between first and second pillar competences

ALAN DASHWOOD

3.1 Introduction

Since the Treaty of Maastricht, the external action of the European Union (EU) has been conducted under the distinct sets of constitutional arrangements found respectively in the EC Treaty (the first pillar) and in Title V and Title VI of the TEU (the second and third pillars). This chapter is more particularly concerned with the relationship between the Union's first pillar competences, exercised through the persona of the European Community (EC) and extending to those fields of external activity for which legal bases exist in the EC Treaty, and its directly exercisable second pillar competence in the field of the Common Foreign and Security Policy (CFSP).[1]

Central to the management of that relationship (as well as of the relationship between first and third pillar competences) is Article 47 of the TEU, found among the Final Provisions in Title VIII of that Treaty. The Article states:

> Subject to the provisions amending the Treaty establishing the European Community, the Treaty establishing the European Coal and Steel Community and the Treaty establishing the European Atomic Energy Community, and to these final provisions, nothing in this Treaty shall affect the Treaties establishing the European Communities or the subsequent Treaties and Acts modifying or supplementing them.

Evidently, the function of Article 47 is to preserve the integrity of the legal order that was brought into being by the EC Treaty, in the face of the new competences conferred upon the Union by the TEU. The main focus of

---

[1] The chapter develops and elaborates ideas that are put forward in a section of A. Dashwood, 'The Law and Practice of CFSP Joint Actions', in M. Cremona and B. de Witte (eds.), *EU Foreign Relations Law: Constitutional Fundamentals* (Oxford: Hart Publishing, forthcoming).

the discussion that follows is to determine how, in practice, the protection thus extended to the external *acquis communautaire* by the TEU itself, can be reconciled with the declared ambition of the same Treaty, in the tenth recital of its preamble, to implement a CFSP, 'thereby reinforcing the identity of the European Union and its independence in order to promote peace, security and progress in Europe and in the world'.

If and when the Treaty of Lisbon (TL) enters into force, the specificity of the Union's CFSP competence will be preserved, indeed strengthened. The issue that is addressed here – as to how CFSP competence interacts with the competences conferred on the Union, in its Community persona, by the EC Treaty – will continue to be posed under the new dispensation, no less starkly though in somewhat different terms, as Marise Cremona has indicated in chapter 2. The conclusions as to that interaction which, it will be argued, can properly be drawn under the existing Treaties, will be examined in the light of the changes envisaged by the TL, in the Epilogue to this chapter.

3.2 Article 47 in its constitutional context

In seeking to understand what Article 47 means by 'affecting the EC Treaty', a first step is to situate the Article in its context within the TEU. There is no warrant in the text of Article 47 itself, or elsewhere in the TEU, for the idea that Article 47 could have the effect of qualifying the natural meaning of other provisions contained in the Treaty. It must be assumed that the authors of the TEU meant what they said in both the common provisions of Title I, and in the provisions of Title V on the scope of the CFSP.

3.2.1 Article 47 and the common provisions of Title I TEU

Close examination of the common provisions contained in Title I TEU tends to confirm the complementary nature of the relationship between EC and TEU competences. It is true that the Communities are explicitly recognised by the TEU as enjoying a certain priority over the other components of the Union. Thus, Article 1(3) TEU defines the Union as being '*founded* on the European Communities, *supplemented by* the policies and forms of cooperation established by this Treaty ... '.[2] In

---

[2] Emphasis added.

addition, Article 2, fifth indent TEU makes it an explicit objective of the Union 'to maintain in full the *acquis communautaire* and build on it with a view to considering to what extent the policies and forms of cooperation introduced by this Treaty may need to be revised with the aim of ensuring the effectiveness of the mechanisms and the institutions of the Community'. At the same time, the reference to 'considering' the possible need for the policies and forms of cooperation introduced by the TEU to be 'revised' is an acknowledgement that any change in the attribution of competences between the pillars would require formal amendment of the Treaties under the procedure of Article 48 TEU. There is an echo here of the principle of conferred powers enshrined in Article 5(1) EC. The commitment to building on the *acquis communautaire* must not be read as an invitation to press aggressively for the extension of Community competences beyond the natural limits set by the language of the legal bases contained in the EC Treaty.

Alongside the protection of the *acquis*, there is the strong statement in Article 2, second indent TEU identifying the CFSP as the principal vehicle for pursuing the objective there set for the Union, of asserting its identity on the international scene; this reflects the recital on the CFSP mentioned above. The common provisions go on to underline the special importance of the principle of consistency as a practical tool for organising the exercise of the diverse competences of the Union in the field of inter-national relations. Article 3(2) TEU provides that '[t]he Union shall in particular ensure the consistency of its external activities as a whole in the context of its external relations, security, economic and development policies', and places responsibility on the Council and the Commission for ensuring such consistency, requiring them to cooperate to that end. The list of external activities in Article 3(2) juxtaposes development policy, which is a first pillar competence, with security policy, which falls under the CFSP and is thus a second pillar competence. It was evidently taken for granted that actions having development objectives are liable to interact with actions having security objectives – otherwise there would be no need to impose on the Council and the Commission a duty to maintain con-sistency between the two policy areas.

What lessons can be drawn from the common provisions with regard to Article 47 TEU? While the Article provides a mechanism for the protection of the *acquis communautaire*, it by no means follows that the external activities the Union is authorised to pursue, respectively, under the EC

Treaty and under Title V TEU are required to take place in hermetically sealed compartments.[3] The principle of consistency assumes, rather, that it is possible and desirable for the different competences to be used in a way that is mutually reinforcing, in the interests of overall policy coherence. The general tenor of the Common Principles favours a pragmatic conception of what may constitute an Article 47 effect, depending on the nature of the particular activities in question; it militates against a strict separation between first and second pillar competences, based on abstract principle.

3.2.2 The scope of the Union's CFSP competence

It is a familiar fact that Title V TEU does not employ the technique of the specific attribution of competences, with numerous individual power-conferring provisions, each constituting the legal basis for a defined field of activity, which is characteristic of the EC Treaty. Instead, the substantive scope of the competence that Title V attributes to the Union is determined by the broadly stated objectives set forth in Article 11(1) TEU, and further clarified with respect to security and defence policy by Article 17(1) and (2) TEU. The difference of approach can be explained, in part, by the specific institutional and procedural arrangements of Title V TEU; these may have been seen by the Member States as sufficient to enable them to protect their respective foreign policy interests, obviating the need for closely circumscribing the powers attributed to the Union at the level of primary law. However, the very nature of foreign and security policy would also help to provide an explanation. There is no way of anticipating in detail the range of actions it may be found appropriate for the Union to take in order, for instance, to safeguard its own security or to help maintain that of the international community.

Article 11(1) TEU provides:

The Union shall define and implement a common foreign and security policy covering all areas of foreign and security policy, the objectives of

---

[3] Cf. Eeckhout's view that 'Article 47 TEU aims to create watertight compartments in the EU vessel between the Community, on the one hand, and CFSP and PJCCM, on the other': P. Eeckhout, *External Relations of the European Union: Legal and Constitutional Foundations* (Oxford: Oxford University Press, 2004), p. 146.

which shall be:

— to safeguard the common values, fundamental interests, independence
  and integrity of the Union in conformity with the principles of the
  United Nations Charter;
— to strengthen the security of the Union in all ways;
— to preserve peace and strengthen international security, in accordance
  with the principles of the United Nations Charter, as well as the principles of the Helsinki Final Act and the objectives of the Paris Charter,
  including those on external borders;
— to promote international cooperation;
— to develop and consolidate democracy and the rule of law, and respect
  for human rights and fundamental freedoms.

To review the Article 11(1) objectives briefly. The first indent is about
safeguarding the very existence of the Union and its moral and political
identity, and the second indent about strengthening the Union's security.
The remaining three indents look beyond the direct interests of the Union
itself, to define its potential contribution as a player on the international
stage: in the maintenance of international peace and security, in promoting international cooperation and in developing and consolidating
democracy, the rule of law and respect for human rights.

Article 17(1) TEU supplements the statement of objectives in
Article 11(1) by making clear that the Union's Title V competence extends
to defence policy. It states that the CFSP 'shall include all questions
relating to the security of the Union, including the progressive framing of
a common defence policy, which might lead to a common defence, should
the European Council so decide'. Further precision is supplied by the
second paragraph of the Article, which says that the questions of security
and defence there referred to 'shall include humanitarian and rescue tasks,
peacekeeping tasks and tasks of combat forces in crisis management,
including peacemaking'. Those are the so-called 'Petersberg tasks', originally identified in 1992 for the (temporarily) revived Western European
Union.[4] In practice, the rapidly evolving European Security and Defence
Policy (ESDP) has so far been concentrated on those tasks; however, as
the phrase 'shall include' indicates, the Union's competence is not confined to them.

---

[4] See paragraph II.4 of the Petersberg Declaration, adopted by the Council of the WEU on
19 June 1992.

Analysis of Article 11(1), together with Article 17(1) and (2), contributes to a proper understanding of Article 47 TEU in two ways.

First, the present drafting of those provisions leaves little room for doubt as to the actual scope of the competence it is intended to confer on the Union. The generality of the reference, in the introductory phrase of Article 11(1), to a CFSP 'covering all areas of foreign and security policy' has been remarked upon, without sufficient acknowledgement of the function served by the list of objectives in the five indents that follow, in determining the scope of the attribution.[5] That qualifying function has been clearer since the reference to 'all areas of foreign and security policy', and the list of CFSP objectives, which were contained in separate paragraphs of Article J.1 in the Maastricht version of the TEU, have been brought together by the Treaty of Amsterdam in the present Article 11(1).[6] When Article 11(1) is considered as a whole, it can be seen that the competence attributed under Title V TEU covers the foreign policy of the Union in a limited and specific sense, namely the political, security and defence aspects of external relations, as distinct from their economic and social aspects.

Second, CFSP competence embraces *all* areas of a foreign, security and defence policy understood in that sense. The plenitude of the attributed competence, within the limits that Article 11(1) itself imposes, is given particular emphasis with respect to security: the second indent of Article 11(1) sets the objective of strengthening the security of the Union 'in *all* ways'; while Article 17(1) states that '*all* questions related to the security of the Union' are included within the CFSP.[7]

Article 47 must be interpreted in a way that allows full value to be given to the strikingly unequivocal language of Articles 11(1) and 17(1) TEU. It cannot have been the intention of the authors of the TEU to allow the scope and effectiveness of the CFSP, as explicitly there defined, to be restricted by Article 47, above all when considerations of the security of the Union, or of international peace and security, are in play.[8]

---

[5] Cf. Eeckhout, *External Relations of the European Union*, p. 141.

[6] A rather more tentative view was expressed by the writer in 'External Relations Provisions of the Amsterdam Treaty', 35 CMLRev. (1998), p. 1019 at pp. 1028 *et seq.*

[7] Emphasis added.

[8] The suggestion that 'the CFSP risks being squeezed between EC and national competences' ignores the plain meaning of these provisions: see Eeckhout, *External Relations of the European Union*, pp. 143 and 150, citing S. Keukeleire, *Het buitenlands beleid van de Europese Unie*, p. 154.

3.3 Article 47 in the case law

At the time when this paper was finally revised, there were only three cases decided by the ECJ in which Article 47 had been directly in issue.[9] These are analysed below. All three of the cases related to instruments adopted under third pillar competences in relation to matters which, it was contended by the Commission, fell within the scope of the Community's competence under the EC Treaty.[10] In addition, still pending before the ECJ was Case C-91/05, was the first case in which the Commission has contested the legality of an act of the Council adopted under the Union's CFSP competence, on the ground that it ought to have been adopted under Community competence (*in casu*, that for development cooperation policy).[11]

3.3.1 The Airport Transit Visas case

In Case 170/96,[12] the Commission brought proceedings under Article 230 EC (then Art. 173 EC) for the annulment of the Council's Joint Action of

[9] See, respectively, nn. 11, 22 and 34.

[10] The converse situation, of a measure that ought not to have been adopted under first pillar competence, is illustrated by Case C-317/04, which was about the Council Decision on the conclusion of an international agreement relating to the transfer of certain data (Passenger Name Records or PNR) held by air carriers to the United States customs authorities: see Case C-317/04, *European Parliament* v. *Council* [2006] ECR I- and the companion Case C-318/04, *European Parliament* v. *Commission* [2006] ECR I-. AG Leger was clear that Article 95 EC had been the wrong legal basis for concluding an agreement the aim and content of which was 'reconciliation of the objective of combating terrorism and other serious crimes with that of protecting airline passengers' personal data' (Opinion, paras. 139 and 140); however, he refrained from indicating what the correct legal basis would have been. The reasoning on this point in the judgment is too meagre to be of relevance to the present discussion.

[11] Case C-91/05, *Commission* v. *Council*, OJ 2005 C 115/10. The disputed measure is Council Decision 2004/833/CFSP of 2 December 2004, OJ 2004 L 359/55. This is one of a series of Decisions implementing Council Joint Action 2002/589/CFSP of 12 July 2002, OJ 2002 L 191/1, which organises contributions by the EU towards combating the accumulation and spread of small arms and light weapons (SALWs). Decision 2004/833 provides for an EU contribution to help with projects in the framework of the Moratorium on the Import, Export and Manufacture of SALWs, which is operated by the Economic Community of West African States (ECOWAS). At the same time as attacking that Decision, the Commission has asked the Court to make a declaration of illegality, pursuant to Article 241 EC, against Joint Action 2002/589. The opinion of AG Mengozzi, recommending that the Commission's action be dismissed, was rendered on 19 September 2007. Judgment has now been given. See the Epilogue to this chapter.

[12] Case C-170/96, *Commission* v. *Council (Airport transit (Visas))* [1998] ECR I-2763; noted by Oliviera, 38 CMLRev. (1999), p. 149.

4 March 1996 on airport transit arrangements.[13] Joint actions were among the instruments provided by Article K.3(2) of the TEU in its Maastricht version for the purpose of attaining the objectives of the then third pillar, which covered cooperation in the fields of justice and home affairs. Based on an initiative by the French Presidency, the act in question was specifically concerned with the visas that nationals of certain third countries may be required to obtain when transiting the airports of Member States. The Commission contended that the Joint Action ought to have been adopted under the then Article 100c EC, which gave the Community competence to determine the third countries whose nationals must be in possession of a visa when crossing the external borders of a Member State.

The *Airport Transit Visas* case clarified the nature of the jurisdiction of the ECJ with regard to Article 47 TEU. At the material time, no jurisdiction existed for the review by the ECJ of the legality of third pillar acts as such. It had been argued by the United Kingdom, which intervened in the case, that the Commission's action was inadmissible, on the grounds that judicial review pursuant to Article 230 EC was available only in respect of acts adopted under legal bases contained in the EC Treaty. In rejecting that contention, Advocate General Fennelly recalled Article 46 TEU (then Art. L), which extends the jurisdiction conferred on the ECJ by the Community Treaties to Article 47 (then Art. M), among other provisions of the TEU. The ECJ's power of judicial review under the Community Treaties, the Advocate General said, had been made available, through the combined effect of Articles 46 and 47, 'so as to ensure respect for the provisions of those Treaties'.[14] Mr Fennelly went on to consider the extent to which the ECJ may examine the content of an act such as the one in issue, in the context of an action for annulment brought under Article 230 EC. His answer was that 'the Court may interpret acts purporting to be adopted under Title VI of the Treaty on European Union, in order to determine whether or not they deal with matters which more properly fall within the Community sphere of competence as determined by Article [47]';[15] and he went on to cite well-known authorities establishing that proceedings under Article 230 EC can be used to review the validity of acts the Member States or the Council purport to have adopted outside the framework of the EC Treaty, which, it is claimed, ought to have

[13] Joint Action 96/197/JAI, OJ 1996 L 63/8.
[14] Opinion, para. 8.   [15] Opinion, para. 11.

been adopted under the appropriate legal basis conferring competence on the Community.[16] A similar conclusion was reached in the judgment of the Court, though more shortly and without citation of authority.[17]

The ECJ now enjoys jurisdiction, pursuant to Article 35(6) TEU, to review the legality of third pillar acts in the form of framework decisions and decisions, on grounds similar to those mentioned in Article 230 EC; and it was under that Article that the proceedings in the subsequent *Environmental Penalties* case were brought.[18] Nevertheless, it remains important that Article 230 EC has been recognised as providing a remedy that enables Article 47 TEU to be legally enforced; not only because an action for annulment under Article 35(6) cannot be brought by the European Parliament or a private party, but also because there is still no jurisdiction for the ECJ to review the legality of second pillar acts, as such.

Besides clarifying the issue of the ECJ's jurisdiction with respect to Article 47 TEU, the *Airport Transit Visas* case provided the first opportunity for an authoritative indication to be given as to the meaning of the requirement imposed by the Article, that nothing in the TEU 'shall affect' the Community Treaties. Advocate General Fennelly expressed the view that 'Article [47] was inserted in the Treaty on European Union with the very purpose of ensuring that, in exercising their powers under Titles V and VI of that Treaty, the Council and the Member States *do not encroach on* the powers attributed to the Communities under the respective founding and amending Treaties'.[19] He continued: 'however clear and unambiguous they may be, the provisions of Title VI may not be applied *so as to restrict in any way* the scope of the provisions of the EC Treaty, interpreted in accordance with the ordinary canons of Community law'.[20] For the Advocate General, it seems, the test showing that a third pillar measure 'encroaches upon' the EC Treaty would be that it has a tendency to 'restrict' the scope of the provisions of that Treaty. Quoting a suggestion made by Denmark, another intervening Member State, 'that the scope of application of each of the relevant provisions has "movable boundaries"', Mr Fennelly said that he disagreed, 'at least in so far as this may imply that the Council would have a discretion to resort to

---

[16] Joined Cases C-181/91 and C-248/91, *Parliament* v. *Council and Commission (Bangladesh)* [1993] ECR I-3685; Case C-316/91, *Parliament v Council (EDF)* [1994] ECR I-625. See Opinion, paras. 14 and 15.

[17] Judgment, paras. 12 to 18.   [18] See n. 22.

[19] Opinion, para. 8, emphasis added.   [20] Opinion, para. 9, emphasis added.

Article K.3 even when the conditions for the application of Article 100c of the Treaty were met'. Echoing the language used by Mr Fennelly, the ECJ defined its task under Article 47 as being 'to ensure that acts which, according to the Council fall within the scope of ... the Treaty on European Union *do not encroach upon the powers conferred by the EC Treaty on the Community*'.[21]

In the event, it was held by the ECJ, following its Advocate General, that there was no encroachment on Article 100c EC, because the situation governed by the Joint Action did not involve the crossing of Member States' external borders by third-country nationals, and was therefore beyond the scope of the competence conferred on the Community by that provision. However, it seems clear from the passages cited above, and from the general tenor of the judgment as well as of the Advocate General's Opinion, that, had there been Community competence under Article 100c to lay down arrangements on airport transit visas, the Joint Action would have been found to 'affect' the EC Treaty within the meaning of Article 47 TEU.

3.3.2 The Environmental Penalties case

Case C-176/03, *Environmental Penalties*,[22] was about a Title VI instrument in the form of a Framework Decision laying down a number of environmental offences, in respect of which the Member States were required to prescribe criminal penalties. The Framework Decision was adopted by the Council on the initiative of Denmark. The Commission considered that the correct legal basis for imposing criminal penalties for the commission of environmental offences was Article 175(1) EC; indeed, it had put forward a proposal for a directive on the protection of the environment through criminal law, which the Council had chosen not to adopt. No less than eleven Member States intervened in the proceedings in support of the Council.

The Opinion of Advocate General Ruiz-Jarabo Colomer analysed in depth the issue as to the existence and scope of Community competence to legislate for the imposition by the Member States of criminal penalties

---

[21] Judgment, para. 16, emphasis added.
[22] Case C-176/03, *Commission* v. *Council (Environmental Penalties)* [2005] ECR I-7879; noted by Tobler, 43 CMLRev. (2006), p. 835.

with a view to the protection of the environment. However, the Advocate General dealt only briefly with Article 47 TEU; he referred to the duty of the Council to refrain from exercising its Title VI powers 'by virtue of the primacy of Community law established by [the Article]',[23] and to the existence of a legal basis for the Community to act with respect to the matters in question as 'cancelling out the powers of the Union'.[24]

The ECJ reiterated the definition of the task imposed upon it by Article 47 TEU, as being to prevent encroachment upon the powers conferred by the EC Treaty on the Community,[25] which meant in the instant case that it was necessary to ascertain whether the relevant provisions of the Framework Decision ought to have been adopted on the basis of Article 175 EC.[26] It recalled that the protection of the environment 'constitutes one of the essential objectives of the Community', as indicated by the express provisions of Articles 2 and 3(1), as well as by Article 6 EC;[27] and that legal bases for Community action on the environment were to be found in Articles 174 to 176 EC.[28] The ECJ then referred to its settled case law, according to which 'the choice of legal basis for a Community measure must rest on objective factors which are amenable to judicial review, including in particular the aim and the content of the measure'.[29] It was clear, the ECJ said, from the title and the first three recitals of the Framework Decision in question, that 'its objective is the protection of the environment'.[30] As to the content of the Framework Decision, while criminal law and procedure did not generally fall within the Community's competence, that did not prevent measures relating to the criminal law of the Member States from being taken, where this was considered necessary to ensure that Community rules on environmental protection were fully effective.[31] It followed that 'on account of both their *aim* and their *content*, Articles 1 to 7 of the framework decision have as their main purpose the protection of the environment and they could have been properly adopted on the basis of Article 175 EC'.[32] Since, therefore, those provisions

---

[23] Opinion, para. 26.   [24] Opinion, para. 27.   [25] Judgment, para. 39.

[26] Judgment, para. 40.   [27] Judgment, paras. 41 and 42.   [28] Judgment, para. 43.

[29] Judgment, para. 45, citing Case C-300/89, *Commission* v *Council* [1991] ECR I-2867 and Case C-336/00, *Huber* [2002] ECR I-7699.

[30] Judgment, para. 46.

[31] Judgment, paras. 48 and 49. As will be noted below, the point is dealt with more superficially than in the Opinion of the Advocate General.

[32] Judgment, para. 51.

encroached upon powers that had been conferred on the Community, and they were not severable, the Framework Decision as a whole was found to infringe Article 47 EC and had to be annulled.[33]

3.3.3 The Ship-source Pollution case

In Case C-440/05,[34] the dispute was about Framework Decision 2005/ 667,[35] providing for the imposition of criminal penalties for the infringement of rules outlawing ship-source discharges of polluting substances into the sea, which were laid down by a companion Community instrument, Directive 2005/35.[36] As a measure forming part of the Community's maritime safety policy, the Directive had Article 80(2) as its legal basis; and it was contended by the Commission that the same legal basis could and should have been used for the adoption of the provisions relating to the criminal character of the infringements, and of the penalties to be prescribed therefore, which were the subject of the Framework Decision.

The ECJ, following Advocate General Mazak, reiterated its reasoning in *Environmental Penalties*, to reach the conclusion that there was indeed Community competence under Article 80(2) EC to adopt Articles 2, 3 and 5 of Framework Decision 2005/667, since those provisions were 'designed to ensure the efficacy of the rules adopted in the field of maritime safety, non-compliance with which may have serious environmental consequences, by requiring Member States to apply criminal penalties to certain forms of conduct'.[37] On the other hand, certain of the provisions of Framework Decision 2005/667 went further than those of the instrument at issue in *Environmental Penalties*, by specifying with some precision '*the type and level* of the criminal penalties to be applied':[38] e.g., it was stated in Article 4(1) that the penalties 'shall include, at least for serious cases, criminal penalties of a maximum of at least between one and three years of imprisonment'; and in Article 4(4), that for offences intentionally

---

[33] Judgment, para. 53. The provisions of the Framework Decision other than Articles 1 to 7 were held by the Court not to be severable.

[34] Case C-440/05, *Commission v Council (Ship-source Pollution)*, judgment of 23 October 2007, not yet reported.

[35] Council Framework Decision 2005/667/JHA of 12 July 2005 to strengthen the criminal law framework for the enforcement of the law against ship-source pollution, OJ 2005 L 255/164.

[36] Directive 2005/35/EC of 7 September 2005 on ship-source pollution and on the introduction of penalties for infringements, OJ 2005 L 255/11.

[37] Judgment, paras. 66 to 69.   [38] Judgment, para. 70, emphasis added.

committed the maximum penalty must be 'at least between five and ten years of imprisonment where the offence caused significant and widespread damage to water quality, to animal or vegetable species or to parts of them and the death or serious injury of persons'. The Court, again following its Advocate General, found that the Community had no competence to adopt such provisions and that consequently their inclusion in Framework Decision 2005/667 did not constitute an infringement of Article 47 TEU.[39] Nevertheless, since those provisions were inextricably linked to elements of the Framework Decision that ought to have been adopted under powers conferred on the Community by the EC Treaty, it was held that the instrument as a whole must be annulled.[40]

3.3.4 Lessons of the case law on the first/pillar third pillar interface

In the *Environmental Penalties* case and again in *Ship-source Pollution*, the ECJ found that both the aim and the content of the provisions of the Framework Decision in question were such as to indicate that the main purpose of those provisions fell within the scope of the specific legal basis provided by the EC Treaty for the protection of the environment (Art. 175 EC); in other words, the very same measure could have been adopted on that legal basis. The case is, therefore, authority for the proposition that the adoption of an act under a TEU competence will 'affect' Article 47 in the intended sense, where an identical act – that is to say, one having not only the same *content* but also the same *aim* – could be adopted under one of the legal bases in the EC Treaty.

The only lesson as to the nature of an Article 47 effect, which can safely be drawn from the case law, is, therefore, the rather narrow one that the EC Treaty is protected against being 'affected' through the direct substitution of a TEU instrument for a Community instrument. For the present, there is no authority as to whether the prohibition of the Article extends to any form of interaction between first pillar competences and second and third pillar competences, other than what may be termed a 'substitution effect'.

---

[39] Judgment, para. 71.
[40] Judgment, paras. 72 to 74.

3.4 The interaction between first and second pillar competences

3.4.1 No identity of objectives between the pillars

A substitution effect in the sense just explained seems unlikely ever to be produced in the interaction between first and second pillar competences, because there is no identity of objectives between the two pillars. This is in contrast to the relationship between first and third pillar competences, which share the establishment of an area of freedom, security and justice as a common ulterior objective.[41]

In the contention of the writer, a clear demarcation *in principle* is intended by the Treaties between the Union's competence under Title V TEU in the domain of the CFSP and the competences in the field of external relations that are conferred on the Community by legal bases in the EC Treaty. Such, at all events, would appear to have been the view of the authors of the Amsterdam Treaty; they chose to preface Article 29 TEU, which proclaims the general objectives of Title VI TEU, with the phrase, '[w]ithout prejudice to the powers of the European Community', but evidently saw no need to include a similar qualification among the provisions of Title V. The contention finds support in the relevant Treaty texts, and it is increasingly being confirmed in legislative practice and by the case law.

Articles 2 to 4 EC are the provisions that lay down the task and activities of the Community, thereby establishing the general parameters of its internal and external competences. They give no hint that action by the Community in the domain of foreign and security policy to which Article V TEU applies, is contemplated as a possibility.

Article 2 EC defines the Community's 'task', in other words the essential purpose it is designed to serve. That task is 'to promote throughout the Community a harmonious, balanced and sustainable development of economic activities, a high level of employment and of social protection, equality between men and women, sustainable and non-inflationary growth, a high degree of competitiveness and convergence of economic performance, a high level of protection and improvement of the quality of the environment, the raising of the standard of living and quality of life, and economic and social cohesion and solidarity among Member States'.

---

[41] See Article 61 EC and Article 29 TEU.

The desirable ends the Community is there called upon to further are exclusively socio-economic in character.

The same focus is evident in the list of 'activities' of the Community in Article 3 EC, as well as in Article 4 EC, which concerns economic and monetary union and the introduction of a single currency. The only external activities explicitly referred to in Article 3 are 'a common commercial policy' under (b), 'a policy in the sphere of development cooperation' under (r), and 'the association of the overseas countries' under (s). It is noteworthy that, in the last-mentioned case, where there might perhaps have been some doubt as to the scope of the activity contemplated, the limitation to socio-economic goals is stated expressly: the specified purpose of association is 'in order to increase trade and promote jointly economic and social development'.

Textual authorisation for pursuing objectives corresponding to those of Article 11(1) TEU is similarly lacking among the power-conferring pro-visions, mostly found in Part Three of the EC Treaty, which constitute the specific legal bases for Community action in the field of external relations. There are a few provisions that might, on a superficial view, appear to contemplate action beyond the socio-economic sphere, but this impres-sion will not withstand close analysis.

Thus, Article 177 EC, which defines the substantive scope of EC development cooperation policy, states in its second paragraph: 'Com-munity policy in this area shall contribute to the general objective of developing and consolidating democracy and the rule of law and to that of respecting human rights and fundamental freedoms'; while Article 181a EC, the legal basis for economic, financial and technical cooperation with third countries other than developing countries,[42] contains similar lan-guage. However, the envisaged 'contribution' by the Community to the general objective set for the Union by the fifth indent of Article 11(1) TEU is not a free-standing competence but rather a consideration that must inform Community policy in pursuing the socio-economic objectives of the envisaged cooperation.[43] The ancillary nature of that contribution is

---

[42] Hereinafter, 'general cooperation'.

[43] The objectives of development cooperation policy are stated by Article 177(1) to be:

— the sustainable economic and social development of the developing countries, and more particularly the most disadvantaged among them;
— the smooth and gradual integration of the developing countries into the world economy;
— the campaign against poverty in the developing countries.

emphasised in the two Regulations that have been adopted in order to organise Community activity aimed at fostering democracy, the rule of law and respect for human rights in third countries; any such operations, it is stipulated, may only be carried on 'within the framework of Community development cooperation policy' or that of general cooperation policy.[44]

Similarly, although they are concerned with the imposition of financial and economic sanctions against third countries, Articles 60 and 301 EC provide further confirmation of the separation intended by the Treaties between competence for external economic relations and competence for external political relations. Under the cross-pillar mechanism that was created by the insertion of the two Articles into the EC Treaty, the role of the Community is purely instrumental. The substantive political decision to interrupt economic relations with a given third country, as a way of putting pressure on its authorities to change some aspect of their behaviour, is adopted under the Union's CFSP competence; and any necessary measures to implement the decision are then taken by the Community.

In recent years, there have been several examples of legislative proposals put forward by the Commission, which were evidently regarded by the Council as over-estimating the scope of application of the EC Treaty, needing therefore to be drastically rewritten before they could be adopted. One example was the proposal that eventually became Council Regulation (EC) 381/2001 of 26 February 2001, creating a rapid reaction mechanism (the RRM Regulation).[45] In the Commission's original conception, the mechanism would have been available to finance 'non-combat activities' (arguably including activities of a military character) having as their

---

At para. 155 of his opinion in Case 91/05, AG Mengozzi states: 'Article 177(1) EC shows that the objectives of the development cooperation policy are primarily economic and social'. In the case of general cooperation, the socio-economic character of the measures authorised by Article 181a is clear from the reference to 'economic, financial and technical cooperation'.

[44] See Council Regulation (EC) 975/1999 of 29 April 1999 laying down the requirements for the implementation of development cooperation operations which contribute to the general objective of developing and consolidating democracy and the rule of law and to that of respecting human rights and fundamental freedoms, OJ 1999 L 120/1; amended by Regulation (EC) 2240/2004 of the European Parliament and the Council of 15 December 2004, OJ 2004 L 390/3. The corresponding measure with respect to general cooperation is Council Regulation (EC) 976/1999 of 29 April 1999, OJ 1999 L 120/8; amended by Regulation (EC) 2241/2004 of the European Parliament and the Council of 15 December 2004, OJ 2004 L 390/6.

[45] OJ 2001 L 57/5.

object, among other things, crisis management and conflict prevention in third countries, with a view to preserving international peace and security. As finally adopted, the Regulation has the much more modest function of supplementing the facilities provided by a number of Community programmes, which are identified in an Annex, where the existing instruments would not allow action to be taken with the requisite urgency. The two Regulations concerning action against anti-personnel landmines in, respectively, developing countries and other third countries (the De-mining Regulations)[46] had a similar legislative history. A Commission proposal that strayed into the field of non-proliferation of landmines was cut down, so as to cover only activities directly connected with resettlement and the resumption of economic activities, such as mine-awareness education, the marking of suspected areas and mine clearance.

An egregious example of a Commission proposal trespassing beyond the limits imposed by the EC Treaty was that for a Regulation establishing an Instrument for Stability, which would have had Article 308 EC as its legal basis.[47] The general thrust of the Instrument was defined in Article 1(1) of the proposed Regulation as being to 'finance measures to promote peace and stability and assure the safety and security of the civilian population in third countries and territories . . . '. The second paragraph of the Article went on to identify the kind of EU policies the Instrument could be used to support, in particular those relating to: the delivery of a response to crisis situations, severe political stability or violent conflict; major challenges to the rule of law in third countries, including the fight against organised crime, trafficking and terrorism; major technological threats with potential trans-border impact, including the promotion of nuclear safety and the fight against weapons of mass destruction; and the development of peacekeeping and peace-support capacity in partnership with international, regional and sub-regional organisations. Clearly, this would have been an instance of the use of Article 308 to pursue political and security objectives exclusive to the CFSP.[48] The Regulation that was finally adopted in November 2006, after more than two years of difficult negotiations, has Articles 179 and 181a EC as its legal bases and explicitly proclaims as its

---

[46] European Parliament and Council Regulation (EC) No 1724/2001 of 23 July 2001, OJ 2001 L 234/1; Council Regulation (EC) No 1725/2001 of 23 July 2001, OJ 2001 L 234/6.

[47] COM(2004)630 final.

[48] The lack of Community competence in such matters was confirmed by the Court of First Instance in its *Yusuf* and *Kadi* judgments, see n. 52.

objective the undertaking of 'development cooperation measures, as well as financial, economic and technical cooperation measures with third countries' by the Community.[49] Article 1(2) goes on to identify two specific aims of the Regulation: 'in a situation of crisis or emerging crisis, to contribute to stability by providing an effective response *to help preserve, establish or re-establish the conditions essential to the proper implementation of the Community's development and cooperation policies*'; and '*in the context of stable conditions for the implementation of Community cooperation policies in third countries,* to help build capacity to address specific global and regional threats having a destabilising effect and to ensure preparedness to address pre- and post-crisis situations'.[50] Possible interaction with second (and third) pillar measures is anticipated by Article 1(3), which provides: '[m]easures taken under this Regulation may be complementary to, and shall be consistent with, and without prejudice to, measures adopted under Title V and Title VI of the EU Treaty'. Thus, in the final version of the Regulation, its nature as an instrument ancillary to the socio-economic objectives of cooperation with third countries has been spelled out, as well as the intention of the Community legislator not to intrude upon the general competence for maintaining international peace and security as such, which belongs to the CFSP.[51]

The conclusion to be drawn from the EC Treaty itself as to the limits of the Community's external relations competences was recently spelled out by the Court of First Instance (CFI) in cases relating to the adoption of coercive financial and economic measures by the EU, pursuant to Resolutions of the United Nations Security Council, against named individuals believed to be associated with Usama bin Laden, the Al-Qaeda network and the Taliban.[52] The fight against international terrorism could not, it was held, 'be made to refer to one of the objects which Article 2 EC

---

[49] See Article 1(1) of Regulation (EC) 1717/2006 of the European Parliament and of the Council of 15 November 2006 establishing an Instrument for Stability, OJ 2006 L 327/1.

[50] Emphasis added.

[51] The writer, nevertheless, continues seriously to doubt whether some of the concrete actions authorised by Articles 3 and 4 of Regulation 1717/2006 have a sufficiently proximate relationship with the socio-economic objectives of EC cooperation policy to justify the choice of Articles 179 and 181a as a joint legal basis.

[52] Case T-306/01, *Yusuf* v. *Council and Commission* [2005] ECR II-3533 and Case T-315/01, *Kadi* v. *Council and Commission* [2005] ECR II-3649; on appeal as, respectively, Case 415/05P and Case 402/05P.

and 3 EC expressly entrust to the Community'.[53] According to the account given in the judgments, the Commission had argued for the existence, in addition to the Treaty objectives articulated in Articles 2 and 3 EC, of 'a more general objective which the Community has to ensure', namely the safeguarding of international peace and security.[54] In support of its contention, the Commission is said to have invoked Articles 3 and 11 TEU, together with the recitals of the preamble to the EC Treaty that speak of 'the solidarity which binds Europe and the overseas countries ... in accordance with the principles of the Charter of the United Nations' and the resolve 'to preserve and strengthen peace and liberty'.[55] The CFI roundly rejected that argument, noting that 'nowhere in the preamble to the EC Treaty is it stated that that act pursues a wider objective of safeguarding international peace and security'. It was certainly a principal aim of the Treaty to put an end to the conflicts of the past between the peoples of Europe by creating 'an ever closer union' among them, but that was without any reference whatsoever to the implementation of a CFSP. The latter policy, the CFI said, 'falls exclusively within the objects of the Treaty on European Union which, as emphasised in the preamble thereto, seeks to *mark a new stage in the process of European integration with the establishment of the European Communities*'.

The reasoning of the CFI seems incontestable. The particular emphasis that is placed, in the second paragraph of Article 3 TEU, on the need for ensuring the consistency of the Union's activities as a whole, would make little sense, if the objectives expressly assigned to the CFSP by Article 11(1) TEU could be read across to the EC Treaty; indeed, were that possible, it is hard to see what role would be left for the Union under Title V TEU. The recitals of the EC Treaty relied upon by the Commission appear no more helpful to its argument. The words omitted from the Commission's citation of the seventh recital refer to ensuring the development of the overseas countries' *prosperity*, thus looking ahead to the socio-economic objectives of association that are specified in Article 3(s) EC; while the eighth recital, as the CFI points out, is manifestly about ending conflicts between the peoples of Europe, by the Member States 'pooling their

---

[53] *Ibid.*, respectively, para. 152 and para. 116. This finding was referred to, with approval, by Advocate General Léger at para. 161 of his Opinion in Joined Cases C-317 *European Parliament* v. *Council* and C-318/04, *European Parliament* v. *Council*, n. 10.

[54] *Ibid.*, respectively, paras. 100 and 153 and paras. 76 and 117.

[55] See the seventh and eighth recitals.

resources' under the arrangements to be set in place pursuant to the Treaty.

Recent authority supporting that analysis is found in the Opinion of Advocate General Mengozzi in Case 91/05. Citing the CFI's *Yusuf* and *Kadi* judgments, the learned Advocate General said:

> ... the preservation of peace and strengthening of international security cannot be made to refer to any of the aims expressly assigned to the Community by Articles 2 EC and 3 EC or, more broadly, to the preamble to the EC Treaty. Even if the preservation of peace and strengthening of international security must inspire action by the Community, they do not fall within the scope of the EC Treaty, but within the objectives of the EU Treaty, in part the CFSP, in accordance with Article 11 (1) EU.[56]

In the result, it is submitted, as regards the relationship between the first and second pillars, Article 47 merely confirms what is already plain from the text of the Treaties themselves: there is no competence under Title V TEU for the Union to adopt measures having the same aim, as well as the same content, as measures that can be adopted under one of the legal bases of the EC Treaty. A genuinely second pillar measure cannot, therefore, be substituted for a genuinely first pillar measure, in the way that was found to have occurred in the *Environmental Penalties* case.

3.4.2 The possibility of an 'overlap effect'

On the other hand, there will sometimes be a degree of overlap between the exercise of CFSP competence and the exercise of Community competences, in the sense that certain actions taken for the purposes of the one, may equally well be taken for the purposes of the other. Such overlap will obviously not occur with respect to European Security and Defence Policy (ESDP) operations of a military character; but, among the growing number of civilian operations that are being mounted in pursuance of Article 11(1) TEU objectives, some are bound to involve activity that might conceivably be carried on in pursuance of different, though complementary, Community objectives.

---

[56] Opinion, para. 159. The different issue, of action tending to preserve peace or strengthen international security, which is taken specifically in furtherance of the socio-economic objectives of development cooperation, is considered below.

The possibility of overlap appears all the more likely if it is accepted that
the notion of development cooperation, as defined by Article 177 EC, can
be understood to have undergone an evolution, so that it now covers
security-related measures with the essential aim of promoting social and
economic development and combating poverty in the countries concerned. This extended interpretation of Article 177 is based on the contention that internal security and stability are an indispensable condition
for implementing a successful development policy (or indeed, for effective
general cooperation pursuant to Article 181a EC).[57] However, this argument, which provides the justification for the activity authorised by
Regulation 1717/2006, must not be pressed too far; taken to its limits, it
could even justify peacekeeping or peace-making operations, which are
clearly beyond the competence of the Community.

A practical illustration of overlapping EC and CFSP competences can
be provided by briefly considering two examples of civilian crisis management operations organised on the basis of a CFSP joint action, which
have both now been completed.

A first example is the EU Rule of Law Mission in Georgia, designated
'EUJUST THEMIS'.[58] According to the 'mission statement' in Article 2(1)
of the Joint Action establishing the operation:

> EUJUST THEMIS shall, in full coordination with, and in complementarity
> to, EC programmes, as well as other donors' programmes, assist in the
> development of a horizontal governmental strategy guiding the reform
> process for all relevant stakeholders within the criminal justice sector,
> including the establishment of a mechanism for coordination and priority
> setting for the criminal justice reform.

Article 2(2) identified some more specific activities that could be undertaken by EUJUST THEMIS. These included providing guidance to
Georgia's new criminal justice reform strategy, supporting the planning
for new legislation, e.g. a Criminal Procedure Code, and supporting the
development of international as well as regional cooperation in the area of
criminal justice.

---

[57] See the Opinion of AG Kokott in Case C-403/05, *European Parliament* v. *Council*, paras. 85–7,
nyr. The views expressed by the learned Advocate General as to the scope of Article 177 EC
were by way of clarification and not directly relevant to the issues before the Court. See also
the Opinion of AG Mengozzi in Case 91/05, paras. 168–172.

[58] Council Joint Action 2004/523/CFSP, OJ 2004 L 228/21.

The objectives of EUJUST THEMIS were laid down by recitals (2) and (3) of the preamble to the Joint Action. According to recital (2), the EU 'aims to support the transition process in Georgia' and 'is committed in particular to continue to assist the new government in its efforts to bring local standards with regard to the rule of law closer to international and EU standards'. Recital (3) noted that '[t]he security situation in Georgia is stable but may deteriorate with potentially serious repercussions on regional and international security and the strengthening of democracy and the rule of law'. The drafting of those recitals recalls the objective of strengthening international security, mentioned in the third indent of Article 11(1) TEU, that of developing and consolidating democracy and the rule of law, mentioned in the fifth indent, and – more obliquely – that of strengthening the Union's own security, mentioned in the second indent, since this could be affected by serious instability in Georgia.

Manifestly, therefore, the mission authorised by the Joint Action was conceived with a view to furthering CFSP objectives; and it was structured as a typical ESDP operation, with a staff of experts seconded from EU Member States or institutions, and with the Political and Security Committee (PSC) exercising political control and strategic direction. However, it appears equally clear that a programme including many of the same elements could have been put together, under a different set of operational arrangements, as a 'contribution' to the strengthening of democracy and the rule of law within the framework of the Community's general cooperation policy. This is demonstrated by the fact that, just a few days after the establishment of EUJUST THEMIS, the Commission announced various projects designed to reinforce the rule of law and democratic processes in Georgia, to be financed on the basis of the Rapid Reactions Mechanism (RRM).[59] Those projects, said the Commission, echoing the words of Article 2 of the Joint Action, would be 'closely coordinated with ... EUJUST THEMIS in order to ensure full complementarity between all the EU actions in support of the rule of law in Georgia'.[60] On that occasion, it seems, the Commission was completely comfortable with the idea that CFSP and EC competences could be exercised in parallel in pursuance of their respective objectives.

A second example of an ESDP operation that might be seen as overlapping, though to a lesser extent, with action capable of being taken in pursuance of Community objectives was the EU Monitoring Mission in Aceh,

---

[59] See n. 45.   [60] IP/04/846 – Brussels, 2 July 2004.

Indonesia (AMM). This was launched in response to an invitation from the Government of Indonesia to the EU and certain Association of South East Asian Nations (ASEAN) countries, to assist it in implementing the Memorandum of Understanding (MoU) incorporating a peace agreement with a former separatist group, the Free Aceh Movement or 'GAM', which had been negotiated in the wake of the tsunami of December 2004.[61]

The issue of competence with respect to the AMM became the subject of a lively debate within the PSC, which was provoked by a Commission proposal that the mission be funded, as an operation linked to development assistance, initially under the RRM and subsequently under the Community's Asia and Latin America programme.[62] The dispute was resolved in favour of establishing the mission on the basis of a CFSP Joint Action,[63] to be financed using appropriations from the CFSP chapter of the Community budget,[64] supplemented by contributions in kind from Member States. That this was legally and politically the appropriate outcome can scarcely be doubted. The main thrust of the AMM was to promote CFSP objectives – a lasting peaceful settlement to the conflict in Aceh and enhanced stability in South East Asia.[65] Recital (7) of the preamble to the Joint Action noted that the mission would 'be conducted in a situation which may deteriorate and could harm the objectives of the Common Foreign and Security Policy as set out in Article 11 of the Treaty'. As for the AMM's mandate, defined by Article 2 of the Joint Action, central features related to matters beyond the competence of the Community, such as monitoring the demobilisation of GAM, monitoring and assisting with the decommissioning and destruction of its weapons, ammunition and explosives, and monitoring the relocation of 'non-organic' military and police forces (i.e. Special Forces and other units of the Indonesian army and police not normally based in Aceh). In addition,

---

[61] An excellent analysis of the AMM was published in December 2005 by the EU Institute for Security Studies: see Occasional Paper no. 61, P.-A. Braud and G. Grevi, 'The EU Mission in Aceh: implementing peace (hereinafter, 'Aceh Occasional Paper'). I am most grateful to Elisa Baroncini of the Dipartimento di Scienze Giuridiche 'A. Cicu', Università degli Studi di Bologna, for having drawn my attention to this publication.

[62] *Ibid.*, pp. 24–7. See Regulation (EEC) 443/92 of 25 February 1992 on financial and technical assistance to, and economic cooperation with, the developing countries in Asia and Latin America, OJ 1992 L 52/1.

[63] Council Joint Action 2005/643/CFSP of 9 September 2005 on the European Union Monitoring Mission in Aceh (Indonesia) (Aceh Monitoring Mission – AMM), OJ 2005 L 234/13.

[64] Consistently with Article 28(3) TEU.   [65] Joint Action 2005/643, Recital (1).

collaboration with the contributing ASEAN countries could be conveniently accommodated within the structure of an ESDP operation.[66]

At the same time, there were some elements of the mandate given to the AMM that could also be addressed by action in pursuance of EC development cooperation objectives. A notable instance was that of the reintegration of former GAM fighters, where the work of AMM monitors on the ground was complemented by the mobilisation of significant amounts of Community aid; interviews with former prisoners, carried out across the entire region, are said to have 'enabled the monitors to gain a much better understanding of the perspectives and priorities of the recipients of aid, as a basis for fine-tuning financial support'.[67] The same account notes the emphasis placed by the Commission itself upon coordinating initiatives with the AMM,[68] just as it did in the case of EUJUST THEMIS.

Nevertheless, it remains a live issue whether ESDP operations like EUJUST THEMIS and the AMM are fully compliant with Article 47 TEU, insofar as they are liable to produce 'overlap effects' of the kind described. To put the point more generally: does the protection afforded by Article 47 go so far as to preclude the adoption of a second pillar measure specifically designed to further one or more of the objectives of Title V TEU, merely because the activity to which it relates might conceivably have been the subject of a measure adopted, in furtherance of a different objective, under one of the legal bases in the EC Treaty; and would that be so, regardless of whether action had actually been taken by the Community or was even contemplated?[69] In other words, does Article 47 still apply, where there is identity of *content* between measures that seem capable of being adopted under different Pillars, but no identity of *aim*?

3.5 Article 47 and the parallelism between first and second pillar competences

In the submission of the writer, the answer to those questions should be that the prohibition of Article 47 TEU does not extend to overlap effects,

---

[66] On the arrangements relating to participation by third States, see Joint Action, Article 10.
[67] Aceh Occasional Paper, pp. 30–1.   [68] *Ibid.*, p. 30.
[69] Such would appear to be the assumption underlying the Commission's case in the proceedings referred to in n. 10.

as between the first and second pillars. It may be permissible, in certain situations, for a measure that is broadly similar in content to be adopted under one competence or the other, or indeed for complementary actions to be taken under both of them. There are both negative and positive reasons that militate in favour of recognising that a degree of parallelism exists between EC and CFSP competences in such areas of overlap.[70]

3.5.1 The negative reason

The negative reason is that the protection of the EC Treaty by Article 47 against overlap effects is simply not necessary.

The adoption of a measure designed to further the foreign policy objectives of the CFSP is unlikely ever to prevent similar action that is deemed appropriate from being taken in furtherance of the socio-economic objectives of the EC Treaty. This is because CFSP competence and the Community competences with which it is most likely to interact, such as those for development cooperation or general cooperation, are non-pre-emptive in character. There is no race to occupy the field, since the exercise of one form of competence leaves open the full range of possibilities for the exercise of the other.

An instructive contrast can be drawn with the interaction between third pillar and first pillar competences that was held to constitute 'encroach-ment' by the former upon the latter in the circumstances of the *Environmental Penalties* case. The Title VI Framework Decision there in issue, if it had been valid, would have had the effect of pre-empting an area of potential legislative activity. So long as it remained in force, no EC regulation or directive relating to the punishment of the offences in question could have been adopted under Article 175, the legal basis for Community measures on the environment, since the existence of two pieces of legislation with similar subject matter would infringe the principle of legal certainty. The third pillar competence was thus effect-ively 'in competition' with an available first pillar competence, in the sense

---

[70] This could perhaps be the answer to Koutrakos's question: 'is it not possible for the coexistence and, furthermore, interaction between the EC and the CFSP rules to be ensured. Rather than two distinct frameworks destined to co-exist in a legally awkward manner because of a political compromise, could the different provisions upon which the Union is based not operate as a dynamic system of interrelated rules?' See P. Koutrakos, *EU International Relations Law* (Oxford: Hart Publishing, 2006), p. 418.

that the exercise of the former would result in the occupation of the field for the time being, excluding or restricting the exercise of the latter. Similarly, in the earlier Case C-170/96, if Community competence had existed under Article 100c for regulating airport transit visas, the adoption of the Joint Action would have prevented that competence from being exercised within the occupied field.

No such encroachment will occur where, owing to the particular nature of the activity to which they relate, second and first pillar competences can be exercised without either of them having a pre-emptive effect. A helpful analogy is available in the case law which establishes that action by the Community in the field of humanitarian aid and development cooperation does not have the consequence of precluding autonomous action by the Member States with respect to the same subject matter, as would be the case in other policy areas.[71] In such areas of parallel competence, which also include general cooperation and research and technological development,[72] there is no necessity to protect the integrity of the Community order by invoking the *AETR* principle,[73] because the first competence in the field, whether Community or Member State, in no way inhibits the future exercise of the other competence.

There is, of course, a distinction between the parallelism of EC/Member State competences that was recognised in the *Bangladesh* and *EDF* judgments,[74] and that of EC/CFSP competences in areas of overlap, such as the circumstances in which the EUJUST THEMIS and AMM operations were mounted: the former provides an instance of parallel competences relating to the same policy area (development cooperation), whereas the latter entails the exercise of *different* competences conferred, respectively, on the Community and the Union, which may in some instances result in the adoption of *similar* actions. However, this is a distinction without a difference. The point is that, in both kinds of case, the respective competences are non-pre-emptive. If the adoption of a measure under Title V TEU in no way inhibits the exercise of a parallel EC competence, there

[71] Joined Cases C-181/91 and C-248/91, *European Parliament* v. *Council and Commission (Bangladesh)* [1993] ECR I-3685; Case C-316/91, *European Parliament* v. *Council (EDF)* [1994] ECR I-625.
[72] The parallel nature of these various competences was explicitly recognised in Article I-14 (3) and (4) CT.
[73] Case 22/70, *Commission Council* [1971] ECR 263.   [74] See n. 15.

cannot be any justification for invoking Article 47. The only constraint should be that imposed by the principle of consistency in Article 3 TEU.[75]

3.5.2 The positive reason

The positive reason for interpreting Article 47 as not prohibiting overlap effects is that such an interpretation is consonant both with the express wording of Articles 11 and 17 TEU and with the *effet utile* of the Union's external relations policy as a whole.

The unequivocal language of Article 11(1) and Article 17(1) TEU, more particularly with respect to security, was noted above. It is a stated objective of the CFSP 'to strengthen the security of the Union *in all ways*';[76] and the CFSP extends to '*all* questions related to the security of the Union'. Preserving peace and strengthening international security are similarly explicit Title V objectives. At the same time, it has been noted that certain security-related activities may be seen as sufficiently proximate to the objectives of Community cooperation policy to be capable of being undertaken on the basis of the competences conferred by Article 177 or Article 181a EC. In the writer's submission, it would defeat the clear intention of Articles 11 and 17 TEU if Article 47 prevented the Council from adopting a CFSP measure, which the Council considered necessary in the interests of the Union's own security and/or the wider interests of international peace and security, merely because the possibility might exist of adopting a measure having similar content in the framework of development cooperation or general cooperation.

Further textual support can be found in the inter-pillar character of the Treaty provisions on developing and consolidating democracy and the rule of law, and respect for human rights and fundamental freedoms. General competence to pursue that objective, which is essentially a political one, belongs within the CFSP, as indicated by the fifth indent of Article 11(1) TEU; however, as we have seen, Community policy in the areas of development cooperation and of general cooperation is required, respectively by Article 177(2) and by Article 181a(1) second subparagraph EC, to 'contribute to' the attainment of the objective. It cannot be the case

---

[75] This line of argument was not accepted by AG Mengozzi in Case 91/05: Opinion, paras. 96–127.

[76] Article 11 (1), second indent.

that Article 47 would preclude the adoption of a CFSP joint action, say, to strengthen the democratic system of certain Middle Eastern countries, merely because parallel action could be taken on the basis of Article 181a: in the first place, the competence conferred by Article 181a, second sub-paragraph is ancillary in character; and, second, the result would be to empty Article 11(1), fifth indent TEU of virtually all its content.

Moreover, practical experience shows that parallel Community and CFSP competences can work well together in furthering the overall objectives of the Union's external action, provided that the Council and the Commission comply with the duty of cooperation, which is imposed on them by Article 3 TEU. The point is vividly illustrated by the EUJUST THEMIS and AMM operations: of the latter, it has been written that 'the Commission's efforts and the AMM mandate can only be regarded as complementary and mutually reinforcing'.[77] On the other hand, any attempt to establish a fixed boundary between EC and CFSP activity would be entirely artificial, giving rise to endless turf wars between the institutions. It would be liable seriously to disrupt the business of developing the foreign policy of the Union and risk constraining its ability to respond flexibly and coherently to international crises.

3.5.3 Exercising parallel first and second pillar competences

It is submitted that, where parallel Community and CFSP competences are available, the decision as to which of them should be exercised, or whether complementary initiatives are called for, should be reached pragmatically in the light of all the circumstances and with due regard to the principle of consistency and the duty of cooperation under Article 3 TEU. The priorities of development cooperation, say, are not the same as those of security policy, and neither are the timetables and procedures for implementing such policies. For instance, it was obviously right to organise the AMM as an ESDP crisis management operation, though one that could be coordinated with the Community's development cooper-ation activity. The integrated approach that was achieved in dealing with the situation in Aceh has been warmly commended, in these terms:

---

[77] Aceh Occasional Paper, p. 29.

Not only is [the AMM] a viable operation with ASEAN partners, but it has brought military, ex-military and civilians together to form a credible and extremely efficient team. The EU has successfully deployed human rights monitors alongside Explosive Ordinance Disposal experts, which constitutes a model for how future ESDP operations could be conducted.[78]

The guiding principle in each case should be to ensure maximum effectiveness in furthering the overall objectives of the Union's external action.

3.6 Epilogue

3.6.1 The ECOWAS judgment

Judgment was given in Case 91/05, commonly referred to as 'the *ECOWAS* case', on 20 May 2008.[79] Contrary to the opinion of AG Mengozzi in Case 91/05, the Court of Justice held that Decision 2004/833 ('the contested Decision') ought to have been adopted under the Community's competence for development cooperation policy, and that it must accordingly be annulled. The ruling turned on the Court's interpretation of the contested Decision as pursuing simultaneously both CFSP objectives and development cooperation objectives, without either of these being incidental to the other; while the particular action that was contemplated (providing funds and technical assistance) was capable of serving both sets of objectives. In a similar situation, where several legal bases in the EC Treaty were concerned, the solution would be to found the instrument in question on all of them; however, in the Court's view, the solution of a cumulative legal basis was precluded by Article 47 TEU. Since, considered in the light of its aim as well as of its content, the Decision could have been adopted as a development cooperation measure, that was what, the case law indicated, should have been done.

If the *ECOWAS* judgment had been available sooner, the main thrust of the argument in this chapter would have been no different. However, it would have been necessary to address some of the unexpected elements of the Court's reasoning, such as the reliance placed on policy documents

---

[78] Aceh Occasional Paper, p. 34.

[79] See n. 11. In Case 91/05, the writer acted for the United Kingdom, which was one of six Member States intervening in support of the Council. The views expressed in this epilogue and throughout the paper are exclusively the writer's own. A brief account of Case 91/05, in similar terms to the above, will be included in the article referred to in n. 1.

(notably the 2006 'Consensus' text),[80] in arriving at a conception of the demarcation between development cooperation competence and CFSP competence that is hard to reconcile with the clear language of Article 177 EC and Article 11 TEU.

Most importantly, there would have been no reason to revise the writer's conclusion as to the existence, even under the present dispensation, of an area of potential 'overlap' between first and second pillar competences, where a measure having a certain *content* may be adopted in furtherance either of a Community *aim* or of a CFSP *aim*. It does not follow from *ECOWAS* that EUJUST THEMIS, still less the AMM, breached Article 47. The trouble with the contested Decision, as understood by the Court of Justice, was that it was pursuing CFSP and development cooperation objectives *simultaneously*. Future accidents could, therefore, be avoided, as long as Article 47 remains in force, by language making crystal clear that the specific and only aim of an arms control measure is the strengthening of international peace and security.

At all events, the significance of the *ECOWAS* case is likely to be short-lived, in view of the changes to the Union structure that the Treaty of Lisbon will bring about.

3.6.2 The interaction between CFSP and TFEU competences under the new dispensation

As already indicated in the Introduction to this chapter, the specificity of the CFSP, as distinguished from the areas of external action provided for by Part V of the TFEU and the external aspects of other Union policies, is to be maintained in the constitutional order resulting from the TL. It is true that there will be a single legal person, the EU, with competence across the whole range of international relations.[81] However, Title I of the TFEU makes very clear that the Union's competence in the field of the CFSP is different in kind from its other competences, which fall into one of the general categories – exclusive, shared or supporting – defined in that Title;[82]

---

[80] Joint Statement by the Council and the representatives of the governments of the Member States meeting within the Council, the European Parliament and the Commission on European Union Development Policy, OJ 2006 C 46/1.

[81] Article 47 TEU revised.

[82] See Articles 2 to 6 TFEU. A similar point is made by Marise Cremona in chapter 2, above, section 2.2.3.

a difference that is emphasised by the retention of the specific provisions on the CFSP in chapter 2 of Title V TEU revised, somewhat spoiling the symmetry of the new Treaty structure.[83] More concretely, the institutional and procedural arrangements applicable to the CFSP retain most of the features that mark the distinctness of the second pillar from the Community model of the first pillar under the existing Treaties – unanimity as the general voting rule for Council decisions, no Commission monopoly of the initiative, exclusion of the European Parliament from formal decision-making, a very restricted jurisdiction for the ECJ. The new Article 24(1), second subparagraph of the TEU revised explicitly draws attention to those particularities, stating that the CFSP 'is subject to specific rules and procedures', and going on to recall the most important of them.

As a result, the implications of deciding whether external action that is contemplated should be taken under CFSP competence or under one of the Union's TFEU competences will continue to be more far-reaching than those of a choice between different legal bases in the TFEU. The issues that are the subject of this chapter will accordingly still be relevant under the new dispensation. However, the conclusions summarised in the preceding section are liable to be affected by two important changes the TL will bring about.

One of these changes concerns the hierarchical relationship between the first (Community) pillar and the second and third (Union) pillars of the existing Treaty structure: the qualified primacy given by the TEU to the first pillar will not be replicated in the new constitutional order. The reference in Article 1 TEU to the Union's being '*founded* on the European Communities, *supplemented by* the policies and forms of cooperation established by this Treaty'[84] disappears from the text of the TEU revised; as also do the references in Articles 2 and 3 TEU to 'building upon the *acquis communautaire*', removing any possible inference that communitarisation even of the CFSP should be an eventual goal. Most significantly for present purposes, Article 47 is to be replaced by Article 40 TEU revised, which makes clear that CFSP competences and the Union's other competences are to be equally protected against each other: the first

---

[83] Apart from Title V TEU, the re-ordering of the Treaties places within the amended TEU the provisions that define the essential nature of the EU, while consigning to the TFEU the legal bases for concrete Union policies, as well as more detailed institutional and procedural provisions.

[84] Emphasis added.

paragraph of the new Article provides that 'the implementation of the [CFSP] shall not affect the application of the procedures and the extent of the powers of the institutions laid down by the Treaties for the exercise of the Union's competences referred to in Articles 3 to 6 of the [TFEU]; while the second paragraph provides that '[s]imilarly, the implementation of the policies listed in those Articles shall not affect the application of the procedures and the extent of the powers of the institutions laid down by the Treaties for the exercise of the Union's competences under this Chapter'.[85]

It follows that the test of a prohibited 'effect' cannot be the same, for the purposes of the first and second paragraphs of Article 40 TEU revised, as it has been recognised by the ECJ to be for the purposes of the present Article 47. We have seen that the ECJ interprets the latter Article as protecting the competences conferred on the Community by the EC Treaty from being 'encroached upon' by the Union's competences under Titles V and VI TEU. Such encroachment – described above as a 'substitution effect' – was found to have occurred in the *Environmental Penalties* and *Ship-source Pollution* cases, because an act having the same aim and content as the third pillar act that was being challenged might conceivably have been adopted under one of the legal bases in the EC Treaty. Evidently, that reasoning cannot apply in relation to a provision offering mutual protection to CFSP competence and the Union's external TFEU competences. Under the new dispensation, the only viable approach will be for the competent institutions to determine where, all things considered, the centre of gravity of a given measure lies.[86]

The other change consists of the omission from the chapter containing specific provisions on the CFSP of the list of objectives presently found in Article 11(1) TEU. The various elements of the Article 11(1) list have been integrated into the general list of objectives of the Union's external action, found in Article 21(2) of the TEU revised.[87] The only guidance as to the scope of the CFSP that will be provided explicitly by the Treaty itself is the definition in Article 24(1), according to which competence in CFSP matters 'shall cover all areas of foreign policy and all questions relating

---

[85] Protection will also be given expressly for the CFSP against the creation of supplementary powers under the amended version of Article 308 EC, found in Article 352 TFEU

[86] See, in the same sense, Marise Cremona in chapter 2, above, section 2.2.3.

[87] More particularly, under points (a), (b) and (c) of Article 21(2).

to the Union's security, including the progressive framing of a common defence policy that might lead to a common defence'. The definition brings together the introductory phrase of Article 11(1) and the opening sentence of Article 17(1) TEU, with the extensive concept of security policy found there.

How will that change impact upon the claim, which has been expressed above with some confidence, that a substitution effect is unlikely ever to be produced in the interaction between first and second pillar competences, there being no identity of objectives between those pillars? Will it be possible to say the same, regarding the future interaction between CFSP competences and external TFEU competences, in view of the common list of objectives laid down by Article 21(2) TEU revised?

On the one hand, it is submitted, in spite of the establishment of the common list, including objectives presently designated as specific to the CFSP, the scope of the competence conferred on the Union by Chapter 2 of Title V TEU revised is still to be understood as confined to 'foreign policy' in the narrow sense explained in section 3.2.2, above – namely, the political, security and defence aspects of international relations. There are two reasons why the reference to 'all aspects of foreign policy' could not be understood in a general sense, as covering the whole range of the Union's competence in the external sphere. One is that a new term – 'the Union's external action' – has been introduced into the amended Treaties precisely for that purpose.[88] The other reason is that, from the new Treaty structure outlined above, it is very clear that the CFSP has been conceived, not as a residual category of external relations competence, but as distinct in principle from the categories of competence defined by Articles 3 to 6 TFEU, which include the legal bases for action by the Union in matters such as trade, development cooperation and general cooperation.[89]

On the other hand, it will no longer be possible to argue that there is a separation intended by the Treaties between competence for external

---

[88] See the heading of Title V TEU revised, as well as Articled 21(3) and Article 22(1), second subparagraph TEU revised, where the CFSP is treated as a specific aspect of the Union's external action. See also the heading of Part Five of the TFEU.

[89] Cf. the explanation suggested by Marise Cremona in chapter 2, above, section 2.2.3, which is based upon the *lex generalis/lex specialis* principle. This seems to the writer hard to reconcile with the express intention to eschew any priority as between CFSP competence and the Union's other external competences.

economic relations and competence for external political relations.[90] The Union is enjoined to pursue the objectives set out in Article 21(2) TEU revised 'in the development and implementation of the different areas of [its] external action covered by this Title and by Part Five of the [TFEU], and of the external aspects of its other policies'. Whatever the external competence in question, therefore, all of the listed objectives are capable in principle of bearing some degree of relevance to its exercise. Though not, of course, the *same* degree of relevance. It will still be the case, for instance, that CFSP competence ought to be used, where action is primarily aimed at furthering one of the broadly political objectives of points (a) to (c) of Article 21(2); whereas competence for development cooperation[91] ought to be used, where action is primarily focused on the development objectives of point (d). Determination of the legal basis for a given external action will, therefore, continue to require consideration of its aim as well as of its content. However, the choice in future may be less clear-cut than under the present dispensation; and there is likely to be a proliferation of 'overlap effects' of the kind discussed in section 3.4.2, above.

Must we, then, anticipate a continuation, even an exacerbation, of the debilitating turf wars between the Commission and the European Parliament, on one side, and the Council and the Member States, on the other, which have bedevilled the Union's external activity in recent years? The answer depends on a further change to be introduced by the TL, namely the establishment of the post of 'double-hatted' High Representative of the Union for Foreign Affairs and Security Policy – at the same time, a top-level Council functionary and a Vice-President of the Commission. It is vital that the first holder of this post should establish an authority across the whole field of the Union's external action, and an independence from sclerotic interests within the institutions, that will enable borderline issues of competence to be resolved in a pragmatic fashion.

---

[90] It appears from the *ECOWAS* judgment that, in the eyes of the Court of Justice, the intended separation is already less clear than the relevant Treaty texts might be thought to indicate.

[91] As provided for in Chapter 1 of Title II of Part Five TFEU.

EC law and UN Security Council Resolutions – in search of the right fit

PIET EECKHOUT

4.1 Introduction

The European Union (EU) has long been a busy international actor. Early on in the development of EC law, the European Court of Justice (ECJ) confirmed that the European Economic Community (EEC) could conclude 'international agreements in most if not all its spheres of activity'. The EEC, later European Community (EC), has made very active use of that international legal capacity. As its activities are ever expanding, the number and scope of the international agreements which the EC concludes increases as well. With the conclusion of international agreements have come questions about the legal effects which such agreements produce. The ECJ had to develop its own doctrine on the matter, and this doctrine cannot be neatly encapsulated in a single concept. It is true that scholars, and at times the ECJ itself, have used the 'direct effect' catchphrase: most international agreements have such direct effect, but some international agreements do not. A more detailed analysis of the relevant law shows, however, that this catchphrase is no more than just that, and may sometimes even be deceptive.[1]

It is not the object of this paper to return to the legal effects which international agreements, as such, produce. The international legal landscape is fast evolving. International treaties are no longer just about relations between international actors. They often include an institutional framework or set up a full-blown organisation. The founding treaties then become living instruments, on the basis of which myriad different

---

[1] P. Eeckhout, *External Relations of the European Union. Legal and Constitutional Foundations* (Oxford: Oxford University Press, 2004), p. 275; cf. J. Klabbers, 'International Law in Community Law: The Law and Politics of Direct Effect', 21 YEL (2002), pp. 263–98.

decisions are adopted. These decisions can be looked at through constitutional law lenses as consisting of legislative-type, executive-type and
judicial-type decisions. These lenses have the merit of signposting us
in the direction of important political concepts such as democracy,
accountability, fundamental rights and respect for the rule of law. It is
further worth adding that, from a material point of view, international
treaty law is increasingly concerned with non-statal actors, such as companies, individuals and NGOs. The International Court of Justice (ICJ)
has recently confirmed that an international treaty may directly confer
rights on individuals.[2] In many ways international law is becoming
another tool for lawmaking sitting side by side and offering many ana-
logies with other tools, in particular the classic exercise of government at
a national level.

The ECJ and the Court of First Instance (CFI) are confronted with this
changing picture. This paper looks at important recent CFI case law on
one very specific corner of that picture: the legal effects in EC law of
United Nations (UN) Security Council Resolutions.[3] In essence, the CFI
decided that EC acts implementing UN Resolutions cannot be reviewed
on grounds of fundamental rights as general principles of Community
law, because this would undermine the binding character of those Resolutions. In so doing, the judges had to find their way through a jungle of
important issues which the fight against terrorism raises, such as: the
status of UN law, particularly in Community law; the powers of the
Security Council; the relationship between the Common Foreign and
Security Policy (CFSP) and action by the EC; the scope for the protection
of fundamental rights and for derogation from those rights.

This paper focuses in particular, on systemic issues concerning the
effects of UN Resolutions in Community law. The CFI judgments are
merely the start of the EU courts' expeditions in this new territory. As with
questions of direct and other effects of international agreements, the
courts have considerable leeway to develop the law: the EC Treaty says
nothing whatsoever on this specific subject. That does not mean that there
are no legal criteria, principles, and even rules, that have a bearing on the

---

[2] ICJ, *La Grand (Germany* v. *US)*, ICJ Reports 2001, p. 494, para. 77.
[3] Other corners include the effects of customary international law, see, e.g. Case C-162/69 *Racke*
v. *Hauptzollamt Mainz* [1998] ECR I-3655 and the effects of WTO dispute decisions, see,
e.g. Case C-377/02 *Van Parys* [2005] ECR I-1465.

matter. In Dworkinian terms, the courts should be looking for judicial replies which best fit both EC and international law, as those are the legal systems in issue.[4] This paper is critical in this respect.[5]

I start by setting out the main components of the CFI's reasoning. The paper then develops a twofold critique, respectively from the international and Community law angles. In its conclusions the paper defends an alternative approach.

4.2 The CFI's approach in Yusuf and Kadi

The CFI's judgments in *Yusuf* v. *Council and Commission* and *Kadi* v. *Council and Commission* have quickly gained notoriety.[6] Those cases were brought by persons suspected of supporting terrorism, and listed as such, not only in an EU Common Position, but also in an EC Regulation freezing their assets.[7] The Common Position and the Regulation reflected UN Security Council Resolutions. The names of the persons involved were listed by the Sanctions Committee set up by those Resolutions. The EC Regulation faithfully followed the ebb and flow of the listing of persons and entities by the UN Committee.

The applicants sought the annulment of the Regulation inter alia on grounds of breach of fundamental rights. I will not set out the CFI's full argument, which is lengthy, but will concentrate on some of the crucial elements in the reasoning.

It is perhaps best to start with the CFI's conclusion on the question of judicial review on grounds of violation of fundamental rights. The CFI considers that the challenged Regulation falls outside the ambit of its judicial review powers, and that it has no authority to call in question, even indirectly, its lawfulness in the light of Community law.[8] This is

---

[4] R. Dworkin, *Law's Empire* (reprint Oxford: Hart Publishing, 1998). The reference to Dworkin seems appropriate as we are dealing with hard cases, in which there is a lot of debate on the grounds of law. I acknowledge that my approach is no more than some kind of Dworkin-lite.

[5] It builds on P. Eeckhout, *Does Europe's Constitution Stop at the Water's Edge?*, 5th Walter van Gerven Lecture (Groningen: European Law Publishing, 2005), pp. 22–7.

[6] Respectively, Case T-306/01 *Yusuf* v. *Council and Commission* [2005] ECR II-3353 and Case T-315/01 *Kadi* v. *Council and Commission* [2005] ECR II-3649. In *Kadi*, an appeal before the ECJ is pending at the time of writing (Case C-402/05 P). I should disclose that I have been consulted by the appellant, Mr Kadi.

[7] Council Regulation 881/2002 OJ 2002 L 139/9.

[8] References here and below are to *Yusuf*, n. 6, para. 276.

remarkable, of course, since the CFI was not dealing with an EU Common Position, but with an EC Regulation, clearly an act of the institutions in the sense of Article 230 EC. The issue is, indeed, not whether an action for annulment can be brought. The issue is rather, in the CFI's conception, that the Regulation implements and applies, in a Community context, Resolutions of the Security Council.

In order to come to this remarkable conclusion, the CFI first considers the relationship between the international legal order under the United Nations Charter and the Community legal order. It opens that analysis by stating that, from the standpoint of international law, the obligations of the EU Member States under the UN Charter clearly prevail over every other obligation of domestic law or of international treaty law, including their obligations under the EC Treaty.[9] That the Charter prevails over other international treaties is of course spelled out by the Charter itself (Art. 103),[10] but the statement that it also prevails over domestic law is more controversial. The CFI explains how this is the case: it simply follows from Article 27 of the Vienna Convention on the Law of Treaties, according to which a party may not invoke the provisions of its internal law as justification for its failure to perform a treaty.

The CFI then points out that this 'primacy', as it calls it, extends to Security Council Resolutions. It subsequently draws attention to Articles 307 and 297 EC. The former provision permits the Member States to give precedence to pre-EC Treaty obligations; the latter recognises that a Member State may be called upon to take measures in order to carry out obligations it has accepted for the purpose of maintaining peace and international security. The CFI concludes that, pursuant both to the rules of general international law and *to the specific provisions of the Treaty*, Member States may, *and indeed must*, leave unapplied any provision of Community law that raises any impediment to the proper performance of their obligations under the UN Charter.[11]

The CFI subsequently admits that the Community, not being a member of the UN, is not directly bound by the Charter as a matter of *international* law. The CFI nevertheless holds that the Community is bound, in the same

---

[9] *Ibid.*, para. 231.

[10] Art. 103 UN Charter reads: 'In the event of a conflict between the obligations of the Members of the United Nations under the present Charter and their obligations under any other international agreement, their obligations under the present Charter shall prevail'.

[11] *Yusuf*, n. 6, paras. 234–40, emphasis added.

way as its Member States, by virtue of the EC Treaty, as a matter of *Community* law. It develops a sophisticated reasoning, referring to the analogy with the *International Fruit Company* judgment where the ECJ held that the General Agreement on Tariffs and Trade (GATT) was binding on the EEC,[12] to come to the conclusion that the Charter is also binding. The consequence is that, first, the Community may not infringe the obligations imposed on its Member States by the Charter or impede their performance and, second, that in the exercise of its powers it is bound to adopt all the measures necessary to enable its Member States to fulfil those obligations.

The CFI considers that it results from all the preceding that there are structural limits on its judicial review capacity. It considers that the institutions, when adopting the Regulation, acted under 'circumscribed powers', with the result that they had no autonomous discretion. Now come the vital paragraphs:

> Any review of the internal lawfulness of the contested regulation, especially having regard to the provisions or general principles of Community law relating to the protection of fundamental rights, would therefore imply that the Court is to consider, indirectly, the lawfulness of those Resolutions. In that hypothetical situation, in fact, the origin of the illegality alleged by the applicant would have to be sought, not in the adoption of the contested regulation but in the resolutions of the Security Council which imposed the sanctions ... In particular, if the Court were to annul the contested regulation ... , although that regulation seems to be imposed by international law, on the ground that that act infringes their fundamental rights which are protected by the Community legal order, such annulment would indirectly mean that the resolutions of the Security Council concerned themselves infringe those fundamental rights. In other words, the applicants ask the Court to declare by implication that the provision of international law at issue infringes the fundamental rights of individuals, as protected by the Community legal order.[13]

This the CFI is not willing to do. It considers that it does not have the jurisdiction to review the Regulation on grounds of general principles of Community law. The CFI does realise that, if it were to stop there, there would be no remedy whatsoever. In the end it finds that there is scope for

[12] Joined Cases 21–24/72 *International Fruit Company* [1972] ECR 1219.
[13] *Yusuf*, n. 6, paras. 266–7.

some measure of judicial review. 'None the less', it states, 'the Court is empowered to check, indirectly, the lawfulness of the Resolutions of the Security Council in question with regard to *jus cogens*, understood as a body of higher rules of public international law binding on all subjects of international law, including the bodies of the United Nations, and from which no derogation is possible'.[14] What is the basis for this jurisdictional competence? Simply the nature of *jus cogens* or peremptory norms under international law. If Security Council Resolutions failed to respect *jus cogens*, however improbable that may be, they would bind neither the Member States of the UN nor, in consequence, the Community. The CFI then reviews the applicants' arguments concerning the right to property, the right to be heard and the right to an effective remedy. I will not analyse this section of the judgments. The conclusion from the review is that there is no violation of *jus cogens*, but it has to be said that the CFI carefully examines the various arguments. This somewhat sweetens the pill of denial of jurisdiction. It is, however, obvious that *jus cogens* does not offer the same standard of review as do general principles of Community law.[15]

The CFI confirmed this reasoning in *Ayadi* and *Hassan*.[16] In those judgments the CFI nevertheless stressed the diplomatic remedies available to persons listed in a UN Resolution, who are able to petition their government to intervene on their behalf at UN level. It highlighted that particular obligations are imposed on the EU Member States when a request for removal from the list is addressed to them. Those obligations stem from their duty to respect fundamental rights as general principles of Community law.[17] The judgments thus appear to shift some of the burden of compliance with fundamental rights from the Community to the Member States.

The most recent CFI judgment, *Organisation des Modjahedines du peuple d'Iran*, offers a remarkable contrast to *Yusuf* and *Kadi*. That case concerned the listing of an organisation, not by the Security Council, but by the EU itself. The CFI annulled the EC act involved (a Council Decision implementing an EC Regulation) because of violations of the

---

[14] *Ibid.*, para. 277.

[15] See, e.g. the discussion on the right to a fair hearing in *Yusuf*, n. 6, paras. 304–31, in particular para. 328.

[16] Case T-253/02 *Ayadi* v. *Council*, judgment of 12 July 2006, paras. 115–17; Case T-49/04 *Hassan* v. *Council and Commission*, judgment of 12 July 2006, paras. 91–3.

[17] *Ayadi*, paras. 144–50; *Hassan*, paras. 114–20.

right to a fair hearing, the right to an effective judicial remedy and the obligation to state reasons.[18]

4.3 Critique from the perspective of international law

Do the judgments in *Yusuf* and *Kadi* fit the system of public international law? At first sight that appears to be so, and one could assess the judgments as follows. The CFI pays its respects to international law. Article 103 of the UN Charter is generally considered to establish an absolute primacy rule in case of conflict between obligations under the Charter and those under other international treaties or agreements.[19] The CFI, commendably, finds a way around the obstacle that the Community is not bound by the Charter as a matter of international law. It extends the *International Fruit Company* reasoning to the UN case. The Member States could not transfer powers to the Community which they themselves do not possess and they have undertaken to ensure that the Community exercises its relevant powers for the performance of their Charter obligations. The judgments, therefore, confirm great respect for international law. Several commentators take that view.[20]

My argument is that such an assessment does not withstand closer scrutiny. True respect for international law does not command the CFI's approach which consists of declaring that a listing in an EC Regulation cannot be reviewed in the light of general principles of Community law.

One should first note that the respect which the CFI pays is remarkable, since it is not imposed by international law as such. The CFI admits that the Charter is not binding on the Community by virtue of international law. It constructs its binding nature on the basis of Community law. I nevertheless concede that the arguments which it advances in support of this construction and the analogy with *International Fruit Company* are

---

[18] Case T-228/02 *Organisation des Modjahedines du peuple d'Iran* v. *Council*, judgment of 12 December 2006.

[19] J. Pauwelyn, *Conflict of Norms in Public International Law* (Cambridge: Cambridge University Press, 2003), p. 99.

[20] C. Tomuschat, case-note, 43 CMLRev. (2006), p. 545; R. H. van Ooik and R. A. Wessel, 'De Yusuf en Kadi-uitspraken in perspectief. Nieuwe verhoudingen in de interne en externe bevoegdheden van de Europese Unie', *Sociaal-economische Wetgeving* (2006), p. 236; P. Stangos and G. Gryllos, 'Le droit communautaire à l'épreuve des réalités du droit international: leçons tirées de la jurisprudence communautaire récente relevant de la lutte contre le terrorisme international', CDE (2006), pp. 466–9.

persuasive. When the Charter was drafted the EEC did not yet exist, and the kind of transfer of powers to an international organisation which EC law implies was difficult to anticipate. The principle that the EC is bound, in areas where powers have been transferred, by some fundamental treaties which are binding on its Member States ensures that such a transfer is accepted at international level instead of creating significant problems.[21]

However, the CFI does not sufficiently explicate what this binding nature of the UN Charter involves. It is necessary to unpack this. The CFI considers that the EC institutions acted 'under circumscribed powers'. But to say that the Charter is binding is not equivalent to excluding judicial review of a Regulation on the basis of the EU's primary law.[22] In international law the binding nature of the Charter is embodied in Article 103 of the Charter, a provision governing conflicts between treaty obligations. It operates for the EU Member States, in the sense that in case of conflict between their obligations under the EC Treaty and those under the UN Charter, the latter must prevail. That is fully accepted and indeed confirmed by Articles 307 and 297 EC. The ECJ has recognised in *Centro-Com*, also a sanctions case, that Community law could not stand in the way of a Member State performing its UN obligations.[23] In that case the ECJ did not accept that certain measures which the United Kingdom had adopted to ensure a better functioning of UN sanctions against Serbia and Montenegro were in conformity with EC trade and sanctions legislation. It nevertheless recognised that, to the extent that those measures were required by the UN Charter, Article 307 EC applied.

Is this dimension of the binding nature of the UN Charter sufficient for excluding judicial review of the Regulation in issue? The CFI considers that the Community may not infringe the obligations imposed on its Member States by the Charter or impede their performance.[24] It is not, however, clear in what way judicial review of a Regulation which implements a UN Resolution would breach that principle. Suppose the CFI had reviewed and annulled the Regulation. The Community law basis for freezing the assets of the various applicants would have disappeared, as the

---

[21] Cf. Eeckhout, *External Relations of the European Union*, pp. 436–9.
[22] In particular, Arts. 6(2) and 46 TEU; see also the next section.
[23] Case C-124/95 *The Queen* ex parte *Centro-Com* v. *HM Treasury* [1997] ECR I-81, para. 61.
[24] *Yusuf*, n. 6, para. 254.

Regulation would have been null and void under Community law. However, the actual freezing measures operate at a national level. The Member States would no longer be bound by the EC Regulation, but they would continue to be bound by their UN obligations. Surely as sovereign States they have the requisite legal means for continuing to apply those measures. There would simply be the same position as in *Centro-Com*. Annulment could by no means mean that the Member States are *prohibited* from freezing the assets of persons listed by the UN. Clearly, the CFI's jurisdiction does not encompass such a prohibition, nor was this argued for by the applicants. From this angle, the imperative to respect international law seems hardly in issue.

There is a second dimension to the binding nature of the UN Charter, imposed as it is, in the CFI's conception, by Community law itself. Without this dimension it could never follow that judicial review is excluded. The CFI's reasoning implies that the conflict provision of Article 103 UN Charter governs conflicts between the EC Treaty and the UN Charter. The EC Treaty demands respect for fundamental rights as general principles of Community law, but this is overridden by the need to comply with the Community's obligations under the UN Charter. Under this second dimension, these conflicts are not those with which the Member States could be confronted. The binding nature of the UN Charter governs *acts of the EC institutions*, not of the Member States; it 'circumscribes' those institutions' powers. They need to ensure that they respect UN Resolutions, even if it means violating general principles of Community law. The courts, likewise, cannot review any such violations which are 'imposed' by a Resolution.

But can we really speak here about a rule governing conflicts between the UN Charter and the EC Treaty? As we have seen it is *Community law itself*, the EC Treaty in other words, which requires that the UN Charter be respected. The conflict we are therefore looking at here is internal to the Community legal system. It is in reality a conflict between the EC law imperative to respect fundamental rights and the EC law imperative to respect UN law. In the second part of this critique I will challenge the CFI's justification for giving priority to the latter imperative, from the standpoint of Community law. For the purpose of my international law critique it is sufficient to note that, what is portrayed as a rule governing conflicts between international law and Community law, is in fact an internal precedence rule. It is in this respect useful to shift the language somewhat. The ECJ has confirmed that the EC Treaty is the constitutional charter of a Community governed by the rule of law.[25] The CFI in *Yusuf* and *Kadi* interprets that constitutional charter as allowing for a breach of the principle that all acts of the institutions are subject to judicial review as regards compliance with fundamental rights as general principles of Community law. We are not talking here about an international conflict rule. We are talking about an internal constitutional carve out, and a very significant one at that.

Since all this is based on the CFI's interpretation of Community law and since the CFI accepts that as a matter of international law the Community is not bound by the UN Charter, it surely cannot be said that international law *requires* this type of respect for the Charter. However, that still leaves the question whether it could not be said that the CFI's approach *promotes* respect for international law. The CFI's decisions may be seen to ensure that UN Resolutions are always heeded and respected, even in the special case of their implementation through a Community Regulation; even in the special case of the Community which is not bound by the UN Charter as a matter of international law.

Again, I would argue that one needs to look below the surface. Does not the CFI in fact translate the conflict rule of Article 103 UN Charter (and the provision in Art. 25 UN Charter according to which UN members agree to accept and implement Security Council Resolutions) into a principle of absolute primacy of Resolutions over all other law, be it international, Community or domestic law? Does this best fit the international legal system? Is that system best construed as including such a principle of primacy to the benefit of the Security Council acting under Chapter VII of the Charter? Is it best construed as including a principle which turns the Security Council into a global supreme legislature, unfettered by any international law constraints?[26] Important though the function of the Security Council no doubt is, I should think that few commentators would defend such an extreme view.[27] Surely the Security

---

[25] Case 294/83 *Les Verts* v. *Parliament* [1986] ECR 1339, para. 23.

[26] Cf. E. Cannizzaro, 'Machiavelli, the UN Security Council and the Rule of Law', Global Law Working Paper 11/05, Hauser Global Law School Program, pp. 20–1.

[27] In the field of terrorism sanctions, the UN itself recognises that the current listing and delisting procedures raise issues, see, e.g. Fifth Report of the Analytical Support and Sanctions Monitoring Team appointed pursuant to Resolutions 1526 (2004) and 1617 (2005) concerning Al-Qaeda and the Taliban and associated individuals and entities, S/2006/750,

Council ought to stay at least within the boundaries of what the UN Charter instructs it to do. There can be intense debate on what those boundaries are, and on whether the Security Council is its own judge in that respect, but I do not think there can be much discussion on the fact that international law is best seen as containing at least some restrictions on what the Security Council is capable of doing.[28]

But, my critical readers will say, this is exactly how the CFI sees it. It recognises that the Security Council is bound by *jus cogens*, by peremptory norms of international law. It in fact reviews the relevant Resolution in the light of *jus cogens*, but comes to the conclusion that no violation occurred.

It is at this juncture necessary to examine the CFI's review on grounds of *jus cogens* in greater depth. The first point to note is that, at a doctrinal level, this review appears to lack coherence. The CFI speaks of *jus cogens*, 'understood as a body of higher rules of public international law binding on all subjects of international law, including the bodies of the United Nations, and from which no derogation is possible'.[29] It finds support in Articles 53 and 64 Vienna Convention on the Law of Treaties (VCLT). This is a classic conception of *jus cogens*. However, in the next paragraph the CFI muddies the waters by stating that 'the Charter of the United Nations itself presupposes the existence of mandatory principles of international law, in particular, the protection of fundamental rights of the human person'.[30] Here, the CFI draws attention to the reference to human rights in the Charter's preamble, and to Chapter I of the Charter, from which it is clear that one of the purposes of the United Nations is to encourage respect for human rights and for fundamental freedoms.

---

20 September 2006, paras. 37–43; see in particular para. 41 which refers to the Secretary-General's position regarding four minimum standards: right to be informed; right to be heard; right to effective review; periodic review by the Security Council; see also Watson Institute for International Studies, *Strengthening Targeted Sanctions Through Fair and Clear Procedures* (Providence: Brown University, 2006). UNSC Resolution 1730 (2006) introduces some improvements, such as the establishment of a focal point to receive delisting requests and the possibility for such requests to be made by individual or group petitioners. It does not, however, establish an independent review procedure.

[28] See, e.g. E. de Wet, *The Chapter VII Powers of the United Nations Security Council* (Oxford: Hart Publishing, 2004), and ch. 5 in particular; Pauwelyn, *Conflict of Norms*, pp. 99–100; M. Shaw, *International Law* (Cambridge: Cambridge University Press, 2003, 5th ed.), pp. 1148–51; D. Akande, 'International Organizations', in M. Evans (ed.), *International Law* (Oxford: Oxford University Press, 2003), p. 285; Bowett's *Law of International Institutions*, P. Sands and P. Klein (eds.) (London: Sweet & Maxwell, 2001), pp. 42–3.

[29] *Yusuf*, n. 6, para. 277.   [30] *Ibid.*, para. 278.

The CFI concludes that those purposes and principles are binding on the members of the UN as well as on its bodies, and that the Security Council's powers of sanction must be wielded in compliance with international law, particularly with the purposes and principles of the UN.[31] In a further paragraph the CFI considers that it should engage in indirect judicial review of the Resolutions in question to see 'whether the superior rules of international law falling within the ambit of *jus cogens* have been observed, in particular, the mandatory provisions concerning the protection of human rights'.[32] It is only if that is the case that a Resolution can be accepted to have binding force.

This is not the place to enter into the debate about the precise scope of *jus cogens*. However, at this point of the development of international law there is clearly a distinction between *jus cogens* and the purposes and principles of the UN, in particular as regards human rights. The very concept of *jus cogens* continues to be contested, and international courts and tribunals appear circumspect about recognising such norms.[33] Most commentators consider that *jus cogens* is limited to norms such as the prohibition on the use of force, the prohibition against slavery, the prohibitions of genocide, torture and racial discrimination.[34] There is definitely no consensus that *jus cogens* extends to the whole of the Universal Declaration of Human Rights, and yet the CFI refers to the right to property in Article 17 of that Declaration and to the right to access to the courts in Article 8.[35] As regards the latter right, the CFI also mentions Article 14 of the International Covenant on Civil and Political Rights.

There are thus two ways of reading the CFI's reasoning. The first is that the CFI puts itself at the vanguard of an extensive and progressive conception of *jus cogens*, a conception which includes human rights norms listed in the Universal Declaration of Human Rights (UDHR) and in the International Covenant on Civil and Political Rights (ICCPR).[36] The second is that the CFI considers that the Security Council is bound by the

---

[31] *Ibid.*, paras. 279–80.   [32] *Ibid.*, para. 282.

[33] D. Shelton, 'International Law and "Relative Normativity"', in Evans, *International Law* n. 28, pp. 153–4.

[34] See, e.g. Restatement (Third) of the Foreign Relations Law of the US, American Law Institute (1987), Vol. 2, 161. For further discussion, see H. Steiner and P. Alston, *International Human Rights in Context* (Oxford: Oxford University Press, 2000, 2nd ed.), pp. 224–36; Shelton, 'International Law', pp. 150–9; Shaw, *International Law*, p. 117.

[35] *Yusuf*, n. 6, paras. 292 and 342.

[36] Cf. van Ooik and Wessel, 'De Yusef en Kadi-uitspraken in perspectief', p. 237.

purposes and principles of the UN which go beyond *jus cogens*, and which include those human rights which the organisation promotes in its various human rights instruments. There is much merit in this second reading. As indicated above, there are surely limits to the powers of the Security Council, and it is conceptually coherent to consider that the human rights norms in UN instruments are among those limits.[37] There is no need for reverting to *jus cogens* as a justification for exploring them. The CFI, however, insists throughout its analysis that it is focusing on *jus cogens*.

Let us now return to the starting point. Does not the CFI's approach promote respect for international law? Does the CFI in fact not manage to have the best of both worlds? It keeps the binding nature of a UN Resolution intact, and yet engages in some measure of review, not on domestic law grounds, but on the basis of international law itself. In doing so it adopts a progressive conception of what *jus cogens* requires.

My argument, instead, is that the CFI's approach has the worst of both worlds. The essence of the problem with which the CFI was confronted is that an individual who is listed in a UN Resolution does not have an effective judicial remedy at the international level. No international court appears to have direct jurisdiction to hear individual challenges to a UN Resolution.[38] That is why relief is sought from municipal courts. I have so far emphasised that the CFI refuses to review on grounds of fundamental rights as general principles of Community law. But as we have just seen, the CFI does review whether the Resolutions themselves comply with *jus cogens*. It calls this an indirect review,[39] but the review is only indirect in the sense that the CFI can only reach the Resolution through the EC Regulation implementing it. The review itself is most direct. It is the lawfulness of the Resolutions in the light of norms of *jus cogens* which is being examined. The radical nature of this review needs to be highlighted. Here is a municipal court, a court of the EU, not a general international court, which in actions brought by individuals against the EU institutions considers itself competent to review a Resolution of the Security Council as to compliance with essential international norms. Community lawyers

---

[37] de Wet, *The Chapter VII Powers*, pp. 191–204; Cannizzaro, 'Machiavelli'; Watson Institute, *Strengthening Targeted Sanctions*, p. 22.

[38] For a discussion of the long-standing debate on the powers of the ICJ in relation to UN resolutions, see Cannizzaro, 'Machiavelli', Section 3; de Wet, *The Chapter VII Powers*, Part I.

[39] *Yusuf*, n. 6, para. 277.

are not unfamiliar with this type of issue. The approach of the CFI is comparable to that of a court at Member State level which would consider itself competent to review the legality of an EC Regulation.

That this claim to jurisdiction over UN Resolutions is disputable and disputed can be seen in the fact that the United Kingdom has cross-appealed this point in *Kadi* – notwithstanding the fact that the CFI concluded that the review in the light of *jus cogens* revealed no unlaw-fulness. Indeed, imagine for a moment that the CFI had come to the opposite conclusion; that it had concluded that the UN Resolutions in issue were unlawful under international law. This could have triggered a severe legal and even political crisis at international level. What this would have meant is that, in view of the lack of legal remedies at an international level, a municipal court considers itself competent to strike down a UN Resolution. Does this best fit the international legal system? Is respect for international law promoted by accepting that municipal courts have the capacity to declare Security Council Resolutions unlawful for violation of *jus cogens*, or of the principles and purposes of the United Nations?

The CFI, of course, did not consider the Resolutions to be unlawful. It is difficult to imagine that it would ever come to that conclusion, and a critical observer may easily conclude that the review on grounds of *jus cogens* is no more than a figleaf.[40] But that is precisely why I consider that the CFI had the worst of both worlds. Its judicial reasoning did not enable the applicants to mount an effective challenge to their listing. This can most clearly be seen when one contrasts *Yusuf* and *Kadi* with the annul-ment in *Organisation des Modjahedines du peuple d'Iran*.[41] Fundamental rights were therefore not effectively protected. And yet the CFI attracted the criticism that it arrogated to itself jurisdiction to review a UN Reso-lution on the basis of *jus cogens*, a jurisdiction which is most disputable.

Time to sum up. The CFI's approach is not required by international law itself. It cannot be justified on the basis that EC law cannot stand in the way of the Member States performing their UN obligations. The latter proposition is undisputed and does not signify that an EC Regulation cannot be reviewed on fundamental rights grounds. The CFI's approach is to construct an internal, constitutional precedence rule: the EC Treaty

---

[40] Cf. Cannizzaro, 'Machiavelli', pp. 18–9; van Ooik and Wessel, 'De Yusef en kadi-uitspraken in perspectief', p. 237.

[41] Cited n. 18.

commands that UN law prevails over respect for fundamental rights. Such a construction cannot be defended with the argument that it promotes respect for international law. It risks turning the UN Security Council into a supreme, unfettered legislature. The CFI nevertheless recognises that there are limits to the Security Council's powers. However, its analysis of those limits is not persuasive and has the worst of both worlds. It arrogates to itself a jurisdiction to review a UN Resolution, a jurisdiction which is clearly disputable; and by not taking this review far enough it exposes itself to the criticism that there is no real scrutiny. My conclusion is therefore that the CFI's reasoning does not fit the rules and principles of international law well enough.

4.4 Critique from the perspective of EC law

Do the judgments in *Yusuf* and *Kadi* fit the EC law system? Do they show that system in its best light?

The above critique from an international law perspective does not examine whether the CFI's approach can be reconciled with specific international law rules and judicial decisions. Indeed, there is very little international law authority on the effect of international law rules in municipal law. This is true also for UN Resolutions. Moreover, the Community, as we have seen, is a special case in that it is not a signatory to the UN Charter, whereas its Member States are. Therefore, public international law provides little direct authority for the issue with which the CFI was faced.

This is different when one turns to Community law. As I will show, there are a number of specific Community law rules and decisions which are relevant to the question at hand. One should therefore first examine whether the CFI's reasoning fits those rules and decisions, whether it matches them or can be reconciled with them. If that were not the case, there would have to be particularly strong reasons for overriding those rules and decisions.

The starting point must be Article 6(2) of the Treaty on European Union (TEU), which confirms that fundamental rights are protected as general principles of Community law. As is well known, this provision codified the ECJ's case law on the matter, but it bears emphasising that respect for fundamental rights is now unequivocally a *Treaty* imperative – an imperative which the EU courts are mandated and instructed to enforce, at least within the scope of EC law.[42] Article 6 TEU in no way qualifies this imperative, which thus appears unconditional. Nor are there any other provisions in either the EU or EC Treaty which contain express derogations from the obligation to respect human rights. There are no provisions which lay down that fundamental rights may be derogated from where this is necessary to respect international law in general, or Security Council Resolutions in particular. Articles 307 and 297 EC, discussed above, are addressed to the Member States, and not to the EC institutions. Those provisions concern Community law in general, and not just fundamental rights.

As regards primary law, it is also worth noting that promoting respect for fundamental rights is an express objective of the CFSP – again without qualification. Article 11(1) TEU provides that one of the five CFSP objectives is 'to develop and consolidate democracy and the rule of law, and respect for human rights and fundamental freedoms'.

The ECJ's case law confirms the above. In *Les Verts*, the ECJ has used particularly strong language to emphasise the institutions' obligation to respect the Treaty and to submit to judicial review: 'the EEC is a Community based on the rule of law, inasmuch as neither its Member States nor its institutions can avoid a review of the question whether the measures adopted by them are in conformity with the basic constitutional charter, the Treaty'.[43] The case law on fundamental rights likewise holds that 'respect for human rights is . . . a condition of the lawfulness of Community acts'.[44] All this is, again, unqualified. All acts of the institutions are subject to review on grounds of respect for fundamental rights.[45]

One cannot fit *Yusuf* and *Kadi* into these rules and decisions with the argument that the CFI was in effect asked to review UN Security Council Resolutions rather than mere EC Regulations. The applicants' actions for annulment were solely directed at those Regulations. They did not seek review of the Resolutions as such, since this is obviously not within the CFI's jurisdiction. The CFI's reference to the institutions' circumscribed powers and its own incapacity to review in the light of fundamental rights, at most points to a principle that the force of international law stands

---

[42] See Article 46(d) TEU.   [43] *Les Verts* v. *Parliament*, n. 25, para. 23.

[44] Opinion 2/94 re Accession to the ECHR [1996] ECR I-1759, para. 34.

[45] It is hardly necessary to point out that the restrictions on standing (Article 230(4) EC) are a mere procedural limit which does not undermine the principle, as such.

in the way of review of a Regulation which copies and implements a particular international rule.

Are there any indications in the ECJ's case law that there is such a principle? Are there indications that the force of international law may trump certain fundamental EC Treaty rules and principles? The opposite is in fact the case. Not only is there a long line of judgments which confirm that, where the institutions conclude an international agreement, they need to respect the limits of the Community's competences and of the division of powers between the institutions. *France* v. *Commission*, a case on an agreement with the US on competition policy matters, confirms that the ECJ is willing to annul the act by which an institution unlawfully concluded an international agreement, even if the agreement is valid and binding under international law.[46] What is more, there is at least one judgment in which the ECJ examined whether certain provisions in a concluded international agreement were in conformity with general principles of Community law, and annulled the act of conclusion after having found that that was not the case: in *Germany* v. *Council*, the ECJ considered that the provisions on the distribution of import licences in the so-called Framework Agreement on bananas, itself part of the EC's tariff schedule at the time of the conclusion of the World Trade Organisation (WTO) Agreement, violated the general principle of non-discrimination. The ECJ annulled the Council decision concerning the conclusion of the Uruguay Round agreements to the extent that the Council approved this Framework Agreement.[47]

The above shows that there are no signs that the force of international law may preclude review on grounds of fundamental rights. The reader may, however, object that one cannot compare the treatment of rules on imports of bananas with the position of a UN Resolution. And it is true that the CFI did not speak about the general force of international law, but focused its reasoning on the overriding character of the UN Charter. Let us therefore further narrow down the issue: are there indications in the case law that UN Resolutions have such force as to preclude review of an EC act implementing them?

Again the opposite is the case. In *Bosphorus*, the ECJ was requested to interpret an EC Regulation implementing a UN sanctions Resolution. The

---

[46] Case C-327/91 *France* v. *Commission* [1994] ECR I-3641.
[47] Case C-122/95 *Germany* v. *Council* [1998] ECR I-973.

provision in issue ordered the impounding of all means of transport, including aircraft, majority owned or controlled by Yugoslav nationals. The question was whether that provision extended to aircraft which was leased to an 'innocent' Turkish charter company. The ECJ decided that it did so extend, basing its interpretation on the text of the UN Resolution (and in line with the interpretation adopted by the UN Sanctions Committee). The ECJ nevertheless went on to examine whether the Regulation, thus applied, violated Bosphorus Airways's fundamental right to property. It came to the conclusion that that was not the case, but only after thorough examination, and there is no indication in the judgment that human rights review was precluded on the ground that the Regulation copied and implemented a UN Resolution.[48]

The analogy with *Yusuf* and *Kadi* is extremely close. While it is correct that in *Bosphorus*, a preliminary ruling case, no express question of validity was raised, but only a question of interpretation, it is clear from the structure of both the Opinion of Advocate General Jacobs and the judgment of the ECJ that the human rights claims advanced by Bosphorus concerned the Regulation's validity.

Both the Advocate General and the ECJ first analysed how the Regulation was to be interpreted *and applied*, without looking at the protection of fundamental rights.[49] They then examined whether the Regulation, as interpreted in the light of the UN Resolution, violated fundamental rights. It is true that the ECJ did not in terms state that it was analysing the validity of the Regulation. However, its judgment is consonant with the more elaborate Opinion of Advocate General Jacobs, which is unambiguous in this respect. The Advocate General stated that 'the question then is whether there is an infringement of the principle of proportionality or of the principle of respect for fundamental rights'. He considered that this part of Bosphorus Airways's claim raised an important issue. He then referred to established Community law principles concerning respect for fundamental rights. The Advocate General pointed out that 'respect for fundamental rights is thus a condition of the lawfulness of Community acts – in this case, the Regulation'.[50] He could hardly have been clearer.

---

[48] Case C-84/95 *Bosphorus* v. *Minister for Transport, Energy and Communications, Ireland and the Attorney General* [1996] ECR I-3953.

[49] *Ibid.*, paras. 31–47 of the Opinion; paras. 8–18 of the judgment.

[50] Opinion, paras. 49–53.

The Advocate General reached the overall conclusion 'that the contested decision did not ... strike an unfair balance between the demands of the general interest and the requirements of the protection of the individual's fundamental rights'.[51] Overall, it is plain that both the Advocate General and the ECJ examined the fundamental rights arguments advanced by Bosphorus Airways. There is no suggestion whatsoever that this examination could not be undertaken on the grounds that the Regulation implemented a UN Resolution.

Nor is it material that the Resolutions and Regulations in *Yusuf* and *Kadi* expressly name and target the applicants, whereas Bosphorus Airways was affected only because it had leased Yugoslav aircraft. In *Bosphorus*, both the ECJ and the UN Sanctions Committee determined that the Regulation, respectively the Resolution, applied to the company. Whether the application of the Regulation and the Resolution to a person is express or implied cannot make any difference as regards the question whether review on the basis of general principles of Community law is possible or not. In *Bosphorus*, too, there was a decision of the UN Sanctions Committee determining that the Resolution applied to the company in question.

Yusuf and *Kadi* do not fit the ECJ's judgment in *Bosphorus*. They could only be made to fit that judgment if one considers that, had the ECJ come to the conclusion that there was a violation of human rights (*quod non*), it would have refrained from declaring the Regulation invalid on the ground that it implemented a UN Resolution; or if one considers that the ECJ was simply seeking to interpret the Regulation in the light of fundamental rights, and was not examining its validity. But such interpretations completely distort the structure and logic of the ECJ's reasoning.

The above analysis shows that *Yusuf* and *Kadi* do not fit the case law of the ECJ on the protection of fundamental rights, on judicial review, and on the force of international law. All acts of the institutions are subject to judicial review on grounds of compliance with fundamental rights. Respect for such rights is a fundamental and unqualified imperative of Community law. That conclusion is reinforced by a number of broader considerations.

One such consideration is that the EU continues to suffer from a democratic deficit, even if one can argue about the extent of that deficit.

---

[51] Opinion, para. 67.

The sanctions policies addressed in this critique do not particularly excel in terms of democratic credentials. The UN Security Council is a purely intergovernmental body. The CFSP Common Positions are adopted by the Council, and so are the actual sanctions Regulations. No parliamentary assembly is directly involved. Nor is there much transparency in the way these decisions are reached. On the contrary, it is one of the central arguments of the litigants in these cases that they have never been informed about the precise nature of the allegations leading to their listing. Protection of fundamental rights is of course no substitute for all of these defects. Yet one can see that such protection is even more needed in cases where the methods under which governmental decisions are taken are questionable from the angle of democratic representation and accountability. As van Gerven has said, the less democratic legitimacy a system possesses, particularly in its legislative branch, the greater the judicial scrutiny the system should be subjected to.[52]

Another important consideration is the central position which the protection of fundamental rights occupies in judicial dialogue concerning the supremacy of EC law. The theme is well-rehearsed, and there is no need here for a full replay. Constitutional courts in several Member States have insisted that the EC needs to ensure an adequate level of human rights protection. They tend to see that as a precondition for their continued willingness not to review EC acts on the basis of domestic constitutional standards (*solange*). The CFI's rulings could undermine this practice of constitutional tolerance.[53] It is in this context necessary to consider the effects of those rulings at a national level. Given that the sanctions are adopted by way of EC Regulations, the full force of EC law supremacy is at work, with no scope whatsoever for courts in the Member States to question their legality.[54] The listing of the individuals concerned cannot be reviewed by national courts. At most those courts could refer a question of validity to the ECJ, but if the ECJ upholds the CFI's reasoning

---

[52] W. van Gerven, *The European Union – A Polity of States and People* (Oxford: Hart Publishing, 2005), p. 63.

[53] The concept was coined by J.H.H. Weiler, 'In defence of the status quo: Europe's constitutional *Sonderweg*', in J.H.H. Weiler and M. Wind (eds.), *European Constitutionalism Beyond the State* (Cambridge: Cambridge University Press, 2003), pp. 15–23.

[54] Case 314/85, *Foto-Frost* v. *Hauptzollamt Lübeck-Ost* [1987] ECR 4199. Cf. A. Garde, 'Is it really for the European Community to implement anti-terrorism UN Security Council Resolutions?', 65 CLJ (2006), p. 284.

the net result is that there will be no court with jurisdiction to review whether the UN sanctions are in conformity with fundamental rights.

What is more, the EU courts are also watched by the European Court of Human Rights (ECtHR). It is perhaps not pure coincidence that it was precisely in *Bosphorus* that the ECtHR recently clarified its approach towards the system of fundamental rights protection in the EU.[55] Subsequent to the ECJ judgment, the company went to Strasbourg, further pursuing its claims based on the right to property, against the Irish Republic and not the EC because the latter is not a party to the European Convention on Human Rights (ECHR). The ECtHR judgment in *Bosphorus* is well-known for accepting that the system of fundamental rights protection in the EC is equivalent to that under the ECHR.[56] Since that is the case, it could be accepted that Ireland needed to act in accordance with its EC law obligations. The ECtHR stated, in general terms, that 'State action taken in compliance with such legal obligations is justified as long as the relevant organisation is considered to protect fundamental rights, as regards both the substantive guarantees offered and the mechanisms controlling their observance, in a manner which can be considered at least equivalent to that for which the Convention provides'.[57] It ruled that EC law generally complies with this standard of equivalence, and that this creates a presumption of compliance with Convention rights. Such a presumption of compliance could be rebutted, but as regards Bosphorus Airways's case the ECtHR stated that it had 'had regard to the nature of the interference, to the general interest pursued by the impoundment and by the sanctions regime and to the ruling of the ECJ (in the light of the opinion of the AG)', and that the presumption of equivalent protection had not been rebutted.[58]

There are several points to be noted in connection with this ruling.[59] First, the ECtHR spoke in general terms when it addressed compliance with legal obligations resulting from membership of an international organisation as a justification for restricting certain fundamental rights. What it said appears to apply to the UN as much as to the EC. The obvious difference is that, in the sphere of sanctions, the UN clearly does not offer substantive guarantees and mechanisms for controlling their observance

---

[55] ECHR, *Bosphorus v. Ireland*, Application No. 45036/98, judgment of 30 June 2005.
[56] *Ibid.*, para. 155.   [57] *Ibid.*   [58] *Ibid.*, para. 166.
[59] See also Watson Institute, *Strengthening Targeted Sanctions*, pp. 22–3.

in the way the EC does. The ECtHR closely examined the EC's judicial system, and there simply is no such system at the UN level to which an individual could turn. Second, the ECtHR did not discuss the UN origin of the sanctions in *Bosphorus* when examining the protection of fundamental rights. However, it was of course fully aware of that origin. The Irish Government had in fact argued that the interference with the company's property rights was justified on the ground of 'compliance with [Ireland's] international obligations', and that 'the margin of appreciation was broad given the strength of the two public interest objectives pursued: the principles of public international law, including *pacta sunt servanda*, pursuant to which the State discharged clear mandatory international obligations following the decisions of the relevant UN and EC bodies (the Sanctions Committee and the ECJ) and participating in an international effort to end a conflict'.[60] The ECtHR chose to concentrate on Ireland's EC law obligations rather than on its UN obligations. If, however, the ECtHR had considered that the binding nature of UN Resolutions trumps ECHR rights, there would have been no need to look at the EC system of fundamental rights protection. Implicitly, therefore, the judgment rejects the kind of reasoning followed by the CFI. The ECtHR may well have refrained from considering the nature of those UN obligations to avoid having to rule that there is no equivalent human rights protection at the UN level. It is not persuasive to argue that the ECtHR did not consider the effect of Article 103 UN Charter, as Ireland expressly referred to its UN obligations. Third, the ECtHR expressly approved the ECJ's reasoning in *Bosphorus*, as well as that of its Advocate General. As we have seen, the Advocate General was very clear about the fact that the sanctions Regulation in issue needed to comply with fundamental rights. The overall conclusion can only be that the CFI's rulings in *Yusuf* and *Kadi* are not consonant with the *Bosphorus* judgment of the ECtHR.

It is clear that *Yusuf* and *Kadi* do not fit the existing rules, principles and decisions governing fundamental rights protection in the EU. They in effect override the existing law. Can that be justified? Such a justification could only be found in the imperative to respect international law. In the previous section that imperative was unpacked in the light of current norms of international law, and found not to provide such a justification. However, let us put that aside for one moment. Could one still not defend

---

[60] *Ibid.*, paras. 112–13.

the position that, in the clash between respect for international law and respect for human rights, the former should prevail, in particular where UN Security Council Resolutions are involved? Is that not a direction which EC law should take?

It is difficult to see any particular justification for this. True, the UN Charter is a cornerstone of the international law edifice, and the Security Council performs a particularly important function. Community law must respect international law, and thus, in particular, UN Resolutions. However, the principle of respect for fundamental rights is, on balance, the stronger imperative, and if it clashes with international law, should override it. It should do so because it is a substantive imperative, an imperative based on the most important values which the European polity should uphold. It should override because it focuses on the unalienable rights of the individual, which must be at the heart of the European Community legal order. It should finally override because the UN legal order itself very much recognises respect for fundamental rights.

My conclusion is therefore that *Yusuf* and *Kadi* do not fit the EC law system, and do not show it in its best light.

4.5 Conclusion: review of EC Regulations implementing UN Resolutions as long as no effective remedy is available at international level

So which approach would provide a better fit? My position is as follows. There is no need to deduce from the binding nature of UN Resolutions that judicial review on grounds of general principles of Community law is excluded. There is no need for considering that review of an EC Regulation which implements a UN Resolution constitutes indirect review of that Resolution; or such indirect review is at any rate no impediment to reviewing the Regulation. Even if the Resolutions are binding under Community law, the international and Community legal orders are distinct, and Community law is autonomous. Public international law recognises this. In a case such as UN terrorism listings, where the individuals concerned have no access to a judicial remedy at international level, it is preferable to emphasise the autonomy of each legal system, international and municipal. Review on the grounds of general principles of Community law would of course have to have regard to the international origin of the listings. There would be little doubt that some degree of deference would need to be shown to the Security Council. This deference, however, cannot stand in the way of the principle of effective judicial review itself. The individual is increasingly a subject of international law, and must thus be guaranteed certain fundamental rights through effective judicial protection. Ideally, international law itself should organise such protection. Where it is lacking, municipal courts have to step into the breach by applying domestic constitutional standards of protection of fundamental rights.[61] This is not optimal, since it puts in jeopardy the uniform implementation of UN Resolutions. It is a second-best solution, but one to be preferred over judicial abdication in the face of the undeniable difficulties which review of UN sanctions represent.

This approach would be consistent with the now firmly established European *solange* tradition. As long as the international legal order does not provide the individual listed in a UN Resolution with an effective remedy, EC law, as a kind of municipal legal system, cannot dispense with review on the basis of its own constitutional standards. Such review is at the very heart of the construction of the 'new legal order' which the EC Treaty represents: both national (constitutional) courts and the ECtHR accept, respectively, the primacy and autonomy of Community law on the condition that fundamental rights are adequately protected.

Furthermore, the EC is in the very comfortable position that such review, if it were to lead to the annulment of an EC Regulation implementing a UN Resolution, would not constitute a breach of international law. As the CFI acknowledged, the UN Charter is not, as a matter of international law, binding on the Community.

Nor should municipal or constitutional review in the light of fundamental rights be seen as conflicting with the binding force of the UN Charter. The EU courts mainly apply the standards of the ECHR. Those standards are comparable to those of the Universal Declaration of Human Rights (UDHR) and of the International Covenant on Civil and Political Rights (ICCPR), which are two UN instruments.[62] Protection of fundamental rights is a core UN Charter objective. Constitutional review would reveal the flaws in the UN system of imposing targeted sanctions, flaws which the UN (or at least some of its organs) recognise. It may provide an impetus to setting up a satisfactory system of independent review at the

---

[61] *Cf.* Cannizzaro, 'Machiavelli', p. 8.
[62] See the analysis in Watson Institute, *Strengthening Target Sanctions*, pp. 10–16.

UN level.[63] Once such a system is in place, municipal courts could defer to it as the *locus* for the protection of fundamental rights.

As long as that is not the case, however, constitutional review is to be preferred over the 'incidental' (but effectively direct) review of the Resolutions on the basis of *jus cogens*. The EU courts' jurisdiction to engage in such review is questionable. It is not consonant with the EC law doctrine of primacy. The ECJ does not accept that national courts rule on the invalidity of EC acts.[64] If it becomes established doctrine that the EU courts may themselves review the validity of international legal norms, would that not risk undermining this *Foto-Frost* principle? Could national courts not be tempted to proclaim that they have jurisdiction to engage in incidental review of EC acts which they are called upon to apply?

At the conclusion of this essay it may be useful to recall what *Yusuf* and *Kadi* are essentially about, namely upholding the rule of law, also in international affairs. It simply cannot be right that an individual's assets are frozen for several years, through an executive decision which cannot be reviewed by a judge, or in judicial-type proceedings. It is no defence to say that Messrs Yusuf and Kadi were able to bring proceedings before the CFI. The judges did not in any way review the basis on which they were listed as individuals supporting terrorism. That cannot be right.

---

[63] Cannizzaro, 'Machiavelli', p. 28.   [64] *Foto-Frost*, n. 54.

Fundamental rights and the interface between second and third pillar

ELEANOR SPAVENTA

It is necessary for him who lays out a state and arranges laws for it to presuppose that all men are evil and that they are always going to act according to the wickedness of their spirits whenever they have free scope.[1]

5.1 Introduction

Following the terrorist attacks perpetrated first against the United States and later against Spain and the United Kingdom, action at international level to combat terrorism has grown steadily. Such action has been taken at both United Nations (UN) and European Union (EU) level in forms previously unknown in the field of international cooperation. In particular, both the UN and the EU have taken upon themselves the task of identifying organisations and individuals that are to be considered as terrorists by international and national communities alike. This process of identification of who or what should be considered a 'terrorist' occurs entirely in executive fora, thus challenging presumptions which have characterised post-war Western democracies as to the division of competences between executive, legislature and judiciary, as well as deeply affecting established systems of checks and balances. Furthermore, such evolution in intergovernmental action has not been matched by a corresponding evolution in the system of judicial protection. Thus, whilst international cooperation in the field of counter-terrorism activity might well be vital to ensure an effective response to the terrorist threat, international organisations are ill equipped, as things stand, to guarantee even the more

I am grateful to Michael Dougan for comments on an earlier draft. The usual disclaimer applies.

[1] N. Machiavelli, *Discorsi sopra la prima deca di Tito Livio*, translated by A. Gilbert (Durham, N.C.: Duke University Press, 1965).

basic rights of individuals and organisations that are targeted through international instruments. The complexity of the interaction between international, European and national law makes it equally difficult for national (and European) judiciaries to intervene in such cases. Those might entail gathering of sensitive evidence possibly relating to another State; problems stemming from hierarchy of norms; inevitable political pressures of compromising the executive's action and its standing in international relations.

In the EU context, the tension between intergovernmental cooperation and effective judicial protection has become manifest following the adoption of a series of counter-terrorism measures, and in particular following the adoption of an EU list of terrorists using a mixed second and third pillar legal basis; and following the adoption of a Community Regulation to freeze the assets of some of the individuals and entities listed in the relevant Common Position. In this sense, the interface between second and third pillar, the instrumental use of Treaty competences to exclude or limit both judicial and democratic accountability, has brought a considerable reduction of fundamental rights standards in the EU. This contribution explores such developments from a fundamental rights perspective. It focuses solely on action taken by the EU on its own account, since action taken by the EU as a result of UN action is extensively explored elsewhere in this book.[2] The overall claim of this contribution is that, given the lack of judicial protection available at EU level, the main responsibility for ensuring effective review in those cases rests with the national courts which have, as a matter of EU law, a duty to ensure that fundamental rights are adequately protected.

5.2 The EU terrorist lists: machiavellian use of competence or genuine counter-terrorist response?

The EU counter-terrorism response resulted in the adoption of a wide-ranging set of measures, spanning from the Framework Decision on Combating Terrorism,[3] to that on the European Arrest Warrant,[4] from

---

[2] See contribution by Piet Eeckhout in this volume.
[3] Council Framework Decision on Combating Terrorism (2002/475/JHA), OJ 2002 L 164/3.
[4] Council Framework Decision 2002/584/JHA on the European arrest warrant and the surrender procedure between Member States, OJ 2002 L 190/1.

the agreement with the United States on extradition,[5] to that on Passenger Name Records.[6] Amongst those measures, the EU has also adopted two Common Positions, which identified certain organisations and individuals as being involved in 'terrorist' acts. The two Common Positions should be distinguished since their status in Community law is different.

   Common Position 2002/402[7] has been adopted to give effect to UN Resolution 1390(2002), the so called Anti-Taliban Resolution.[8] According to the latter, the UN Sanctions Committee draws up a list of those individuals and organisations who are alleged to be linked to the Taliban, Al-Qaeda and the like. National authorities must then take action to freeze the assets of those listed in the UN list. In order to give effect to the UN Anti-Taliban Resolution, the EU has adopted the above-mentioned Common Position, and a Community Regulation requiring the freezing of assets of those entities/individuals identified by the UN Sanctions Committee. We are not concerned with this Common Position, since, as said above, this is examined elsewhere in the book.

   The other instrument which contains a list of alleged terrorists (including organisations) is Common Position 2001/931.[9] This instrument is broadly speaking aimed at implementing UN Security Council

---

[5] Agreement on extradition between the European Union and the United States of America, OJ 2003 L 181/27; see generally J. Wouters and F. Naert, 'Of Arrest Warrants, Terrorist Offences and Extradition Deals: an Appraisal of the EU's Main Criminal Law Measures against Terrorism after *11 September*', 41 CMLRev. (2004), p. 909.

[6] Agreement on extradition between the European Union and the United States of America, OJ 2003 L 181/27; see also Agreement on mutual legal assistance between the European Union and the United States of America, OJ 2003 L 181/34; Agreement between the European Union and the United States of America on the processing and transferring of passenger name record (PNR) data by air carriers to the United States, OJ 2006 L 298/29. For a rather critical appraisal of the agreement, see the debate in front of the plenary session of the European Parliament, *Use of Passenger Data*, debate of 11 October 2006, Document of 16/10/06, 13991/06 PE 326. The first PNR agreement had been adopted using Community competence and was annulled for lack of competence, Joined Cases C-317 and 318/04 *European Parliament* v. *Council and Commission* (2006) ECR I-4721. For this reason, the Council had to re-adopt the agreement relying on third pillar competence (Art. 38 TEU read in conjunction with 24(4) TEU). As a result, the agreement cannot be challenged in front of the ECJ, since the latter has no jurisdiction in relation to such matters.

[7] Common Position 2002/402/CFSP concerning restrictive measures against Osama bin Laden, members of the Al-Qaeda organisation and the Taliban and other individuals, groups, undertakings and entities associated with them and repealing Common Positions 96/746/CFSP, 1999/727/CFSP, 2001/154/CFSP and 2001/771/CFSP, OJ 2002 L 169/4.

[8] UN Security Council Resolution 1390(2002).

[9] Common Position 2001/931/CFSP on the application of specific measures to combat terrorism, OJ 2001 L 344/93.

Resolution 1371(2001),[10] the general anti-terrorist Resolution, which
provides that States must fight terrorism by adopting a series of measures,
including the prevention and suppression of the financing of terrorist acts,
the criminalisation of the financing of terrorist acts and the freezing of
assets of those in any way connected with a terrorist activity. The general
anti-terrorism Resolution, however, fails to define what is to be understood as a 'terrorist act' since agreement could not be reached on that
point. Furthermore, in relation to this measure, there is no prior identification at UN level of those individuals and entities which should be
subjected to restrictive measures.

Common Position 2001/931 has been adopted using a mixed second
and third pillar competence, since it relates to two different types of
terrorist organisations/individuals: one part of the list relates to those
alleged terrorists who have a link with a third country, i.e. whose alleged
activity is external to the EU borders; the other part of the list is concerned
with alleged terrorists whose activity is wholly internal to the EU. The
distinction between 'foreign linked' and 'home' terrorists is important
because for the former, the Council was able to use Common Foreign and
Security Policy (CFSP) competence (Art. 15 TEU) and therefore rely on
the passarelle clause contained in the EC Treaty (Arts. 301 and 60 EC,
complemented by Art. 308) in order to trigger the Community competence to adopt a Regulation to freeze the assets of those identified in the
list.[11] Like in the case of the UN-derived Regulation, residual competence
of the Community was necessary to adopt the Regulation, since the
freezing order does not specifically concern 'third countries'.

In relation to home terrorists, the Council had to rely on Article 34
TEU, thus adopting the act using police and judicial cooperation in
criminal matters competence. Since in this case there was no 'foreign'
element involved, the Council considered that there was no possibility of
justifying action at CFSP level. Given that this part of the list was adopted
using third pillar competence, the Community could not enact a freezing
Regulation as there is no passarelle clause bridging the first and third
pillars. As a result, there is no direct 'legal consequence' arising from
being included in the EU domestic list: there is no freezing of assets at

---

[10] UN Resolution 1373(2001), 28 September 2001.
[11] Council Regulation 2580/2001 on specific restrictive measures directed against certain persons
and entities with a view to combating terrorism, OJ 2001 L 344/70.

Community level, and the only obligation imposed upon Member States by the Common Position is that of affording 'each other the widest possible assistance in preventing and combating terrorist acts' and to 'fully exploit' their existing powers in relation to enquiries and proceedings conducted in relation to any of the organisations or individuals listed in the Annex to the Common Position.[12] Common Position 2001/931 appears then to be, for home-related terrorists, little more than a naming and shaming instrument. Such naming and shaming is obviously not without consequences for those therein mentioned; however, even if such consequences might be very serious, there is no possibility in relation to this list to bring review proceedings in front of the European courts. Title VI of the EU Treaty does not provide for the possibility to bring direct proceedings for annulment of third pillar instruments. Thus, individuals listed in the Common Position cannot challenge either the legality of the Common Position, or their inclusion in the list. Furthermore, third pillar Common Positions are excluded from the limited preliminary ruling jurisdiction of the Court.[13]

Common Position 2001/931 and Regulation 2580/2001 therefore raise considerable problems since the EU's system of judicial protection seems, when available at all, inadequate to the task of protecting individuals from executive action. We will first consider the problems raised by Regulation 2580/2001, then turn to the problems faced by those whose name has been included in the home-terrorist list.

5.3 Expanding Community competence beyond Community objectives: the adoption of Regulation 2580/2001

Individuals and organisations whose alleged terrorist activity takes place outside the territory of the EU are identified by the Council in a list annexed to Common Position 2001/931. Such list is drawn up 'on the basis of precise information or material in the relevant file which indicates that a decision has been taken by a competent authority'. The competent authority is a 'judicial authority' or, where judicial authorities have no competence, 'an equivalent competent authority in that area'.[14] The decision might concern the instigation of investigations, prosecutions or

---

[12] Article 4 Common Position 2001/931/CFSP.   [13] Article 35 TEU.
[14] Article 1(4) Common Position 2001/931.

condemnation for terrorist acts. Article 1(6) provides that such list must be reviewed at regular intervals, and at least once every six months, to ensure that there are grounds for keeping individuals and entities on the list. According to Article 2 Common Position 2001/931, the European Community must order the freezing of the funds of those identified in the list. This has been done by means of Regulation 2580/2001 which provides for the freezing of assets of those identified in a list drawn up by the Council acting in unanimity in accordance with the provisions of Common Position 2001/931. De facto the list drawn in the Common Position is then replicated, for those who have a foreign link, in a Community instrument for the purpose of freezing assets. The first problem that arises in relation to Regulation 2580/2001 relates to whether the Community had competence to enact such measure.

As mentioned above, Regulation 2580/2001 was adopted using two legal bases: Article 60 read in conjunction with Article 301 EC, which provide the bridge between CFSP and the Community; and Article 308 EC, which provides for the residual competence of the Community. The reason for the dual legal basis is that Article 60 EC refers to measures on the movement of capital and payments as regards 'third countries concerned'. Thus, in relation to those individuals and entities that do not have a specific connection with a third country, there was no other competence in the EC Treaty than the Community residual competence. In the *Yusuf* and *Kadi* cases,[15] the Court of First Instance (CFI) found that in relation to the UN-derived lists, the Community had competence to adopt a Regulation which provides for the freezing of assets of listed entities and individuals, even when such entities and individuals did not have a connection with third countries.

In the CFI's opinion, such competence could not rest on Articles 301 and 60 EC alone, since those provisions require the measure to be adopted in relation to third countries. Whilst such a link with third countries is present in relation to so-called smart sanctions, i.e. sanctions that target specific individuals which have dealings with, or economic activities directed at, the third country which is being sanctioned, such is not the

---

[15] Case T-306/01 *Yusuf and Al Barakaat v. Council and Commission* (2005) ECR II-3533; Case T-315/01 *Kadi v. Council and Commission* (2005) ECR II-3649; the two rulings are virtually identical for what we are concerned and, therefore, thereafter we will refer solely to the *Yusuf* ruling.

case when the individual or organisation targeted cannot be clearly linked with a third country. That was the case in relation to the Anti-Taliban Regulation since, following the regime change, the Taliban did not have a specific connection with the Afghan Government. The CFI also found that Article 308 EC, which provides for the residual competence of the Community, could not be relied upon, by itself, as a legal basis for the Regulation freezing the assets of those identified in the list. In order to rely on Article 308 EC, it is necessary to link the action taken to one of the objectives of the Community; however, the CFI found that neither the CCP, nor the free movement of capital or the risk of a distortion of competition, could be relied upon to establish such a link. Further, the CFI held that Article 308 EC cannot be of help in 'giving the institutions general authority to use that provision as a basis with a view to attaining one of the objectives of the Treaty on European Union'.[16] Otherwise, the CFI reasoned, the specificity of the pillars would be compromised and the Community would gain competence in all matters covered by the second and third pillar.

However, the CFI then found that a cumulative reading of Articles 308, 301 and 60 EC, was capable of establishing Community competence to adopt a Regulation freezing the funds of individuals who had no connection with a 'third country'. In order to make such finding, the CFI reasoned as follows. Articles 60 and 301 EC are 'quite special provisions': they establish the passerelle between the CFSP and the Community, and when action is taken under those provisions, the action is in fact that of the Union not that of the Community. The CFI then remarked how, according to Article 3 TEU, the Union is to be served by a single institutional framework, and how it has to ensure consistency of its external activities as a whole. It then continued: 'Now, just as the powers provided for by the EC Treaty may be proved to be insufficient to allow the institutions to act in order to attain, in the operation of the common market, one of the objectives of the Community, so the powers to impose economic and financial sanctions provided for by Articles 60 EC and 301 EC, namely, the interruption or reduction of economic relations with one or more third countries, especially in respect of movements of capital and payments, may be proved insufficient to allow the institutions to attain *the objective of the CFSP, under the Treaty on European Union, in view of*

---

[16] Case T-306/01 *Yusuf and Al Barakaat* v. *Council and Commission* (2005) ECR II-3533, para. 136.

which those provisions were specifically introduced into the EC Treaty.'[17]
For this reason, the Community had competence to enact the contested
Regulation.

The CFI's purposive reasoning is very interesting: the creation of the
bridge between two pillars, which are otherwise linked only by the common provisions of the TEU, allows for a greater flow than appears at first
sight. Thus, Article 308 EC can be used to attain the objectives set out in
Articles 301 and 60 EC. Pragmatically, one might well agree with the CFI
and note that when those provisions were drafted the world was a very
different place. It is not surprising, then, that the drafters did not provide
for the possibility to enact sanctions against individuals and entities acting
on their own accord, since the situation warranting those types of sanctions had not yet presented itself. However, the principle of attributed
powers is not only a fundamental constitutional principle of the Treaty, it
is also a guarantee for national parliaments, and for the democratic
process as a whole. This was made clear in Opinion 2/94 where the ECJ
held that Article 308 EC 'cannot serve as a basis for widening the scope of
Community powers beyond the general framework created by the provisions of the Treaty as a whole and, in particular, by those that define the
tasks and the activities of the Community'.[18] By allowing the use of that
provision to widen the bridge between the two pillars for the attainment of
CFSP objectives, rather that for the attainment of Community objectives
'in the course of the operation of the common market', the CFI, however,
did exactly that: it broadened the scope of Community competence.
In such delicate matters, where individual rights are at stake, this result
might be seen as not entirely satisfactory, not the least since it prevented a
national debate as to whether such type of sanctions should be enacted
by the Community and whether, if so, special guarantees should not
accompany Community action. In this respect, the CFI failed to notice
that the expansion of Community competence in this case would entail
a 'modification of the system for the protection of fundamental rights',
since it affects the guarantees of effective judicial protection provided for
in domestic systems;[19] that it clearly had 'fundamental institutional

---

[17] Case T-306/01 *Yusuf and Al Barakaat* v. *Council and Commission* (2005) ECR II-3533, para. 163.
[18] Opinion 2/94 *Accession of the Community to the European Convention for the Protection of Human Rights and Fundamental Freedoms* (1996) ECR I-1579, para. 30.
[19] *Ibid.*, para. 35.

implications' for the Member States,[20] since it affected the right and duty of national parliaments to scrutinise executive action in a field which affects individual rights, and that therefore it went beyond the scope of Article 308 EC.

For the time being, however, the issue of competence should be treated as a fait accompli also in relation to Regulation 2580/2001, since the fact that the Regulation at issue in *Yusuf* was implementing (indirectly) a Security Council Resolution played no part in the CFI's assessment of the Community competence to act.

It is now time to turn our attention to more substantive issues in relation to the listing process and to the judicial remedies available to those who are included in the list. We will first consider the list as attached to Regulation 2580/2001, then turn to the list annexed to Common Position 2001/931. Whilst, as we have seen above, the list in the former reproduces partially the list in the latter, the legal issues the two raise are different since in relation to the latter there is no jurisdiction of the European courts.

5.4 The right to effective judicial protection and the foreign terrorist list

As mentioned above, the Community judicature has full jurisdiction, both in direct actions and in preliminary rulings, in relation to the list of 'foreign' terrorists attached to Regulation 2580/2001.[21] Thus, there is as much access to the judicature as it is possible in the Community system and the individual is not deprived of judicial protection. The problem, however, is whether such protection is truly effective and whether it is substantive, as well as formal.

A recent ruling of the CFI might serve to illustrate the problem. In the *Organisation des Modjahedines du peuple d'Iran* (OMPI),[22] the claimants

---

[20] *Ibid.*, para. 35.

[21] Those listed in the annex to the Regulation are deemed to be directly and individually concerned for the purposes of Article 230 EC, see, e.g. Case T-228/02 *Organisation des Modjahedines du peuple d'Iran*, judgment of 12 December 2006. This said, the question of standing might still be problematic in relation to organisations, see, e.g. T-299/02 *PKK and KNK v. Council* (2005) ECR II-539, overruled by C-229/05P *PKK and KNK v. Council*, judgment of 18 January 2007, nyr.

[22] Case T-228/02 *Organisation des Modjahedines du peuple d'Iran*, judgment of 12 December 2006.

brought proceedings against the Council challenging the legality of their inclusion in the list annexed to Common Position 2001/931, as well as their inclusion in the list annexed to Regulation 2580/2001, which had the effect of freezing their assets. It appears from the case that the decision to include the applicants in such lists was instigated by the United Kingdom, which also included them in its own terrorist list. In challenging their inclusion in the lists, the claimants relied on several pleas, amongst which the most relevant for our analysis are infringement of the right to a fair hearing; infringement of essential procedural requirements; infringement of the right to effective judicial protection; infringement of the presumption of innocence; and a manifest error of assessment.

The process of 'listing' is surrounded by a certain secrecy. According to Common Position 2001/931, the list is drawn on the basis of 'precise information or material in the relevant file which indicated that a decision has been taken by a competent authority' in respect of those concerned. And, a 'competent authority' means a judicial authority or, when such authority does not have competence, an 'equivalent' competent authority. De facto it appears that persons and organisations are placed on the EU and EC lists at the request of one of the Member States, and that the Council exercises only a formal power of scrutiny.[23] Those who are to be included on the list have no right to submit observations either before or after having been placed on the list; and might well not be aware of the reason that led to their inclusion, or of the authority (and the Member State) that instigated the listing.[24] Indeed, since inclusion is at the request of the Member States, the Council itself might not be in a position to

---

[23] On this point, see E. Spaventa, 'Fundamental what? The difficult relationship between foreign policy and fundamental rights', in M. Cremona and B. de Witte (eds.), *EU Foreign Relations law: Constitutional Fundamentals* (Oxford: Hart Publishing, forthcoming); and also I. Tappeiner, 'The fight against terrorism. The lists and the gaps', *Utrecht Law Review* (2005), p. 97, also available at: www.utrechtlawreview.org.

[24] Following the CFI ruling in Case T-228/02 *Organisation des Modjahedines du peuple d'Iran*, judgment of 12 December 2006, nyr, the Council has indicated that it is going to 'provide a statement of reasons to each person and entity subject to the asset freeze, wherever that is feasible, and to establish a clearer and more transparent procedure for allowing listed persons and entities to request that their case be re-considered', EU Council Secretariat Factsheet 'Judgement of the Court of First Instance in the OMPI case T-228/02'. And in the Notice for the attention of those persons/groups/entities that have been included by Council Decision 2006/1008/EC of 21 December on the list of persons, groups and entities to which Regulation 2580/2001 applies (OJ 2006 C 320/02), the Council expressly stated that it is open to those listed to request a statement of reasons when the statement had not already been provided.

declare the information requested, either because that information does not appear in the file, or because disclosure might prejudice security interests of the Member State concerned. Furthermore, in at least one instance, the inclusion of an individual in the list appears to have been at the request of a third country.[25]

In analysing the lawfulness of the OMPI's inclusion in the list, the CFI, most likely mindful of the political minefield in which it had landed, limited its observations to issues of procedural propriety. The CFI started by finding that both the right to a fair hearing, the obligation to state reasons and the right to effective judicial protection all applied in the context of the decision to freeze funds.

Acknowledging that the listing procedure initially takes place at the national level, the CFI held that the right to be heard played first (and foremost) in the context of the national procedure.[26] However, it should be noted, that such a right does not stem from Community law since, prior to the adoption of the decision which leads to inclusion in the list, the matter can be said to fall exclusively within national law. In contrast to the substantive obligations imposed upon Member States in relation to the delisting process at UN level,[27] it is unlikely that Community law might be of use in increasing (or establishing) procedural guarantees at this stage of the domestic procedure. However, once the person/organisation is or has been included in the Community list, Community law imposes upon the Council a duty to respect Community law rights, including those rights deriving from the general principles. In defining the extent of such rights, the CFI substantially accepted the argument put forward by the United Kingdom to the effect that it is not for the Council to decide whether the proceedings conducted at national level are well-founded and whether the claimant's fundamental rights were respected in that context. Thus, the

---

[25] See, e.g. the transcript of comments on combating the financing of terrorism made by Alan P. Larson, Under Secretary for Economic, Business, and Agricultural Affairs, in testimony before the House (Congress) Committee on Financial Services on 19 September 2002, available at: http://useu.usmission.gov/Dossiers/Terrorist_Financing/Sep1902_Larson_Testimony.asp; 'The European Union has worked with us to ensure that nearly every terrorist individual and entity designated by the United States has also been designated by the European Union', and also the testimony of Juan C. Zarate (Deputy Assistant Secretary, Executive Office) *Terrorist financing and financial crime*, US Department of the Treasury, Senate Foreign Relations Committee, 18 March 2003, JS-139, available at http://www.ustreas.gov/press/releases/js139.htm.

[26] Case T-228/02, para. 119.

[27] Case T-253/02 *Ayadi* v. *Council*, judgment of 12 July 2006, nyr.

claimant's rights in relation to the inclusion in the EU list is limited to a right to make their views known about the legality of such inclusion, i.e. whether there is a decision of a competent authority and whether the material in the file shows that such a decision was taken by a competent authority, etc. Furthermore, the complainants also gain a right to be notified of the evidence adduced against them (or such evidence as there is in the file) before, or soon after, their inclusion, or their reinclusion in the list. And, the Council has a duty to state the reasons which led it to include the person in the list. Such rights can, however, be curtailed for overriding reasons of public interest, and in particular for reasons relating to national security. Further, the CFI also clarified that it must be put in a position to actually review the lawfulness of the inclusion in the list: in the case at issue, neither the United Kingdom nor the Council had provided it or the claimant with sufficient information as to either the authority which had taken the decision, or the reasons that led Council to include the applicant in the list. Furthermore, the CFI also found that OMPI's right to be heard had been violated; for these reasons, the decision to include the OMPI in the list was quashed.

The *OMPI* ruling is very complex, and it falls beyond the scope of this contribution to provide a detailed analysis of it. However, a few remarks are worth making. From a fundamental rights perspective, the CFI's approach is of course to be welcomed since it sets at least some procedural limits to be respected by the executive when imposing economic sanctions on individuals. And, it also makes clear that violation of such procedural guarantees might lead to the annulment of the decision to include a person/organisation in the list. However, it should be noted that the CFI refused to engage in a substantive review of the reasons which led to inclusion, and also indicated that such substantive review would never fall among its tasks. In the CFI's view, such substantive review is a matter for the competent authority at national level. Furthermore, the CFI excluded that Council has a duty to scrutinise the national authority's decision to include someone in the list.

The effect of this finding is to establish a system of quasi-automatic recognition of decisions taken by authorities in the Member States, and possibly also in third countries. Whilst admittedly such recognition is not automatic, since a Council decision is still necessary, the CFI's statement to the effect that even the Council is not required to look at the substantive reasons that led to the national decision is not very satisfactory, especially when one considers it together with the statement that Council should not even look at whether the fundamental rights of the parties have been respected at national level. This might of course lead to decisions taken in breach of fundamental rights (and yet in conformity with national law) to be given a pan-European effect, without any possibility of redress. And, this would presumably be the case even when the decision had been taken by an authority of a third country, even in instances in which the third country's standard of fundamental rights protection falls below that guaranteed by the EU. In a field like terrorism, where the very definition and decision as to what and who constitutes a terrorist might be politically motivated, this is a regrettable state of affairs. This is even more the case since such pervasive effects in national law were achieved without a clear Parliamentary mandate and through an expansive interpretation of Community competence.

In any case, and regardless of any misgivings one might have about both the Community regime and the *OMPI* ruling, it should be queried how effective the jurisdiction of the Community courts is. At the time of writing, the ruling of the CFI had yet to be given effect: the OMPI was still listed in the Annex to Regulation 2580/2001 and its assets were still frozen.[28] Furthermore, the Council has indicated that it did not consider that the ruling applies to the list annexed to the Common Position since the CFI did not annul the applicant's inclusion in that list. Whilst it is true that the CFI could not comment upon the legality of the inclusion of the OMPI in the list annexed to the Common Position, since it has no jurisdiction over such instruments, the obligation to respect fundamental rights applies also to CFSP and third pillar instruments by virtue of Article 6 TEU and of the general principles of EU law. The finding that the applicants' fundamental rights had been infringed applies a fortiori to the list adopted in the context of the Common Position, and, if anything, it applies even more strongly in that context *because* of the lack of jurisdiction of the Community courts. However, the Council made clear that it has no intention of taking the OMPI off that list.[29] In its press release the Council also indicated that the freezing of funds did no longer apply to OMPI. This notwithstanding, the Council has failed to amend the list

---

[28] Cf. A. Rettman, 'EU backing down on terror list secrecy', *EUobserver*, 16 January 2007.
[29] EU Council Secretariat Factsheet *Judgment of the Court of First Instance in the OMPI Case T-228/02*, para. 3.

annexed to the Regulation.[30] This poses some not insignificant problems for the authorities and banks which have to comply with the freezing order: theoretically, once an act has been declared null by a competent court, and lacking a statement of continued validity pending the adoption of a new and valid act, that act is legally non-existent.[31] Practically, however, it is likely that those who have to execute the freezing order will be unwilling to take the risk of releasing the assets without having received clear instructions to that end. The only concession that the Council has made to the CFI ruling was to issue a notice concomitant to the Decision which added some people and entities to the list annexed to Regulation 2580/2001.[32] In such notice, the Council alerted those included in the new list to their right to request reasons, to their right to apply to Council for a decision to reconsider, and to their right to bring Article 230 EC review proceedings in front of the CFI.

Finally, there is an open question as to whether the EU terrorist lists should be considered as still in force. As said above, Article 1(6) of Common Position 2001/931, which applies also to Regulation 2580/2001, provides that the names in the list should be reviewed at regular intervals and *at least* once every six months 'to ensure that there are grounds for keeping them on the list'. There are two questions, closely interconnected, in relation to this provision: first, does the review necessarily take the form of a new decision, or can it be seen as simply a confirmatory act? And second, what is the legal consequence of failure to carry out the review?

As for the first point, Council practice indicates that a new decision must be taken, when the review is carried out, in relation to *all* entities listed. Thus, the Council has so far updated the list by means of Common Positions and decisions (for that annexed to the Regulation) which

---

[30] Council Decision 2006/1008 of implementing Article 2(3) of Regulation 2580/2001 on specific restrictive measures directed against certain persons and entities with a view to combating terrorism, OJ 2006 L 379/123.

[31] Of course, the CFI ruling does not affect freezing of funds pursuant to national law, see, e.g. Hansard 8 January 2007, reply by Mr McNulty to a question posed by Mr David Jones 'The Court of First Instance did not rule on the substantive question as to whether People Mojahedin Organisation of Iran is a terrorist group; its judgement was on EU procedures, and as such has no effect on the UK's domestic proscription arrangements.'

[32] Notice for the attention of those persons/groups/entities that have been included by Council Decision 2006/1008/EC of 21 December on the list of persons, groups and entities to which Regulation 2580/2001 applies, OJ 2006 C 320/3.

repealed the previous instruments.[33] This practice is consistent with a purposive interpretation of Article 1(6), since the review establishes a guarantee for those listed and it cannot be interpreted as being a mere formal requirement. Such interpretation seems also consistent with the CFI ruling in the *OMPI* case, since the CFI has indicated that the decision to keep someone on the list following the review is to be considered a new decision so that those included have a right to be heard in relation to that decision. Furthermore, if the duty to review implies the duty to adopt a new decision in respect of all applicants, then it means that, in contrast to the UN list, unanimity is required to place someone on the list, and not to strike someone off.[34]

The second interpretative problem relates to the legal value of the lists in the event in which six months elapse without Council having adopted a new decision. This was the situation at the time of writing since the last decisions in respect of the lists were taken in May 2006.[35] Article 1(6) does not appear to introduce an automatic sunset clause, i.e. it does not state that the Common Position and decisions which contain the list have a validity limited to six months. However, the wording of that provision suggests that the review should be considered an essential procedural requirement, non-compliance with which renders the decision open to legal challenge after the expiry of the six-month term. The duty to review is in fact phrased in mandatory terms, so that there seems to be no discretion vested in the Council as to when, and whether, to engage in the review process. Furthermore, this interpretation is also in line with the very purpose of the review which is aimed at ensuring that

[33] Last updates, Council Common Position 2006/380/CFSP of 29 May 2006 updating Common Position 2001/931/CFSP on the application of specific measures to combat terrorism and repealing Common Position 2006/231/CFSP, OJ 2006 L 144/25; and Council Decision 2006/379 of 29 May 2006 implementing Article 2(3) of Regulation 2580/2001 on specific restrictive measures directed against certain persons and entities with a view to combating terrorism and repealing Council Decision 2005/930, OJ 2006 L 379/123.

[34] And this might well be the reason why Council has failed to review the May lists: thus it might be that agreement could not be reached on whether to keep on the list some of those therein listed.

[35] Council Decision 2006/379 of 29 May 2006 implementing Article 2(3) of Regulation 2580/2001 on specific restrictive measures directed against certain persons and entities with a view to combating terrorism and repealing Council Decision 2005/930, OJ 2006 L 379/123; and Council Common Position 2006/380/CFSP of 29 May 2006 updating Common Position 2001/931/CFSP on the application of specific measures to combat terrorism and repealing Common Position 2006/231/CFSP, OJ 2006 L 144/25. The fact that the lists have not been renewed is all the more serious given the change in composition of Council following the accession of Bulgaria and Romania.

the detrimental effects that such decisions have on individuals and organisations are truly kept to the minimum necessary for the protection of the public interest.

5.5 The right of effective judicial protection and the domestic terrorist list

It is now time to consider the problems arising from the EU domestic terrorist list. In relation to those individuals and organisations who have no link with a third country, no freezing Regulation could be adopted since there is no passarelle clause between the third and the first pillar. Thus, and as said at the beginning, the EU domestic terrorist list is little more than a naming and shaming exercise: individuals and organisations are put on the list, their assets are not frozen since there is no competence to do so at EU level, and the only obligation falling upon Member States is to 'fully exploit', upon request, their existing powers in accordance with EU law and international conventions.[36] Thus, the inclusion in the EU list does not impose upon the Member States an obligation to outlaw the organisations therein listed; or for those Member States which have proscription lists at domestic level, an obligation to transpose the EU list in their own domestic instrument;[37] and there is no duty to freeze the assets of those individuals and organisations which are identified in the Common Position. Given the fact that Member States are under no duty to take specific action against those listed in the Common Position, one could well wonder why such listing was deemed necessary at European level. Similar cause for perplexity is provoked by the decision to adopt such a list using a Common Position, the only Title VI instrument which is entirely excluded from the, already limited, jurisdiction of the ECJ.[38] After all, Common Positions are policy instruments which, according

---

[36] Article 4 Common Position 2001/931/CFSP.

[37] *Cf.* in the UK, the Anti-Terrorism Act 2006, and 2000, and the list of the proscribed groups, available at: http://www.homeoffice.gov.uk/security/terrorism-and-the-law/terrorism-act/proscribed-groups. Several of the groups which are listed in Common Position 2001/931 as amended, are not listed in the UK list.

[38] I have argued elsewhere that Common Position 2001/931 is, at least so far as concerns home terrorists, a decision and as such it is subject to the (voluntary) jurisdiction of the ECJ, see Spaventa 'Fundamental what?', cited; see also Advocate General Mengozzi's opinion in Case C-355/04 P *Segi et al* v. *Council*, delivered 26 October 2006, case still pending at the time of writing.

to Article 34(2)(a) TEU should define 'the approach of the Union to a particular matter'. Furthermore, the European Parliament has no role to play in the adoption of Common Positions, unlike for decisions and framework decisions where it has a right to be consulted. Given that the choice of a policy instrument to identify individuals and organisations seems rather ill-fitted with the aim pursued by the measure, one could well wonder whether such choice was not driven by the desire to limit democratic and judicial scrutiny.

Since there is no jurisdiction of the European courts, the only avenue open to applicants wishing to be delisted is that of pursuing their case in front of the national courts. However, action in front of national courts might well not be particularly effective not the least since, even should the national court make a finding favourable to the person/entity listed, that finding would not have effects beyond the domestic jurisdiction. We are first going to analyse the obstacles to effective judicial protection, to then turn to the assessment of the powers and duties of the national courts under EU law.

The first hurdle that the applicant needs to overcome is that of establishing standing in front of a national court: in most jurisdictions standing is conditional upon there being a challengeable act to attack. In relation to the EU list, however, that might not be the case since the 'naming and shaming' is self-executing, i.e. it does not necessarily need implementation at national level. Its purpose is achieved by virtue of its very existence. And, as we have seen in the previous sections, the fact that inclusion in the list should follow a decision taken by a 'competent authority' is not in itself guarantee of it being a challengeable decision. First, it seems that the competent authority might be external to the EU. Second, the applicant might well be in the dark as to which authority, and which Member State, has taken the decision concerning him/it. As we have seen in the *OMPI* case, one of the reasons which led the CFI to quash the inclusion of the applicant in the list was the fact that neither the Council nor the United Kingdom could, or wanted to, disclose the identity of the 'competent authority' which had initially taken the decision which determined the OMPI's inclusion in the list. Third, even when the authority is known to the applicant, the information upon which inclusion in the list is based might not have been disclosed. In this respect, it should be considered whether the *OMPI* ruling imposes substantive duties of disclosure upon national authorities and/or Council.

Here we should distinguish the case in which the applicant challenges the original decision taken before its inclusion in the EU list[39] from the case in which the applicant challenges such decision after having been included in such list. The distinction is important since in the former situation the matter is wholly regulated by national law and European law cannot be of assistance. In the latter case, however, the issue clearly falls within the scope of European law and, for this reason, some procedural guarantees should apply as a matter of EU law. In this respect it is worth recalling the ruling in *Ayadi*.[40] That case concerned the inclusion of the applicant in the list annexed to the Anti-Taliban Regulation, i.e. the Regulation adopted in order to give effect to the UN Anti-Taliban Resolution. As said above, individuals and organisations whose assets are to be frozen are identified by the UN Sanctions Committee, and the UN list is then transposed in a Union and Community instrument. Competence to strike people off the list rests with the UN Sanctions Committee and the delisting procedure can be triggered only by a State which makes representations on behalf of the applicant. In *Ayadi*, the CFI clarified that Member States have substantive obligations in relation to the delisting process (such as the duty to consider the applicant's case; the duty to allow for judicial review of the decision not to make representations at UN level, etc.) and that such obligations are binding upon national authorities by virtue of Community law, following the established principles according to which, when Member States have a discretion in implementing Community law, they have a duty to comply with fundamental rights as general principles.

The reasoning in *Ayadi* can be transposed to the EU list, even lacking the Community courts' jurisdiction. Thus, the national authority which has taken the initial decision should be under the same obligation as those outlined by the CFI in relation to Council in the *OMPI* ruling. Once the organisation/individual has been put on the EU list, the matter falls within the scope of EU law and for this reason the procedural and fundamental rights guarantees imposed by EU law must apply to proceedings at national level also in respect to the national competent authority. As a result, it can be argued that, as a matter of EU law, such an authority has a duty to state the reasons which led it to take the decision (subject to the

---

[39] See to this effect the *obiter dictum* in Case T-228/02, para. 119.
[40] Case T-253/02 *Ayadi* v. *Council*, judgment of 12 July 2006, nyr.

public security caveat) and that fundamental rights as general principles of EU law apply in full. Finally, and as mentioned above, the *OMPI* ruling applies also to the Common Position. Whilst the Community courts lack jurisdiction to enforce such obligations, Council should consider itself bound by it and therefore individuals and organisations listed in the Common Position should have a (non-enforceable) right to a statement of reasons from Council as well as a right to be heard.

Leaving aside the practical difficulties that might arise in accessing a national court, there are serious problems as to the extent to which the national court could extend its review beyond the decision of the national authority. In this respect, one should consider Advocate General Mengozzi's opinion in the case of *SEGI*. SEGI is an alleged terrorist organisation fighting for Basque independence which was included in the list attaching to Common Position 2001/931. SEGI first brought its case in front of the ECtHR, which refused jurisdiction on the grounds that the issue was one of potential, rather than actual, violation of fundamental rights.[41] It then brought proceedings for damages in front of the CFI which dismissed the action for manifest lack of jurisdiction. In an *obiter dictum*, the CFI acknowledged that probably no judicial remedy would be available to the applicant in relation to its inclusion in the EU list.[42] In his opinion in the appeal to the CFI ruling, Advocate General Mengozzi focused on the latter *obiter* to express his views on the duties of national courts in relation to third-pillar instruments especially, if not only, when the European courts lack jurisdiction. In particular, he was concerned with the non-availability of an action for damages in relation to EU law. Relying on the fact that the EU is, by express provision of the TEU, bound by fundamental rights and the rule of law, the Advocate General argued that the fact that the European courts lacked jurisdiction did not imply that there was no judicial remedy available. Rather, by relying on the duty of loyal cooperation which applies also to the third pillar,[43] Mr Mengozzi found that 'in the context of the third pillar of the Union as well it is for the Member States to establish a system of legal remedies and procedures which ensure respect for the right to effective judicial protection and for their courts to interpret and apply

---

[41] Decision declaring the inadmissibility of the case *Segi and Gestoras pro-Amnistia* v. *15 States of the European Union*, appl. No. 6422/02 and 9916/02, 23 May 2002.

[42] Case T-388/02 *Segi et al* v. *Council*, order of 07/06/04, appeal pending (Case C-355/04 P), para. 38.

[43] Case C-105/03 *Pupino* (2005) ECR I-5285.

the national procedural rules governing the bringing of actions in such a way as to ensure such protection'.[44] Furthermore, the Advocate General argued that national courts should consider themselves competent to declare a third pillar instrument invalid, even when they are able to refer the matter to the ECJ. Thus, the principle established by the CFI in *Foto-Frost* should not apply to the third pillar since in the latter, unlike in the Community pillar, there is no complete system of legal remedies and there is no system to ensure the uniform application of EU law. As a result, in the Advocate General's opinion, not only do individuals have a right to seek annulment of a Common Position which concerns them, but also have a right to damages which must be considered as inherent in the TEU. And in relation to those matters the standard of fundamental rights protection to be applied is (or should be) that of EU law, rather than that of national constitutional law.

The arguments put forward by Advocate General Mengozzi are compelling and it is to be seen whether the ECJ will be willing to espouse them in a ruling which would arguably go beyond its jurisdiction. Even were that the case, it is clear that given the institutional structure of the third pillar, the only means of guaranteeing effective judicial protection are in the hands of national courts. And, as argued by Mr Mengozzi, the need to ensure such a protection in relation to EU instruments should be seen as an obligation placed upon national courts directly by the EU system.

As well as the arguments outlined above, there are other considerations which could lead the national courts to take as active role as possible in relation to these matters.

First, one could argue that the Council Common Position is ultra vires since its adoption conflicts with Article 6 TEU which is a provision binding on the EU institutions regardless of whether the European courts have jurisdiction in assessing the breach. Thus, it could be argued that the very adoption of an act at EU level which has detrimental effects on individuals, and which does not provide for an effective system of judicial protection that includes the possibility of challenging the evidence upon which the inclusion in the list has been decided, constitutes a breach of the right to effective judicial protection guaranteed by the Treaty. In such a case, and in the absence of jurisdiction of the European courts, it would fall upon national judiciaries to declare such Act legally void (in its

---

[44] Opinion in Case C-355/04, para. 107.

entirety and not only in relation to the person who has brought the challenge). And, in this respect, the ruling of the CFI was a lost opportunity since, had it put fundamental rights before political considerations, it should have declared the entire Regulation unlawful, possibly leaving the Member States a reasonable time to enact national rules freezing the assets of those on the list to avoid the danger of a general defreezing order. The same reasoning could also be made at national level, by relying on national constitutional law rather than EU law. In this respect, the doctrines of limited conferral of power espoused by the German and Italian Constitutional courts in the 1970s should be revived in relation to third pillar instruments.[45] As long as the EU does not guarantee fundamental rights protection to a level comparable to that guaranteed in national law, the national constitutional courts should retain the last word as to the compatibility of EU instruments (not only third pillar instruments but even second pillar) with their constitutional guarantees. And, similarly, this line of reasoning should be followed by the ECtHR which should clearly state that the (rebuttable) presumption of equivalent protection between the Community and Convention system does not apply in relation to acts of the European Union.[46]

Second, the national courts could rely on the *Yusuf* ruling in relation to Common Position 2001/931, so as to justify the scrutiny of the compatibility of the Common Position with fundamental rights as general principles of EU law. In *Yusuf*, the CFI held that it could not assess the validity of the Regulation at stake, since it was implementing a Security Council Resolution. Since the Council had no discretion as to whether to include Mr Yusuf in the list, then the CFI could not assess the compatibility of the Regulation with the general principles of Community law, as that would have implied the review of the UN Council Resolution with Community law, something that the CFI felt was not possible. However, the CFI also held that it was in its power to assess the compatibility of the

[45] See German Constitutional Court rulings in *Internationale Handelsgesellschaft* CMLRep. (1974), p. 540 (*Solange I*); *Steinike und Weinlig* CMLRep. (1980) p. 531; *Brunner and others* v. *EU Treaty* 31 CMLRev. (1994), p. 57; and the Italian Constitutional Court rulings Sentenza 7/3/64, n. 14 (in F. Sorrentino, *Profili Costituzionali dell'Integrazione Comunitaria* (Torino: Giappichelli Editore, 1996, 2nd ed.), pp. 61 *et seq.* and *Società Acciaierie San Michele* v. *High Authority* (judgment of 27 December 1965, n. 98), CMLRep. (1967), p. 160.

[46] See Case *Bosphorus etc* v. *Ireland* (Appl. No. 45036/98), judgment of 30/6/05, note J.-P. Jacqué *Revue trimestrielle de droit européen* (2005), p. 756.

Regulation with the principles of *jus cogens* which bind the Security Council. If such reasoning is transposed to the EU system then, even should we find that the principle of supremacy applies also in relation to EU instruments and, therefore, such instruments cannot be assessed having regard to national constitutional law, it would be open to national courts to assess the validity of the Common Position in relation to fundamental rights as general principles of EU law. Again, since the principle of effective judicial protection is a principle of EU law, then the national courts would be entitled (as well as required) by EU law to take a proactive stance and assess whether inclusion in the list is justified.

This said, the situation is extremely unsatisfactory. The Council's response to the *OMPI* ruling, as well as its delay in renewing the existing list,[47] do not indicate a willingness to react to judicial assessments of the compatibility of the list with fundamental rights. Furthermore, a ruling at national level would not have effects beyond the jurisdiction of the court which issued the judgment and for this reason its effects in relation to EU instruments would be significantly limited, unless the Council were to be willing to act promptly to modify the list following a ruling of a national court to that effect.

5.6 Conclusions

The practice of identifying individuals and organisations as terrorists in a European instrument is obviously problematic from a fundamental rights perspective. The exercise of EU competence in this instance has considerably reduced, if not altogether eliminated, the possibility of a meaningful democratic debate about how best to address the terrorist threat and how to strike a reasonable balance between counter-terrorism action and the fundamental rights of those concerned. Furthermore, the Council's decision to use EU competence in such matters might well raise some questions as to whether the Member States acted instrumentally to avoid both democratic and judicial scrutiny. In this respect, consider the oddity of the domestic terrorist list: individuals and organisations are identified as terrorists in

---

[47] EU officials allegedly said that the non-renewal of the list within the prescribed time is simply a 'procedural problem', source *EUobserver*, 16 January 2007, 'EU backing down on EU terror list secrecy'. Mr Piris, Legal Adviser to the Council, allegedly held that the *OMPI* ruling concerned the preceding list and not the May list.

such a list, and yet the Member States are under no obligation to take action against such individuals/organisations. Given that the UN anti-terrorism Resolution requires States to act against terrorist organisations and individuals, one could well argue that the lack of action in respect of those entities and individuals is in breach of international law. The suspicion that inclusion in the EU domestic list might be politically motivated thus looms large in one's mind. If it is established that those people and entities are linked to terrorism, then action should be taken. Or else they should not be placed on the list. In any event, it is inexcusable that Union competence should be used so as to deprive individuals of their right to effective judicial protection.

In relation to the use of Community competence to provide for the freezing of assets of the foreign-linked 'terrorist', the fundamental rights issue might seem at first sight less pressing. After all, in those cases the Community judiciary has full jurisdiction. However, and leaving aside the issues arising from an extensive interpretation of Community competence to the detriment of individual rights, the *OMPI* ruling is evidence of the Community courts' unwillingness to exercise meaningful judicial scrutiny. Furthermore, Council has so far refused to take any steps to comply with that ruling; in a national context, such defiance would have been unthinkable; in the EU, allegedly based on the rule of law, it is all too possible.

6

The EU as a party to international agreements: shared competences, mixed responsibilities

RAMSES A. WESSEL

6.1 Introduction

The question of whether the European Union (EU) is competent to enter into international agreements with third States and other international organisations in the non-Community areas has been subject to intense debate ever since the negotiations on the Maastricht Treaty. The main controversy behind the debate was (and to some extent still is) the unclear legal status of the EU. While the Treaty of Lisbon (TL) clearly confirms the international legal personality of the Union (Art. 47 TEU revised), the current Treaty regime remains silent on this question.[1]

This has not prevented the EU from engaging actively in legal relations with third States and other international organisations. By now the EU has become a party to some 90 international agreements. With the increasing legal activity of the EU on the international plane, particularly reflected in the coming of age of the European Security and Defence Policy (ESDP),[2] the question of its legal accountability becomes more prominent. Whereas the international legal responsibility of the European *Community* has been subject to extensive legal analysis,[3] the same does not hold true for the

The author wishes to thank Steven Blockmans for his useful comments on an earlier draft.

[1] Nevertheless, 'As time goes by, the debate seems ever more irrelevant', as Eeckhout rightly observes. Eeckhout also points to the consensus on this issue in academic circles, see P. Eeckhout, *External Relations of the European Union: Legal and Constitutional Foundations* (Oxford: Oxford University Press, 2004), p. 155. Cf. also the views by (the Council's Legal Counsel) R. Gosalbo Bono, 'Some Reflections on the CFSP Legal Order', 43 CMLRev. (2006), pp. 354–5.

[2] More extensively, M. Trybus, *European Union Law and Defence Integration* (Oxford: Hart Publishing, 2005); and R.A. Wessel, 'The State of Affairs in EU Security and Defence Policy: The Breakthrough in the Treaty of Nice', *Journal of Conflict & Security Law* (2003), pp. 265–88.

[3] See for a recent overview Eeckhout, *External Relations of the European Union.*

European *Union*.[4] It is unclear whether the EU as such may be held accountable for any wrongful act. While there are good reasons to assume that the EU already enjoyed an international legal status from the outset,[5] this does not imply that its external relations regime is therefore also comparable to the rules we know from Community law. The general perception is that the relationship between the EU and its Member States in the Common Foreign and Security Policy (CFSP or second pillar) – and to a lesser extent in the Police and Judicial Cooperation in Criminal Matters (PJCCM or third pillar) – is still clearly different from the relation the same Member States maintain with the European Community, and that, therefore, different rules apply in relation to the legal effects of agreements concluded by the EU.[6]

Both the conclusion of international agreements by the EU and its international activities in relation to military missions, as well as some decisions related to the suppression of international terrorism call for a fresh look at the relation between the EU and its Member States in terms of international responsibility. If Henry Kissinger were in office, he would have every reason to raise the question 'Whom should I sue?', now that his famous question on the telephone number of Europe has been answered by the availability of the number of the High Representative for CFSP, Javier Solana. Indeed, it is in the external political (foreign affairs) and security relations in particular that the complex relationship between the EU and its Member States presents itself in its full dimension. The purpose of this contribution is to present a meaningful way to answer questions regarding the legal accountability of the EU in the area of foreign, security and defence policy, while acknowledging the important role of the Member States in this area. The division of powers between the EU and its Member States is a central issue in the analysis. After all, the Treaty provides that the EU 'shall assert its identity on the international scene, in

---

[4] See, however, F. Naert, *International Law Aspects of the EU's Security and Defence Policy* (Dissertation to be defended at the University of Leuven, 2008); as well as S. Blockmans, *Tough Love: The European Union's Relations with the Western Balkans* (The Hague: T.M.C. Asser Press, 2007).

[5] R.A. Wessel, 'The International Legal Status of the European Union', EFARev. (1997), pp. 109–29; see also 'Revisiting the International Legal Status of the EU', 5 EFARev. (2000), pp. 507–37.

[6] See, in general, E. Denza, *The Intergovernmental Pillars of the European Union* (Oxford: Oxford University Press, 2002); see, nevertheless, for the legal development of CFSP: Gosalbo Bono, 'Some Reflections'.

particular through the implementation of a common foreign and security policy' (Art. 2), but 'the Member States shall support the Union's external and security policy actively and unreservedly in a spirit of mutual solidarity' (Art. 11(2)).

In order to place the developments in a broader context, I will first investigate the division of external competences in the area of the CFSP and the more recent ESDP (Section 6.2). Section 6.3 will subsequently deal with the different types of agreements concluded by the EU. This will be followed, in Section 6.4, by an analysis of the role of the Member Sates in these agreements. Finally, Section 6.5 will be used to draw some conclusions on the responsibility of the EU and/or its Member States on the basis of the agreements.

6.2 Shared competences in European foreign policy

In the absence of case law in the non-Community areas of the EU, the question has arisen how the competences in this field are divided between the two distinct levels of governance. Research over the past decade pointed to a clear distinction between the competences of the Member States and the competences of the EU. Obviously, there is a difference between the 'States', as represented by the Heads of State as the original 'contractors', and the 'European Union' they created. While the Treaty on some points shows ambiguity, a separate role of the EU, alongside the actions of the Member States, has been accepted from the outset.[7]

With regard to international agreements concluded by the EU, Article 24 TEU is the applicable provision. This provision is modelled after Article 300 EC, as indicated for instance by its paragraph 6,[8] and has undergone changes with the Nice Treaty revision.[9] However, as will be

---

[7] See for references R.A. Wessel *The European Union's Foreign and Security Policy: A Legal Institutional Perspective* (The Hague, Kluwer Law International, 1999). More recently: Gosalbo Bono, 'Some Reflections', p. 253, who observes a certain development: 'it clearly became an international organisation, separate from the European Communities and the Member States'.

[8] Compare with Article 300(7) EC.

[9] Namely the inclusion of paragraph 6 and an extension of qualified majority voting, see E. Regelsberger and D. Kugelmann, 'Article 24 EUV para. 1', in R. Streinz, *EUV/EGV* (Munich: Beck, 2003); as well as I. Österdahl, 'The EU and Its Member States, Other States, and International Organisations – The Common European Security and Defence Policy after Nice', *Nordic Journal of International Law* (2001), pp. 341–72.

shown below, there are clear differences between Community and EU procedures. Article 24 TEU provides:

1. When it is necessary to conclude an agreement with one or more States or international organisations in implementation of this Title, the Council, acting unanimously, may authorise the Presidency, assisted by the Commission as appropriate, to open negotiations to that effect. Such agreements shall be concluded by the Council acting unanimously on a recommendation from the Presidency.
2. The Council shall act unanimously when the agreement covers an issue for which unanimity is required for the adoption of internal decisions.
3. When the agreement is envisaged in order to implement a joint action or common position, the Council shall act by a qualified majority in accordance with Article 23(2).
4. The provisions of this Article shall also apply to matters falling under Title VI. When the agreement covers an issue for which a qualified majority is required for the adoption of internal decisions or measures, the Council shall act by a qualified majority in accordance with Article 34(3).
5. No agreement shall be binding on a Member State whose representative in the Council states that it has to comply with the requirements of its own constitutional procedure; the other members of the Council may agree that the agreement shall nevertheless apply provisionally.
6. Agreements concluded under the conditions set out by this Article shall be binding on the institutions of the Union.

The scope of this provision extends to police and judicial cooperation in criminal matters, as the cross-references in Articles 24 (CFSP) and 38 (PJCCM) indicate. This turns the provision into the general legal basis for the EU's treaty-making, which may even be used to conclude cross-pillar (second and third) agreements.[10] The debate on whether such agreements are concluded by the Council on behalf of the EU or on behalf of the Member States[11] seems to be superseded by practice now that the EU has become a party to a number of international agreements on the basis of

---

[10] See the 2006 Agreement between the European Union and the United States of America on the processing and transfer of passenger name records (PNR) data, which is based on Decision 2006/729/CFSP/JHA of the Council of 16 October 2006, OJ 2006 L 298. This refers to both Articles 24 and 38.

[11] See more extensively Wessel, 'The International Legal Status'.

Article 24.[12] And, even before that it was clear that 'it would hardly be persuasive to contend that such treaties are in reality treaties concluded by individual Member States'.[13]

Nevertheless, the regime of Article 24 reflects the multilevel character of the external relations regime.[14] The Nice Treaty underlined the separate competence of the Union to conclude treaties. According to modified paragraphs 2 and 3 of Article 24, the Council shall still act unanimously when the agreement covers an issue for which unanimity is required for the adoption of internal decisions, but it will act by a qualified majority whenever the agreement is envisaged to implement a Joint Action or Common Position. Finally, paragraph 6 sets out that the agreements concluded by the Council shall be binding on the institutions of the EU. This explicitly hints at the possibility of the EU having obligations under international law as distinct from the obligations of the Member States.[15]

While 'mixity' has become the solution in the Community to overcome the division of competences,[16] the international agreements concluded

[12] See, however, some early agreements which mention 'The Council of the European Union' as the contracting party, including the 1999 Agreement with Republic of Iceland and the Kingdom of Norway, and the 2000 Agreement with Republic of Iceland and the Kingdom of Norway.

[13] C. Tomuschat, 'The International Responsibility of the European Union', in E. Cannizzaro (ed.), *The European Union as an Actor in International Relations* (The Hague: Kluwer Law International, 2002), p. 181. Cf. also Eeckhout, *External Relations of the European Union*, p. 159; P. Koutrakos, *EU International Relations Law* (Oxford: Hart Publishing, 2006), pp. 406–9 and Gosalbo Bono, 'Some Reflections', pp. 354–6.

[14] See more extensively R.A. Wessel 'The Multilevel Constitution of European Foreign Relations', in N. Tsagourias (ed.), *Transnational Constitutionalism: International and European Perspectives* (Cambridge University Press, 2007), pp. 160–206.

[15] Nevertheless, some Member States (still) hold to the view that the Council concludes agreements on their behalf, rather than on behalf of the Union, see S. Marquardt, 'La capacité de l'Union européenne de conclure des accords internationaux dans le domaine de la coopération policière et judiciaire en matière pénal', in G. De Kerchove and A. Weyembergh (eds.), *Sécurité et justice: enjeu de la politique extérieure de l'Union européenne* (Brussels: Editions de l'Université de Bruxelles, 2003), p. 185. See the same contribution for arguments underlining the view that the Council can only conclude these agreements on behalf of the EU, Cf. also S. Marquardt, 'The Conclusion of International Agreements Under Article 24 of the Treaty on European Union', in V. Kronenberger (ed.), *The European Union and the International Legal Order: Discord or Harmony?* (The Hague: Asser Press, 2001), pp. 333–50; D. Verwey, *The European Community, the European Union and the International Law of Treaties* (The Hague: Asser Press, 2004), p. 74; and R.A Wessel 'Revisiting the International Legal Status of the EU'.

[16] On mixity, see Eeckhout, *External Relations of the European Union*, Chapter 7; A. Dashwood, 'Why continue to have mixed agreements at all?', in J.H.J. Bourgeois, J.-L. Dewost and M.-A. Gaiffe (eds.), *La Communauté européenne et les accords mixtes* (Brussels: Presses Interuniversitaires Européennes, 1997), pp. 93–9; A. Rosas, 'Mixed Union – Mixed Agreements', in M. Koskenniemi (ed.), *International Law Aspects of the European Union* (The Hague: Martinus

under CFSP are – perhaps ironically – *exclusively* concluded by the EU.[17] It would, of course, go too far to conclude on an exclusive competence for the Union on this basis. In fact the whole system of CFSP as described above seems to point to the existence of 'shared', or better, 'parallel' competences: both the EU and its Member States seem to be competent to conclude treaties in the area of CFSP (including ESDP). This implies that, once the EU has concluded an international agreement, there is no direct legal relationship between the Member States and the contracting third party.

At the same time, it may be argued that the so-called *Haegeman* doctrine is not only applicable to the Community but also to the EU and that the agreements form an 'integral part of the Union's legal order'.[18] The reference in Article 24(6) TEU that the agreements bind the institutions supports this view. In this respect, the principle of consistency as reflected in Articles 1, 3 and 11 TEU should also be mentioned.[19] The notion that '[t]he Union shall in particular ensure the consistency of its external activities as a whole' (Art. 3 TEU) could link the EU agreements to agreements or other external actions based on the EC Treaty. It is disputed whether we are dealing with a justiciable principle.[20] The principle of consistency may be regarded as a special form of the loyalty principle laid

Nijhoff Publishers, 1998), pp. 125–48; N.A. Neuwahl, 'Joint Participation in International Treaties and the Exercise of Power by the EEC and its Member States: Mixed Agreements', 28 CMLRev. (1991), pp. 717–40; and on responsibility in these cases, see in particular E. Neframi, 'International Responsibility of the European Community and of the Member States under Mixed Agreements', in Cannizzaro (ed.), *The European Union as an Actor*, pp. 193–205.

[17] As the 2004 Agreement with the Swiss Confederation concerning the latter's association with the so-called Schengen *acquis* shows, combined EC/EU agreements are possible (see Section 6.4.3). A similar construction has been debated for the 2006 Cooperation Agreement with Thailand. In the end, however, the agreement was concluded as a traditional Community/Member State mixed agreement; see D. Thym, 'Die völkerrechtlichen Verträge der Europäischen Union', *ZaöRV* (2006), p. 909. A similar debate took place on the EU's accession to the ASEAN Treaty of Amity and Cooperation. As the relevant documents (such as Council Doc. 15772/06) are not in the public domain, the final outcome is not yet clear.

[18] As provided by the ECJ in relation to international agreements concluded by the European Community: Case 181/73 *Haegeman* [1974] ECR 449 and Case 104/81 *Kupferberg* [1982] ECR 3641, see in the same line Thym, previous note, p. 38.

[19] See more extensively R.A. Wessel 'The Inside Looking Out: Consistency and Delimitation in EU External Relations', 37 CMLRev. (2000), pp. 1135–71; as well as 'Fragmentation in the Governance of EU External Relations: Legal Institutional Dilemmas and the New Constitution for Europe', in J.W. de Zwaan *et al.* (eds.), *The European Union – An Ongoing Process of Integration, Liber Amicorum Fred Kellermann* (The Hague: Asser Press, 2004), pp. 123–40.

[20] See, for instance, B. Weidel, 'The Impact of the Pillar Construction on External Policy', in S. Griller and B. Weidel (eds.), *External Economic Relations and Foreign Policy in the European Union* (Vienna: Springer Verlag, 2002), p. 34.

down in Article 10 EC, as it emphasises institutional coordination and
the coordination of actions among institutions and Member States
(Section 6.4.3).[21]

6.3 Agreements concluded by the European Union

6.3.1 Conclusion of agreements by the Council

The Treaty regime in Article 24 TEU is reflected in the way this provision
has been used by the EU in practice. Recent research by Thym reveals that
the procedure through which agreements are concluded confirms the
central position of the EU's institutions and organs at all stages of the
decision-making process.[22] The usual procedure is that the Council
authorises the Presidency 'to designate the person empowered to sign the
Agreement in order to bind the European Union'. Agreements are
negotiated by the Presidency (often 'assisted by the Secretary-General/
High Representative'). After discussion of the draft agreement in a
Council working party, together with the decision by which it is to be
adopted, the agreement follows the normal route through the Council's
preparatory organs. The decision to conclude the Agreement is finally
taken by the Council in a separate Decision on the basis of Article 24
(or in the case of PJCCM Article 38). It is striking that the Council
Decision not only allows for the conclusion (signing) of the agreement,
but at the same time provides the ratification of the agreement: the
decision is used to 'approve the Agreement on behalf of the European
Union' and to 'authorise to sign the agreement in order to bind the
European Union'.[23] The actual signing of the agreement may be done by
the President of the Council (when this can take place during a session of
the Council), by the Secretary-General/High Representative, or by a
Special Representative present in the third country.[24] A distinction

---

[21] In addition, its influence is reflected in the context of the unity of law, which is generally seen
as a guiding obligation in relation to the interpretation of Community law rather than overall
Union law.

[22] See Thym, 'Die völkerrechtlichen', pp. 870–75.

[23] Cf. Council Decision 2005/851/CFSP of 21 November 2005 concerning the conclusion of the
Agreement between the European Union and Canada establishing a framework for the
participation of Canada in the European Union crisis management operations, OJ 2005 L 315.

[24] See for the dates of the entry into force of the agreements the Agreements database, available
at: http://www.consilium.europa.eu/cms3_applications/Applications/accords/search.asp.

between adoption and ratification is, however, made in the decisions related to third pillar agreements. A reason seems to be that in these cases some Member States invoked Article 24(5): 'No agreement shall be binding on a Member State whose representative in the Council states that it has to comply with the requirements of its own constitutional procedure' (Section 6.4.1).

It is indeed striking that all agreements are concluded by the 'European Union' only; the Member States are not mentioned as parties. This clearly deviates from earlier arrangements in which the EU was merely used to coordinate the external policies of the Member States.[25] Indeed, throughout the text of the current agreements, rights and obligations are related to the EU and the other party. The standard formula reads as follows: 'The EUROPEAN UNION, on the one hand, and [THIRD COUNTRY or INTERNATIONAL ORGANISATION], on the other hand, hereinafter referred to as the 'Parties', HAVE AGREED AS FOLLOWS: ... '. In exceptional circumstances, the Agreement is based on an Exchange of Letters, in which case the High Representative acts as the legal representative of the EU. Even in that case, however, the formal conclusion of the agreement is decided upon by the Council. Thus, the entire decision-making process as well as the conclusion of the agreement does not reveal a separate role for the Member States. Apart from the references to the EU in both the texts and the preamble of the agreements and the fact that adoption and ratification is done 'on behalf of the Union', this is confirmed by the central role of the Union's institutions and organs (including the Presidency, the Council's working parties and the Council Secretariat), and the final publication in the L-series of the Official Journal (decision on *inter se* agreements of the Member States are published in the C-series).[26] Indeed, 'fairly strange operations would be needed to demonstrate that a treaty concluded under such circumstances has instead created legal bonds between the

---

[25] The prime example is formed by the *Memorandum of Understanding on the European Union Administration of Mostar*, which was concluded by the 'The Member States of the European Union acting within the framework of the Union in full association with the European Commission'; signed in Geneva on 5 July 1994. The Agreement was signed by the Presidency after approval by the Council on the basis of the very first CFSP Decision: 93/603/CFSP of 8 November 1993, OJ 1993 L 286; see also J. Monar, 'Editorial Comment – Mostar: Three Lessons for the European Union', 2 EFARev. (1997), pp. 1–6.

[26] More extensively, see Thym, 'Die völkerrechtlichen', p. 873.

third party concerned and each one of the Member States of the European Union'.[27]

The international agreements to which the EU has become a party may largely be categorised as follows:

1. agreements between the EU and a third State on the participation of that State in an EU operation;
2. agreements between the EU and a third State on the status or activities of EU forces;
3. agreements between the EU and a third State in the area of PJCCM;
4. agreements between the EU and a third State on the exchange of classified information;
5. agreements between the EU and other international organisations;
6. agreements between the EU and a third State in the form of an Exchange of Letters;
7. joint Declarations and Memoranda of Understanding between the European Union and a third State;
8. agreements concluded by European Union agencies.

6.3.2 Agreements on the participation of a third state in an EU operation

The establishment of military and police missions on the basis of the ESDP called for agreements between the EU and non-Member States willing to participate in the mission. The lion's share of agreements to which the EU is a party fall into this category. Thus, agreements have been concluded with European third States (Albania, Ukraine, Norway, Turkey, Iceland, Switzerland). With non-European third States (Canada, New Zealand, Argentina, Morocco, Chile, the Russian Federation) as well as with most States that acceded to the EU in 2004 and 2007, prior to their accession. Some agreements have been concluded in the form of an Exchange of Letters (see Section 6.3.6).

The purpose of the agreements is to fix obligations between the EU and the third State participating in an EU mission. Recurring elements in these agreements are the association of the third State with relevant decisions of the EU, the status of personnel and forces, the exchange of classified

---

[27] Tomuschat, 'The International Responsibility', pp. 181–2.

information, the chain of command and financial aspects. In all cases the framework is set by the Joint Actions and other Decisions forming the basis of the operation. The third State accepts the obligation to place its participation within that framework and to transfer the operational control to the EU Head of Mission (in case of civilian crisis management operations) or the EU Operation Commander (in case of military crisis management operations). Nevertheless, all forces and personnel remain under the full command of their national authorities.[28] In relation to the exchange of information, the third State ensures that, when it handles EU classified information in the context of the operation, it respects the relevant principles and standards. Regarding the financial aspects, the third participating State assumes all the costs associated with its participation in the operation, apart from the costs that are subject to common funding.

The agreement also ensures that there are no differences in the legal status of EU Member States and third States in a mission, as both 'shall have the same rights and obligations in terms of the day-to-day management of the operation'.[29] This is reflected in the fact that, although military missions fall under the political control of the Political and Security Committee, a 'Committee of Contributors', in which all participating States have a seat:

> will play a key role in the day-to-day management of the operation; the Committee will be the main forum where contributing States collectively address questions relating to the employment of their forces in the operation; the Political and Security Committee, which exercises the political control and strategic direction of the operation, will take account of the views expressed by the Committee of Contributors.[30]

For the present article, the most relevant parts are to be found in the sections on the status of personnel and forces and the chain of command. The 2005 agreement with Canada, for instance, provides that 'Canada shall exercise jurisdiction over its personnel participating in the EU crisis management operation' and that 'Canada shall be responsible for

---

[28] Cf. Articles 6 and 10 of the Agreement between the European Union and Canada establishing a framework for the participation of Canada in the European Union crisis management operations, OJ 2005 L 315/21.

[29] *Ibid.*

[30] See PSC Decision BiH/3/2004 of 29 September 2004 on the setting-up of the Committee of Contributors for the European Union military operation in Bosnia and Herzegovina (2004/739/CFSP), preamble.

answering any claims linked to its participation in an EU crisis management operation, from or concerning any of its personnel'.[31] Questions of
liability seem to be out of the hands of the EU as the participating third
State remains fully responsible for actions of its own personnel and forces.
Indeed, the agreements explicitly regulate a possible liability, although one
may argue that the following (standard) clause counts only when a
liability of the participating State has been established; it does not exclude
possible liability of the EU:

> In case of death, injury, loss or damage to natural or legal persons for the
> State(s) in which the operation is conducted, Canada shall, when its liability
> has been established, pay compensation under the conditions foreseen in
> the agreement on status of mission/forces.[32]

In any case, it is made clear that there shall be no claims between the
participating States in an EU operation. Thus, the agreement with Canada
provides that 'Canada undertakes to make a declaration as regards the
waiver of claims against any State participating in an EU crisis management operation' and '[t]he European Union undertakes to ensure that
Member States make a declaration as regards the waiver of claims against
Canada'.[33] While earlier agreements left the liability question in the dark,
formulas such as this one have become a standard clause in all agreements
on the participation of third States in EU operations.

6.3.3 Agreements on the status or activities of EU forces

A smaller number of agreements relate to the regulation of the status and
activities of the EU in the State where the mission is established. These
agreements are usually referred to as SOFAs (Status of Forces Agreements)
or SOMAs (Status of Mission Agreements).[34] So far, for this purpose,
agreements have been concluded with the former Yugoslav Republic of
Macedonia, Georgia, Congo, Indonesia, the Federal Republic of Yugoslavia
(before its dissolution), Bosnia and Herzegovina, and Albania.

---

[31] Agreement between the European Union and Canada establishing a framework for the
participation of Canada in the European Union crisis management operations, OJ 2005 L 315/
21, Article 3(3) and (4).
[32] *Ibid.*, para. 5.   [33] *Ibid.*, paras. 6 and 7.
[34] Model SOFAs and SOMAs exist for police (EU Doc. 14612/4/02 REV 4, 29 April 2003),
civilian and military ESDP missions (not in the public domain, but see EU Doc. 8720/05 and
EU Doc. 8886/05, 18 May 2005).

These agreements address a number of issues. First, they provide that EU personnel shall respect the laws and regulations of the Host Party.[35] At the same time, the Host Party shall respect the autonomy and the unitary and international nature of the EU mission. Other rules and agreements relate to the identification of EU personnel, headquarters and means of transportation; the facilitation by the Host States of the crossing of the border, the movement and the presence on its territory of EU troops; the employment of local personnel, the security of EU personnel, and the access to information and communications.

Central to the agreements are the provisions on immunities and privileges of EU personnel. In the 2005 Agreement with the Democratic Republic of Congo, for instance, it is provided that 'EUPOL Kinshasa (the name of the EU mission) shall be granted the status equivalent to that of a diplomatic mission under the Vienna Convention on Diplomatic Relations.'[36] The usual issues around immunities and privileges are regulated: immunity from the criminal, civil, and administrative jurisdiction of the Host Party; inviolability of premises, archives and documents and correspondence; exemption from all national and communal dues and taxes of imported goods and services, etc. Similar agreements are included on the immunities and privileges of EU personnel.[37] The frequent granting of privileges and immunities equivalent to that of a diplomatic mission and diplomatic personnel is quite unusual, in particular for larger military missions such as Concordia.[38]

Reliance on the Vienna Convention on Diplomatic Relations, rather than on the SOFA regime developed in the UN framework seems to be typical of many EU missions, but not of all. Thus European Union Force (EUFOR) Althea in Bosnia and Herzegovina operates on the terms of its predecessor and uses the SOFA agreed on between NATO and Bosnia Herzegovina. Similarly, the SOFA of the United Nations Organisation Mission in the Democratic Republic of Congo (MONUC) was declared

---

[35] With the exception of the very first SOFA on the EU Police Mission in Bosnia and Herzegovina (2003), which lacks a provision on applicable law, see also F. Naert, 'ESDP in Practice: Increasingly Varied and Ambitious EU Security and Defence Operations', in M. Trybus and N. White (eds.), *European Security Law* (Oxford University Press, 2007), pp. 225–48.

[36] Agreement between the European Union and the Democratic Republic of Congo on the status and activities of the European Union police mission in the Democratic Republic of the Congo (EUPOL Kinshasa), OJ 2005 L 256/58.

[37] *Ibid.*, paras. 5 and 6.   [38] Naert, *International Law Aspects*, Chapter 2.

applicable to the EU mission in 2006 by the Security Council and comparable regulations may be found in relation to EU mission agreements with Indonesia (Aceh) and Gabon (on Congo).[39]

In relation to the division of powers between the EU and the Member States, it is furthermore notable that immunities can be waived by the Secretary General/High Representative. In the agreement with Congo this is phrased as follows:

> The Secretary General/High Representative shall, with the explicit consent of the competent authority of the Sending State or the sending EU institution, waive the immunity enjoyed by EUPOL Kinshasa personnel where such immunity would impede the course of justice and it can be waived without prejudice to the interests of the EU.[40]

While these arrangements may give the impression that neither the EU nor its Member States is responsible in case of any wrongful act by the mission or its personnel, the agreements do include a provision on the basis of which separate regulations are to be made between the Head of Mission and the administrative authorities of the Host Party. These agreements entail procedures for settling and addressing claims, but are not in the public domain. In the words of the Congo Agreement they, however, do not deal with claims 'arising out of activities in connection with civil disturbances, protection of the EUPOL Kinshasa or its personnel, or which are incidental to operational necessities'.[41] Indeed, in general, claims arising out of activities in connection with the operation are not the subject of reimbursement by participating States or the EU.[42] Special arrangements are created for other claims compensations and can be found in the more recent mission agreements. While in most cases a special claims commission will deal with the claims, the agreement with Gabon even introduces an 'arbitration tribunal' for claims above € 40,000. On the basis of paragraph 5 of the Agreement:

> The arbitration tribunal shall be composed of three arbitrators, one arbitrator being appointed by the Host State, one arbitrator being appointed by EUFOR and the third one being appointed jointly by the Host State and

---

[39] Cf. also Thym, 'Die völkerrechtlichen', p. 879.

[40] Agreement between the European Union and the Democratic Republic of Congo, Article 6, paragraph 2. This provision was first used in the SOMA for the 2004 EU Proxima Mission in FYROM, OJ 2004 L 16/66.

[41] *Ibid.*, Article 14.   [42] Cf. also F. Naert, n. 4, Chapter 2.

EUFOR. Where one of the parties does not appoint an arbitrator within two months or where no agreement can be found between the Host State and EUFOR on the appointment of the third arbitrator, the arbitrator in question shall be appointed by the President of the Court of Justice of the European Communities.[43]

Claims up to € 40,000 are to be settled by diplomatic means between the host states and EU representatives.

In general, it is striking that the SOFAs and SOMAs frequently grant privileges and immunities to the operations and missions, to the same extent as is normally done to diplomatic missions and diplomatic personnel. In the UN, for instance, full diplomatic status is reserved for top officials of a mission only. The provision in, for instance, the UN Model SOFA, that forces shall be under the exclusive jurisdiction of their sending State, is omitted in the EU agreements. While the possibility of a waiver may compensate for this, it is not expected that contributing States grant this waiver very easily as local jurisdictions – when they exist at all – may not function in accordance with international human rights standards.[44] Hence, while the SOFAs and SOMAs do deal with claims procedures, the question of a division between EU and Member States responsibilities is not regulated in any clear way. Nevertheless, the agreements provide that claims shall be submitted to the EU mission or operation. Thus, the 2005 EU Model SOFA (Art. 15) provides that claims 'shall be forwarded to EUFOR via the competent authorities of the Host State'. When no amicable settlement can be found 'the claim shall be submitted to a claims commission composed on an equal basis of representatives of EUFOR and representatives of the Host State'. In the case of a dispute, it shall be settled by diplomatic means 'between the Host State and EU representatives' or by an arbitration tribunal composed of arbitrators appointed by the Host State and the EU mission. The EU Model SOFA even foresees a role of the ECJ, to appoint the third arbiter when both parties cannot agree on the appointment of this

---

[43] Agreement between the European Union and the Gabonese Republic on the status of the European Union-led forces in the Gabonese Republic (14 June 2006). This agreement was necessary in view of the stationing of the EU-led operation EUFOR RD Congo on the territory of the Gabonese Republic.

[44] See Naert, 'ESDP in Practice'; see paras. 27 and 47(b) of the UN Model SOFA, UN Doc. A/45/594, 9 October 1990.

person.[45] As shown above, this possibility was already used in the Gabon agreement.

The EU as such thus seems to play a pivotal role in the claims procedure and no direct formal contacts are planned between the Host State and any EU Member State. Any legal duties the contributing States may have, thus seem to be regulated through the EU. Nevertheless, Member States have not been willing to waive any *rights* that they have on the basis of international law. Article 17(2) of the Model SOFA provides:

> Nothing in this Agreement is intended or may be construed to derogate from any rights that may attach to an EU Member State or to any other State contributing to EUFOR under other agreements.

There are no reasons, however, not to apply the regular financial distribution system for common costs to claims compensation as well. The special ATHENA system invented for the allocation of costs can be used for a fair distribution.[46]

A final point – which cannot be dealt with in the limited scope of this contribution – is the absence in the agreements of any reference to the applicability of international humanitarian law. While, by now, this has become standard practice in relation to UN missions,[47] international humanitarian law is assumed to be mentioned in non-public documents related to military missions only (such as the Operation Plan or the Rules of Engagement).[48]

---

[45] As a procedure before the ECJ to hold the EU liable seems to be excluded because of the lack of a treaty basis, plaintiffs have no possibilities to use the regular (Community) procedures (Arts. 235 and 288 EC) in this regard. Cf. in general also M.-G. Garbagnati Ketvel, 'The Jurisdiction of the European Court of Justice in Respect of the Common Foreign and Security Policy', 55 ICLQ (2006), pp. 77–120.

[46] Also Thym, 'Die völkerrechtlichen', p. 880.

[47] See in particular the quite (in)famous *UN Secretary-General Bulletin on Observance by United Nations forces of international humanitarian law*, UN Doc. ST/SGB/1999/13, 6 August 1999, available at: http://www.un.org/peace/st_sgb_1999_13.pdf; as well as M.C. Zwanenburg, *Accountability of Peace Support Operations: Accountability under International Humanitarian Law for United Nations and North Atlantic Treaty Organisation Peace Support Operations* (Leiden: Martinus Nijhoff Publishers, 2005), p. 70 and D. Shraga, 'UN Peacekeeping Operations: Applicability of International Humanitarian Law and Responsibility for Operations-Related Damage', 94 AJIL (2000), pp. 406–12.

[48] See Naert, *International Law Aspects*, Chapter 3. In this respect Naert points to Article 6 TEU, which at least reflects the Union's respect for fundamental rights.

6.3.4 Agreements in the area of PJCCM

So far, only a limited number of agreements have been concluded by the European Union on the basis of Article 38 EU, the specific legal basis for the conclusion of international agreements in the 'Third Pillar'. Article 38 EU reads:

> Agreements referred to in Article 24 may cover matters falling under this title.[49]

In 2003, the EU concluded two agreements with the United States, one on mutual legal assistance and one on extradition.[50] While the EU Member States have not become a party to these agreements (Art. 2 provides: '"Contracting Parties" shall mean the European Union and the United States'), these two agreements have established a complex legal regime in which the Member States do have rights and obligations as well. This is particularly clear in the provisions on the application of the Agreement in relation to (already existing or new) bilateral extradition or mutual legal assistance treaties with the US. These provisions lay down the rules of application of the Treaty and divide the competences between the EU and its Member States. In fact, these two agreements with the US reveal a marginal role for the EU as such: most rights and obligations rest on the 'State', which may either be an EU Member State or the US. An example may be found in Article 10 of the extradition agreement:

> If the requested State receives requests from the requesting State and from any other State or States for the extradition of the same person, either for the same offence or different offences, the executive authority of the requested State shall determine to which State, if any, it will surrender the person.

---

[49] See also P. De Koster, 'Bref état des lieux sur les accords de coopération conclus sur la base de l'article 38 du traité UE', in De Kerchove and Weyembergh (eds.), n. 21, pp. 195–9; see in general on the third pillar S. Peers, *EU Justice and Home Affairs Law* (Oxford: Oxford University Press, 2006).

[50] Both Agreements are published in OJ 2003 L 181; see on the negotiations and the content of the agreements G. Stessens, 'The EU–US Agreements on Extradition and on Mutual Legal Assistance: how to Bridge Different Approaches', in De Kerchove and Weyembergh, *Sécurité et justice*, pp. 261–73. Stessens points to the fact that certain results in these agreements would have been unattainable for individual states in bilateral agreements with the US.

Similar references to State obligations may be found in the Treaty on Mutual Legal Assistance, as its Article 4 shows:

> Upon request of the requesting State, the requested State shall, in accordance with the terms of this Article, promptly ascertain if the banks located in its territory possess information on whether an identified natural or legal person suspected of or charged with a criminal offence is the holder of a bank account or accounts. The requested State shall promptly communicate the results of its enquiries to the requesting State.

Formally, however, the Member States are not bound by the agreements vis-à-vis the United States; they only have obligations to uphold the Treaty provisions in relation to the EU. This is confirmed by the fact that the US thought it necessary to ask for written instruments in which the Member States stated that they considered themselves bound by the agreements.[51] This may very well be the reason for the somewhat peculiar provision in joint Article 3(2)(a) of the Agreements, on the basis of which the European Union 'shall ensure that each Member State acknowledges, in a written instrument between such Member State and the United States of America, the application ... of its bilateral mutual legal assistance treaty in force with the United States of America'. As we seem to be dealing with what are clearly 'shared' or 'parallel' competences, a mixed agreement should have been the obvious solution. This way the new agreement could have replaced the original bilateral treaties, rather than making them part of a new complex system.[52]

A perhaps even more complex legal regime is created when both the European Union and the European Community enter into an agreement with a third party. In 2004, the EU (on the basis of Arts. 24 and 38 EU) and the EC concluded an agreement with the Swiss Confederation concerning the latter's association with the implementation, application and development of the so-called Schengen *acquis*.[53] While rights and obligations rest mainly on the Institutions (the Commission and the Council), there

---

[51] See Marquardt, 'The conclusion of International Agreements', p. 193; and J. Monar, 'The EU as an International Actor in the Domain of Justice and Home Affairs', 9 EFARev. (2004), pp. 395–415.

[52] See also Thym, 'Die völkerrechtlichen', p. 890; Marquart (2003), 'The conclusion of International Agreements', p. 193 and T. Georgopoulos, 'What Kind of Treaty-Making Power for the EU?', 30 ELRev. (2005), p. 207.

[53] See Council Decisions 2004/849/EC and 2004/860/EC of 25 October 2004. These decisions are published in OJ 2004 L 368/26 and OJ 2004 L 370/78 respectively. The Agreement (13054/04) is available at the Public Register of the Council only.

are occasional references to the Member States. This confirms that, despite the different procedural rules, 'cross-pillar mixity' is possible.[54]

A similar situation is created by the 2004 Agreement between the EU and the Republic of Iceland and the Kingdom of Norway.[55] This agreement relates to the application of certain provisions of the 2000 Convention on Mutual Assistance in Criminal Matters between the EU Member States. The purpose of the Agreement with Iceland and Norway is to extend the scope of the earlier Convention to these two States. Nevertheless, it is not the Member States that enter into a new agreement, but the EU, which means that a legal relation is established between the EU and Iceland/Norway only. On a more substantive note, however, it is clear that – as phrased by Article 1 – the original Convention 'shall be applicable in the relations between the Republic of Iceland and the Kingdom of Norway and in the mutual relations between each of these States and the Member States of the European Union'.

It seems that in these cases the EU and its contracting party agreed on some role for the EU Member States. While legally the Member States have not entered into any treaty obligation, their rights and duties follow from the agreement the organisation of which they are a member concluded with a third State. While this sheds a new light on the binding nature of EU decisions vis-à-vis the Member States, on a political note one may argue that the decision to conclude the Treaty was taken by the Council, in which all of them have a seat. From a legal perspective, the distinction between the Council as Institution and the Member States should be upheld, as Member States may only be addressed on an individual basis by a third State when their obligations have explicitly been regulated in the agreement. In all cases it is made clear, however, that the agreements can be terminated by the Contracting Parties (i.e. the EU and the other party) only. The same seems to hold true for any modification of the agreements.

6.3.5 Agreements on the exchange of classified information

With a small number of third States, the EU entered into an agreement on the establishment of security procedures for the exchange of classified information (see the Agreements with Norway, Croatia, Ukraine, Romania, and Bosnia and Herzegovina). In contrast to the agreements discussed

[54] Cf. Eeckhout, *External Relations of the European Union*, p. 184.   [55] OJ 2004 L 26/1.

above, these agreements do not create separate rights and duties for the Member States. Again, they are concluded by the EU, and they even explicitly provide:

> For the purposes of this Agreement, 'EU' shall mean the Council of the European Union (hereafter Council), the Secretary General/High Representative and the General Secretariat of the Council, and the Commission of the European Communities (hereafter European Commission).

Hence, the obligations rest on the Parties only and in case of any violation of the procedures by an EU Member State, the third party will have no choice but to address the EU Institutions.

The Agreements form good examples of cross-pillar decision-making as the decisions by which they are adopted are based on both Articles 24 and 38.[56] In 2003, the Council adopted a model for this type of agreement.[57]

6.3.6 Agreements between the EU and other international organisations

The first agreement concluded between the EU and another international organisation was the 2002 'Berlin Plus' Agreement with the North Atlantic Treaty Organisation (NATO), which allows the EU to draw on NATO military assets.[58] This agreement, however, was not based on Article 24 EU and a decision to conclude this agreement was never adopted by the Council. It was merely announced at the 2002 Copenhagen European Council after it was signed by NATO's Secretary-General George Robertson and the EU's High Representative for CFSP Javier Solana.[59] As the prescribed procedures have not been followed, it is doubtful whether this is more than a gentlemen's agreement.[60] However, this does not

---

[56] See, for instance, Decision 2004/731/EC (*sic!*) of the Council of 26 July 2004 concerning the conclusion of the Agreement between the European Union and Bosnia and Herzegovina on security procedures for the exchange of classified information, OJ 2004 L 324/15.

[57] See Agreement on security procedures for the exchange of classified information with Bulgaria, Romania, Iceland, Norway, Turkey, Canada, the Russian Federation, Ukraine, the United States of America, Bosnia and Herzegovina, and FYROM. Council authorisation to Presidency to open negotiations in accordance with Articles 24 and 38 of the TEU, Council Doc. 13819/03 (not public).

[58] Published in 42 ILM (2003), p. 242.

[59] See M. Reichard, 'Some Legal Issues Concerning the EU–NATO Berlin Plus Agreement', *Nordic Journal of International Law* (2004), pp. 37–67.

[60] *Ibid.* Reichard concludes that ' "Berlin Plus" is nothing but a non-binding agreement', although 'legally binding force may arise for some of its contents through estoppel'. The letters

simplify matters. The 'Berlin Plus' Agreement forms the basis of all EU–NATO military cooperation and it would be difficult to disregard the mutual rights and obligations in practice. In any case, it seems fair to conclude that the agreement was concluded between the two organisations and that all possible controversies will have to be settled between the secretaries-general of the two organisations. The Member States are bound only through their organisations.

Article 24 is referred to in the subsequent 2003 Agreement between the EU and NATO on the security of information.[61] The Agreement establishes a procedure to protect and safeguard classified information being exchanged between the two organisations. Again, the Member States play no role in this Agreement as it only creates rights and obligations for both organisations (in the case of the EU specified as the Council, the Secretary-General/High Representative, the General Secretariat and the Commission). This is made even more explicit in the 2006 Agreement between the International Criminal Court and the EU on cooperation and assistance:[62]

> For the purposes of this Agreement, 'EU' shall mean the Council of the European Union (hereafter Council), the Secretary-General/High Representative and the General Secretariat of the Council, and the Commission of the European Communities (hereafter European Commission). *'EU' shall not mean the Member States in their own right.*[63]

The clear division between the EU and its Member States returns in subsequent provisions, in which it is said that the Agreement shall only relate to EU documents and not to documents originating from an individual Member State.

6.3.7 Agreements in the form of an Exchange of Letters

Occasionally, agreements are not concluded in the form of a single document, but on the basis of an Exchange of Letters between the EU and a third State. Apart from the form, there do not seem to be any differences

---

from both Secretaries-General which formed the basis for the agreement had to be retrieved by Reichard using the Council's procedure for disclosing information. In his book, Reichard also refers to and reproduced letters between the EU Presidency and the CFSP High Representative, see M. Reichard, *The EU–NATO Relationship – A Legal and Political Perspective* (Aldershot: Ashgate, 2006), pp. 400–2.

[61] OJ 2003 L 80/35.   [62] OJ 2006 L115/49.   [63] Article 2(1), emphasis added.

with the regular agreements concluded by the EU.[64] In the Decisions taken by the Council to approve the agreements, Article 24 is explicitly mentioned as the legal basis. Thus, in 2002 for instance, the Council approved of an agreement between the EU and the Republic of Lebanon on cooperation in the fight against terrorism.[65]

More recently, this form of instrument was used to establish an agreement with Indonesia on an EU Monitoring Mission in Aceh and to allow for the participation of a number of third States in this mission. Thus, apart from the agreement on the tasks, status, privileges and immunities of the Aceh Monitoring Mission and its personnel (the so-called SOMA),[66] agreements in the form of an Exchange of Letters were concluded with Brunei, Singapore, Malaysia, Thailand and the Philippines.[67] In these cases, also, it is made clear that the EU as such becomes a party to the agreement and that possible obligations of the Member States are the concern of the EU. Thus, the 2005 Agreement with Thailand, for instance, provides that:[68]

> The European Union shall ensure that its Member States make, on the basis of reciprocity, a declaration as regards the waiver of claims, for the participation of the Kingdom of Thailand in the AMM.

The declaration itself is annexed to the agreement:

> The EU Member States applying the Joint Action [...] on the EU Monitoring Mission in Aceh (Aceh Monitoring Mission – AMM) will endeavour, insofar as their internal legal systems so permit, to waive as far as possible claims against the Kingdom of Thailand for injury, death of their personnel, or damage to, or loss of, any assets owned by themselves and used by the AMM.

The Council Decision approving the agreements authorises the Presidency to designate the person(s) empowered to sign the Agreement in the form of an Exchange of Letters to bind the EU. The fact that the Presidency leaves the Exchange of Letters as well as their signing to the Secretary

---

[64] Indeed, it is generally held that there is no difference in the legal status between single document agreements and agreements in the form of an Exchange of Letters, see J. Klabbers, *The Concept of Treaty in International Law* (The Hague: Kluwer Law International, 1996).

[65] Doc. 7494/02, to be found in the Council's register.   [66] OJ 2005 L 288/59.

[67] See for the Council Decision, Doc. 12321/05. The agreements may also be found in the Council's register.

[68] Doc. 12321/05, 4 October 2005.

General/High Representative, Javier Solana, may again be seen as underlining the institutional role of the EU. While the Member States are of course involved in the adoption of the Decision approving the Agreement, their role is less visible in both the negotiation and the conclusion of the Agreements.

6.3.8 Joint declarations and memoranda of understanding

Irrespective of the fact that the Council's agreements database lists some Joint Declarations between the EU and third States as 'agreements', one may doubt whether they need to be mentioned here. All Joint Declarations seem to be lacking a 'consent to be bound' on the side of the parties and the form clearly differs from the other texts, while Article 24 is not referred to as the legal basis. Nevertheless, the Declarations seem to create new 'institutional facts' and rights and duties for the signatories. Thus, in the 2005 EU–Afghanistan Joint Declaration, Afghanistan and the EU agree to form a new partnership and even refer to this as an 'agreement'.[69] Both parties undertake clear commitments. Similar wording was used in, for instance, the 2005 EU–Iraq Joint Declaration on Political Dialogue or the 2004 Joint Declaration of the People's Republic of China and the European Union on Non-Proliferation and Arms Control.[70]

The legal status of 'Memoranda of Understanding' (MOU) is even less clear. On some occasions the EU has made use of this instrument. An example is formed by the 2006 MOU on a Strategic Partnership between the EU and the Republic of Azerbaijan in the field of energy.[71] As no reference is made to Article 24 or any other legal basis, we have to assume that we are not dealing with a formal agreement (in the sense that a 'consent to be bound' is lacking), but with a form of cooperation which may result in a formal legal relationship at a later stage. In any case, it is clear that the MOU is concluded between the third State and the EU as the commitments are all related to the EU and the MOU is signed 'on behalf of the European Union'.[72]

---

[69] Doc. 14519/05, 16 November 2005.

[70] Doc. 12547/05, 21 September 2005 and Doc. 15854/04, 8 December 2004, respectively.

[71] Available at: http://register.consilium.europa.eu/pdf/en/06/st14/st14323.en06.pdf.

[72] See also n. 25.

6.3.9 Agreements concluded by EU agencies

Although the scope of this contribution does not allow a detailed analysis of the role of the EU agencies, their treaty-making competences should not be neglected. The EU agencies enjoy an independent international legal personality, which also allows them to enter into agreements with third States and other international organisations. Formally, these agreements thus fall outside the scope of this contribution; after all, they are not concluded by the EU itself.

The prime example of an agency which has concluded a number of international agreements is Europol.[73] Apart from the cooperation agreement with the United States,[74] Europol concluded agreements with a number of European and non-European third States, with EU bodies and other international organisations.[75] A similar position is taken by Eurojust, the body established in 2002 to enhance the effectiveness of the competent authorities within Member States when they are dealing with the investigation and prosecution of serious cross-border and organised crime.[76] In 2005, cooperation Agreements were concluded with Romania and Iceland.[77] A final agency in the third pillar area is the European Police College (CEPOL), which was granted legal personality in 2004.[78] In June 2006 the European Police Academy concluded cooperation agreements with Iceland, Norway and Switzerland.[79]

In the second pillar, the agencies also enjoy a separate legal personality.[80] But, so far, the European Defence Agency, the European Institute for

---

[73] See for its legal status Article 26 of the first Europol Convention of 10 March 1995 (entry into force 1 October 1998), OJ 1995 C 316/2; more extensively C. Rijken, 'Legal Aspects of Cooperation between Europol, Third States, and Interpol', in Kronenberger, n. 21, p. 587.

[74] See N. Lavranos, 'Europol and the Fight Against Terrorism', 8 EFARev. 2003, p. 259.

[75] A list of agreements is available at: http://www.europol.europa.eu/index.asp?page=agreements.

[76] See Article 1 of Council Decision 2002/187/JHA by which Eurojust was established, OJ 2002 L 63/1.

[77] See Eurojust Press Release of 2 December 2005, available at: http://www.eurojust.europa.eu/press_releases/2005/02-12-2005.htm.

[78] See Decision 2004/566/JHA of the Council of 26 July 2004, OJ 2004, L 251/19 as well as Decision 2005/681/JHA of the Council of 20 September 2005, OJ 2005 L 256/63.

[79] See Thym, 'Die völkerrechtlichen', p. 893 who refers to Council Documents 9259/06, 9265/06 and 9179/06 for the draft versions.

[80] See respectively Decision 2004/551CFSP of the Council of 12 July 2004, OJ 2004 L 245/17; Joint Action 2001/544/CFSP of the Council of 20 July 2001, OJ 2001 L 200/1; and Joint Action 2001/555/CFSP of the Council of 20 July 2001, OJ 2001 L 200/5.

Security Studies and the European Union Satellite Centre have not entered into international agreements.[81]

6.4 The role of the Member States in the agreements

6.4.1 National constitutional approval

One of the main issues in the debate on the question of whether the Council concludes the agreements on behalf of the EU or on behalf of the Member States was related to Article 24, paragraph 5:

> No agreement shall be binding on a Member State whose representative in the Council states that it has to comply with the requirements of its own constitutional procedure; the other members of the Council may agree that the agreement shall nevertheless apply provisionally.

This provision was often read in conjunction with Declaration No. 4 adopted at the Amsterdam IGC:

> The Provisions of Article J.14 and K.10 [now Articles 24 and 38] of the Treaty on European Union and any agreements resulting from them shall not imply any transfer of competence from the Member States to the European Union.

However, neither in theory, nor in practice these provisions limited the treaty-making capacity of the EU. Article 24 provides that the Council concludes international agreements after its members (the Member States) have unanimously agreed that it can do so.[82] On the basis of paragraph 5, Member States may invoke their national constitutional requirements to prevent becoming bound by the agreement, but this does not affect the conclusion

---

[81] See on the European Defence Agency M. Trybus, 'The New European Defence Agency: A Contribution to a Common European Security and Defence Policy and a Challenge to the Community *Acquis*?', 43 CMLRev. (2006), pp. 667–703.

[82] The explicit reference to the unanimity rule (as a *lex specialis*) seems to exclude the applicability of the general regime of constructive abstention in cases where unanimity is required as foreseen in Article 23 TEU. Furthermore, as indicated by G. Hafner, 'The Amsterdam Treaty and the Treaty-Making Power of the European Union: Some Critical Comments', in G. Hafner *et al.*, *Liber Amicorum Professor Seidl-Hohenveldern – In Honour of his 80th Birthday* (The Hague: Kluwer Law International, 1998), p. 279. The application of the constructive abstention to Article 24 would make little sense, since Article 24 already provides the possibility of achieving precisely the same effect insofar as Member States, by referring to their constitutional requirements, are entitled to exclude, in relation to themselves, the legal effect of agreements concluded by the Council.

of the agreement by the EU. While on some occasions the issue was raised,[83] it has obviously not precluded the conclusion of these agreements.

One may argue that when agreements are not binding on Member States that have made constitutional reservations, *a contrario*, agreements *are* binding on those Member States that have not made this reservation. While this may hold true for the relation between the Member State and the EU, it cannot be maintained vis-à-vis the third State or other international organisation. After all, no treaty relationship has been established between the Member States and this party, and unless the agreement explicitly involves rights and/or obligations for Member States in relation to the other party there is no direct link between them. In case Member State participation is necessary for the EU to fulfil its treaty obligations, the other party seems to have to address the EU, which, in turn, will have to address its Member States.

The above-mentioned Declaration No. 4 on the negation of a transfer of competences does not seem to conflict with this distinct treaty-making capacity of the EU. Since the right to conclude treaties is an original power of the EU itself, the treaty-making power of the Member States remains unfettered and, indeed, is not transferred to the EU. Therefore, the Declaration can only mean that this right of the EU must not be understood as creating new substantive competences for it.[84] Through the Council Decision, Member States have been provided with an opportunity to set limits to the use by the EU of its treaty-making capacity, both from a procedural and a substantive perspective.

The fact that the EU becomes a party to the agreement (and not its Member States), is underlined by the way the agreements come into force. Many agreements use the following provision on the entry into force:[85]

> This agreement shall enter into force on the first day of the first month after the Parties have notified each other of the completion of the internal procedures necessary for this purpose.

---

[83] See Marquardt, 'The conclusion of International Agreements', p. 182, who refers to Germany and France. More extensively: R.A. Wessel and G. Fernandez Arribas, 'EU agreements with third countries: Constitutional reservations by Member States', in S. Blockmans (ed.), *The European Union and International Crisis Management: Legal and Policy Aspects* (The Hague: T.M.C. Asser Press, 2008).

[84] As submitted by Hafner, 'The Amsterdam Treaty' p. 272.

[85] See, for instance, the 2005 Agreement between Romania and the European Union on security procedures for the exchange of classified information, OJ 2005 L 118/47.

However, so far, the 'internal procedures' on the side of the EU seem to relate to the necessary decision of the Council and not to any national constitutional procedure in the Member States. In other cases, the entry into force is even more simple:[86]

> This Agreement shall enter into force on the first day of the month after the Parties have signed it.

It goes beyond the scope of this contribution to investigate the parliamentary procedures related to these agreements in all 27 Member States, but based on some discussions it seems that Member States generally do not consider the EU agreements relevant to be put through their regular parliamentary procedure.[87] As ratification by the Governments of the Member States is not required for agreements concluded by the EU, their constitutional requirements simply do not apply. At least in the Netherlands the agreements are not considered to be in need of parliamentary approval as the Kingdom of The Netherlands is not a party. For the same reason the agreements are not published in the national official journal of treaties concluded by the Kingdom, the *Traktatenblad*. An exception was made for the two agreements concluded with the United States in the area of PJCCM, because these could be considered to complement or even amend existing bilateral treaties with the US. However, the position of the Netherlands was not exceptional: all Member States – with the exception of Austria, Estonia, France and Greece – made a constitutional reservation. The same situation occurred in relation to the conclusion of the agreements with Iceland and Norway, while eight Member States invoked Article 24(5) in relation to the agreement with Switzerland.[88] This clearly differentiates the third pillar agreements from the ones concluded under CFSP. In these cases, again, the question becomes relevant why the EU and its Member States

---

[86] See for instance the 2006 Agreement between the International Criminal Court and the European Union on cooperation and assistance, OJ 2006 L 115/ 49.

[87] This is confirmed by G. de Kerchove and S. Marquardt, 'Les accords internationaux conclus par l'Union Européenne', *Annuaire Français de Droit International* (2004), p. 813: ' . . . dans la pratique suivie jusqu'à présent aucun Åtat membre n'a invoqué le respect de ses règles constitutionnelles lors de la conclusion par le Conseil d'accords dans le domaine de la PESC'. More extensively: Wessel and Fernandez Arribas, 'EU Agreements with third countries'.

[88] *Ibid.*, pp. 813 and 823. In these cases the Council decided to have a procedure in two stages, allowing for Member States to follow domestic parliamentary procedures; see Conclusions of the Council of 6 June 2003, Doc. 10409/03 of 18 June 2003; Cf. also Monar, 'The EU as an International Actor' and Georgopoulos, 'What kind of', p. 193.

have not opted for the same construction that has proven its value under
Community law: the 'mixed agreement'.

6.4.2 The role of the Member States in agreements concluded by international organisations

The question of the distinction between an international organisation and its
Member States in international law is a classic in the law of international
organisations. The general opinion is that international organisations are
separate legal entities that have their own legal responsibilities under
international law. Usually, the principles of the law of state responsibility
apply by analogy to international organisations.[89] At the same time, States
may not use the creation of international organisations to escape their own
responsibilities. Their involvement may flow from: (i) the fact that they may
have established an international organisation without binding it to their
own international obligations; (ii) their own conduct in the framework of
the organisation; or (iii) issues related to complicity or control of an
international organisation by a State.[90] These propositions were recently
summarised by Brölmann as follows:

> 1. International organisations are separate legal creatures, and thus not
> entirely open in the way of classic international law relations; 2. they are not
> entirely closed in the way of states either; 3. they are thus (perceived as)
> transparent, layered legal entities; 4. consensual, equality branches of the
> law such as the law of treaties have difficulty accommodating this quality;
> 5. endeavours in this regard are made nonetheless, although not rendered
> explicit; 6. the legal system – in this case the law of treaties – ultimately
> prevails, as the legal order of necessity sets the term for participation of legal
> subjects.[91]

The latter proposition points to the fact that the international law of
treaties works with closed entities. Indeed, under treaty law the international parties should not be bothered with the complexity of the
EU's institutional set-up. International organisations, just like States, are

---

[89] See, for instance, M. Hirsch, *The Responsibility of International Organisations Toward Third Parties: Some Basic Principles* (Dordrecht: Kluwer, 1995); Zwanenburg, *Accountability* n. 47, p. 70 and the references made there.

[90] For a recent survey of the different arguments, see Naert, *International Law Aspects*, Chapter 3.

[91] C. Brölmann, *The Institutional Veil in Public International Law: International Organisations and the Law of Treaties* (Oxford: Hart Publishing, 2007).

seen as unitary actors and may in general not invoke internal issues to escape treaty obligations. One problem, however, is that international organisations are not a party to the 1969 Vienna Convention on the Law of Treaties and that the 1986 Convention between States and International Organizations or Between International Organizations has not yet entered into force (apart from the fact the EU has not signed this agreement). For treaty law to be applicable, it has, thus, to be established that the relevant provisions are part of customary law.[92] Nevertheless, the 1986 Convention is generally used as a framework for doctrine to settle issues related to the conclusion of treaties by international organisations.

The distinct role of the Member States in the agreements concluded by their organisation was one of the most difficult issues to settle in the 1986 Convention. In the end, a rather general provision was devoted to this issue only: Article 74(3):

> The provisions of the present Convention shall not prejudice any question that may arise in regard to the establishment of obligations and rights for States members of an international organization under a treaty to which that organization is a party.

This provision seems to pay respect to the internal legal order of the organisation, in particular in conjunction with Article 5:

> The present Convention applies to any treaty between one or more States and one or more international organizations which is the constituent instrument of an international organization and to any treaty adopted within an international organization, without prejudice to any relevant rules of the organization.

However, it would go too far to conclude on a priority of the internal rules of the organisation (for instance in relation to the extent its Member States are bound by an agreement) on the basis of these provisions. In fact, attempts to introduce in the Convention separate rights and obligations

---

[92] Customary international law is generally believed to apply to international organisations as well, see H.G. Schermers and N.M. Blokker, *International Institutional Law* (Leiden: Martinus Nijhoff Publishers, 2005), p. 988. One of the best arguments in this regard is also reproduced by Naert, *International Law Aspects*, 2007, Chapter 3: 'It is submitted that the better basis for holding that international organisations are bound by (relevant) customary international law (subject to necessary modifications) is the argument that this simply derives from their international legal personality.' Indeed, as one could argue, participation in the international legal order implies being subject to its rules.

for Member States on the basis of treaties concluded by the organisation (either through the constituent instrument of the organisation or a subsequent unanimous decision) have failed.[93] And, indeed, other provisions in the 1986 Convention underline the 'dualist' approach. Thus, both Articles 27 (Internal law of States, rules of international organisations and observance of treaties) and 46 (Provisions of internal law of a State and rules of an international organisation regarding competence to conclude treaties) do not allow for a party to rely on its internal law as a ground for non-compliance or for challenging the validity of its consent to be bound.[94] This would prevent the EU to, for instance, invoke implementation problems or constitutional reservations at the level of the Member States as a ground for non-compliance vis-à-vis the other party.

This does not mean that Member States may simply ignore agreements concluded by their international organisation. Apart from the three possible grounds mentioned above, it is generally held that at least the internal rules of the organisation may extend some duties of the organisation to the Member States,[95] which may lead to 'a good faith duty not to hinder the organisation to give effect to agreements it has lawfully entered into'.[96] In the case of the EU, the loyalty obligation in Article 11, paragraph 2 could be used to build on this idea (see Section 6.4.3).

In relation to the responsibility of Member States for any actions of their international organisation, there is considerable disagreement between authors, in particular when no express clause in relation to their responsibility for conduct of the organisation has been included in the constituent treaty.[97] Both international practice and case law are limited, and, when available, not always consistent. Usually a balance is sought

---

[93] See on the history of this provision and the proposed far-reaching draft articles which underlined a distinct position of the Member States: Brölmann, *The Institutional Veil*, pp. 273–90.

[94] *Ibid.*, pp. 292–5.

[95] See, for instance, Schermers and Blokker, *International Institutional Law*, p. 1143.

[96] Naert, *International Law Aspects*, Chapter 3.

[97] The topic is currently on the agenda of the International Law Commission. See the interesting reports by Special Rapporteur G. Gaja on the Responsibility of International Organisations, available at http://www.un.org/law/ilc/. The accountability of international organisations was also addressed by the International Law Association, see its Final Report (2004) on this issue, reproduced in *International Organizations Law Review*, 2004; also K. Wellens, *Remedies against International Organisations* (Cambridge: Cambridge University Press, 2002) and I.F. Dekker, 'Making Sense of Accountability in International Institutional Law', *Netherlands Yearbook of International Law* (2005), pp. 83–118.

between the separate international legal personality of an organisation (and its connected individual responsibility) and the need to protect the other party in situations where no remedies exist for the harm inflicted upon it. This was reflected in the 1995 Report of the *Institut de Droit International* (IDI) on this issue. Rapporteur Higgins took the view that:

> by reference to the accepted sources of international law, there is no norm which stipulates that Member States bear a legal liability to third parties for the non-fulfilment by international organisations of their obligations to third parties.[98]

A minority of the members of the IDI, however, held that, in principle, there is a Member State liability. It seems fair to conclude, however, that the majority of writers agrees on the presumption that Member States are not liable for any conduct of the organisation, but that this resumption may be rebutted.[99]

With regard to the EU these questions may, in particular, return in relation to the ESDP missions. The practice in other organisations underlines the difficulty to come up with clear-cut answers. In a recent study on the accountability under international law of UN and NATO peace support operations, Zwanenburg concluded that state practice in connection with UN peace support operations demonstrates that the conduct of national contingents in these operations is attributed to the UN or NATO because the contingents have been placed at the disposal of the organisation.[100] Thus, there is a presumption that a contingent is placed at the disposal of the organisation and this is rebutted only if it is established that the troops in question were acting in fact on behalf of a troop contributing State. For some ESDP missions (i.e. where one Member State acts as a leading nation) this could imply a responsibility for the troop contributing State.[101] In any case, practice seems to support the view that Member State responsibility is secondary to the responsibility of the organisation. In the case of the UN, claims in relation to the conduct of a UN peace support operation have so far been addressed to

---

[98] Droit IDI 66-I (1995) 415, para. 113.
[99] It goes beyond the scope of this contribution to go into detail, see for a rather extensive analysis Zwanenburg, *Accountability of Peace Support*, Chapter 2.
[100] *Ibid.*, pp. 130–4.
[101] See on the varying character of the ESDP missions Naert, *International Law Aspects*.

the organisation.[102] In the *Use of Force* cases of the Federal Republic of Yugoslavia against ten NATO members before the International Court of Justice, the arguments used related to the role of the troop contributing States in the command and control of the operation, as well as to the idea that the actions of the NATO command structure are imputable jointly and severally to individual Member States (the so-called 'piercing the institutional veil' argument).[103]

6.4.3 Binding nature of the agreements under Union law

In Section 6.2 it was argued that there are no reasons not to apply the *Haegeman*-doctrine to the agreements concluded by the EU and to regard them as forming 'an integral part of Union law'. Indeed, the reference in Article 24(6) TEU that the agreements bind the institutions supports this view.[104] The remaining question, however, is whether this indeed means that Member States are automatically bound by the agreements as a matter of EU law, or that perhaps even a 'direct effect' of the agreements can be construed. Afterall, this would place the Member States in a different position towards the agreements than in other international organisations. In the European Community, Member States do have special obligations on the basis of agreements concluded by the Community.[105] After all, Article 300(7) EC clearly provides that agreements shall be binding on the Institutions *and* the Member States and, in *Kupferberg*, the Court held:

> In ensuring respect for commitments arising from an agreement concluded by the Community Institutions the Member States fulfil an obligation not only in relation to the non-member country concerned but also and above all in relation to the Community which has assumed responsibility for the due performance of the agreement.[106]

Irrespective of the fact that the past 15 years have blurred the distinction between Community law and the law of the other Union Pillars (see also Section 6.4.4), judgments such as in *Haegeman* and *Kupferberg* explicitly

---

[102] Zwanenburg, *Accountability of Peace Support*, p. 339.

[103] *Ibid.*, pp. 340–1.   [104] See also Thym, 'Die völkerrechtlichen', p. 38.

[105] See in general on this issue for instance V. Lowe, 'Can the European Community Bind the Member States on Questions of Customary International Law?', in Koskenniemi, *International Law*, pp. 149–68.

[106] Case 104/81 *Kupferberg* [1982] ECR 3641, para. 13.

related to the 'autonomous legal order' of the Community and it cannot easily be argued that all differences have disappeared. EU law can still be seen in distinction to Community law, which implies that the legal nature of agreements that form part of EU law should be judged first and foremost on the basis of the EU legal order. Hence, Article 300(7) EC does not apply and Article 24(6) TEU provides that EU agreements are binding on the Institutions, without a reference to the Member States. While there are good reasons to assume that decisions in the non-Community parts of the EU are also binding on the Member States and that they cannot be ignored in their domestic legal orders,[107] it is not at all obvious that the principles of 'direct effect' and 'supremacy' form part of EU law.[108] This implies that the domestic effect (applicability) of the agreements depends on national (constitutional) arrangements. As we have seen, the practice of the PJCCM agreements indeed reveals that Article 24(5) TEU is used in a way to allow national parliaments to allow their governments to approve of the treaty before the EU adopts the final ratification decision.

On the other hand, it is also questionable whether one can still maintain the view that under CFSP and PJCCM no sovereign rights were trans-ferred to the Union and that therefore Member States have retained complete freedom to enter into international agreements on issues already covered by EU agreements.[109] Elsewhere, we have argued that the CFSP normative order does indeed restrain the external competences of the Member States and that the primary CFSP norms entail a consultation obligation which cannot be ignored by Member States without a complete denial of the *rationale* behind CFSP. In addition, Member States' specific obligations under the CFSP title should be interpreted in the light of the general loyalty obligation to support the Union's CFSP (Art. 11(2) TEU). This obligation becomes more substantive once the Union has acted, and given the proximity between the provisions of Article 11(2) TEU and Article 10 EC respectively, there are reasons to interpret the former in the light of the latter's interpretation. In addition, in a situation of parallel

---

[107] See more extensively R.A. Wessel *The European Union's Foreign and Security Policy: A Legal Institutional Perspective*, Chapter 5.

[108] Cf. Also K. Lenaerts and T. Corhaut, 'Of Birds and Hedges: the Role of Primacy in Invoking Norms of EU Law', 31 ELRev. (2006), pp. 287–315.

[109] *Cf.* Thym, 'Die völkerrechtlichen', p. 904: 'Hiernach besitzen die Mitgliedstaaten die rechtliche Möglichkeit, innerstaatlich und im völkerrechtlichen Verkehr auch Regelungen zu treffen, die im Widerspruch zu ihren unionsrechtlichten Verpflichtungen stehen.'

competences, the nature of the EU competence involved should be considered, and, in particular, its possible pre-emptive effect. Indeed, it seems too early completely to rule out exclusivity in the field of CFSP. After all, the (international) legal status of agreements concluded by the EU could be deprived of any effect if they would allow Member States to conclude agreements which would depart from established EU law.[110]

6.5 Conclusion: mixed responsibilities for the Union and its Member States?

Both legal analysis and recent case law provide a mixed picture of the possible responsibilities of the Member States on the basis of international agreements concluded by the EU. So far, agreements concluded under Article 24 and/or Article 38 TEU are concluded by the EU only; the EU Member States are not contracting parties. This explains why no ratification procedures take place on the basis of domestic constitutional provisions. The possibility of invoking Article 24(5) on domestic constitutional requirements remains open, but should not be equalled with ratification and does not legally stop the EU from concluding the agreement. In practice, national parliamentary involvement seems to have been limited to third pillar matters (police and judicial cooperation in criminal matters), because of the separate role of the Member States in those agreements.

The conclusion not to deviate from the general starting point in international institutional law by arguing that the EU is itself primarily responsible for the implementation of the agreement seems therefore justified. The Member States did indeed allow the EU to become a party to the agreements, but this does not mean they themselves have entered into a legal relationship with the third States or international organisations.

Nevertheless, agreements concluded by the EU also bind the Member States indirectly. Clear examples can be found in the third pillar agreements on the basis of which member States have obligations as well. More in general, the agreements concluded by the EU seem to be restraints on Member State competences to conclude new agreements covering the same issues. Both Article 10 EC and Article 11(2) TEU seem to call for a

---

[110] C. Hillion and R.A. Wessel, 'Restraining External Competences of EU Member States under CFSP', in: M. Cremona and B. de Witte (eds.), *EU Foreign Relations Law – Constitutional Fundamentals* (Oxford: Hart Publishing, 2008).

loyal attitude of the Member States with regard to agreements adopted (or planned) by the EU. Member States do seem to remain free to conclude agreements in the same domain that do not conflict with existing EU agreements, but in case of a conflict between an agreement concluded by the EU and a bilateral agreement between an EU Member State and a third party, there are reasons to give priority to the former.[111] This is in clear contradiction to rules of general treaty law, as reflected in particular by Article 30 of the 1969 Vienna Convention (which is believed to form part of customary law). After all, treaty law has a clear preference for the application of the *lex posterior* principle. However, holding on to this principle would allow EU Member States to conclude agreements with third parties and to circumvent the agreements concluded by the EU, which would violate the loyalty principle as a central element in the cooperation between the EU and its Member States. One could argue, indeed, that this restraint boils down to a 'tacit recognition of the supremacy of obligations arising out of the second and third pillar over obligations arising under other obligations',[112] calling for an obligation for the Member States to try and solve the conflict with the third party.

In general, the question remains whether the EU and a third State are competent at all to commit EU Member States when the latter have not become a party to the agreement. In some cases, Member States have been given special responsibilities in the agreements. However, even in these cases, the presumption seems that the other contracting party has no legal right to directly approach EU Member States with regard to these matters, unless a special procedure to this has been established in the agreement. In any case, the EU does not seem responsible for actions by third States participating in an operation. In the separate agreements with these States, responsibility has been placed in the hands of the contributing State. With a view to the fact that these States participate in an EU operation and that their only legal relation is with the EU, it would be better when the EU would at least be the formal addressee of any claims as the host State should not be bothered with the complex composition of an EU mission.[113] Claims could then be

---

[111] See also Marquardt, 'The Conclusion of International Agreements', p. 191.

[112] J. Klabbers, 'Restraints on the Treaty-Making Powers of Member States Deriving from EU Law', in E. Cannizzaro (ed.), *The European Union as an Actor*, p. 169.

[113] Cf. C. Tomuschat, n. 13, p. 183: 'third States do not need to proceed to lengthy investigations to find out who was competent *de jure*. They may address any possible claims to the entity that has acted *de facto*.'

handled internally, either between the EU and its own Member States or between the EU and a participating third state.

Returning to the renewed 'Kissinger question': it seems that responsibility should first of all be sought at the level of the EU as this is the only contracting party. International treaty law seems to point to the presumption that Member States are not liable for any conduct of the organisation. This presumption may, however, be rebutted and in the case of the EU no provisions or procedures on the non-contractual liability exist and a collective responsibility may be the result. An example could be the inability of the EU to live up to either its obligations arising out of the agreement or to more general (customary) obligations for instance related to the protection of human rights. Some recent case law could be interpreted as supporting this view.[114]

In practice, situations in which the question of international responsibility needed to be answered have not yet come up. Generally, claims – for instance related to the liability of a military mission – are dealt with within a private law system and borne by the responsible national contingent in a mission. This may very well flow from the fact that even Member States themselves have not concluded on their own immunity and accept responsibility for their behaviour in EU operations. While concrete issues are thus settled on a case-by-case basis, Naert recently presented some more general rules of guidance in these matters.[115] In his view, Member States remain responsible for any violation of their own international obligations, including through or by the EU, whenever the opposite would lead to an evasion of their international obligations. This view comes close to the one held by the ECtHR in relation to the protection of human rights and the requirement of equal protection by the international organisation to prevent responsibility on the side of the Member States.[116]

---

[114] See in particular Case T-49/04 *Hassan*, para. 116 and Case T-253/02 *Ayadi*, judgments of 12 July 2006, nyr. The CFI held that: 'the Member States are bound, in accordance with Article 6 EU, to respect the fundamental rights of the persons involved, as guaranteed by the ECHR and as they result from the constitutional traditions common to the Member States, as general principles of Community law'.

[115] Naert, *International Law Aspects*, Chapter 3.

[116] Cf. in particular the *Bosphorus* case, 30 June 2005. Statements like this could be interpreted as pointing to a responsibility on the side of Member States for agreements concluded by the Union, and come close to a remark on the nature of CFSP made by the ECHR in the *Segi* case, in which it held that 'CFSP decisions are . . . intergovernmental in nature. By taking part in

This 'piercing of the institutional veil' may certainly be required from a practical point of view. After all, it remains difficult to sue international organisations even if they have violated agreements to which they are a party. On a more principal note, however, the question remains whether holding the Member States responsible is legitimate, taking into account the fact that in almost all cases the EU agreements have not even been dealt with at the domestic level: national parliamentary involvement has been excluded and governmental involvement has been limited to a vote as a member of one of the organisations institutions. Indeed, the differences with the Community are clear: the Union does not conclude mixed agreements and unlike Article 300(7) EC, Article 24(6) TEU explicitly relates the binding nature of the agreements to the Institutions. The conclusion could therefore be that in cases where the Union is simply not able and/or willing to answer any legitimate demands of a third party, the proper route for the EU would nevertheless be to accept responsibility at the international level and to seek compensation on the basis of internal EU law in relation to its own Member States. After all, to conclude with a politico-legal statement:

> An entity discarding any notion of liability for its conduct could not be taken seriously in international dealings. As strange as it may seem, the capacity to incur international responsibility is an essential element of the recognition of international organisations in general and of the European Union in particular as entities enjoying personality under international law.[117]

---

their preparation and adoption each State engages its responsibility. That responsibility is assumed jointly by the States when they adopt a CFSP decision.' Application No. 6422/02, *Segi and Gestoras Pro-Amnistia and others* v. *15 States of the European Union*, 23 May 2002. See more extensively E. Cannizzaro, 'Panorama – International Responsibility for Conduct of EU Member States: The Bosphorus Case', *Rivista di diritto internazionale* (2005), pp. 762–6; and the annotation by D. Scott, 43 CMLRev. (2006).

[117] Tomuschat, 'The International Responsibility', p. 183.

The Common Commercial Policy enhanced by the Reform Treaty of Lisbon?

PETER-CHRISTIAN MÜLLER-GRAFF

7.1 Introduction

The Common Commercial Policy (CCP) of the European Community (EC) is loaded with great expectations. These expectations envisage a strong role for the Community in shaping the rules of international trade that are essential to the sustainable economic and social prosperity of its Member States in a globalised world.[1] Whether the Constitutional Treaty with its creation of a new Union[2] would foster this path and close the gap between the developing world trade system and the power of the European Community,[3] was the subject of much discussion and critical analysis.[4] In the aftermath of the stalemate of the ratification procedure caused by the referendums in France and in the Netherlands, this topic has transformed first into the question of whether the non-ratification of the Constitutional Treaty would impede the pursuit of a legitimate and effective CCP in a globalised economy and now into the question whether the Reform Treaty

---

[1] See recently H.G. Krenzler and C. Pitschas, 'Die Gemeinsame Handelspolitik im Verfassungsvertrag – ein Schritt in die richtige Richtung', in C. Hermann, H.G. Krenzler and R. Streinz (eds.), *Die Außenwirtschaftspolitik der Europäischen Union nach dem Verfassungsvertrag* (Baden-Baden: Nomos, 2006), p. 11.

[2] P.-C. Müller-Graff, 'Institutional Changes in the Constitutional Treaty – A Reason for its Rejection?', in A. Albi and J. Ziller (eds.), *The European Constitution and National Constitutions* (Alphen aan den Rijn: Kluwer Law International, 2007), p. 215. The external relations of the projected new Union were the subject of several working groups of the European Convention.

[3] See H.G. Krenzler and C. Pischas, *Europarecht* (2001), p. 460.

[4] See n. 1; see also C. Hermann, 'Die Außenhandelsdimension des Binnenmarktes im Verfassungsentwurf – von der Zoll– zur Weltordnungspolitik', *Europarecht* (2004), pp. 192 *et seq.*; J. Monar, 'Die Gemeinsame Handelspolitik der Europäischen Union im EU-Verfassungsvertrag: Fortschritte mit einigen neuen Fragezeichen', *Außenwirtschaft* (2005), p. 99; M. Krajewski, 'External Trade Law and the Constitutional Treaty: Towards a Federal and More Democratic Commercial Policy?', 42 CMLRev. (2005), p. 91; M. Cremona, 'The Draft Constitutional Treaty: External Relations and External Action', 40 CMLRev. (2003), p. 1347.

of Lisbon (TL) enhances the potential of the CCP. In the context of a comparison of the TL with the current primary Community law, three particular aspects are addressed here: the scope and categorisation of competences, the overarching primary law context and the rules governing how competences are exercised.

7.2 Scope and categorisation of competences

Turning first to the CCP competences as envisaged by the TL, the projected novelties concern both the scope and categorisation of competences.

7.2.1 Scope of competences

Concerning the substantive scope of competences in the CCP, two features characterise the TL: the perpetuation of the *acquis* and its further extension.

The perpetuation of the *acquis* is laid down in Article 207(1) TFEU (corresponding to Art. III-315(1) CT). The substantive part of this paragraph is no different from the present Article 133(1) EC[5] and lists five fields as subjects of the CCP, which is based on uniform principles: changes in tariff rates; the conclusion of tariff and trade agreements; the achievement of uniformity in measures of liberalisation; export policy; and measures to protect trade, such as those to be taken in the event of dumping and subsidies.

This list is not only perpetuated by the new Article 207(1) TFEU but it is also enriched by the explicit mention of three new areas in this Article: the conclusion of agreements in relation to trade in services;[6]

---

[5] For the legal situation after the Treaty of Amsterdam, see e.g. M. Cremona, 'EC External Commercial Policy after Amsterdam: Authority and Interpretation within Interconnected Legal Orders', in: J.H.H. Weiler (ed.), *The EU, the WTO and the NAFTA: Towards a Common Law of International Trade?* (Oxford: Oxford University Press, 2000), pp. 5 *et seq.*; M. Cremona, 'Rhetoric and Reticence: EU External Commercial Policy in a Multilateral Context', 38 CMLRev. (2001), p. 359. For the novelties of the Treaty of Nice, see e.g. C. Hermann, 'Common Commercial Policy after Nice: Sisyphus Would Have Done a Better Job', 39 CMLR (2002), p. 7; H.G. Krenzler and C. Pitschas, 'Progress or Stagnation? The Common Commercial Policy after Nice', 6 EFARev. (2001), p. 312. As a coherent treatise, see e.g. P. Eeckhout, *External Relations of the European Union. Legal and Constitutional Foundations* (Oxford: Oxford University Press, 2004).

[6] See Pitschas, 'Der Handel mit Dienstleistungen', in Hermann *et al.* (eds.), *Die Außenwirtschaftspolitik*, p. 99.

the commercial aspects of intellectual property;[7] and foreign direct investments.[8] Such an extension, however, will not necessarily come into being without a hitch. In particular, whether the latter term should be interpreted in its strictest or in its broadest sense became already the subject of dispute in Article III-315(1) CT and will require clarification.[9] But, at least in principle, the main subject matter of the World Trade Organisation (WTO)[10] is matched by the new formulation.[11] The area of transport services will remain mostly unaffected by the Reform Treaty, because it is subject to special rules[12] that do not deviate from the relevant primary law as it stands today.[13]

7.2.2 Categorisation of competences

Concerning the legal character of the Union's competences in terms of the category of competences in CCP, the present principle of exclusivity is explicitly affirmed, but its limits are reduced.

Explicit affirmation of the principle

The doctrinal and judicial categorisation of this competence in the EC Treaty is explicitly affirmed in Article 3(1) TEU revised (corresponding to Art. I-13(1) CT), which ranks this as one of the six exclusive competences of the Union. It designates an outstanding role for the Union: side by side with the customs union, the establishment of the competition rules necessary for the functioning of the Internal Market, monetary policy (for the Member States whose currency is the euro), the conservation of marine biological resources under the common fisheries policy, and the conclusion of certain international agreements which affect the exercise of the Union's internal competences. As a matter of course, therefore, the

---

[7] See T. Müller-Ibold, 'Handelsaspekte geistigen Eigentums sowie Investitionen', in Hermann *et al.* (eds.), *Die Außenwirtschaftspolitik*, p. 117.

[8] See previous note, p. 126.

[9] H.G. Krenzler and C. Pitschas, 'Die Gemeinsame Handelspolitik nach dem Entwurf des Europäischen Verfassungsvertrags – ein Schritt in die richtige Richtung', *Recht der Internationalen Wirtschaft* (2005), pp. 805 *et seq.*

[10] On this aspect, see e.g. contributions of E.-U. Petersmann and M. Hilf, in P.-C. Müller-Graff (ed.), *Die Europäische Gemeinschaft in der Welthandelsorganisation* (Baden-Baden: Nomos, 2000).

[11] See C. Vedder, 'Ziele der Gemeinsamen Handelspolitik und Ziele des auswärtigen Handelns', in Hermann *et al.* (eds.), *Die Außenwirtschaftspolitik*, p. 51 ('Deckungsgleichheit').

[12] Article 205(5) TFEU; corresponding to Article III-315(5) CT.   [13] Article 133(6) EC.

principle of subsidiarity as defined in Article 5(3) TEU revised (corresponding to Art. 10(3) CT) will not apply since, by its very nature, it only applies to those areas that do not fall within the Union's exclusive competence. This holds true for the full range of this competence which is defined by the TL – for the first time – as primary law. It follows that bilateral agreements on the protection of direct investments between one Member State and a third country may well be affected by the new Treaty depending upon the definition of the scope of foreign direct investment concerned.

Reduction of limits

It follows from the substantive extension of the scope of the European competence for the CCP, that the present limits on the Community's exclusive character, as it stands today, would effectively be abandoned. Unlike the present very complex Article 133(5) to (7) EC, the new Article 207 TFEU (corresponding to Art. III-315 CT) contains no language that hints at a non-exclusive competence which would be subject to the principle of subsidiarity and which might entail specific procedures.[14] This particularly affects the negotiation and conclusion of agreements in the fields of trade in services and the commercial aspects of intellectual property. Under the present law, agreements relating to trade in cultural and audiovisual services, educational services, and social and human health services, are classified as falling within the shared competence of Community and Member States (Art. 133(6)(2) EC). However, this present form of shared competence in the EC Treaty is not identical to the definition of shared competence in the new Article 2(2) TFEU (corresponding to Art. I-12(2) CT), which provides that the Union and the Member States may legislate and adopt legally binding acts in that area, but also that Member States shall exercise their competence to the extent that the Union has not exercised, or has decided to cease exercising, its competence.

In comparison, the meaning of shared competence under Article 133 EC is different in that negotiation of such agreements requires the common accord of the Member States and also that such agreements must be concluded jointly by the Community and the Member States. Article 207 TFEU (corresponding to Art. III-315 CT) does not perpetuate this device.

---

[14] However, the projected Protocol on the Application of the Principles of Subsidiarity and Proportionality applies also in respect to the principle of proportionality.

Negotiations and conclusion of agreements are brought within the full scope of the Union's competence in commercial policy.[15] Consequently, all basic WTO-related subject matters would not only fall within the competence of the Union but within its exclusive power.

Again, an important exception arises in the area of international agreements in transport services. Article 207(5) TFEU (corresponding to Art. III-315(5) CT) explicitly stipulates that agreements in this area shall be subject to the specific transport provisions of Article 90 *et seq.* TFEU (corresponding to Art. III-236 *et seq.* CT) and Article 218 TFEU (corresponding to Art. III-325 CT). These provisions fall into shared competence in the sense of Article 4(2)(g) TFEU (corresponding to Art. I-14(2)(g) CT). The general provision on the negotiation and conclusion of international agreements (Art. 218 TFEU; corresponding to Art. III-325 CT) applies to these agreements. Here, the requirement of mixed agreements survives in all cases where the transport policy fulfils more than a simple subordinate or ancillary function. This confirmation of the status quo has been criticised in legal writing but it cannot be considered as unreasonable if the structure of external competence mirrors the internal competence structure of the Union.[16] Hence, on the basis of the internal order of competences within the Union, the mixed procedure would continue to be required where agreements involve competences of the Member States that are considered to be an equally important part thereof.

7.3 Overarching primary law context

Moving on to the overarching primary law context of the European competence in commercial policy, these new features again become evident by comparison with the present situation. Already the Constitutional Treaty aimed at achieving consistency of the CCP with the overarching context of policies of the Union. This objective of consistency is perpetuated by the TL. It is characterised by a fan of various means employed to achieve this consistency. This fan includes more systematisation for consistency, more substantive consistency and more consistency at institutional level.

---

[15] Article III-315(3) to (5) CT.
[16] See for this pattern in the scheme of competences in external relations P.-C. Müller-Graff, 'Die primärrechtlichen Grundlagen der auswärtigen Beziehungen der Europäischen Union', in P.-C. Müller-Graff (ed.), *Die Rolle der erweiterten Europäischen Union in der Welt* (Baden-Baden: Nomos, 2006), p. 24.

7.3.1 More systematisation to achieve consistency

The overall structure of the new text is systematic in its approach. The current split between Community and Union law in the field of external relations and, in particular, between the supranational CCP (Art. 131 *et seq.* EC) and the intergovernmental Common Foreign and Security Policy (CFSP) (Art. 11 *et seq.* EU), would systematically have been brought under one and the same title by the Constitutional Treaty, namely 'The Union's External Action' (Art. III-292 *et seq.* CT). However, this move would not have overcome the differences in the legal nature of the available instruments, nor the differences in legal categories of competence between CCP (exclusive competence) on the one hand, and CFSP (shared or specific) on the other.[17] In the TL the current systematic split is perpetuated, however overarched by the corresponding titles 'General Provisions on the Union's External Action and Specific Provisions on the Common Foreign and Security Policy' (Art. 21 *et seq.* TEU revised) and External 'Action by the Union' (Art. 205 *et seq.* TFEU).

The rationale behind the provisions governing the Union's External Action in the Constitutional Treaty was to move from general rules to more specific ones, thereby applying the classical method of continental codification. This was illustrated by the fact that the provisions having general application (Art. III-292 *et seq.* CT) related to seven specific topics: CFSP; CCP; cooperation with third countries and humanitarian aid; restrictive measures; international agreements; international organisations; and the solidarity clause. As a matter of course, this was, in the first place, only a formal structure.

7.3.2 The obligation of substantive consistency

Besides the mentioned systematic device for more consistency, the Constitutional Treaty also obliged the Union to pursue more substantive

---

[17] The proper qualification of the Union's competence in matters of common foreign and security policy under the Constitutional Treaty has caused some irritation. While the specific position in Article I-16 CT might have supported the opinion that common foreign and security policy constitutes a specific type of competence which cannot be aligned with the pattern of 'exclusive, shared or supportive et al.' categories (Arts. I-13, I-14, I-17 CT), the wording of Article I-13(1) CT ('The Union shall share competence with the Member States, where the Constitution confers on it a competence which does not relate to the areas referred to in Articles I-13 and I-17') allowed an understanding of Article I-16 CT as a shared competence.

consistency. Article III-292(3) CT provided that the Union should ensure consistency between the different areas of its external action and other policies. Article 21(3) TEU revised exactly follows this objective. While 'consistency' is an abstract word, its meaning in this context conveys the understanding that external relations measures should not conflict with each other.[18] Moreover, a binding set of overarching principles and objectives is listed in the very first article of the provisions of general application (Art. 21 TEU revised; corresponding to Art. III-292 CT). They refer to the general objectives of external relations as enshrined in Article 3 (5) TEU revised; corresponding to I-3(4) CT) and include upholding and promoting the values and interests of the Union and, by so doing, contribute to peace, security, the sustainable development of the Earth, solidarity and mutual respect among peoples, protection of human rights and strict observance and development of international law. The basic notion of the observance of international law as enshrined in the Westphalian Peace Treaty in 1648,[19] is intended to generate mutual reliability and trust. The Union shall respect these principles in developing and implementing the different areas of the Union's external action covered by the Titles on external action in the TEU and the TFEU and the external aspects of its other policies (Art. 21(3)(1) TEU revised; corresponding to Art. III-292(3)(1) CT). The objective of substantive consistency is explicitly affirmed in the chapter on the CCP itself by the obligation of the Union that this policy shall be conducted in the context of the principles and objectives of the Union's external action (Art. 207(1) and 205 TFEU; corresponding to Art. III-315(1) CT).

Scholarly debate on these novelties in the Constitutional Treaty has thrown up concerns that the inclusion of the CCP into the overall context of external relations potentially deforms and weakens the CCP.[20] It is argued that in a situation of tension between the CCP and CFSP, Member States will play the decisive role, through the European Council, in

---

[18] See P.-C. Müller-Graff, 'Europäische Politische Zusammenarbeit und Gemeinsame Außen- und Sicherheitspolitik: Kohärenzgebot aus rechtlicher Sicht', *Integration* (1993), p. 147.

[19] See B. M. Kremer, *Der Westfälische Friede in der Deutung der Aufklärung* (Tübingen: Mohr Siebeck, 1989).

[20] See e.g. J. Monar, 'Die Gemeinsame Handelspolitik der Europäischen Union im EU-Verfassungsvertrag', pp. 99, 106 *et seq.*; J. Monar, 'Die Gemeinsame Handelspolitik und das Primat der Gemeinsamen Außen- und Sicherheitspolitik im Verfassungsvertrag', in Hermann *et al.* (eds.), *Die Außenwirtschaftspolitik*, p. 87; Vedder, *Ziele der Gemeinsamen Handelspolitik and Ziele des auswärtigen Handelns*, p. 53.

defining the yardsticks of consistency as laid down in Article 22 TEU revised; corresponding to Art. III-293(1) CT).[21] It is true that the influence of the Commission is limited but it must not be forgotten that the Commission and the High Representative of the Union for Foreign Affairs and Security Policy may submit joint proposals to the Council.[22] However, it has to be kept in mind that the obligation to 'embed' the commercial policy within the general foreign policy is not something entirely new. The Maastricht Treaty on European Union already introduced the consistency obligation with the words (now Art. 3 TEU) that 'the Union shall in particular ensure the consistency of its external activities as a whole in the context of its external relations, security, economic and development policies'.[23]

Apart from this, the TL adds a new element to the consistency obligation, namely a new legal character. The consistency obligations of the present Articles 3 and 1(3) TEU do not have the quality of Community law but that of classical international law. In contrast, the new consistency obligation for the CCP implied in Article 207(1) TFEU by reference to Article 21(3) TEU revised shares the present Community law nature of this policy. Consequently this consistency obligation falls under the power of judicial review by the European Court of Justice (ECJ).[24]

7.3.3 Institutional means for consistency

The objective of achieving overall consistency is completed by a new institutional device. It is true that, as outlined above, the present single institutional framework already explicitly provides for the consistency and continuity of the activities carried out in order to attain given objectives.[25] It is also primary law that the Council and the Commission are responsible for ensuring the consistency of the external activities of the Union.[26]

Nevertheless, a new institutional element is added by the TL to the existing system of safeguarding substantive consistency as a result of

---

[21] See Krenzler and Pitschas, *Die Gemeinsame Handelspolitik*, p. 803.

[22] See Article 22(2) TEU revised; corresponding to Article III-293(2) CT.

[23] For this obligation of consistency of the external relations see n. 19; see also Krenzler and Pitschas, *Die Gemeinsame Handelspolitik*, p. 803.

[24] The present Article 46 TEU does not contain Article 3 TEU on its list.

[25] See Article 3(1) TEU.   [26] See Article 3(2) TEU.

creating the office of the High Representative of the Union for Foreign Affairs and Security Policy. The TL explicitly provides that the Council and the Commission shall be assisted by this new office in ensuring consistency between the different areas of its external action and between these and its other policies.[27] Certainly, while 'assistance' is a vague word, the general task of the new office is much stricter. The High Representative 'shall' ensure this consistency (Art. 18(4) TEU revised; corresponding to I-28 CT). Moreover, he 'shall' be responsible within the Commission for responsiblities incumbent on it in external relations and for coordinating other aspects of the Union's external action. Hence, the coordination task confers upon the High Representative a potentially strong position. This is underlined by his power to qualify an international agreement as exclusively or principally relating to the CFSP (Art. 218(3); corresponding to III-325 CT). This in turn determines who is responsible for the purposes of submitting recommendations for negotiations to the Council: the Commission or the High Representative.[28] It is obvious that these provisions leave ample leeway for political discretion and that all this can hardly be controlled neither by law nor consequently by the ECJ for that matter except perhaps in obvious cases of circumvention. But they could also put the High Representative in a schizophrenic institutional dilemma. It is almost inevitable that he would be challenged as to his talent to combine and marry together the views of the Commission and the Member States. It is far from clear what effects this device would have on the CCP, but it offers perhaps a potential for a more streamlined Union external policy.

As a consequence, concerns have also been expressed about this institutional connection between commercial policy and general foreign policy.[29] The basic argument is that the double function of the High Representative in the Commission (as Vice-President) and in the Council (as Chairman of the Council for Foreign Affairs) might infringe the autonomy and supranationality of the Union's commercial policy. Such an eventuality cannot be dismissed outright. However, the obvious counter-question is whether an autonomous commercial policy could fit

---

[27] See Article 21(3)(2) TEU revised; corresponding to Article III-292(3)(2) CT.

[28] Despite of this power, Article 40 TEU revised (corresponding to Art. III-308 CT) provides a barrier to changes of internal procedures.

[29] For example J. Monar, *Die Gemeinsame Handelspolitik.*

with the idea that the Union speaks with one voice in international relations.[30] Merging the Community and the Union into a consistent, overarching entity is not a simple technocratic exercise: it holds implications for trade policy in the wider world context and its emancipation from pure economic assessments. In view of the political challenges of trade globalisation, this seems to be a relatively modern approach when compared to a simple concept of free trade in the sense of a heralding motto like 'All economics is global'. In this context, it is worth recalling here a small booklet of quotations of the former speaker of the US House of Representatives, Tip O'Neill, bearing the title 'All politics is local'.[31] In short, while the emphasis on consistency might weaken the potential of an allegedly pure commercial external action, it could also strengthen a more comprehensive political approach by the Union to its external relations. The recent negotiations with Iran on a trade agreement clearly illustrate this point: their outcome heavily depends on the parallel negotiations on an agreement concerning Iran's nuclear activities.

7.4 Rules governing the exercise of competences

Turning to the last issue, the rules on how competences are exercised in the area of the CCP, the TL introduces certain developments compared to those under the current primary law. These concern: substantive limits, the relationship between the institutions, and the rules of decision-making within the Council.

7.4.1 Substantive limits

As a matter of course, the exercise of competence in the CCP shall not affect the delimitation of competences between the Union and the Member States and shall not lead to harmonisation of legislation by or to regulatory provisions of the Member States insofar as the TL excludes

---

[30] For this 'one voice'-concept, see Articles 3(5); 21 TEU revised (corresponding to Art. I-3(4); III-292 CT); M. Jopp, 'Ideen und Realitäten im Verfassungsprozeß am Beispiel der Reformansätze für GASP und EVSP', in, Müller-Graff (ed.), Die Rolle der erweiberten Europoischen Union in der Welt (Baden-Baden: Nomos, 2006), pp. 46 et seq.

[31] T. O'Neill and G. Hymel, All Politics is Local and Other Rules of the Game (New York: Times Books, 1994).

such harmonisation (Art. 207(6) TFEU; corresponding to III-315(6) CT).[32] In other words, the TL will not change the present situation.[33]

7.4.2 The relationship between institutions

The relationship between the institutions in the area of CCP will change under the Reform Treaty in two respects: it will shift more power to the European Parliament (1) and will improve inter-institutional cooperation (2).

More 'parliamentarism'

The shift towards more 'parliamentarism' is the consequence of the projected increase of competences of the European Parliament. This shift is the result of three devices.

The first is the link of the European Parliament to international negotiations. The Commission is obliged to report regularly to the European Parliament on the progress of negotiations (Art. 207(3)(3) TFEU; corresponding to III-315(3)(3) CT), not just to the special committee set up by the Council.

The second device is the procedure of legal implementation. Article 207(2) TFEU simply states that regulations[34] shall establish the measures defining the framework for implementing the common commercial policy. This provision will trigger two mechanisms in the system of the Reform Treaty increasing the role of the European Parliament. First, the *procedure of adoption of regulations* will imply the joint adoption by the European Parliament and the Council under the so-called 'ordinary legislative procedure'[35] (which resembles the present co-decision procedure under which the European Parliament has the power to veto a proposal).[36] The second mechanism derives from the fact that the regulations for implementing an international agreement would affect *the conclusion of these agreements*. It is true that the new Treaty confers upon the Council, acting upon a proposal from the negotiator, the competence

---

[32] The exclusion of harmonisation resembles one element in the definition of the category of competence of the Union to carry out actions to support, coordinate or supplement the actions of the Member States in Article 2(5)(2) TFEU (corresponding to Art. I-12(5)(2) CT).
[33] See Article 133(6) EC.   [34] Article 288(2) TFEU.
[35] Article 294 TFEU (corresponding to Art. III-396 CT).   [36] See Article 251 EC.

to adopt a decision concluding the agreement.[37] However, in several cases listed in Article 218 TFEU; corresponding to Art. III-325 CT), the Council is obliged to obtain the consent of the European Parliament, including for agreements in fields subject to the ordinary legislative procedure.[38]

But even in cases where no implementation would be required by way of legislative measures to be taken within the ordinary legislative procedure, the consent of the European Parliament would have to be obtained by the Council before a decision concluding the agreement could be adopted – except where these relate exclusively to the CFSP[39] – particularly in the context of agreements having important budgetary implications for the Union and for 'agreements covering fields to which either the ordinary legislative procedure applies, or the special legislative procedure where consent by the European Parliament is required' (Art. 218(6) TFEU; corresponding to Art. III-325(6) CT). Such strengthened involvement of the European Parliament will anchor its role as sentinel and guardian of supranational procedures and would counterbalance any concerns[40] that the High Representative might 'intergovernmentalise' the CCP.

The High Representative of the Union for Foreign Affairs and Security Policy

The shift towards more inter-institutional cooperation is spurred on by the creation of the office of the High Representative of the Union for Foreign Affairs and Security Policy, having as its main task of conducting the Union's common foreign and security policy. Nevertheless, in its additional functions and in its double institutional link to the Commission and the Council, this office operates under the general legal and political obligation of the Union to guarantee consistency in external relations.[41] As a result, it shall be responsible, not only for the compatibility of the CCP with the objectives of the general foreign policy but also for the compatibility of the general foreign policy with the objectives of the common commercial policy. This provides an opportunity for an intensive cooperation between Council and Commission in issues concerning the CCP.

---

[37] Articles 207(3) and 218(6)(1) TFEU (corresponding to Art. III-315(3) and III-325(6)(1) CT).
[38] Article 218(6)(2) TFEU (corresponding to Art. III-325(6)(2) CT).
[39] Article 207(3) and 218(6)(2) TFEU (corresponding to III-315(3); III-325(6)(2) CT).
[40] See n. 20.   [41] See Article 21(3) TEU revised; corresponding to Article III-292(3) CT.

7.4.3 Decision-making within the Council

Finally, another significant development will affect the rules of decision-making within the Council. The TL will considerably increase the number of cases where decisions could be taken by qualified majority voting.[42] This mode of decision-making would even be the principle for the negotiation and conclusion of commercial agreements (Art. 207(4) TFEU; corresponding to Art. III-315(4) CT).

However, contrary to what the Convention's working groups and the Convention itself had decided, there are still exceptions to this. Unanimity is still required for certain subjects of CCP.[43] They concern three groups of agreements. First, agreements in the fields of trade in services and the commercial aspects of intellectual property, as well as foreign direct investment, where such agreements include provisions for which unanimity is required for the adoption of internal rules. This exception reasonably safeguards in the same subject matter the parallelism of the rules of decision in its internal and external dimension.[44] The second group of exceptions comprises agreements in the field of trade in cultural and audiovisual services, where these risk prejudicing the Union's cultural and linguistic diversity. This meets an important concern. In view of the substantive purpose of this exception, the last word on the assessment as to whether an agreement falls within this category of risk should be left to the discretion of any of those Member States that are culturally or linguistically concerned.[45] The third group of exceptions is marked by agreements in the field of trade in social, education and health services, where these risk seriously disturbing the national organisation of such services and prejudice the responsibility of Member States to deliver

---

[42] For this increase already in the Constitutional Treaty see K.H. Fischer, *Der Europäische Verfassungsvertrag* (Baden-Baden: Nomos, 2005), pp. 27 and 101.

[43] See on this point also previous note, p. 30.

[44] For the reasonableness of this structural pattern, n. 18.

[45] Against this solution and for a common risk assessment by all Member States, see Krenzler and Pitschas, 'Die Gemeinsame Handelspolitik', p. 808; but this view has the unreasonable consequence that already the opposition of any one single Member State against affirmatively assessing a risk for the cultural and linguistic diversity could override a Member State which is specifically concerned and would then subject the decision on the negotiation and conclusion of an agreement to qualified majority voting. This might jeopardise the diversity of languages within the Union and privilege few of them in the long run.

them. Ultimately, whether an agreement gives rise to such a risk is left to the discretion of the specific Member State concerned.[46]

Critics of these exceptions assume that the negotiating power of the Union is seriously threatened by them.[47] Even if this were true, it has to be remembered that the concept of the Union as envisaged by the TL (and already by the Constitutional Treaty) is not that of a (federal) State;[48] the Union will retain the character that the Community and the Union have under primary law currently.[49] It seems convincing, therefore, that the Union's internal structure is mirrored by the rules of decision-making within the Council regarding the conclusion of agreements involving or touching upon essential features of a Member State. This demonstrates again that the CCP should not be conceived of and conducted in an isolated way by concentrating only on external trade aspects. The implications of commercial policy for other areas must be taken into account and this will contribute to a more comprehensive and coherent Union level approach to the challenges of the wider world context.

7.5 Conclusion

The general conclusion is that the TL follows the path of the Constitutional Treaty in general[50] and in the new potential for evolution of the CCP in particular. In view of the challenges that Member States are facing in the wider world context, the new devices will, no doubt, enhance the possibilities of the CCP in the interest of the European Union and its Member States.

---

[46] This opinion is shared by Krenzler and Pitschas, 'Die Gemeinsame Handelspolitik', p. 809.

[47] See previous note, p. 811.

[48] See e.g. P.-C. Müller-Graff, 'The Process and Impact of EU Constitution-making: 'Voice and Exit'', in D. Curtin, A. E. Kellermann and S. Blockmans (eds.), *The EU Constitution: The Best Way Forward?* (The Hague: Asser Press, 2005), p. 73; P.-C. Müller-Graff, 'Systemrationalität in Kontinuität und Änderung des Europäischen Verfassungsvertrags', *Integration* (2003), p. 302.

[49] For this aspect in the present state of primary law of the EC/EU, see e.g. P.-C. Müller-Graff, 'The German Länder: Involvement in EC/EU Law and Policy Making', in S. Weatherill and U. Bernitz (eds.), *The Role of Regions and Sub-national Actors in Europe* (Oxford: Hart Publishing, 2006), p. 105.

[50] See P.-C. Müller-Graff, *Die Zukunft des Europäischen Verfassungstopos und Primärrechts nach der Deutschen Ratspräsidentschaft*, Lecture, 26 June 2007, Humboldt University, Berlin, available at www.whi.berlin.de.

The extent to which the EC legislature takes account of WTO obligations: jousting lessons from the European Parliament

JACQUES BOURGEOIS AND ORLA LYNSKEY

8.1 Introduction

The debate on the direct effect of World Trade Organisation (WTO) law within the European Union (EU) is one which has been ongoing at judicial, political and academic levels since the establishment of the WTO over a decade ago. This debate has been fuelled by the dissident opinions voiced within the European Court of Justice[1] (ECJ), and by novel opportunities arising for the ECJ to nuance its already complicated jurisprudence, *Van Parys*[2] being a case in point. The extent to which the EC judicature takes account of WTO obligations has, therefore, been subject to much scrutiny.[3] The same cannot, however, be said about the Community legislature. It would appear at the outset that more often than not in the course of the decision-making process, those that are opposed to legislative proposals will invoke WTO incompatibility arguments. However, this issue needs to be analysed in further detail. This contribution therefore sets out to examine precisely this question: to

---

[1] See in this regard opinions of Advocate General Cosmas in C-183/95 *Affish* v. *Rijksdienst Keuring Vee en Vlees* [1997] ECR I-4315; Advocate General Tesauro in C-53/96 *Hermès* v. *FHT* [1998] ECR I-3603; Advocate General Elmer in C-365/95 *T. Port* v. *Hauptzollamt Hamburg-Jonas* [1998] ECR I-1023 and Advocate General Alber in C-93/02 *Biret International* v. *Council* [1997] ECR I-10499.

[2] C-377/02 *Van Parys* v. *Belgische Interventie- en Restitutiebureau* [2005] ECR I-1465.

[3] For a more recent study on this topic, see P.J. Kuijper and M. Bronckers, 'WTO law in the European Court of Justice', 42 CMLRev. (2005), p. 1313; see also J. Bourgeois, 'The European Court of Justice and the WTO: Problems and Challenges', in J. Weiler (ed.), *The EU, the WTO and the NAFTA: Towards a Common Law of International Trade* (Oxford: Oxford University Press, 2000).

what extent does the EC legislature take into account substantive WTO obligations when legislating?[4]

An exhaustive analysis of this question would necessitate examining the legislative history of all Community legislation. Furthermore, several situations would need to be distinguished: those situations where in the course of the decision-making process draft legislation was amended or provisions dropped on account of WTO obligations, those situations where objections based on WTO obligations were consciously put aside during the process, those where no thought was given to possible inconsistency with the WTO Agreements and, finally, those where WTO considerations were taken into consideration. Such information is very difficult to unearth. The authors have in this regard been in contact with several EU officials in order to identify legislation which has proven difficult to adopt in this context.[5] Indeed, we queried how often potential conflicts between a measure contemplated by the EC/EU and WTO obligations have arisen, how often measures adopted by the EC/EU appeared subsequently to be in conflict with WTO obligations, and whether there have been cases in which a measure was proposed and/or adopted by the EC/EU after the issue of conflict with WTO obligations was raised. The only information available on this issue is found in Council minutes, parliamentary questions, debates and opinions of the last decade. Uncovering this information is a laborious task and even then the results are not conclusive. Therefore, to facilitate our analysis of this question our research has been circumscribed and only select EC measures will be looked at in the light of this research question. The measures concerned have not been chosen at random. Rather, we have chosen to analyse the EC measures which have given rise to complaints before the

---

[4] A similar project entitled 'The impact of the WTO on EU Decision-Making' has been undertaken by G. DeBurca and J. Scott. This chapter is found in DeBurca and Scott (eds.), *The EU and the WTO. Legal and Constitutional Issues* (Oxford: Hart Publishing, 2001). Our work differs from that work insofar as a different research framework and different measures have been used to examine what is essentially the same research question.

[5] A representative, involved in the enactment of trade legislation, of the European Parliament, the Council of the European Union and the European Commission respectively have been contacted in this regard. One filled out questionnaire was returned, for which we are grateful. The answers given in this questionnaire were nevertheless couched in very vague and general terms and therefore were of little use in determining key pieces of legislation which have posed EC/WTO related difficulties in recent years. And all this despite the fact that an interested MEP would probably have no difficulty obtaining answers to such a questionnaire.

WTO over the last decade to determine the extent to which the EC legislature considered itself bound by WTO rules when enacting them.

To date, 56 WTO disputes have been initiated against the EC. Of these 56 disputes, certain concerned EC measures whilst others concerned EC Member State measures.[6] Moreover, a number of these disputes related to anti-dumping duties imposed following an alleged violation of the Anti-dumping Agreement, countervailing measures as permitted by the Subsidies and Countervailing Measures (SCM) Agreement or safeguarding measures imposed in accordance with the General Agreement on Tariffs and Trade (GATT). The relevant clauses of these WTO agreements are almost always literally reproduced in the provisions of the EC basic regulations.[7] Hence, these disputes will not be dealt with here as they concern interpretations of EC measures adopted in accordance with EC Regulations which were worded in an equally vague manner as the corresponding WTO Agreements. Thus, it is somewhat inevitable that when the EC is taking measures based on these basic Regulations it will take account of its WTO obligations.[8]

It is, therefore, more interesting to focus on non-trade defence measures. This will lead to a more representative picture of the extent to which the EC legislature takes WTO obligations into account. However, rather than

---

[6] Six of the disputes have concerned EC Member State measures: WT/DS7 (EC – Scallops (Canada) 5 August 1996), WT/DS12 (EC – Scallops (Peru) 5 August 1996), WT/DS14 (EC – Scallops (Chile) 5 August 1996), WT/DS115 (EC – Measures Affecting the Grant of Copyright and Neighbouring Rights 6 January 1998), WT/DS124 (EC – Enforcement of Intellectual Property Rights for Motion Pictures and Television Programs 30 April 1998) and WT/DS135 (EC – Asbestos, 18 September 2000, 12 March 2001). Three disputes are hybrid in nature in that they concern the 'Airbus saga' where national measures which had EC approval were challenged as being contrary to WTO; DS172 (EC – Measures Relating to the Development of a Flight Management System, 21 May 1999), DS316 (EC – Measures Affecting Trade in Large Civil Aircraft, reports not yet circulated) and DS347 (EC and Certain Member States – Measures Affecting Trade in Large Civil Aircraft (Second Complaint), not yet circulated). It was argued in these disputes that, in any event, it was the EC that was responsible for these Member State measures as the EC is the legal entity party to the WTO Agreements.

[7] Moreover, the preambles of the basic Anti-dumping Regulation, the Regulation implementing the SCM Agreement and that which governs the EC's import regime all contain explicit references to the EC's WTO obligations. It is also noteworthy that, as it is explicitly stated in these Regulations that they implement WTO law, according to the *Nakajima* line of jurisprudence, they are directly effective. For an analysis of this line of case law, see n. 3.

[8] This does not exclude the possibility that disputes over the interpretation of WTO Agreements arise between the EC and the other WTO Members. A prime example of this is WT/DS141 (EC – Anti-dumping duties on imports of cotton-type bed-linen from India, 30 October 2000, 1 March 2001).

treating each of these cases individually, we would like to highlight some specific measures which have been subject to repeated challenge over the past decade and to analyse the extent to which the EC legislature has been aware of WTO considerations when enacting them. In this regard, we will focus on the following measures: the Bananas dispute, biotechnology measures, measures taken in the framework of the common organisation of the cereals market, measures on export subsidies for sugar and, finally, measures on the designation/indication of geographical origin.

It will be seen that although the fact that WTO obligations have been taken into account is not always explicitly stated in the measures concerned, WTO awareness is now more present than ever.[9] However, this contribution will illustrate that this awareness does not always necessarily lead to increased compliance with WTO measures.[10]

8.2 The Bananas dispute

8.2.1 Background to the dispute

The background to the EC Bananas saga is by now well documented.[11] The EC introduced Council Regulation 404/93[12] to establish a common market organisation for bananas, the most significant provisions of this Regulation concerned imports from third countries. These provisions protected EC and African, Caribbean and Pacific Group of States (ACP) bananas by introducing different measures for so-called 'dollar bananas', i.e. bananas

---

[9] Whether this awareness stems from the fact that the legislature is now more savvy regarding trade concerns or because of the rise in costs compliance with WTO rules entails for certain industries is difficult to discern.

[10] Indeed, this is perhaps a foreseeable conclusion given that in a report issued by the European Parliament in 1997, the Parliament clearly implies that although the EC, unlike its Member States, does not have an explicit 'sovereignty shield' against the GATT such a 'shield' implicitly exists thanks to the limitations on direct effect imposed by the ECJ's jurisprudence, see 'Report on the relationships between international law, Community law and the constitutional law of the Member States', Committee on Legal Affairs and Citizen's Rights, rapporteur: S. Alber, 24 September 1997. Drawing this inference and the terms in which it is worded to its logical conclusion it is clear that the Parliament sees, or at least saw, a need to defend EC interests from the GATT with the help of a 'shield'. A lowest common denominator approach to compliance with WTO obligations could therefore have been predicted.

[11] For a more detailed background of this dispute, see notably F. Breuss, S. Griller and E. Vranes, *The banana dispute: an economic and legal analysis* (Vienna: Springer, 2003).

[12] Council Regulation 404/93 of 13 February 1993 on the common organisation of the market in bananas, OJ 1993 L 47/1.

produced in Latin America. The Regulation introduced an annual tariff quota for imports from third countries, with imports in excess of this quota being subject to a prohibitively high tariff. However, the Regulation distinguished between third-country imports in general and those coming from ACP countries which were free from customs duties. Further to this restriction, access to the tariff quota for third-country importers was subject to a licensing system. Non-ACP third-country importers could acquire only 66.5 per cent of these licences with the remainder being available for purchase by ACP importers who could then profitably trade them. The system put in place by Regulation 404/93 was challenged under the GATT, the panel favouring the complainants. The adoption of this report was, however, blocked by the EC. Nevertheless, the fact that the Regulation was challenged under the international trading system did bring about changes to the EC regime. The EC negotiated a 'Banana Framework Agreement' with several Latin American States and set the result of these negotiations out in its schedule of tariff concessions. Council Regulation 3290/94[13] and Commission Regulation 478/95[14] integrated this change in the EC's schedule of tariffs into the EC legal order. In addition, the EC received a waiver under the Uruguay Round Agreements with respect to the Lomé Convention. It transpired, however, that the legitimacy of the EC's banana regime was not yet beyond question. Following a challenge before the WTO, the Appellate Body found that the allocation of tariff quotas to exporting countries breached Article XIII GATT. The licence allocation system violated Article III:4 (national treatment) and I:1 (Most Favoured Nation). The licence allocation system also amounted to a violation of General Agreement on Trades in Services (GATS) Article XVII on national treatment.[15] Further EC legislation ensued in an attempt to render the EC's regime WTO compliant. Council Regulation 1637/98,[16] which was implemented by Commission Regulation

---

[13] Council Regulation 3290/94 of 22 December 1994 on the adjustments and transitional arrangements required in the agriculture sector in order to implement the agreements concluded during the Uruguay Round of multilateral trade negotiations, OJ L 349/23.

[14] Commission Regulation 478/95 of 1 March 1995 on additional rules for the application of Council Regulation 404/93 as regards the tariff quota arrangement for imports of bananas into the Community and amending Regulation 1442/93, OJ 1993 L 49/13.

[15] WT/DS16 (EC – Regime for the Importation, Sale and Distribution of Bananas, no panel established nor settlement notified).

[16] Council Regulation 1637/98 of 20 July 1998 amending Regulation 404/93 on the common organisation of the market in bananas, OJ 1992 L 210/28.

2362/98, was enacted. The US, and other Contracting Parties,[17] alleged, however, that these Regulations did not amount to full compliance; the Dispute Settlement Body (DSB) agreed.[18] Consequently, the EC legislature was once again compelled to act[19] and Council Regulation 2587/2001,[20] which amended the original Regulation attacked before the GATT, Regulation 404/93, was the result. Given that the EC bananas regime has been under the watchful eye of other GATT, and then WTO parties, for more than a decade, the extent to which the EC legislature took into account WTO obligations when enacting this final compliance measure is interesting to gauge.

8.2.2 The seeds are sown for Council Regulation 2587/2001

The bananas dispute left the EC legislature in a tricky situation. Following on from the first negative result of the WTO dispute settlement proceeding, the legislature was of the opinion that its enactment of Regulation 1637/98 brought the EC's regime into compliance with the world trading system. In this regard, it is hardly surprising that the European Parliament encouraged the Commission to stand strong in the face of the banana regime's second WTO challenge. In a resolution,[21] issued on the 11 March 1999, the Parliament stated that it 'firmly supports the Commission in its strategy in the banana dispute with the U.S., based on the strict adherence to the rules and procedures of the WTO'.[22] Indeed, the Parliament saw it as the role of the Commission to defend the right of the EC to satisfy its development commitments to ACP countries and

---

[17] DS27, European Communities – Regime for the Importation, Sale and Distribution of Bananas (Complainants: Ecuador, Guatemala, Honduras, Mexico, United States), 5 February 1996.

[18] The threat of US retaliation was not without difficulties. The EC–bananas III case was the first one in which the so-called 'sequencing' issue came to a head. This problem has arisen as neither Article 21.5 DSU, which sets out a compliance determination procedure, nor Article 22 DSU, on the procedure for compensation and the suspension of concessions, stipulates the order in which resort should be had to these procedures. In EC–bananas, the US contested that the compliance procedure should appear first in the sequence. This is a matter which remains unresolved, available at: http://www.wto.org/english/tratop_e/dispu_e/disp_settlement_cbt_e/c6s10p2_e.htm.

[19] This is so in particular as the US had taken retaliatory measures in the interim.

[20] Council Regulation 2587/2001 of 19 December 2001 amending Regulation 404/93 on the common organisation of the market in bananas, OJ 2001 L 345/13.

[21] Available at: http://trade.ec.europa.eu/doclib/docs/2003/december/tradoc_114961.pdf.

[22] Ibid., Section C 8.

certain other regions. In further resolutions that year, the Parliament's emphasis was not so much on compliance with the EC's WTO obligations however, as on the Community's interest in protecting the privileged relations between it and ACP banana importers. In the May 1999 Resolution on the Transatlantic Economic Partnership and EC–US trade disputes, the Parliament stated that 'the EU will have to be careful, when choosing a new type of banana import regime, to ensure that the economies of its remote banana producing regions and the ACP states, which are heavily dependent on exporting to the Community market, are not affected and that the interests of those banana producers are safeguarded as far as possible'.

The Council was not as verbose about its views on the matter and the Agricultural Committee, which convened on 19 December 2000, accepted the proposal set forward by the Commission. Just over one year later, the Council adopted Regulation 216/2001[23] without debate. This lack of debate in the Council should not, however, be taken as an indication that this Regulation, adopted to comply with WTO obligations, was acceptable to all. The Commission had not stood as strongly in the face of the second challenge to the EC's regime as the Parliament had originally anticipated. Thus, the European Parliament protested vigorously against the Commission's proposal. Thus, upon reading it, the Parliament restated its opposition to 'many aspects of the Commission's package of reforms intended to bring the EC's banana import regime into line with world trade rules, in particular the automatic abolition of tariff quotas in 2006'.[24] Earlier that year, the Parliament had proposed to the Commission that a transitional period of ten rather than six years be put in place so as to give the producers time to adapt to the new system.[25] The Commission refused to take this submission into account, leading to the Parliament's final unfavourable opinion. Nor was the Council obliged to take account of the Parliament's opinion as the measure was adopted on the basis of the consultation procedure. The Council, therefore, also overlooked the Parliament's opinion, favouring the introduction of a common customs tariff for the bananas concerned by 1 January 2006.

[23] Council Regulation 216/2001 of 29 January 2001 amending Regulation 404/93 on the common organisation of the market in bananas, OJ 2001 L 31/2.

[24] CNS/1999/0235: 14/12/2000 – EP: position, 1st reading or single reading, available at: http://www.europarl.europa.eu/oeil/FindByProcnum.do?lang=2&procnum=CNS/1999/0235.

[25] CNS/1999/0235: 13/04/2000 – EP: partial vote, 1st reading.

What is noteworthy about this scenario is that the Council championed Community compliance with WTO obligations while the Parliament did all in its power to safeguard what it considered to be traditional Community interests.

8.3 Biotechnology measures

There were several EC measures at issue in the 'Biotech' dispute,[26] the history of which is as follows. In August 2003, a WTO panel was established to consider the consistency of various measures taken by the EC and its Member States with WTO rules.[27] Three types of measures were challenged in this case, the first type of measure challenged, the alleged EC moratorium on approvals of biotech products, being the most interesting for our purposes.[28] The United States alleged in their request for consultations that the EC had applied a de facto moratorium on the approval of biotech products since October 1998 and had thus suspended both its consideration of applications for biotech products under the EC approval system and the granting of such approval. Indeed, it was contended that a number of applications for the placement of biotech products on the market had been blocked in the approval process under EC legislation and that final approval had never been considered. It was thus argued by the United States that imports of its agricultural and food products had been restricted contrary to the WTO Agreements.

The European Commission did little to conceal its disappointment, perhaps even resentment, that the United States resorted to WTO action in such a sensitive field. Indeed, the position of the EC with regard to the challenge was made abundantly clear in its submissions to the panel: 'It is not the function of the WTO Agreement to allow one group of countries to impose its values on another group. Nor is it the purpose of the WTO

---

[26] For a detailed analysis of the issues at stake in this dispute, see L. Boisson de Chazournes and M. Mbengue, 'GMOs and Trade: Issues at Stake in the EC Biotech Dispute', *Review of European Community and International Environment Law* (2004), pp. 289–305.

[27] WT/DS293/1, EC – Measures Affecting the Approval and Marketing of Biotech Products, Request for Consultations by Argentina, 21 May 2003.

[28] The second type of measures challenged were the various product-specific EC measures related to the approval of biotech products. The third were the various national measures enacted or put in place by EC Member States related to the import and/or marketing of biotech products. This final type of measure is not of interest for our purposes.

Agreement to trump the other relevant rules of international law which permit – or even require – a prudent and precautionary approach.'[29]

It is also clear that the EC was of the opinion that not only was the resort to international trade rules misguided in the light of the measures in question but also that such resort was unjustified given that the EC believed its measures were in line with its WTO obligations. Trade Commissioner Pascal Lamy firmly asserted this at the time: 'The EU's regulatory system for GMO's authorization is in line with WTO rules: it is clear, transparent and non-discriminatory. There is therefore no issue that the WTO needs to examine. The US claims that there is a so-called moratorium but the fact is that the EU has authorized GM varieties in the past and is currently processing applications. So what is the real US motive in bringing the case?'[30] Without getting involved in the conspiracy theories hinted at by the then trade Commissioner, it is submitted that this statement seems to illustrate at least that the EC believed in good faith that its actions complied with WTO obligations. What will now be examined is whether this was the case; in other words, whether the EC legislature took account of the EC's WTO obligations when it enacted the legislation that is at the root of this dispute.

The primary pieces of legislation concerned in this dispute were Regulation 258/97[31] concerning novel foods and novel food ingredients and Directive 2001/18[32] on the deliberate release into the environment of genetically modified organisms.[33] An analysis of the legislative path followed by the former measure leads one to the conclusion that the EC legislature took no account of WTO obligations when enacting it. WTO considerations, although not expressly mentioned in the latter, were at least indirectly

---

[29] EC Measures Affecting the Approval and Marketing of Biotech Products, First Written Submission by the European Communities (17 May 2004).

[30] 'European Commission regrets US Decision to file WTO Case on GMOs as misguided and unnecessary', Brussels, Press Release (13 May 2003).

[31] Regulation 258/97 of the European Parliament and of the Council of 27 January 1997 concerning novel foods and novel food ingredients, OJ 1997 L 43/1.

[32] Directive 2001/18 of the European Parliament and of the Council of 12 March 2001 on the deliberate release into the environment of genetically modified organisms, OJ 2001 L 106/1.

[33] The other legislation referred to in this case has subsequently been repealed; Council Directive 90/220 of 23 April 1990 on the deliberate release into the environment of genetically modified organisms, OJ 1990 L 117/15, Commission Directive 94/15 of 15 April 1994, which amended Directive 90/220 by adapting it to technical progress for the first time and Commission Directive 97/35 of 18 June 1997, adapting to technical progress for the second time Council Directive 90/220, OJ 1997 L 169/72.

considered, recital 13 of the Commission's proposal for Directive 2001/18 stating that, 'The content of this Directive duly takes into account international experience in this field and international trade commitments and the Cartagena Protocol.'[34] However, no reference was made to the EC's WTO obligations in the common position on the Directive adopted by the Council, nor was there any reference to it in the European Parliament's resolution of 12 April 2000. Indeed, when the European Parliament adopted the report of Mr David Robert Bowe in February 2001, it was the question of the EC's internal position regarding genetically modified organisms, rather than any debate concerning the global trading system which dominated the Parliament's focus.[35]

What is interesting to note, however, is that much more thought was given to WTO rules by the legislature when enacting Regulation 1830/2003,[36] which amended Directive 2001/18/EC. The Parliament suggested that the Commission's proposal, which states that the system of identifiers should take account of developments in international fora, be elaborated upon. The Parliament recommended the addition of the phrase 'ensuring the reciprocal and complementary nature of the relevant international agreements, in particular between the WTO agreements and the Protocol on Biosafety'.[37] This amendment was justified by the Parliament on the ground that 'the European Union must carry out its own legislative process in line with the Cartagena Protocol and the international market by developing dialogue, in particular with the developing countries, in all the world fora set up to regulate the use of GMOs'.[38] Of even more interest

---

[34] n. 32, recital 13. The reference to the Cartagena Protocol was introduced by the Parliament in its recommendation for second reading on the Council common position for adopting a European Parliament and Council directive on the deliberate release into the environment of genetically modified organisms and repealing Council Directive 90/220 (11216/1/1999 – C5-0012/2000 – 1998/0072(COD)), 23 March 2000. The Parliament had the opportunity at this point to simultaneously introduce an express reference to the WTO but it did not do so.

[35] The European Parliament adopted the Directive on its third reading. The compromise reached at conciliation on genetically modified organisms (GMOs) was endorsed by 338 votes to 52 with 85 abstentions.

[36] Regulation 1830/2003 of 22 September 2003 concerning the traceability and labelling of genetically modified organisms and the traceability of food and feed products produced from genetically modified organisms and amending Directive 2001/18, OJ 2003 L 268/24.

[37] Report issued by the European Parliament on the proposal for a European Parliament and Council regulation concerning traceability and labelling of genetically modified organisms and traceability of food and feed products produced from genetically modified organisms which would amend Directive 2001/18 COM(2001)182 – C5-0380/2001.

[38] Ibid.

is the fact that the Parliament signalled a potential WTO violation which the Regulation could give rise to: '[i]n the event that the EU unilaterally applies traceability and labelling requirements to imported products and carries out checks without an adequate scientific basis, it may create a trade dispute with third countries which results in the matter being referred to the WTO'.[39]

It can thus be concluded that although the EC legislature originally paid little or no heed to WTO considerations when enacting legislation to regulate the trade of Genetically Modified Organisms (GMOs), increasing attention is now being paid to such considerations in this field. While this is, of course, a welcome development, given that the EC considers that the safety of GMOs for 'the environment, human health and animal health should be assessed on a case by case basis'[40] and that it has consistently made it clear that 'every country has the sovereign right to make its own decisions on GMOs in accordance with the values prevailing in its society',[41] this is perhaps not an issue on which it should easily crumble to external trade pressures. Indeed, the EC legislature would do well to bear the fallout following its change of heart on the European Leghold Trap Regulation[42] in mind before caving in too easily to pressure from other WTO Members on the biotechnology issue.

The so-called 'Leghold Trap Regulation' had a twofold purpose; it banned the use of leghold traps within the EC and it envisaged an import ban on 13 species of fur and fur products from countries that had not banned the use of such traps.[43] This ban was to enter into force on 1 January 1995, or one year after that at the latest. The US and Canada were particularly affected by this ban as almost 50 per cent of North American fur was imported into the EC at some stage of the production process. Given that the Tuna-Dolphins report, issued after the adoption of the Regulation but before its implementation, threw the GATT compatibility of the EC measure into question, it came as no surprise when,

---

[39] *Ibid.*   [40] 'Europe's rules on GMOs and the WTO', Memo 06/61, Brussels, 7 February 2006.

[41] *Ibid.*

[42] Council Regulation 3254/91 of 4 November 1991 prohibiting the use of leghold traps in the Community and the introduction into the Community of pelts and manufactured goods of certain wild animal species originating in countries which catch them by means of leghold traps or trapping methods which do not meet international humane trapping standards, OJ 1991 L 308/1.

[43] S. Princen, 'EC Compliance with WTO Law: The Interplay of Law and Politics', 15 EJIL (2004), p. 555.

in 1994, consultations were requested by Canada in a first step towards the introduction of a formal trade complaint against the EC. Contemporaneously, amendments to the regulation proposed by the Commission at the behest of US lobbyists[44] were rejected by the European Parliament, a staunch defender of animal rights. Realising that the Regulation's amendments was not on the cards although the WTO compatibility of the act was questionable, the Commission embarked on a different route. Agreements on humane trapping standards, which were exempt from the scope of the Regulation, based on Article 300 EC, were thus negotiated with the trade partners concerned. By opting for this route, the Commission avoided EC involvement in a trade dispute before the WTO. It also reduced the role of the European Parliament to nought as the consultation procedure was used to bring certain countries outside the scope of the Regulation. The Council was therefore the final hurdle which needed to be crossed to undermine the impact of this legislation. Following the formation of a blocking minority in the Council in its Environmental Ministers composition, the matter was shifted to the General Affairs Council which approved the agreement with Canada first and with the US shortly thereafter. Thus, although the import ban was in the end adopted, the end result arguably falls short of the desired result as the 'shadow of WTO law' had a considerable impact on the whole affair.[45] It is difficult to imagine how the Parliament could defend its position any better on the biotechnology issue.[46] It may well be for the Council to take a firmer stance and to have the courage of its convictions to weather any ensuing WTO storms.

---

[44] *Ibid.* The US and Canadian governments focused their lobbying efforts on the then DG I (Trade) and put pressure on the Commission by highlighting that (a) it was unlikely to win the case as it had argued against the use of unilateral trade measures in both the *Tuna-Dolphin* case and in the Uruguay Round negotiations and (b) that with the imminent advent of the WTO the EC would no longer be able to unilaterally block the establishment of dispute resolution panels or the adoption of their reports.

[45] *Ibid.*

[46] It should be noted that the Commission stood firmly behind the decision to conclude these 'exemption agreements'. Sir Leon Brittan, former Vice-President of the Commission, stated that 'the regulation itself made it quite clear that an option – and, I would suggest, a preferable option – was for there to be an agreement on trapping standards. The reason why that option was put in was because such an agreement would secure an improvement in animal welfare, whereas a ban would totally fail to do so. That is why we make no apology for the fact that we have negotiated with Canada, the Russian Federation and the United States', Debates in the European Parliament, 11 June 1997, available at: http://www.europarl.europa.eu/debats/debats?FILE=97-06-11LEVEL=DOC&GCSELECTCHAP=13&GCSELECTPERS=289.

8.4 Measures enacted in the framework of the common organisation of the cereals market

Since the inception of the WTO, several complaints have been made about the legislative measures taken by the EC in the framework of its common organisation of a market in cereals. Having analysed the legislative history of these challenged measures, it would appear that no consideration whatsoever was given to WTO obligations when enacting them. It is, therefore, noteworthy that the new Regulation on the common organisation of the cereals market, Council Regulation 1784/2003,[47] makes several explicit references to the WTO.[48] It is also worth mentioning that these references are made despite the insistence of the parliamentary committee concerned[49] that they be toned down to a certain extent. For example, in its opinion on the Regulation, the European Parliament recommended that what is now recital 8 be amended. This recital stipulates that 'The creation of a single Community market for cereals involves the introduction of a trading system at the external frontiers of the Community. . . . The trading system should be based on the undertakings accepted under the Uruguay Round of multilateral trade negotiations.' The Committee on Agriculture and Rural Development recommended that this reference to 'undertakings accepted under the Uruguay round' be removed. It also recommended that some text be inserted which would state that the trading system at the external frontiers should 'guarantee the Community preference'. This suggestion was not taken on board by the Council who retained the original formulation in the final version of the Regulation. The Parliamentary Committee also urged the Council to remove the reference to the WTO in what was then recital 12 of the Regulation. The Commission had proposed that the recital state 'For the most part, the customs duties applicable to agricultural products under the World Trade Organisation (WTO) agreements are laid down in the common customs tariff.' The Parliament recommended instead that this recital read 'For the most part, the customs duties applicable to agricultural products are laid down in the common customs tariff.' The Committee

---

[47] Council Regulation 1784/2003 of 29 September 2003 on the common organisation of the market in cereals, OJ 2003 L 270/78.

[48] See recitals 10, 13, 17 and Articles 17 and 22.

[49] Report on the proposal for a Council regulation on the common organisation of the market in cereals (COM(2003)23 – C5-0042/2003 – 2003/0008(CNS)) Committee on Agriculture and Rural Development, Rapporteur: D. Souchet, 21 May 2003.

justified both of these recommendations on the grounds that whilst the EU does and should honour its international undertakings, the objectives of the common agricultural policy are laid down by Article 33 of the Treaty and not by the WTO. Therefore, while one part of the Community legislature refused to acknowledge that the Community had to a certain extent ceded dominion in this field, the other insisted that this be expressly recognised.

Another amendment suggested by the Parliament was that the wording of the following recital be changed: 'Provisions for granting a refund on exports to third countries, based on the difference between prices within the Community and on the world market, and falling within the limits set by the WTO Agreement on agriculture, should serve to safeguard Community participation in international trade in cereals.'

The Parliament again wanted to remove the reference to the WTO and to put more emphasis on the Community's interests. It suggested the following formulation: 'Provisions for granting a refund on exports to third countries, based on the difference between prices within the Community and on the world market facilitate Community participation in international trade in cereals.' Export refunds should be 'managed in keeping with the objectives of the CAP, in the interests of European operators and with a view to establishing a fair price on the internal market'. The change in formulation was justified by contending that it would render the wording clearer. This justification was obviously unsatisfactory for the Council who once again did not integrate the Parliament's suggested changes into the final version of the legislative text. It would thus seem that the final document is a lot more 'WTO-friendly' than the Parliament had hoped.

The parliamentary rapporteur observed how important it was for the EC to keep its policies in compliance with the international rules and stated that any change in the EC's CAP would have a direct effect on current WTO negotiations on various trade distorting measures. He remarked that 'although the principal purpose of the CAP is not to take account of the EU's position in the WTO, it is important that all the Union's policies are coordinated appropriately'. That progress had been made in this regard was noted: 'since 1992, the shift from price support to direct farming aid – from the "amber box" to the "blue box" in WTO terminology – has been a cornerstone of EC CAP policy. This follows the EC's commitment to non-trade distorting internal subsidies and the gradual liberalisation of all markets.' Yet, that there was more progress to be made was also highlighted. The rapporteur issued the reminder that 'not all the concerns of the EC citizens can be met by relying on market forces alone' and that the EC would need to make a more concerted effort to tackle issues such as food safety, protection of the environment and rural development in the future WTO negotiations.

This is another example of a field in which the Parliament is aware of the EC's WTO commitments but refuses to explicitly draw consequences from this awareness. It is left to the Council, which in this case seems decidedly more WTO-friendly, to ensure that the Community's WTO obligations are reflected in the legislation.

8.5 Measures on export subsidies for sugar

The EC is by far the largest sugar beet producer in the world, producing over 17 million metric tons per annum, thereby comparing to the levels produced by Brazil and India the world's largest producers. This high level of production means that there is a structural surplus in the EC. As a result, the EC put in place a particular regime for this market essentially based on the establishment of support prices,[50] production quotas to limit over-production, tariffs and quotas on imports from third countries, and subsidies to export surplus production out of the EC.[51] These policies are administered based on the classification of sugar as A quota, B quota or C sugar. A quota sugar is the quota which is determined on the basis of domestic consumption and B quota sugar is the additional amount permitted to fulfil export potential. Domestic prices for A and B sugar are maintained by a host of government measures and in addition these categories receive direct export subsidies. C sugar is the production which exceeds the quota and therefore must be sold outside the EC without the aid of a subsidy. It was this regime which was successfully challenged before the WTO in April 2005.[52] The panel concerned found that EC sugar producers were able to produce and export sugar at below the total cost of production due to the cross-subsidisation of C sugar by A and B sugar.

---

[50] A minimum price to growers of sugar beet, and a guaranteed price to support the market.

[51] European Commission Report, 'The European Sugar Sector; its importance and its future', June 2005.

[52] WT/DS265 (EC – Export Subsidies on Sugar (Australia), 15 October 2004, 28 April 2005) WT/DS266 (EC– Export Subsidies on Sugar (Brazil), 15 October 2004, 28 April 2005) and WT/DS283 (EC – Export subsidies on sugar (Thailand) 15 October 2004, 28 April 2005).

It held that 'A, B or C sugar are part of the same line of production and thus to the extent that the fixed costs of A, B or C are largely paid for by the profits made on sales of A and B sugar, the EC sugar regime provides the advantage which allows EC sugar producers to produce and export C sugar at below total cost of production.'[53] Thus, even in the absence of direct export subsidies, export subsidisation was held to exist. The Appellate Body upheld the Panel's finding in this regard.

Whilst the EC legislature took into account its WTO obligations when enacting Regulation 1260/2001[54] which put in place this regime, it obviously failed to do so to a sufficient extent. The European Parliament, who was entitled to give an opinion on this Regulation in accordance with the consultation procedure, voted overwhelmingly against the Commission proposal primarily on the grounds that the period for the enforcement of the Regulation should be much longer. It did consistently state throughout its report, however, that 'it is pointless to attempt to anticipate the results of the agricultural negotiations under way at the WTO without knowing the commitments made on behalf of all the world's sugar-producing countries'. This assumption was then used to support its contention that 'the duration of the regulation should be extended so that it expires in 2006 at the same time as the Berlin Agreement, pending the signature of a new agricultural agreement under WTO auspices'.[55] WTO considerations never featured expressly in the Council meetings leading up to the conclusion of Regulation 1260/2001.[56] Recital 10 of the Regulation, contested before the WTO, acknowledges that the WTO Agreements necessitate the progressive reduction of export support; it failed to consider however that by cross-subsidising C sugar the EC could be found to breach its WTO quota obligations. One should however recognise that this cross-subsidising objection was not obvious; the interpretation in *Canada-Dairy Products*[57] of the Agreement on Agriculture came as a surprise to more than one observer.

---

[53] *Ibid.*

[54] Council Regulation 1260/2001 of 19 June 2001 on the common organisation of the markets in the sugar sector, OJ 2001 L 178/1.

[55] Report on the proposal for a Council regulation on the common organisation of the Markets in the sugar sector (Regulation 2038/1999) (COM(2000)604 – C5-0534/2000 – 2000/0250 (CNS)) Committee on Agriculture and Rural Development, Rapporteur: Joseph Daul, 28 February 2001.

[56] See in this regard the minutes of Council meeting 2360, 19 June 2001.

[57] WT/DS/103 Canada-Dairy (15 October 2004, 28 April 2005), see n. 63.

In the light of the results of this WTO dispute, a major overhaul of the EC sugar regime was deemed necessary. Although change was always on the cards as the current regime expired on 30 June 2006, the EC found itself with a difficult choice to make. The exports of C sugar benefiting from prohibited export subsidies must have been either put to an end or the subsidisation by way of cross-subsidisation must have been ended. The prohibition of export subsidies would have meant that the EC would be in breach of its agreements with ACP countries and India[58] whilst the end of cross-subsidisation would have necessitated the end of subsidisation for A and B quotas.[59] Given this choice, not only did the EC decide to reduce the price of white sugar by 39 per cent, it also made the decision to restructure its sugar market. A key element of this reform, which came into force on 1 July 2006, was the establishment of a restructuring fund financed by sugar producers to sponsor this restructuring process. The EC's objective is to reduce the quota by approximately 6 million tonnes over a four-year transition period in order to guarantee market balance. Consequently, by the start of the 2006/2007 marketing year on 1 July 2006 quotas were reduced by 1.5 million tonnes. Each tonne of quota renounced was compensated with €730 from the restructuring fund.[60]

It is expected that the first year of the reformed sugar regime will prove difficult given that the EC will have to limit its export possibilities to comply with the international trade regime.[61] It is, therefore, interesting to note the extent to which these obligations, as opposed to the

[58] The Protocol on sugar attached to the 1975 Lomé Agreement (between the EC and ACP countries) sets out a commitment by the EC to buy certain quantities of sugar at guaranteed prices and a commitment by the ACP signatory countries to supply that sugar. Under the Lomé Agreement, duty free import quotas are allocated for 1.3 million tonnes per year. An identical agreement to this Protocol (involving 10,000 tonnes per year) was concluded at the same time with India. These agreements contributed to the sugar surplus within the EC which was further aggravated by the WTO's condemnation of the EC's export regime. An obvious solution for the EC would be to breach these international agreements in an attempt to comply with the WTO reports.

[59] S.J. Powell and A. Schmitz, 'The Cotton and Sugar Subsidies Decisions: WTO's Dispute Settlement System Rebalances the Agreement on Agriculture', 10 *Drake Journal of Agricultural Law* (2005), available at: http://papers.ssrn.com/sol3/papers.cfm?abstract_id=814764.

[60] This is also the level 2007/08, but the restructuring aid then falls to 625 €/t in 2008/09 and 520 €/t in 2009/10, the fourth and final year.

[61] Press Release, CAP Reform: EU agriculture ministers adopt groundbreaking sugar reform, IP/06/194, Brussels, 20 February 2006.

Community interest, featured in the enactment of the legislation putting the regime in place, that is to say Council Regulation 318/2006.[62]

In its draft opinion on the Regulation,[63] the Parliamentary Committee on International Trade made two main assertions. The first thing the Committee argued was that the aforementioned proposed price cuts were excessive and thus contrary to one of the Common Agricultural Policy's core objectives, namely to ensure a fair standard of living for European farmers. The Committee Rapporteur pointed out that the WTO's Appellate Body 'did not find that the EC's high intervention prices for sugar violated the Community's obligations under the WTO Agreement on Agriculture'.[64] The second assertion made was that C sugar should be eliminated from the European regime. In this regard, the Parliamentary Report recommended that additional quotas not be allocated to Member States that produced C sugar in the past. Not only would to do so provide further incentives for the production of surplus sugar, it would also be contrary to the WTO ruling on export subsidies. The Parliament was therefore clearly working on the theory that an elimination of the C sugar category alone would be sufficient to comply with the panel and Appellate Body rulings. The Council did not deem this to be sufficient, however, and insisted on cutting the reference price of all sugar. The Council may well have been conscious of the situation in which Canada found itself in the dairy products dispute over Canada's two-tiered pricing system for dairy products.[65] Canada had amended its pricing system to supposedly bring it into accordance with the Agreement on Agriculture following unfavour-able panel and Appellate Body reports. However, the amended pricing system was also held to facilitate export subsidies contrary to WTO law. Both New Zealand and the US therefore lodged a request with the DSB to take retaliatory action against Canada by suspending tariff concessions up to the value of the damage calculated to be caused to them by Canada's illegal dairy export subsidy regime. These requests were referred

---

[62] Council Regulation 318/2006 of 20 February 2006 on the common organisation of the markets in the sugar sector, OJ 2006 L 58/1.

[63] Draft opinion of the Committee on International Trade for the Committee on Agriculture and Rural Development on the proposal for a Council regulation on the common organisation of the markets in the sugar sector (COM(2005)0263 – C6-0243/2005 – 2005/0118(CNS)) Draftsman: Béla Glattfelder.

[64] *Ibid.*

[65] Canada – Measures affecting the Importation of milk and the exportation of dairy products, n. 57.

to arbitration and a mutually agreed solution was subsequently reached. In this way, Canada avoided retaliatory action on the part of its trading partners.[66] The EC legislature, in particular the Council, chose not to hedge its bets in this regard.

8.6 Measures concerning the indication of geographical origin

Within the EC there are several Regulations in place which are designed to provide protection for geographic indications.[67] Regulation 2081/92[68] is one such regulation. This piece of legislation provides protection for designations of origin (PDO) and for geographical indications (PGI) of agricultural products and foodstuffs. Crucially, a name cannot be registered for a PDO or a PGI if a similar trademark already exists. This refusal is nonetheless subject to the proviso that usage of the earlier trademark by a subsequent user would lead to confusion regarding the identity of the product due to its reputation or the length of time this trademark has been in use by it. The Regulation is therefore designed to ensure that the geographical designations which it covers within the Community are subject to uniform protection. In this regard, it provides for a system of Community registration for those products which fall within its scope. Products which do not fall within its scope, on the contrary, are subject to the national protection which a Member State confers on geographical designations and are therefore governed by the national law of that Member State and confined to the territory of that Member State.

The US contended[69] that EC Regulation 2081/92, as amended, does not provide national treatment with respect to geographical indications and does not provide sufficient protection to pre-existing trademarks that are similar or identical to a geographical indication. This contention was

---

[66] Available at http://www.mfat.govt.nz/Treaties-and-International-Law/Trade-law-and-free-trade-agreements/0-Canada-Dairy.php.

[67] For further see the website of the UK Patent Office, available at: http://www.ukpats.org.uk/patent/p-applying/p-should/p-should-otherprotect/p-should-otherprotect-geographic/p-should-other-protect-geographic-europe.htm.

[68] Council Regulation 2081/92 of 14 July 1992 on the protection of geographical indications and designations of origin for agricultural products and foodstuffs, OJ 1992 L 208/1.

[69] WT/DS/174 (EC – Protection of Trademarks and Geographical Indications for Agricultural Products and Foodstuffs (US), 15 March 2005). Australia contested the same measure in DS/290 (EC – Protection of Trademarks and Geographical Indications for Agricultural Products and Foodstuffs (Australia), 15 March 2005).

upheld by a WTO panel. The EC then enacted Council Regulation 510/2006[70] to bring the EC regime into compliance. Whether or not the EC has in fact complied with its WTO obligations has been called into question by Australia and the US. These parties both disagree that the EC has fully implemented the DSB's recommendations and rulings and have therefore invited the EC to take account of their comments and to revise its newly promulgated Regulation. It is thus useful to examine the extent to which the EC legislature took account of its WTO obligations, in particular the WTO Appellate Body ruling, when adopting this legislation.

In its opinion on Regulation 510/2006,[71] the European Parliament suggested several amendments and additions to the Commission's proposal in order to render the Regulation more WTO compliant in general. For example, Parliament suggested that a new recital be added to those proposed by the Commission which would state that 'The strengthening of the Community policy on designations of origin and geographical indications requires, additionally to the clarification and simplification referred to in this Regulation, the negotiation of a multilateral register under WTO auspices, with the objective of ensuring the durability of the policy.' The Parliament also suggested that the Regulation be amended to stipulate that 'Traditional geographical or non-geographical names designating an agricultural product or a foodstuff originating in a region or a specific place which fulfil the conditions referred to in the second and third intents of paragraph 1(a) shall also be considered as designations of origin or geographical indications.' Consequently, Parliament proposed that geographical indications be included in this paragraph since ensuring that products which do not qualify for PDO status should be eligible for PGI status if they match the definition laid down in 1(b) 'can only contribute to securing recognition of the PDO/PGI scheme in connection with the WTO negotiations'.[72] A similar addition was made in part 3 of Article 2 for the same reasons. In his comments, the rapporteur explicitly

---

[70] Council Regulation 510/2006 of 20 March 2006 on the protection of geographical indications and designations of origin for agricultural products and foodstuffs, OJ 2006 L 93/12.

[71] Report on the proposal for a Council regulation on the protection of geographical indications and designations of origin for agricultural products and foodstuffs (COM(2005)0698 – C6-0027/2006 – 2005/0275(CNS)).

[72] Report on the proposal for a Council regulation on the protection of geographical indications and designations of origin for agricultural products and foodstuffs (COM(2005) 0698 – C6-0027/2006 – 2005/0275(CNS)) Committee on Agriculture and Rural Development, Rapporteur: Friedrich-Wilhelm Graefe zu Baringdorf (23/02/2006).

acknowledged that the issue of geographical indications is one which has
long been a 'bone of contention' with the EC's trading partners in the
WTO. The rapporteur also notes that the EC was engaged in WTO action
on this point and that, although the EC regulation was not inconsistent
with WTO obligations on the majority of points criticised, certain
improvements could still be made. He noted in particular that the WTO
dispute settlement reports compelled the EC 'to improve access by third
country nationals to the EC system and to place those nationals on an
equal footing with EC citizens, particularly with regard to the application
procedure and the right to object'. The rapporteur, however, considered
that the relevant adjustments form a substantial part of the legislative
proposal he was considering and was also pragmatic in his remarks. He
noted that 'geographical indications are a key issue in the fundamental
debate being held about applying conditions on standards to trade in
agricultural products and foodstuffs within the context of the WTO' and
that the WTO challenge was more a matter of principle for the US and
Australia than a matter of need.

Thus, it can be seen that the EC legislature was more mindful of WTO
considerations when adopting this legislation on geographic indications
than it had previously been. As can be deduced from the Parliamentary
Committee report, however, the EC's motives for this had less to do with
WTO compliance than with the defence of EC interests. The EC aims to
negotiate an extension of the Agreement on Trade Related Aspects of
Intellectual Property Rights (TRIPS) register to include foodstuffs and
other agricultural products and improving the WTO compatibility of its
existing legislation in this field can only further its negotiating powers.

8.7 Conclusion

Having examined the legislative history of the five Community measures
chosen as case studies, some brief conclusions can be reached.

First, it is clear when looking at the time of adoption of various
measures that increasing attention is being paid to WTO concerns by the
EC legislature. The legislation on the common organisation of the cereals
market is an appropriate example.

Second, it would appear from the examples examined in this chapter
that the Parliament consistently seeks to defend Community interests over
WTO interests at all costs. In the bananas dispute, Parliament advocated

that the transitional period for the new regime be extended to protect Community interests and thus further delay full WTO compliance. Parliament illustrated its wariness regarding unbridled market forces in the cereals case study warning that not all the concerns of the EU citizens can be met by relying on market forces alone. In the sugar dispute it urged the Commission to reconsider the proposed price cuts, introduced for WTO compliance reasons, claiming that they were excessive. This may not be surprising given that, as mentioned at the beginning of this chapter, Parliament implied that denying WTO law direct effect in the European legal order would effectively shield Community interests. The Council, on the other hand, appears to have been a more robust advocate of compliance with WTO obligations, sometimes even to the detriment of the Community interest the Parliament seeks to protect. Indeed, this also may not come as a surprise given its intergovernmental nature. An example has cropped up recently which will put this theory to the test. The Commission has proposed a Regulation banning the placing on the market and importing and exporting of cat and dog fur.[73] This proposal inevitably poses trade-related problems. The Commission has confidently stated that the import ban is in conformity with Article XX(a). Yet, this is highly debatable. While the Parliament will undoubtedly give its support to the proposal, the support of the Council may not be as forthcoming. Given that the Regulation will be adopted using the co-decision procedure, the extent to which trade concerns will contribute to the inter-institutional wrangling will be interesting to observe.

---

[73] Proposal for a Regulation of the European Parliament and of the Council banning the placing on the market and the import and export from the Community of cat and dog fur and products containing such fur COM(2006)684 final.

PART II

Bilateral and regional approaches

The relations between the EU and Switzerland

CHRISTINE KADDOUS

9.1 Introduction

The Swiss Confederation, located in the very heart of the European continent, is not a member of the European Union (EU), nor indeed of the European Economic Area (EEA). Even so, Switzerland's relations with the EU are dense and intense and in constant evolution. They have been developed in an ad hoc way and are founded on specific institutional mechanisms. Some 20 agreements of primary importance, together with one hundred or so secondary agreements are linking Switzerland with the EU today.[1]

The aim of this contribution is to examine Switzerland's relations with the EU from a legal point of view. After a brief look at the history of these relations, which should help to better understand their specificity, the basic contents of each of the two main groups of bilateral agreements (the Bilateral Agreements I and II), their institutional framework and their characteristics will be studied in order to determine their position in the EC legal order. These Agreements will then be examined in the light of the EEA Agreement, before a global appraisal of the legal and political situation is made in order to determine the main options for future Swiss European policy.

9.2 Historical background

Switzerland, as a country that has traditionally been neutral, at the end of World War II and in the context of the Cold War, refrained from full participation in the process of integration which started in Western

---

[1] For a list of these agreements, see C. Kaddous and M. Jametti Greiner (eds.), *Accords bilatéraux II Suisse – UE et autres Accords récents*, Dossier de droit européen n° 16 (Basel-Brussels-Paris: Helbing-LGDJ-Bruylant, 2006), pp. 929–46.

Europe. Preferring to concentrate on economic integration, in 1960 Switzerland acted together with the United Kingdom, Denmark, Norway, Sweden, Austria and Portugal to launch the European Free Trade Association (EFTA).[2] Next came the signing of a Free Trade Agreement with the European Economic Community (EEC) in 1972, abolishing tariff barriers on industrial products between the two parties.[3]

In 1986, the Single European Act[4] opened the way for a single market in the EEC with the so-called 'four freedoms': free movement of persons, goods, services and capital. Switzerland and the other EFTA members launched negotiations with the EEC at the end of the 1980s, which led to the creation of the EEA, including the same four freedoms. However, this attempt to integrate with the Single European Market was rejected by the Swiss electorate in a referendum on the EEA Agreement in 1992.[5] This was mainly due to certain institutional features that were perceived as a limitation on the sovereignty of the people, in particular in relation to the principle of direct democracy.

Following this 'no' to any multilateral approach in the relations with the EC, the Swiss Government (the 'Federal Council'), froze the application for EU membership that it had submitted in May 1992. It then adopted the approach of conducting bilateral negotiations with the EU in key sectors. After lengthy negotiations, seven agreements were signed in 1999 – the Bilateral Agreements I or *Bilaterals I* – and approved by a large majority in a referendum in May 2000.[6] These Agreements cover Free Movement of Persons, Overland Transport, Air Transport, Agriculture, Research, Technical Barriers to Trade and Public Procurement,[7] and came

---

[2] Convention establishing the European Free Trade Association of 4 January 1960, published in the Systematic Collection (SC) of Swiss Law under 0.632.31. This Convention has been updated and incorporates all amendments up to May 2005.

[3] Agreement of 22 July 1972 between the Swiss Confederation and the European Economic Community, OJ 1972 L 300/189; also published in the SC of Swiss Law under 0.632.401. There is also an Agreement between the European Economic Community and the Swiss Confederation concerning direct insurance other than life insurance signed in 1989, OJ 1991 L 205/2; SC 0.961.1.

[4] Single European Act, OJ 1987 L 169/5.

[5] The EEA Agreement of 2 May 1992, OJ 1994 L 1/3, was defeated because it only received 49.7 per cent of the votes with seven cantons voting in favour.

[6] On 21 May 2000, the Swiss people approved the agreements by 67.2 per cent.

[7] They are published in the OJ 2002 L 114/1, and in the SC under different numbers according to their context. Agreement on the Free movement of Persons between the European Community and its Member States on the one part, and the Swiss Confederation, on the other part, of 21 June 1999, OJ 2002 L 114/6; SC 0.142.112.681; Agreement between the European Community and the

into force on 1 June 2002. The Agreement on Free Movement of Persons (FMP Agreement) is implemented in stages, with a transitional period in which the Swiss labour market is opened to nationals of the EU Member States on a gradual basis subject to strict controls.[8] Time has shown that these seven agreements are beneficial to both the EU Member States and Switzerland.

A further round of negotiations – the so-called *Bilaterals II* – was completed at the political level on 19 May 2004. This produced new agreements in eight other sectors: cooperation in the fields of Police, Justice, Asylum and Migration (Schengen/Dublin), Taxation of Savings, Fight against Fraud, Processed Agricultural Products, Environment, Statistics, Media, Education, Vocational Training, Youth and Pensions.[9] They have had the effect of extending and systematising the conventional framework of the relations with the EU, and developing the cooperation beyond purely economic aspects in fields such as internal security, asylum, environment, statistics and culture. These agreements were endorsed by the Swiss Parliament in December 2004. At the instigation of some 50,000 petitioners opposing Switzerland's participation in the Schengen/Dublin cooperation, a referendum was mounted but on 5 June 2005 the electorate voted in favour of Swiss participation in Schengen/Dublin.[10]

The enlargement of the EU in 2004 only necessitated amendments to one of the agreements of the package of the Bilateral Agreements I, i.e. the FMP Agreement, because it was a mixed one concluded on the part of the EU by the European Community and its Member States. On 25 September

---

Swiss Confederation on the Carriage of Goods and Passengers by Rail and Road of 21 June 1999, OJ 2002 L 114/91, SC 0.740.72; Agreement between the European Community and the Swiss Confederation on Air Transport of 21 June 1999, OJ 2002 L 114/73; SC 0.748.127.192.68; Agreement between the European Community and the Swiss Confederation on Trade in Agricultural Products of 21 June 1999, OJ 2002 L 114/132, SC 0.916.026.81; Agreement on Scientific and Technological Cooperation between the European Community and the Swiss Confederation of 21 June 1999, OJ 2002 L 114/468, SC 0.420.513.1; Agreement between the European Community and the Swiss Confederation on Mutual Recognition in relation to Conformity Assessment of 21 June 1999, OJ 2002 L 114/369, SC 0.946.526.81; Agreement between the European Community and the Swiss Confederation on Certain Aspects of Government procurement of 21 June 1999, OJ 2002 L 114/430, SC 0.172.052.68. See also the Message of the Federal Council, which is the Swiss Government, to the Parliament of 23 June 1999, Federal Journal (FJ) 1999, 6128 *et seq.* that gives details of explanatory report for each agreement.

[8] Article 10 FMP Agreement.

[9] The Bilateral Agreements II were signed 26 October 2004. Some of them are in force, others not yet. For the references of publications, see n. 68 *et seq.*

[10] The Swiss people approved the Schengen/Dublin Association Agreements by 54.6 per cent.

2005, Swiss voters approved the extension of that Agreement to include the ten new EU Member States.[11] The other six agreements of 1999 were automatically extended as they fell fully within the exclusive competence of the EC. Since 1 January 2007, the EU has enlarged with Romania and Bulgaria and now comprises 27 Member States. New negotiations have been launched with Switzerland in order to extend the FMP Agreement to the two new EU members.

Switzerland's policy towards the EU is also based on solidarity. An important aspect of this is the financial support, which is intended as a gesture of solidarity towards the ten new EU Member States but also as a contribution to reduce economic and social inequalities in the enlarged EU.[12] This support towards the ten new EU Member States was approved by the Swiss people on 26 November 2006.

9.3 The Bilateral Agreements between the EU and Switzerland

Switzerland is very close to the EU geographically,[13] culturally[14] and economically.[15] Both are founded on common fundamental values such as democracy, human rights and the rule of law. Despite the rejection of the EEA Agreement in 1992, the relations between the EU and Switzerland have been intensified through the Bilateral Agreements of 1999 and 2004, which cover globally more than 15 different fields.

From a legal point of view, six out of the seven agreements of the Bilateral Agreements I are concluded between the EC and Switzerland. The FMP Agreement, being the exception, was concluded between the Community, its Members States and Switzerland. Consequently, this Agreement has been ratified not only by the EC but also by all the EU Member States in accordance with their respective constitutional

---

[11] The extension of the FMP Agreement and the revision of accompanying measures were approved by the Swiss population by 56 per cent.

[12] The Federal Act on Cooperation with Eastern Europe was approved by the Swiss people with 53.4 per cent.

[13] Neighbouring States of Switzerland are Austria, France, Germany and Italy and they are all members of the EU. Liechtenstein is a contracting party to the EEA Agreement.

[14] According to Article 4 of the Switzerland Federal Constitution of 18 December 1998, SC 101, the national languages are: German, French, Italian and Romansh. It is worth noting that three of them are official languages of the EU.

[15] In fact, the European Union is by far the most important trading partner of Switzerland.

requirements. The FMP Agreement is a mixed agreement because the EC is not exclusively competent with regard to the free movement of persons but shares this competence with its Member States.

The Bilateral Agreements II are concluded between the EC and Switzerland, with the exception of the Schengen Agreement, the Agreement concerning the Fight against Fraud and the one on Pensions of Retired Officials. The Schengen Agreement presents the particularity of being a 'cross-pillar' agreement, concluded by the EU, the EC and Switzerland. The 'anti-fraud' Agreement is a mixed agreement between the EC and its Member States, on the one hand, and Switzerland on the other. The Pensions Agreement binds the European Commission to Switzerland.

Apart from these Bilateral Agreements containing international obligations in relation to EC law, the Federal Council decided *unilaterally* in 1988[16] to bring Swiss legislation with international implications in line with European standards in order to reduce the differences between the Swiss legal order and that of the EC/EU. Since then, the 'autonomous adaptation' of Swiss legislation to EU regulations and standards, without any treaty obligation, is often reverted to and will remain important in the future for those matters not covered by the Bilateral Agreements I and II.[17]

9.3.1 Bilateral Agreements of 1999 (Bilateral Agreements I)

The Bilateral Agreements I fall into three categories:[18] an *integration* agreement (the Agreement on Air Transport); a *cooperation* agreement (the Agreement on Scientific and Technological Cooperation), and five *liberalisation* agreements based on the *equivalence of legislation* in the Contracting Parties (the FMP Agreement, the Agreement on the Carriage of Goods and Passengers by Rail, the Agreement on Mutual Recognition in relation to Conformity Assessment, the Agreement on Trade in

---

[16] FJ 1988 III 388.

[17] On this question, see C. Kaddous, 'L'influence du droit communautaire sur l'ordre juridique suisse', in *Mélanges en l'honneur de M. l'Avocat Général Léger. Le droit à la mesure de l'homme* (Paris: Pédone, 2006), pp. 407–23; W. Wiegand and M. Brülhart, *Die Auslegung von autonom nachvollzogenem Recht der Europäischen Gemeinschaft*, Swiss Papers on European Integration (1999), vol. 23, pp. 29 *et seq.*

[18] These agreements bind Switzerland to the EC and to its Member States for the FMP Agreement; Switzerland to the EC and to the Euratom Community for the Agreement on Scientific and Technological Cooperation, and Switzerland to the EC for the remaining five Agreements.

Agricultural Products, and the Agreement on Certain Aspects of Government Procurement).

Aims and contents

This part of the study deals with the objectives and main content of each of the Bilateral Agreements I. It provides an overview of their main characteristics, as well as the fields covered by these international instruments.

The Agreement on Free Movement of Persons   The aim of this Agreement is to accord to Swiss nationals and nationals of the EU Member States the rights of entry, residence and access to work as employed persons, establishment on a self-employed basis and the right to stay in the territory of the Contracting Parties. The Agreement also facilitates the provision of services in the territory of the Contracting States, and, in particular, liberalises those of brief duration (for a maximum period of 90 days per calendar year). It also guarantees the right of entry into, and residence in, the territory of the Contracting Parties to persons not exercising an economic activity in the host country. Finally, it affords the same living, employment and working conditions as those accorded to nationals. All these rights are provided on the basis of the non-discrimination principle on grounds of nationality. However, one of the essential characteristics of the Agreement is that the free movement of persons is liberalised progressively, in stages, over a period of 12 years.[19]

The Agreement also provides for the coordination of social security systems[20] and contains the same principles as those in force within the EU concerning mutual matters for recognition of diplomas so as to make it easier for Swiss and EU nationals in the partner territories to access and pursue activities as employed and self-employed persons, as well as to provide services.[21] The Agreement also makes provision for the acquisition of immovable property insofar as it is linked to the exercise of other rights conferred by the Agreement itself.[22]

---

[19] Article 10 FMP Agreement, see D. Grossen, P. Gasser and D. Veuve, in D. Felder and C. Kaddous (eds.), *Accords bilatéraux Suisse – EU (Commentaires)*, Dossier de droit européen n° 8 (Basel-Brussels: Helbing & Lichtenhahn-Bruylant, 2001), pp. 259–311.

[20] Article 8 FMP Agreement and Annex II, under which the Contracting Parties apply between each other the coordination system applicable in the EU Member States or equivalent rules.

[21] Article 9 FMP Agreement and Annex III.

[22] Article 25 of Annex I, see F. Schobi, in Felder and Kaddous (eds.), *Accords bilatéraux*, pp. 417–34.

The FMP Agreement is one of liberalisation based on the equivalence of legislation, in which the Contracting Parties have expressed in the preamble of the Agreement their desire to bring about free movement of persons on the basis of the rules applying within the EC.[23] As already mentioned, it is a mixed agreement because its scope exceeds the Community competence in this field.

Switzerland and the EU agreed to extend this agreement in 2004. In an additional protocol, separate transitional regulations were laid down in relation to the new EU Member States. This transitional system provides for a gradual and controlled opening of the Swiss labour market to workers from the new Member States. Labour market restrictions (priority for Swiss nationals, quotas, controls on salary and working conditions) may continue to apply until 30 April 2011.[24]

The Agreement on Air Transport The Agreement acknowledges the integrated nature of international civil aviation and establishes rules within the area covered by the EC and Switzerland without prejudice to those contained in the EC Treaty, in particular to existing Community competences under the competition rules set out in Articles 81 and 82 EC, as well as under all relevant competition rules derived therefrom.

It provides for the basis of reciprocity for access of Swiss companies to the EU's deregulated civil aviation market. The traffic rights are attributed progressively to Swiss airline companies (these constitute the air transport freedoms[25]). Switzerland thus takes over, in essence, the same legal provisions as if it had joined the EU, with certain restrictions to take account of the fact that the various rights are granted on a step-by-step basis. The third and fourth freedoms are applicable as of the entry into force of the Agreement (1 June 2002), the fifth and seventh two years later

---

[23] See also the Joint Declaration on the application of the Agreement, according to which the Parties will undertake to apply to nationals of the other Contracting Party the *acquis communautaire*, as provided in the Agreement.

[24] Extension Protocol, signed 26 October 2006, OJ 2006 L 89/30; OC (Swiss Official Collection) 2006 995. The negotiations on the extension of the Agreement for Romania and Bulgaria have not yet started.

[25] 1st freedom: right to overfly; 2nd freedom: non-commercial stopover; 3rd freedom: Zurich–Paris; 4th freedom: Paris–Zurich; 5th freedom: Zurich–Paris–Madrid (with possibility of taking passengers on board in Paris whose destination is Madrid); 6th freedom: Paris–Geneva–Vienna; 7th freedom: Paris–Madrid; 8th freedom: Paris–Lyon (so-called cabotage, i.e. domestic flight by a foreign company).

(1 June 2004). The application of the eighth is currently negotiated between the Contracting Parties.[26]

Discrimination on the ground of nationality is prohibited.[27] Swiss individuals and companies are placed on an equal footing with nationals of EU Member States and companies incorporated in the EU as far as the freedom of establishment and of investment in the area of civil aviation are concerned.[28]

The specificity of this is that Switzerland applies Community law and that generally it reproduces the provisions applicable within the EU. Seen from this perspective, the Agreement is clearly one of *integration* aimed at harmonising the rules applicable to aviation within Europe. Switzerland has committed itself to adopting the relevant Community law provisions, the application and interpretation of which belong to the competent institutions of the Contracting Parties, subject to the prerogatives of the European Commission and of the European Court of Justice (ECJ) as provided for in Community law.

Homogeneity of current and future rules within the Contracting Parties is of utmost importance. This idea has been clearly expressed in the preamble, which mentions the Contracting Parties' desire, 'in full deference to the independence of the courts', to prevent divergent interpretations and to arrive at an interpretation of the provisions of the Agreement, together with the corresponding provisions of Community law substantially reproduced in the Agreement, which is as uniform as possible.[29]

The Agreement on the Carriage of Goods and Passengers by Rail   The objective of this Agreement is to coordinate overland transport policy between Switzerland and the EU Member States. This policy comes within the scope of a more sensitive approach to the environment, by aiming to

---

[26] For further details on the content of the Agreement, see A. Auer, U. Haldimann and S. Hirsbrunner, in Felder and Kaddous (eds.), *Accords bilatéraux*, pp. 435–80; R. Dettling-Ott, 'Abkommen über den Luftverkehr', in D. Thürer, R. Weber and R. Zäch (eds.), *Bilaterale Verträge Schweiz–EG* (Zurich: Schulthess, 2002), pp. 459–514.

[27] Article 3 Agreement.   [28] Articles 4 and 5 Agreement.

[29] This Agreement also contains provisions on the relations with other States and international organisations. In principle, the Contracting Parties remain independent in their relations with third States and in their participation in international organisations. However, some coordination is to take place within the framework of the Joint Committee (Arts. 24 to 27 Agreement).

reconcile the efficiency of transport systems with environmental concerns, in particular in the Alpine region.

It aims to liberalise access to the transport market for the carriage of goods and passengers by road and rail, 'in such a way as to ensure the more efficient management of traffic using routes which, from a technical, geographical and economic viewpoint, are the most suitable for all the modes of transport covered by the Agreement'. This liberalisation has been implemented gradually and reciprocally, on a step-by-step basis, and will be completed at the latest by 2008.

The Agreement gave rise to an increase in weight limits applicable to lorries transiting through Switzerland from 28 to 34 tonnes in 2001 and to 40 tonnes in 2005 (end of the transit agreement[30]), with a simultaneous increase in road taxes, to support the transfer of trans-Switzerland heavy goods traffic from the road to the railway. It also allows Swiss transport companies to access the market under similar conditions as those enjoyed by companies established in the EU. During the transitional phase, Switzerland established an annual quota for transit of 40-tonne lorries crossing the Swiss Alps, and tax advantages for trucks transporting light goods or travelling empty.[31] As of 2005, the overland transport market is entirely deregulated, meaning that Swiss transporters are free to transport goods from one EU Member State to another without having to pass through Switzerland ('grand cabotage').[32] The 'polluter pays' principle is enshrined in the Agreement insofar as Swiss road taxes are calculated according to the distance travelled and the level of polluting emissions of heavy goods vehicles.

To a certain extent this Agreement constitutes an implicit recognition by the EC that the objectives pursued by the Swiss transport policy lie fully within its own transport policies.

Agreement on Mutual Recognition in relation to Conformity Assessment   The objective pursued by this Agreement is the elimination of technical barriers to the trade in industrial goods between the EC and Switzerland. In order to avoid duplication of procedures, it provides for the

---

[30] Agreement of 5 May 1992 between Switzerland and the EEC on the overland transport of goods, SC 0.740.71.

[31] Article 8 Agreement.

[32] For further details on the content of this Agreement, see M. Friedli, J.-C. Schneuwly *et al.*, in Felder and Kaddous (eds.), *Accords bilatéraux*, pp. 481–548.

mutual recognition of conformity tests, certification and approval of products by each Contracting Party on the basis of the regulations of the other party or on the basis of the regulations of the same party insofar as they are found to be equivalent.[33] Products can thus be certified by conformity assessment bodies recognised in Switzerland and can then be sold on the Community market without any further certification, and vice versa.

Should legislation of the Contracting Parties be deemed not to be equivalent, the products destined for the Swiss and Community markets will be subject to double certification under both Swiss and Community regulations. Both certifications can, however, be given by the same accreditation body.[34] The Contracting Parties' authorities designate a number of, mostly private, certification bodies that are authorised to assess, in the country of origin, the conformity of the concerned goods with the regulation of the other State.[35]

The Agreement does not reproduce the 'Cassis de Dijon' principle, because this would have required institutional arrangements exceeding the scope of the bilateral negotiations.[36] However, the Swiss Government is currently considering introducing this principle unilaterally into its national legal order,[37] which would raise many legal and political issues.

In December 2006, the Contracting Parties agreed to revise the Agreement of 1999 in order to improve its implementation and to abolish the 'origin clause' that limited the scope of the Agreement to products originating in the Contracting Parties. This revision took effect on 27 February 2007.[38]

Here, again, this is a liberalisation agreement based on the equivalence of legislation of the Contracting Parties. Contrary to the WTO Agreement

---

[33] Article 1(2) Agreement; see also Article 3 and Annex I, which defines the 15 product sectors covered by the Agreement.

[34] For further details on the content of the Agreement, see O. Zosso and H. Hertig, in Felder and Kaddous (eds.), *Accords bilatéraux*, pp. 549–76.

[35] Article 5 Agreement.

[36] See *Message relatif à l'approbation des accords bilatéraux entre la Suisse et la CE*, 23 June 1999, FJ 1999 5440, p. 5522. This principle is, however, applicable within the EEA Agreement. On the applicability of the 'Cassis de Dijon' principle within the realm of the EC–Switzerland 1972 Free Trade Agreement, see O. Jacot-Guillarmod, *Le juge national face au droit européen*, Dossier de droit européen n° 3 (Basel: Helbing & Lichtenhahn, 1993), p. 235 and cited references.

[37] See *Report of the Federal Council* on the 'Cassis de Dijon' Principle, of 23 September 2005. This project concerns the revision of the Swiss Federal law on Technical Barriers to Trade, SC 946.51.

[38] Agreement revising the Agreement between the European Community and the Swiss Confederation on mutual recognition in relation to conformity Assessment, OJ 2006 L 386/51; SC 0.946.526.81.

on Technical Barriers to Trade, which only makes recommendations regarding the recognition of conformity assessment carried out in other countries, the current Agreement contains binding rules.[39]

The Agreement on Trade in Agricultural Products   The Agreement aims to reinforce free trade relations between the EC and Switzerland by improving the access of agricultural products to the market.[40] This liberalisation agreement, based on the 'equivalence of legislation', takes into account the rights and obligations of the Parties under the WTO Agreement. It is not applicable to processed agricultural products as defined in the 1972 Free Trade Agreement.[41]

Consisting of two parts, the first relates to tariff concessions (quantitative aspects) and the second aims to reduce technical barriers to trade of certain products (qualitative aspects). As far as the improvement of access to the Contracting Parties' markets is concerned, the Agreement provides for a number of tariff concessions in a variety of different sectors: dairy products, horticulture, fruit and vegetables, bovine and porcine meat, as well as wine specialities. These concessions consist of reductions and eliminations of customs duties or of tariff quotas.

As for the quantitative aspects, it concerns the elimination of technical barriers to trade in the following areas: cheeses, plant health, animal feed, seeds, wine-sector products, spirit drinks and aromatised wine-based drinks, organic products, marketing standards for fresh fruit and vegetables, and animal health.[42]

The Agreement on Certain Aspects of Government Procurement   The objective of the Agreement consists of harmonising government procurement systems in the EC and Switzerland, and of further opening public sector procurement markets of the Contracting Parties. It is a liberalisation

---

[39] *Message of the Federal Council* of 23 June 1999, FJ 1999 5533.

[40] 'Agricultural products' are understood as those enumerated in Chapters 1 to 24 of the International Convention on the Harmonised Commodity Description and Coding system, RS 0.632.11.

[41] However, given the importance of the trade of these products for Switzerland, the Contracting Parties have provided for further negotiations in this field, see the *Message* of 23 June 1999, FF 1999 5536 and the declaration, p. 5546.

[42] For further details on the content of the Agreement, see P. Aebi, M. Botsch *et al.*, in Felder and Kaddous (eds.), *Accords bilatéraux*, pp. 577–619; R. Senti, 'Abkommen über den Handel mit landwirtschaftlichne Erzeugnissen', in Thürer, Weber and Zäch (eds.), *Bilaterale*, pp. 579–634.

agreement based on the equivalence of legislation comprising two parts: the first is a follow up of the 1994 WTO Agreement on Public Procurement Markets (APM)[43] to further the objectives of the APM through bilateral negotiations; the second part goes beyond the level of freedom of access foreseen in the APM and aims to reach a high level of commercial liberalisation comparable to that in place within the EC.

The Agreement concerns only certain aspects of public procurement, as it already takes into account the APM applicable within the WTO. In practice, the combination of the two (APM and bilateral agreement) results in a complete reciprocal opening up of the Contracting Parties' respective public procurement markets. It extends the liberalisation achieved through the APM to districts and local authorities, and opens markets in excess of a threshold value, for public or private sector companies operating in the field of transport by rail, telecommunications, or gas and heat procurement, for private sector companies supplying water or electricity, and for public transport.[44]

The principle of non-discrimination is applicable to public procurement markets[45] and provisions are made for a right of appeal.[46] Besides the classical judicial means of challenging the procurement procedures, the Contracting Parties have agreed to establish an independent authority, where it does not already exist, that is competent to initiate proceedings or take administrative or judicial action against the Covered Entities in the event of a breach of this Agreement.[47] In the EC, this role is played by the European Commission. In Switzerland, the *Conférence des gouvernements cantonaux* and the *Federal Council* gave a special commission the task of implementing and surveying the correct application and respect of Switzerland's international duties in matters relating to public procurement markets.[48]

---

[43] The EC and Switzerland are parties to this Agreement, which entered into force on 1 January 1996, SC 0.632.231.42.

[44] For further details on the content of this Agreement, see L. Wasecha, E. Bollinger and R. Mayer, in Felder and Kaddous (eds.), *Accords bilatéraux*, pp. 633–82; G. Biaggini, 'Abkommen über bestimmte Aspekte des öffentlichen Beschaffungswesen', in Thürer, Weber and Zäch (eds.), *Bilaterale*, pp. 307–78.

[45] Article 6 Agreement.   [46] Article 5 Agreement.   [47] Article 8 Agreement.

[48] This Commission was created on 3 April 1996 and has the task of ensuring the respect on every level of Switzerland's international duties. This entity must be in a position to hear any complaints on the proper application of the Agreement, see *Message of the Federal Council* of 23 June 1999, FJ 1999 5517.

The Agreement on Scientific and Technological Cooperation The object of the Agreement was the participation of Switzerland in the Fifth EU Framework Programme for Research and Development (1998–2002) and the corresponding Euratom programme.[49] All specific programmes and means available were opened to researchers, universities, companies and private parties established in Switzerland. The Agreement put researchers from the EU and Switzerland on an equal footing. Swiss participants can initiate collaboration, manage and coordinate a project. Likewise, researchers established in the EU were able to participate in Swiss research programmes and projects.[50]

These programmes expired at the end of 2002, as did the 1999 Agreement. A new Agreement was concluded in 2004 in order to participate in the Sixth Framework Programme. On 25 June 2007, this last Agreement has been renewed for the Seventh Framework Programme,[51] which runs from 2007–2013.

Legal bases and competences

For the 1999 Bilateral Agreements, the choice of the legal basis in the EC Treaty was founded on political rather than legal considerations. From a strictly legal point of view, these agreements had to be concluded under the specific provisions of the EC Treaty relating to the different fields covered by the agreements, i.e. Articles 39, 43, 49 and other EC provisions for Free Movement of Persons, Articles 71 EC for Air Transport, and so forth.[52]

However, instead of adopting this position, a political solution has been found in order to simplify the ratification process in the Community legal order. These agreements have been considered as 'association agreements' in the sense of Article 310 EC. Although this provision was not listed as a legal basis in the proposal of the European Commission to the Council concerning the conclusion of the seven agreements,[53] the Commission specified in its explanatory report to the proposal that,

---

[49] This programme aims to ensure the security of nuclear fusion facilities, see the *Message* of the Federal Council of 23 June 1999, FJ 1999 5440.

[50] For further details on the content of the Agreement, see C. Kleiber and C. Von Arb, in Felder and Kaddous (eds.), *Accords bilatéraux*, pp. 683–702.

[51] The Agreement has to be renewed for each generation of the Framework Programmes, see Article 9 Agreement.

[52] C. Kaddous, 'Les accords sectoriels dans le système des relations extérieures', in Felder and Kaddous (eds.), *Accords bilatéraux*, p. 88.

[53] COM(1999)229 final.

in view of the 'package character' of the agreements and their institutional provisions, the consent of the European Parliament according to Article 300(3)(2) EC was necessary. A further consequence of the qualification of these Bilateral Agreements as association agreements, was the requirement of a unanimous decision of the Council according to Article 300(2)(1) EC.

The replacement of the initial substantive provisions of the EC Treaty as legal bases for the conclusion of the Agreements by Article 310 EC did not affect the distribution of powers between the EC and the Member States,[54] taking into account that only the FMP Agreement is indeed a mixed agreement; the others are concluded, as was already mentioned, by the EC, without the Member States being a party to them.

Institutional framework

In accordance with the principles of public international law,[55] the Contracting Parties of the Bilateral Agreements I are responsible for the implementation and application of the treaties on their own territory. There is one important exception to this principle in the Agreement on Air Transport, in which the Parties stipulated that the rules set out in the Agreement are without prejudice to those in the EC Treaty, in particular to those regarding competition (in particular, Articles 81 and 82 EC and the competition rules derived therefrom).

Unlike the EEA Agreement[56] and other association agreements with several common organs, the institutional framework of the Bilateral

---

[54] On the scope of Article 310 EC, see, e.g. C. Kaddous, 'Le droit des relations extérieures dans la jurisprudence de la Cour de justice', Dossier de droit européen n°6, 1998, pp. 218–24; P. Eeckhout, *External Relations of the European Union. Legal and Constitutional Foundations* (Oxford: Oxford University Press, 2004), pp. 103–6.

[55] Articles 26 and 27 Vienna Convention on the Law of Treaties, United Nations Treaty Series, vol. 1155, p. 331; SC O.111.

[56] On the EEA Agreement, see, e.g. O. Jacot-Guillarmod (ed.), *Accord EEE. Commentaires et réflexions. EWR-Abkommen. Erste Analysen. EEA Agreement. Comments and reflexions* (Zürich: Schulthess/Stämpfli, 1992), pp. 49–75, p. 55; S. Norberg, K. Hökborg *et al.* (eds.), *EEA Law. A Commentary on the EEA Agreement* (Stockholm: Fritzes, 1993); S. Norberg, 'The Agreement on the European Economic Area', 29 CMLRev. (1992), pp. 1171–98; R. Zach, D. Thürer and R. Weber (eds.), *Das Abkommen über den Europäischen Wirtschaftsraum – Eine Orientierung* (Zürich: Schulthess, 1992); P.-C. Müller-Graff and E. Selving (eds.), *EEA–EU Relations* (Berlin: Verlag Arno Spitz, 1999); C. Baudenbacher, P. Tresselt and T. Örlygsson (eds.), *The EFTA Court. Ten Years on* (Cambridge: Hart Publishing, 2005); M. Johansson, U. Wahl and U. Bernitz (eds.), *Liber Amicorum in Honour of Sven Norberg. A European for all Seasons* (Brussels: Bruylant, 2006).

Agreements I is limited. Based on classical intergovernmentalism (except for the Air Transport Agreement), cooperation within the Agreements is made through Joint Committees, in charge of the administration and surveillance of their application. A Joint Committee is set up for every agreement; it is composed of representatives of the Contracting Parties and the decisions are taken by consensus. The Committee is the forum for the exchange of views and information between the Contracting Parties. It shall make recommendations and, in specific cases provided for in the agreements, it disposes of a decision-making power. For example, in the FMP Agreement, the Joint Committee is authorised to modify the Annexes II and III of the Agreement but it has no competence to change the main text of the Agreement or Annex I.[57]

There is no joint judicial body or tribunal to supervise the correct application and uniform interpretation of the agreements. Consequently, it is possible that different courts of the Contracting Parties, which are institutionally independent, take different decisions within their own legal system.[58] However, courts in the EU Member States may submit a question for preliminary ruling to the ECJ in accordance with Article 234 EC. Within the EU, uniformity in the application of the bilateral agreements is guaranteed by the ECJ.[59]

Exceptionally, in the Agreement on Air Transport, the provisions on competition shall be applied and controlled by the Community institutions in accordance with Community rules. In fact, there is a case pending before the Court of First Instance (CFI) between Switzerland and the Commission in relation to the Agreement on Air Transport concerning Zurich Airport.[60]

Reference to the case law of the ECJ

The objective of 'equivalence of legislation' or 'homogeneity' (as far as the Air Transport Agreement is concerned) is very important for the proper

---

[57] Article 18 FMP Agreement.
[58] B. Spinner, 'Rechtliche Grundlagen und Grenzen für bilaterale Abkommen', in D. Felder and C. Kaddous, n. 17, p. 15; also T. Jaag, 'Institutionen und Verfahren', in D. Thürer et al., Bilaterale Verträge Schweiz-EG, Ein Handbuch (Zurich: Schulthess, 2002), pp. 39–64, p. 45; S. Breitenmoser, 'Sectoral Agreements between the EC and Switzerland: Contents and Context', 40 CMLRev. (2003), pp. 1137–86.
[59] See Case 181/73 Haegeman [1974] ECR 449; see also Case 12/86 Demirel [1987] ECR 3719.
[60] Case T-319/05 (originally C-70/04), Swiss Confederation v. Commission, pending.

functioning of the Bilateral Agreements I. However, only two of them contain express provisions on taking into account the ECJ case law: the FMP and the Air Transport Agreements.

Article 16(2) of the FMP Agreement provides that, insofar as the application of the Agreement involves concepts of Community law, account shall be taken of the relevant ECJ case law rendered prior to the date of its signature. Case law after that date shall be brought to Switzerland's attention. At the request of a Contracting Party, the Joint Committee shall determine the implications of such case law. A similar system is provided for in the Air Transport Agreement.[61] Despite the fact that the other agreements of the Bilateral Agreements I do not contain such reference to the case law of the ECJ, it must be stressed that in order to preserve the *effet utile* of the Agreements, the administrative and judicial authorities designed to apply these texts are encouraged to ensure as uniform an interpretation and application of the rules as possible, the content of which is substantially equivalent to provisions of Community law.

Development of the law

One of the main reasons for the rejection of the EEA Agreement by the Swiss people was its dynamic character, i.e. the obligation to adopt the future *acquis communautaire* in the dynamic and homogenous EEA.[62] Therefore, the Bilateral Agreements I only require the mutual recognition of equivalent legal provisions.

The 1999 Bilateral Agreements have no dynamic character.[63] Only the *acquis communautaire* as it stood prior to the date of their signature and to which reference is made, will be applied in the relations between the Contracting Parties. For example, in the FMP Agreement, the case law of the ECJ

---

[61] For the Air Transport Agreement, the system of reference to Community law is provided in Article 1(2).

[62] On the homogenous character of the EEA Agreement, see, e.g. O. Jacot-Guillarmod, 'Préambule, objectifs et principes (Arts 1–7 EEE)', in *Accord EEE. Commentaires et réflexions. EWR-Abkommen. Erste Analysen. EEA Agreement. Comments and reflexions* (Zürich: Schulthess/Stämpfli, 1992), p. 55; M. Cremona, 'The *Dynamic and Homogeneous* EEA: Byzantine Structures and Variable Geometry', 19 ELRev. 1994, pp. 508–26; C. Baudenbacher, 'Between Homogeneity and Independence. The Legal Position of the EFTA Court in the European Economic Area', Columbia Journal of European Law (1997), pp. 169–227.

[63] D. Felder, 'Appréciation juridique et politique du cadre institutionnel et des dispositions générales des accords sectoriels', in Felder and Kaddous (eds.), *Accords bilatéraux*, p. 128; T. Jaag, 'Institutionen und Verfahren', in D. Thürer, R. Weber and R. Zäch (eds.), *Bilaterale*, pp. 39–65.

and of the CFI as established after 21 June 1999 must be brought to Switzerland's attention through the Joint Committee.[64] It is then for the Committee to determine the implications of such case law. Similarly, if one of the Contracting Parties initiates new legislation it shall inform the other party through the Joint Committee, which shall hold an exchange of views on the implications of such an amendment for the proper functioning of the Agreement.[65] Since the references in the Bilateral Agreements are static, a change in the EU legislation does not automatically bring about a change in the Bilateral Agreements I.

Amendments to the Agreements only enter into force after the respective internal ratification procedures have been completed on both sides. Merely technical adjustments and amendments to the *acquis communautaire* (such as acts listed in the annexes) may nevertheless be adopted by decision of the Joint Committee and enter into force immediately thereafter.[66]

'Guillotine clauses'

As a consequence of the principle of 'appropriate parallelism' introduced by the EC, the Bilateral Agreements I are interconnected by the so-called 'Guillotine clause'.[67] This means that all the 1999 Bilateral Agreements could only enter into force all together at the same time and would also all come to an end if any of them is terminated or not renewed. Thus, the Agreements cease to apply six months after receipt of notification of nonrenewal or termination. Cancellation of one Agreement has direct consequences for the effectiveness of the other Agreements of the *Bilaterals I*.

9.3.2 Bilateral Agreements of 2004 (Bilateral Agreements II)

The 2004 Bilateral Agreements allow the relations between the EU and Switzerland to intensify in fields which go beyond purely economical interests, such as internal security, asylum, environment and culture. All of them, except the Agreement on the Fight against Fraud and the Schengen Agreement, are Community Agreements that fall within the exclusive competence of the Community. The Agreement on the Fight against Fraud

---

[64] Article 16(2) FMP Agreement.   [65] Article 17(2) FMP Agreement.
[66] Article 18 FMP Agreement.
[67] See, for example, Article 25(4) FMP Agreement; Article 36(4) Agreement on Air Transport.

is a mixed Agreement and the Schengen Agreement has the characteristic of being concluded, on the Union side, by the EU *and* the EC.

Aims and contents

Like the 1999 Agreements, the 2004 Bilateral Agreements can be put into three categories. The Schengen/Dublin Association Agreements are *integration* agreements, providing for the adoption of the *acquis communautaire*, as defined in the annexes and allowing Switzerland certain rights in decision-shaping for the future developments in these two Agreements. Other Agreements are based on *cooperation* and cover Statistics, Fight against Fraud, Taxation of Savings, MEDIA programmes, Environment and Pensions. The 1999 and 2004 Research Agreements also belong to this category.[68] Finally, the Agreement on Processed Agricultural Products is based on *trade liberalisation* and modifies the 1972 Free Trade Agreement between Switzerland and the EC.[69]

The Agreement on Processed Agricultural Products   This Agreement, in force since 30 March 2005, revises the 2nd protocol to the 1972 Free Trade Agreement and sets the tariffs applicable to processed agricultural products, that is to say second transformation tier products of the food industry, such as chocolate and biscuits, or icecream.[70] Agricultural raw materials, or products that have undergone first transformation immediately produced from raw materials, such as meat products, milk powder, cheese, flour, crystallised sugar, oils and fats do not belong to this category. The Agreement, which mainly concerns a price compensation mechanism, aims to make it easier to compensate the large differences in the price of raw materials in Switzerland and the EU.

The Agreement on Cooperation in the Field of Statistics   The Agreement on Cooperation in the Field of Statistics, in force since 1 January

---

[68] These two Agreements are not formally part of the series of Bilateral Agreements. They are published at SC 0.420.513.1. For further information, see P.-E. Zinsli, in Kaddous and Jametti Greiner (eds.), *Accords bilatéraux*, pp. 901–10.

[69] See n. 3.

[70] Agreement between the European Community and the Swiss Confederation amending the Agreement between the European Economic Community and the Swiss Confederation of 22 July 1972 as regards the provisions applicable to processed agricultural products, OJ 2005 L 23/19; SC 0.632.401.23; see *Message of the Federal Council* of 1 October 2004, FJ 2004, 5927 *et seq.*

2007, formalises the already tight relationship between Eurostat and the Swiss Federal Statistics Bureau (*Office fédéral de la statistique*).[71] It guarantees the progressive harmonisation of statistics between Switzerland and the EU and greatly improves comparability of data in vital areas such as trade relations, employment markets, social security, transport, planning and environment.

The Agreement in the Field of Environment   The Agreement, in force since 1 April 2006, concerns Swiss participation in the European Environment Agency (EEAg) and in the European environmental information and observation network (EIONET).[72] The task of the EEAg, created at the beginning of the 1990s,[73] is to produce objective, reliable and comparable information aimed at all the actors that have a role to play in the implementation of European policy in environmental matters. Given the cross-border nature of environmental issues, the EEAg must work in cooperation with other States in Europe. Switzerland remains the only western European country which does not participate in the EEAg's network and it was in the joint interest of the Contracting Parties that a solution be found to change this. Participation in the EEAg reinforces Switzerland's contribution to environmental protection efforts and allows it to participate actively in the strategy and research projects at a European level.

The MEDIA Agreement   The object of this Agreement, which was in force since 1 April 2006, was Switzerland's participation in European MEDIA Plus and MEDIA Training Programmes[74] aimed at audiovisual

[71] Agreement between the EC and the Swiss Confederation on cooperation in the field of statistics, OJ 2006 L 90/2; SC 0.431.026.81; see also the *Message of the Federal Council* of 1 October 2004, FJ 2004, 5973 *et seq.*

[72] Agreement between the European Community and the Swiss Confederation concerning the participation of Switzerland in the European Environment Agency and the European Environment Information and Observation Network, OJ 2006 L 90/37; SC O.814.092.68; see the *Message of the Federal Council*, FJ 2004, 6001 *et seq.*

[73] Council Regulation 1210/90 of 7 May 1990 on the Establishment of the European Environment Agency and the European Environment Information and Observation Network, OJ 1990 L 120/1, last modified by Parliament and Council Regulation 1641/2003 of 22 July 2003, OJ 2003 L 245/1; see contribution by K. Inglis in this volume.

[74] Council Decision 2000/281 of 20 December 2000, on the implementation of a programme to encourage the development, distribution and promotion of European audiovisual works (MEDIA Plus – Development, Distribution and Promotion) (2001–2005), OJ 2000 L 336/82, as modified by Decision 846/2004, OJ 2004 L 157/4; see also Parliament and Council Decision 2001/163 of 19 January 2001, on the implementation of a training programme for

production.[75] MEDIA Plus supports the development, distribution and promotion of audiovisual productions. It supports producers in the elaboration of scenarios and the choice of teams during production plan development and budgeting for the production of test and promotional films. MEDIA Training helps industry professionals with their training. The programme subsidises training schools giving courses in digital production or in scenario conception. Through this Agreement, Switzerland participates in all MEDIA programmes, and is the first European State to take part in it without being a member of the EEA or a candidate for EU membership. The Swiss participation was envisaged until the end of 2006, which coincided with the expiry date of the programmes. A new agreement was signed in October 2007. It envisages the participation of Switzerland in MEDIA 2007,[76] for the period 2007–2013. It is provisionally applied as from 1 September 2007.

The Agreement concerning the Pensions of Retired Officials   This Agreement between the European Commission and the Swiss *Federal Council*, in force since 31 May 2005, aims to avoid the double taxation of officials who have retired from the European Institutions and are living in Switzerland.[77]

The Schengen/Dublin Association Agreements   Two Agreements are envisaged for this area: an Association Agreement between Switzerland, the EU and the EC covering the field of the Schengen Convention,[78] and another between Switzerland and the EC related to the field of asylum.[79]

---

professionals in the European audiovisual programme industry (MEDIA – Training) (2001–2005), OJ 2001 L 26/1, as modified by Decision 845/2004, OJ 2004 L 157/1.

[75] Agreement between the European Community and the Swiss Confederation in the audiovisual field, establishing the terms and conditions for the participation of the Swiss Confederation in the Community programmes MEDIA Training, OJ 2006 L 90/23; SC 0.784.405.226.8; see also *Message of the Federal Council* 2004, 6021 *et seq.*

[76] Agreement between the Swiss Confederation and the European Community in the Audiovisual Field, Establishing the Terms and Conditions for the participation of the Swiss Confederation in the Community Programme MEDIA 2007, OJ 2007 L 330/11; SC 0.784.405.226.8.

[77] This Agreement is published in the SC 0.672.926.81; no reference of publication in the OJ.

[78] Proposal for a Council Decision on the conclusion, on behalf of the European Community, of the Agreement between the European Union, the European Community and the Swiss Confederation concerning the latter's association with the implementation, application and development of the Schengen *acquis*, COM(2004)593 final.

[79] Proposal for a Council Decision on the conclusion, on behalf of the European Community of the Agreement between the European Community and Switzerland concerning the criteria and mechanisms for establishing the State responsible for examining a request for asylum lodged in a Member State or in Switzerland.

Both agreements follow the model used for Norway and Iceland in 1999.[80] The association includes the implementation, application and development of the Schengen *acquis*, as well as the application of the criteria and mechanisms for establishing which State is responsible for examining a request for asylum lodged in an EU Member State or in Switzerland.

The two Agreements were worked out so as to take into account certain specificities of Swiss constitutional law. They allow Switzerland to participate fully in the cooperation established through the Schengen and Dublin instruments. Switzerland does have the right to participate in the decision-making process for the development of the *acquis*. It is thus represented in the working groups of the Council active in the areas covered by Schengen and Dublin, and is associated with the work of the Committees assisting the Commission in the same fields. The Agreements are based on the adoption by Switzerland of the Schengen and Dublin *acquis*, as defined in the relevant annexes of the two association agreements.[81] As to the future development of the *acquis*, Switzerland was given two years to make independent and informed decisions as to whether it wishes to adopt the new act into Swiss law (Norway was given a maximum of six months, and Iceland four weeks). This period will permit Switzerland to comply with its ordinary legislative procedure and involve its democratic institutions (Federal Council, Parliamentary approval and referendum, if necessary). Adoption does not follow automatically but must first be approved every time by the Swiss legislature. Switzerland will also be able to apply the *acquis* on a temporary basis, if possible by the means available through the Federal

---

[80] Agreement concluded by the Council of the European Union and the Republic of Iceland and the Kingdom of Norway concerning the latter's Association with the Implementation, Application and Development of the Schengen *acquis*, of 18 May 1999, OJ 1999 L 176/36; this Agreement as well as other relevant texts in matters of Schengen are published in C. Kaddous, *Union européenne. Communauté européenne. Recueil de textes* (Bern-Brussels-Paris: Stämpfli-Bruylant-LGDJ, 2004), p. 834. Agreement between the European Community and the Republic of Iceland and the Kingdom of Norway concerning the Criteria and Mechanisms for Establishing the State Responsible for Examining a Request for Asylum lodged in a Member State or in Iceland or Norway, OJ 2001 L 93/40.

[81] An exception to the adoption of future *acquis* is provided for in Article 7(5) of the Agreement. It concerns the search and seizure requests for offences in direct taxation which, had they been committed in Switzerland, would not have been punishable by detention under Swiss law. This is to be read in relation with the Agreement on the Taxation of Savings, see n. 88.

Constitution.[82] But the non-adoption of a new act could lead to the suspension, termination or annulment of these Agreements.[83]

The Agreement on the Fight against Fraud   Under this Agreement, which is not yet in force, the Contracting Parties agree to fully cooperate in administrative and judicial matters pertaining to fraud and other criminal activities, including in areas such as customs duty and the indirect taxation in trade of goods and services.[84] Cooperation in matters of money laundering will be greatly improved and will concern important fraud and smuggling cases.

Administrative cooperation will be granted in accordance with the standards of the Convention on mutual assistance and cooperation between customs administrations.[85] Judicial cooperation by means of coercive measures (search and seizure) will be subject to the dual criminality requirement as set out in Article 31 of the Agreement provision corresponding to Article 51 of the Convention Implementing the Schengen Agreement.[86]

The scope of the Agreement is limited to indirect taxation, subsidies and public procurement offences. Indirect taxes include, for example, customs duties, value added taxes, and specific excise duties on alcohol, tobacco and petrol. Direct taxes are excluded from the scope of application of the Agreement.

The Agreement on the Taxation of Savings   This Agreement, in force since 1 January 2005, aims at the adoption by Switzerland of measures equivalent to those applicable within the EC under Directive 2003/48,[87] in

---

[82] If Switzerland cannot apply the contents of the *acquis* on a provisional basis, the EU and EC may take proportionate measures to ensure the proper functioning of the association, see Article 7(2)(b) of the Schengen Association Agreement, and Article 4(3) of the Dublin Association Agreement.

[83] Article 7(4) of the Schengen Association Agreement and Article 4(6) of the Dublin Association Agreement. For further details on these questions, see the *Message of the Federal Council* of 1 October 2004, FJ 2004 5756, n° 2.6.7.5.

[84] Proposal for a Council Decision on the conclusion of the Agreement between the European Community and its Member States, on the one part, and the Swiss Confederation, on the other part, to counter fraud and all other illegal activities affecting their financial interests, COM(2004)559 final; see also *Message of the Federal Council* 2004, 6127 *et seq.*

[85] So-called 'Naples II' Convention, OJ 1998 C 24/2.   [86] OJ 2000 L 239/19.

[87] Council Directive 2003/48 of 3 June 2003 on Taxation of Savings Income in the form of interest payments, OJ 2003 L 157/38.

order to guarantee an effective taxation of savings income in the form of interest payments.[88] Switzerland undertakes to introduce a withholding tax on all interest payments from a non-Swiss source made by a paying agent located on Swiss territory, to a natural person domiciled for tax purposes in an EU Member State. This withholding tax, which will be raised incrementally to 35 per cent, may be replaced by a voluntary disclosure by the beneficial owner expressly authorising his or her paying agent in Switzerland to report the interest payments to the competent authority of his or her State. Switzerland undertakes to provide administrative assistance on request to EU Member States in cases of tax fraud or the like, provided it concerns interest payments falling within the Agreement's scope of application. The introduction of an automatic system for the exchange of information between taxation authorities is not envisaged in the Agreement because it would be irreconcilable with banking secrecy in tax matters. The Agreement also provides for the sharing of withholding tax between the EU Member States and Switzerland on a 75:25 per cent basis. The Contracting Parties further undertake to renounce, on a reciprocal basis, taxation on the payment of dividends, interests and royalties between affiliated companies.

The Exchange of Letters concerning the participation in educational, vocational training and youth programmes   Through an Exchange of Letters, the Swiss State Secretary for Education Research and the European Commission's Director General of Education and Culture have agreed on the modalities of the meetings to take place after the adoption of the second set of the Bilateral Agreements.[89] These meetings serve the exchange of information on the existing *Socrates, Leonardo da Vinci* and *Youth* programmes, and on the subsequent programmes; they contribute to the preparation of Swiss participation in the next generation of programmes, as of 2007.[90] This Exchange of Letters is not an agreement in the legal sense of the term; it is rather a declaration of intent.

---

[88] Agreement between the European Community and the Swiss Confederation providing for measures equivalent to those laid down in Council Directive 2003/48/EC on taxation of savings income in the form of interest payments – Memorandum of Understanding, OJ 2004 L 385/30; SC 0.642.026.81; see also *Message of the Federal Council* of 1 October 2004, FJ 2004, 6163 *et seq.*

[89] See *Message of the Federal Council* of 1 October 2004, FJ 2004 5614, no. 1.1.

[90] On the next generation of programmes for 2007–2013, see J. Burri, in Kaddous and Jametti Greiner, *Accords bilatéraux*, pp. 803–22.

Since the signing of the Decision establishing the *Lifelong Learning* and
Youth in Action programmes at the end of 2006,[91] the Swiss Federal Council
adopted the mandate to start up negotiations with the EU on 1 March 2007.
The EU mandate is in place since 30 January 2008 and the negotiations
should start in the first half of 2008. It is not clear whether the participation
of Switzerland will start in the course of 2008 or at the beginning of 2009.
Until then, Switzerland will continue to participate in EU education programmes indirectly, in the framework of individual projects and on the basis
of an agreement with project coordinators or partner institutions.

Legal bases and competences

Contrary to the 1999 Agreements, all founded on Article 310 EC, those of
2004 are based on specific provisions of the EU and/or EC Treaties.[92] The
question of the competences to conclude the Bilateral Agreements II and
the determination of the appropriate legal basis fed the discussions between
the Community institutions, particularly in relation to the Schengen
Association Agreement. In June 2002, the Council of the European Union had
decided to authorise the Commission and the Presidency to negotiate a single
agreement between the Community and the Union, on the one hand, and
Switzerland, on the other. The EU is competent on the basis of Article 38 EU
for all the aspects of the Schengen *acquis* relevant to the third pillar of the EU
Treaty and the EC is competent for all the aspects relevant to the first pillar of
the EU Treaty. The Commission tried to oppose – unsuccessfully – resorting
to a 'cross-pillar' agreement 'EC–EU' (mixed agreement of second generation)
and favoured the conclusion of a mixed agreement 'EC–Member States' or of
two parallel agreements: one concluded by the EC and the other by the EU.

The Commission invoked different arguments for this approach. As
Articles 24 and 38 EU only authorise the conclusion of agreements
covering fields relevant to the Common Foreign and Security Policy
(CFSP) and the Police and Judicial Cooperation (PJC), there is something of a risk that the constitutional reservation of Article 24 EU might
prevent the entry into force of the Community parts of the Agreement.
However, it must be recalled that this risk also exists in relation to 'first
generation' mixed agreements as one Member State may jeopardise the

[91] European Parliament and of the Council Decision 1720/2006 of 15 November 2006
establishing an action programme in the field of lifelong learning, OJ 2006 L 327/45.
[92] See C. Kaddous, 'La place des Accords Bilatéraux II dans l'ordre juridique de l'Union
européenne', in Kaddous and Jametti Greiner, *Accords bilatéraux*, p. 72.

entry into force of the Agreement if it fails to ratify it, which would render the provisional application of the Community parts of the Agreement null and void.[93] The practice of the qualified majority rule, for the conclusion of purely Community agreements (Art. 300(1) EC), is absorbed by the requirement of unanimity for the adoption of agreements founded on Article 24 EU. This is an unfortunate effect of the contamination of the Community procedures by the EU Treaty conclusion procedures. Moreover, the European Parliament is placed in a complex situation in which it is asked to give an opinion on or give its assent to, the Community parts of the agreements while it is excluded from giving such an opinion on those parts of the agreements falling under the scope of Article 24 and 38 EU. Finally, the following questions concerning the legal effects of 'second generation' mixed agreements are relevant: is the ECJ competent to interpret and apply the non-Community parts of such an agreement and may individuals invoke the provisions of such an agreement?[94]

At first sight, whether to conclude two parallel agreements (Commission approach) or to conclude a unique 'cross-pillar' agreement (Council approach), the complexity of the questions remains because it is linked to the structure of the pillars and to the complementarity of the EU and EC competences in areas covered by the Schengen Convention.[95]

Institutional framework

All the agreements of the Bilateral Agreements II, except the Association Agreements to Schengen and Dublin, are based on intergovernmental cooperation that operates through Joint Committees responsible for the

---

[93] J.-V. Louis, 'Les accords conclus au titre des 2ème et 3ème piliers', in J.-V. Louis and M. Dony (eds.), *Commentaire J. Mégret. Relations extérieures* (Brussels: Editions de l'Université, 2005), p. 329.

[94] These questions will be studied at Section 9.3.3.

[95] As of today, the Commission proposed approving the Schengen Association Agreement by way of two separate decisions: one in relation to the conclusion of the Agreement in the name of the Community for all the aspects relevant to the first pillar of the EU Treaty, and the other in relation to the conclusion in the name of the EU for all the aspects of Schengen relevant to the third pillar. The Schengen Association Agreement is concluded on the basis of Articles 62, 63, 66, 95 EC and 38 EU. The ratification procedure has been achieved on the part of the EU on 1 February 2008 and the agreements have been in force since 1 March 2008. See Council Decision of 28 January 2008 on the conclusion on behalf of the European Union of the Agreement between the European Union, the European Community and the Swiss Confederation on the Swiss Confederation's association with the implementation, application and development of the Schengen acquis, OJ 2008, L 53/50.

administration and surveillance of the Agreements' application. It must be mentioned, however, that the Taxation of Savings and Pensions Agreements do not set up a joint committee.

In principle, the Joint Committees have the same powers as in the Bilateral Agreements I.[96] They are also competent to settle disputes between the Contracting Parties.[97]

In the Schengen and Dublin Agreements, the Joint Committees have a specific structure. Their meetings take place at different levels: Ministers, senior officials or experts.[98] These Committees constantly review the evolution of the case law of both the ECJ and the Swiss courts relating to the provisions of the Agreements.[99] These Committees have an important power, particularly where new acts have not been incorporated into the Swiss internal legal order.[100]

At the same time, Switzerland has the right to submit statements or written observations to the ECJ in cases where a court in a Member State has made a reference to the ECJ for a preliminary ruling for the interpretation of the Agreements.[101]

The Taxation of Savings Agreement, which does not set up a Joint Committee, provides that where the Swiss competent authorities and one or more of the other competent authorities of a Member State disagree as to the interpretation or application of the agreement, they shall endeavour to resolve this by mutual agreement.[102] The administration of the Agreement takes place by mutual agreement between the competent authorities of the Contracting Parties and the same holds true for any disagreement that arises as to the interpretation and application of the Agreement. This means of administration and settlement of disputes in a

---

[96] See Section 9.3.1, Institutional Framework.

[97] See, for example, Article 40 Agreement concerning the Fight against Fraud.

[98] See Article 3(1) and (5). For further details on this question, see the contribution of S. Gutzwiller, 'Komitologie und Gemischte Ausschüsse im Rahmen der Assoziierung der Schweiz an Schengen/Dublin', in Kaddous and Jametti Greiner (eds.), *Accords bilatéraux*, pp. 245–66.

[99] Article 8(1) Schengen Association Agreement and with a formulation a bit different without incidence however on the substance, Article 5(1) of the Dublin Association Agreement.

[100] Article 7(4) and (10) Schengen Association Agreement and Article 4(7) Dublin Association Agreement.

[101] Article 8(2) Schengen Association Agreement and Article 5(2) Dublin Association Agreement.

[102] Article 12 Agreement.

diplomatic manner and on an ad hoc basis between the Parties seems also to constitute the foundation of the Pensions Agreement.[103]

Implementation and surveillance

The Contracting Parties shall take all appropriate measures to ensure the fulfilment of the obligations arising out of the Agreements and shall refrain from any measures which would jeopardise attainment of the objectives of the Agreements.[104] This formula repeats the application of the principle *pacta sunt servanda* according to which every treaty in force is binding upon the Parties to it and must be performed by them in good faith (Art. 26 Vienna Convention of 1969 and of 1986) and of the principles of autonomy and sovereignty of the Parties. More details have been brought in the Bilateral Agreements II, particularly in the Taxation of Savings Agreement which expressly mentions that Switzerland shall take the measures necessary to ensure that the tasks required for the implementation of the Agreement are carried out by paying agents established within the territory of Switzerland and which specifically provides for provisions on procedures and penalties.[105]

Principle of 'equivalence of legislation'

The principle of 'equivalence of legislation' of the Contracting Parties is fundamental to the proper functioning of most of the Bilateral Agreements II (Taxation of Savings, Environment and Media). By this means, the Contracting Parties safeguarded their legislative autonomy with the requirement of maintaining the equivalence of their legislation. This task is facilitated by the introduction of reciprocal information procedures and, in certain cases, of consultation when one of the Contracting Parties envisages amending its legislation on a point regulated by the agreements.[106] Consequently, the evolution of legislation has to be taken into account regularly in such a way as to avoid any divergence between Swiss law and the law of the EU in the fields regulated by the agreements.

---

[103] Despite the fact that the text of the Agreement does not envisage specific provisions in that field.

[104] See Article 10 Agreement on Cooperation in the area of Statistics and Article 15 of the Agreement in the field of Environment.

[105] Article 1(5) Agreement.

[106] See, for example, Article 4 of the Agreement in the field of Statistics.

Otherwise, the proper functioning and the efficiency of these texts would seriously be jeopardised.

Principle of the 'acceptance of the *acquis*'

The Schengen and Dublin Association Agreements are founded on the principle of 'acceptance of the *acquis*'. Switzerland shall accept the *acquis* in these fields as it stood at the moment of the signature of the agreements (26 October 2004),[107] as well as its future development. However, Switzerland safeguarded a measure of autonomy insofar as it may decide independently whether it will or will not accept new developments of the Schengen or Dublin *acquis*. The refusal to so accept may lead, in certain circumstances, to the termination of the agreements.

Unlike the FMP Agreement of 1999, these agreements do not take into account any case law of the ECJ prior to the date of signature of the agreement. This is largely because case law in this field is scarce and plays less of a role compared to the case law on the free movement of persons and, also, the ECJ has less jurisdiction than in other matters.[108] However, the Contracting Parties clearly indicated in these two agreements their objective of ensuring the most uniform possible application and interpretation of the *acquis* provisions.[109]

With this aim in mind, the Joint Committees shall keep under constant review, developments in the ECJ and Swiss case law. A mechanism of regular mutual transmission of such case law is set up. Furthermore, Switzerland shall report each year to the Joint Committee on the way in which its administrative authorities and courts have applied and interpreted the provisions of the Schengen and Dublin Association Agreements.[110] In case of a substantial divergence between the ECJ case law and that of Swiss courts, or a substantial divergence in the application of the Agreements' provisions between the authorities of the Member States

---

[107] The relevant Acts and measures are enumerated in Annexes A and B Schengen Association Agreement and in Article 1(1) Dublin Association Agreement.

[108] See the competence of the ECJ on the basis of Articles 68 EC and 35 EU in comparison with the classical competences of the ECJ according to Articles 220 *et seq.* EC. For the relevant case law, see Cases C-187/01 and C-385/01 *Gözütok* [2003] ECR I-1345; Case C-105/03 *Pupino* [2005] ECR I-5285; see also Case C-77/05 *United Kingdom* v. *Council of the European Union*, [2007] nyr; Case C-137/05 *United Kingdom* v. *Council of the European Union*, [2007] nyr; Case C-467/05 *Ministero Pubblico* v. *Giovanni Dell'Orto*, [2007] ECR-I-5557.

[109] Article 8 Schengen Association Agreement and Article 5 Dublin Association Agreement.

[110] Article 9 Schengen Association Agreement and Article 6 Dublin Association Agreement.

concerned and the Swiss authorities, the Joint Committees must resolve the problem. They have two months to ensure a uniform application and interpretation by the Contracting Parties.[111] If they are unable to do so, the dispute settlement procedure is triggered, with all that this implies, potentially even leading to the termination of the Agreement.[112]

Development of the law

As with the 1999 Agreements, the Bilateral Agreements II are static and based on the recognition of equivalent legal provisions. There is, however, the important exception of the Schengen and Dublin Association Agreements which provide that Switzerland accept the Schengen and Dublin *acquis* as well as their future developments. Despite this obligation, Switzerland has safeguarded the autonomy of its decisions as it decides independently whether to accept or refuse new developments in the Schengen or Dublin *acquis*. The refusal to accept future *acquis* may lead, in certain circumstances, to the termination of the Agreements. There is no decision-making right as such, only a formal right to participate in decision-shaping within the EU relevant working groups.

Special clauses

Unlike the Bilateral Agreements I, the second set of Agreements do not contain a guillotine clause. There is no legal link between the different agreements, except between the Schengen and Dublin Agreements, which will enter into force and/or terminate simultaneously.[113]

9.3.3 Bilateral Agreements I and II and the Community legal order

Bilateral Agreements I and II, like all international agreements concluded by the EC, shall be binding on the institutions and on Members States according to Article 300(7) EC. This provision means that these agreements, as of their entry into force, form an integral part of Community law in accordance with the *Haegeman* judgment of 1974.[114] In general,

---

[111] Article 9(2) Schengen Association Agreement and Article 6(2) Dublin Association Agreement.

[112] Article 10 Schengen Association Agreement and Article 7 Dublin Association Agreement.

[113] Article 15(4) Schengen Association Agreement and Article 14(2) Dublin Association Agreement.

[114] Case 181/73 *Haegeman*, n. 59.

Community agreements, as well as mixed agreements, do have the same status in the Community legal order, especially as concerns provisions falling under the Community competence.[115] If they do not fall under the Community competence, which is the case of certain provisions of the FMP Agreement as well as of the Agreement on the Fight against Fraud, do these provisions form an integral part of Community law?

This issue was studied for the first time in the *Demirel* judgment of 1987[116] in relation to the competence of the ECJ to interpret the provisions on the free movement of workers in the Association Agreement with Turkey. Whereas the German and British Governments took the view that, in case of mixed agreements, the ECJ's interpretative jurisdiction does not extend to provisions whereby Member States have entered into a commitment with regard to Turkey in the exercise of their own powers, the ECJ considered that it was competent to interpret the provisions in question and concluded that its jurisdiction was not determined by the question of who is finally competent to implement the Agreement.

We share the position adopted by the ECJ in this ruling concerning mixed agreements.[117] It is, indeed, difficult to conceive that the status of provisions, being part of an agreement, could vary according to the fact that these provisions fall under the Community competence or under the competence of the Member States. This would run counter to the principle of uniformity of application of agreements in the EU and that the ECJ should ensure. While the ECJ asserted in the *Dior* judgment of 2000[118] that, acting in cooperation with the courts and tribunals of the Member States pursuant to Article 234 EC, it is in a position to ensure a uniform interpretation of Article 50 of the TRIPs,[119] it took an ambivalent position on the question of the recognition of direct effect in establishing a distinction in terms of whether it concerned a field 'to which TRIPs applies and in respect of which the Community has already legislated' or a field 'in respect of which the Community has not yet legislated and which

---

[115] See also Case C-13/00 *Commission* v. *Ireland* [2002] ECR I-2943, para. 14; Case 459/03 *Commission* v. *Ireland* [2006] ECR I-4635, para. 84.

[116] Case 12/86 *Demirel* [1987] ECR 3719.

[117] The ECJ confirmed its position in Case C-53/96 *Hermès* [1998] ECR I-3603. The question was whether the provisional measures adopted in order to put an end to the sell of counterfeit ties of the trademark *Hermès* fell within the scope of the definition of 'provisional measure' provided for in Article 50 of TRIPs.

[118] Joint Cases C-300/98 and C-392/98, *Dior* [2000] ECR I-11307.

[119] See previous note, para. 38.

consequently falls within the competence of the Member States'.[120] In this last hypothesis, it allows potentially divergent positions by the Member States on the question of the direct effect of TRIPs provisions and seems, therefore, to accept a breach in the principle of the uniform application of mixed agreements.

Even if certain inconsistencies may appear in the case law of the ECJ, the Bilateral Agreements I and II, whether they are Community agreements or mixed agreements, should have the same status in the Community legal order. They should form an integral part of it from the moment of their entry into force and the ECJ should have jurisdiction to interpret them. In particular, if the ECJ were to decide on its jurisdiction with regard to the FMP Agreement or to the Agreement on the Fight against Fraud, it should no doubt adopt the same position as in the *Demirel* and *Hermès* judgments.

The Schengen Association Agreement raises other questions as it presents the characteristic of having been signed at the same time by both the EU and the EC. According to Article 24(6) EU, agreements based on Articles 24 and 38 EU, are binding on the institutions of the EU. This formula is similar to that of Article 300(7) EC.[121] However, the ECJ has not rendered similar rulings to those of *Haegeman* of 1974 or *Commission* v *Ireland* of 2002. It must be emphasised that according to Article 46 EU the ECJ has no jurisdiction to interpret and apply the agreements concluded in the fields of CFSP and PJC unless the question concerns the limits between the pillars.[122]

The role of the ECJ varies according to the pillars: complete jurisdiction in the Community field,[123] a less extensive jurisdiction in the third pillar (PJC) and no jurisdiction in the second pillar (CFSP). This situation will, without any doubt, raise sensitive questions once the ECJ is asked to interpret and apply the Schengen Association Agreement because it will have to decide on its jurisdiction in relation to the 'cross-pillar' Agreement, the content of

---

[120] *Ibid.*, para. 39.

[121] Except that Article 24 EU does not specify that these agreements are binding on the Member States of the EU. However, this has no effect on the status of these agreements in the legal order of the EU.

[122] Case C-170/96 *Commission and Parliament* v. *Council* [1998] ECR I-2763, para. 16: 'it is the task of the Court to ensure that acts which, according to the Council, fall within the scope of Article K.3(2), of the Treaty on European Union do not encroach upon the powers conferred by the EC Treaty on the Community'.

[123] It must, however, be noted that the ECJ has special competences in accordance with Article 68 EC.

which is found in both the Community pillar and the third pillar of the EU Treaty. The proposals for decisions on the signature of the Agreement indicate, through a reference to Council Decision 1999/436,[124] which parts of the Schengen *acquis* covered by the Agreement fall under the scope of the EU Treaty and which parts fall under the EC Treaty. This could be very useful to the ECJ in order to determine the scope of its jurisdiction.

In addition to the case where it is interpreting the Agreement, the ECJ may also be required, in accordance with Articles 68 EC or 35 EU, to decide on provisions belonging to the Schengen *acquis* whether they are Acts mentioned in Annex A, such as the Convention implementing the Schengen Agreement, or acts of the EU and of the EC listed in Annex B of the Schengen Association Agreement. Such case law will be transmitted to the Contracting Parties through the Joint Committee in charge of ensuring the most uniform possible application and interpretation of the '*acquis*' provisions. In this way, the ECJ could be put in the position of exercising an 'indirect' competence on the interpretation of the non-Community parts of the Schengen Association Agreement.

Interpretation of the Agreements by the ECJ

In the *Haegeman* case,[125] the ECJ confirmed its jurisdiction to give preliminary rulings concerning the interpretation of provisions of international agreements concluded by the EC.[126] This preliminary ruling is also relevant for other types of procedures provided for in the EC Treaty.[127] The ECJ may be called upon to interpret an international agreement in actions for annulment,[128] actions for failure to act, enforcement actions against Member States,[129] cases introduced on the basis of Article 241 EC, or applications for an opinion on the compatibility of an international agreement with the provisions of the EC Treaty according to Article 300(6) EC.[130]

---

[124] Council Decision 1999/436 of 20 May 1999 determining, in conformity with the relevant provisions of the Treaty establishing the European Community and the Treaty on European Union, the legal basis for each of the provisions and decisions which constitute the Schengen *acquis*, OJ 1999 L 176/17.

[125] See *Haegeman* judgment, n. 59.

[126] For a more recent example, see Case C-377/02 *Van Parys* [2005] ECR I-1465.

[127] J. Rideau, 'Les accords internationaux dans la jurisprudence de la Cour de Justice des Communautés européennes', RGDIP (1990), pp. 289–418, p. 343.

[128] Case C-69/89 *Nakajima* [1991] ECR I-2069.

[129] See Case C-475/98 *Commission* v. *Austria* [2002] ECR I-9797.

[130] Opinion 1/03 (New Lugano Convention) [2006] ECR I-1145.

The ECJ shall ensure the uniform interpretation and application of international agreements on the territory of the EU Member States[131] even where such exceptions do exist as mentioned.[132] However, the uniformity sought by the ECJ does not inevitably extend beyond the frontiers of the EU since partner Contracting Parties have no obligation to take into account the interpretation given by the ECJ. This phenomenon has been highlighted in relation to the Free Trade Agreement between the EC and Switzerland of 1972. The ECJ and the Swiss Federal Tribunal had diverging interpretations as to the direct effect of the Agreement.[133] Nevertheless, a recent judgment of the Federal Tribunal seems to indicate an evolution in this field.[134] In any case, a difference in interpretation of the same text, unsatisfactory from the legal as well as from the economic point of view, should be avoided whether it concerns the Free Trade Agreement of 1972 or the Bilateral Agreements I or II.

Subject to the comments made in relation to the Schengen Association Agreement, the ECJ should declare itself competent to interpret the Bilateral Agreements I and II since these are, in the same way as other international agreements, acts of the institutions of the Community. The uniformity of interpretation guaranteed at Community level through Article 234 EC does not extend to Switzerland. For this reason, the Bilateral Agreements I and II should be interpreted homogeneously in their entirety by the relevant authorities. This is particularly important for the FMP Agreement as well as for the Schengen and Dublin Association Agreements in which the Contracting Parties are convinced of the need to ensure as uniform an interpretation and application of the *'acquis'* provisions as possible.[135] The Joint Committees are continuously examining the evolution of the case law of the ECJ as well as that of the Swiss courts.

---

[131] Case C-104/81 *Kupferberg* [1982] ECR I-3641; Case C-61/94 *Commission* v. *Germany* [1996] ECR I-4012, para. 16.

[132] See our comments on the *Dior* judgment, n. 118.

[133] See the judgment of the Swiss Federal Tribunal, ATF 105 II 49 *Bosshard* v. *Sunlight (Omo)* of 25 January 1979 and the *Austrian Case Austro-Mechana* of 10 July 1979. On the case law of the Federal Tribunal in relation to the Free Trade Agreement, see Jacot-Guillarmod, *Le juge national*, pp. 128–40.

[134] Case 1 A. 71/2004 of 8 March 2005 rendered in the field of the protection of environment, in which the Federal Tribunal applied the Free Trade Agreement between Switzerland and the Community without making any reference to its contrary previous case law.

[135] See Article 8 Schengen Association Agreement and Article 5 Dublin Association Agreement.

The solution in these two Association Agreements is not identical to that provided for in the FMP Agreement, which makes reference in Article 16(2) to the need to take into account the relevant case law of the ECJ prior to the signature of the Agreement. This obligation has not been extended to the case law of the ECJ after the date of signature, since it would have meant that Switzerland should submit to 'foreign judges'. However, it is interesting to note that the Swiss Federal Tribunal did not hesitate to take inspiration from judgments of the ECJ issued after the signing date which confirm or specify prior case law.[136]

It appears that the three Agreements follow the same objective of taking into account the case law of the ECJ but by means of different approaches. Under the 1999 Agreement, case law prior to the signing date of the Agreement is taken into account and new case law is transmitted to Switzerland by the Joint Committee which determines its implications. Under the 2004 Agreements there is an exchange of the case law, an annual report is provided and any dispute about the Agreements' application is resolved within the framework of the Joint Committee. Furthermore, the Association Agreements enable Switzerland to submit statements or written observations to the ECJ in cases where a court in a Member State has referred questions to the ECJ for preliminary rulings on the interpretation of the provisions referred to in Article 2 of the Agreement.[137] This right of Switzerland to intervene followed an amendment of the ECJ Statute (Art. 23), which became effective in 2002.[138]

The other Bilateral Agreements II do not expressly mention the objective of homogeneity. However, we would strongly plead in favour of uniformity of interpretation and application of these Agreements founded on the principle of 'equivalence of legislation'. In fact, if a provision of an international agreement has a substantially equivalent content to a provision of EC law and if the objective of the agreement is identical or

---

[136] See, for example, ATF 130 II 1, ATF 130 II 113 and recently the judgment 2 I.753/2004 of 29 April 2005. However, a limit has been fixed in relation to the definition of Union citizenship, see ATF 130 II 113(6). For a detailed analysis of these questions, see C. Kaddous and C. Tobler, 'Chronique droit européen: Suisse–Union européenne', RSDIE (2005), pp. 611–40; see also F. Filliez and H. Mock, 'La Suisse et l'Union européenne: état des lieux d'une relation sui generis', Journal des Tribunaux. Droit européen (2006), pp. 161–8.

[137] Article 8(2) Schengen Association Agreement and Article 5(2) Dublin Association Agreement. These provisions are similar to those of the Norway and Iceland Agreements.

[138] Council Decision 2002/653 of 12 July 2002 amending the Protocol under the Statute of the Court of Justice of the European Communities, OJ 2002 L 218/1.

similar to that of the EC Treaty, the first provision should in principle receive the same interpretation as the second, otherwise the *effet utile* of the provision would not be ensured.[139]

It should be noted that the solutions negotiated between the Contracting Parties are not legally satisfactory insofar as they only contribute to avoiding differences of interpretation and application without guaranteeing 'full' homogeneity. They present the significant advantage of respecting the independence of the administrative and judicial authorities of the Contracting Parties. The future and proper functioning of these agreements will depend on the decision of the Swiss political authorities to accept or reject the future *acquis* in the framework of Schengen and Dublin as well as on the position of the administrative and judicial authorities that will be interpreting the provisions of the Bilateral Agreements II.

Direct effect of the Agreements

The doctrine of direct effect (or direct applicability) in EC law has been set down by the ECJ in the *Van Gend en Loos* judgment of 1963.[140] Direct effect can be defined as a characteristic of a Community rule which confers the capacity to create rights and obligations upon individuals.

The question of direct effect is of great importance because if an agreement is interpreted as only creating rights and obligations between the Contracting Parties, its effectiveness is obviously more limited than if it were to create rights and obligations that individuals could enforce before their national authorities.

According to settled case law, the ECJ considers that a provision of an international agreement must be regarded as having direct effect when, 'regard being had to its wording and the purpose and nature of the agreement itself, the provision contains a clear and precise obligation which is not subject, in its implementation or effects, to the adoption of any subsequent measure'.[141] These principles are applicable to the Bilateral Agreements, since they do not specify the effect of their provisions in the legal orders of the Contracting Parties. This question is resolved on the EC side, by the competent jurisdiction, in particular by the ECJ and by the national courts

---

[139] See our comments on the identical or divergent interpretation of EC Community Law and international agreements in Kaddous and Felder, *Accords bilatéraux*, pp. 103 *et seq.*

[140] Case 26/62 *Van Gend en Loos* [1963] ECR 6.

[141] Case C-12/86 *Demirel* [1987] ECR 3719, para. 14.

which are responsible, under Article 10 EC, to ensure the legal protection that persons derive from the direct effect of EC provisions law.[142] This means that the administrative and judicial authorities will be bound to recognise the direct effect of certain provisions of the Bilateral Agreements. For example, as far as Schengen is concerned, direct effect can be recognised as regards: Article 2(1) (no checks of persons at the internal borders); Article 40(3)(e) (prohibition of entry into private homes and places not accessible to the public), or Article 51 (judicial assistance in criminal matters) of the Convention implementing the Schengen Agreement.[143] The same holds true for Article 5 (1)(2) (transmission of information and evidence) or Article 30(3) (presence of the authorities of the requesting Contracting Party and the use of transmitted information as evidence) the Agreement on the Fight against Fraud.

In a parallel and independent manner, the question of direct effect will have to be resolved by the Swiss administrative and judicial authorities that will have to interpret and apply the provisions of the Bilateral Agreements. As far as the Schengen and Dublin *acquis* are concerned, the most important direct applicable provisions should be properly published in Switzerland.[144]

Cases pending before the ECJ/CFI

To date, the ECJ has once ruled on Bilateral Agreement between the EU and Switzerland. However, another case is pending which concerns a dispute with Germany in relation to Zurich Airport (Agreement on Air Transport).[145] The case ruled by the CFI concerned the wine produced in the Swiss Commune de Champagne (Agreement on Agriculture).[146] In its order, the CFI declared inadmissible the action whereby a number of natural and legal persons sought annulment of the Council decision approving the international agreement between the European Community and the Swiss

---

[142] Case 33/76 *Rewe* [1976] ECR 1989, para. 5; Case C-213/89 *Factortame* [1990] ECR I-2433, para. 19.

[143] One must notice the particular situation of the character of the Schengen Association Agreement which falls under the third pillar of the EU Treaty as an application of Article 34 (2) EU. There is an exclusion of direct effect for decisions and framework decisions in the EU legal order. On this question, see Case C-105/03 *Pupino* [2005] ECR I-5285. The annex in Schengen does not give any details in this regard. The question arises whether the Swiss Federal Tribunal will interpret the effects of these decisions and framework decisions in accordance with the case law of the ECJ.

[144] Message of the Federal Council of 1st October 2004, FJ 2004, 5923; see also the Federal Statute of 18 June 2004 on the Federal Law Collections and Federal Journal ('Feuille fédérale'), SC 170.512.

[145] Case T-319/05 (originally C-70/04) *Swiss Confederation* v. *Commission*, pending.

[146] Case T-212/02 *Commune de Champagne* v. *Council and Commission* [2007] nyr.

Confederation on trade in agricultural products. The CFI emphasised that a unilateral Act of the Community cannot create rights and obligations outside the Community territory defined in Article 299 EC. Only the international agreement, which is not amenable to appeal, is capable of producing legal effects on Swiss territory, in accordance with the specific rules of that State and once it has been ratified according to the procedures applicable in that State, Thus, the contested decision had no legal effect on Swiss territory and was therefore not capable of altering the legal position of the applicants on that territory. A third case concerned the FMP Agreement, but this reference for a preliminary ruling was removed from the register in August 2006.[147] In this last case a national court had submitted questions on the interpretation of Article 9(1) of Annex I of the FMP Agreement and whether the periods of employment in Switzerland before the entry into force of the FMP Agreement should be taken into account when calculating the remuneration of contractual public servants working in Austria at the time. Many employees from Tirol worked in the health sector in Switzerland before 1 June 2002, the date of entry into force of the Agreement. These periods had not been taken into account for the purposes of calculating their remuneration. The ECJ would have had to take position on its own jurisdiction to interpret the FMP Agreement, on the possible direct effect of one of the Agreement's provisions as well as on the scope of these provisions. The Advocate General, who had already given his opinion before the case was withdrawn, pleaded in favour of the ECJ's jurisdiction, of the direct effect of Article 9(1) of Annex I and of an interpretation of the relevant provision in a manner identical to that given in relation to Article 39 EC.[148]

9.4 A comparison between the Bilateral Agreements and the EEA Agreement

In this part of the study we will compare the Bilateral Agreements with the EEA in order to specify the differences and similarities of the two systems, the first being founded on a 'bilateral' relation, whereas the second is based on 'multilateral' cooperation with the EU.

---

[147] Case C-339/05 *Zentralbetriebsrat der Landeskrankhäuser Tirols* v. *Land Tirol*, removed by Order of 4 August 2006, OJ 2006 C 294/35. The opinion of Advocate General Damaso was delivered on 6 June 2006.

[148] See the Opinion, previous note, paras. 35 *et seq.*

9.4.1 Aims and contents

After 1992, the Bilateral Agreements were seen as a substitute for the EEA Agreement. With the sector by sector approach covering some 20 important fields,[149] they constitute an original and unique form of 'cooperation/integration' in the EU's external relations'. Three areas are not covered in the EEA Agreement, i.e. Fight against Fraud, Schengen/Dublin cooperation and Taxation of Savings.

However, membership of the EEA would mean larger participation in the EC Internal Market as well as in certain flanking areas, which are necessary for the proper functioning of a homogeneous area. The EEA Agreement includes free movement of services (not limited as in the FMP Agreement to 90 days per calendar year) covering, in particular, financial services and telecommunications, free movement of capital as well as rules on competition, State aid and company law.

In the Bilateral Agreements, competition rules are not included, with the exception of the Agreement on Air Transport, for which the European Commission and the ECJ have jurisdiction to ensure its correct interpretation and application.

Furthermore, the EEA Agreement contains rules in the fields of consumer protection, environment, intellectual property, social policy, economic and social cohesion, which are absent in the Bilateral Agreements. Another difference between the Bilateral Agreements and the EEA Agreement, mentioned before, is the 'Cassis de Dijon' principle, which is part of the EEA and which Switzerland intends to introduce unilaterally.[150]

9.4.2 Institutional framework

Unlike the EEA Agreement, the institutional framework of the Bilateral Agreements is limited and creates no new institutions. There is no judicial body or tribunal to supervise the correct application and uniform interpretation of the agreements. Cooperation in principle is made through Joint Committees, in charge of the administration and surveillance of the application of the agreements, with decisions taken by consensus. The mechanism is therefore much 'lighter' than that provided for in the EEA, which is based on a two-pillar structure with EEA–EFTA institutions

---

[149] See n. 1.   [150] See n. 36 and 37.

matching those on the EU side, including the EFTA Court and EFTA Surveillance Authority.[151]

9.4.3 Application of EC law, development of the law and reference to ECJ case law

Unlike the EEA Agreement, the Bilateral Agreements have no dynamic character. Only the '*acquis communautaire*' prior to the signature of the Agreements and to which reference is made, is applied in the relations between the Contracting Parties.[152] This means that a change in EU legislation does not automatically bring about a change in the Bilateral Agreements. However, the principle of 'equivalence of legislation' acts here as an incentive to the parallel evolution of the two legal orders. In that respect, Switzerland preserved its legislative autonomy and its sovereignty better than it would have been able to in the EEA Agreement. With an evolving character in which the common rules are continuously updated, the EEA is founded on the principle of the 'acceptance of the *acquis*' and aims to create a homogeneous area. The EFTA States have a 'quasi-obligation' to accept the future development of the *acquis* relevant to the EEA. They may refuse a new act but such a refusal must be collective and may entail the suspension of the Agreement in the absence of a contrary decision by the EEA Joint Committee. This is because the EFTA States speak with one voice, which may be something of a handicap if the interests are heterogeneous and thus limits the possibility for an EFTA State to assert its specific interests.

The objective of 'equivalence of legislation' in the Bilateral Agreements and of 'homogeneity' in the EEA Agreement (and the 1999 Air Transport Agreement) is of the utmost importance for the proper functioning of these agreements. Therefore, the reference to the case law of the ECJ is central. However, as explained earlier, the degree of the obligation 'of taking into account' varies from one agreement to another. In the FMP Agreement, account shall be taken of the case law issued prior to the signature of the Agreement. In the EEA Agreement, the same rule is set out in Article 6 but

---

[151] For further details on the EFTA Surveillance Authority and the EFTA Court, see S. Norberg, 'The EEA Surveillance System', in Jacot-Guillarmod, *Accords EEE*, pp. 589–602; L. Sevon and M. Johansson, 'The Protection of the Rights of Individuals Under the EEA Agreement', 24 ELRev. (1999), pp. 373–86.

[152] Exception of the Schengen/Dublin Association Agreements.

solutions have been negotiated since Opinion 1/91,[153] to secure the uniform interpretation and application of the EEA also in respect to the case law dating from *after* the entry into force of the Agreement.[154]

9.4.4 Participation in the EU legislative process

Taking into account the sectoral character of the Bilateral Agreements and the fact that they do not constitute an acceptance of the *acquis communautaire*, with the exception of the Agreement on Air Transport and to a certain extent the Schengen/Dublin Agreements,[155] Switzerland is not in a position to participate in *all* the EC Committees participating in the administration and the development of the *acquis*. However, it has obtained the right for its representatives to participate as active observers in the meetings of important committees in the fields of research, air transport, social security, recognition of diplomas[156] and Schengen and Dublin.[157] In all of these cases, Swiss representatives have a right to take the floor but not to vote.

In the EEA Agreement, the EFTA States are associated in the Community legislative process in the fields covered by the Agreement but at different levels of participation depending on the type of the EC Committee involved. The EC was keen, in the EEA Agreement, to safeguard its autonomy of decision.[158] The EFTA States have the opportunity to influence the shaping of EEA-relevant legislation, i.e. EC legislative proposals in the preparatory stage. This is enshrined in the EEA Agreement as a right for representatives of the EFTA States to participate in experts groups of the European Commission and to submit comments on upcoming legislation.[159] While the EFTA States use these opportunities to actively shape legislation, they have little influence on the final decision on

---

[153] Opinion 1/91 (EEA Agreement) [1991] ECR I-6079.

[154] Article 3(2) of the Agreement between the EFTA States on the establishment of a surveillance Authority and a Court of Justice, OJ 1994 L 344/3.

[155] See the contribution of S. Gutzwiller, *Komitologie und Gemischte Ausschüsse im Rahmen der Assoziierung der Schweiz an Schengen/Dublin*, n. 98.

[156] Council Declaration annexed to the Final Act of signature of the Agreements of 1999.

[157] Article 6 Schengen Association Agreement and Article 2 Dublin Association Agreement.

[158] For further comments on the institutional system of the EEA, see D. Felder, 'Structure institutionnelle et procédure décisionnelle de l'EEE', in Jacot-Guillarmod (ed.), *Accord EEE*, pp. 571–87; A. Toledano Laredo, 'The EEA Agreement: an overall view', 29 CMLRev. (1992), pp. 1199–213.

[159] Articles 100 and 101 EEA.

the EU side. They may neither sit nor vote in the European Parliament or at the Council level.

Generally speaking, one may consider the consultation and information process which has been set up for the EFTA countries to be 'better' than that provided for in the Bilateral Agreements because it allows participation in the EU legislative process in a larger number of fields. However, it must be observed that the 'decision-shaping' in the EEA Agreement is more limited than that in the Schengen and Dublin Agreements at the stage of a proposal of the Community's legislative. No more than an information and consultation process within the Joint Committee is provided for in the EEA Agreement (Art. 99(3)), whereas in the other Agreements Switzerland is associated in the discussions with the members of the Council of the European Union (Arts 3 to 6 Schengen Agreement).[160]

In any case, the EFTA States as well as Switzerland do not benefit from the same rights as the EU Member States in the legislative process simply because 'co-decision' only occurs in the hypothesis of accession to the EU.

9.5 Conclusion

As it appears from this study, the relations between the EU and Switzerland are of great complexity because of the identity and specificity of this country located in the middle of Europe. Despite the fact that it shares with the EU values such as freedom, democracy and a social market economy, it chooses to develop its European policy on the basis of cooperation characterised by a pragmatic approach.

After the rejection of the EEA Agreement by the Swiss population, the Federal Council has pursued its relations with the EU through bilateral agreements. It has suspended but not withdrawn its application for full membership of the EU. The 1999 Bilateral Agreements were a solution in order to bridge the gap between the European and the Swiss markets. The second series of Agreements concluded in 2004 went beyond the purely economic aspect of Swiss–EU relations and covered fields like asylum, environment, statistics and culture. Globally, the Bilateral Agreements constitute a helpful intermediate or transitional step for a country like Switzerland, which for different reasons of democratic and institutional

---

[160] T. Blanchet, 'Le succès silencieux de dix ans d'espace économique européen: un modèle pour l'avenir avec d'autres voisins?', in Johansson, Wahl and Bernitz (eds.), *Liber Amicorum*.

structures is not yet ready or willing to embark on the path of European integration with the EU Member States.

However, the question remains whether this network of bilateral agreements is adequate to respond to the needs created by growing relations with an enlarged and increasingly integrated EU. The EEA Agreement does not appear to be attractive enough to be considered as a better solution than the 'step-by-step' approach of pursuing Swiss European policy, despite the fact that it is considered a success by the EEA EFTA members. At the same time, for the Swiss Government, accession is a long-term option alongside others such as the creation of a customs union, the improvement of the existing institutional framework, the creation of a bilateral association, the option of the EEA as a form of multilateral cooperation or even the scenario of a differentiated integration.[161] For the Federal Council, the purpose of Swiss foreign policy is to defend the national interests, whether they are specific (maintenance of independence and security, prosperity, defence of economic interests abroad, etc.) or whether they pursue more general objectives (promotion of international law and human rights, the peaceful coexistence of peoples, etc.). As far as Switzerland's European policy is concerned, its objectives can to a great extent be achieved in the present circumstances through the existing agreements, their adaptation and continuous extension to meet new requirements, as well as by following 'autonomous policies' that do not prejudice future decisions.[162] In the opinion of the Swiss Government, the bilateral route should be continued as long as certain conditions are met. That is to say the possibility for Switzerland to participate to a certain extent in EU decision-making, the readiness of the EU to find solutions with Switzerland on the basis of bilateral agreements in various sectors and, finally, an economic context that does not appear unfavourable from the Swiss point of view, particularly with regard to monetary matters. As a matter of fact, it is obvious that Switzerland is not able to influence all of these conditions. Furthermore, one might assert that if these conditions were to change, and one can already see some changes on the EU side, Switzerland would be led to adapt its instruments of European policy.

---

[161] See the *Europe 2006 Report* of the Swiss Government of 28 June 2006, FJ 2006 6461, Chapter 2.
[162] On the principle of 'autonomous adaptation' of Swiss legislation to European Standards, see n. 17.

Whatever possible future scenarios, the short-to-medium term priorities of Switzerland are the effective implementation of the existing Bilateral Agreements (and the ratification of the pending agreement on Fight against Fraud) as well as the adaptation or renewal of existing ones, the development of contractual relations in areas where this seems appropriate and possible (for example Galileo, electricity, public health) and the contribution of the country to the reduction of economic and social inequality in Europe. It is quite difficult to determine the priorities of the EU with regard to Switzerland. For the moment, both sides are busy studying the ways to improve the institutional structure of the Bilateral Agreements in order to counter their main disadvantages such as their complexity, the existence of so many different Joint Committees in parallel (almost a Joint Committee per Agreement) bringing the risk of a not always efficient and coherent approach, and last but not least the static character of the Agreements in contrast to the EU legislation in constant evolution. Such a common project would certainly contribute to a better equilibrium and would facilitate the proper functioning of the Agreements. It would at the same time 'restructure' the relations between the EU and Switzerland for the benefit of both Parties.

10

The relations between the EU and Andorra, San Marino and Monaco

MARC MARESCEAU

10.1 Introduction

Writing on the relations between the EU and Andorra, San Marino and Monaco is not an easy exercise.[1] Various aspects make these relationships very complex. An important one has to do with history, whether or not in combination with geography. It is simply impossible to examine the relationships between the EU and, for example, Andorra, without explaining why Andorra is where it is and how it comes that this piece of land in the heart of the Pyrenees is neither France nor Spain and not part of the EU. But entering into the unique and often fascinating history of micro-States in a contribution like this is an almost impossible venture. Constraints of various natures impose all kinds of limitations and the reality is such that only a very fragmented picture of the relevant historical facts can be provided. Nevertheless, the very short historical background to each of the three micro-States should help to elucidate their specificity in their present relations with the EU.

One of the characteristics common to all of the European micro-States is the very special relationship with their immediate neighbour or neighbours; this very often also explains why their neighbours did not absorb them. But this common feature is at the same time the characteristic which makes

The author had the opportunity to discuss with H.E. the Ambassador of Andorra, Mrs Carme Sala; H.E. the Ambassador of San Marino, Mr Gian Nicola Fillipi Balestra; and H.E. the Ambassador of Monaco, Mr Jean Pastorelli, various aspects covered in this paper. He would like to express his gratitude for these very useful discussions. All views and opinions expressed in the paper are the responsibility of the author alone.

[1] A first attempt was 'Les micro-états européens et l'Union européenne: une relation de proximité sous tension?', in *Les dynamiques du droit européen en début du siècle. Etudes en l'honneur de Jean-Claude Gautron* (Paris: Pédone, 2004), pp. 751–75. The present contribution is a more elaborated and updated study.

it very difficult to make generalisations. While it seems to a large extent correct to say that 'the level of independence of a micro-State depends on the will of the larger neighbouring State',[2] it is also a fact that the history of each micro-State is quite different and very closely intertwined with the political, economic and legal background of the region in which it is located. Consequently, the overall picture of each of the micro-States' relationships with the EU is a diversified one. Each has gradually developed its own bilateral framework with the EU, sometimes at the initiative of the EU, sometimes at its own initiative. There seems to have been little or no concertation among the micro-States themselves on their possible relations with the EU, except perhaps regarding some developments related to the Treaty establishing a Constitution for Europe. But a lack of concerted action by Andorra, San Marino and Monaco (and also Liechtenstein) in developing their own relations with the EU does not prevent these countries from having formal or/and informal contacts with each other, for example, through their official representations accredited to the EU in Brussels.

The EU too, for its part, has never had a well-defined global policy approach towards these small grey spots which have remained outside the enlarged EU. The EU has other priorities, and most of its initiatives towards micro-States have been developed on a purely ad hoc basis. This is, of course, in the light of what has just been mentioned, perfectly understandable. However, one important exception to this state of affairs is the EU initiative in the field of taxation of savings income which will be examined in more detail later in this contribution. All micro-States, in one way or another, are known for their low level of taxation and/or accommodating fiscal laws. For the first time in the history of the external relations of the EU, the micro-States were subjected equally to a well-conceived EU political strategy in this respect.

This contribution first examines each of the three European micro-States' specific relationships with the EU. As was already mentioned, because of their different histories, the individual legal frameworks show a great diversity. Therefore, the analysis of the relationships of each micro-State with the EU starts with a short introduction to the historical and political background of the micro-State in question in which the relations

---

[2] See J. Duursma, *Fragmentation and the International Relations of Micro-States. Self-determination and Statehood* (Cambridge: Cambridge University Press, 1996), p. 433.

with the neighbouring State or States, in all cases EU Member States, occupy a prominent place. Not all legal instruments governing the relations between the EU and the micro-States are included in this part. Sections 10.3 and 10.4 deal with a number of important bilateral agreements with the micro-States or other initiatives, involving the EU and/or its Member States and affecting the micro-States. Section 10.3 concerns, more specifically, the monetary dimension of the relationships and the various initiatives taken in this respect, while in Section 10.4 the position of the micro-States in the EU's fiscal policy is briefly examined. However, the separation between the different parts in this contribution should not be taken too strictly. The 'micro-States' specificity' remains very much a determining factor for what is covered in all the different parts, but in Section 10.3 and Section 10.4 the focus is more on global EU policies. For example, when the EU approached Andorra for the conclusion of an agreement on taxation of savings income, Andorra insisted on a 'package'-strategy allowing also for negotiations on other subjects of interest for the Principality. In other words, negotiation and acceptance of certain specific arrangements falling under the global EU approach, including also their timing, are not always disconnected from other initiatives.

10.2 The micro-States' specificity as a determining factor in their relations with the EU

Among the European micro-States, one in particular occupies a substantially different position to the others. While the three micro-States examined in this contribution have gradually developed or are developing their own bilateral relations with the EU, Liechtenstein, for its part, is a participant in the European Free Trade Association (EFTA) framework and is the only micro-State which is a full member of the European Economic Area (EEA). Certainly, this does not necessarily exclude the conclusion of specific bilateral arrangements, but on the whole the picture of Liechtenstein's relations with the EU is considerably different from that of the other micro-States. This, together with reasons related to available space in this volume, explains why the relations with Liechtenstein are not included in this contribution. They form part of a separate study which will be published elsewhere. The relations between Andorra and San Marino and the EU probably have the most in common but nevertheless vary in various important aspects. Monaco, because of its extremely small size and above all because of its very close relationship to France, is in itself a special case in the peculiar world of micro-States.

10.2.1 Andorra

Background

The principality of Andorra with a territory of 468 km^2 is no doubt the giant of the European micro-States. In terms of geographical extent, it is more than 200 times the size of Monaco, and it is greater than Malta,[3] which is now an EU Member State.[4] Also, as far as population is concerned, Andorra is the largest European micro-State with more than 70,000 inhabitants[5] but it remains far behind Malta, which has around 400,000 inhabitants.

Andorra's history is particularly complex and goes back well into the Middle Ages. Its existence, as independent territory, finds its origin in the continuous struggle between the Count of Foix (South of France) and the Bishop of Urgell (a city in the North of Catalonia). In 1278 and 1288 arbitrations led to a compromise between the civil and religious powers involved in the dispute and the system of *Pareatges* ('Paréages') was introduced. The *Pareatges* established co-sovereignty by the Bishop and the Count and granted certain rights to the co-sovereigns in a number of areas, including the military and the administration of justice. Andorrans paid tribute – the *quèstia* – to the Count and the Bishop, although the most important thing was that the two powers renounced to conquer or incorporate in their own respective territories, the territory that is now Andorra. It is this arrangement which constitutes, to use the expression of Mateu and Luchaire, Andorra's birth certificate.[6] The fact that there was not a single prince but *two* co-princes is the main explanation for Andorra's unique status in international law. Often through a very subtle play of diplomacy, including sometimes playing off the one against the

---

[3] The surface of Malta is 316 km^2.   [4] Since 1 May 2004.

[5] The majority of the population in Andorra is of Spanish nationality (38 per cent); the Andorrans represent 36 per cent of the inhabitants. Other nationalities are Portuguese (11 per cent), French and others (15 per cent), see *L'Andorre en chiffres 2005*, Ambassade de la Principauté d'Andorre en France, Govern d'Andorra, Ministeri de Finances, Servei d'Estudis, n.d., p. 21.

[6] M. Mateu and F. Luchaire, *La Principauté d'Andorre. Hier et aujourd'hui* (Paris: Economica, 1999), p. 19.

other, Andorra has survived for more than seven centuries.[7] In 1993 Andorra adopted a modern constitution offering all the characteristics of a parliamentary democracy with the application of the rule of law and fundamental rights and freedoms, while preserving a number of its historical specificities. Some basic elements of the *Pareatges* are maintained, the most important being the confirmation that the Co-Princes, that is to say the Bishop of Urgell and the President of the French Republic,[8] are jointly and indivisibly, the *Cap de l'Estat* (Head of State) in their personal and exclusive right (Art. 43). Their powers are identical and they are the symbol and guarantee of the permanence and continuity of Andorra as well as of Andorra's independence. The *Coprínceps* (Co-Princes) sanction and enact the laws and they express the consent of the State to honour its international obligations.[9] The *Consell General* (General Council), composed of directly elected members, represents the Andorran people[10] and the Government is politically responsible to the *Consell General.*

[7] See, for example, M. Mateu and F. Luchaire, previous note, pp. 21–45. It is interesting to note how this 'Andorran specificity' was perceived in the (rare) accounts of Andorra by foreign observers particularly in the nineteenth century. For a curious but interesting account by an American traveller, see B. Taylor, *The Republic of the Pyrenees. Andorra 1867*, re-edited in *L'Andorra dels viatgers. Els Americans, 1*, Ministeri d'Afers Exteriors, Andorra, 2002. For another comment, see 'La République d'Andorre', *L'Illustration européenne*, 1870–1871, pp. 123–4, which notes that Andorra, notwithstanding its very small size, 'a toujours fait preuve [of the necessary energy] pour conserver intacte son indépendance, au milieu des crises nombreuses qu'ont traversées ses puissants voisins, la France et l'Espagne'.

[8] Sometimes political events taking place with Andorra's neighbours, in particular France, affected certain aspects of the implementation of the *Pareatges*. For example, in the seventeenth century the rights of the Count of Foix were transferred to the King of France. After the French Revolution and after a period of great uncertainty, Napoleon re-established the *quèstia* and agreed to restore the former administrative, commercial and police framework. After 1815, King Louis XVIII became Co-Prince of Andorra and later the President of the French Republic assumed the function of Co-Prince. This is still the situation today.

[9] If one of the Co-Princes is impaired to do so, the signature of the other Co-Prince together with the countersignature of the Head of Government, is sufficient (Art. 45(3)). On the specific position of the Co-Princes when Andorra negotiates agreements in areas indicated in Article 64(1) of the Constitution affecting the relations with the neighbouring States, see J.-C. Colliard, 'L'État d'Andorre', *Annuaire français de droit international* (1993), p. 387, who qualifies the power of the Co-Princes, for the category of agreements mentioned, as 'un véritable droit de *véto*'; on the position of the French Co-Prince in general, see also F. de Saint-Sernin, 'Le Président de la République française, coprince d'Andorre', *Revue des deux mondes*, Numéro spécial 'Visages de l'Andorre' (2001), pp. 18–25.

[10] Half of the representatives are elected on the basis of a national single constituency, half are elected by the seven *Parròquies* ('parishes' in the sense of 'municipalities').

Even if Andorra was never occupied by one of its neighbours or 'integrated' into the territory of one of its neighbours, its international legal capacity remained uncertain. For a very long time, the only international instruments worth mentioning in which Andorra was involved were the commercial agreements, concluded in 1867 through an Exchange of Letters with Spain and France.[11] It was only far into the twentieth century that the question of Andorra's international legal status became a highly debated matter. This was particularly the case after 1980, when the calls of the Andorran people for domestic reform and modernisation of the Andorran institutions and political structures also became more and more outspoken.[12] Interestingly enough, this went together with a strong economic development of the Principality,[13] mainly as a result of a rapidly growing tourist sector bringing millions of visitors to Andorra every year.[14] One of the Principality's many attractions for these visitors is its low indirect taxation.

One serious difficulty facing Andorra in its attempt to acquire international legal personality has been the position of the French Government which refuted such personality on the grounds that Andorra was only 'a territory' and not a sovereign State. In 1971, the French Cour de Cassation, while recognising that 'les vallées d'Andorre' did benefit from certain privileges, still stated that they neither constituted a State nor a subject of international law ('les vallées d'Andorre . . . ne constituent ni un Etat, ni une personne de droit international'[15]). Clearly, in this view, it was only the French President, as Co-Prince of Andorra, who could decide whether an international agreement had to be applied in the territory.[16] Consequently, any international activity or representation of Andorra needed to be organised through the French Co-Prince.

---

[11] See P. Raton, *Le statut international de la Principauté d'Andorre*, Andorra, Govern d'Andorra, n.d., 2nd ed., pp. 21–2.

[12] See Mateu and Luchaire, *La Principauté d'Andorre*, n. 6, pp. 58–60.

[13] See A. Pintat, 'L'engagement international de l'Andorre', *Revue des deux mondes*, n. 9, pp. 27–34.

[14] In 2004 Andorra received 11.6 million tourists, see *L'Andorre en chiffres*, n. 5, p. 37.

[15] Judgment of 6 January 1971, *Recueil Dalloz-Sirey*, 1971, p. 338, with annotation by J.-C. Sacotte. Further in the judgment the Cour de Cassation seems to confuse the specific role of the French President as Co-Prince of Andorra with that of the French State.

[16] For a detailed and critical analysis of the classic French position, see N. Marquès, *La reforma de les institucions d'Andorra (1975–1981). Aspectes Interns i Internacionals* (Lleida: Virgili & Pagès, 1989), pp. 252–71.

Gradually, this monolithic interpretation was challenged by leading international law experts.[17] But, perhaps even more importantly, the other Co-Prince, the Bishop of Urgell, was no longer prepared to follow the French interpretation and pleaded more and more openly for the recognition of the Principality's international personality in its own right.[18]

In analysing the bilateral relations between the EU and Andorra, the commercial Agreement of 1990 constitutes a historical point of departure. Its origin, context and contents, as well as its domestic constitutional and international repercussions, are hereunder briefly examined. This is followed by an analysis of the 2004 Cooperation Agreement concluded with the EC. Other agreements or negotiations on agreements with the EC are included in Sections 10.3 and 10.4 of this contribution.

The 1990 Agreement with the EEC

Origin and context   The decisive and international breakthrough of Andorra came in 1990, when it succeeded in signing a bilateral agreement with the EEC, the first bilateral agreement since the 1867 Exchange of Letters with its neighbours. Today, this international legal instrument remains the main but not sole bilateral legal framework with the EC. The establishment of the EEC, of which Andorra's neighbour, France, was a founding member, had already resulted in a number of anomalies with regard to the legal regime of the trade relations between the EEC and Andorra.[19] While these anomalies might still be tolerated as long as France remained the only neighbour of Andorra in the EC, the situation changed dramatically with the prospect of accession of Spain to the EC. Spain was by far Andorra's largest trading partner and the 1867 bilateral Exchange of Letters could no longer continue to govern their bilateral trade relations. In a Joint Declaration on future trade arrangements with Andorra,

---

[17] See, for example, K. Zemanek, *Le statut international d'Andorra. Situation actuelle et perspectives de réforme* (Andorra: Casa de la Vall, 1981), p. 187.

[18] For the position of the Bishop rejecting the monopoly of the French Co-Prince in external matters, see N. Marquès, *La Reforma*, n. 16, pp. 270–1.

[19] An interesting but unpublished PhD thesis on the relations between the EEC and Andorra before the conclusion of the 1990 Agreement, is that of P. Klaoussen, *Les effets de l'intégration communautaire sur le régime juridique des échanges commerciaux de l'Andorre*, Université de Toulouse I, 1989, p. 230. For the author's analysis of these anomalies, see in particular pp. 66–87.

included in one of the Annexes to the Accession Treaty for Spain and Portugal, it was explicitly stipulated that 'an arrangement governing trade relations between the Community and Andorra will be finalised within a period of two years of the date of entry into force of the Act of Accession and will be intended to replace the national arrangements at present in force'. The existing national arrangements were supposed to continue to be applied until the new bilateral arrangement came into force. Needless to say, this Declaration offered on a golden plate a unique opportunity for Andorra to affirm itself internationally. Since a bilateral agreement with the EEC was envisaged, this would mean recognition of Andorra's international legal personality by the EEC. Moreover, indirectly, such a move would undoubtedly substantially contribute to the recognition of Andorra's legal personality worldwide.

Before Spain's signature of the Accession Treaty, the Andorran Government had already taken the initiative in 1982 urging the Co-Princes to support direct exploratory contacts between the Government and the European Community in order to assess the economic consequences of a possible accession of Spain to the EC.[20] In the light of what has been explained above, it is clear that a serious obstacle for any move forward remained the French position on direct bilateral negotiations between Andorra and the EC. But another major hurdle was the question who was to represent Andorra, if such bilateral contacts were to be established. There were no constitutional provisions on the conclusion of agreements and practice was lacking. Fortunately for the Principality, when solutions for these questions became unavoidable, that is to say in the second half of the 1980s and early 1990s, the time had never been so propitious for a resolute step in the direction of the 'andorisation' of the Principality's external relations. Indeed, in France, even if at least initially, the Quai d'Orsay still preferred to continue to defend the traditional French view on the representation of Andorra internationally, it was not a secret that the then French Co-Prince, President Mitterand, was not unsympathetic to the Andorran cause.[21] This had been made clear by the President

---

[20] See Declaration of the Andorran *Cap de Govern* (Head of Government) M. Oscar Ribas, quoted in R. Poy, *El Repte, Records d'un cap de Govern d'Andorra* (Andorra: Fundació Julia Reig, 2001), pp. 57–8.

[21] For a very interesting account and analysis of the history of the 1993 Constitution in relation to the position of the French Co-Prince, see Colliard, 'L'État d'Andorre', n. 9, pp. 367–92, who emphasises that in general the French Co-Princes were more in favour of democratic and

himself on the occasion of the remittance of the *quèstia* in 1989, while the negotiations between Andorra and the EC were pending, when he stated that, as regards the institutional reforms in Andorra, he was open towards any solution which responded to the profound aspirations of the Andorran people domestically as well as internationally. In other words, also for President Mitterand, constitutional and international emancipation seemed to go hand in hand. With regard to the ongoing negotiations with the EC, he expected that the coming agreement would take into account Andorra's legitimate interests and such an agreement would at the same time also facilitate, to use the President's words, 'l'indispensable désenclavement d'Andorre dans l'Europe d'aujourd'hui'.[22]

It is evident that such a strong and unequivocal position by the French Co-Prince constituted an invaluable support for the Andorran delegation negotiating the agreement with the EC. It must also be said that the composition of this delegation had already been a complicated matter in itself and in the end a large delegation composed of representatives of the Government, the Co-Princes, the French Ministry of Foreign Affairs, Andorran officials and ad hoc experts, negotiated this historical agreement. Expectations were very high since the ultimate objective of the negotiations was nothing less than a customs union between Andorra and the EEC. Although the recognition of Andorra's international personality remained a difficult political and legal question, astonishingly, negotiations did not concentrate on this aspect at all. In the formal bilateral negotiations the matter was not even raised and, apparently, a political compromise had been reached on this delicate issue before the real negotiations started. The European Commission, which logically was the negotiator for and on behalf of the Community, preferred to tackle the genuine substantive issues – after all, the main objective of the agreement was to establish a customs

---

constitutional reforms than the Bishop. The democratic dimension of the institutional changes in Andorra constituted an essential element of President Mitterand's favourable disposition towards these changes and in this context Colliard also quotes the President who had noted, at the remittance of the *quèstia* in 1991, that the preparatory works for the constitution incorporated 'des principes aussi fondamentaux que l'instauration d'un Etat de droit démocratique et souverain', p. 385; also comments in R. Poy, *El somni. Records d'un cap de Govern d'Andorra* (Andorra: Fundació Julià Reig, 2004), p. 121–2; on this point see also Mateu and Luchaire, *La Principauté d'Andorre*, n. 6, pp. 64–5. In France, between 1986 and 1988, it was the period of the 'cohabitation'.

[22] See Présidence de la République, 'Allocution prononcée par Monsieur François Mitterand, Président de la République à l'occasion de la remise de la *quèstia* andorrane', Palais de l'Elysée, 17 novembre 1989.

union – and, apparently, it was also the Council's and Commission's idea to conclude the agreement with Andorra through a mere Exchange of Letters, instead of a 'classical' bilateral agreement. The reasons invoked for this procedure were the flexibility of the legal instrument 'Exchange of Letters' together with the specificities of Andorra's legal status. Certainly, Andorra would have preferred a more classic legal format for the Agreement, especially in the light of the importance of its substantive objective, above the not very convincing legal justification of the choice of the legal instrument used by the EC. But even if the agreement was agreed upon via the 'Exchange of Letters' procedure, it would then nevertheless constitute Andorra's biggest international achievement ever in its history. In other words, the Agreement would be a real constitutional and international 'primeur' for the Principality. Finally, in 1989 the Andorran delegation and the European Commission were able to reach agreement on the substance and the Agreement was signed in 1990.[23] The substantive legal bases used by the EC for the conclusion of this agreement were Articles 113 and 99 EEC. The reason that Article 99, on harmonisation of turnover taxes, was also deemed necessary, in addition to the basic Treaty provision on commercial policy, remains somewhat unclear, unless perhaps the arrangements on 'allowances' (see *Contents* below) justified it. An immediate consequence of this choice was that the Agreement required unanimity among the Member States for its conclusion. An interesting side effect of the conclusion of this Agreement on the basis of the unanimity rule within the Council was that *all* the Member States also, even if only indirectly, recognised Andorra's international legal personality.

Contents   The Agreement establishes a customs union between the EC and Andorra covering the Chapters 25 to 97 of the Harmonised System (industrial products). There is free movement of goods covered by these Chapters, provided they are produced in the Community or in the Principality, including those obtained wholly or in part from products coming from third countries and in free circulation in the Community or in Andorra. Free movement of goods applies equally to goods which come

---

[23] For text, see OJ 1990 L 374/14. The Agreement entered into force on 1 July 1991. From the Andorran side the Agreement has three signatures: one for the President of the French Republic as Co-Prince of Andorra, one for the Bishop of Urgell as Co-Prince of Andorra, and one for the Government of Andorra.

from third countries and are in free circulation in the Community or in Andorra (Art. 3). Logically, the free movement principle covers the elimination of certain duties and charges having equivalent effect to customs duties as well as quantitative restrictions and measures having equivalent effect (Art. 9). Andorra had to align its laws to the EC laws on imports of goods from third countries (Art. 7). The first Joint Committee EEC–Andorra established an inventory of Community legal acts to be applied by Andorra.[24] An important consequence of this commitment was that tariff preferences granted by the EC to third countries also have to be applied by Andorra. Processed agricultural products falling within the chapters mentioned above are not subject to duties on the fixed component but to the variable component that continues to apply to products covered by the Chapters 1 to 24 of the Harmonised System (agricultural products). Agricultural products do not come within the scope of the customs union. They are not totally excluded from the Agreement, however, and if they originate in Andorra, are free from import duties on imports in the Community (Art. 11). For imports into Andorra of agricultural products originating in the Community, the Community's CAP refunds apply and Andorra is entitled to levy import duties on such products.[25]

The Agreement contains specific provisions on trade in tobacco. Article 12(2) provides that Andorra grant a preferential tariff of 60 per cent of the normal customs duty applicable to certain tobacco products manufactured in the Community from raw tobacco as compared to imports of the same products from third countries. The origin of this special treatment of certain tobacco from Community origin is to be found in the situation that existed before the signature of the 1990 Agreement when arrangements with the French SEITA and Spanish TABACALERA existed in Andorra, granting preferential tariffs to cigarettes and tobacco manufactured by these two companies.[26]

---

[24] See Decision 2/91, Joint Committee EEC–Andorra, OJ 1991 L 250/24 and later repealed and replaced by Decision 1/2003, Joint Committee EC–Andorra, OJ 2003 L 253/3.

[25] Andorra's import duties are very low, except for tobacco and beverages.

[26] SEITA and TABACALERA were for a very long time national legal monopolies in respectively France and Spain for the production and wholesale distribution of tobacco products. These legal monopolies are now abolished but the arrangements with Andorra on import of tobacco of Community origin which had been made while both companies still enjoyed this status continue to be applicable.

The Agreement further provided that for a period of five years the Community was authorised, acting on behalf of and for Andorra, to put into free circulation goods with destination Andorra and originating in third countries (Art. 8(1)). Since 1 July 1996 this is done by Andorra itself.[27] Not to be underestimated either is the part of the Agreement concerning the allowances ('*les franchises*') for travellers entering the Community from Andorra allowing imports of goods of a strictly non-commercial nature. Generally speaking, the total value of the goods that may be imported free of import duties, turnover tax and excise duties is three times the value granted by the Community to travellers from other third countries. There are, however, quantitative limits on certain products, such as milk products, tobacco, alcohol, coffee, tea and perfume. In addition, the Agreement provides for the application of the principle of non-discrimination in the field of indirect taxation on products (whether included in the customs union or not) of one Contracting Party compared to similar products from the other Contracting Party (Art. 15). Finally, it is worth mentioning that the Agreement contains a Joint Statement regarding the provisions in the Agreement on movement of goods, stipulating that where they are similar to the EEC Treaty, the Contracting Parties' representatives in the Joint Committee 'shall undertake to interpret the former, within the scope of this Agreement, in the same way as the latter are interpreted in trade within the European Economic Community'.

Today, the 1990 Agreement is still in force and is to the satisfaction of both parties. A few minor problems have arisen regarding the application of the rules of origin for goods not covered by the provisions on the customs union (for example, regarding madeleine cakes, bovines, the concept 'sufficient working or transformation'), but on the whole there have been few problems. There is one important exception, however. In the second half of the 1990s the so-called tobacco war broke out between the EC and Andorra. Andorra was accused of being a source of intensive smuggling of cigarettes manufactured under licence in Andorra or manufactured in non-member States of the EU, imported into Andorra, and then exported to the EU, particularly Spain. Large quantities of cigarettes were indeed confiscated, mainly by the Spanish customs authorities but also by customs authorities of some other Member States. According to the EC, the quantities of tobacco imported into or manufactured in Andorra were far exceeding what was

---

[27] Decision 1/96, Joint Committee EC–Andorra, OJ 1996 L 184/79.

necessary for the estimated local consumption and for duty free sales to tourists. In 1997, for example, the EC tax receipt losses as a result of cigarettes smuggling were estimated at 400 million ECU and according to the European Commission, there was 'a lack of appropriate legislative instruments in Andorra to prevent and combat fraud'.[28] One of the interesting legal questions in the dispute was whether the concerned Andorran exports in themselves constituted a violation of the 1990 Agreement. Whatever the legal interpretation of the two Parties, the strong pressure exercised by the EU, and Spain in particular, through very tight controls at the border, led the Andorran Government to take unilateral measures in 1999 in the form of legislation to combat customs fraud and penalise smuggling.[29] Since then, no serious problems with the EU seem to have arisen regarding tobacco exports from Andorra nor indeed in the bilateral trade relations as a whole. However, the Court of Auditors of the EC has criticised the provisions of the 1990 Agreement EEC–Andorra in general, emphasising that the vast majority of goods imported into Andorra were not for consumption in Andorra itself but rather for sale to tourists who in turn were largely reimporting these goods back into the Community. The Court of Auditors, therefore, suggested that 'it might be more appropriate to base the systems in Andorra [and San Marino] on the rules and levels attributable to the actual consumption of goods'. While accepting 'a formula of population ratios taking tourists into account', the Court nevertheless concluded that there appeared 'to be a need for a review of such arrangements [as in the Agreement with Andorra] in the light of the single market'.[30] It thus implied that a renegotiation of the 1990 Agreement would be required. The Commission did not specifically address this suggestion in its reply, but responded in more broad terms that certain arrangements entered into with some micro-States 'have historical and/or political origins'. The Commission '[was] therefore trying to find appropriate means of reconciling the historical and political interests in question and the financial interests of the Community's own resources'. The Commission also emphasised 'that the financial impact of these exceptional situations on the Community is

---

[28] European Commission, *Protection of the financial interest of the Communities. Fight against fraud. Annual Report 1997*, COM(98) 276, p. 19.

[29] See the laws on customs fraud and on control of sensitive goods of 4 March 1999 and on penal sanctioning of smuggling of July 1999.

[30] See Special Report No 2/93 on the customs territory of the Community and related trading arrangements accompanied by replies of the Commission, OJ 1993 C 347/1.

negligible'.[31] The historical, geographical and political specificities together with the negligible economic repercussions on the EU as a whole, are indeed convincing arguments in favour of maintaining a special relationship with Andorra and other European micro-States.

Before entering into some of the constitutional and international implications of the 1990 Agreement, one specific trade aspect was organised in a separate legal instrument and deserves mention here. In 1997, a Protocol with the EC on veterinary matters was signed to supplement the 1990 Agreement.[32] Its main objective is 'to maintain traditional flows of trade in live animals and animal products between Andorra and the European Community'.[33] Basically, Andorra undertakes in this Protocol to apply Community veterinary rules. The list of Community veterinary provisions to be applied is drawn up by the Joint Committee set up by the 1990 Agreement. The Protocol is of prime importance for the agricultural sector, as well as for the application of animal and food safety laws in Andorra and is interesting from a legal point of view. Various Decisions of the EC–Andorra Joint Committee have further implemented Community legislation in these areas.[34] Decision 1/2005 of the Committee is of particular relevance because it deals with the position of Andorra towards the basic Community Regulation 178/2002 laying down the general principles and requirements of food law, establishing the European Food Safety Authority and procedures in matters of food safety.[35] It also lays down the conditions of Andorra's participation in the Community's 'rapid alert system'.[36]

Constitutional and international implications   The 1990 Agreement EEC–Andorra had important consequences domestically as well as externally. It was an important step towards the modernisation of Andorra's institutions and, as already mentioned, in 1993 a modern written constitution was adopted. The 1993 Constitution clearly and unambiguously formulated Andorra's independence and, most importantly, its external legal capacity. On this last aspect, the impact of the conclusion of the 1990 Agreement was simply colossal. While Andorra had been one of the

---

[31] See previous note, p. 27.   [32] OJ 1997 L 148/16.   [33] See Preamble of the Protocol.
[34] See Decision 2/1999, OJ 2000 L 31/84; Decision 1/2001, OJ 2002 L 33/35; Decision 2/2003, OJ 2003 L 269/38.
[35] For text, see OJ 2002 L 31/1, amended by Regulation 1642/2003, OJ 2003 L 245/4.
[36] OJ 2005 L 318/26.

European micro-States with the most uncertain or most fragile external legal personality, the Agreement now implied that it was treated by the EC as a full-fledged third State. With, in the past, one big neighbour claiming to have exclusivity over Andorra's international relations, the conclusion of a bilateral agreement with the EEC meant a dramatic turning point and a fact of immense historical importance for the Principality.[37] After the conclusion of this Agreement, it seems that France no longer insisted on representing Andorra internationally. The conclusion of the 1990 Agreement in combination with the 1993 Constitution were the beginning of a rapidly and universally recognised international presence of Andorra, including inter alia membership of the UN, the Council of Europe, opening of various embassies and representations abroad, among them the opening in Brussels of a mission accredited to the EU. Andorra is an observer in the WTO but not yet a member.[38]

Another very important milestone in the development of Andorra's external relations was the trilateral agreement signed with Spain and France on 1 June in 1993 on good neighbourly relations, friendship and cooperation.[39] This agreement, which ultimately consecrates Andorra's external capacity and is therefore the most important ever signed with its neighbours, has far-reaching effects indeed. First, it takes account of the specific geographic situation of Andorra and its historical traditions and recognises in Article 1 the Principality of Andorra as a sovereign State. In addition, the integrity of the Principality is guaranteed. It is important to note that the trilateral agreement refers to the importance of the 'European context' in which relations among the parties are developed. Moreover, the Parties commit themselves to settling any differences that might arise, taking into consideration the obligations undertaken within the framework of the European Community (Art. 4). Since the signature of this agreement,

---

[37] See also the declaration of the then Head of Government, M. Oscar Ribas, at the moment of ratification of the Agreement, in Poy, *El somni*, p. 108.

[38] Andorra applied for WTO membership in 1997 and there have been several meetings of the Working Party on the Accession of Andorra. Bilateral contacts on market access have taken place and Andorra has made offers in goods and services. The dialogue continues but there seems to be no hurry for a quick decision on accession. Questions have been asked in the meetings of the Working Party on the compatibility of WTO rules with the 1990 Agreement which, as was already mentioned, excludes from the customs union agricultural products, see, e.g. Working Party on the Accession of Andorra, Meeting of 7 August 2000, WT/ACC/AND/8, pp. 59–60.

[39] For text, see *Journal Officiel de la République Française*, 1995, no. 35.

various other bilateral and trilateral agreements have been signed by Andorra with one or both of its neighbours.[40]

The 2004 Cooperation Agreement

The 2004 Cooperation Agreement signed between the EC and Andorra[41] is the result of two phases of negotiations.[42] The first began in 1997 and although negotiations had been smooth, the agreement could not be finalised mainly because of the tobacco war, mentioned above. In 2002, negotiations resumed.[43] This move was not disconnected from complex bilateral negotiations on other matters, in particular on the taxation of savings income (see Section 10.4). The main objective of the 2004 Agreement is to strengthen and deepen the existing bilateral relations. The Agreement, which in no way amends or affects the 1990 Agreement, covers a wide variety of specific areas for cooperation, including environment, communications, information, culture, education, training and youth, social aspects, health, trans-European networks, transport and regional policy. The Agreement contains a non-discrimination clause for workers with Andorran nationality legally resident in an EU Member State and for workers having the nationality of a Member State legally resident in Andorra as regards working conditions, pay and redundancy (Art. 5), but there are no provisions on movement of persons or right of establishment. It is too early to make an assessment of the real impact of the Agreement on the bilateral relations and, so far, few initiatives for concrete implementation have been taken.[44] One of its advantages is that it offers a broad legal basis for cooperation, which, moreover, the parties may extend by mutual consent through the conclusion of agreements on specific matters (Art. 8).

---

[40] See, for example, the trilateral 2000 Convention on entry, movement, stay and establishment of nationals of the Contracting Parties; for text, see *Journal Officiel de la République Française*, 6 August 2003, no. 180.

[41] For text, see OJ 2005 L 138/23. The Agreement entered into force in 2005.

[42] See M. Maresceau, 'Informe sobre el projecte d'Acord de cooperació entre la Comunitat Europea i Andorra', in *Els acords polítics amb Europa 2001–2005* (Andorra: Govern d'Andorra, Ministeri d'Afers Exteriors, 2005), pp. 47–51.

[43] For an overview of the negotiations in both phases, see V. Pou i Serradell, *Els nous acords Andorra – Unió Europea* (Andorra: Crèdit Andorrà, 2006), pp. 98–105.

[44] The first meeting of the Cooperation Committees, set up by the Agreement, took place on 25 November 2005.

From an EC law point of view, the 2004 Cooperation Agreement is of a non-mixed character and this may seem astonishing at first sight in the light of the social provisions which it contains and which previously implied the need for the co-signature of the EU Member States. Although there is no formal explanation provided by the EU why the Agreement is not also signed by the EU Member States, it is probably because Article 137 EC, as amended by the Nice Treaty, allows the Community to support and complement the activities of the Member States in the field of social policy, including 'conditions of employment for third country nationals legally residing in Community territory'. The Cooperation Agreement is based on multiple legal sources, of which the Council Decision of 10 May 2005 on the conclusion of the Agreement mentions no less than ten substantive provisions of the EC Treaty. The Commission had also suggested that the Agreement be based on Article 300(2)(1) EC and Article 300(3)(2) EC as procedural sources, which meant that the European Parliament was supposed to give its opinion. However, Parliament modified the proposed legal bases and replaced those proposed by the Commission by Article 310 EC, which is the EC Treaty provision on 'association'. Parliament invoked the far-reaching competences of the cooperation committee which had been set up by the Agreement and, as such, in the view of the Parliament, should be seen as 'a specific institutional framework' requiring the *assent* of the Parliament in accordance with Article 300(3) EC. Parliament's approach, however, appeared to be somewhat overdone. For the sole sake of guaranteeing its own prerogatives and in a unilateral gesture, the imposition by Parliament of Article 310 EC as a legal basis for a cooperation agreement, albeit a broad one, seemed neither appropriate nor desirable given that at various levels in Andorra itself, it had been a matter of discussion whether the Principality should seek associate status with the EC or not, but this had not been settled and nor was this decision linked with this particular cooperation agreement.[45] Certainly, the Cooperation Agreement is not necessarily an end in itself and broader and deeper cooperation and perhaps association or another form of close relationship are not to be excluded in the future. But before such a step

---

[45] Although it must be said that a similar practice has occurred in some other instances, for example, regarding the *Bilaterals I* with Switzerland (see contribution by C. Kaddous in this volume), which were also based on Article 310 EC, while the agreements, individually or as a whole, were not association agreements and while the issue of possible 'association' of Switzerland with the EC had never been part of any bilateral discussion between Switzerland and the EC.

could seriously be contemplated by Andorra, a broad political debate and large political consensus on the relationship with the EU as a whole and, in particular, on the place of Andorra in Europe, would appear indispensable.

10.2.2 San Marino

Background

The Republic of San Marino, with a territory of 61 km^2 and approximately 30,000 inhabitants, located in the North of Central Italy, is probably one of the oldest independent European republics. The fourth century, when Marino – later San Marino – founded a Christian community in what is now San Marino, is often mentioned as the beginning of the history of San Marino. Whether this is legend or reality will not be answered here, but it can be said that it has indeed been something of a miracle that San Marino has remained standing throughout its history as an independent State[46] while the mighty and less mighty city-States and republics in its neighbourhood disappeared as independent entities one after the other. San Marino even survived the process of unification of Italy.[47] Today, San Marino is a sovereign State but it has no formal written constitution. The Republic has a unique institutional structure and since 1974 a 'modern' Declaration of the citizens' rights and fundamental principles on the organisation of the Republic has been applicable.[48] This Declaration also

---

[46] On the history of the Republic and how it survived the big and small turbulences around it, see inter alia, A. Garosci, *San Marino. Mito e storiografia tra i libertini e il Carducci* (Milano: Edizioni di Comunità, 1967), p. 387. An old but still readable work on the general history of San Marino is that by H. Hauttecoeur, *La République de San Marino* (Brussels: Havermans, 1894), see in particular the pages on 'the conquest' of the Republic by Cardinal Cesare Borgia, the son of Pope Alexander VI, in the beginning of the sixteenth century (pp. 95–102) and on Cardinal Alberoni's occupation of San Marino in 1739–1740, which lasted a few months (pp. 135–54). Both occupations were particularly dangerous episodes for San Marino's existence as an independent State.

[47] In the period of the *Risorgimento*, Garibaldi, who in 1849 had found refuge in San Marino when in great difficulty against the Austrians, later, when he successfully united Italy, left San Marino untouched as an independent State, see P. Franciosi, 'Garibaldi e la Repubblica di San Marino', in *Scritti Garibaldini* (San Marino: Biblioteca di San Marino, 1982), pp. 85–146.

[48] Just to give an illustration, the Head of State is double-headed with two *Capitani Reggenti*, appointed by the *Consiglio Grande e Generale* (Great General Council) which is composed of members elected by general suffrage, who take their decisions based on collegiality, see Article 3 of the 'Dichiarazione dei diritti dei cittadini e dei principi fondamentali dell'ordinamento sanmarinese'. On the constitutional system, see G. Guidi (ed.), *Piccolo Stato, costituzione e connessioni internazionali. Atti del convegno dell'Associazione di diritto pubblico comparato ed europeo. San Marino. Collegio Santa Chiara, 21–22 giugno 2002* (Turin: Giappichelli, 2003), pp. 121–75. The text of the 1974 Dichiarazione (with amendments) is reproduced at pp. 299–303.

stipulates that 'constitutional laws' ('*leggi costituzionali*') can be enacted (Art. 3 bis). The international legal personality of San Marino is well-established and unchallenged. San Marino has developed a wide range of official bilateral relations with third countries and is also a member of many international organisations, such as the Council of Europe since 1988 and the UN since 1992. San Marino is not a member of WTO. Probably, the size of its territory, its fully enclaved status, its participation in a customs union first with Italy and later with the EC, make WTO membership if not superfluous, at least burdensome, while the practical effects of such membership for the Republic remain negligible. San Marino already had a diplomatic mission accredited to the EC in 1983 and has the longest European diplomatic practice in Brussels of the four European micro-States.

An important point of reference, from the point of view of this contribution, is the 1939 Agreement between San Marino and Italy on friendship and good neighbourly relations.[49] As a result of this Agreement, San Marino became part of the Italian customs territory. The Italian authorities collected the duties on imports of goods destined for consumption in San Marino and on an annual basis sent a flat-rate compensatory amount to the authorities in San Marino. The 1939 Agreement remained applicable after the fall of Mussolini. After the entry into force of the EEC Treaty it came within the scope of the then Article 234 EEC (now Art. 307 EC),[50] which stipulates that the rights and obligations arising from agreements concluded *before* the entry into force of the EEC Treaty between one or more Member States on the one hand, and one or more third countries on the other hand, are not affected by the provisions of the EEC Treaty.

The 1991 Agreement on Cooperation and Customs Union   The customs regime resulting from the 1939 Agreement lasted until 1 December 1992, the date of entry into force of the Interim Agreement on trade and

---

[49] In the period between the two World Wars, San Marino, while remaining an independent State, had also adopted fascism. It was with the fascist government of San Marino that the Italy of Mussolini concluded the 1939 Agreement. Mussolini, during his reign, left San Marino untouched. On San Marino's fascist period, see P. Sabbatucci Severini, 'Un microstato e il suo tutore: San Marino e l'Italia. 1861–1960', in *Il piccolo Stato. Politica storia diplomazia. Atti del convegno di studi. 11–13 ottobre 2001* (San Marino: AIEP, 2004), pp. 261–9.

[50] Since San Marino is not a Member State of the EU, the duties levied by Italy on imports with destination San Marino cannot be considered as Community own resources. A complex legal dispute has arisen on the status of the customs duties collected by Italy, on behalf of San Marino, before the entry into force of the Interim Agreement in 1992, see Case C-10/00 *Commission* v. *Italy* 2002 ECR I-2357.

trade-related matters between the EC and San Marino.[51] This Agreement incorporated the trade and trade-related provisions of the 1992 Agreement on cooperation and customs union signed between San Marino and the EEC and its Member States.[52] The mixed nature of this last Agreement, with its lengthy ratification procedures in the EU Member States, explained the need for a separate Interim Agreement which could be concluded rapidly since for 'trade and trade-related matters' the Community has exclusive competence. When the 1992 Cooperation Agreement entered into force in 2002, it replaced the Interim Agreement.

Apart from the agreements with San Marino on the use of the euro and on taxation of savings income which are further examined, the 1992 Agreement on Cooperation and Customs Union is the only important bilateral legal framework that should be mentioned. It consists of three substantive parts. The most important is that on the establishment of the customs union (Arts. 2–13). A few comments on this part are provided further below. A second part concerns the promotion of cooperation in a number of sectors including industry, environment, tourism, communication, information and culture (Arts. 14–18). The scope of cooperation can be extended by mutual consent (Art. 19). A third part is devoted to social provisions, including cooperation in the field of social policy (Arts. 20–22). Workers having San Marino nationality employed in a Member State shall be free from discrimination based on nationality in relation to its own nationals as regards working conditions or remuneration. This non-discrimination principle also applies in the field of social security. San Marino, for its part, applies the non-discrimination principle to workers from the EU Member States employed in its territory. It is the inclusion of these provisions in the Agreement which explains why, when the Agreement was signed, the mixed procedure for its conclusion was followed. But this procedure would also lead to an exceptionally long and difficult road for approval in all the Member States, complicated by the fact that the EU further enlarged in the course of this process and additional ratifications were necessary. In the end, the ratification procedure would last no less than eleven years, which is the longest ever for a mixed

---

[51] For text, see OJ 1992 L 359/13.
[52] For text, see OJ 2002 L 84/43. Strangely enough, the official title of the Agreement omits 'the Member States' while they were formally 'Contracting Parties' to the Agreement.

agreement. The provisions on cooperation, though in force since 2002, seem to have had only limited effect in practice and not a single implementing decision seems to have been taken by the Cooperation Council in any of the areas for cooperation.

The provisions on the customs union are of considerable importance, of course. All products covered by Chapters 1 to 97 of the Common Customs Tariff, that is to say also agricultural products (unlike the customs union with Andorra), fall within the scope of the provisions of the customs union (Art. 2). The provisions on the establishment of the customs union are identical or very similar to those of the customs union with Andorra, and it is obvious that this Agreement inspired the Agreement with San Marino.

Similarly to what was laid down in the Agreement with Andorra, San Marino authorised the Community, for a period of five years and even beyond, if no agreement could be reached, 'acting on behalf of, and for, San Marino, to carry out customs clearance formalities, in particular release for free circulation of products sent from third countries to San Marino'. Thus far, and in contrast with what happened in the case of Andorra, the transfer of these competences to the authorities of San Marino has not taken place, which means that all third-country goods destined for San Marino are first customs-cleared by Italian or other Member States' customs authorities. Consequently, goods originating in non-EC countries with the destination of San Marino cannot cross the Community without first being put into free circulation. In other words, San Marino itself does not collect duties or charges on its imports. For the Republic to assume this responsibility would have meant a sufficiently large and well-trained customs staff. This is probably the main explanation why the San Marino authorities have not insisted on the implementation of this provision of the Agreement. It should be added that goods originating in San Marino are automatically considered as being in free circulation.

In 2002, the Government of San Marino published a policy paper on its relations with the EU.[53] While acknowledging that the 1992 Cooperation and customs union Agreement had contributed to facilitating its participation in the Internal Market, difficulties remained and, on the whole, as was already mentioned, the results of the Agreement have been limited. The Agreement may, therefore, have to be extended and new forms of bilateral cooperation may be necessary. It is interesting to note that the

---

[53] http://ec.europa.eu/comm/external_relations/sanmarino/doc/aidememoire.pdf.

Memorandum signals that it is 'important to thoroughly consider all implications – which the Republic cannot and does not intend to circumvent – of a possible membership in the European Union for a country which, in terms of territorial extension and population, is a microstate and wants to preserve its own identity. Such implications would not only affect the Republic of San Marino, but also the European Union.' With this statement, San Marino was the first European micro-State not to formally exclude a possible EU membership option and this view has very recently gained momentum. On 27 August 2007, San Marino informed the EU Presidency that it wants to achieve increasing integration with the EU in the light of a possible application for EU membership. This initiative is not (yet) a formal application for membership. It remains to be seen how the EU intends to respond to this move and in the conclusions of this study we come back to this point.

10.2.3 Monaco

Background

Monaco with its 2 km^2 is the second smallest micro-State in the world (Vatican City is the smallest) and has a population of around 33,000 of which only 16 per cent have Monegasque nationality (47 per cent French, 16 per cent Italian and 21 per cent other nationalities). Monaco is a hereditary and constitutional monarchy. The 1962 Monegasque Constitution, reviewed in 2002, stipulates that Monaco is a sovereign and independent State. However, Monaco has exceptionally close relations with its neighbour, France, which implies inter alia the inclusion of French officials in very high official posts in Monaco. For example, the *Ministre d'Etat* (Minister of State), presiding the *Conseil de Gouvernement* (Governmental Council), is a French national (but since 2002 it might have been a Monegasque national). This and other links with France could have been an obstacle to its acceptance as a truly independent State but the Principality has nevertheless gradually been able to receive international recognition of its independent status. Monaco has been a member of the United Nations since 1993 and became, after thorough screening,[54] a member of the Council of Europe in 2004. Monaco is not a member of the WTO.

---

[54] See G. Grinda, 'Le processus d'adhésion de Monaco au Conseil de l'Europe: incidences sur l'ordre juridique de la Principauté', *Revue de Droit Monégasque* (2005), pp. 25–58.

The history of Monaco is closely connected with that of the Grimaldi dynasty. Already by the end of the thirteenth century the Grimaldi family was in possession of Monaco. In the second half of the fifteenth century, Monaco's independence was recognised, but in order to survive as an independent entity it needed to sign various agreements accepting protection from foreign powers (Spain, France and Sardinia). In 1793, Monaco was annexed by France but in 1814 was granted independence, with the King of Sardinia exercising his protection, and this was confirmed and reinforced in 1815 by the Congress of Vienna.[55] In 1861, after the County of Nice had become part of France, a considerable portion of the territory of Monaco (the cities of Roquebrune and Menton) became part of France.[56] Monaco signed an agreement with France in the same year and the latter became not only its sole neighbour, but also its supervisor. In 1865, a customs union was established. In 1918, still during World War I, an Agreement between France and Monaco was signed under strong pressure from France. France agreed to guarantee the independence, sovereignty and integrity of Monaco. However, the 1918 Agreement also considerably affected Monaco's external capacities, was close to establishing a French 'protectorate' and offered a legal basis for a possible 'permanent intervention' in the affairs of the Principality.[57] While Article 1 stipulated that Monaco exercises its sovereign rights 'in perfect conformity' with the political, military, maritime and economic interests of France, Article 2 unequivocally linked Monaco's external relations to those of the French Republic, since Monaco needed for the development of its international relations prior approval ('*entente préalable*') from the French Government. France agreed to 'facilitate' Monaco's participation at its side ('*à ses côtés*') at international conferences and institutions. The 1930 Treaty[58] provided a legal basis allowing French officials to occupy various high posts in the Monegasque civil service, including that of Head of Government. In 1963, after a bitter dispute between the two Parties over the fiscal laws in Monaco, a series of

---

[55] On the 'protection' of Monaco after the French Revolution and First Empire, see L.H. Labande, *Histoire de la Principauté de Monaco* (Monaco: Editions de l'Imprimerie Nationale de Monaco, 1934), pp. 383–476.

[56] On this episode, see J.-J. Antier, *Le Comté de Nice* (Paris: Editions France-Empire, 1972), pp. 303–20.

[57] See J.-B. Robert, *Histoire de Monaco* (Paris: PUF, 1997, 2nd ed.), pp. 91–2 and p. 101.

[58] For text, see *Journal Officiel de la République Française*, 1935, p. 1931.

agreements were signed, among them an agreement on neighbourhood relations and mutual administrative assistance.[59]

On 24 October 2002, a new bilateral cooperation agreement between France and Monaco was signed.[60] Its main aim was 'to modernise' the existing bilateral relationships, especially the 1918 Agreement.[61] As far as the external relations of the Principality are concerned, France commits itself to take Monaco's fundamental interests into consideration, while Monaco undertakes to conduct its international relations regarding fundamental issues in convergence with those of the French Republic through appropriate concertation (Art. 2).[62] Certainly, the new agreement no longer uses the 1918 expressions '*parfaite conformité*' and '*entente préalable*', although there is still strong emphasis on 'concertation' and 'convergence' with France. Torelli interprets these references as '*la contrepartie de l'abandon de la France de ses privilèges*'.[63] Moreover, Article 1(2) of the 2002 Treaty stipulates, in general terms, that in the exercise of its sovereign rights Monaco will align its policies with the fundamental interests of France in the fields of politics, economics, security and defence. Notwithstanding the fact that for Monaco

---

[59] For text, see *Journal Officiel de la République Française*, 1963, p. 412. For an in-depth legal analysis of the crisis between Monaco and France in 1962 and 1963 and the agreements signed between the two Parties in 1963, see J.-P. Gallois, *Le régime international de la Principauté de Monaco* (Paris: Pédone, 1964), pp. 150–215.

[60] For text, see *Journal Officiel de la République Française*, 7 January 2006, p. 309.

[61] A review of the 1918 Agreement had also been strongly suggested in the Report of two judges at the European Court of Human Rights, Mr A. Pastor Ridruejo and Mr G. Ress, on the conformity of the Monegasque legal order with the Council of Europe fundamental principles and prepared at the request of the Bureau of the Assembly of the Council of Europe. The Report, rather rapidly, concluded that Monaco was 'irrefutably an independent sovereign State with regard to international relations'. Monaco was a member of the UN, and was therefore 'being recognised as an independent sovereign State by the organised international community as a whole'. However, the Report also observed that the exercise of this sovereignty was subject to significant limitations as a result of bilateral treaties with France and considered as highly desirable, that the Treaties of 1918 and 1930 be amended, see AS/Bur/Monaco (1999) 1 rev. 2, 25 July 1999. The Opinion of the Parliamentary Assembly of the Council of Europe reiterated many of the suggestions contained in the Report and insisted also strongly on the introduction of changes in the established practice, based on the Franco-Monegasque Treaty of 1930, which resulted in reserving senior Monegasque Government and civil servants posts to French officials. Depriving Monegasque citizens from such posts 'runs counter to the principle of non-discrimination', see Opinion No. 250 (2004).

[62] Article 2(1) of the 2002 Agreement reads as follows: 'la Principauté de Monaco s'assure par une concertation appropriée et regulière que ses relations internationales sont conduites sur les questions fondamentales en convergence avec celles de la République Française'.

[63] M. Torelli, 'Un nouveau cadre conventionnel entre la France et Monaco: le traité du 24 octobre 2002', *RGDIP* (2003), pp. 7–30, in particular p. 23.

the 2002 Agreement constitutes a considerable qualitative improvement compared with the 1918 Agreement,[64] the impression remains that the bilateral relations France–Monaco continue to have primacy over Monaco's external relations as a whole.[65]

The continuing 'patronage' of Monaco by France, under the 2002 Agreement in an intensity which is undoubtedly different from that established by the 1918 Agreement, cannot be denied. Even if the 2002 Agreement has been qualified as '*un traité respectueux de la souveraineté monégasque*'[66] aiming at enhancing bilateral cooperation – and Monaco's membership of the Council of Europe may help to consolidate the acquired greater liberty of action – at the same time the very close relationship France–Monaco – no other European micro-State is so closely linked with its neighbour – remains probably the explanation, or at least one of the explanations, why, up until now, no bilateral agreement of a general nature between Monaco and the EC has been signed. Monaco is already part of the Community customs territory and applies the customs code as applied in France, while French customs officials are in charge of the customs controls of the territory of Monaco.[67] The unilateral integration of Monaco in the customs territory of the Community had already materialised in 1968 with Regulation 1496/68 of 27 September 1968,[68] and this was recalled in subsequent Regulations, the latest one being Regulation 2913/92 of 12 October 1992 establishing the Community Customs Code.[69] In addition, it should also be mentioned that Monaco follows the French VAT regime.

The 2003 Agreement on the application of certain Community acts

Being included in the Community customs territory of the EC means that Monaco applies EC law regarding the customs union. Consequently,

---

[64] See G. Grinda, *La Principauté de Monaco, L'Etat, son statut international, ses institutions* (Paris: Pédone, 2005), pp. 34–5, who emphasises that the 2002 Agreement more strongly relies on the principle of equality among States in comparison to the 1918 Agreement.

[65] Professor Torelli's remark is in this context eloquent where he compares the 2002 Agreement with the 1993 trilateral Agreement between Andorra and its two neighbours which explicitly refers to the European context of the trilateral relations (see n. 39). In the lack of such a reference in the 2002 Agreement 'on pourrait y voir le maintien du bilatéralisme le plus strict', n. 63, p. 16.

[66] Expression is from Grinda, *La Principauté de Monaco*, n. 64, p. 34.

[67] Customs Convention of 18 May 1963, *Journal Officiel de la République Française*, 27 September 1963, no. 8679.

[68] OJ 1968 L 238/1.   [69] OJ 1992 L 302/1, Article 3(2)(b).

Monaco applies the EC rules regarding free movement of goods.[70] The same holds true for the common customs tariff on imports from non-EC Member States, but preferential agreements concluded by the EC with third countries do not apply to goods originating in Monaco. The Community customs territory does not cover external trade. In other words, goods originating in Monaco do not have Community origin but as a result of Monaco being in the Community customs territory, they benefit from free movement inside the EU. However, even in the EU they may nevertheless encounter obstacles, in particular where the Community has established specific rules for the harmonisation of the laws of the Member States. Such rules go beyond the rules that Monaco applies as being part of Community customs territory. This explains why the Principality signed a bilateral agreement with the EC in 2003 – the first in the history of its relations with the EU – 'on the application of certain Community acts on the territory of the Principality of Monaco'.[71]

The Agreement aims at facilitating economic activities and trade in the field of medicine for human and veterinary use, cosmetic products and listed medical devices. It makes the Community acts covering these fields and incorporated in the Annex of the Agreement applicable on the territory of Monaco. The acts in question are applicable in the legal order of Monaco without further legislative or administrative intervention. Moreover, it is also stipulated in Article 1 of the Agreement that 'such rules must be interpreted in accordance with the case law of the Court of Justice of the European Communities'. The main significance of this Agreement is that it gives manufacturers in Monaco greater legal certainty regarding the access of their products to the EU market. In the light of the special relationship between Monaco and France, the Monegasque authorities, in order to preserve uniform interpretation in accordance with the case law of the ECJ, 'may have recourse to their special administrative relationship with the French Republic' (Art. 2(2)). This may be helpful where Monaco itself does not possess the required infrastructure, laboratories, know-how, etc. for the required tests and verifications. A Joint Committee EC–Monaco – also the first established in the relations EU–Monaco – is responsible for the management and proper implementation

---

[70] See G. Vandersanden, 'L'application du droit communautaire sur le territoire de la Principauté de Monaco', *Revue de Droit Monégasque* (2000), pp. 176–9.
[71] OJ 2003 L 332/42.

of the Agreement. This Committee also acts as a dispute settlement body and its jurisdiction has a draconian dimension: if a dispute is brought before it, it is forced to find a solution within the foreseen procedure and time limits since failing to do so signifies the end of the Agreement (Art. 4(3)). Clearly, the assumption is that neither the spirit nor the text of the Agreement lends to flexibility in application and it is in the interests of both parties that the provisions of the Agreement are strictly applied.

Monaco and the Schengen Agreement   Monaco concluded a bilateral agreement with France in 1963 on entry, stay and establishment of foreigners.[72] With this agreement, Monaco, as a third State, occupies a very special position regarding the movement of persons with a Member State of the EU. Basically, Monaco allows the French authorities to decide about immigration into Monaco, the reason being that there is no control of persons at the French-Monegasque border. Monaco only has a common border with France and France is therefore its only neighbour. However, Monaco has direct access to the Mediterranean sea and, moreover, has a heliport. While overland visitors to Monaco must proceed via France and satisfy the French immigration laws, the possibility of direct access to Monaco by air or sea has necessitated some specific measures.

As far as travel through France is concerned, an important landmark was the 1985 Schengen Agreement. The border between France and Monaco would, in principle, have become the Schengen external border. This, however, would have meant that the 1963 bilateral agreement between France and Monaco on free movement of persons was rendered inapplicable. A pragmatic and legally workable solution has been found in order to maintain the free movement regime. In its Decision of 23 June 1998 on Monegasque residence permits, the Schengen Executive Committee recalled in the preamble that 'freedom of movement between France and Monaco was instituted prior to the entry into force of the Convention implementing the Schengen Agreement' and '[that] the Contracting Parties to the Convention implementing the Schengen Agreement have not called into question these rules on freedom of movement'. Moreover, 'on the basis of the Agreement on Good Neighbourly Relations between France and Monaco of 18 May 1963, as revised and supplemented by an Exchange of Letters between France and Monaco

---

[72] See reference, n. 59.

of 15 December 1997, the French authorities apply the rules and checks laid down in the Convention implementing the Schengen Agreement when carrying out checks on the entry, stay and establishment of foreign nationals in the Principality of Monaco'. As a result of this specific situation the Schengen Executive Committee decided inter alia to incorporate Monegasque residence permits in the French section of Annex IV to the Common Consular Instructions. Moreover, Monaco-Heliport and Monaco Port de la Condamine were added to the authorised external border crossing points of the Schengen Common Manual.[73]

10.3 The use of the euro in San Marino, Monaco and Andorra

None of the European micro-States has its own official national currency and they all used on their territory one of the neighbours' currency.[74] San Marino used the Italian lira and Monaco the French franc, while Andorra used both the Spanish peseta and the French franc (Liechtenstein uses the Swiss franc). The legal base for the use of the neighbour's currency was in each case the monetary convention which each had concluded with its respective neighbours. However, the use of the peseta and French franc in Andorra was not based on conventions concluded by Andorra with its neighbours; Andorra was using these currencies on a purely de facto basis. The introduction of the euro in EU Member States necessarily affected the use of the currency in the three micro-States.

A Declaration attached to the Final Act to the Treaty of Maastricht provided that the existing monetary conventions between Italy and San Marino and Vatican City, and between France and Monaco remained unaffected by the EC Treaty 'until the introduction of the ECU as the single currency of the Community'. In the meantime, the Community undertook the commitment 'to facilitate such renegotiations of existing arrangements as might become necessary as a result of the introduction of the ECU as a single currency'. On 31 December 1998, the Council took the necessary decisions on the position to be adopted by the Community regarding the monetary relations with San Marino and Monaco.[75] Interestingly, in the negotiation of a monetary convention on the use of

---

[73] For text, OJ 2000 L 239/11.

[74] This part of the contribution is largely based on the study mentioned at n. 1, pp. 766–8.

[75] Decisions 1999/36 and 1999/97, OJ 1999 L 30/31 and L 30/33. Also for the Vatican City a decision was adopted, OJ 1999 L 30/35.

the euro, it was France that was asked to negotiate with Monaco and Italy with San Marino, both on behalf of the Community. The reasons for this unusual step were, as far as Monaco is concerned, the fact that France had 'particular monetary links with the Principality of Monaco which are based on various legal instruments'. Moreover, financial institutions located in Monaco had the potential right to access the refinancing facilities of the Banque de France and they also participated in some French payment systems under the same conditions as French banks. Given the historical links between France and the Principality, it was therefore considered 'appropriate that France negotiates and may conclude the new agreement on behalf of the Community'.[76] For San Marino a largely similar reasoning was followed, also invoking inter alia, 'the historical links' between Italy and San Marino in order to have the convention negotiated and concluded by Italy on behalf of the Community. Each within their sphere of competence, the European Commission and the European Central Bank were associated with these negotiations. The derogation from the classical negotiation procedure of Article 300 EC did not constitute a problem from a legal point of view since Article 111(3) EC explicitly makes such derogation possible. The negotiations with the two small States were successfully concluded in 2001.[77]

As a result of these conventions, San Marino and Monaco are entitled to use the euro as their official currency and they granted legal tender status to euro banknotes and coins as from 1 January 2002.[78] Both countries abstain from issuing national banknotes or coins unless on the basis of an agreement with the Community. They are allowed to issue a specific amount of euro coins every year as determined in the respective conventions.[79] San Marino is allowed to continue to issue gold coins denominated in scudi, while Monaco may issue euro collector coins under certain conditions. These coins for

---

[76] See preamble Council Decision of 31 December 1998 on the position to be taken by the Community regarding an agreement concerning the monetary relations with the Principality of Monaco, OJ 1999 L 30/31.

[77] For text of the Convention with San Marino, see OJ 2001, C 209/1 and with Monaco, OJ 2002 L 142/59.

[78] On these agreements, see also 'Monetary and exchange rate arrangements of the Euro Area with selected third countries and territories', European Central Bank, *Monthly Bulletin*, 2006, pp. 90–3.

[79] For San Marino the amount is €1,944,000 a year; while for Monaco this is 1/500th of the amount of coins minted in the same year by France. This difference is a consequence of the previous bilateral agreements with Italy and France.

collection purposes do not have legal tender status in the Community. It is to be noted that the monetary convention with Monaco is more detailed and in some ways also more rigid than that with San Marino, one of the reasons being that credit institutions and other financial institutions established in Monaco are subject to the same rules as those established in France for the purposes of prudential supervision of credit institutions and the prevention of systemic risks to payment and securities settlement systems.[80] Monaco must cooperate in good faith with France 'in order to ensure that the law applicable in Monaco in the areas covered by this Agreement will at all times be identical, or where appropriate, equivalent to the law applicable in France'. The Agreement with San Marino provides for the possibility that credit institutions in San Marino will also have access to the Euro Payments Area system although to date no such access has been established.

As was already mentioned, Andorra has used the euro as its currency since 1 January 2002 on the basis of a unilateral decision. The reason why Andorra has never concluded a monetary convention with its neighbours is probably that it would have been a delicate matter to choose a particular neighbour because of the constitutional structure of co-principality. However, the reason suggested by the European Central Bank that 'Andorra did not become a sovereign State till 1993'[81] is a somewhat simplistic interpretation of Andorra's complex constitutional status. This said, in 2003 the Andorran authorities proposed to the Community to conclude a monetary convention. This request was linked with the 'taxation of savings income' package (see Section 10.4). The EC's acceptance to open negotiations was made dependent on the initialling by Andorra of the 'taxation of savings income' Agreement and on Andorra's undertaking to ratify that Agreement.[82]

---

[80] See Article 11(2) of the Agreement. The Agreement contains in Annexes references to the EC legislation which must be applied by Monaco. These Annexes can later be updated; for an application, see Commission Decision 2 August 2006, OJ 2006 L 219/23.

[81] See Opinion of the ECB of 1 April 2004 on the position to be taken by the Community as regards an agreement concerning the monetary relations with Andorra, Council, 2 April 2004, ECOFIN 122 UEM 56.

[82] This condition imposed on Andorra is somewhat astonishing, since, regardless of the conclusion of the taxation of savings income Agreement (see n. 90), it would appear also to be in the interest of the Community that when third countries use the euro, there is an agreement laying down the terms of such use, see also Opinion of the ECB of 1 April 2004 on the position to be taken by the Community as regards an agreement concerning the monetary relations with Andorra, Council, 2 April 2004, ECOFIN 122 UEM 56. The ECB noted 'that it would be in the Community's interest to open negotiations on a monetary agreement with Andorra' and considered 'that a third country should only introduce the euro following agreement with the Community'.

Absence of ratification would have meant suspension of the negotiations on the monetary agreement. Ratification by Andorra took place on time and the negotiations for a monetary convention were opened at the end of 2004. This time it is the European Commission acting for the Community that negotiates this agreement, in association with Spain and France as well as with the European Central Bank for matters falling within its competence.[83] At the time of writing, no monetary convention on the use of the euro has yet been signed and the Principality is adopting appropriate legislative measures for the application of the relevant Community legislation.

10.4 Bilateral agreements on taxation of savings income

Within the EU it has been particularly difficult to tackle taxation policies of the Member States from the point of view of fair competition. The reason for this difficulty has to do with the need for unanimity. However, an important political landmark was the 2000 Santa Maria da Feira European Council which agreed on a global package of measures regarding taxation.[84] While the main objective of the EU initiative was in the first place to reach a commitment on automatic exchange of information among the EU Member States, it soon appeared necessary, at least for a transitional period, to apply different measures to three of the EU's own Member States, but considered to be equivalent as providing automatic information. Belgium, Luxembourg and Austria were indeed allowed to apply a withholding tax on interest income that is paid to nationals resident in other EU Member States. The rate was determined as 15 per cent for the period 1 July 2005 to 30 June 2008 and 20 per cent for the period 1 July 2008 to 30 June 2011. From 1 July 2011 onwards 35 per cent tax will be levied. A difficulty in this respect was that not only EU Member States had to be taken into consideration but also non-EU States qualified as 'key third countries'. These countries were identified as Switzerland and also the four European micro-States (Andorra, San Marino, Monaco and Liechtenstein), which for the first time in their history received the honour of being called 'key third countries' by

---

[83] See Council Decision of 11 May 2004 on the position to be taken by the Community regarding an agreement concerning the monetary relations with the Principality of Andorra, OJ 2004 L 244/47.

[84] See Annex IV to the Santa Maria da Feira European Council Conclusions.

the EU.[85] Thus, in parallel with the discussion within the EU on the proposal for a taxation of savings income directive, agreements with the key third countries were negotiated to establish equivalent measures. As a matter of fact, a political compromise with Switzerland was already reached in March 2003 in the context of a negotiation-package, called *Bilaterals II*.[86] This made it possible to go ahead with the Council Directive 2003/48/EC on taxation of savings income in the form of interest payments which was formally adopted on 3 June 2003,[87] before any of the four micro-States had signed an agreement with the EC. The preamble to the Directive stated that as long as the United States, Switzerland and the four European micro-States did not apply measures equivalent to or the same as those provided for in the Directive, capital flight towards these countries 'could imperil the attainment of the objectives of the Directive'. Consequently, there ought to be synchron-isation of application of the measures by the EU Member States with those equivalent measures applied by the third countries concerned. Article 17(2) of the Directive explicitly stipulated that Member States shall apply the provisions of the Directive from 1 January 2005, later extended to 1 July 2005, provided that 'the Swiss Confederation, the Principality of Liechtenstein, the Republic of San Marino, the Princi-pality of Monaco and the Principality of Andorra apply from that same date measures equivalent to those contained in this Directive in accordance with agreements entered into by them with the European Community, following unanimous decisions of the Council'.[88]

Needless to say, the Swiss decision to agree to sign an agreement with the EC on taxation of savings income (hereafter Taxation Agreement) unleashed enormous pressure on the European micro-States and they had no option other than also to sign similar agreements. When the EU demanded the signature of such an Agreement, some micro-States, however, proposed other subjects for negotiation. Initially, the idea of forming negotiation-packages was not very much appreciated and certainly not favoured by the

---

[85] Similar measures had to be applied by territories or dependencies of the Member States.

[86] On these Agreements, see contribution by C. Kaddous in this volume.

[87] For text, OJ 2003 L 157/38. For an analysis, see D. Berlin, 'La fiscalité de l'épargne dans l'Union européenne. Histoire d'une harmonisation en voie de disparition', *Journal des Tribunaux, Droit européen* (2003), pp. 162–8.

[88] The application of the Directive was not made dependent on an agreement on equivalent measures with the US, which had declined to sign an agreement with the EC.

EU, but it was also difficult for the EU to categorically ignore or simply reject any request of the micro-States for other negotiations to be opened or existing ones widened. Andorra, for example, insisted on a true package-strategy, in particular to push forward with the Cooperation Agreement, to initiate negotiations on a monetary convention on the use of the euro and to facilitate the movement of Andorran citizens across EU external borders.[89] Other micro-States emphasised the need for further cooperation in specific areas such as, for example, in the field of services. The package-approach received a degree of formal recognition through acknowledgements made in the Memorandums of Understanding, signed on the occasion of the sig-nature of the Taxation Agreements themselves. But even if no mention of certain requests were made in these Memorandums, they could still de facto be handled in separate negotiations. In the end, the Taxation Agreements with the four micro-States were all signed in 2004 and are virtually all identical.[90] They lay down the principle that the paying agent (bank/financial institution) in the States concerned will withhold a tax on interest payments similar to the one mentioned regarding the three EU Member States derogating from the principle of automatic exchange of information. The retention tax will not be applied to EU resident taxpayers authorising

---

[89] At a meeting of the Strategic Committee on Immigration, Frontiers and Asylum (SCIFA, 6 October 2004, Doc. 13020/1/04), a favourable and pragmatic response was given to the Andorran request – a similar request had later also been formulated by San Marino – to facilitate the crossing of external EU borders by Andorrans and nationals of San Marino. The Presidency invited the Member States to inform their border guards that citizens of Andorra and San Marino are allowed to use 'EU corridors' at the external borders, except when such use could give rise to delays for EU citizens. However, neither Andorra nor San Marino have concluded an agreement with the EC on free movement of persons and consequently nationals of the two countries are not 'persons enjoying the Community right of free movement' within the meaning of Regulation 562/2006 of the European Parliament and the Council of 15 March 2006 establishing a Community Code on the rules governing the movement of persons across borders (Schengen Borders Code, OJ 2006 L 105/1), in particular Article 9(2). Liechtenstein nationals, via the EEA, clearly fall within the category of Article 9(2) and are allowed to use the 'EU corridors'. However, it should be noted that Regulation 562/2006 also explicitly deals with the question of stamping travel documents of third-country nationals and that it stipulates that no entry or exit stamp shall be affixed 'to documents enabling nationals of Andorra, Monaco and San Marino to cross the border' (Art. 10(3)(e)). It is not clear from the wording of the Regulation whether and to what extent the SCIFA initiative has had an impact on the formulation of Article 10(3)(c). It is too early to assess to what extent nationals of Andorra and San Marino are allowed to make use of the 'EU corridor'.

[90] For the text of these Agreements, see with Andorra, OJ 2004 L 359/32 and OJ 2005 L 114/9; San Marino, OJ 2004 L 381/34 and OJ 2005 L 114/11; Monaco, OJ 2005 L 19/53 and OJ 2005 L 110/40. All these agreements have entered into force.

the paying agent in Andorra, Monaco, San Marino (and also Liechtenstein) to disclose information on the interest payment to his tax authorities. There is no automatic exchange of information and in this way the principle of bank secrecy is largely maintained. However, the agreements concluded do allow for exchange of information upon request. The EU's neighbours have agreed to grant exchange of information on request concerning the income covered by the Agreements on conduct constituting 'tax fraud under the laws of the *requested State* or the like'.[91] It is the laws of each of the contracting States that determine the meaning of 'tax fraud' and a number of micro-States even had to introduce this notion into their domestic legislation. 'The like' only includes 'offences with the same level of wrongfulness as is the case for tax fraud under the laws of the requested State'.

As just mentioned, the Taxation Agreements are all accompanied by a Memorandum of Understanding (MoU) signed by the EC, the Member States[92] and each of the four micro-States.[93] In the MoUs, it is stated that the Taxation Agreement *and* the MoU constitute 'an acceptable agreement', while three of them (with Monaco, San Marino and also Liechtenstein) even use the expression '*balanced* and acceptable agreement',[94] protecting the interests of the contracting parties. All MoUs further stipulate that the contracting parties shall apply the arrangements in good faith and shall refrain from unilateral action which might jeopardise them without due cause. At first sight, the 'balanced' nature of the Taxation Agreement is not evident to everybody and it looks very much like a dictated and imposed text by the EC. Elements of a 'balanced' nature and/or elements making the arrangements 'acceptable' can only be seen in conjunction with the broader political negotiation-packages that some micro-States have managed to negotiate in parallel or at least to a large degree alongside the negotiations of the Taxation Agreement itself. Andorra, for example, as was already mentioned, insisted on the opening of negotiations for a monetary agreement on the use of the euro and this, together with the signing of the Taxation Agreement, was seen, as is stated

---

[91] Emphasis added.

[92] The MoUs refer, among other things, to the possible conclusion of bilateral agreements between the micro-States and EU Member States or to certain undertakings by the Member States, except the one with Monaco, which does not contain such references to Member States and which is only signed by the EC.

[93] Also the Taxation Agreement with Switzerland was accompanied by a MoU.

[94] Emphasis added.

in the MoU with Andorra, '[to] constitute a significant step in the deepening of cooperation between the Principality and the European Union'. Some of Andorra's other requests were not formalised in the MoU but nevertheless largely agreed on a case-by-case basis.

The MoU with Andorra also mentions a specific obligation for Andorra. Andorra undertook to introduce into its domestic legislation the concept of 'crime of tax fraud, consisting at least of the use of documents which are false, falsified, or recognised as being incorrect in terms of their content, which intend to deceive the tax authorities in the field of taxation of savings income'. Clearly, the definition of tax fraud is only relevant for the purposes of the application of the Taxation Agreement. This limitation of the scope of the concept 'tax fraud' is also to be found in the MoUs with the other micro-States. In some MoUs, references were further made to enlarging cooperation in the field of financial and insurance services (San Marino, Monaco) or to increase with the EU Member States further economic or fiscal cooperation (Andorra).

For the EU, it is certainly a success to have been able to establish a network of Taxation Agreements with Switzerland, the four micro-States and to obtain similar commitments from the many dependencies and territories. However, it is too early to make an assessment of the concrete results obtained. One of the problems is that not all off-shore centres in the world have signed similar agreements with the EC and escape routes continue to exist. In particular, the EU has so far been unable to include in its scheme a number of important centres such as Hong Kong and Singapore, two dangerous places from the point of view of tax avoidance because of their potential capacity to undermine the EU's fiscal objectives.[95]

10.5 Conclusion

As was made clear throughout this study, the relations between the EU and the European micro-States will always be of a great complexity because of the specificity of these States. In one way or another, all the European micro-States share the same existential concern about their place and role as very small entities on a European continent, that is today so largely interdependent and integrated in the EU. But having the enlarged EU on their doorstep, makes the relations with this vast

---

[95] See *Financial Times*, 13 October 2006, 'Hong Kong ready to reject EU call on tax avoidance'.

neighbour a permanent but at the same time also more 'anonymous' challenge than previously experienced in their relationships with their close historical neighbour or neighbours. One of the possible future scenarios is that the micro-States could face more indirect and sometimes more direct pressure from this omnipotent neighbour. Was the EU's taxation of savings income initiative a sign of the first and clear writing on the wall for such a new EU orientation towards micro-States? Or was it rather a coincidental combination of different factors in domestic and external EU policy?

From the point of view of the micro-States, the fact that the Treaty establishing a Constitution for Europe has been rejected was not a good thing. As is well known, Article I-57 foresaw a specific provision on the relations between the EU and its neighbours, stipulating that 'the Union shall develop a special relationship with neighbouring countries', founded on the values of the EU and characterised by close and peaceful relations based on cooperation. Article I-57 did not specifically address the relations with the neighbouring micro-States but a Declaration on Article I-57 made it clear that the EU was willing to take into account 'the particular situation of the small-sized countries which maintain specific relations of proximity with it'. Fortunately, the TL has kept these references intact in the new Article 8 EU Treaty and in a Declaration on this provision. Once the revised Treaty has been ratified, Article 8, combined with the Declaration, will provide for the possibility of a specific legal basis to develop the relations between the EU and the micro-States as EU neighbours. So far, various existing channels that have been set up with the EU have already allowed a degree of specificity for the micro-States. But can the existing bilateral networks, whether upgraded or not, continue to be adequate or do they need to be replaced by more global, and perhaps more institutionalised, legal and political frameworks? Is accession to the EU in the long run a realistic alternative for the micro-States?

Until now, accession of micro-States to the EU has never seriously been contemplated by the EU nor the micro-States, with the possible exception of San Marino. However, if the EU were increasingly to be tempted to exert pressure on its very small neighbours, this might provoke possible applications for EU membership from them. Fully fledged accession would, next to the fact that at present the EU is not in the mood for further enlargements, almost certainly create immense institutional and legal complications for the EU, unless a specific format of membership status could be found for these small States. Past EU accession practice leaves little space for special forms or types of accession adapted to the specific needs of very small States. While it is true that not much is eternal in EU policy, it is also true that attitudes among micro-States themselves towards EU accession are not very precise and vary considerably. For example, as already mentioned, San Marino now seems to be moving towards fuller integration in the EU, not excluding membership. The interesting thing of San Marino's move is that it might force the EU to reflect in depth on its relations with the micro-States as a whole. Moreover, San Marino's initiative may well also affect the other micro-States' position towards the EU. In the hypothesis that San Marino were to apply formally for EU membership, it might be a complicated matter for the EU to reject this application. Indeed, at first sight, very little can be invoked against this application, except that San Marino is so small that it may perhaps never have the capacity to apply the *acquis communautaire* fully. Be this as it may, other micro-States that have not (yet) considered EU membership will certainly follow the EU–San Marino relations closely, even if membership is still something difficult for them to imagine. But whatever the micro-States' views on EU accession, as the closest neighbours of the EU, micro-States are all well aware that they cannot isolate themselves from the world around them and that they have necessarily to align their laws and regulations to (very) large parts of the EU substantive *acquis*. Certainly, they are themselves best placed to make an assessment as to the degree and intensity of this alignment, while preserving those fundamental elements which characterise their own identity and specificity. In this context, it should also be observed that aligning laws and regulations to those of the EU is not only limited to micro-States alone. Also, larger EU neighbours such as Norway or Switzerland, whether they like it or not, are even much more exposed in the very same exercise.

One thing remains frustrating for those involved in only 'aligning', whether it concerns small or larger neighbours of the EU: none may participate in the EU legislative process itself and, consequently, their impact on EU decision-making is non-existent, or virtually so. In these circumstances, the best option for the micro-States at present, and most likely also for the EU, is to establish well-conceived and well-structured networks of agreements or a comprehensive agreement because this seems to offer both parties the best armour for protecting their respective interests. In this respect, the former Head of Government of Andorra,

M. Oscar Ribas, has observed that the micro-States may lack the capacity to adopt the whole *acquis communautaire*, and even compliance with the full Internal Market *acquis* might already be a difficult matter, in particular with regard to the right of establishment.[96] In this view, a *preferential association agreement* or an *ad hoc accession* would be the best options for the recognition of the micro-States' specificity. In terms of substance, the two concepts are perhaps not fundamentally different but EU membership, be it on an ad hoc basis, would necessarily imply greater involvement for the micro-States in the operation of the EU than would any form of association. Whatever possible future scenarios, it should not be forgotten that already today, sophisticated political and legal frameworks are in place. This is certainly the case for Liechtenstein which was not examined in this contribution. But also Andorra and San Marino have a special relationship with the EU. Both form a customs union, only for industrial products in the case of Andorra but for all products in the case of San Marino, while Monaco is included in the customs territory of the Community and applies the EC law regarding the customs union. These arrangements constitute very far-reaching forms of trade integration and on the whole have been working very well. With Andorra and San Marino there is also a legal framework for establishing advanced cooperation in various areas. However, on the ground, concrete implementation proves difficult and the EU's partners have voiced disappointment about this. Important cooperation initiatives do not come from the EU other than when the EU absolutely wants something for itself. The message is clear: if the micro-States want enhanced cooperation they have to take the initiative themselves and thoroughly prepare cooperation dossiers. But even then it might still be difficult to predict whether the EU is willing to respond effectively to these expectations. Framing those expectations in an ultimate objective of accession, as San Marino seems to be doing now, may perhaps lead to enhanced consideration of the micro-States specificity by the EU whether in an (adapted) accession or cooperation/association module.

A last word on the impact of the EU on the micro-States' status internationally. It has been mentioned how important in this respect the

---

[96] O. Ribas Reig, *La integración en la UE de los microestados históricos europeos en un contexto de globalización* (Barcelona: Real Academia de Ciencias Económicas y Financieras, 2005), pp. 89–90.

emerging relationship with the EU/EC has been for some micro-States. Probably Andorra was the greatest beneficiary since, as was explained before, as a result of the 1990 Agreement with the EEC, the lasting uncertainty concerning its international legal personality was definitively removed. Agreements between the EC and other micro-States did not necessarily have the same effect. For San Marino (and also for Liechtenstein) there was no issue of international legal personality to be settled. In addition, it should be stressed that the relations EU–micro-States are not simply complementary to the bilateral relations between the micro-States and their historical neighbour(s) but that the relations with the EU also contribute to achieve a better equilibrium in the structure of the micro-States' external relations. The relations with the EU indeed help to readjust the previously often monolithic nature of the relations with the historical neighbours. But, whatever the EU's actual or potential contribution to a more effective and more balanced external policy of the micro-States, this should not be interpreted or perceived as being in conflict with the relations with the historical neighbour(s). Good relations with the 'old' neighbour(s) will always remain a *conditio sine qua non* for stability and prosperity of the micro-States.

11

The EU's Neighbourhood Policy towards Eastern Europe

CHRISTOPHE HILLION

11.1 Introduction

The increasing use of instruments that are not explicitly envisaged by the Treaty on European Union is one of the recent trends in the EU external relations. 'Action plans', 'partnerships', 'road maps', 'agendas' and the like have proliferated, particularly in the glossary of the Union's international action. Such atypical devices have in common a non-legally binding nature, a relative immunity to the usual competence-squabbling that characterises the EU system of external relations,[1] and, yet, they have an ability to stimulate change in the existing relationship between the EU and its partners. However problematic it can be in terms of legal certainty, transparency and accountability, the use of unorthodox formula of external action may allow the EU to carve out more coherent and effective foreign policies, thereby fulfilling its general objective of 'assert[ing] its identity on the international scene'.[2]

The 'European Neighbourhood Policy' (ENP) is a particularly glowing example of this trend. Initiated jointly by the External Relations' Commissioner and the High Representative for the Common Foreign and Security Policy (CFSP),[3] the ENP has developed in a piecemeal fashion outside the

The author thanks Dr Anne Myrjord for all her helpful suggestions and support. All mistakes are mine only.

[1] See contributions by A. Dashwood and R. Wessel in this volume; see also C. Timmermans, 'The uneasy relationship between the Community and the second pillar of the Union: back to the Plan Fouchet?', *Legal Issues of Economic Integration* (1996), p. 66.

[2] Article 2 TEU.

[3] See in this regard the Joint Letter of Commissioner Patten and HR Solana on Wider Europe available at: http://ec.europa.eu/world/enp/pdf/_0130163334_001_en.pdf. For a detailed account of the origins and development of the ENP, see e.g. E. Lannon and P. Van Elsuwege, 'The EU's emerging Neighbourhood Policy and its potential impact on the Euro-Mediterranean

Treaty framework,[4] to become one of the key EU external actions.[5] It is a comprehensive policy whereby the enlarged Union seeks to ensure security, stability and prosperity around itself,[6] by stimulating political and economic reforms in its neighbouring countries, in return for closer relations.[7]

The instruments and techniques the EU employs to carry out its neighbourhood policy greatly reminds of the so-called 'pre-accession strategy' through which it orchestrated candidate countries' extensive transformation in the period 1997–2004/07. Seen as a good template for stimulating reforms, the pre-accession *methodology* is not only used to prepare countries for membership,[8] it is now extensively relied upon to transform the EU neighbours into a 'ring of [EU] friends'.

The purpose of the present paper is to examine the ENP as a novel form of EU external action towards its East European neighbours, Ukraine and Moldova in particular.[9] It will first present the ENP as an integrated policy of the Union. It will then show that this new policy metamorphoses the existing EU relations with those States, based on the Partnership and Cooperation Agreements (PCAs),[10] by using some of the techniques of the pre-accession

partnership', in P. Xuereb (ed.), *Euro-Med Integration and the 'ring of friends': The Mediterranean's Europe Challenge* (Malta: European Documentation and Research Centre, 2003), vol. IV, p. 21.

[4] Communication from the Commission to the Council and the European Parliament–Wider Europe–Neighbourhood: A New Framework for Relations with our Eastern and Southern Neighbours, COM(2003)104; Communication on the European Neighbourhood Policy – Strategy Paper; COM(2004)373; Communication from the Commission to the Council and the European Parliament on strengthening the European Neighbourhood Policy, COM(2006)726. Other ENP primary documents are available at: http://ec.europa.eu/world/enp/documents_en.htm#5.

[5] Communication to the Commission from Commissioner Ferrero Waldner, 'Implementing and promoting the European Neighbourhood Policy', SEC(2005)1521.

[6] The ENP covers Algeria, Armenia, Azerbaijan, Belarus, Egypt, Georgia, Israel, Jordan, Lebanon, Libya, Moldova, Morocco, Palestinian Authority, Syria, Tunisia and Ukraine.

[7] GAERC Conclusions, 14 June 2004, p. 11.

[8] The pre-accession strategy notably concerns Croatia, Turkey and Macedonia as official candidate States available at: http://ec.europa.eu/enlargement/countries/index_en.htm.

[9] The eastern dimension of the ENP is intended equally to cover Belarus 'as soon as the country indicates a willingness to move towards true democracy, human rights and rule of law' (Commissioner Ferrero Waldner, 21/11/2006; IP/06/1593). It was also deemed to cover the Russian Federation (COM(2003)104, p. 4), but the latter has instead favoured a 'strategic partnership' with the EU; see contribution by P. Van Elsuwege in this volume; C. Hillion, 'The Russian Federation', in S. Blockmans and A. Łazowski (eds.), *The European Union and its Neighbours* (The Hague: Asser Press, 2006).

[10] PCA between the European Communities and their Member States on the one hand, and Ukraine on the other, OJ 1998 L 49/1; PCA between the European Communities and their Member States on the one hand, and Moldova on the other, OJ 1998 L 181/1.

strategy. A third part explores the future prospects of the ENP, in the light of the current discussions on a new EU agreement with Ukraine.

11.2 An integrated EU external action

Since it represents a pivotal inspiration for the development of the ENP, the EU enlargement policy should be recalled in its key substantive and institutional features (1). Against this background, it will be suggested that, like enlargement, the ENP is an all-encompassing and integrated EU policy (2).

11.2.1 Enlargement: an EU policy par excellence

The EU enlargement policy towards central and eastern European countries (CEECs) is regarded as a successful foreign policy.[11] Indeed, it has been remarkably efficient in stimulating profound reforms in the countries concerned. Such efficiency derives from incentives offered by the EU, namely the promise of accession (the proverbial 'carrot'), but, arguably, it also stems from the integrated and thus coherent character of the policy, both in substantive and institutional terms.

Enlargement is an integrated policy in that it entails the projection of the entire EU *acquis* towards the applicant State. To become a Member State, the candidate must accept all EC norms, as well as the CFSP and PJCCM (Police and Judicial Cooperation in Criminal Matters) *acquis*.[12] The classical division into EU 'pillars' is thus irrelevant in the enlargement process, for the latter is all-encompassing by definition. In other words, and as indeed suggested by the inclusion of its legal basis (Art. 49 TEU) in the Final Provisions of the TEU, enlargement is an 'un-pillarised' policy of the EU, thus immune to 'pillar politics'.[13]

---

[11] See COM(2003)104, p. 5; see also e.g. M. Cremona, 'Enlargement: A Successful Instrument of Foreign Policy?' in T.Tridimas and P. Nebbia (eds.), *European Union Law for the Twenty-First Century: Rethinking the New Legal Order* (Oxford: Hart Publishing, 2004), vol. 1, p. 397; Report of W. Kok to the European Commission, *Enlarging the European Union – Achievements and Challenges*, Florence, Robert Schuman Centre for Advanced Studies, European University Institute, 2003, p. 4.

[12] Further on accession conditions: F. Hoffmeister, 'Earlier enlargements', in A. Ott and K. Inglis (eds.), *Handbook on European Enlargement* (The Hague: Asser Press, 2002), p. 90; C. Hillion, 'The Copenhagen criteria and their progeny', in C. Hillion (ed.), *EU Enlargement – A Legal Approach* (Oxford: Hart Publishing, 2004), p. 3.

[13] See C. Hillion, *The European Union and its East-European Neighbours – A laboratory for the organisation of EU external relations* (Oxford: Hart Publishing, forthcoming).

The all-encompassing character of the enlargement process is epitomised by the EU 'pre-accession strategy'. This ad hoc strategy,[14] developed specifically to prepare the accession of the CEECs, transformed the existing contractual relations between the EU and these countries (viz. the 'Europe Agreements' based on Art. 310 EC) into pre-accession devices.[15] It also established, through the novel 'accession partnership',[16] a system of EU monitoring of the candidates' adaptation to all EU membership requirements.[17] In particular, individual 'accession partnerships' were drafted by the Commission to set out a list of principles, objectives and priorities on which the candidate's adaptation efforts should concentrate to meet all EU accession conditions, be they economic, political or legal. The candidate's performance in meeting those targets was assessed by the Commission and recorded in comprehensive annual progress reports, on the basis of which the Council would thereafter adjust the pace of the accession process, as well as the allocation of the specific financial assistance to prepare membership.[18] The Commission was thereby granted a pivotal position in implementing the enlargement policy, broadly defined by the European Council. Acting well beyond its conventional role of 'guardian of the [EC] Treaty', it promoted, and controlled, the future members' progressive application of the wider *EU acquis*.[19]

---

[14] For a detailed analysis of the pre-accession strategy, see M. Maresceau, 'Pre-accession', in M. Cremona (ed.), *The enlargement of the European Union* (Oxford: Oxford University Press, 2003), p. 9.

[15] M. Maresceau and E. Montaguti, 'The relations between the European Union and central and eastern Europe: a legal appraisal', 32 CMLRev. (1995), p. 1327.

[16] Council Regulation 622/98 on assistance to the applicant States in the framework of the pre-accession strategy, and in particular on the establishment of Accession Partnerships, OJ 1998 L 85/1.

[17] On Accession Partnership and conditionality, see H. Grabbe, 'A Partnership for *Accession*? The Implications of EU Conditionality for the Central and East European Applicants', *Working Paper no. 99/12*, EUI Robert Schuman Centre for Advanced Studies, 1999; K. Inglis, 'The pre-accession strategy and the accession partnerships', in Ott and Inglis, *Handbook*, p. 103; T. Haenebalcke, K. Inglis and E. Lannon, 'The Many Faces of EU Conditionality in Pan-Euro-Mediterranean Relations', in M. Maresceau and E. Lannon (eds.), *The EU's Enlargement and Mediterranean Strategies: A Comparative Analysis* (Basingstoke: Palgrave, 2001), p. 97; C. Hillion, 'EU shapes for Eastern Enlargement', *EU Focus*, 1998, p. 3.

[18] Article 4 of Council Regulation 622/98 establishes a system whereby the Council, on a proposal from the Commission, can review the pre-accession financial assistance, if progress in meeting the accession requirements is found to be insufficient.

[19] In its annual reports, the Commission provides an assessment of the candidates' progress in meeting all the accession conditions (Copenhagen criteria), including those of a political nature, such as the protection of minorities. It also supervises the candidates' progress in

Both in substantive and institutional terms, it appears that the enlargement policy articulated through the pre-accession strategy, is an all-encompassing EU policy, rather than an EC external action and/or a CFSP/PJCCM measure. Based on atypical instruments, it generated a new dynamic in the EU–CEECs relationship. It also entailed new roles for the EU institutions, and novel forms of interactions between them, foreign to the procedures set out in the Treaty.[20] As such, the enlargement policy is regarded, notably by the Commission, as an attractive model for organising, beyond the enlargement context, the EU external action towards the neighbouring countries.

11.2.2 An integrated policy inspiring the ENP

While not designed to prepare membership,[21] the ENP borrows several elements of the enlargement policy.[22] To begin with, the ENP involves the EU as a whole. The policy is conceived as an all-encompassing promotion of EU norms and standards towards the neighbours.[23] In particular, the ENP promotes legislative and regulatory approximation to selected EC standards in return for 'a stake in the internal market', ultimately to create an

---

adopting the *acquis* in Justice and Home Affairs, and CFSP; see Chapters 24 and 27 of the regular reports for each candidate country. As regards more particularly the scrutiny of the political conditionality, see A. Williams, 'Enlargement of the Union and human rights conditionality: a policy', 25 ELRev. (2000), p. 601; K. Smith, 'The evolution and application of EU membership conditionality', in Cremona (ed.), *The enlargement*, p. 105; D. Kochenov, *The Failure of Conditionality*, Groningen, PhD Dissertation, 2007.

[20] It should be noted that the 2003 Accession Treaty has partly maintained this extraordinary role for the Commission, by endowing it with the power to adopt specific safeguard measures in the field of Justice and Home affairs, with no equivalent in the context of the TEU; see Article 39 of the Act of Accession, OJ 2003 L 236/33. Further: K. Inglis, 'The Union's fifth accession treaty': New means to make enlargement possible', 41 CMLRev. (2004), p. 937; E. Lannon, 'Le Traité d'adhésion d'Athènes: Les négociations, les conditions de l'admission et les principales adaptations des traités résultant de l'élargissement de l'UE à vingt cinq Etats membres', CDE (2004), pp. 15; C. Hillion, 'The European Union is dead. Long live the European Union . . . A Commentary on the Accession Treaty 2003', 29 ELRev. (2004), p. 583.

[21] See the evolving formulations of the disconnection between the ENP and membership prospect, in the various communications of the Commission: COM(2003)104, p. 5; COM (2004)373, p. 3; COM(2006)726, p. 2.

[22] Further: J. Kelley, 'New Wine in Old Wineskins: Policy Adaptation in the European Neighbourhood Policy', 44 JCMS (2006), p. 29; A. Magen, 'The Shadow of Enlargement: Can the European Neighbourhood Policy Achieve Compliance?', Stanford, *CDDRL Working Papers*, Nr 68, 2006; S. Lavenex, 'EU external governance in wider Europe', *Journal of European Public Policy* (2004), p. 680.

[23] COM(2004)373.

'economic community' between the EU and the ENP partners.[24] It also covers political issues, insisting, for instance, on the neighbours' respect for the fundamental rights advocated by the EU, while calling for stronger cooperation in CFSP matters in the form of, for instance, further involvement of East European countries in European Security and Defence Policy (ESDP) operations, and stronger cooperation in Justice and Home Affairs.

Indeed, the Commission has emphasised that the ENP is 'a comprehensive policy integrating related components from all three *pillars* of the Union's present structure'.[25] It offers 'a means for an enhanced and more focused policy approach of the EU towards its neighbourhood, bringing together the principal instruments at the disposal of the Union and its member States [and] contribute[s] to further advancing and supporting the EU's foreign policy objectives'.[26] Indeed, the ENP represents a regional implementation of the European Security Strategy.[27]

The projection of the EU as an integrated normative whole is not only reflected in the list of objectives of ENP. It is also evidenced and articulated by the 'action plans' (APs) the EU adopted for each ENP country.[28] Based on prior Commission 'Country Reports' on the political, economic, social and legislative situation of the ENP partners,[29] each AP establishes a list of specific priorities for reform on which the partner concerned should mobilise its resources, in return for a closer relationship with the EU.[30] '[C] overing a number of key areas for specific action',[31] those priorities are nonetheless comprehensive in their coverage and in their ambitions.[32] They

---

[24] COM(2006)726, p. 5.   [25] COM(2004)373, p. 6.   [26] COM(2004)373, p. 8.

[27] The ESS ('A Secure Europe in a Better World' (available at: http://ue.eu.int/uedocs/cmsUpload/ 78367.pdf) endorsed by the European Council in 2003 calls for 'a ring of well governed countries to the East of the European Union and on the borders of the Mediterranean with whom we can enjoy close and cooperative relations'. Further: M. Cremona and C. Hillion, '*L'Union fait la force*? Potential and Limitations of the European Neighbourhood Policy as an Integrated EU Foreign and Security Policy', *EUI Law Working Papers* 2006/39.

[28] Except in relation to Algeria, Belarus, Libya and Syria. APs available at: http://ec.europa.eu/ world/enp/documents_en.htm. Further, on the APs, C. Hillion, '*Thou shalt love thy neighbour*: the draft European Neighbourhood Policy Action Plan between the EU and Ukraine', in A. Mayhew and N. Copsey (eds.), *Ukraine and European Neighbourhood Policy* (Brighton: Sussex European Institute, 2005), p. 17.

[29] Commission Staff Working Paper: European Neighbourhood Policy, Country Report – Ukraine; SEC(2004)566; Commission Staff Working Paper: European Neighbourhood Policy, Country Report – Moldova; SEC(2004)567. Other Country Reports available at: http://ec. europa.eu/world/enp/documents_en.htm.

[30] COM(2004)373, p. 3.   [31] COM(2004)373, p. 3.

[32] E.g. GAERC Conclusions, 16 June 2003 and 14 June 2004.

relate to 'political dialogue and reform; trade and measures preparing partners for gradually obtaining a stake in the EU's Internal Market; justice and home affairs; energy, transport, information society, environment and research and innovation; and social policy and people-to-people contacts'.[33]

The Neighbourhood Policy is thus comprehensive in scope. But it is also integrated in its institutional set up. Not founded on any particular legal basis, the ENP took shape through ad hoc interplays between the Commission (particularly DG external relations) and the Council (including the High Representative (HR) for CFSP), with the blessing of the European Council.[34] Such atypical interactions are not only apparent in the setting up of the ENP, they are also evident in the conduct of the policy, and notably at the level of the *elaboration* and *suivi* of the APs.

The *elaboration* of the AP was mainly the work of the Commission, 'in cooperation with the HR for CFSP for CFSP matters', and in consultation with the country concerned. In the case of Ukraine, the process of consultation started in January 2004 and lasted until September of the same year. Six meetings took place to discuss the draft AP proposed by the Commission, represented at the level of the Deputy Director General of DG External Relations, with the Ukrainian Deputy Foreign Minister. The Commission was then alone in representing the EU. Indeed, in contrast to the negotiations of classical EC external agreements, it did not have any particular 'negotiating mandate' from the Council.[35] Instead, the content of the drafts forwarded to the Ukrainian authorities, and the EU position during the 'negotiations' were essentially the product of the Commission's own initiative. This novel procedure was, however, suspended in March, for two months, after some Member States objected that the Commission should not negotiate the AP on its own, and certainly not the latter's non-EC elements. Hence, when the EU consultations with Ukraine resumed, the EU delegation comprised not only a Commission official, but also a representative of the Council Secretariat General, and a representative of the EU Presidency.[36]

---

[33] COM(2004)373, p. 3.

[34] See e.g. European Council Conclusions, 12–13 December 2002; European Council Conclusions, 19–20 June 2003; European Council Conclusions, 16–17 October 2003; European Council Conclusions, 17–18 June 2004; European Council Conclusions, 16–17 June 2005; European Council Conclusions, 15–16 December 2005; European Council Conclusions, 15–16 June 2006.

[35] Cfr. Article 300 EC.   [36] Interviews, Ukrainian officials, January 2007.

Once completed,[37] each of the APs was presented by the Commission to the Council,[38] which swiftly endorsed them.[39] Formally, the Council was asked by the Commission to adopt a 'decision on the position to be adopted by the Communities and its (sic) Member States within the [PCAs] Cooperation Council[s] ... with regard to the adoption of a Recommendation on the implementation of the ... Action Plan'.[40] Interestingly, the Commission proposed that the decision be based not only on Article 2(1) of the Council and Commission decision on the conclusion of the Partnership and Cooperation Agreement (PCA),[41] but also on Article 15 TEU concerning CFSP Common Positions. The Commission's proposal thereby confirmed the comprehensive and inter-pillar character of the APs.

Having been endorsed by the Council, the APs were eventually presented to the respective EU–Ukraine and EU–Moldova Cooperation Councils for approval,[42] as a 'recommendation on the implementation' of the ... Action Plans.[43] Based on PCA Cooperation Councils' recommendations, the APs,

---

[37] The Commission endorsed the AP on 9 December 2004: Communication from the Commission to the Council on the Commission proposals for Action Plans under the European Neighbourhood Policy (ENP), COM(2004)795.

[38] The APs were also transmitted to the European Parliament, the Economic and Social Committee, and the Committee of the Regions for information.

[39] GAERC Conclusions, 13 December 2004.

[40] Commission Proposal for a Council Decision on the 'position to be adopted by the Community and its Member States within the cooperation Council established by the (PCA) ... with regard to the adoption of a Recommendation on the implementation of the EU–Moldova Action Plan', COM(2004)787; Commission Proposal for a Council Decision on the 'position to be adopted by the Community and its Member States within the cooperation Council established by the (PCA) ... with regard to the adoption of a Recommendation on the implementation of the EU–Ukraine Action Plan', COM(2004)791.

[41] Council and Commission Decision of 26 January 1998 on the conclusion of the Partnership and Cooperation Agreement between the European Communities and their Member States, of the one part, and Ukraine, of the other part, OJ 1998 L 49/1; Council and Commission Decision of 28 May 1998 on the conclusion of the Partnership and Cooperation Agreement between the European Communities and their Member States, of the one part, and the Republic of Moldova, of the other part, OJ 1998 L 181/1.

[42] The Council invited the Committee of Permanent Representatives to prepare the necessary decisions enabling the Cooperation Councils with the respective ENP partners to confirm these action plans and to launch their implementation. As pointed out by the Council, it is only a *confirmation*. The APs were in practice already 'agreed' with the partner countries concerned even before the Commission, as a college, had formally adopted them on 9 December 2004.

[43] Recommendation 1/2005 of the EU–Ukraine Council of 21 February 2005 on the implementation of the EU/Ukraine Action Plan; Recommendation 1/2005 of the EU–Moldova Cooperation Council of 22 February 2005 on the implementation of the EU/Moldova Action

like the individual accession partnerships adopted by the Commission for each candidate,[44] do not have legally binding effect.[45] They are 'political documents',[46] whose implementation is not subject to prior formal ratification by the 'parties'.

As regards the *suivi*, the ENP foresees that the Commission is responsible for drawing up periodic progress reports on the overall implementation of the APs, in cooperation with the HR for CFSP 'on issues related to political dialogue and cooperation, and the CFSP'.[47] These reports are to be transmitted to the Council which decides (in tandem with the European Council) on the development of the Partnerships, on the potential review of the financial assistance, and as the case may be, on opening negotiations with a view to establishing a 'European Neighbourhood Agreement'.[48]

The foregoing suggests that the ENP involves *sui generis* interplays among the EU institutions. Foreign to the classical Treaty procedures, this institutional set-up reproduces, to a considerable extent, the ad hoc interactions of the pre-accession strategy, while elaborating upon them. The cooperation between the HR for CFSP and the Commission is particularly noticeable in this regard as it tends to foreshadow the merger of the two functions envisaged in the Treaty of Lisbon.[49] More generally, aimed at handling the multi-faceted external implications of the 2004/07 enlargement, the neighbourhood policy is an integrated action of the *Union*. As such, it benefits, to some extent at least, from the immunity to the 'pillar politics' that often characterise the EU system of external relations, thereby enhancing the coherence of the Union's action towards its neighbours.

Plan. The recommendation contains a sole Article whereby the Cooperation Council recommends that the Parties implement the AP which is annexed thereto.

[44] E.g. 1999 Accession Partnership for Poland available at: http://ec.europa.eu/enlargement/archives/pdf/dwn/ap_02_00/ap_pl_99_en.pdf.

[45] The Mediterranean APs were also adopted as recommendations by the Association Council established by the Euro-Mediterranean Association Agreements, despite such Councils having a power to adopt binding decisions (e.g. Art. 83 of EMAA with Morocco, OJ 2000 L 70/2). Had they been adopted in the form of a decision, APs would have formally become part of the Community legal order, with potentially far-reaching legal implications, notably direct effect (see Case C-192/89 *Sevince* [1990] ECR I-3461).

[46] See introduction of the EU/Moldova AP.

[47] See GAERC Conclusions, 13 December 2004; and Conclusions of the subsequent December 2004 European Council.

[48] See further Section 11.4.   [49] Article 18 TEU revised.

11.3 Adapting existing relations to the needs of an enlarged EU

In addition to its integrated structure, the ENP is also characterised by its capacity effectively to modify the perspective of existing agreements, despite its non-legally binding nature. More particularly, through the ENP, the PCAs with Ukraine and Moldova are being embedded into an all-encompassing EU foreign policy perspective. The ENP thereby triggers a (unilateral) reorientation of the Partnerships (a). It also introduces a close EU monitoring of the ENP countries' implementation of the PCA (b), thus preparing the grounds for establishing a new generation of bilateral agreements.

11.3.1 A 'political reorientation' of the PCAs

As stipulated in the AP, 'the ENP opens new partnership (sic)'. Indeed, through the neighbourhood policy, the EU is revisiting the objectives of the Partnerships based on the PCAs, and transforms the latter into a means to achieving the EU's foreign policy objective of establishing a ring of stable, secure and prosperous friends.

According to the PCA with Ukraine, the Partnership aims:

to provide an appropriate framework for the political dialogue between the Parties allowing the development of close political relations;

to promote trade and investment and harmonious economic relations between the Parties and so to foster their sustainable development;

to provide a basis for mutually advantageous economic, social, financial, civil scientific technological and cultural cooperation;

to support Ukrainian efforts to consolidate its democracy and to develop its economy and to complete the transition into a market economy.[50]

The ENP goes far beyond these fairly general objectives.[51] It offers the ENP partners 'the prospect of a stake in EU internal market, and further integration and liberalisation to promote the free movement of persons,

---

[50] Article 1 PCA Ukraine; also Article 1 PCA Moldova.

[51] In the case of Ukraine, the ENP objectives also surpass those of the 1999 Common Strategy, OJ 1999 L 331/1. Further, on these objectives: M. Maresceau, 'EU Enlargement and EU Common Strategies on Russia and Ukraine: An Ambiguous Yet Unavoidable Connection', in Hillion (ed.), *EU Enlargement*, p. 181.

goods, services and capital (four freedoms)',[52] as well as the possibility 'to participate progressively in key aspects of EU policies and programmes' in return for their concrete political and economic reforms.[53] Indeed, it refers to 'a ring of countries, sharing the EU's fundamental values and objectives, drawn into an increasing close relationship, going beyond cooperation to involve a significant measure of economic and political integration',[54] hence exceeding the PCA's aim of 'a gradual rapprochement between the Ukraine and a wider area of cooperation in Europe and neighbouring regions'.[55]

While the EU reformulates the established Partnerships' objectives through the ENP, the latter does not, however, intend, at least initially, to replace the PCAs.[56] Rather, like the pre-accession strategy did in relation to the Europe Agreements, the ENP triggers a 'political reorientation' of the existing contractual framework between the EU and the East European countries.[57] Without being formally renegotiated, the terms of the PCAs are being further articulated to fit in the overall EU policy framework set out by the ENP. Indeed, the latter seeks, particularly through the APs,[58] to ensure fulfilment of the Partners' PCA obligations.[59] For example, the EU/Ukraine AP seeks 'full implementation of PCA commitments in the sphere of trade in goods'.[60] With respect to the conditions affecting establishment and operation of companies, the AP also calls for 'the full implementation of title IV, chapter II of the PCA, and in particular of the most favoured nation and national treatment principles'.[61]

More than simply articulating the PCA, the AP occasionally revisits its provisions. For instance, the APs with Ukraine and Moldova not only require the fulfilment of the PCA commitments regarding movement of workers, they also elucidate what the commitments are, and how they

---

[52] COM(2003)104, p. 4.   [53] COM(2004)373, p. 8.   [54] COM(2004)373, p. 5.

[55] See preamble of the PCA with Ukraine.

[56] Indeed, the EU continues to consider the PCA as a 'valid basis of EU–(eastern neighbours) cooperation'; COM(2004)787 (Moldova), p. 8; COM(2004)791 (Ukraine), p. 7.

[57] The concept of political reorientation was initially employed to characterise the effect of the pre-accession strategy on the existing relations between the EU and the CEECs, namely the Europe Agreements, see Maresceau and Montaguti, 'The relations'; K. Inglis, 'The Europe Agreements compared in the light of their pre-accession reorientation', 37 CMLRev. (2000), p.1173.

[58] The draft recommendations on the implementation of the APs, as proposed by the Commission contain a 'sole article' which stipulates that the implementation of the AP is 'directed towards attainment of the objectives of the PCA', see COM(2004)787 (Moldova), p. 6; COM(2004)791(Ukraine), p. 6.

[59] COM(2004)373, p. 3.   [60] Pt. 2.3(1) EU/Ukraine AP.   [61] Pt. 2.3(2) EU/Ukraine AP.

should be fulfilled. In particular, the APs foresee that to comply with the PCA labour provisions, the partners have to 'ensure full application of the best endeavour clause by abolishing all discriminatory measures based on nationality which affect migrant workers, as regards working conditions, remuneration and dismissal'.[62] In legal terms, a 'best endeavour' clause, such as the one included in the PCA workers' provisions, does not by definition establish an obligation of result.[63] In requiring the 'abolishing' of all discriminatory measures, the APs seem to say otherwise. Notwithstanding the apparent contradiction in terms of these provisions, they suggest that the AP hardens up some of the PCA's obligations, albeit through non-legally binding instruments.

The reformulation of the PCA carried out through the ENP also concerns the degree and intensity of ENP partners' legislative approximation. While the PCA merely foresees that Ukraine and Moldova should 'endeavour to ensure that their legislation will gradually be made compatible with that of the Community',[64] the ENP in general, and the AP in particular, are set to advance the process approximation of their legislation, norms and standards with those of the European Union,[65] and to reinforce their administrative and judicial capacity to ensure the effectiveness of the legal adaptation.[66] In the same vein, Community assistance through the European Neighbourhood and Partnership Instrument (ENPI) is to be used to support measures aimed 'at promoting legislative and regulatory approximation towards higher standards in all relevant areas and in particular to encourage the progressive participation of partner countries in the internal market and the intensification of trade'.[67]

The ENP therefore seeks to support the East European States' fulfilment of their obligations under the PCAs, but in the all-encompassing perspective of the neighbourhood policy. Rather than replacing the Agreements, the APs set out concrete priorities, targets and steps with a view to giving practical guidance to the East European authorities to enhance their compliance with

---

[62] E.g. Pt. 2.3(4) EU/Ukraine AP; Pt. 2.4.4. EU/Moldova AP.

[63] See in this regard Opinion of Advocate General Stix-Hackl in Case C-265/03 *Simutenkov* [2005] ECR I-2579; Annotation, CMLRev. (2008), p. 815.

[64] Article 50 PCA Moldova; Article 51 PCA Ukraine.

[65] E.g. Pt. 1 – 'New Partnership, economic integration and cooperation perspective', EU/Ukraine AP and Pts 1 'Introduction' EU/Moldova AP (also pt 20).

[66] E.g. Pt. 1 – 'Priorities for action', EU/Ukraine AP and EU/Moldova AP.

[67] Article 2, ENPI Regulation, OJ 2006 L 310/3.

the rules of these Agreements, as restated in the light of the ENP objectives. Indeed, as suggested earlier, the ENP has the effect of widening the relationship. The CFSP, as well as the 'Justice and Home Affairs' dimensions of the Partnerships,[68] are developed and strengthened,[69] in line with the ambitions set out in the ENP. For instance, the EU/Moldova AP foresees that particular attention should be paid to 'sustained efforts towards a viable solution to the Transnistria conflict'. It also provides that Moldova should continue administrative reform and strengthening of local self-government, in line with European standards, notably those contained in the European Charter on Local Self Government. In the field of judicial cooperation, the AP enjoins the Moldovan authorities to 're-examine and amend the law on the organisation of the judiciary with a view to ensuring its independence, impartiality and efficiency, including clarification of the procedure for appointment and promotion, statutory rights and obligations of judges'.[70] In the same vein, Ukraine should ensure implementation of its recent reforms of civil, criminal and administrative codes and codes of procedure, based on European standards; and continue the reform of the prosecution system in accordance with the relevant Council of Europe Action Plan.[71]

Thus, through the ENP, the EU reformulates the objectives of the Partnerships, widens the latter's scope and revisits some of their provisions with a view to guiding and enhancing the partners' compliance, as a means to achieving the ENP objectives. This reorientation is backed-up by a new system of monitoring, inspired by the pre-accession strategy, which coupled with incentives, is deemed to instil dynamism in the relationship.

11.3.2 Including compliance incentives and monitoring in the partnerships

Each AP establishes 'a benchmarked roadmap in bringing about needed reforms'.[72] Carrying out those reforms is the key for the ENP partner to

---

[68] See e.g. Pt. 2.4. EU/Ukraine AP. A specific action plan on Justice and Home Affairs with Ukraine was set out on 10 December 2001, and cooperation in this field continues to be based on this specific AP, though supplemented by the ENP Action Plan. See in this regard the press release following the meeting on JHA of the EU Troika and Ukraine, 29 March 2004, available at: http://ue.eu.int/ueDocs/cms_Data/docs/pressdata/en/er/79718.pdf.

[69] E.g. Pt. 2.1. EU/Ukraine AP.   [70] Pt. 2.1.2 EU/Moldova AP.   [71] Pt. 2.1. EU/Ukraine AP.

[72] Address by J. Solana, 'The role of the EU in promoting and consolidating democracy in Europe's East' at the *Common Vision for a Common neighbourhood Conference* (Vilnius, 4 May 2006).

get 'closer to the European Union', by way of integration into European programmes and networks,[73] increased assistance and enhanced market access.[74] Moreover, the ENP foresees the future establishment of a 'European Neighbourhood Agreement' which would replace the present bilateral agreements,[75] 'upon fulfilment of the objectives and actions contained in the ... Action Plan'.[76] As suggested by the Commission, 'the speed and intensity of this process [of rapprochement] will depend on the will and capability of each partner country to engage in this broad agenda'.[77]

Indeed, the partners' fulfilment of the AP priorities is closely assessed and monitored on a basis of a system tested earlier in the context of the pre-accession strategy. In principle, the monitoring takes place within the PCAs' institutional frameworks.[78] Partner countries are asked to provide detailed information, 'as a basis for this joint monitoring exercise'.[79] But as indicated earlier, the evaluation of the Partners' performance is ultimately recorded in periodic progress reports drafted by the Commission, in cooperation with the HR for CFSP.[80] These reports are then transmitted for examination to the Council,[81] which should then decide on the development of the Partnerships.

---

[73] See in this regard: Communication from the Commission to the Council and to the European Parliament on the general approach to enable European Neighbourhood Policy partner countries to participate in community agencies and community programmes, COM(2006)724.

[74] For the complete list of incentives, see COM(2004)373, pp. 8–9.

[75] COM(2004)373, p. 5.   [76] Pt. 1 (Introduction) EU–Ukraine AP.

[77] See e.g. Commission Staff Working Paper 'European Neighbourhood Policy – Country Report – Moldova; SEC(2004)567. Though not legally binding, the APs do influence the policy-making in the countries concerned. For example, the government's programme of Ukrainian Prime Minister Tymoshenko included several priorities foreseen in the AP, such as customs reforms or fight against corruption.

[78] The involvement of the PCA's institutions in the monitoring process is also typical of the pre-accession strategy. Council Regulation 622/98 establishing the Accession Partnership which foresees that 'the role played by the bodies set up by the EAs is central to ensuring the proper implementation and follow up of these action plans', see 11th Recital of the Preamble, OJ 1998 L 85/1.

[79] COM(2004)373, p. 10.

[80] The first batch of 'progress reports' was published on 4 December 2006, as part of an overall Commission Communication 'on strengthening the European Neighbourhood Policy'. The reports are available at: http://ec.europa.eu/world/enp/pdf/sec06_1505-2_en.pdf (Ukraine); and http://ec.europa.eu/world/enp/pdf/sec06_1506-2_en.pdf (Moldova).

[81] See GAERC Conclusions, 22 January 2007.

As the Commission points out:

> When the monitoring process demonstrates significant progress in attaining the priorities which have been set, these incentives can be reviewed, with a view to taking further steps along the path to greater integration with the internal market and other key EU policies. The process is a dynamic one, with the Action Plans constituting an important first step.[82]

In particular, in speaking of a possible future agreement with East European countries, the Council predicated the opening of negotiations on the Partners' addressing the political priorities of the AP,[83] a conditionality that is reminiscent of the evolution of the Copenhagen political criteria into 'admissibility condition', i.e. for opening accession negotiations.[84] The deepening of the bilateral relationship is equally subject to the Partners' commitment to promote market oriented economic reforms,[85] and cooperation on key foreign policy objectives such as counter-terrorism and non-proliferation of weapons of mass-destruction. Its performance also influences the EU allocation of funds, particularly under the ENPI.[86] Constituting the financial incentive for global reform of

---

[82] COM(2004)373, p. 9.

[83] The Joint Statement of the EU–Ukraine Summit of December 2005 reads as follows: 'EU leaders confirmed their commitment to initiate early consultations on a new enhanced agreement between EU and Ukraine to replace the Partnership and Cooperation Agreement, as soon as the political priorities of the Action Plan have been addressed', available at: http://europa.eu/rapid/pressReleasesAction.do?reference=PRES/05/337&format=HTML&aged=0&language=EN&guiLanguage=en.

[84] Further: M. Cremona, 'Accession to the European Union: Membership Conditionality and Accession Criteria', *Polish Yearbook of International Law* (2002), pp. 234–8. C. Hillion, 'Enlargement of the European Union – A legal perspective', in A. Arnull and D. Wincott (eds.), *Accountability and Legitimacy in the European Union* (Oxford: Oxford University Press, 2002), p. 401.

[85] As well as to the partner's accession to the WTO, see 'EU-Ukraine start negotiations on new Enhanced Agreement', available at: http://www.europa.eu/rapid/pressReleasesAction.do?reference=IP/07/275&format=HTML&aged=0&language=EN&guiLanguage=en.

[86] Article 28 of the ENPI Regulation (OJ 2006 L 310/1) provides that where a partner country fails to observe the principles set out in the ENPI, the Council, acting by a qualified majority on a proposal from the Commission, may take appropriate steps in respect of any assistance granted to the partner country under the ENPI Regulation. Such conditionality is without prejudice to the provisions on the suspension of aid in partnership and cooperation agreements which provide that respect for human rights and democratic principles constitute an essential element of the Agreement. Any violation of such an essential element may lead to the immediate suspension of the PCA. Further: M. Cremona, 'Human rights and democracy clauses in the EC's trade agreements', in N. Emiliou and D. O'Keeffe (eds.), *The European Union and world trade law* (Chichester: Wiley, 1996), p.62; C. Hillion, 'Introduction to the Partnership and Cooperation Agreements', in A. Kellermann, J. De Zwaan and J. Czuczai

the ENP countries, it embodies a system of sanction in case progress is lacking, a system that was foreshadowed by the pre-accession strategy, and more specifically the accession partnerships.[87]

Through a blend of incentives, strengthened monitoring and potential financial sanctions, the ENP introduces more dynamism in the existing Partnerships. The latter become all the more dynamic that, as suggested above, the ENP envisages their potential upgrading through the conclusion of a new agreement. The ENP thereby turns the PCA into a transitional arrangement.

11.4 Towards a new generation of bilateral agreements

The EU policy papers on the neighbourhood policy evoke the establishment of a 'European Neighbourhood Agreement' that would replace the existing bilateral arrangements, but without specifying what it would consist of.[88] Rather, and in contrast to the AP, the scope (a) and nature (b) of this new arrangement appear to be determined through bilateral discussions between the Union and the neighbours concerned, as suggested by the negotiations between the EU and Ukraine.[89]

11.4.1 A contractual widening and deepening of the existing relationship

According to the Commission, the envisaged agreement should include provisions for the purposes of establishing a Free Trade Area (FTA), and possibly a 'deep' and 'comprehensive' FTA,[90] by opposition to 'simple and shallow' FTA.[91]

(eds.), *EU enlargement – The Constitutional Impact at EU and National Level* (The Hague: Asser Press, 2001), p. 215.

[87] See Section 11.2.1.   [88] COM(2004)373, p. 5.

[89] 'Commission proposes negotiating directives for enhanced agreement with Ukraine', IP/06/1184; 13/09/2006: http://europa.eu/rapid/pressReleasesAction.do?reference=IP/06/1184&format=HTML&aged=0&language=EN&guiLanguage=en; see 'EU-Ukraine start negotiations on new Enhanced Agreement': http://www.europa.eu/rapid/pressReleasesAction.do?reference=IP/07/275&format=HTML&aged=0&language=EN&guiLanguage=en.

[90] COM(2006)726, pp. 4–5.

[91] Further on these concepts, see M. Emerson (ed.), *The Prospect of Deep Free Trade between the European Union and Ukraine* (Brussels: Centre for European Policy Studies, 2006).

A *comprehensive* FTA is conceived as encompassing liberalisation of trade in goods and services, in compliance with the relevant GATT and GATS requirements.[92] The EU trade relations with East European countries would thereby be significantly deepened. Essentially inspired by the Most Favoured Nation principle, the PCAs with Moldova and Ukraine only contain a 'rendez-vous' clause whereby the parties agreed merely to *discuss* the feasibility of an FTA, without any commitment to establish it.[93]

A *deep* FTA refers to the important role regulatory approximation would play in the new relationship. Such approximation is set to supplement the abolition of tariffs, entailed by the establishment of a classical FTA, with a reduction of non-tariff (i.e. technical)[94] barriers by fostering the adoption, by the ENP partners, of EC-compatible or equivalent standards. The new agreement would thereby consolidate a process already furthered under the APs,[95] with a view to promoting economic integration between the EU and the ENP partners, and to preparing the grounds for the latter's ultimate participation in the internal market.

If it were to establish such a deep and comprehensive FTA, the new agreement would bring about considerable widening and deepening of EU *trade* relations with its East European neighbours, though it should be recalled that the FTA, and a fortiori a deep FTA, will not be put in place overnight. As illustrated by the old Europe Agreements (EAs),[96] additional years may be needed after the agreement's entry into force for the FTA to be fully operational. Indeed, the economic situation of the partners is liable to determine how quickly such an FTA might be set up.

---

[92] See Article XXIV GATT and Article V GATS, respectively. Further: P. Van Den Bossche, *The Law and Policy of the World Trade Organization: Text, Cases and Materials* (Cambridge: Cambridge University Press, 2005), p. 658.

[93] Article 4 PCA Ukraine. Further from this author: 'Partnership and cooperation agreements between the EU and the NIS of the ex-Soviet Union', 3 EFARev. (1998), p. 399; R. Petrov, 'The Partnership and Cooperation Agreements with the Newly Independent States', in Ott and Inglis, *Handbook*, p. 175.

[94] E.g. technical norms and standards, sanitary and phytosanitary rules, competition policy, enterprise competitiveness, innovation and industrial policy, research cooperation, intellectual property rights, trade facilitation, customs measures and administrative capacity in the area of rules of origin, good governance in the tax area, company law, public procurement and financial services, COM(2006)726, p. 4.

[95] This legal approximation also builds on the provisions on legislative cooperation in the PCAs (e.g. Article 50 PCA Moldova, and Article 51 PCA Ukraine). Further: R. Petrov, 'Recent Developments in the Adaptation of Ukrainian Legislation to EU Law', 8 EFARev. (2003), p. 125.

[96] E.g. Europe Agreement establishing an association between the European Communities and their Member States, of the one part, and the Republic of Poland, of the other part, OJ 1993 L 348/2.

Beyond the deepening of trade relations, the new agreement is deemed to trigger 'enhanced cooperation' in various fields, such as energy, environment, transport and education. Building on the AP and on other existing arrangements,[97] it is envisaged that such enhanced cooperation would also cover other aspects of EU external relations such as CFSP and ESDP cooperation, as well as cooperation in the area of freedom, security and justice.[98] Potentially covering the whole breadth of EU activities, the new agreement would consolidate and codify the comprehensive dimension, explored earlier, of existing relations between the EU and its East European countries.[99] What the EU precisely means by 'enhanced cooperation' however remains to be seen. This enhancement will only be genuine if it is clearly articulated in the language of the agreement's provisions.

11.4.2 An all-encompassing Association Agreement?

Contrary to the APs, the new agreement is meant to be binding.[100] Yet thus far, neither the Commission nor the Council have given any indication as to its precise legal basis. One could nonetheless foresee that the 'enhanced' or 'neighbourhood' agreement take the form of an association agreement based on present Article 310 EC, potentially close although not necessarily identical to the EAs. This proposition finds support first, in the terminology of several ENP documents and second, in the inherent logic of the policy.

---

[97] E.g. Agreement between the European Union and Ukraine establishing a framework for the participation of the Ukraine in the European Union crisis management operations, OJ 2005 L 182/28; Agreement between the European Union and Ukraine on security procedures for the exchange of classified information, OJ 2005 L 172/83; Agreement between the European Community and Ukraine on certain aspects of air services, OJ 2006 L 211/23; Agreement between the European Community and the Government of Ukraine on trade in certain steel products, OJ 2005 L 232/22; Agreement renewing the Agreement on cooperation in science and technology between the European Community and Ukraine, OJ 2003 L 267/31. The new agreement will also build upon soft law instruments; e.g. the EU Action Plan on Justice and Home Affairs of 10 December 2001, OJ 2001 C 77/1.

[98] In this regard, see 'Commission proposes negotiating directives for enhanced agreement with Ukraine', n. 89.

[99] See Cremona and Hillion, 'L'Union' n. 27.

[100] Support can be found in the procedure followed by the Commission in launching the discussion with the Council on the future agreement (see 'Commission proposes negotiating directives for enhanced agreement with Ukraine', n. 89); and by the terminology of COM (2006)726, p. 4.

Association Agreements have been defined by the ECJ in the *Demirel* judgment,[101] which states that an 'association agreement creat[es] special, privileged links with a non-member country which must, at least to a certain extent, take part in the Community system'. Suggesting that the new agreement could be an association thus defined, the Commission Strategy Paper of 2004,[102] as well as the subsequent Council Conclusions endorsing it,[103] explicitly refer to a 'privileged relationship' between the EU and its neighbours,[104] while the introductory section of the APs with Ukraine and Moldova, respectively, hints at the progressive establishment of *privileged* links. Furthermore, the ENP perspective of moving the EU relationship with its neighbours beyond cooperation to a 'significant measure of economic and political integration',[105] and the possibility for neighbouring countries progressively to take part in key aspects of EU policies and programmes,[106] including participation in relevant Community and Union agencies,[107] seem to echo the formula used by the Court when articulating the concept of association.[108]

Indeed, any agreement 'below' association would not be perceived as an 'enhanced' contractual relationship. To begin with, there is no longer any justification for maintaining an alternative arrangement to association (i.e. PCA) vis-à-vis East European States with which the EU aims at developing a close relationship. Arguably, there used to be such an explanation. At the

---

[101] Case 12/86 *Meryem Demirel* v. *Stadt Schwäbisch Gmünd* [1987] ECR 3719. Further on association agreements, see the contributions in M.-F. Christophe-Tchakaloff (ed.), *Le concept d'association dans les accords passés par la Communauté: essai de clarification* (Brussels: Bruylant, 1999).

[102] COM(2004)373 final, p. 3.

[103] GAERC Conclusions, 14 June 2004 (10189/04; Presse 195).

[104] In the same vein, the ENPI Regulation includes in its Preamble the notion of 'privileged relationship' between the EU and its neighbours; while the Resolution of the European Parliament on the European Neighbourhood Policy (P6_TA(2006)0028) talks about 'privileged relations'.

[105] COM(2004)373 final, p. 5; though the Council more cautiously refers to 'gradual economic integration and deepening of political *cooperation*' (emphasis added); GAERC Conclusions, 22 January 2007; see pt. 2, second indent (5463/07; Presse 7).

[106] COM(2004)373 final, p. 8.

[107] Further, in this regard: Communication from the Commission to the Council and to the European Parliament on the general approach to enable ENP partner countries to participate in Community agencies and Community programmes, COM(2006)724 final.

[108] Article 8(1) TEU revised foresees that the Union 'shall develop a *special relationship* with neighbouring countries'. Para. 2 of Article 7a suggests that it can take the form of 'specific agreements with the countries concerned', which 'may contain reciprocal rights and obligations as well as the possibility of undertaking activities jointly'.

start of the nineties, the EU Member States were not yet determined to enlarge the EU to the CEECs. In this context, the EAs were conceived by some Member States as an *alternative to accession*, as indeed suggested by the preamble of the EAs with Poland and Hungary, and by the Commission's initial communication on the new type of association.[109] Consequently, the EU had to 'package' the EA as a special and exclusive breed of association agreement to make it less unpalatable for the CEECs. Including the former Soviet republics in the already widening bundle of EAs[110] would have, allegedly, diminished their exclusive character, and diluted their political value.[111] Indeed, following the 1993 Copenhagen European Council, a direct link was eventually established between the EAs and accession, making an EA-like treatment ever more inaccessible for 'non-CEECs'. Now that all the EA States have become members of the EU, the initial rationale for not granting Ukraine or Moldova an association agreement has vanished. Association is thus available.

The second argument which may prevent the EU from proposing an agreement that falls short of establishing an association with Moldova and Ukraine stems from its existing relations with the southern ENP States, namely the Euro-Mediterranean Agreements.[112] These agreements *are* association agreements. Unless the EU seeks to dilute the Euro-Mediterranean *acquis*, which would be contrary to the logic of the ENP, it is unlikely that the current relationship is going to be downgraded. In other words, the new EU agreement with the southern neighbours would, at any rate, be an association. Against this background, the EU arguably has to offer East European partners an enhanced agreement that, at the very least, matches the type of relations it has with the southern

---

[109] Commission 'Communication on Association agreements with the Countries of Central and Eastern Europe: a General Outline'; COM(90)398. Further e.g. M. Maresceau, 'A legal analysis of the Community's Association Agreements with central and eastern Europe: general framework, accession objectives and trade liberalisation', in S.V. Konstadinidis (ed.), *The legal regulation of the European Community's external relations after the completion of the internal market* (Aldershot: Darmouth Press, 1996), p. 125.

[110] EAs were being concluded with Bulgaria, Romania, the Baltic States and eventually Slovenia.

[111] It was also felt on the EC side that the post-soviet States (the so-called 'Newly-Independent States') should be approached differently from the CEECs, because of their potential re-integration, e.g. in the form of the Commonwealth of Independent States. Further: J. Raux, 'Les instruments juridiques de la Communauté avec les Etats de l'Europe de l'Est', in J.-C. Gautron (ed.), *Les relations Communauté européenne – Europe de l'Est* (Paris: Economica, 1991), p. 41.

[112] See contribution by E. Lannon in this volume.

Mediterranean States. Establishing a less ambitious relationship with East European countries would undermine the coherence of the ENP. Incidentally, it would also diminish the value of the EU's declared ambition to 'build an increasing close relationship' with Ukraine and Moldova,[113] as well as its acknowledgement of the latter's European aspirations.[114] Indeed, it could be recalled, particularly for those Member States that remain undecided, if not reluctant to conceive of Ukraine's and Moldova's eligibility for membership to the Union,[115] that association does not automatically mean accession. After all, Latin American countries have concluded association agreements with the Community.[116]

While the new EU agreement with the East European neighbours should, almost inexorably, take the form of an association agreement its likely all-inclusive scope, both in terms of objectives and content, may mean that the *Union* might become a concluding party to the new agreement, alongside the Community and the Member States. This point is not contradicted by the Council decision on the negotiating directives, which refers to an 'enhanced agreement between the *European Union* and Ukraine' (emphasis added).[117] Such a cross-pillar framework agreement would be among the first of this kind in the typology of EU external agreements and, arguably, a way symbolically to materialise the EU ambition of going beyond and above the existing relationship.[118] Also, it could make the new agreement more appealing to the East European States that are keen on developing an ever closer relationship with the EU.

---

[113] GAERC Conclusions, 22 January 2007, pt. 2, second indent (5463/07, Presse 7).

[114] This European perspective of Ukraine was recognised by the EU notably in the EU Common Strategy on Ukraine, OJ 1999 L 331/1; the EU/Ukraine Action Plan; and in the GAERC Conclusions, 22 January 2007, pt. 1 (5463/07; Presse 7). A similar perspective was recognised in relation to Moldova, as recalled by the EU/Moldova AP.

[115] *Agence Europe* No. 9349, 23 January 2007, p. 5.

[116] See e.g. Agreement establishing an association between the European Community and its Member States, of the one part, and the Republic of Chile, of the other part, OJ 2002 L 352/1.

[117] GAERC Conclusions, 22 January 2007 (5463/07, Presse 7); see in this regard: J. Raux, 'Towards a pan-Euro-Mediterranean strategy: association of proximity', in Maresceau and Lannon, *The EU's Enlargement*, p. 42; J. Raux, 'Association et perspectives partenariales', in Christophe-Tchakaloff (ed.), *Le Concept*, p. 89.

[118] Indeed, it would not be the first time that the EU–Ukraine relations would be used as a *laboratory* for testing new formula of EU external relations (e.g. Common Strategies, Partnership and Cooperation Agreements); further from this author, *The European Union and its East-European Neighbours – A laboratory for the organisation of EU external relations* (Oxford: Hart Publishing, forthcoming).

Beyond the questions of legal basis and label of the EU agreement with its neighbours, the thorny issue of procedure for concluding it has to be examined. In EU external relations, the rule appears to be as follows: the more ambitious the agreement, the more difficult its conclusion. In particular, concluding an association agreement requires a unanimous vote within the Council,[119] and the assent of the European Parliament (EP).[120] Furthermore, assuming that the new agreement covers most areas of EC external relations, including areas of shared competence (e.g. environment, social policy), it is likely to be *mixed*. As such, it will have to be concluded by the EC together with its Member States, and will therefore require the ratification by all 27 Member States – if not more by the time of its conclusion. Numerous national interests,[121] as well as the concerns of the EP, will thus have to be thoroughly considered, particularly during the negotiations.[122]

Indeed, if it were to establish enhanced cooperation in all EU external policies, as suggested earlier, the new agreement could theoretically be concluded as 'a cross-pillar agreement' by the Community and the EU, on the basis of present Articles 300(3)(2) EC and Article 24 TEU, respectively.[123] Choosing this complex legal basis would involve distinct procedural arrangements. In particular, the provisions relating to EC competence (exclusive and possibly shared) would fall to be negotiated by the Commission (possibly with Member States for areas of shared competence), while parts of the agreement on cooperation in CFSP and PJCCM[124] matters could be negotiated by the EU Presidency, assisted by

---

[119] Article 300(2) EC.   [120] Article 300(3), (2) EC.

[121] As epitomised by the Polish veto on the start of negotiations of a new post-PCA agreement with Russia.

[122] On the complexities of mixed agreements, see e.g. J. Heliskoski, *Mixed agreements as a technique for organizing the international relations of the European Community and its Member States* (The Hague: Kluwer Law International, 2001); D. O'Keeffe and H. Schermers (eds.), *Mixed agreements* (Deventer: Kluwer Law, 1983).

[123] There have been discussions about cross-pillar agreements in the context of the EU accession to the ASEAN Treaty of Amity and Cooperation (TAC) as suggested by Council doc. 16042/ 06 of 30 November 2006 entitled 'Draft Council authorization to the Presidency and the Commission to negotiate the accession to ASEAN Treaty of Amity and Cooperation (TAC) by the EU and EC respectively' (non-public); on the other hand, the adoption of mixed EC–EU instruments might be less plausible following the *ECOWAS* judgment of 20 May 2008, C-91/05, nyr.

[124] For PJC matters, Article 38 TEU would have to be added to Article 24 TEU.

the Council's Secretariat.[125] Even if it were decided (as is the normal practice with classic mixed agreements)[126] to ask the Commission to act as sole negotiator on behalf not only of the Community and the Member States, but also of the EU, such a decision would not in any event prejudge the question of the competence of the Community, the Member States or the EU on particular issues. In other words, the draft agreement would still have to be concluded by the EC, the EU, together with the Member States, in their individual fields of competence. Such complex procedure could lead to some squabbling referred to in the introduction, notably between the Commission and the Council, as to which parts of the agreement relate to the competence of the EC, the EU, and the Member States, respectively.[127] In other words, the immunity to pillar politics gained from the non-legal nature of the initial ENP instruments, might be the *quid pro quo* for more legal certainty.

The foregoing suggests that, at least for procedural reasons, the EU may be in a difficult position to offer an ambitious agreement that would match the objectives of its ENP, not to mention the neighbours' expectations.[128] Unless pragmatic arrangements are found to ensure a solid and coherent EU position,[129] a bundle of bilateral sectoral agreements could be explored as an alternative to an all-encompassing framework agreement, although this fallback arrangement would need to be spearheaded by an overall institutional framework.

11.4.3 A lasting arrangement?

The Council and the Commission acknowledge that the 'new enhanced agreement shall not prejudge any possible future developments in

---

[125] The Council's adoption of negotiating directives was not clear on the question of who is going to negotiate the Agreement. It merely mentions that negotiations were due to be launched at the 'EU–Troika Ukraine Ministerial meeting' of February 2007.

[126] For instance, for the negotiations of the WTO Agreement; see in this regard: Opinion 1/94 *WTO* [1994] ECR I-5267.

[127] On such EU/EC competence battle, see e.g. Case C-176/03 *Commission* v. *Council (Environmental penalties)* [2005] ECR I-7879 and Case 91/05 *Commission* v. *Council (ECOWAS)* nyr. The European Parliament could also get involved in such power politics as it has done in the past, though not entirely successfully, see Cases C-317/04 and 318/04, *Parliament* v. *Council (PNR)*, judgment of 30 May 2006, nyr; see contribution by A. Dashwood in this volume.

[128] On Ukraine's reactions to the EU current position, see *EUobserver*, 21 January 2007.

[129] Further: M. Petite, 'Current Legal Issues in the External Relations of the European Union', *EUI Law Working Papers*, 2006/38.

EU–Ukraine relations'.[130] The EU nonetheless favours an agreement that is long-lasting, rather than limited in time and thus opened to early renegotiation.[131] This requires an agreement adaptable to change, which in turns notably depends on the institutional framework to be set up by the new agreement.

In particular, the vitality of the relationship would be fostered if, in contrast to the PCAs, the agreement were to establish an organ (e.g. an association council)[132] endowed with a full-fledged decision-making power and clear tasks. In effect, alongside timelines and transition periods, for instance to establish an FTA, association agreements often include enabling clauses, entrusting the association council with the power to elaborate and strengthen the relationship through binding decisions.[133] The relationship thereby evolves without the parties having to renegotiate the whole agreement, with all the procedural pitfalls that such process entails.

It should be recalled that such decision-making power is already conferred upon the EMAs' association councils,[134] which in itself is an argument in favour of granting a similar power to the future EU–East European organs.[135] Indeed, giving the neighbours the possibility to take part in the development of the *acquis* would contribute to fulfilling the ENP objective of involving them in Community and Union policies,[136] and incidentally give more substance to the ENP 'joint ownership' mantra.[137] The Commission evoked in its legislative and work programme

[130] GAERC Conclusions, 22 January 2007 pt. 2, last indent.

[131] It remains to be seen whether that option would be positively perceived by the ENP partners, particularly the Ukraine, in view of its membership aspirations.

[132] Such an organ would most likely be supported by other committees (including parliamentary committees) and sectoral sub-committees.

[133] Thus, the development of the movement of workers between the Community and Turkey, and the establishment of an EC–Turkey customs union have depended significantly on the decisions adopted by the Association Council established by the Ankara Agreement.

[134] E.g. Article 80 EMA Morocco.

[135] Cf. the argument of consistency invoked under Section 2.A.

[136] Moreover, provided they meet certain conditions, the binding decisions adopted by such a body could be guaranteed before Member States' jurisdictions thereby also involving citizens in the EU rapprochement with its neighbours, see in this regard, the European Court of Justice's numerous judgments of the EC–Turkey association council e.g. Case 192/89 *Sevince* [1990] ECR 3461. Note that direct effect of the rules underpinning the new relationship does not depend on the adoption of additional measures by an organ, such as an association council. As well-established, the provisions of the agreement itself may have direct effect (Case C-63/99 *Głoszczuk* [2001] ECR I-6369; Case C-171/01 *Wählergruppe Gemeinsam* [2003] ECR I-4301 and Case C-265/03 *Simutenkov* [2005] ECR I-2579).

[137] COM(2004)373, p. 8.

that it would 'prepare the grounds for a *renewed* institutional arrangement with . . . Ukraine' (emphasis added).[138] It however remains to be seen whether such 'renewal' entails endowing the new institution with decision-making power.

11.5 Conclusion

The ENP embeds the existing relationship between the EU and its East European partners into a new perspective. Through the use of atypical instruments, inspired by the ad hoc techniques for preparing accession, the policy has been partly shielded from the pillar politics that are so typical of the EU system of external relations, thereby carrying the promise of coherence and integration in the EU action towards its neighbours. Also, it allows a subtle reorientation and reformulation of the relationship, without the Parties having gone through the formal negotiation of a new agreement.

Though conducive to better institutional coherence, reliance on the enlargement tool-kit for developing a policy whose ultimate aim is to establish a new generation of agreement is not unproblematic. Indeed, coherence gains may be eroded by the upcoming conclusion of neighbourhood/enhanced agreements, and the consequent comeback of more classical methods of EU external relations shaping. The next generation of agreements between the EU and its East European neighbours is envisaged to go 'above and beyond' existing arrangements. Time will tell whether these ambitions will be reflected by the objectives and nature of the new agreements, and matched by their detailed content. At any rate, if the agreements are to constitute a genuine enhancement of the relationship, their provisions, and the rights and obligations they contain, will have to substantiate such improvement. This point is particularly true for those countries that have a membership agenda, like Ukraine and Moldova. Moreover it is essential for the overall credibility of the ENP. Yet, given its complex external relations system, and the current period of introversion it is passing through, the EU might be in a tricky position to deliver.

---

[138] Communication from the Commission: 'Unlocking Europe's full potential – Commission Legislative and Work Programme 2006', COM(2005)531, p. 10.

The four Common Spaces: new impetus to the EU–Russia Strategic Partnership?

PETER VAN ELSUWEGE

12.1 Introduction

One year before the EU accession of ten new Member States, the May 2003 Saint-Petersburg EU–Russia Summit launched the aim of creating four Common Spaces, namely a Common Economic Space; a Common Space of Freedom, Security and Justice; a Common Space of External Security and a Common Space of Research and Education, including Cultural Aspects.[1] The Council and the Commission later confirmed the EU's intention to develop the Common Spaces concept as 'an extensive basis' for strengthening the EU–Russia Strategic Partnership.[2] The central aim of this new framework is to reinforce the bilateral relationship on the basis of a mutually agreed agenda for further action. In this respect, the May 2005 Moscow EU–Russia Summit adopted a single package of road maps with approximately 400 points for regulatory cooperation.[3]

This first manifestation of a joint, issues-based agenda – replacing the EU's 1999 unilateral Common Strategy – has opened a new chapter in EU–Russia relations. Possible linkages between different action points open up new opportunities for pragmatic cooperation and progress. The

---

[1] Whereas the four Common Spaces concept has been officially launched at the 2003 St Petersburg EU–Russia Summit, a Franco-German 'non paper' discussed with Russian officials in the context of the Iraq crisis formed the basis for this arrangement; see 'Franco-German plan sees visa free travel for Russians', *EUobserver*, 16 March 2003; T. Gomart, 'Le Partenariat entre l'Union Européenne et la Russie à l'épreuve de l'elargissement', *Revue du Marché commun et de l'Union européenne* (2004), p. 351.

[2] Commission Communication on Relations with Russia, COM(2004)106, 9 February 2004; Council Report on the implementation of the Common Strategy of the European Union on Russia, 10601/04, 16 June 2004.

[3] Conclusions fifteenth EU–Russia Summit, Moscow, 10 May 2005, available at: http://ec.europa.eu/comm/external_relations/russia/summit_05_05/index.htm.

parallel conclusion of two bilateral agreements on visa facilitation, a long-standing Russian desire, and readmission, an old priority for the EU, illustrates the potential of this new approach.[4] This observation, however, does not conceal the existence of numerous question marks surrounding the Common Spaces programme. A first major question entails the legal nature of the Common Spaces and the framework for the implementation of the road maps. In this respect, the legal options after the expiry of the Partnership and Cooperation Agreement deserve particular attention. Second, the relationship between the Common Spaces and other EU foreign policy instruments, such as the Northern Dimension and the European Neighbourhood Policy, has to be addressed. Last, but not least, the question remains as to how the accession of the Central and Eastern European countries affects the EU's relations with Russia. This contribution aims to address these questions in order to assess the potential added value of the Common Spaces on the road towards, in the words of the Commission, 'a genuine Strategic Partnership based on positive interdependence'.[5]

12.2 The EU–Russia Strategic Partnership and the challenge of enlargement: sowing the seeds for the common spaces agenda

12.2.1 The PCA extension dilemma: limits of a unilateral approach

The bilateral Partnership and Cooperation Agreement (PCA), signed in Corfu on 24 June 1994 and in force since 1 December 1997, marked the beginning of a new legal relationship between the EC/EU and the Russian Federation.[6] From the outset, however, it was clear that the PCA *as such*

---

[4] Both agreements have been signed at the May 2006 Sochi EU–Russia Summit and entered into force on 1 June 2007. Agreement between the European Community and the Russian Federation on the facilitation of the issuance of visas to the citizens of the European Union and the Russian Federation, OJ 2007 L 129/27. Agreement between the European Community and the Russian Federation on readmission, OJ 2007 L 129/40.

[5] Commission Communication on Relations with Russia, COM(2004)106, p. 1.

[6] Agreement on Partnership and Cooperation between the European Communities and their Member States, of the one part, and the Russian Federation, of the other part, OJ 1997 L 327/3. During the first years after the disintegration of the Soviet Union, the legal framework of the relations between the EC and Russia was based on the old EEC–USSR Trade and Co-operation Agreement, OJ 1990 L 68/2.

was unable to handle the multifaceted and cross-pillar challenges of EU–Russia cooperation. For this reason, the June 1999 Cologne European Council adopted the Common Strategy on Russia (CSR) on the legal basis of Article 13 EU, introduced by the Treaty of Amsterdam.[7] This unilateral CFSP instrument, which expired in June 2004, identified the EU's ambitions for the development of its 'Strategic Partnership' with Russia. Despite high expectations and good intentions, the CSR scarcely concealed the lack of strategic vision on the part of the EU. Perhaps the most astonishing feature of the EU's external relations vis-à-vis Russia has been the virtual absence of the enlargement dimension.[8] The limits of this policy became obvious in the political and legal discussions surrounding the extension of the PCA to the new Member States.[9] For the EU, the conclusion of a protocol to the PCA providing for such an adaptation was seen as a technical and automatic operation. Russia, however, claimed compensation for the alleged negative consequences of enlargement and proceeded from the assumption that extending the PCA to the new Member States was a good opportunity to negotiate this question. In this respect, Moscow presented to the EU in January 2004 a list of 14 concerns, mainly of an economic nature but also including the politically sensitive issue of protection of the sizeable Russian-speaking minorities in Estonia and Latvia.[10] Remarkably, a similar list was submitted to the Commission in 1999.[11] In addition, Russia's Medium-Term Strategy on Relations with the EU (2000–2010) also included a specific chapter on 'securing the Russian interests in an expanded European Union', which inter alia referred to a possible refusal to extend the PCA.[12] In spite of these clear requests from the Russian side to proactively discuss the consequences of enlargement in the framework of

---

[7] Common Strategy of the European Union of 4 June 1999 on Russia, OJ 1999 L 157/1.

[8] See e.g. M. Maresceau, 'EU Enlargement and EU Common Strategies on Russia and Ukraine: An Ambiguous yet Unavoidable Connection', in C. Hillion (ed.), *EU Enlargement. A Legal Approach* (Oxford: Hart Publishing, 2004), pp. 181–219.

[9] Pursuant to Article 6(2) of the 2003 and 2005 Acts of Accession, the accession of new Member States to mixed agreements required the conclusion of protocols between the Council, acting unanimously on behalf of the Member States, and the third country concerned, OJ 2003 L 236/34 and OJ 2005 L 157/30.

[10] 'Russia critical of minorities treatment in new EU Member States', *EUobserver*, 19 January 2004.

[11] 'Russia seeks new Commission's understanding on enlargement request', *Uniting Europe*, 1999, 66, pp. 3–4.

[12] Medium-term Strategy for Development of Relations between the Russian Federation and the European Union (2000–2010), available at: http://ec.europa.eu./external_relations/russia/russian_medium_strategy/.

the 'Strategic Partnership', the EU preferred a 'wait-and-see' approach, which led to a crisis in bilateral relations.[13]

Confronted with the lack of strategic planning and its corresponding inertia in solving long-standing issues, the December 2003 European Council instructed a general revision of 'all aspects of the Union's relations with Russia'.[14] The European Parliament Committee on Foreign Affairs, Human Rights, Common Security and Defence, produced a first recommendation on 2 February 2004,[15] which was followed by a Commission Communication[16] and an assessment report of the Council.[17] The self-evaluation revealed numerous weaknesses of the EU–Russia Strategic Partnership. First, the inability of the EU to speak with one voice in order to send clear and unambiguous messages to Russia undermined the credibility of the EU's position. The controversial statements of the Italian Prime Minister Silvio Berlusconi, acting as President of the Council at the November 2003 Rome EU–Russia Summit, in defence of Russia's behaviour in Chechnya and against the official EU position, clearly illustrated this problem.[18] Second, the CSR entailed a great number of objectives but lacked a concrete, issues-based strategic agenda and clear priorities. The task of transforming the broadly defined objectives into operational action points was attributed to each incoming Council Presidency. In practice, however, the six-months Presidency work plans

---

[13] Russia's more assertive stance on enlargement and insufficient progress on key issues such as Siberian overflight rights, ratification of the Kyoto Protocol, conclusion of a readmission agreement and Russia's WTO accession talks, in combination with worries concerning Chechnya and tendencies of growing authoritarianism in Moscow after the detention of Yukos chairman Michail Chodorkovsky, led to a crisis atmosphere by the end of 2003. When speaking in the European Parliament after the November 2003 Rome EU–Russia Summit, Commissioner Günter Verheugen described the state of EU–Russia relations as follows: 'We have very many action plans but hardly any action. We have grand strategies but small deeds. We have visions but little practice. That is my assessment, and the Russian side agreed with it', Debates of the European Parliament, 19 November 2003.

[14] Presidency Conclusions Brussels European Council, 12–13 December 2003, *Bulletin EU*, 12/2003, I.24.67.

[15] Report with a proposal for a European Parliament recommendation to the Council on EU–Russia Relations, A5-0053/2004.

[16] Communication from the Commission to the Council and the European Parliament on Relations with Russia, COM(2004)106, 9 February 2004.

[17] Council of the European Union, 'Relations with Russia – Assessment Report', 6472/04, 19 February 2004.

[18] The European Commission and the European Parliament clearly distanced themselves from Berlusconi's remarks, see *Agence Europe*, 8 November 2003, p. 5. Arguably, this controversy formed the immediate cause for the December 2003 European Council conclusions on Russia.

became 'routine exercises' without many practical effects.[19] Third, the highly developed institutional framework of the Strategic Partnership, with numerous joint bodies and meetings, was not always very effective. This could be attributed to a lack of coordination between the different institutions and pillars. Fourth, and this was perhaps the most important conclusion, the EU and Russia failed to produce a common agenda for cooperation. Both partners mainly proceeded on the basis of unilateral strategies with a different focus. In particular, Russia's ambition to be treated as an equal partner of the EU seemed difficult to reconcile with the asymmetric approach of the CSR.[20]

In the months before enlargement, all EU institutions recognised the limits of a unilateral policy towards Russia and suggested measures to establish a more coherent and effective bilateral relationship. In the short term, the transformation of the Cooperation Council into a Permanent Partnership Council (PPC) was recommended. The suggestion that the PPC should act as 'a clearing house for all issues of EU–Russia cooperation' remained vague but essentially addressed the need for more cross-pillar coordination.[21] For this reason, the PPC meets more frequently and in different formats. Significantly, Russia and the EU disagreed on the appropriate composition of this body. Whereas Russia proposed a 25+1 format, reflecting the sort of arrangement it has with NATO, the EU insisted that Russian ministers would meet only a troika of EU representatives.[22] This discussion reflected, once again, the difficulty of reconciling Russia's wish to be treated as an equal partner and the EU's complex institutional structures, which exclude third parties from internal decision-making. Moreover, fears that Russia could exploit divisions between the EU Member States strengthened the EU's principled position.[23] In the end, Russia accepted the troika formula. Depending upon the subject under discussion, PPC meetings bring together ministerial representatives from Russia, the EU Presidency, the incoming EU Presidency and a European

---

[19] Council of the European Union, 'Common Strategies: Report by the Secretary-General/High Representative', 14871/00, Brussels, 21 December 2000, p. 4.

[20] H. Haukkala, *Two Reluctant Regionalizers? The European Union and Russia in Europe's North*, UPI Working Papers (Helsinki: Finnish Institute of International Affairs, 2001), pp. 7–8.

[21] Council Report on the implementation of the Common Strategy of the European Union on Russia, 10554/03, Brussels, 16 June 2003.

[22] K. Barysch, 'EU–Russia Relations. The EU Perspective', in D. Johnson and P. Robinson (eds.), *Perspectives on EU–Russia Relations* (London: Routledge, 2005), p. 31.

[23] *Ibid.*

Commissioner. This mechanism allows full discussion on issues where the EC/EU and its Member States share competence. The first meeting of the PPC in the Foreign Minister format took place in Luxembourg on 27 April 2004 and finalised the deal on the extension of the PCA. To date, PPC meetings have also been organised in the fields of justice and home affairs, energy and transport.

Apart from the short-term institutional rearrangements, the Commission confirmed the intention to elaborate the concept of the four Common Spaces as the new long-term strategic framework for EU–Russia relations. Significantly, it used the prospect of a Joint Action Plan, which had been proposed by the Russian side in April 2000, as leverage to solve the PCA extension dilemma.[24] Only a few days before the accession of the new Member States on 1 May 2004 both parties managed to find a mutually acceptable solution in the form of a 'Protocol to the PCA to take account of enlargement' and a 'Joint Statement on EU enlargement and EU–Russia relations'.[25] This combination of a short legal document and a wider political statement signalled Russia's formal consent with the enlargement of the EU. A similar formula was used for the accession of Romania and Bulgaria.[26]

12.2.2 The legal and political consequences of the PCA extension

The application of PCA rules to Russia's relations with the new EU Member States has important legal consequences. The Most Favoured Nation principle (Art. 10(1)), for instance, rules out the application of double customs standards, which characterised Russia's trade relations

[24] The Commission explicitly stated that 'the EU should not engage in substantive discussions with Russia on the Action Plan before agreement is reached on PCA extension'. Communication from the Commission to the Council and the European Parliament on relations with Russia, COM(2004)106, 9 February 2004, p. 7.

[25] Protocol to the Partnership and Cooperation Agreement (PCA) between the European Communities and their Member States, of the one part, and the Russian Federation, of the other part, to take account of the accession of the Czech Republic, the Republic of Estonia, the Republic of Cyprus, the Republic of Hungary, the Republic of Latvia, the Republic of Lithuania, the Republic of Malta, the Republic of Poland, the Republic of Slovenia, and the Slovak Republic to the European Union, OJ 2006 L 185/17; Joint Statement on EU Enlargement and EU–Russia Relations, Brussels, 27 April 2004, UE-RU 1003/04.

[26] Protocol to the Partnership and Cooperation Agreement (PCA) between the European Communities and their Member States, of the one part, and the Russian Federation, of the other part, to take account of the accession of the Republic of Bulgaria and Romania to the European Union, OJ 2007 L 119/32; Joint Statement on EU Enlargement and Russia–EU Relations, Luxembourg, 23 April 2007, 8747/07.

with Estonia and Latvia before enlargement. Russian citizens of the latter countries can now directly invoke the PCA's non-discrimination provision (Art. 23) as far as their conditions of employment, remuneration or dismissal are concerned.[27] Finally, the PCA transit rules (Arts. 12, 19 and 78) are highly significant for regulating the transit of goods between mainland Russia and Kaliningrad.[28] The Joint Statement addresses Russia's concerns in this respect and includes other political guarantees. It is noteworthy, for instance, that Russia, as a non-WTO member, is not legally entitled to any compensation for loss of market access on the basis of Article XXIV(6) GATT 1994.[29] The Joint Statement, however, indirectly applies this WTO principle as the EU confirmed that 'compensatory tariff adjustments accorded in the context of EU enlargement through modifications of the EU tariff schedule will be applied on an MFN basis to the advantage of Russian exporters'.[30]

Apart from other economic and technical issues, inter alia dealing with the level of import tariffs, veterinary certifications or the export of Russian steel, the Joint Statement also addresses the question of minority protection. A diplomatic compromise formula does not name any countries – an explicit requirement of Estonia and Latvia – but proclaims in rather general terms that the parties 'welcome EU membership as a firm guarantee for the protection of human rights and the protection of persons belonging to minorities' and 'underline their commitment' in this respect.[31] A concrete consequence of this commitment has been the establishment of a regular EU–Russia human rights dialogue after the November 2004

---

[27] See Case C-265/03 *Simutenkov* [2005] ECR I-2579. Significantly, the PCA is only relevant for legally employed Russian citizens and not for the approximately 500,000 non-citizens or 'aliens' living in both countries. Their legal status in the EU is essentially based upon Council Directive 2003/109/EC of 25 November 2003 concerning the status of third-country nationals who are long-term residents, OJ 2004 L 16/44, see P. Van Elsuwege, *Russian-speaking Minorities in Estonia and Latvia: Problems of Integration at the Threshold of the European Union*, ECMI Working Paper No. 20 (Flensburg: ECMI, 2004), available at: http://www.ecmi.de/download/ working_paper_20.pdf.

[28] The legal importance of the PCA for regulating the transit of goods to Kaliningrad forms a plausible explanation for Russia's swift ratification of the PCA extension protocol. The latter provisionally entered into force on 1 May 2004 in anticipation of the ratification procedures. The Russian Duma ratified the Protocol in October 2004.

[29] On the application of this Article in the context of EU enlargement, see M. Cremona, 'The Impact of Enlargement: External Policy and External Relations', in M. Cremona (ed.), *The Enlargement of the European Union* (Oxford: Oxford University Press, 2003), pp. 186–96.

[30] Joint Statement on EU Enlargement and EU–Russia Relations, n. 25.

[31] *Ibid.*

The Hague EU–Russia Summit where it was explicitly recognised that respect for human rights, including the rights of persons belonging to minorities, constitutes a basic principle of EU–Russia cooperation in the field of freedom, security and justice.[32] Hence, EU enlargement reinforces the human rights dimension of the EU–Russia Strategic Partnership.[33] In practice, however, the discussions are largely confined to standard diplomatic statements.

The economic and political priorities identified in the Joint Statement confirm the multidimensional character of the Strategic Partnership, including competences of the Community, the Union and the Member States. The ambition to create four Common Spaces can be perceived as an attempt to ensure cross-pillar coherence in the EU's external relations with Russia. For this reason, the EU pursued a 'package approach' in the negotiations on the Common Spaces road maps.[34] The latter, adopted at the May 2005 Moscow EU–Russia Summit, replace the CSR as the strategic framework for EU–Russia relations.[35] Hence, the question arises as to what extent this new framework can provide added value in comparison to the previous situation.

12.3 The four Common Spaces: an innovative instrument of the EU's external relations?

The concept of 'common spaces' is not as new as it may sound at first. In a sense it reminds of the old Gorbachev rhetoric of a 'common European house'. Moreover, the integration of Russia into 'a common European

---

[32] Presidency Statement on EU–Russia Human Rights Consultations, Brussels, 1 March 2005, 6198/05.

[33] Significantly, the EU–Russia Partnership entailed an important human rights dimension from the outset. Of particular importance is, for instance, Article 6 PCA, which states that 'the parties endeavour to cooperate on matters pertaining to the observance of the principle of democracy and human rights, and hold consultations, if necessary, on matters related to their due implementation', see on this point C. Hillion, 'Russian Federation', in S. Blockmans and A. Lazowski (eds.), *The European Union and its Neighbours. A Legal Appraisal of the EU's Policies of Stabilisation, Partnership and Integration* (The Hague: Asser, 2006), pp. 480–4.

[34] D. Lynch, 'Struggling with the Indispensable Partner', in D. Lynch (ed.), *What Russia sees*, Chaillot Paper 74 (Paris: European Union Institute for Security Studies, 2005), p. 132.

[35] The Council decision of June 2004 not to renew the extension of the CSR signalled a further commitment to proceed with the Common Spaces concept. See Council report on the implementation of the Common Strategy of the European Union on Russia, 10601/04. Originally, the plan was to adopt the Common Spaces road maps on the occasion of the November 2004 The Hague EU–Russia Summit but mutual disagreements delayed the adoption of the agenda to the May 2005 Moscow EU–Russia Summit.

economic and social space' formed one of the principal objectives identified in the CSR. In order to give this idea a more concrete content, the
October 2001 EU–Russia Summit established – on the basis of Article 93
PCA – a joint High Level Group (HLG), which presented a concept paper
on a Common European Economic Space (CEES) to the November 2003
Rome EU–Russia Summit.[36] Significantly, the word 'European' has been
dropped in the framework of the four Common Spaces. This change does
not affect the basic objective of this rather ambiguous project, which is to
establish 'an open and integrated market between the EU and Russia,
based on the implementation of common and compatible rules and regulations'.[37] The Common Economic Space (CES), however, has a broader
scope, including policy sectors such as telecommunications, transport,
energy, space and environment, which did not figure so explicitly in the
CEES. Significantly, Article 55(2) PCA includes a largely comparable list of
areas for legislative approximation. It is noteworthy that the CES road map
avoids references to the one-sided approximation of Russia's legislation to
EU standards – as is provided under Article 55 PCA – but employs more
neutral terms such as 'regulatory convergence' or 'the elaboration of
common approaches'. To a certain extent, the CES thus appears to be a
'rhetorical exercise', repackaging old ambitions in a new, equivocal dis-
course. In practice, however, it seems that also within the CES concept the
burden of legal adaptation essentially falls on Russia.[38]

The other Spaces also proceed from ideas laid down in previous documents. The Common Space on Freedom, Security and Justice (CSFSJ), for
instance, builds upon the EU–Russia Action Plan on organised crime[39] and
proceeds from the intention of judicial cooperation in civil and criminal
matters laid down in the CSR. The road map for the CSFSJ includes a long
list of actions and objectives including inter alia the exploration of an
EU–Russia agreement on mutual legal assistance – reflecting the EU's
agreement with the United States[40] – and enhanced cooperation of Russian
institutions with EU agencies such as Eurojust and Europol.

---

[36] Joint Statement 12th EU–Russia Summit, Rome, 6 November 2003, available at: http://ec.
europa.eu/comm/external_relations/russia/summit11_03/1concl.pdf.

[37] *Ibid.*　　[38] Hillion, 'Russian Federation', p. 494.

[39] European Union Action Plan on Common Action for the Russian Federation on Combating
Organised Crime, OJ 2000 C 106/5.

[40] Agreement on Mutual Legal Assistance between the European Union and the United States of
America, OJ 2003 L 181/34.

Of particular importance is the recognition of visa-free travel as a long-term perspective as well as the inclusion of a specific section on the fight against terrorism. Both priorities are new in comparison to the CSR and illustrate the potential of cross-fertilisation between the different spaces. The fight against terrorism, in particular, links the CSFSJ to the Common Space on External Security (CSES).

The road map for the CSES reflects the general political dialogue provisions of the PCA (Art. 6), in particular the ambition to 'bring about an increasing convergence of positions on international issues of mutual concern'. It also builds upon the CSR section on 'political and security dialogue' and, in particular, on Russia's involvement in joint foreign policy actions. In this respect, the June 2002 Seville European Council laid down arrangements for consultation and cooperation between the EU and Russia on crisis management. This allowed Russia's participation in the EU Police Mission in Bosnia and Herzegovina.[41] The road map for the CSES includes some specific measures aiming at streamlining and improving the framework for joint crisis management operations, inter alia in 'regions adjacent to the EU and Russian borders'. The main point of discussion remains Russia's insistence to be involved at the various stages of the decision-making process. The EU has consistently rejected such far-reaching proposals. The Common Spaces' road map only provides for a general 'exchange of views' and the potential development of 'principles and modalities for joint approaches in crisis management'. At present, a policy dialogue is developing, notably through regular meetings between the Ambassador of Russia in Brussels and the EU Political and Security Committee Troika.[42]

Finally, the Common Space on Research and Education, including Cultural Aspects (CSRE) gives some concrete substance to the loose PCA provisions on science and technology (Art. 62), education and training (Art. 63) and cultural cooperation (Art. 85) as well as to the general ambitions of the CSR concerning the involvement of Russia in exchange programmes for students and young scientists and Russia's interest in the participation of Russian scientists and scientific centres in EU research and education programmes laid down in its Medium-Term Strategy for

---

[41] Agreement between the European Union and the Russian Federation on the participation of the Russian Federation in the European Union Police Mission (EUPOL) in Bosnia and Herzegovina (BiH), OJ 2003 L 197/38.

[42] European Commission Factsheet, 'EU–Russia Common Space on External Security', available at: http://ec.europa.eu/comm/external_relations/russia/summit_11_06/ext_security.pdf.

relations with the EU. The integration of Russia in a European Higher Education Area in accordance with the main provisions of the Bologna process is an ambitious objective of the CSRE, which is probably the least sensitive space from a political point of view but potentially the most important in terms of promoting 'people-to-people' contacts and mutual understanding.

Whereas the four Common Spaces are apparently mainly inventories of existing objectives, their added value essentially lies in the adoption of road maps with some concrete action points. The establishment of a European Studies Institute in Moscow as part of the CSRE or the envisaged creation of a EuroMeSCo type of cooperation in the field of security and foreign policy[43] are, for instance, interesting innovations. In comparison to the CSR, the Common Spaces agenda comprises a more detailed and structured overview of the remaining challenges of EU–Russia cooperation. Numerous provisions, however, remain rather vague and are sometimes encapsulated in a meaningless diplomatic language. It is, therefore, noteworthy that the Council has adopted a more specific 'action oriented paper' on the implementation of the CSFSJ.[44] This internal EU document clearly spells out the EU's priorities in compliance with the Strategy for the External Dimension of Justice and Home Affairs, adopted by the Council in December 2005,[45] and could form an interesting model for the implementation of the other Common Spaces. By comparison with the old practice of six months' Presidency work plans, it contributes to a more coherent and consistent approach in the EU's relations vis-à-vis the Russian Federation. The Commission and the Council Secretariat systematically monitor the implementation of the action oriented paper and report to the Justice and Home Affairs (JHA) Council and the General Affairs and External Relations Council (GAERC) every 18 months. In the intermediate period, regular meetings between the Presidency, the Council Secretariat, the Commission and interested Member States are scheduled.

---

[43] EuroMeSCo stands for Euro-Mediterranean Study Commission and is a network of independent research institutes and academic centres dealing with foreign policy analysis and research into security issues. It was established in 1996, in the framework of the Euro-Mediterranean Partnership; more information available at: http://www.euromesco.net.

[44] Council of the EU, 'Action oriented paper on implementing with Russia the Common Space of Freedom, Security and Justice', Brussels, 28 November 2006, 15534/1/06.

[45] Council of the EU, 'A Strategy for the External Dimension of JHA: Global Freedom, Security and Justice', Brussels, 15446/05, 6 December 2005.

Another major difference is the fact that the Common Spaces are common to the EU and Russia whereas the CSR was a unilateral EU document and, as such, only common among the EU Member States. Accordingly, the Common Spaces better reflect Russia's insistence on 'equal partnership'. The parallel conclusion of bilateral agreements on readmission and visa facilitation at the May 2006 Sochi EU–Russia Summit clearly illustrates the added value of this new approach. Attempts to conclude an 'isolated' readmission agreement, as envisaged in the CSR, turned out impossible given Russia's reluctance to engage in any kind of arrangement without guarantees of efficient border control at its Eastern borders and reciprocal advantages in terms of facilitated travel to the EU.[46] A transitional period of three years regarding the readmission of third-country nationals or stateless persons coming from countries with which Russia has not concluded bilateral treaties or arrangements on readmission solved the first concern. The facilitated procedures for issuing short-term visas, i.e. for intended stays of no more than 90 days, for Russian citizens travelling to Schengen countries and vice versa addressed the second request. The visa exemption for holders of diplomatic passports and the waiving of the fixed visa fee of €35 for certain categories of persons was of particular importance for the Russian side.[47] Hence, this package deal reveals the pragmatic nature of EU–Russia relations on the basis of the Common Spaces agenda in comparison to the unilateral approach of the CSR.

A third remarkable difference between the CSR and the four Common Spaces relates to the legal basis of the strategic agenda. The CSR formed a Treaty-based instrument of the EU's external relations (Art. 13 EU) whereas the Common Spaces emerged as a '*sui generis*' solution for the lack of progress in bilateral relations. Accordingly, the possibility provided by Article 23 EU to adopt CFSP instruments by qualified majority such as joint actions, common positions and any other decisions on the basis of the Common Strategy no longer applies. The Common Spaces road maps have been adopted in the framework of an EU–Russia Summit and, therefore, have a political significance comparable to the Joint Statement on EU enlargement. Hence, the road maps do not replace the PCA as the basic legal framework for bilateral EU–Russia relations but rather supplement the latter agreement with a long list of practical measures.

---

[46] Maresceau, 'EU Enlargement', p. 211.
[47] See Article 6 of the visa facilitation agreement, OJ 2007 L 129/30.

Similar to the CSR, the institutional and legal framework of the PCA forms the primary instrument for the implementation of the identified priorities.[48] The EU and Russia, however, agreed at their May 2006 Sochi Summit to work towards a new basic treaty, anticipating the expiry of the first period of validity of the PCA in November 2007.

12.4 Towards a new legal framework for the implementation of the Common Spaces road maps: challenges ahead

The PCA has been concluded for an initial period of ten years. Article 106 PCA provides for an automatic annual renewal of the agreement unless either side informs the other party of its denunciation at least six months before the expiry date. Whereas, from a legal point of view, the PCA can therefore continue to apply after 30 November 2007, a revision of this framework agreement is recommendable for a number of reasons. Most obviously, the context of EU–Russia relations has changed considerably since the entry into force of the PCA in 1997. On the one hand, the EU accession of new Member States, including three former Soviet republics, and the further extension of the EU's competences after the adoption of the Treaties of Amsterdam and Nice increased the significance of the EU as a key legal, political and economic partner for Russia. On the other hand, Russia itself transformed from a passive observer into an assertive neighbour with strategic energy resources and a renewed activism on the international political level. Reflecting this evolution, the level of bilateral cooperation has gradually extended beyond the scope of the PCA, with more than 40 dialogues on various policy domains and the conclusion of sector-specific bilateral agreements. Moreover, important changes have been introduced without formally amending the PCA such as inter alia the recognition of Russia's market economy status in 2004 or the transformation of the Cooperation Council into the Permanent Partnership Council. Several of the PCA provisions have, therefore, already become outdated. Given the numerous GATT/WTO provisions in the PCA,[49] Russia's WTO accession will make the agreement virtually redundant.

---

[48] Presidency Conclusions Brussels European Council (25–26 March 2004), *Bulletin EU*, 3/2004, I.24.76.

[49] See J. Lebullenger, 'Un Accord de partenariat confronté aux règles du GATT et de l'OMC', in J. Raux and V. Korovkine (eds.), *Le Partenariat entre l'Union Européenne et la Fédération de Russie* (Rennes: Apogée, 1998), pp. 199–215.

Another weakness of the PCA as the legal basis for implementing the Common Spaces programme is the relative lack of provisions concerning cooperation on second and third pillar issues.[50] In addition, the PCA does not allow for the adoption of legally binding decisions within the Cooperation Council, now turned into the Permanent Partnership Council (Art. 90). Finally, Moscow seems not very satisfied with the asymmetric nature of the PCA and, in particular, with the provision on unilateral legal approximation (Art. 55). For this reason, in 1999 Russia suggested 'the joint elaboration and conclusion of a new framework agreement on Strategic Partnership and cooperation in the 21st century'.[51] After the adoption of the Common Spaces road maps, Russian Foreign Minister Sergey Lavrov reiterated the need for a new legal framework replacing the PCA and reflecting the equal partnership between the EU and Russia.[52] On 3 July 2006, the European Commission launched the first step in this direction with the adoption of the draft negotiating directives for 'an updated and more ambitious framework for the EU–Russia relationship'.[53] Poland, however, vetoed the planned opening of the negotiations at the November 2006 Helsinki EU–Russia Summit in response to Russia's ban on the import of Polish meat imposed in November 2005 on health and food safety grounds. In the opinion of Poland, the actions undertaken by Moscow are not proportionate to the irregularities found and, therefore, infringe Article 19 PCA, which forbids the use of veterinary and phyto-sanitary restrictions on trade between the parties in an arbitrary and unjustified manner.[54] This trade dispute clearly illustrates the limits of the

---

[50] To a certain extent, this has been solved through the mixed character of the PCA, which allows the interconnection of the different pillars of the Union. The majority of PCA provisions, however, concerns trade and economic issues, see C. Hillion, *The Evolving System of European Union External Relations as Evidenced in the EU Partnerships with Russia and Ukraine*, PhD thesis, Leiden, 2005.

[51] 'Medium-Term Strategy for Development of Relations between the Russian Federation and the European Union (2000–2010)', available at: http://ec.europa.eu/external_relations/russia/russian_medium_term_strategy/.

[52] Transcript of remarks and replies to media questions by Russian Minister of Foreign Affairs Sergey Lavrov after round table meeting in international affairs committee of the State Duma of the Russian Federation, Moscow, 28 November 2005, 2533-23-11-2005, available at: http://www.ln.mid.ru.

[53] European Commission approves terms for negotiating new EU–Russia Agreement, Brussels, 3 July 2006, IP/06/910.

[54] Council of the EU, 'Problems in exports of meat, meat products and plant products to the Russian Federation', Brussels, 16 November 2005, 14533/05.

PCA, and in particular its loose dispute settlement procedure.[55] It also announces a very difficult negotiating process for defining a legal framework for EU–Russia relations in the post-PCA period.[56] Generally speaking, the following main options can be distinguished: (i) the PCA can be radically replaced by another document; (ii) the PCA can be extended with amendments (PCA+); or (iii) the PCA can be abandoned in order to proceed on the basis of joint political declarations and sectoral agreements as is, for instance, the case in the relations with the EU's other global strategic partner, the United States.[57]

12.4.1 Scenario 1: a new comprehensive framework agreement

The European Commission's ambition to draft 'an agreement which covers the whole range of EU–Russia cooperation' raises interesting legal questions. The inclusion of all policy areas covered in the four Common Spaces almost necessarily requires a 'multi-pillar agreement', concluded by both the EC and the EU, given that it will contain provisions falling under the EC and EU Treaty rules. To date, an example of such a specific case of 'cross-pillar mixity' is provided in the Agreement between the EU, the EC and the Swiss Confederation concerning the latter's association with the implementation, application and development of the Schengen *acquis*. Given the different procedures for the conclusion of agreements under the Community and Union pillars, as well as differences in terms of legal effect and jurisdiction of the ECJ, this agreement has been adopted by two separate Acts, one based on the Community Treaty and the other on Articles 24 and 38 of the Treaty on European Union.[58]

---

[55] Article 101 PCA only provides for the settlement of disputes on the basis of 'recommendations'. Conciliators may be appointed but their recommendations are not binding upon the Parties. In December 2003, the Cooperation Council adopted the rules of procedure for the settlement of disputes under the PCA, UE-RU 1001/1/03. This mechanism has, however, not been used or even contemplated in the Polish meat row.

[56] The Samara EU–Russia summit of 18–19 May 2007 could not produce a solution to the dispute between Poland and Russia. Accordingly, negotiations on a new framework agreement have not yet started at the time of writing of this contribution.

[57] For further reflections on the options for the post-PCA period, see M. Emerson (ed.), *The Elephant and the Bear Try Again. Options for a New Agreement between the EU and Russia* (Brussels: CEPS, 2006), p. 108.

[58] Council Decision 2004/849/EC of 25 October 2004, OJ 2004 L 368/26 and Council Decision 2004/860/EC of 25 October 2004, OJ 2004 L 368/78.

This complex procedure is not without consequences. One of the main problems is to find a balance between the roles of the various institutions in the negotiating process. It is illustrative that the competence question already gave rise to discussions between the Commission and the Council before the start of the negotiations with Russia.[59] Moreover, Article 24(5) provides that, for the conclusion of agreements on CFSP matters, Member States can invoke 'requirements of its own constitutional procedure' during the negotiations implying that in this case, the agreement shall not be binding on the Member State in question. It seems obvious that this might create problems regarding the application of the entire cross-pillar agreement.[60] A potential solution could, therefore, be to leave these sensitive areas out of the new agreement and to conclude separate agreements in these policy areas in parallel. Even in the hypothesis of a separate agreement on second and third pillar issues, the inclusion of policy areas going beyond the EC's exclusive competences implies that also the Member States will have to be involved in the conclusion and ratification procedure of a new EC–Russia framework agreement. This traditional form of mixity entails well-known problems concerning the entry into force and legal effect of the agreement.[61]

Another question concerns the legal basis of the new agreement from an EC point of view. One of the options could be to transform the PCA into a 'Strategic Association Agreement', based on Article 310 EC.[62] Apart from the symbolic importance of this 'upgrading' of the bilateral relationship, the possibility to adopt binding decisions within the association council would certainly be a major improvement from a legal point of view. On the other hand, the asymmetric nature of association agreements, based upon approximation to EU rules and policies, might be difficult for Russia to accept politically. For this reason, the 1999 Medium-term Strategy

---

[59] A. Beatty, 'Council and Commission clash over Russia talks', *European Voice*, 28 September 2006.

[60] J.-V. Louis, 'Les accords conclus au titre des deuxième et troisième pilliers', in J.-V. Louis and M. Dony, *Le droit de la Communauté européenne* (Brussels: Editions de l'Université de Bruxelles, 2005), pp. 328–9.

[61] P. Eeckhout, *External Relations of the European Union. Legal and Constitutional Foundations* (Oxford, Oxford University Press, 2004), pp. 215–25; M. Maresceau, 'Bilateral Agreements concluded by the European Community', *Collected Courses of the Hague Academy of International Law*, 2006, vol. 309, pp. 207–11.

[62] M. Vahl, 'Whither the Common European Economic Space? Political and Institutional Aspects of Closer Economic Integration between the EU and Russia', in T. De Wilde D'Estmael and L. Spetschinsky (eds.), *La politique étrangère de la Russie et l'Europe. Enjeux d'une proximité* (Brussels: Lang, 2004), p. 178.

explicitly ruled out Russia's accession to or 'association' with the EU. Accordingly, the examples provided by the old Europe Agreements, the European Economic Area Agreement or Euro-Mediterranean Association Agreements do not provide blueprints for EU–Russia relations.

An alternative could be a less ambitious agreement, including only a limited number of priority areas. With regard to the CES, a 'comprehensive Free Trade Agreement' covering goods, services, investment and a set of common regulatory principles has been suggested.[63] It is noteworthy that the Common Spaces road maps do not refer to the perspective of free trade. It is, however, not a secret that the creation of a free trade area is a primary objective after Russia's accession to the WTO. Importantly, a far-reaching trade agreement with Russia cannot exclude the energy question. Particularly after Russia's refusal to ratify the multilateral Energy Charter Treaty, which inter alia includes important provisions on free transit, investment and competition, it is the ambition of the European Commission and the EU Member States to include those principles in the post-PCA agreement.[64] It is questionable whether Russia will be prepared to introduce the most sensitive ECT provisions through this back door. In any event, it seems that a far-reaching trade agreement might exceed the EC's exclusive competence in the area of Common Commercial Policy[65] and does, therefore, not necessarily avoid the above-mentioned challenges of mixity. Hence, a continuation of the PCA – at least in the short term – or a PCA+, focusing on the institutional mechanisms for the implementation of the Common Spaces, cannot be excluded and forms a 'fall-back option' should no agreement be reached on the more substantial issues under discussion.

12.4.2 Scenario 2: updating the PCA to the realities of the Common Spaces agenda

Article 4 PCA provides that 'the parties undertake to examine together, by mutual consent, amendments which it may be appropriate to make to

---

[63] European Commission factsheet, 'EU–Russia Common Economic Space', prepared for the November 2006 EU–Russia Summit, available at: http://ec.europa.eu/comm/external_relations/russia/summit_11_06/com_eco_space.pdf.

[64] Communication from the Commission to the European Council, *External Energy Relations – From Principles to Action*, COM(2006) 590 final, Brussels, 12 October 2006, p. 3.

[65] On the competence question in matters of commercial policy, see Eeckhout, *External Relations*, pp. 9–57.

any part of the Agreement in view of changes in circumstances, and in particular in the situation arising from Russia's accession to the GATT/ WTO'. This often forgotten provision of the PCA allows adapting the agreement to the changing context of EU–Russia relations without negotiating an entirely new treaty. The modernisation of the current framework while preserving the legal continuity of the PCA avoids complex competence questions and retains the most important elements of the existing partnership such as the directly applicable rights of Russian nationals legally employed on the territory of an EU Member State or the multilevel institutional framework. On the other hand, the absence of any specific amendment procedure in the PCA implies that changes can only be made on the basis of bilateral protocols. The example of the PCA extension protocol has illustrated that this is not always an easy option. The question is, however, whether a comprehensive framework treaty is necessary at all. Apart from the legal problems regarding the formal conclusion and ratification of such agreements in a Union of 27 Member States, the example of the PCA illustrates that this exercise often results in 'long-winding and pretentious texts that are thin or devoid of legally binding-substance'.[66] For this reason, it has been argued that the future of EU–Russia relations would be served better by concrete, sector-specific agreements and political declarations or dialogues.[67]

12.4.3 Scenario 3: a network of political dialogues and sectoral agreements

The archetype of this third scenario is the EU–US Transatlantic Partnership. The absence of a comprehensive framework agreement did not prevent the development of close relations in various areas on the basis of a dense network of bilateral agreements and a multilevel political dialogue established on the basis of political declarations. In this respect, the Joint EU–US Action Plan, accompanying the New Transatlantic Agenda, is not so dissimilar from the road maps of the Common Spaces. Another interesting example is provided by the EU's relations with Switzerland on the basis of large package deals of interconnected bilateral agreements. In

[66] M. Emerson, F. Tassinari and M. Vahl, 'A New Agreement between the EU and Russia: Why, What and When?' in Emerson (ed.), *The Elephant*, p. 62.
[67] *Ibid.*

the Common Spaces road maps there are many issues of mutual interest that could be linked together in a similar way. The joint conclusion of the readmission and visa facilitation agreements can be seen as an example of such a practice.

Table 1. *Bilateral agreements between the EC/EU and Russia as provided for in the Common Spaces road maps*

Agreement on investment-related issues	Common Economic Space
Agreement on veterinary certification*	Common Economic Space
Agreement on fisheries	Common Economic Space
Agreement on Galileo/GLONAS cooperation	Common Economic Space
Agreement on customs cooperation	Common Economic Space
Agreement on trade in nuclear materials	Common Economic Space
Agreement on readmission*	Common Space of Freedom, Security and Justice
Agreement on visa facilitation*	Common Space of Freedom, Security and Justice
Agreement on mutual legal assistance	Common Space of Freedom, Security and Justice
Agreement on cooperation between the European Police Office (EUROPOL) and the Russian Federation*	Common Space of Freedom, Security and Justice
Agreement between Eurojust and the Russian Federation	Common Space of Freedom, Security and Justice
Agreement on judicial cooperation in criminal matters	Common Space of Freedom, Security and Justice
Agreement on information protection	Common Space of Freedom, Security and Justice
Agreement on science and technology cooperation*	Common Space on Research and Education, including Cultural Aspects

*this agreement has already been concluded[68]

The extension of the network of bilateral EC/EU–Russia agreements (see Table 1) is certainly a central ambition of the Common Spaces agenda. The examples of the EU's relations with important partners such as the

[68] For an overview, see the Agreements Database of the Council of the EU, available at: http://eur-lex.europa.eu/en/accords/accords.htm.

United States or Switzerland prove that stable bilateral relations are possible without an overarching framework agreement. It is, however, difficult to return to such a situation in the case of Russia. A simple termination of the PCA without replacement by a new treaty could be interpreted as a step back. The clear commitments to human rights, including the protection of minorities, the directly applicable non-discrimination provision for legally employed workers, and the multilevel institutional framework are all important chapters of the PCA-*acquis*. The inclusion of such principles in a legally binding text is important from the perspective of legal certainty. Hence, a relatively short, long-term and legally binding treaty focusing on the main principles and objectives while leaving the more detailed policy plans to separate agreements, seems to be the most realistic option. In comparison to the PCA, a focus on equal partnership in the spirit of the four Common Spaces and the inclusion of new priority areas (energy, fight against terrorism, mutual legal cooperation, education and culture, etc.) can be expected.

12.5 The Common Spaces in relation to the Northern Dimension and the European Neighbourhood Policy: a confirmation of the 'equal partnership' approach

The Common Spaces agenda not only creates a new context for the EU's unilateral and bilateral policy vis-à-vis the Russian Federation but also significantly affects the multilateral Northern Dimension (ND).[69] At the fourth ND Ministerial Meeting of 21 November 2005, the Foreign Affairs Ministers of the EU Member States, Russia, Iceland and Norway, together with the European Commissioner for External Relations and Neighbourhood Policy, agreed to reshape the ND into the 'political and operational framework for promoting the implementation of the EU–Russia Common Spaces at regional/sub-regional/local level'.[70] In this context, a new long-term 'ND Policy Framework Document' and a 'Political Declaration on the ND Policy' have been adopted in the margins of the

---

[69] The ND officially entered the EU's institutional setting in 1999 on the initiative of the Finnish EU Presidency as a 'policy framework' aiming at 'better coordination' and 'synergies' between existing cooperation programmes in the North of Europe. For more information concerning the development of the ND policy, see H. Ojanen (ed.), *The Northern Dimension: Fuel for the EU?* (Helsinki, Finnish Institute of International Affairs, 2001), p. 262.

[70] Guidelines for the Northern Dimension Policy from 2007, 14358/1/05, 18 November 2005.

November 2006 Helsinki EU–Russia Summit.[71] The active involvement of Russia in the preparation of the new ND basic texts as well as the explicit recognition that the ND is based on an equal partnership between the EU, Iceland, Norway and Russia are important innovations compared to previous practice. During the ND's formative years, Russia had always been largely excluded from decision-making. In particular, the dominant role of the EU institutions in the preparation and adoption of the ND Action Plans virtually limited Russia's role to that of an external observer with only a limited, consultative role.

The 'restyled' ND policy is no longer based on three-year action plans but operates on the basis of general policy guidelines defined by bi-annual ND ministerial meetings bringing together representatives of the four partners. Similar meetings at the senior official level take place at least every alternate year and, in order to provide continuity, a Steering Group of experts from the four partners meets three times a year. The implementation of the ND objectives is essentially based on the creation of sector-specific partnerships[72] and the financing of concrete projects approved within the meetings of foreign ministers or senior officials. The equal representation of Russia within those decision-making bodies and ND partnership institutions forms an interesting innovation and an attempt to ensure the 'joint ownership' of the ND policy. It is in line with the new approach represented by the Common Spaces road maps and allows for pragmatic cooperation in areas of mutual interest. Finally, the new ND and the Common Spaces agenda form an alternative to the EU's more unilateral and conditionality based European Neighbourhood Policy (ENP).

From the outset, the EU's position on the inclusion of Russia within this new policy framework has been somewhat ambiguous. Whereas the first Council conclusions identified Russia as 'a key partner' rather than a target country of the ENP,[73] later Commission documents explicitly

---

[71] Available at: http://ec.europa.eu/comm/external_relations/ north_dim/doc/frame_pol_1106.pdf.

[72] To date, a Northern Dimension Environmental Partnership and a Northern Dimension Partnership on Public Health and Social Well-being has been established whereas a new ND Transport and Logistics Partnership is envisaged. For comments, see P. Van Elsuwege, 'The Common Spaces in EU–Russia Relations and the Future of the Northern Dimension', in C. Archer (ed.), *The Northern Dimension of the European Union: Glancing Back, Looking Forward. Proceedings from the Northern Dimension Network* (Kaunas: Kaunas University Press, 2007), pp. 37–46.

[73] Council of the EU, General Affairs and External Relations, Brussels, 18 November 2002, 14183/02, p. 13.

included Russia within the geographic coverage of this policy.[74] Moscow, however, rejected negotiations on an ENP Action Plan due to the conditional and asymmetrical nature of this instrument. The joint elaboration of road maps for the implementation of the Common Spaces formed an acceptable alternative to the dominant position of the Commission in the drafting and monitoring of the ENP Action Plans. Moreover, it underlines Russia's special status in comparison to the other neighbouring countries included in the broad ENP concept. The Common Spaces alternative, however, does not imply that the ENP has become completely irrelevant for EU–Russia relations. The issues discussed within the Common Spaces framework are largely similar to those dealt with in the ENP context. For this reason, the European Neighbourhood and Partnership Instrument (ENPI), which replaces the old TACIS financial instrument from 1 January 2007 onwards, also covers Community assistance to Russia.[75] Comparable to the mechanism of the ENP, financial cooperation will be targeted at meeting the objectives defined in the Common Spaces road maps. It is noteworthy that also in respect of financial cooperation, 'full ownership' on the part of Russia is a key priority for the future. In a special report, the European Court of Auditors concluded that efficiency of the use of TACIS funds in the Russian Federation has been very low due to a lack of real dialogue between the Commission and the Russian authorities.[76] Hence, the active involvement of Russian representatives in project identification and implementation is an essential condition to the successful realisation of the Common Spaces agenda.

12.6 Conclusion: challenges and opportunities surrounding the Common Spaces concept

The re-definition of the EU–Russia Strategic Partnership along the lines of the four Common Spaces has raised mixed reactions. On the one hand,

[74] Communication from the Commission to the Council and the European Parliament, 'Wider Europe – Neighbourhood: A New Framework for Relations with our Eastern and Southern Neighbours', COM(2003)104 final, 11 March 2003.

[75] Regulation 1638/2006 of the European Parliament and of the Council of 24 October 2006 laying down general provisions establishing a European Neighbourhood and Partnership Instrument, OJ 2006 L 310/1.

[76] Court of Auditors, Special Report No. 2/2006 concerning the performance of projects funded under TACIS in the Russian Federation, OJ 2006 C 119/1.

the Common Spaces road maps have been criticised for their lack of substance and fuzzy language.[77] On the other hand, it has been argued that 'they can bring new momentum to stalled cooperation processes'.[78] It might be too early to make a final assessment of this new concept but it is obvious that the Common Spaces represent a number of new character-istics and recent trends in EU–Russia relations. The road maps constitute a first attempt to create a joint, issues-based agenda for future cooperation replacing the EU's unilateral Common Strategy. 'Equal partnership' and 'joint ownership' are the new keywords denominating the relations between the EU and Russia. Whereas this rhetoric cannot conceal that, in practice, legal approximation will essentially be based upon the *acquis communautaire*, there is a growing understanding that Russia's involve-ment in policy formulation and priority identification is a necessary prerequisite to making progress. Accordingly, the Common Spaces agenda reveals an evolution towards more pragmatic cooperation.

The adoption of a wide-ranging list of action points allows progress in areas where Russia and the EU have a clear common interest. The joint conclusion of bilateral agreements on visa facilitation and readmission but also Russia's ratification of the Kyoto protocol, the bilateral deal on Russia's WTO accession, the envisaged abolition of Siberian overflight rights and new initiatives in the ND framework, provide good examples of this pragmatic approach. Whereas the PCA continues to exist, for the time being, as the general legal framework agreement of the EU–Russia Stra-tegic Partnership, it is obvious that more flexible political declarations adopted in the context of the biannual EU–Russia summits gain importance. The extension of the PCA on the basis of a short legal protocol and a more extensive political joint statement is a case in point. The introduction of the Common Spaces road maps and the adoption of the ND policy framework document are other illustrations of this tendency. In addition, the Common Spaces road maps indicate an ambition to extend the network of legally binding sector-specific bilateral agreements.

The Common Spaces provide for a general political framework or 'package', reflecting the multidimensional nature of the EU–Russia Strategic

---

[77] M. Emerson, 'EU Russia Four Common Spaces and the Proliferation of the Fuzzy', *CEPS Policy Brief*, May 2005, available at: http://shop.ceps.be/BookDetail.php?item_id=1224.

[78] K. Barysch, 'The EU and Russia: From Principle to Pragmatism?', *Centre for European Reform Policy Brief*, November 2006, available at: http://www.cer.org.uk/pdf/ EU_russia_barysch_final_10nov06.pdf.

Partnership. Whereas this approach has some potential to provide added value, the new agenda also faces a number of challenges. From a legal point of view, the uncertain future of the PCA and the absence of joint decision-making bodies is certainly a factor to be reckoned with. There is an obvious risk that the negotiation of a post-PCA agreement will give rise to new tensions between the various actors involved. Politically speaking, the historically strained relations between Russia and the new Central and Eastern European Member States, in particular the Baltic States and Poland, might complicate pragmatic progress on substantive issues. The May 2007 Samara EU–Russia Summit, for instance, has been over-shadowed by Moscow's disputes with three new Member States, i.e. the ban on Polish meat, the removal of a Soviet war memorial in the Estonian capital Tallinn and the disruption of oil supply to Lithuania. For the first time, the EU and Russia did not even agree on the terms of a Joint Statement.

The insistence of Polish and Baltic MEPs on Russia's recognition of the Soviet occupation of the Baltic States is another very sensitive issue. The response of Commissioner Ferrero-Waldner that it is up to historians to clarify the past and that the EU's priority must be to look to the future, illustrates the understanding that raising this question as a condition for cooperation might paralyse the entire Strategic Partnership.[79] Issues such as Russia's behaviour in Chechnya or respect for civil liberties can, however, not be avoided. The mysterious murders of Anna Politkovskaya and Aleksandr Litvinenko raise questions about growing authoritarian tendencies in Russia. Hence, the main challenge will be to find a balance between a politically inspired, value-based approach and an economically motivated, pragmatic relationship.

Another topical question potentially affecting the Common Spaces is Russia's ambition to create a Single Economic Space (SES) together with Ukraine, Kazakhstan and Belarus.[80] The European Commission rather diplomatically observed that the implications of the SES 'will need to be examined carefully in terms of their possible impact on work on the Common Economic Space and on a possible future FTA'.[81] It seems

---

[79] Debates of the European Parliament, 25 May 2005, available at: http://www.europarl.europa.eu.

[80] On this initiative, see S. Glinkina and L. Kosikova (eds.), *Development of Common Economic Space of Russia, Ukraine, Belarus and Kazakhstan in the context of EU Enlargement* (Moscow: Russian Academy of Sciences, 2006), available at: http://indeunis.wiiw.ac.at.

[81] Communication from the Commission to the Council and the European Parliament on relations with Russia, COM(2004)106, p. 2.

obvious that a competitive integration project on the EU's eastern borders, which does not depart from the *acquis communautaire*, gives rise to
serious legal obstacles. It also raises questions in the light of Ukraine's
ambition of close relations to and even membership of the EU. There is,
in other words, a potential clash of geopolitical visions that could be
detrimental for the general development of EU–Russia relations.

The EU's ability to speak with one voice in order to send clear and
unambiguous messages to Russia seems to be a crucial determinant for
developing a genuine Strategic Partnership. Russia's threat to ban all EU
meat imports after the accession of Bulgaria and Romania and the suggestion to conclude bilateral certification agreements with individual EU
Member States, points at a potential Russian 'divide and rule' policy. The
refusal of the EU Member States to conclude such bilateral deals paved the
way for an EC–Russia memorandum on this issue and avoided the
scenario of a divided Community.[82] Of utmost importance is also the
development of a common external energy policy. From a legal point of
view, this ambition provides a highly significant example of the interconnection between the Community's competences under the first pillar[83]
and the Common Foreign and Security Policy. Accordingly, the Energy
Policy for Europe (EPE) – launched at the March 2006 European Council
in a reaction to Russia's gas dispute with Ukraine – requires the
involvement of both the European Commission, the High Representative
for the CFSP and the EU Member States. The EU's dependence on supplies from Russia in combination with the dominant role of Russia's state-
owned oil and gas companies, *Transneft* and *Gazprom*, implies that energy
will be – more than ever – a key issue of the EU–Russia Strategic Partnership. Russia's refusal to ratify the Energy Charter Treaty and the
construction of a new gas pipeline bypassing the Baltic States and Poland
explains the insistence of the latter countries on legally binding commitments from Russia in questions of energy transit and liberalisation.
The ability of the EU to present a common position on the principles for a
future energy partnership with Russia, to be considered in the framework

---

[82] H. Mahony, 'Russia and EU reach deal on meat imports', *EUobserver*, 20 December 2006.

[83] Notwithstanding the absence of a specific legal basis for a European energy policy, the EC
Treaty provisions on the internal market, competition, Common Commercial Policy,
environment and transport all relate to the energy field. It is noteworthy that, in contrast to
the current situation, the Treaty of Lisbon provides for a specific legal basis for the EU's energy
policy (Title XXI).

of the post-PCA agreement, will therefore be an interesting test case. Finally, the future internal developments in Russia constitute a crucial factor for the successful implementation of the Common Spaces agenda. Of particular importance will be the 2008 Russian presidential elections and the question of how Putin's successor will evaluate the importance of close relations with the EU. In any event, it seems obvious that Russia will always require special treatment in the EU's external relations.

The EU's Strategic Partnership with the Mediterranean and the Middle East: a new geopolitical dimension of the EU's proximity strategies

ERWAN LANNON

13.1 Introduction

For the first time ever, the European Commission, the Presidency of the Council and the Secretary General/High Representative for Common Foreign and Security Policy (CFSP) have designed a comprehensive framework towards the Mediterranean and the Middle East, two regions that previously had been artificially disconnected in the EU's external relations strategies.

Since the freeze of the Euro-Arab Dialogue in the mid-1980s, the relations of the Member States with the Arab world were not based on a single framework. Seven so-called 'Arab Mediterranean countries' (Algeria, Egypt, Jordan, Lebanon, Morocco, Syria and Tunisia) benefited from the Global Mediterranean Policy. Mauritania, Somalia, and Sudan were considered as belonging to the African, Caribbean and Pacific (ACP) group of countries and therefore included under the Lomé Convention's framework. Bahrain, Kuwait, Oman, Qatar, Saudi Arabia and the United Arab Emirates benefited, for their part, from a specific contractual relationship established between the EC and the members of the Gulf Cooperation Council. This approach was considered, by the members of the Arab League, as leading to a 'balkanisation' of the Arab world. The launching of the Euro-Mediterranean Partnership (EMP) at the Barcelona Conference in November 1995 was innovative in that it welcomed the new Palestinian Authority among the southern Mediterranean partners. Nevertheless, the Arab League continued to criticise the EU for not developing a comprehensive Euro-Arab strategy.

Therefore, when the Member States decided, in 2003, to launch a new initiative towards the Middle East, this 'Euro-Arab' issue was discussed at

EU level. A good illustration of this fact is that the first report on this new European Middle East initiative was entitled *Strengthening the EU's partnership with the Arab World.*[1] However, we will see that the final version of the *Strategic Partnership with the Mediterranean and the Middle East* does not cover all Arab countries but only the majority of them (16[2] out of 22 members of the Arab League Charter). It is noteworthy also that three non-Arab countries namely Israel, Iran and Turkey, are also included among the beneficiaries of this Strategic Partnership.

This Euro-Arab issue was not the only motive for developing a new European strategy towards the Middle East. The 2004 *big bang* enlargement raised the issue of the definitive limits of the enlargement process, of the ultimate borders of the EU and, consequently, of its present and future neighbours. The idea of creating a buffer zone to surround the enlarged EU is linked with the notion of a 'European hinterland'. The EU is in fact trying to develop its relations with and to assert is influence on countries and regions not only in its immediate vicinity but also towards the 'neighbours of its neighbours'. The idea being that those countries belong to the same geopolitical area.

One of the first signs of this was the extension of the European Neighbourhood Policy (ENP) to the Southern Caucasus.[3] The development of border control/management cooperation within the framework of both EMP and ENP is a second important indicator that the EU Member States would like their partners to play the role of a buffer zone notably against the increasing migratory pressure from Africa but also from the Middle East (Afghanistan, Iran, Iraq and Pakistan). The third indicator is precisely the creation of the *Strategic Partnership with the Mediterranean and the Middle East* (SPMME).

The purpose of this contribution is to study the genesis of the SPMME, its methodology and objectives and to assess its potential. In order to do so the main reports that led to the creation of this new Strategic Partnership are analysed. The main agreements concluded with the Middle

---

[1] Joint Commission/High Representative report on 'Strengthening the EU's partnership with the Arab World' annexed to the Note from the Secretariat General of the Council of the European Union, 15945/03, PESC 791, Brussels, 9 December 2003.

[2] Algeria, Morocco, Tunisia, Egypt, Jordan, Lebanon, Palestinian Authority, Syria, Bahrain, Oman, Qatar, Kuwait, Saudi Arabia, UAE, Yemen, Iraq.

[3] Armenia, Azerbaijan and Georgia. Communication of the Commission, 'European Neighbourhood Policy Strategy Paper', COM(2004)373 final, p. 10.

East countries and the new EU's financial instruments will also be taken into consideration.

13.2 The genesis of the Strategic Partnership with the Mediterranean and the Middle East

It was at the June 2003 Thessaloniki European Council that the Member States asked the Commission and the CFSP High Representative to formulate a 'detailed work plan . . . , taking full account of existing policies and programmes and in particular the Barcelona Process and the New Neighbours Initiative' with a view to strengthening its partnership with the Arab world.[4]

13.2.1 The Preliminary Report on 'Strengthening the EU's partnership with the Arab World'

The Joint Commission/High Representative Preliminary Report entitled *Strengthening the EU's partnership with the Arab World*,[5] introduced by a letter of President Prodi, the High Representative and Commissioner Patten, was presented on 9 December 2003 to the Council of Ministers. It should be stressed again that originally, in 2003, it is the Arab world and more precisely the '22 signatory parties of the Arab League Charter', that were the primary concern of this new approach and not the Middle East as such. The introductory letter refers, for example, to 'a clear focus on the objective of political, social and economic reform in the Arab World'. In other words, the Report also tackled the situation of five Arab countries (Comoros, Djibouti, Mauritania, Somalia and Sudan) that are considered by the EU as belonging to the ACP group of countries.[6] The report does recognise that 'from a strictly political point of view, relations with the ACP belong to a different set of problems' and that there will be 'two main lines of action for the EU in its relations with the Arab countries, the Mediterranean line and the Wider Middle East'.[7]

---

[4] Presidency Conclusions, Thessaloniki European Council, 19 and 20 June 2003, points 66–7.
[5] Joint Commission/High Representative Report on 'Strengthening the EU's partnership with the Arab World', annexed to the Note from the Secretariat General of the Council of the European Union, 15945/03, PESC 791, Brussels, 9 December 2003.
[6] African, Caribbean and Pacific Countries.
[7] Joint Commission/High Representative Report, n. 5, p. 7.

The Preliminary Report mentioned two non-Arab countries – Iran and Israel – but, at that time, Turkey was not included among the beneficiaries of the new strategy. As far as Iran is concerned, it is stated that 'recent developments point towards the need to establish a regional stability strategy for this group of countries which, with the addition of Iran, could be defined as the *"Wider Middle East"*.[8] The report further considered that after the fall of Saddam Hussein, it was essential for the success of the reconstruction efforts to have an 'adequate security environment, a strong and vital UN role, a realistic schedule for the handing over of political responsibility to the Iraqi people, and the setting up of a transparent multilateral trust fund to channel support from the international community'. In addition, restoration of stability and order was also considered as an 'essential element for achieving international security'.[9] Clearly the idea was thus to develop a long-term approach for social, economic and political reconstruction in Iraq.[10]

For the members of the Gulf Cooperation Council[11] (Bahrain, Kuwait, Oman, Qatar, Saudi Arabia and the United Arab Emirates), the situation differs in that, for a number of years, EU Member States have developed a relation with this regional economic grouping. The same applies to Yemen (see Section 13.4.1).

Regarding the crucial Israeli–Palestinian issue, it was recalled that the Israeli–Palestinian conflict deserved 'special reference'. The resolution of the Arab–Israeli conflict was considered as being a 'strategic priority for the EU'[12] (see also the principles defined by the Interim Report).

---

[8] *Ibid.*, p. 7.   [9] *Ibid.*, p. 6.   [10] *Ibid.*, p. 10.

[11] The Cooperation Council for the Arab States of the Gulf (formerly named and still commonly called Gulf Cooperation Council (GCC)) was created in May 1981. The unified economic agreement between the countries of the Gulf Cooperation Council was signed in November 1981. The GCC Charter states that the basic objectives are to 'effect coordination, integration and inter-connection between Member States in all fields, strengthening ties between their peoples, formulating similar regulations in various fields such as economy, finance, trade, customs, tourism, legislation, administration, as well as fostering scientific and technical progress in industry, mining, agriculture, water and animal resources, establishing scientific research centres, setting up joint ventures, and encouraging cooperation of the private sector'. Cooperation Council for the Arab States of the Gulf, Secretariat General, 'Introduction: The Concept and Foundations', available at: http://www.gcc-sg.org/Foundations.html.

[12] 'Strengthening the EU's partnership with the Arab World', op. cit., p. 7. According to the 1995 Barcelona Declaration the Euro-Mediterranean initiative was 'not intended to replace the other activities and initiatives undertaken in the interests of the peace, stability and development of the region, but that it will contribute to their success. The participants support the realisation of a just, comprehensive and lasting peace settlement in the Middle East based

13.2.2 The Interim Report on an 'EU Strategic Partnership with the Mediterranean and the Middle East'

A second *Interim Report on an EU Strategic Partnership with the Mediterranean and the Middle East* was presented in March 2004.[13] Its geographical scope, relationship with other EU frameworks and its principles and priorities for action deserve special attention.

The geographical coverage of the SPMME and bridges with the EMP, ENP and the Cotonou Agreement

The Interim Report emphasised that the primary focus of the Strategic Partnership will be the countries of North Africa and the Middle East.[14] In other words, the ACP Arab countries were definitely excluded from the scope of the new Strategic Partnership with one exception: Mauritania. Being a member of the Arab Maghreb Union, Mauritania was to be 'included in the current initiative taking full account of existing instruments, i.e. the Cotonou Agreement and the structures emanating from it'.[15] This is not a real novelty. Because it belongs to the Arab Maghreb Union (AMU), Mauritania had already been associated to the Global Mediterranean Policy, the Renewed Mediterranean Policy and the Euro-Mediterranean Partnership but the result of regional cooperation projects was negligible due to the tensions resulting from the Western Sahara conflict.

A major novelty of this report was that, contrary to the report on *Strengthening the EU's partnership with the Arab World*, Turkey was explicitly included in the SPMME together with all the Mediterranean partners covered by the Euro-Mediterranean Partnership.[16] In fact, the passage from a 'Euro-Arab' to a 'North Africa-Middle East' approach necessarily implied the inclusion of Turkey as this candidate country for EU membership will remain a full member of the Euro-Mediterranean Partnership until its (still hypothetical) formal EU accession. In this context, it is interesting

---

on the relevant United Nations Security Council resolutions and principles mentioned in the letter of invitation to the Madrid Middle East Peace Conference, including the principle land for peace, with all that this implies', Barcelona Declaration, 28 November 1995, available at: http://ec.europa.eu/comm/external_relations/euromed/bd.htm.

[13] 'Interim Report on an EU Strategic Partnership with the Mediterranean and the Middle East', annexed to the Note of the Council General Secretariat, 7498/1/04 REV 1, Brussels, 19 March 2004, Euromed Report n° 73, available at: http://ec.europa.eu/comm/external_relations/euromed/publication/euromed_report73_en.pdf.

[14] *Ibid.*, p. 3.   [15] *Ibid.*, p. 7.   [16] *Ibid.*, p. 5.

to note that if originally Turkey was formally excluded from ENP because of its 'candidate country' status, it is now associated to the ENP. In fact, the December 2006 Communication of the European Commission on 'Strengthening the European Neighbourhood Policy' stated that regarding regional cooperation with the 'partner countries around the Black Sea (whether under the ENP, or in the case of our relations with Russia under the Strategic Partnership and with Turkey as a candidate country), the EU should be fully inclusive, whatever the formal context of its bilateral relations with these countries'.[17]

The inclusion of Turkey into the SPMME and its late association to the ENP thus confirms Turkey's strategic location and potential role in the region and gives more consistency to the ENP-EMP-SPMME triangle.

Principles for action and priorities

In the Interim Report, 11 principles for action as well as a number of priorities for the SPMME are listed. Among them one should note down that the EU 'will avail of opportunities provided through the dialogue in partnership to promote its concerns regarding respect for human rights and the rule of law' and will support 'internally driven reforms in the economic, political and social spheres through engagement with state and civil actors'. This kind of priority must be considered while keeping in mind that they apply to countries such as Iran, Iraq, Saudi Arabia or Yemen which are not models in the field of human rights, the rule of law or as far as 'women's empowerment' is concerned. Last, but not least, the solution of the Arab–Israeli conflict is not considered as being a precondition for implementing reforms in the Arab world.

As far as the methodology is concerned, flexibility is the first keyword as the EU will implement the *Strategic Partnership for the Mediterranean and the Middle East* through 'existing instruments and, where appropriate, new instruments'. As far as the Mediterranean countries are concerned,

---

[17] Communication of the European Commission on: 'Strengthening the European Neighbourhood policy', Brussels, 4 December 2006, COM(2006)726 final, pp. 10–11. The Commission Communication further specifies that 'in addition, and building on these closer contacts, it will be useful to establish a regular dialogue with BSEC at Foreign Minister level, which would help implement and develop further the Union's Black Sea regional policy ... The Commission intends to address the question of strengthened Black Sea dialogue further in a separate Communication next year. The "Black Sea Synergy" should take account of other regional initiatives, such as the Baku initiative in the transport and energy fields.'

'the Work Programme for the Mediterranean countries should draw on the implementation of the EU's Neighbourhood Policy'.[18] Second, differentiation between the Mediterranean countries and countries 'East of Jordan' is, for obvious reasons, also a key element, the idea being to work on two parallel tracks seeking articulation between various actions in the region where appropriate.

Third, the joint ownership principle is also central as reforms can only succeed if they are generated from within the societies and are not to be imposed from the outside. In this regard, the March 2004 European Council, in welcoming the Interim Report, underlined the importance of 'intensive consultation with the countries involved'. The European Council also recalled the 'readiness of the EU to work with the US and other partners in cooperating with the region'.[19]

13.3 The Final Report of June 2004: the East of Jordan Track

Taking into account the discussion by the Permanent Representatives Committee (COREPER) on 3 June 2004 and the drafting suggestions made at that meeting, the Final Report on the *Strategic Partnership with the Mediterranean and the Middle East* was transmitted by the Presidency again to the COREPER in June 2004,[20] then to the Council of Ministers and finally to the European Council.

13.3.1 The SPMME as an 'Overall Strategic Framework'

Obviously the *Strategic Partnership with the Mediterranean and the Middle East* is very much an example of soft law. By endorsing the SPMME, the June 2004 European Council gave it a clear political legitimacy.[21] In this regard, it is noteworthy to recall that the founding Act of the Euro-Mediterranean Partnership, the November 1995 Barcelona Declaration, was also not a legally binding document that was not even signed by the partners. Its main orientations were previously endorsed by the

---

[18] Interim Report on the SPMME, n. 13, p. 9. For the impact on the financial instruments, see 13.3.2.

[19] Presidency Conclusions of the Brussels European Council 25–6 March 2004, points 59–61.

[20] 'Final Report on an EU Strategic Partnership with the Mediterranean and the Middle East', annexed Note 10246/04 from Presidency to COREPER/Council on, Brussels, 8 June 2004.

[21] See point 68.

June 1995 Cannes European Council (as the EU negotiating position) and its results approved by the December 1995 Madrid European Council, as the Barcelona Declaration was annexed, as such, to the Presidency Conclusions.[22]

It is also interesting to compare the *Strategic Partnership with the Mediterranean and the Middle East* with the ENP. The strategy for the latter is based on a series of European Council Presidency Conclusions and on Communications (including Strategy Papers) and Country Reports (CRs) prepared by the European Commission. On the basis of these *unilateral* CRs, the European Commission then prepares a draft Action Plan that is discussed with the beneficiary and, if possible, more informally with representatives of civil society of the partner. Afterwards, the draft Action Plans are submitted to the Council of Ministers for approval. Finally, they are forwarded to the main institutional bodies of the Euromed Association Agreements, the Association Councils, where they are adopted *via* a *recommendation* (and not a *decision*). Therefore the Action Plans are also not legally binding documents, contrary to what the Commission proposed originally. More precisely, Commission had suggested that the Action Plans be adopted by means of a *decision* of the Association Council. Moreover, in practice their 'bilateral nature' depends on the real input of the beneficiaries (government and civil society) in the process of drafting the document.

In fact, there is a general tendency to favour soft law operational instruments and to use already existing bilateral frameworks but without excluding the possibility of concluding new agreements in the future. New financial instruments adopted on the basis of Council regulations provide legal certainty as far as financial procedures are concerned. Nevertheless, the general idea seems to be to favour, circumstances allowing, the creation of 'umbrella frameworks' or 'overall strategic frameworks' that are not legally binding. The set of political objectives, guidelines and benchmarks, can therefore be adapted and updated regularly without using a heavy administrative machinery.

---

[22] See the Presidency Conclusions of the Cannes European Council, 26–7 June 1994, part B, document entitled 'Euro-Mediterranean Conference in Barcelona: Position of the European Union'; see also the Presidency Conclusions of the Essen European Council, 9–10 December 1994, Annex V: 'Council report for the European Council in Essen concerning the future Mediterranean Policy'. For the Madrid European Council of 15–16 December 1995, see Annex 11: 'Mediterranean-Barcelona Declaration'.

This kind of approach raises the problem of using existing agreements for implementing the various strategies and of the compatibility of their objectives with the new multilateral frameworks. For instance, during a Public Hearing held at the European Parliament in 2006, the Algerian Ambassador mentioned that, in his opinion, there was a lack of consistency between, on the one hand, the objectives of the Euro-Mediterranean Association Agreement concluded with Algeria and, on the other hand, of the ENP. He concluded that Algeria was not interested in participating in ENP.[23] In fact, it is the methodology of ENP, based on the pre-accession strategy model, that was severely critised. The new *Strategic Partnership with the Mediterranean and the Middle East* is obviously not perceived by the EU partners in the same way. The main reason for this is that the SPMME draws its inspiration from the Euro-Mediterranean Partnership and is not based on the pre-accession strategy model, as is the case of the ENP.

13.3.2 *Additional clarifications and new trends*

The Final Report clarified the fact that the SPMME is based on two distinct tracks. The first 'Mediterranean track' relies on EMP and ENP while the second 'East of Jordan Track' embrace the six Members of the Gulf Cooperation Council together with Iran, Iraq and Yemen. This double track approach is certainly consistent as it establishes a triangular relationship between the EU on the one hand, and the Mediterranean and the East of Jordan countries on the other hand. The creation of a comprehensive approach regarding the whole region from Morocco to Iran and Iraq together with the whole Arabian peninsula, is a clear sign that the EU is developing a new geopolitical approach. But this geographical extension is not the only novelty.

Among the new trends that were consolidated in the Final Report, one should highlight, first of all, the establishment of an approach based on three complementary strategies: EMP, ENP and SPMME. Second, the resolution of the Arab–Israeli conflict is at the heart of the preoccupations but is not a precondition for launching reforms in the Arab world. Third, the social reforms are key elements of the strategy (including educational and women's empowerment).

---

[23] See *Agence Europe* n° 9269, 21 September 2006, p. 3.

Another key priority is cooperation in the field of security and defence and more particularly on issues such as non-proliferation, counter-terrorism and security dialogue.[24] The inclusion of an EU standard clause on non-proliferation of Weapons of Mass Destruction in all new third-country agreements as well as the establishment of expert sub-committees under the association and other third-party agreements is a novelty in this regard.[25] Last, but not least, the SPMME will be reinforced through the conclusion of new bilateral agreements with the East of Jordan countries (GCC, Iran, Iraq).

13.4 Instruments and perspectives offered to the East of Jordan Track

In this section we will briefly analyse the agreements concluded with the East of Jordan countries and the possibilities offered to Iran and Iraq. Then, we will examine the new financial instruments created by the EC in the framework of the new financial perspectives.

13.4.1 Bilateral and regional agreements (to be) concluded with the beneficiaries of the 'East of Jordan Track'

Countries already benefiting from a contractual relation with the EC: the GCC and Yemen

As far as the GCC is concerned, a 'Cooperation Agreement between the European Economic Community, of the one part, and the countries parties to the Charter of the Cooperation Council for the Arab States of the Gulf ... of the other part' was signed in 1989.[26] Article 11(1) of this agreement is devoted to trade aspects. In this field, the objective is to promote the 'development and diversification of the reciprocal commercial

---

[24] Including encouragement to partners to consider confidence building measures such as notification of exercises, exchanges of military observers.

[25] See E. Lannon 'La dimension Sécurité Défense de la Politique Européenne de Voisinage', in M.-F. Labouz, C. Philip and P. Soldatos (eds.), *L'Union européenne élargie aux nouvelles frontières et à la recherche d'une politique de voisinage* (Brussels: Bruylant, 2006), pp. 181–208.

[26] 'Cooperation Agreement between the European Economic Community, of the one part, and the countries parties to the Charter of the Cooperation Council for the Arab States of the Gulf (the State of the United Arab Emirates, the State of Bahrain, the Kingdom of Saudi Arabia, the Sultanate of Oman, the State of Qatar and the State of Kuwait) of the other part', OJ 1989 L 54/3.

exchanges' between the Parties to the 'highest possible level'. Furthermore, paragraph 2 already envisaged the possibility to negotiate an agreement 'aimed at the expansion of trade', a clear although indirect reference of the possibility of concluding a free trade agreement in the future. As recalled by the European Commission, free trade agreement negotiations were initiated in 1990 but soon came to a standstill. In 1999, the negotiations regained momentum after the GCC's declaration to create a GCC customs union.[27]

As underlined by the European Commission, the 'aftermath of the Iraq war and EU efforts towards the establishment of an EU Strategic Partnership for the Mediterranean and the Middle East provoked a renewed interest in EU–GCC relations'. The Commission is therefore seeking to enhance cooperation with the GCC within the framework of the new SPMME. According to the European Commission, such an enhanced cooperation will also 'open up possibilities to support the region's domestic reform efforts including areas such as education or human rights'.[28] On 21 September 2006, the Foreign Ministers Troika meeting with the members of the GCC reconfirmed the commitment to conclude the negotiations concerning a new Free Trade Agreement.

It was in 1984 that relations between the EEC and the Yemen Arab Republic were formalised within a 'Development Cooperation Agreement'. Following the unification of Yemen, the 1984 Cooperation Agreement was *extended* in March 1995 and a Framework Cooperation Agreement was signed in November 1997. It is interesting to mention Article 9 on 'Regional cooperation' as the 1984 Agreement already envisaged 'activities designed to develop cooperation between the Republic of Yemen and its neighbours' and more specifically a 'coordination with the Community's decentralised cooperation programmes with the Mediterranean and GCC countries'.[29] However, it was only in 2004 that the bilateral political dialogue, focusing on democracy, human rights, democratisation and cooperation in the fight against terrorism, was launched.[30] Also interesting is the 'Evolutive

---

[27] In November 2005, the 13th round of EU–GCC FTA negotiations took place, see European Commission, 'The EU & the Gulf Cooperation Council (GCC) – Overview', available at: http://ec.europa.eu/comm/external_relations/gulf_cooperation/intro/index.htm.

[28] *Ibid.*

[29] 'Cooperation agreement between the European Community and the Republic of Yemen', OJ 1998 L 72/18.

[30] See 'Joint Declaration on Political Dialogue between the European Union and the Republic of Yemen', Brussels, 6 July 2004, available at: http://ec.europa.eu/external_relations/yemen/intro/joint_decl_06-07-04.pdf.

clause' of Article 16 allowing for the extension and reinforcement of this Agreement. Thus, the agreement can easily be adapted to the new ambitions of the SPMME.

Countries of the East of Jordan Track not yet benefiting from an agreement with the EC: Iran and Iraq

Regarding Iran, the Final Report on the SPMME mentioned that nego-tiations were pending for a Trade and Cooperation Agreement as well as for a parallel political agreement and that the EU was also engaged in a 'Comprehensive Dialogue and a Human Rights Dialogue with Iran'.[31] In fact, during the preparations of the SPMME in 2003 and early 2004, the EU developed an active diplomacy to persuade Iran to comply with relevant UN Security Council Resolutions calling for a stop to uranium enrichment activities. Of course, the increasingly tense situation since the outcome of the Iranian general elections in early 2004 had been held under conditions that were criticised by the EU and 'had left the potential deepening of ties between the European Union and Iran behind initial expectations'.[32]

In December 2006, the European Council expressed 'its concern about the negative impact of Iranian policies on stability and security in the Middle East' and decided to cancel the meeting of the EU–Iran human rights dialogue due to the Iranian Government's 'recent statements con-cerning the EU and individual Member States, as well as its threats towards Israel, and the continuing deterioration of human rights and political freedoms of its citizens'.[33]

Until the resolution of the nuclear issue and a radical change in the external strategy of Iran it seems doubtful that the Member States will reactivate the talks on a trade and cooperation agreement. The provisions of the SPMME in the field of security and defence are therefore very relevant here. A regional security dialogue on confidence building measures, for example, remains of fundamental importance.

At present there is no agreement between the EC and its Member States, on the one hand, and Iraq, on the other hand, but in 2005 the European

---

[31] *Ibid.*

[32] European Commission, DG External Relations, 'EU Iran Relationships – Overview', available at: http://ec.europa.eu/external_relations/iran/intro/index.htm.

[33] Presidency Conclusions Brussels European Council, 'Declaration on Iran', Annex III, 14–15 December 2006.

Commission proposed negotiating directives for a Trade and Cooperation Agreement. By entering into negotiations for contractual relations with Iraq, the EU aims to promote institutional and socio-economic reforms. Another important element of this agreement will be to develop bilateral trade relations in conformity with WTO rules while ensuring a 'minimum level of predictability, transparency and legal certainty for economic operators'.[34] However, the current situation in Iraq is too confused to envisage the conclusion of such an agreement in the near future.

13.4.2 The financing instruments for development cooperation and economic cooperation

Following complex discussions between the European Parliament, the Council and the Commission, a new framework for providing assistance was proposed in order to make the Community's external assistance more effective.

Seven main Regulations have been adopted in this regard. Regulation 1085/2006[35] establishes an Instrument for Pre-Accession (IPA) for Community assistance to candidate and potential candidate countries; Regulation 1638/2006[36] lays down general provisions establishing a European Neighbourhood and Partnership Instrument (ENPI); Regulation 1934/2006[37] establishes a financing instrument for cooperation with industrialised and other high-income countries and territories; Regulation 1905/2006 establishes a financing instrument for development cooperation;[38] Regulation 1717/2006[39] establishes an instrument for stability; Regulation 1889/2006[40] establishes a financing instrument for the promotion of democracy and human rights worldwide while Regulation 1257/96[41] concerns humanitarian aid.[42]

For the East of Jordan countries of Iraq, Iran, the six members of the GCC and Yemen, two of the above-mentioned regulations must be taken into account. The first is Regulation 1905/2006 establishing a financing instrument for development cooperation. According to its Annex I, this

---

[34] European Commission, 'EU and Iraq launch negotiations for a Trade and Cooperation Agreement', IP/06/1585, Brussels, 20 November 2006.

[35] OJ 2006 L 210/82.   [36] OJ 2006 L 310/1.   [37] OJ 2006 L 405/40.

[38] OJ 2006 L 378/41.   [39] OJ 2006 L 327/1.   [40] OJ 2006 L 386/1.   [41] OJ 1996 L 163/1.

[42] The Regulation establishing an instrument for nuclear safety cooperation will be adopted at a later date.

Table 1. *Beneficiaries and type of financing instruments (2007–2013)*

Strategies/Beneficiaries	Type of financing instrument under the new financial perspectives (2007–2013)
SPMME	
Mediterranean Track (EMP): Algeria, Morocco, Tunisia, Egypt, Israel, Jordan, Lebanon, PA, Syria, (Libya)	Regulation 1638/2006 laying down general provisions establishing a European Neighbourhood and Partnership Instrument (ENPI).
– East of Jordan Track: Bahrain, Oman, Qatar, Kuwait, Saudi Arabia, UAE	Regulation 1934/2006 establishing a financing instrument for cooperation with industrialised and other high-income countries and territories
Yemen, Iran, Iraq (together with again Oman and Saudi Arabia)	Regulation 1905/2006 establishing a financing instrument for development cooperation
Pre-accession strategy: Turkey	Regulation 1085/2006 establishing an Instrument for Pre-Accession Assistance (IPA)
– Cotonou Convention: Mauritania	Regulation 1905/2006 establishing a financing instrument for development cooperation

Regulation applies to Iran, Iraq, Oman, Saudi Arabia and Yemen. Noteworthy is that Mauritania is incorporated in Annex II of the Regulation on the 'OECD/DAC list of ODA recipients' as this country belongs to the Least Developed Countries category and therefore benefits from a special treatment.

The second regulation to be taken into account as far as the 'East of Jordan' countries are concerned, is Regulation 1934/2006 establishing a financing instrument for cooperation with industrialised and other high-income countries and territories. According to this Regulation Bahrain, Kuwait, Oman, Qatar, Saudi Arabia and the United Arab Emirates are among the beneficiaries together with countries such as the US or Canada. It must be stressed that Saudi Arabia and Oman are referred to in both Regulations 1934/2006 and 1905/2006.

Table 1 (above) provides an illustration of the new situation for the Mediterranean, the Middle East and other Arab countries as far as financing instruments are concerned.

The complexity of the financing system, as demonstrated in the table, is striking. Therefore one of the main challenges for the Council of Ministers and the European Commission will be to respect the duty of implementing consistent proximity strategies as a number of horizontal, cross-border and trans-regional programmes complement the four main financing instruments mentioned in the table.

13.5 Conclusion

All things considered, the *Strategic Partnership with the Mediterranean and the Middle East* is the broadest EU's proximity strategy in terms of beneficiaries: Iran, Iraq, six members of the Gulf Cooperation Council, Yemen, eight Arab partners of the EMP, Turkey, Mauritania and Israel (having in mind the possibility offered to Libya). In other words it comprises a total of 47 members (20 partners and 27 Member States).

Certainly, the launching of the *Strategic Partnership with the Mediterranean and the Middle East* is a clear indication of the willingness of the EU to play an enhanced political and economic role in the Middle East. The conclusion of a new generation of agreements will consolidate this process. In this regard, positive developments have been recorded as far as the GCC and Yemen are concerned.

The Strategic Partnership set up by the EU has the potential to become a major instrument for implementing, together with the governments and civil societies of the Middle East, the required political and socio-economic reforms. The challenges are numerous but it offers an umbrella framework for developing, step-by-step, a genuine Middle East strategy.

Seen in this context, the progress achieved by the EU is considerable if one recalls that, in 1991, the Member States of the EEC were not even invited to the Madrid negotiations on the Middle East. Clearly, the Strategic Partnership is also a reminder of how Europe, the Mediterranean and Middle East are joined together both by geography and shared history.

However, the global framework created by the EU in its proximity remains extremely complex. To illustrate this the position of three countries can be mentioned. First of all Turkey, incorporated in the EU pre-accession strategy, remains a full member of the Euro-Mediterranean Partnership and is associated to European Neighbourhood Policy and *Strategic Partnership with the Mediterranean and the Middle East*. Second,

EU–Russia relationships are based on a specific Strategic Partnership but Russia benefits from the European Neighbourhood and Partnership Instrument. Finally, Mauritania is included in the Cotonou framework, associated to the *Strategic Partnership with the Mediterranean and the Middle East* and has an observer status within the framework of the Euro-Mediterranean Partnership. It remains to be seen, therefore, whether in the future the European Commission will manage to implement all these differentiated proximity strategies in a consistent manner.

14

The EU's transatlantic relationship*

GÜNTER BURGHARDT

14.1 Introduction: fundamentals of an enduring relationship

The fundamentals of the EU–US relationship can be summarised as follows:

- Since its inception post World War II, the European unification process has been embedded within a strong transatlantic dimension [Marshall-Plan (1947); Truman/Eisenhower/Monnet; Kennedy/Hallstein].
- Today, the EU–US relationship is still the most powerful, the most comprehensive and the strategically most important relationship in the world. The EU and the US combine some 60 per cent of the world's GDP, with the EU having overtaken the US numbers of around US$10 trillion recently. They represent around 40 per cent of world trade in goods and even more in services. They hold 80 per cent of the global capital markets. They are each other's main trading partner and source, as much as recipient, of foreign direct investment.
- There is scarcely an issue that does not involve the transatlantic relationship – from Afghanistan to biotech, from WTO negotiations to counter-terrorism, from data privacy to aircraft – the EU and US are involved bilaterally, regionally or globally. Europe matters to America, and America matters to Europe, because of major converging concerns, largely compatible values and overlapping interests. The EU and the US share common objectives with regard to coherent strategies for the promotion of peace, stability and economic development around the globe. There is – in the short and medium term – no alternative to the EU–US relationship.
- 'Europeanism' and 'Atlanticism' do not stand in opposition to each other. European integration and transatlantic cooperation constitute a synergetic unity. A capable unified Europe strengthens the transatlantic relationship and can support the US. A weak, divided Europe, however, weakens the transatlantic partnership and with it the US.

*This text was completed in April 2007.

- A balanced transatlantic partnership does not require 'less' America but 'more' Europe. It needs a less 'imperialistic' America and a more efficient, more 'relevant' Europe. On the one hand, the EU has to reinforce its institutional and operational capacities to strengthen its role as an efficient international actor. On the other hand, the US has to unambiguously reach out to the EU as a collectively respected partner.

- The EU and the US would both benefit from a dialogue on their respective security strategies, including a common threat analysis, and a genuine effort to close the gap between the US doctrines of preemption and preeminence and the EU doctrine of effective multilateralism. The overriding objective should be a fully complementary and internationally legitimised conceptual and strategic approach in the fight against terrorism. Meaningful EU/US consultations should precede and, wherever possible, be followed by joint action based on the complementarity of US and European capabilities combining hard and soft power.

- There would be no America without Europe and there would be no free, prosperous and united Europe without America. Together, Europe and America can achieve almost anything; divided, they risk failing in many things and, as formulated by former Secretary of State Colin Powell: 'When we quarrel we make headlines, when we work together, we make progress!'[1] A solid, well functioning transatlantic relationship remains indispensable to tackle current economic and security challenges.

- After a period of unprecedented transatlantic disagreement and estrangement during the first George W. Bush Administration, a new sense of realism has emerged since the start of President Bush's second term. The results of the November 2006 mid-term elections have dramatically reinforced that pattern. Both sides should now fully avail themselves of the new momentum to effectively take the next decade of transatlantic partnership forward, politically by updating the now ten-year-old New Transatlantic Agenda, and economically by working towards a barrier-free transatlantic economic area. The next transatlantic changeovers in 2009, when the inauguration of a new US President will coincide with a renewal of key EU institutions, could provide an opportunity for such truly comprehensive review of the 'state of the (transatlantic) union'.

---

[1] Former Secretary of State Colin Powell during the EU/US Ministerial meeting at the Department of State on 18 December 2002.

14.2 The three post-World War II phases of the transatlantic relationship

Transatlantic relations are based upon two pillars: NATO and the bilateral relations between the European Union and the countries of North America – the US, Canada, and, for the sake of completeness, Mexico – with the EU–US partnership occupying a pivotal role.

Any review of the EU's external relations would be incomplete without discussing the vital partnership between the EU and the United States of America, the oldest and strategically most important chapter of the EU's gradually and painstakingly evolving external policies. This is, of course, based on the close historical and cultural roots and affinities between the 'old' and the 'new' world: not only is 'America a child of Europe' (Hallstein), and are 'America and Europe family' (Einstein), but the US also stood at the cradle of the very beginnings of Europe's post-World War II (WWII) unification process. An EU–US partnership is the backbone of any EU foreign policy strategy, although the transatlantic relationship over the past 50 years went through ups and downs hitting occasional bumps in the road. The recent most profound crisis over America's unilateral decision to wage all out 'war on terror', based on President Bush's polarising neo-conservative doctrine of 'prevention, preemption and preeminence', the extensive reliance on US military power, his 'axis of evil' rhetoric leading to the invasion of Iraq and the overly simplistic approach to the complexity of Middle East policies, has put an unprecedented strain on the relationship. However, the partnership between Europe and the United States must endure, not because of the immense achievements in the past, but because the common future depends on it.

Thus, the recent divide did not arise because of poor atmospherics or miscommunication. It arose because of one side taking action strongly opposed by the other, or declining to join in actions that the other strongly favours. Unilateral American policies sparked divisions among Europeans. European distrust, in turn, convinced American neoconservatives of the need to impose their agenda and to divide Allies into 'those who are with us and those who are against us', through 'coalitions of the willing', not of the convinced.

In hindsight, transatlantic relations can be divided into three broad phases:

• From the early beginnings in the late 1940s to the end of the Cold War in 1989;

- From 'Eleven/Nine', 1989, to 'Nine/Eleven', 2001; and
- From post Nine/Eleven to today's era of New Realism.

During the entire period, a transatlantic agenda emerged, reflecting both Europe's ever stronger capabilities as well as its apparent deficiencies. Dozens of sectoral or issue specific agreements were reached representing an impressive transatlantic *acquis*. While no single overarching EU–US Partnership Treaty[2] has so far been a realistic option, the mechanics of transatlantic dialogue and consultation have gradually been agreed upon, with the Transatlantic Declaration of 1990 and the New Transatlantic Agenda of 1995 codifying the main institutional arrangements and principal fields of cooperation and common action. In addition to that, cooperation did not just cover bilateral matters, but was extended to the many international fora, from the WTO, the UN family of organisations to the G7/G8, and ultimately NATO, in line with the EU's evolving international role and capabilities.

The unprecedented coincidence in transatlantic changeover in the autumn of 2004, with the Barroso Commission starting on 1 November, the re-election of President Bush for a second term on 2 November, and a newly elected European Parliament and US Congress, provided a unique opportunity to re-energise the transatlantic agenda on the basis of a return to some degree of normality. Already during the three summits of June 2004,[3] the working atmosphere had been characterised by a noticeable change of tone. From its very start, the second Bush Administration signalled an end to its tactics of polarisation, in particular with regard to the EU, as the traditional 'indispensable partner' of the 'indispensable nation'.[4] US military overstretch, soaring financial cost and budgetary deficits, moral discreditation and a crisis of legitimacy of US international

---

[2] An idea supported at regular intervals by the European Parliament, and more recently developed in the reports by Elmar Brok *on improving EU–US relations in the framework of a Transatlantic Partnership Agreement* of May 8, 2006 (A6-0173/2006), and by Erika Mann *on EU–US Transatlantic Economic Relations* of April 20, 2006 (A6-0131/2006).

[3] The G8 Summit under US Chairmanship in Sea Island, Georgia; the annual bilateral EU/US Summit in Dromoland Castle, Ireland, under Irish EU Council Presidency; and the NATO Summit in Istanbul, Turkey.

[4] America, the 'indispensable nation' is a term coined by President Clinton and generally attributed – and often used – by Secretary of State Albright. Portraying the EU as the 'indispensable partner' is an intellectual liberty of my own making, much to the satisfaction of Madeleine Albright with whom I was proud to enjoy many stimulating conversations and a personal friendship throughout my term in Washington DC.

action relying on the use of military power with no solution to the new threats in sight became the driving forces in favour of the search for New Realism.

President Bush's visit of the European institutions in Brussels in February 2005, President Barroso's early invitation to the White House on 18 October 2005 and the EU/US June 2005 Washington and June 2006 Vienna Summits, have put the broad EU–US agenda with its strategy, foreign policy, economic cooperation and global issues chapters back on track. On the institutional side, however, it appears questionable at present whether public doubts in the acceptance of US leadership and recent set backs in further European integration with the ratification of the EU's Constitutional Treaty on hold, will allow major advances in updating the ten-year-old New Transatlantic Agenda into a new partnership agreement or transatlantic 'declaration of interdependence'.

Looking further ahead, a new opportunity might be provided by the next transatlantic changeovers in 2009. A new US Administration, together with the renewal of EU institutions, important ongoing changes in Member States' political leaderships and, hopefully, the implementation of major reinforcements in the EU's foreign policy machinery could create the much-needed momentum leading to a thorough update of transatlantic mechanisms and agendas.

14.3 From the early beginnings to the end of the Cold War (1947 to 1989)

From its inception, the process of European integration had a transatlantic dimension. Europe's 'Founding Fathers' revolutionary post-World War II project aiming at replacing a failed system of absolute national sovereignty by a community of nation states pooling sovereignty through common rules and institutions, had the full support of the United States in the spirit of the 'founding brothers' of the American Constitution of 1787.

In contrast to the end of World War I, the US assumed the role of an active, protecting power and mediator in Europe, and for that purpose remained present as 'a power in Europe' without being a European power. Reconstruction and stabilisation of Western Europe became an indispensable building block of the US doctrine of containment and dissuasion of the communist threat. From the Truman/Eisenhower/Monnet via the Kennedy/Hallstein, the Reagan/Bush/Delors interaction up to the Clinton era, the US had been instrumental in supporting the concept of an organised and structured transatlantic relationship based on a military alliance, NATO – with the US the dominant member – and on an evolving partnership between the United States and the emerging EU.

The Marshall-Plan (1947) helped the devastated European economies to recover. Schuman and Monnet closely cooperated with the Truman and Eisenhower Administrations based on their common World War II experience. George Ball, an American lawyer and later Under-Secretary of State under Kennedy, had an office at the *Commissariat au Plan* advising Monnet on the European Coal and Steel Community (ECSC) Treaty.[5] The US in the last year of the Truman Administration was the first third country to provide the ECSC with formal international recognition when Monnet received a dispatch from President Truman's Secretary of State Dean Acheson[6] on his first day in office as President of the ECSC's High Authority.[7] President Eisenhower followed up in 1953 with the accreditation of a US Ambassador, the first full diplomatic representative ever to a European Institution.[8] Monnet reciprocated by opening an ECSC information office in Washington DC in 1954,[9] partly to offset

[5] George Ball describes his intimate relationship with Jean Monnet and his active involvement 'as a private American lawyer' with the Schuman Plan negotiations in a detailed chapter of his memoirs: *The Past Has Another Pattern* (New York: Norton, 1982), pp. 69–99.

[6] Dean Acheson's memoirs *Present At The Creation* (New York: Norton, 1969) is another invaluable source of information about the US role as a deeply dedicated 'midwife' during the early stages of European unification.

[7] This was the first formal diplomatic note addressed by a foreign government to a European Community institution. The written statement to the effect that the United States henceforth intended to deal with the ECSC High Authority on all matters of its competence constituted the first act of international recognition by a third country.

[8] David Bruce, the first US Ambassador accredited to the European Coal and Steel Community, was a top professional diplomat with a uniquely distinguished career, having been Ambassador to Paris, London and Bonn. His almost daily reports to the State Department and to the White House about the implementation of the ECSC Treaty and the ongoing negotiations on a European Defence Community form a remarkable part of any archive about Europe's early days. During my term, a full documentation has been assembled at the European Commission Washington Delegation offices, drawing on the State Department and Library of Congress archives, as well as on documents collected by the Universities of Georgetown (where Hallstein had delivered a series of lectures explaining the European process), Princeton and Yale.

[9] This office started operating initially from within the premises of George Ball's law firm and was directed by a locally hired American journalist. Monnet thought that explaining the complex process of European integration to American decision makers was best done by an American. Over the decades the office evolved into a fully fledged 'Delegation', as the Commission preferred to call what is today a de facto European Union Embassy. Since the early 1990s, the Head of Delegation has the status of Ambassador accredited to the US President. In May 2004, on the

US disappointment over the failure of the European Defence Community in the French Assembly, which had strong US support. The regular visits of the first President of the European Commission Walter Hallstein to Washington, and his conversations with President Kennedy inspired the latter to deliver a visionary speech on Independence Day 4 July 1962 in Philadelphia with the twin proposal of a 'transatlantic partnership of equals' and a 'Declaration of Interdependence' between the 'New World' and the 'New Europe' should the European agenda successfully materialise. And it was President Kennedy who advocated strongly with Prime Minister MacMillan the need for the UK to join the European Communities, including the unavoidable acceptance of the EC's not so popular Common Agricultural Policy – a rare example of far-sighted leadership.[10]

The web of consultations and agreements of all sorts got richer with the European Communities implementing the Paris and Rome Treaties. Consultations with the US Administrations were conducted by the Commission and culminated in yearly 'High Level' meetings between teams led by the US Secretary of State and the Commission President. Delors reinforced the momentum by turning the tide from the Europessimism of the late 1970s/early 1980s to the Single European Act of 1985 and the 1992 project to completing the Internal Market while regularly keeping in touch with Presidents Reagan and Vice President, and later President Bush '41'.[11] Delors' early visit to President Reagan at the White House in April 1985 greatly facilitated US understanding for the Commission President's 'Agenda 1992' – although it could not entirely dissipate American initial fears of a 'Fortress Europe' – and was instrumental for getting the Uruguay Round of multilateral trade negotiations off the ground, the prelude to the setting up of the WTO in 1995.

occasion of Schuman Day and of the EU's historical eastern enlargement, the fiftieth anniversary of European presence in Washington was celebrated in the Benjamin Franklin rooms of the US Department of State with Secretary Colin Powell and myself exchanging speeches to mark the event (available at: http://www.eurunion.org/delegati/040506gb.htm). For the first time ever, the European Union anthem was played in those official reception rooms, and a US Secretary of State paid tribute to the blue flag with the 12 golden stars at his headquarters. We ended the ceremony wishing that Benjamin Franklin's 300th birthday in 2006 might coincide with the entry into force of the first EU Constitutional Treaty, accompanied by a solemn declaration on the transatlantic relationship . . . (!).

[10] See Ball, *The Past*, pp. 213–22.

[11] The acronyms 'Bush "41"' and later 'Bush "43"' (the respectively forty-first and forty-third US President under the 1787 Constitution) is widely used as a distinction between Bush 'father' and Bush 'son'.

The April 1985 Reagan/Delors meeting in the White House was the opening set for regular and close consultations throughout the decade of three subsequent Delors Commission Presidencies.[12] They provided the ground for the European side to fully assume its role, in almost intimate interaction with the Bush/Baker team, when the fall of the wall and the dissolution of the Soviet Union opened the prospect of 'Europe whole and free', a notion coined by President Bush in 1989. I should like to point to two out of several not so widely publicised events that illustrate the central role played by a Commission President at a turning point of European history. The high regard Delors had acquired and the confidence placed in his unpretentious intellectual leadership led President Bush to stop over in Brussels on 4 December 1989 on his way back to Washington from his Summit meeting with President Gorbachev in Malta, not only to inform NATO partners but also to brief Delors and to seek his support for what would later be known as the four basic principles of the 'Europe whole and free' agenda. My notes from that meeting at Stuivenberg Castle close to Brussels still make fascinating reading; and I remember the – unusual – White House press *communiqué* after the meeting, pointing to the fact that this was the third meeting between Presidents Bush and Delors within a year and expressing President Bush's appreciation for Delors' personal contribution and insight.

The political concept Bush had pieced together appeared simple and ingenious: equal respect for the two fundamental and yet not always easily reconcilable Helsinki principles relating to the recognition of existing borders and to the right for self determination, the perspective of German unification in the context of European integration and of the North Atlantic Alliance, and a massive and coordinated effort of economic and financial support for the new democracies in central and eastern Europe.

Bush sought Delors' support for an agenda to which not all European leaders had yet whole-heartedly adhered, as the subsequent December 1989 Strasbourg European Council meeting with Mitterrand in the chair had famously shown. Already in July 1989, at the G7 *Sommet de l'Arche* in Paris, Bush had joined forces with Chancellor Kohl and the Canadian

---

[12] Jacques Delors served two full terms from, respectively, 1985–8 and 1989–92, extended by two more years from 1993–4 in view of the nomination of a new Commission under the amended rules of the Maastricht Treaty to take office with the enlargement from 12 to 15 Member States.

Prime Minister Mulroney to convince a reluctant Mitterrand (in the chair as the G7 host) and a more than sceptical UK Prime Minister Thatcher that Delors should be tasked with the coordination of what would become the 'G24' financial assistance effort for Europe's liberated new democracies.

In a way, the subsequent EU pre-accession and then accession process leading to the EU's eastern enlargement on 1 May 2004 had its early roots at that memorable G7 dinner on 14 July 1989 at the Hotel de la Marine overlooking the Place de la Concorde, and which was surrounded by the gorgeous festivities of the bicentenary of the French Revolution, so ably orchestrated by Mitterrand's Sherpa Jacques Attali. What was most remarkable was the deep familiarity, knowledge about and appreciation by the US leadership of the role assumed by the nascent European institutions, and more particularly by the European Commission in those creative moments of Europe's history.[13]

14.4 From 'Eleven/Nine' 1989 to 'Nine/Eleven' 2001

The fall of the Berlin Wall on 9 November 1989 thus symbolised the greatest common achievement of the US and Europe. It resulted from the successful combination of US determination, based on its military power, and from the attractiveness of the model of European integration to the peoples under communist rule. The post-eleven/nine 1989 agenda, 'Europe whole and free and at peace with itself' would not have been possible with the US or Europe acting alone.

The end of the Cold War led to significant transformations of the geopolitical environment. A complex, much more unpredictable multipolar security landscape, had replaced the bipolar structure of confrontation between two rival power blocs. Transatlantic relations saw themselves confronted with new security threats: international terrorism; proliferation of weapons of mass destruction; failed states; regional conflicts; the first Gulf war and the Balkan wars.

---

[13] A much later testimony of the then US leaders' state of mind concerning the process of European unification has been recorded by Wilfried Martens, a former Belgian Prime Minister, in his recently published autobiography, *De Memoires. Luctor et Emergo* (Tielt: Lannoo, 2006), pp. 602–3. During a private event in a Flemish provincial town in July 1999, attended by Reagan, Bush, Thatcher and Martens, the discussion was about whom they considered the greatest political personality in Europe after the war. While Thatcher naturally concluded on Winston Churchill the three other discussants agreed on Jean Monnet.

Both, those changes in the geopolitical environment, and Europe's expanding capabilities as a global political and strategic actor led to a positive reassessment of the EU–US relationship at the end of the Cold War. European integration had created the indispensable context, which led the 'Four plus Two' negotiations to a successful conclusion. As described above, the Bush (father) Administration very early in the process recognised those fundamental facts. Benefiting from President Bush and Secretary Baker's close personal relations with Commission President Delors, both teams engaged in what have probably been among the most productive moments of the EU–US relationship.

As a result, the 1990 Transatlantic Declaration (TAD), ultimately agreed in the margins of the November Conference on Security and Cooperation in Europe (CSCE) Summit at the Paris Kleber Conference Centre,[14] for the first time defined the principles for EU–US cooperation and consultation in a single and comprehensive formal document. On substance, the two sides agreed to inject fresh momentum into cooperation on transatlantic and global trade and economic relations – with the US side putting an end to the 'Fortress Europe' criticism in relation to the EU's '1992' project of completing its Internal Market. The TAD agenda also covered the EU's nascent foreign policy cooperation, which had been institutionalised for the first time in the 'Single European Act', signed on 28 February 1986 and entered into effect on 1 July 1987 covering issues such as the fight against terrorism and the proliferation of weapons of mass destruction, while military matters were excluded at the explicit request of the US negotiators.[15] On procedure, the TAD established a mechanism for consultations

[14] Interestingly enough the EU/US bilateral Declaration saw the light at a moment when the transformation from the CSCE to the OSCE, another 'transatlantic' multilateral organisation, coincided with the signing of the OSCE 'Charta for a New Europe' (not the polemic neoconservative caricature of Rumsfeld, but a memorable European–American historic achievement).

[15] While the US had actively supported the European Defence Community Treaty in the early 1950s, their attitude had changed with the subsequent incorporation of Germany into NATO and WEU. Henceforth, US negotiators traditionally maintained that military security matters were issues to be discussed with Allies in NATO. A particularly robust and somewhat undiplomatic expression of this stance was the Dobbins/Bartholomew memorandum in the spring of 1991 addressed to EU Member States, members of NATO during the Inter-governmental Conference leading to the conclusion of the Maastricht European Union Treaty in December 1991. That demarche resulted in strengthening the hand of those Member States that took minimalist positions towards the common security and defence articles of the Treaty, in particular its Article J 4, the complex architecture of which can be partly attributed to the pressure exercised by the US.

at all levels, including biannual summits, ministerial and working level meetings, as well as regular briefings with the European Political Cooperation structures. On the European side, the TAD committed the Commission as well as the Member States through the respective Council Presidencies. The earlier format of 'High Level Consultations'[16] were discontinued and replaced, at the initiative of the Commission, by regular 'sub-cabinet meetings' to cover the various working level contacts on the many issues of community competence.

In 1995, the New Transatlantic Agenda (NTA) together with a Joint Action Plan completed and reinforced the 1990 agenda and mechanisms in response to EU developments under the Maastricht Treaty, signed on 7 February 1992 and entered into force on 1 November 1993, the gradual implementation of the EU's Common Foreign and Security Policy (CFSP), the enlargement and pre-accession processes and the EU's gearing up to its 'Agenda 2000' agreed at the December 1995 Madrid European Council. Again, progress in transatlantic relations went hand in hand with the dynamics of European integration and intergovernmental cooperation. The NTA was concluded three years into President Clinton's first term and reflected his Administration's decisive involvement in the first Balkan War which was brought to an end, that same year, with a peace accord negotiated on a US military base in Dayton, Ohio. The NTA's objective was to move from consultation under the TAD to a new level of cooperation and common action, including, this time, all aspects of security and defence policies.

Until today, the NTA presents the most comprehensive 'constitutional basis' of EU–US cooperation. It provides an institutionalised framework for official EU–US interactions: regular meetings at the Presidential, Ministerial and working levels. The NTA's four main goals: promoting peace, stability, democracy and development; expanding world trade and economic growth; meeting global challenges (including cooperation fields such as environment protection, protection of public health and law enforcement issues); and building ties between EU and US representatives from business, academic, consumer, labour, environment and government circles [including the Transatlantic Legislators' Dialogue (TLD) and the Transatlantic Business Dialogue (TABD)]. The Joint EU–US Action Plan comprised some 150 specific actions to which the EU and the

---

[16] See 14.3.

US have committed themselves (these range from reducing barriers to transatlantic trade and investment to promoting links between colleges and universities).

In the context of the NTA, the Transatlantic Economic Partnership (TEP) was launched at the EU–US London summit in 1998 to reduce many of the remaining barriers to the free flow of commerce and to facilitate conducting business across the Atlantic. The TEP is an extension of the approach taken in the NTA, including both bilateral and multi-lateral elements. Bilaterally it aims at tackling technical barriers to trade through the expansion of Mutual Recognition Agreements (MRAs) and other measures. Multilaterally, its purpose is to further stimulate liberalisa-tion by joining forces on international trade issues. The TEP also provides for an 'early warning system' to share information on regulatory initiatives with a view to containing disputes, particularly in the area of food safety.

The Bonn Declaration adopted at the 1999 EU–US summit in Bonn presented another step forward from the NTA.[17] Both sides explicitly committed themselves to a 'full and equal partnership' in economic, political and security affairs. Embedded in the NTA process, the Bonn Declaration outlined how the EU and the US wanted to shape their relationship over the decade ahead.

These arrangements were more recently stepped up by further economic initiatives launched in consecutive Summit meetings from 2001 until today: the Positive Economic Agenda (PEA) launched in 2002, including Guidelines on Regulatory Cooperation and Transparency and the Financial Markets Regulatory Dialogue. They clearly illustrate the comprehensiveness of the EU–US economic relationship which goes far beyond occasional, although highly publicised, trade disputes and is supported by close to 50 individual sector or issue-specific agreements and administrative arrangements, insti-tutionalised dialogues and regulatory cooperation activities at all levels between the US Administration and the European Commission.

A particularly successful cooperation has developed over the years in the area of competition policy. Contrary to the public perception following a few controversial and highly publicised cases, close links have been established between the European Commissioner in charge of

---

[17] Again, this additional building block in the transatlantic architecture coincided with an important American political and security commitment in Europe, three years into President Clinton's second term, when the US helped to bring the second Balkan war in Kosovo to an end.

antitrust matters and his two US counterparts, the US Department of Justice and the Federal Trade Commission (FTC). During my tenure, the 10th anniversary of the EU/US 1991 Cooperation Agreement was celebrated in Washington at the EU Commission's Kalorama Residence with Commissioner Mario Monti and successive teams of Attorney Generals and Chairmen of the FTC in attendance. When GE/Honeywell and Microsoft were hotly discussed in public, Mario Monti also found a way to discuss matters quietly on the Hill with members of Congress led by Senators DeWine and Kohl.

All in all, the EU–US economic relationship holds important lessons for both the EU's policy aspirations and a well functioning transatlantic partnership. European and American economies have become more intertwined and interdependent after the end of the Cold War. The years since the Cold War – when the 'glue' of the Cold War partnership supposedly loosened transatlantic relations – marked actually one of the most intense periods of transatlantic integration ever. The economic relationship became a stabiliser of the overall relationship. Particularly in the areas of trade and competition policies, and regulatory cooperation, EU–US interaction reached an unprecedented level of intensity that has earned the EU collective respect as an equal partner by Administration, Congress and the business community. In a nutshell, it is widely recognised that the transatlantic economy constitutes the most globalised part of the global economy.

A profound change of direction in the overall transatlantic relationship marked the start of President G.W. Bush's first term in early 2001. While EU/US partnership had generally grown ever closer until the end of the Clinton era, President Bush '43' started off by disavowing an important number of international commitments, including the Kyoto Protocol and the International Criminal Court Treaty. At the same time, the EU and the US had decided, not entirely convincingly, to reduce the number of Summit meetings from two to a single one per year. When the first – now annual – EU/US Summit took place in June 2001, in Göteborg, Sweden, the US President faced harsh criticism from the 16 members of the European Council.[18] These developments led to growing tensions with

---

[18] This was the first ever meeting at Summit level, where the US President met all 16 members of the European Council (the 15 Heads of State or Governments and Commission President Prodi) collectively. The Summit also had another historic significance since it coincided with the first bilateral visit of a US President to Sweden.

the EU during the first eight months preceding nine/eleven 2001, when the terrorist attacks on New York and Washington with their tectonic geo-political effects marked a crucial crossroads not only for the bilateral EU–US relationship.[19]

14.5 From Nine/Eleven 2001 to today's New Realism

The unprecedented terrorist attacks on the United States' mainland on 11 September 2001 profoundly and abruptly changed America's trad-itional sense of invulnerability and security at home.[20] The collapse of the Twin Towers represented a widely underestimated turning point in America's foreign and security policy – America was, and still considers itself to be, 'at war'.

When the Presidents of the European Council and of the European Commission, Verhofstadt and Prodi, visited President Bush in the Oval Office on 27 September, 2001, they expressed Europe's unreserved soli-darity with the US and proposed to start working on a common agenda. President Bush readily replied that the dramatic nature of this challenge to the entire civilised world 'provides us with a new opportunity to work together'. Sadly, that opportunity was not fully grasped. While transat-lantic cooperation in the areas of justice and home affairs successfully extended into a wide range of subjects covered on the Washington end by the Department of Justice and by the newly created Homeland Security Department, the US-led 'war on terror' quickly divided the international community and drove a wedge right through the EU membership. After a period of international unity focusing on Afghanistan, the US resumed a policy of unilaterally determining the agenda, preferring to assemble

---

[19] Condoleezza Rice, the then National Security Adviser, would stress at later lunches with the EU Heads of Mission in Washington DC, how much the President had disliked the 'Gothenburg bashing'. The atmospherics had been badly affected to a degree that might explain Mrs Rice's harsh language when she informed the Heads of Mission at the first post-Göteborg joint lunch at Ambassador Eliasson's Residence during Sweden's Council Presidency that 'Kyoto was dead upon arrival'.

[20] I was able at first hand to witness the dramatic impact of these earthshaking events in Washington. While briefing the members of the European Parliament's Delegation for Relations with the US Congress in the press room of the Commission Delegation in the early morning of September 11, news came in about a plane having hit the North Tower. Switching on our TV screen we followed the day's incredible events. Our first meeting with Congressional counterparts in an almost deserted Capitol Hill was a deeply moving experience. In this hour of tragedy 'we were all Americans'.

ad hoc 'coalitions of the willing' to partnerships of equals and 'tool boxes' to permanent Alliances.[21]

In retrospect, nine/eleven had the effect of amplifying a policy mix based on a number of factors which presidential speech writers are nowadays eager to call the 'Bush doctrine': the ideology of the neo-conservative foreign policy school; reliance on the military superiority of the world's sole hyper-power with a defence budget bigger than all other countries' defence budgets combined; the religiously motivated missionary zeal of America as the chosen country called by history and divine providence to defend freedom and democracy, God's gift to mankind; unconditional support for the policies of Israeli Governments, allied with the large 'reborn Christian' constituencies in the American 'bible belt'; an oversimplified and devastatingly polarising distinction between right and wrong, good and evil; and a refusal to let 'others' have a say in determining America's course of action. Hand in hand with a naïve and badly informed comparison between bringing regime change and democracy to Iraq and the wider Middle East and the successful and peaceful post-World War II transformations in Germany and Japan, and inspired by a quick and easy 'mission accomplished' mentality, it has become increasingly evident that the foreign policy experiments of the Bush Administration will probably have to be remembered as counting among the most problematic periods of contemporary American history.[22] The mounting number of self-critical publications and the growing intensity of the domestic debate, however, are a hopeful and healthy sign of America's inherent power to ultimately adjust an unhappy course of action. The more recent experience from the July 2006 Lebanon war has sent an additional formidable message to all

---

[21] There was a similar effect on the EU's internal developments: Cooperation in Justice and Home Affairs, a long time neglected 'third pillar', picked up momentum and benefited a broad transatlantic anti-terrorism agenda while the EU's foreign policy chief Javier Solana was quickly made to understand that, in the absence of EU common positions, he was to practise the art of making himself invisible. Later on, in an article of the *International Herald Tribune*, dated 12 August 2006, he is quoted as follows: 'It would have been absurd to think that I could resolve the situation publicly. Sometimes you have to know . . . that means disappearing at the right time.' The exemplary cooperation between Commissioner Vittorino and the EU Counter-Terrorism Coordinator G. de Vries, on the one hand, and Homeland Security Secretary Rich as well as Attorney General Ashcroft, on the other, became a noteworthy success story in transatlantic cooperation.

[22] Winston Churchill famously had this to say about US foreign policy: 'America will always do the right thing, after having exhausted every other alternative.' And: 'However brilliant your strategy, you may care occasionally to look at the results.'

sides that military power alone is insufficient to solve problems in the absence of a broader therapy addressing the root causes.

The EU, for reasons of its own shortcomings, proved unable to respond collectively as a Union. Its members split into those who decided to follow and those who opposed the US, advocating a more comprehensive and internationally legitimised approach of what Europe prefers to call 'fight against terrorism' as opposed to 'war on terror'. This did not, however, prevent the EU and the US from signing important agreements on a number of homeland security and counter-terrorism measures and to continue working together on Afghanistan and other international hot spots, crucial achievements that have continued without interruption – despite the most serious worsening of the transatlantic political climate over the war in Iraq.

While, as a consequence, for much of 2002 and 2003, the general tenor of EU–US relations remained uneasy and combative, 2004 had seen some of the rifts beginning to settle. In the US, after a period of patriotic conformism and almost zero tolerance for criticising a President at war, the Commander in Chief, critical voices took issue with the course of US foreign policy and its negative effects on America's public image. Increasingly, the case was made for America to reach out to its partners, and notably the EU. The neoconservative agenda of preemption and preeminence, of 'the mission determining the coalition' had obviously met with limits of military, financial and moral overstretch. Foreign policy uncharacteristically dominated the presidential campaign of 2004 in a country deeply divided.

On the EU side, lessons had been learned as well. It had become clear that no single Member State on its own was able ultimately to influence the Washington decision-making process, and that only collective engagement together with enhanced capabilities could make an impact. Moreover, putting aside past differences over the war had to make room for the need to address together post-Saddam Iraq as part of the problems of the wider Middle East, a region closer to Europe than to the US. The triple, G8, EU/US, and NATO, Summit Meetings in June 2004[23] displayed a new sense of realism, articulated in a quite substantive set of seven policy declarations at the EU–US meeting.

The unique coincidence in transatlantic changeovers in November 2004, a newly elected European Parliament in June 2004, the Barroso

---

[23] See n. 3.

Commission starting its mandate on 1 November 2004 coinciding with President Bush's re-election for a second term, together with Congressional elections on 2 November 2004, provided for an opportunity on both sides to reassess the state of the transatlantic relationship and to re-energise the transatlantic agenda in the areas of the economy, foreign and security policies and the strengthening of the consultative mechanisms.

A first strong gesture was the visit by President Bush to EU Head-quarters in Brussels on 22 February 2005. The summit meeting with the 25 EU Heads of State or Government and Commission President Barroso reviewed the main priorities on the international agenda, including the Middle East, Iraq, Iran, the Barcelona Process, the Balkans and Russia, and global economic and environmental issues. On this occasion, the EU and the US reaffirmed their commitment to transatlantic partnership, 'irreplaceable and vital' to meeting common challenges.

Four months later, the June 2005 Summit in Washington DC adopted joint declarations on the promotion of democracy, the Middle East, UN reform, counter-terrorism and non-proliferation, and Africa. A central part of the Summit's agenda was the strengthening of economic cooperation. The Summit launched an 'EU–US Initiative to Enhance Transatlantic Economic Integration and Growth' and agreed to boost trade and investment between the EU and the US by, inter alia, setting up a 'High Level Regulatory Cooperation Forum' to facilitate regulatory cooperation. A '2005 Roadmap for Regulatory Cooperation' set the priorities for a number of sectors and specific issues, thus tying the efforts to complete a transatlantic business-friendly regulatory environment in with and reinforcing the EU's own Lisbon agenda.

On 18 October 2005, Commission President Barroso's invitation to the White House – the first such bilateral visit of a Commission President to the White House for many years – added to the list of conciliatory gestures. Discussions focused on the WTO Doha Round, transatlantic economic issues and the promotion of democracy around the world.

All in all, 2005 had seen a determined and systematic effort to change the rhetoric and to discontinue a policy of polarisation, a necessary condition for putting a transatlantic agenda back on track and onto the radar screen.

Clearly, the biggest progress so far has been made with respect to economic cooperation. On 30 November 2005, following on from commitments made at the EU–US summit, the EU side hosted a first informal

EU–US Economic Ministerial meeting bringing together relevant members of the Commission, Member States (Ministers representing three successive Council Presidencies) and a US team led by the Secretary of Commerce. Issues discussed included Intellectual Property Rights (IPR), regulatory cooperation, trade and security, and innovation.

At the June 2006 Vienna EU/US Summit, the atmosphere was forward looking (President Bush: 'What is past is past and what's ahead of us is a hopeful democracy in the Middle East'). The four broad agenda items, foreign policy cooperation with a particular focus on the Middle East; confronting global challenges; energy security; and economic and trade issues were dealt with constructively. Where differences remained, 'we disagreed in an agreeable way'.[24] The Summit mandated another Economic Ministerial meeting to implement the broadened 'Roadmap for EU/US Regulatory Cooperation' annexed to the Vienna Declaration. The second US/EU Economic Ministerial took place in Washington on 9 November 2006 and was co-chaired by the US Secretaries of Commerce Gutierrez and of Energy Bodman with the Commission Vice President Verheugen and the Finnish Minister for Trade attending on the EU side. The agenda routinely covered a number of regulatory issues, with a specific focus on renewable and alternative energy matters. There is clearly a need for creating additional momentum in order to further broaden and deepen the economic agenda.[25]

At the time of completion of this text, Chancellor Merkel's recent transatlantic economic initiative seems to be making good progress. Energy and climate change policy were among the new priorities for regulatory cooperation against the background of the Action Plan adopted by the Spring EU Council on 8/9 March.

With regard to foreign and security policy, much, of course, depends on the EU's ability to pursue its course towards more effective diplomatic and security structures and assets. Only with the further reinforcement of its 'hard' power capacities will the EU's impressive 'soft' power resources gain the full credit they deserve. At the same time, it is up to America to review the principles underpinning their foreign and security policy. However, that is frankly a debate that the EU can only hope to influence by getting its own act together. More fundamentally, EU–US partnership

---

[24] President Bush at the post Summit Press Conference.
[25] The next EU/US Summit meeting was scheduled to take place on 30 April 2007.

will require a better meeting of minds on strategy. Post 9/11, the dominating agendas of our respective political systems are different, as illustrated by the gap between the September 2002 and March 2006 US National Security Strategy documents based on the doctrine of preemption and preeminence,[26] and the December 2003 EU Security Strategy based on effective multilateralism. The EU's 'post-1989' agenda focuses on peace by nation building with internationally legitimated use of force as a measure of last resort. This agenda rests on the bitter experience of centuries of wars that have brought Europe close to destruction. The US 2001 'war on terror' agenda is about regaining invulnerability at home by exercising on a global basis what America considers its sovereign rights. Simply speaking, the peoples of Europe, knowing by experience that there is no absolute protection against terrorist acts, feel themselves largely at peace, reconciled, seeking to export stability across their borders, while America feels itself at war.

14.6 Conclusion

Today, the US margin of manoeuvre is restricted as a consequence of military overstretch, financial deficits, the loss of the moral high ground and the deep damage done to the US Administration's image in the world.

An intensely self-critical internal debate in the US – as mentioned above – again is about the need for stable partnerships, with the EU first in line. The library of recent foreign policy publications[27] argues that the

---

[26] The US National Security Strategy was updated in March 2006, expanding on and assessing the 2002 version. 'America is at war' remains the major focus while the threat analysis is zooming in on the problem of Iran's nuclear ambitions and identifying Iran as the country likely to present the single greatest future challenge. Most commentators have severely criticised the document as more of the same with William Pfaff stating that 'intellectual poverty is the most striking quality of the new statement' revealing 'a lumpy stew of discredited neoconservative ideas', see *International Herald Tribune*, 20 March 2006.

[27] Among early assessments about the growing transatlantic crisis as a result of neoconservative unilateralism are: J. Nye, *The Paradox of American Power – why the world's only superpower can't go it alone* (Oxford: Oxford University Press, 2002); C. Kupchan, *The End of the American Era* (New York: Knopf, 2002); and C. Prestowitz, *Rogue Nation – American Unilateralism and the Failure of Good Intentions* (New York: Perseus, 2003). A comprehensive 'examination of what has gone wrong in the fragile US/Europe Alliance – and how to make it right' is *Allies at War – America, Europe, and the Crisis over Iraq* by P. Gordon and J. Shapiro (New York: McGraw-Hill, 2004). Other key contributions include: Z. Brzezinski, *The Choice – Global Domination or Global Leadership* (New York: Basic Books, 2004); H. Kissinger and L. Summers, *Renewing the Transatlantic Partnership* (New York: Council on Foreign Relations, 2004);

neoconservative 'Bush Doctrine' lies in tatters, and that the US image in the rest of the world has shifted from the Statute of Liberty and the 'Shining city on the hill'[28] to the hooded prisoner at Abu Ghraib. Headlines such as Anatol Lieven's 'Decadent America must give up imperial ambitions'[29] dramatically illustrate the depths of new American soul searching. The outcome of the June 2006 war between Israel and Lebanon reinforces the lesson that the use of military power alone – without at the same time dealing with the root causes of Middle East problems – far from solving those underlying issues, only increases anger and frustration, and provides a breeding ground for more conflict instead of leading to much needed reconciliation.

The increasingly disastrous situation in Iraq together with unprecedented low approval numbers for the Bush Administration have translated into the dramatic power shift as a result of the 7 November 2006 mid-term elections. The Democrats' taking over of the majority in both the House and the Senate, as well as among State Governors, is putting President Bush under severe pressure to diversify his sources of advice. The departure of Secretary Rumsfeld, an icon of the Iraq strategy, and the central role of the Iraq Study Group led by former Secretary Baker illustrate the fact that without a change of course in US Middle East Policy over the two years the GOP's stand in the 2008 elections would seem to be becoming extremely critical.[30]

G. Soros, *The Bubble of American Supremacy* (New York: Public Affairs, 2004); S. Serfaty, *The Vital Partnership – Power and Order, America and Europe Beyond Iraq* (Lanham: Rowan and Littlefield, 2005); F.G. Burwell, D.C. Gompert *et al.*, *The Transatlantic Transformation: Building a NATO/EU Security Agenda* (Washington: The Atlantic Council of the US, 2006). Francis Fukuyama's *America at the Crossroads – Democracy, Power, and the Neoconservative Legacy* (Yale: Yale University Press, 2006), provides an in-depth analysis of the dominant foreign policy school at the heart of the Bush Administration. Another turn in the doctrinal debate is *Ethical Realism – a Vision for America's Role in the World* (New York: Pantheon Books, 2006), co-authored by the leftist Anatol Lieven and the conservative John Hulsman, looking back longingly to the kind of self-confident multilateral commitment of the cold war Eisenhower and Truman Administrations as an inspiration for present day's policy-makers.

[28] John Winthrop's famous saying in June 1629 upon arriving with the Pilgrim Fathers on the shores of what is now Massachusetts: 'Consider that we shall be as a city upon a hill, the eyes of all people upon us' can rightly be seen as the foundation of America's soft power, the aspiration of freedom and liberty, the pursuit of happiness in the land of unlimited opportunities, a soft power so badly eroded over the past years.

[29] *Financial Times,* 29 November 2005.

[30] In almost perfect timing with the run-up to the mid-term elections Bob Woodward, the author of *Bush at War* (New York: Simon and Schuster, 2002) and of *Plan of Attack* (New York: Simon and Schuster, 2004), had come out with his third national bestseller *State of*

Fighting terrorism and preventing the proliferation of weapons of mass destruction, dealing with the world's many trouble spots, engaging in nation building where States have failed or have been destroyed, all this and more requires the combined and complementary blend of European, mainly soft, and American, primarily hard, power. Although transatlantic partnership will necessarily continue to show some degree of asymmetry, it must be based on mutual respect and the realistic assumption that agreement will not always be possible on all issues and that, therefore, any disagreements must be managed equally respectfully.

There have been regular suggestions that such management should be based on a strengthened set of bilaterally agreed rules, of developing the present mechanisms, the Transatlantic Declaration of 1990 and the New Transatlantic Agenda of 1995, into some form of Treaty. It appears questionable whether public doubts in the acceptance of US leadership and recent setbacks in further European integration with the ratification of the EU's Constitutional Treaty on hold, will allow major advances soon in updating the ten-year-old New Transatlantic Agenda into a new partnership agreement and/or transatlantic 'Declaration of Interdependence'. Present circumstances may suggest that such high profile proposition might not be achievable in the very near future. It, however, remains a necessary step to be undertaken when conditions might become more favourable on both sides in the perspective of transatlantic changeovers by 2009.

Geopolitical developments over the next decades, from accelerating economic globalisation to the emergence of new political power centres, will, however, make the case for transatlantic partnership between the 'New World' and the 'New Europe', as the backbone of the multipolar global system, ever more compelling. While the most recent transatlantic survey has shown again that confidence in the leadership of the present US Administration has pursued its steep descent,[31] the June 2006 Bertelsmann/

Denial (New York: Simon and Schuster, 2006). All three widely marketed publications describe in remarkable detail the neoconservative foreign policy decision-making process post September 11 to today's Iraq conundrum, and have no doubt played their part in shaping informed public opinion. After 'Watergate', surely another important example of the maturity of the American democratic process.

[31] Transatlantic Trends 2006, a project of the German Marshall Fund of the United States and the Compagnia di San Paolo, with additional support provided by Fundação Luso-Americana, Fundación BBVA, and the Tipping Point Foundation, Washington DC and Brussels, 6 September 2006. Available at: http://www.transatlantictrends.org/trends/doc/2006_TT_Key %20Findings%20FINAL.pdf.

Emnid international survey about 'World powers in the twenty-first century' concludes that despite its worsened negative image, the US will remain in overall demand as a principal international force of order.[32] The US, as much as the EU, will have to engage in serious homework for transatlantic partnership to remain the prominent mutually attractive policy option in the longer term. The US, the 'more perfect Union', will need to actively regain full credibility in relation to its conduct of international affairs. The EU will have to convincingly prove that its determination to evolve towards 'an ever closer Union' is unaffected by the recent setbacks over the failed ratification of its Constitutional Treaty. The 'Berlin Declaration' agreed upon by EU leaders on 25 March 2007 on the occasion of the 50th anniversary of the Rome Treaties includes a commitment to 'placing the European Union on a renewed common basis before the European Parliament elections in 2009'. If successful, the EU's capacity to act as a major international player would be greatly enhanced. An EU foreign minister, working under the dual authority of a more continuous European Council President, as well as of the Commission President, would considerably streamline transatlantic communication and common action. The EU's growing capabilities and collective experience in security and defence would open the perspective for NATO to evolve towards a more appropriate European American Treaty Organisation. The longer-term goal of achieving a barrier free transatlantic market by 2015,[33] as well as closer ties between legislators in a Transatlantic Assembly bringing together the European Parliament and the US Congress,[34] would all appear attractive building blocks for a Transatlantic Partnership Treaty to be initiated as of 2009.

---

[32] Bertelsmann Stiftung/TNS Emnid, Berlin, 2 June 2006.

[33] An initiative long-time advocated by fora such as the Transatlantic Policy Network and officially put on the agenda by Chancellor Merkel and Commission President Barroso at their respective White House meetings with President Bush in January 2007.

[34] The newly-elected democratic leadership in both the House and the Senate might be more open in future to strengthening regular ties with the European Parliament under its new President HansGert Poettering.

PART III

Selected substantive areas

With eyes wide shut: the EC strategy to enforce intellectual property rights abroad

INGE GOVAERE

15.1 Introduction

Intellectual property (IP) protection has gradually occupied a more and more prominent role in the external relations of the EC.[1] Over the last couple of years an important shift is noticeable in the objectives sought to be achieved by the EC, in particular as it interacts with and within the dynamic international context created by the World Trade Organisation (WTO) Agreement on Trade Related Aspects of Intellectual Property (TRIPS Agreement).[2] The conclusion of the latter in 1994 was itself testimony to the more long-standing and still ongoing objective of the EC – and the US – to eliminate piracy and counterfeiting at the source.[3] The

---

[1] On the linkage made between EC external (trade) policy and IP protection, in particular as leading up to the conclusion of the TRIPS Agreement, see earlier work: I. Govaere, 'Intellectual Property Protection and Commercial Policy', in M. Maresceau (ed.), *The European Community's Commercial Policy after 1992: The Legal Dimension* (Deventer: Kluwer Academic Publishers, 1993), pp. 197–222; I. Govaere, 'Trade-Related Aspects of Intellectual Property Rights: The EC Dichotomy Uncovered', in T. Flory (ed.), *La place de l'Europe dans le commerce mondial* (Luxembourg: Institut Universitaire International Luxembourg, 1994), pp. 161–215.

[2] On the early interaction between TRIPS and regional trade areas, including the EC, see M. O'Regan, 'The Protection of Intellectual Property, International Trade and the European Community: The Impact of the TRIPS Agreement of the Uruguay Round of Multilateral Trade Negotiations', *Legal Issues of European Integration* (1995), pp. 1–51; I. Govaere, 'Convergence, Divergence and Interaction of Regional Trade Agreements and the Agreement on Trade-Related Aspects of Intellectual Property Rights (TRIPs)', in P. Demaret, J.-F. Bellis and G. Garcia Jimenez (eds.), *Regionalism and multilateralism after the Uruguay Round* (Brussels: European Inter-university Press, 1997), pp. 465–94.

[3] Much has been written about the difficult negotiating history, the underlying objectives and content of the TRIPS Agreement, see among others F.K. Beier and G. Schricker (eds.), *GATT or WIPO* (Weinheim: VCH, 1989); H. Paemen and A. Bensch, *Du GATT à l'OMC: La Communauté européenne dans l'Uruguay Round* (Leuven: Leuven University Press, 1995); C. Correa

minimum levels of worldwide harmonisation imposed by the TRIPS Agreement on all WTO members were to render it possible for (EC) IP holders to prohibit the very production of products without their consent in third countries of exportation. The beneficial effect for the EC was double. Exports markets would be secured through the possibility of obtaining 'islands of exclusivity' for IP holders worldwide. Less counterfeit and pirated products would be imported into the EC so that less pressure would be put on the EU external frontier controls. The practice turned out to be somewhat different. For the year 2002, for instance, figures advanced with respect to the number of counterfeit and piracy products intercepted at the EU external frontiers were still as high as 85 million, with an increase between 1998 and 2002 of 800 per cent.[4] In 2005, about 75 million counterfeit articles were seized according to the EC Customs statistics.[5]

An important oversight at the time of the conclusion of the TRIPS Agreement was the failure to anticipate the natural correlation between, on the one hand, little enthusiasm of certain (especially developing) States to contract obligations under the WTO to enact IP legislation and, on the other hand, a poor implementation and enforcement record. It is well-known that the TRIPS Agreement was at first sight successfully concluded as part of a wider package deal. Its inherently coercive nature put the obligation on all WTO members to adopt an important body of IP legislation, without allowing for substantive derogations for the developing or least-developed countries. At best, the latter could benefit from a longer transitional period of ten years which, by a decision of 29 November 2005,

---

and A. Yusuf, *Intellectual Property and International Trade: The TRIPS Agreement* (London: Kluwer Law International, 1998); K. Maskus, *Intellectual Property Rights in the Global Economy* (Washington: Institute for International Economics, 2000); D. Gervais, *The TRIPS Agreement: Drafting History and Analysis* (London: Sweet & Maxwell, 2003, 2nd ed.); C. Cottier and P. Mavroidis, *Intellectual Property: Trade, Competition and Sustainable Development* (Ann Arbor: The University of Michigan Press, 2003).

[4] EC Commission, *EU strategy to enforce Intellectual property rights in third countries – facts and figures–November 2004*, see website DG Trade, available at: http://trade.ec.europa.eu/doclib/ docs/2004/november/tradoc_119828.pdf. It should nonetheless be mentioned that these startling figures may at least in part also be due to a better understanding of the problem by EU customs officials and increased control at the EU external borders subsequent to the adoption of the Counterfeit Regulation 3295/94 of 22 December 1994, OJ 1994 L 341/8. This is now repealed and replaced by Council Regulation 1383/2003 concerning customs actions against goods suspected of infringing certain intellectual property rights and the measures to be taken against goods found to have infringed such rights, OJ 2003 L 196/7.

[5] See website DG Trade, available at: http://trade.ec.europa.eu/doclib/docs/2007/february/ tradoc_133204.pdf.

was for the least-developed countries further extended until 1 July 2013.[6] Most WTO members are now formally in compliance with the TRIPS obligation to enact the necessary IP legislation. Yet this does not suffice. It soon became apparent that there is a crucial problem in terms of a poor implementation and enforcement record, especially – if by no means limited to – developing countries. In the US it was considered that an appropriate response would comprise a mixed approach whereby convincing developing countries that the TRIPS Agreement is also in their best interests, in terms of technology transfer, creating incentives to develop new medicine and preventing public health hazards of defaulting products, is combined with targeted litigation.[7] Also the EU responded through the elaboration of a *Strategy for the Enforcement of Intellectual Property Rights in Third Countries* on 10 November 2004 (hereafter: 'IP Enforcement Strategy').[8] It is useful first of all to briefly set out the stated objectives and actions taken so far under this IP Enforcement Strategy (15.2). This will be followed by some critical reflections about what is left unsaid in the strategy paper (15.3). Three issues in particular will be underlined, namely the competence of the EC to develop such a strategy, the interference with public policy choices and flexibility mechanisms under the TRIPS Agreement, and the ensuing paradoxical consequences in terms of EC trade policy especially with respect to pharmaceutical products.

15.2 The IP enforcement strategy: stated objectives and mechanisms

Underlying the elaboration of the IP Enforcement Strategy paper is the European Commission's findings that violations of IP rights continue to increase in spite of the adoption of minimum harmonisation of IP

---

[6] For the decision and the text thereof, see WTO Press/424 of 29 November 2005. A further extension of the deadline until 2016, specifically for patents for pharmaceutical drugs in least-developed countries, was already accepted by the DOHA WTO Ministerial Declaration on the TRIPS Agreement and Public Health, adopted on 14 November 2001, WT/MIN(01)/DEC/2 of 20 November 2001.

[7] See, for instance, C. Levy, 'Implementing TRIPS – a Test of Political Will', *Law and Policy in International Business* (2000), pp. 789–95; C. Levy, J. Gorlin and G. Ritter, 'Panel II: Agreement on Trade-Related Intellectual Property Rights (TRIPS)', *Law and Policy in International Business* (2000), pp. 797–9. On the contested use of US s. 301, see C. Arup, 'TRIPs: Across Global Fields of Intellectual Property', *European Intellectual Property Review* (2004), pp. 8–10.

[8] See website DG Trade, available at: http://trade.ec.europa.eu/doclib/docs/2005/april/tradoc_122636.pdf.

legislation by the WTO members. Instead of trying to identify the root causes for the reluctance of certain countries to also effectively comply with such IP standards,[9] the Commission rather argues that this makes it 'essential for the European Union to increasingly focus on vigorous and effective implementation of the enforcement legislation'[10] specifically in third countries. The stated objectives of the IP enforcement strategy thus elaborated are fourfold: provide for a long-term action in view of the goal to achieve a significant reduction of IP violations in third countries; describe, prioritise and coordinate mechanisms to achieve that end; provide information of actions available to IP holders; and enhance cooperation on this matter with IP holders.[11] Similarly, as for other important and topical issues of the external relations of the EC, such as the protection of human rights, it is also here emphasised that the focus of the EC approach should lie on 'positive and constructive efforts'.[12] Also now, the Commission proposes to combine the following five methods at the disposal of the EC in order to achieve an adequate level of IP enforcement in third countries.

15.2.1 Targeting countries

First and foremost, it should be recalled that counterfeit and piracy is not a problem specific to a clearly identified and limited number of countries. On the contrary, it affects most, if not all, countries worldwide, including the EU and the US.[13] In order to pursue an effective strategy, it is nonetheless held to be crucial from the outset to introduce a mechanism in the form of a periodical *Survey on Enforcement of Intellectual Property Rights in Third Countries*. The purpose is to identify priority countries that

---

[9] See Section 15.3.2.   [10] IP Enforcement Strategy, p. 3.   [11] *Ibid.*, p. 3.

[12] *Ibid.*, p. 4. On the issue of human rights in the external relations of the EC, see I. Govaere and A. Van Bossuyt, 'Le commerce à visage de plus en plus humain? Les droits de l'homme dans la politique commerciale commune', in M. Candela Soriano (ed.), *Les droits de l'homme dans les politiques de l'Union européenne* (Brussels: Larcier, 2006), pp. 225–54. There are other striking similarities in the more general external relations approach and methodology when comparing IPR and human rights, such as the use of a combination of methods and in particular the thematic 'human rights' or 'IPR' political dialogue with certain identified countries such as China, see Section 15.2.4.

[13] See, for instance, the Notification of a Mutually Agreed Solution between the US and the EC-Denmark concerning the TRIPS obligation of the latter to make available prompt and effective measures affecting the enforcement of IP rights, WT/DS83/2, IP/D/9/Add.1 of 13 June 2001.

will be targeted by the EC's 'positive and constructive' approach, which in spite of appearances may not be called 'a blacklist', at least not officially.[14] As a result of the October 2006 Enforcement Survey, the EC now identifies three categories of countries in order of importance of counterfeit and piracy infringements.[15] China is the one and only country listed in category 1 and is thus currently the main priority for the EC. This does not really come as a surprise as China alone accounts for two thirds of counterfeit and pirated products entering the EC. Category 2 identifies countries that have concluded preferential agreements with the EC including a high IP standard obligation, but with serious deficiencies in IP enforcement. Here we find Russia, Ukraine, Chile and Turkey. The third category is constituted by the Association of Southeast Asian Nations (ASEAN) (in particular, Thailand, Malaysia, Indonesia, the Philippines and Vietnam), Mercosur (in particular Brazil, Argentina and Paraguay) and Korea. The common feature here is that these are countries or regions that may in the near future develop closer trade relations with the EC, which would then necessarily need to include a higher focus on IP enforcement issues.[16]

15.2.2 Trade preferences as a leverage for TRIPS-plus

As may already be inferred from the criteria used for the division of targeted countries in categories, both *bilateral (trade) and multilateral (TRIPS) agreements* are considered to be an important tool to improve the enforcement of IP protection in third countries, also in the future. This clearly shows that the entry into force of the TRIPS Agreement did not meet the expectations of a truly multilateral, instead of the prior bilateral and unilateral approach employed by both the EC and the US,[17] in order to force, especially developing, countries to modify their IP laws. On the contrary, it appears that bilateral and unilateral pressure may still be used inter alia by the EC and the US to force compliance with higher IP standards

---

[14] IP Enforcement Strategy, p. 5.

[15] See website DG Trade, available at: http://ec.europa.eu/trade/issues/sectoral/intell_property/survey2006_en.htm.

[16] *Ibid.*

[17] For EC statements to that effect, see the 'Guidelines and Objectives proposed by the European Community for the Negotiations on Trade Related Aspects of Substantive Aspects of Intellectual Property Rights' of 7 July 1988 in Breier and Schricker (eds.), *GATT or wipo* p. 325.

and better IP enforcement than provided for under TRIPS.[18] Prior to the TRIPS Agreement the EC inserted in most bilateral agreements a provision calling upon the signatory parties to introduce and maintain the same level of IP standards and enforcement as the EC. In particular, before the enactment in 2004 of the Enforcement Directive[19] it was not always apparent what the internal EC point of reference precisely was. In order to strengthen such clauses it is now envisaged to clearly define what the EU considers to be the highest international IP standards and to stipulate what kind of effort is required. In the same vein, the Commission intends to raise enforcements concerns more systematically at Summit meetings as well as in the respective Councils and Committees created by the various bilateral agreements.[20]

Such an approach based on the increased use of substantive and institutional arrangements in agreements concluded by the EC is obviously meant to impose so-called TRIPS-plus obligations on the third countries concerned. It should nonetheless be recalled that in the past this has also backfired for the EC Member States. In particular, the express reference to the Paris Act of the Berne Convention in Article 5 of Protocol 28 of the Agreement on European Economic Area was successfully invoked by the Commission against Ireland,[21] where earlier proposals to adopt unilateral EC measures to oblige Member States to comply with the Paris Act had met with little enthusiasm in the Council.[22] Similar to the TRIPS Agreement, bilateral agreements may thus provide the basis for what could be called 'external harmonisation' of EC law in the field of IP. Furthermore, there is no apparent reason why the IP clauses in bilateral agreements could not be used by third countries against the EC and its Member States in case of non-compliance or deficiencies in IP enforcement.

---

[18] For examples of such bilateral agreement of the EC and the US, see P. Drahos, 'BITs and BIPs, Bilateralism in Intellectual Property', *Journal of World Intellectual Property* (2001), pp. 792–807.

[19] Directive 2004/48 of 29 April 2004 on the Enforcement of Intellectual Property Rights, OJ 2004 L 157/45.

[20] IP Enforcement Strategy, p. 6.

[21] Case C-13/00 *Commission* v. *Ireland* [2002] ECR I-2943.

[22] For the Commission (Amended) Proposal for a Council Decision, whereby obligations under TRIPS were forwarded, see COM(92)10 final of 14 February 1992. Instead, a non-binding Council Resolution was adopted, see OJ 1992 C 138/1. On this matter, see Govaere, 'Convergence, Divergence', pp. 475–7.

15.2.3 Towards a TRIPS-plus Agreement

The EC bilateral agreements approach goes beyond the TRIPS Agreement when it calls for respect of the highest IP standards, as opposed to the already high minimum standards set in the latter. It is significant that the IP Enforcement Strategy Paper indicates that the EC will not only monitor TRIPS compliance, especially by priority countries, and consult with other trading partners in the TRIPS Council with respect to insufficient implementation of TRIPS obligations. It will also consult other trading partners with respect to a possible extension of current TRIPS obligations, leading to a so-called TRIPS-plus Agreement,[23] in particular when the EC has already adopted such higher standards. A perfect example concerns Article 51 TRIPS which currently only obliges member countries to adopt border measures relating to the import of counterfeit and pirated products. The EC will endeavour to extend this obligation to cover also export and transit of such products. In other words, it wishes to align TRIPS obligations to the enlarged scope of the EC Counterfeit and Piracy Regulation as adopted in 2003.[24] The new EU–US Joint Strategy of 20 June 2006, joining their forces in what is called 'the global fight against counterfeit and piracy theft'[25] as well as the *Joint Communication from the EC, US, Japan and Switzerland to the TRIPS Council on IPR Enforcement* of 16 October 2006,[26] show that the EC's consultations with its most important trading partners are already in a well-advanced stage.

15.2.4 IP political dialogue: a rather meagre carrot, a sizeable stick

Besides the specific bilateral or multilateral agreement-based approach, the Commission also points to the need for a more horizontal approach.

---

[23] On the current debate on the future direction of TRIPS towards a TRIPS-plus or TRIPS-minus, see also T. Dreirer, 'Shaping a Fair International IPR-Regime in a Globalized World', in I. Govaere and H. Ullrich (eds.), *Intellectual Property, Public Policy and International Trade*, Peter Lang, 2007, p. 232. For US actions in the direction of TRIPS-plus, see Arup, '*TRIPS*' pp. 8–10.

[24] Regulation 1383/2003 on customs actions against goods suspected to constitute counterfeit and piracy (repealing and replacing the former Counterfeit Regulation 3295/94), OJ 2003 L 196/7.

[25] See website DG Trade, available at http://trade.ec.europa.eu/doclib/docs/2006/june/tradoc_129013.pdf. Pursuant to this on 1 February 2007 the 'EU/USA review progress in joint anti-competitive drive and plan to expand work in 2007', see http://ec.europa.eu/trade/issues/sectoral/intell_property/p010207_en.htm.

[26] See website DG Trade, available at: http://trade.ec.europa.eu/doclib/docs/2006/october/tradoc_130863.pdf.

The issue of adequate and effective IP protection at the source is to be systematically addressed as a priority concern in *political dialogue* with all third countries and in all possible international fora. Similarly, as for the human rights dialogue, the Commission proposes to repeat the message '*improve your IP enforcement*' as frequently and at as high a level as possible.[27] It will thereby be conveyed to third countries that enforcement of IP is mostly in the mutual interest. Next to the more general political dialogue including IP, also examples of more advanced political dialogue specifically on IP issues are to be found. Noteworthy is for instance the 'EU–Japan Joint Initiative for IPR enforcement in Asia' which was decided as early as 2003 at the EU–Japan Summit.[28] But more attention is usually paid to the very important annual 'EU–China Dialogue on Intellectual Property', as it concerns the one and only category 1 priority country. This IP dialogue was agreed upon in October 2003 and inter alia led to the creation of the 'EU–China IP Working Group' in July 2004.[29]

Counter-arguments of third countries pertaining to the lack of sufficient financial or technical means to enforce IP effectively are countered by the EC willingness to offer assistance – for instance in the form of training of officials – in accordance with the recipient's needs.[30] Yet, with this rather meagre carrot comes an important and potentially sizeable stick. It is equally made clear that the EC will not hesitate to undertake action in the face of deficient enforcement that harms EC IP holders' interests, inter alia through an application of the Trade Barriers Regulation.[31] The philosophy behind it is that there needs to be a threat of a sanction in order to render

---

[27] IP Enforcement Strategy, p. 7.   [28] *Ibid.*

[29] The first meeting of the EU–China IP Working Group took place in October 2005, the second meeting on 6 June 2006. It is also significant that an IP expert has been appointed at the Commission Delegation in Beijing in April 2006. For details, see the website of the Commission, available at: http://ec.europa.eu/trade/issues/sectoral/intell_property/ipr_china_en.htm.

[30] IP Enforcement Strategy, p. 8. For instance, between 2002 and 2005 a total of €5,600,000 was allocated to a first specific IPR programme with China, whereas from mid-2007 a further €11,000,000. is foreseen for a second IPR programme with China. For the period 1996–2006, €7,500,000 support was given in the framework of a specific IPR programme with ASEAN. For these and other figures on 'EU Support in the Field of IPR', see website DG Trade, available at: http://trade.ec.europa.eu/doclib/docs/2006/august/tradoc_129556.pdf.

[31] IP Enforcement Strategy, p. 10. The Trade Barriers Regulation is Council Regulation 3286/94, OJ 1994 L 349/71 as last amended by Council Regulation 356/95 of 20 February 1995 amending Regulation 3286/94 laying down Community procedures in the field of the Common Commercial Policy in order to ensure the exercise of the Community's rights under international trade rules, in particular those established under the auspices of the World Trade Organisation (WTO), OJ 1995 L 41/3.

the rule effective. The possibility of sanctioning non-compliance with EC expectations will not remain a dead letter. This is illustrated by the fact that since 1996 there are already several cases under the Trade Barriers Regulations related to problems of IP protection for EC industry abroad.[32]

15.2.5 Public-private partnership building

In order to gain the upper hand in the fight against counterfeit and piracy, the Commission also conceives of the creation of a rather unique and new public-private partnership. This implies inter alia the creation of local IP networks involving various entities confronted with counterfeit and piracy issues, such as companies, associations and chambers of commerce, which are to be supported by Directorate General (DG) Trade.[33] Not only does the Commission rely on information supplied by those private entities to formulate its policies and course of action, it also intends to positively engage in raising awareness of IP holders as well as consumers and users in third countries. An important tool in this respect is the *Guidebook on Enforcement of Intellectual Property Rights* which was announced in the IP Enforcement Strategy paper[34] and publicised on the Commission website on 18 April 2005.[35] The Commission approach also has an introspective edge to it through advocating more structural cooperation and enhanced transparency – mainly on the basis of the newly created webpage – of the Commission services dealing with IP enforcement

---

[32] For instance, the following cases all relate to alleged deficiencies in IP protection in third countries (OJ reference is to initiation of examination procedure): Two cases against Canada relating to lack of protection of geographical indication of 'Bordeaux' and 'Médoc' wine (OJ 2002 C 124/6) and 'Prosciutto di Parma' (OJ 1999 C 76/6); against Turkey for measures on imports of pharmaceutical products (OJ 2003 C 311/31); against the US with respect to licensing of musical works (OJ 1997 C 77). Also under the predecessor of the Trade Barriers Regulation, the so-called New Commercial Policy Instrument, was action undertaken on the basis of alleged infringement of IP standards obligations by third countries. For instance, a procedure was initiated on 20 July 1991 (OJ 1991 C 189) under the New Commercial Policy Instrument and was further administrated under the TBR against Thailand for Piracy of sound recordings. The procedure was finally suspended on 20 December 1995, following the entry into force of a new copyright legislation in Thailand and the creation of a court specialised in IP infringements (OJ 1996 L 11). For other early cases under the New Commercial Policy Instrument, see I. Govaere, 'Intellectual Property Protection and Commercial Policy', in M. Maresceau (ed.), n. 1, pp. 197–222.

[33] IP Enforcement Strategy, p. 11.   [34] *Ibid.*, p. 12.

[35] See website DG Trade, available at: http://ec.europa.eu/trade/issues/sectoral/intell_property/guidebook.htm.

issues. This aspect is considered to be crucial for the efficacy of the IP Enforcement Strategy and, in particular, to render this public-private partnership operational. Annex 1 of the IP Enforcement Strategy paper lists as many as eight different Commission DGs each with their specific responsibility for different aspects of IP enforcement, namely DG Trade, DG Internal Market (MARKT), DG Agriculture (AGRI), DG Taxation and Custom Union (TAXUD), DG Justice and Home Affairs (JAI), DG Development (DEV) and DG External Relations (RELEX), and finally DG Enterprise (ENTR),[36] so that the importance of this point can hardly be overestimated.

15.3 Turning a blind eye

The IP enforcement strategy may in the end turn out to be successful in achieving its main objective of increasing the level of IP enforcement in third countries. In particular as a similar message and strategy is actively and sometimes jointly pursued by other industrialised countries, such as the US and Japan. The strategy does not, however, indicate any legal basis for the prescribed course of action (point A). Similarly, it does not question whether there are – or should be – alternatives to the chosen path. Instead, it very much looks like the aim and method easily coincide and translate into a simple and straightforward slogan: 'Enforce the enforcement of IP protection.'

Little or no regard is being paid to identifying potential root causes for poor IP enforcement in third countries. Yet ignoring the problem in the IP enforcement strategy does not mean that the problem ceases to exist and can be ignored in practice. At least one such root cause appears to be linked to the fact that the original TRIPS agreement was drafted – or at least interpreted – in such a way as to unduly favour private interests (of inter alia EC industry) above public interests (of especially developing countries). The access to essential medicine debate is illustrative in that regard. It has led to a renewed discussion in the framework of the current WTO DOHA round about the scope and implications of TRIPS and, in particular, the overriding need to safeguard public policy choices and flexibility mechanisms. The question is whether the so-far negotiated solution, consisting first in the waiver of August 2003 followed by the

---

[36] IP Enforcement Strategy, Annex 1, Background, p. 19.

important amendment to the TRIPS Agreement decided upon in December 2005, is sufficient in that respect (point B).

The IP enforcement strategy also says nothing about the sometimes paradoxical consequences of an approach which is based predominantly on enforcement of private interests of the IP holders whilst turning a blind eye to the root causes relating to the public interest in third countries. The preamble of the TRIPS Agreement mentions among its objectives inter alia of reducing distortions to international trade, whereas the guiding General Agreement on Tariffs and Trade (GATT) principles of National Treatment and Most-Favoured-Nation Treatment not surprisingly occupy a prominent role also in the TRIPS Agreement.[37] It is rather puzzling to find that, in the end, the solution found in the framework of the WTO in order to allow IP holders of the industrialised countries to enforce to a maximum extent IP protection in third (developing) countries appears to be the introduction of a two-tiered trading system. In the EC this has recently led to the adoption of trade measures facilitating, if not stimulating, IP holders to engage in tiered pricing as well as compulsory licensing of patents for the export of certain pharmaceutical products to countries with public health problems. This is necessarily coupled with a prohibition agains (re-)importing such (pharmaceutical) products into the EC, thus in essence impeding rather than enhancing international trade in certain well-defined IP protected products. This calls for a brief analysis of the implications of full enforcement of IP rights abroad on market access in the EC (point C).

15.3.1 Dispensing with a legal basis

If the effects on the EC itself are clearly trade-related, it is significant that nowhere is an indication to be found as to the legal basis for the adoption of the IP enforcement strategy paper, or any course of action to be taken thereunder. In view of the principle of conferred competence of the EC[38] this is to be deeply deplored, even though strictly speaking the strategy paper is of course not a legally binding instrument. The aim, as the names suggests, is to formulate a strategy or an operational policy, which

---

[37] Articles 3 and 4 TRIPS, respectively.
[38] Article 5 EC Treaty reads: 'The Community shall act within the limits of the powers conferred upon it by this Treaty and of the objectives assigned therein.'

presupposes the existence of an identifiable competence for the EC to undertake action in that field. The use of non-binding instruments to formulate an external policy whilst dispensing with the obligation to formally anchor any EC action to the Treaty is not specific to IP issues. It is a more and more recurrent technique used also in relation to other less clear-cut fields in terms of division of competence, such as human rights protection.[39]

The external competence of the EC in matters of IP protection is indeed still not totally clear-cut. It should be recalled that the European Court of Justice (ECJ) in its well-known Opinion 1/94 relating to TRIPS has held that only border measures relating to counterfeit and piracy came within the exclusive competence of the EC under the Common Commercial Policy heading.[40] For the remaining – and most important – part TRIPS has shared competence for the EC and the Member States subject to the doctrine of implied powers. It is interesting to note that the ECJ acknowledged that specific action aimed at raising the level of IP protection in third countries had already been undertaken prior to TRIPS on the basis of Article 133 EC, inter alia through the use of the former New Commercial Policy Instrument. The ECJ simply underlined that such an institutional practice could not serve as a binding precedent to conclude the TRIPS Agreement on the basis of Article 133 alone. In particular, as the latter also implied harmonisation of IP laws of the EC Member States.[41]

It is uncertain what lessons may be drawn from Opinion 1/94 for the IP enforcement strategy. The first troubling feature is the reference to prior 'institutional practices' in the external action of the EC. Did the ECJ mean to indicate that the earlier measures were based on Article 133 EC 'in practice' but not necessarily correctly so from a legal perspective? The fact is that the legal basis of such measures targeting deficiencies in IP protection in third countries was never challenged before the ECJ and was also not the focus of the Article 300(6) EC request leading to Opinion 1/94. Or is it to be understood from Opinion 1/94 that Article 133 EC may be used to target IP protection in third countries but no longer when such measures also affect the EC and its Member States?[42] If so, what could possibly be the justification for such a distinction? In Opinion 1/94, the ECJ clearly underlined that through the sole use of Article 133 EC to conclude

[39] See Govaere and Van Bossuyt (Le commerce), pp. 225–54.
[40] Opinion 1/94 [1994] ECR I-5267, para. 55.   [41] Paras. 61–7.   [42] Paras. 63 and 67.

TRIPS, internal EC procedures for harmonisation of IP legislation could be circumvented.[43] This was not totally convincing as it seems to confuse implied powers and CCP reasoning.[44] In the same Opinion 1/94, a similar argument of the Council was quite rightly rejected with respect to Agriculture, Sanitary and Phytosanitary measures and Technical Barriers to Trade.[45] Also, in the later *Energy Star Agreement* Case, the ECJ expressly dismissed the argument that the need for different internal decision-making procedures forms an obstacle to the sole use of Article 133 EC externally.[46] Be that as it may, it is a fact that even after Opinion 1/94 the Trade Barriers Regulation, with a sole legal basis of Article 133 EC, continues to be used to target inter alia third countries' deficiencies in securing effective rights for EC IP holders, a practice which until now has gone largely unchallenged.[47]

Regard should also be had to the dynamic nature of EC external competence. Finding that the EC may exercise external competence in IP-related matters, if not under the CCP then by virtue of the implied powers doctrine, is today far less troublesome than at the time when the WTO Opinion was delivered. In Opinion 1/94 the ECJ succinctly held that internal IP harmonisation mainly related to trade marks, whereas in other areas of IP protection no harmonisation was envisaged.[48] The situation has rapidly evolved since then. The entry into force of the TRIPS Agreement in itself represented an important 'external harmonisation' of IP laws of the EC Member States, paving the way for the adoption of additional EC IP harmonisation measures. An important breakthrough in that respect came about in 2004 – the same year as the IP enforcement strategy under discussion here – with the adoption of the above-mentioned EC *IP enforcement Directive* on the basis of Article 95 EC.[49] The latter is in the first place addressed to the EC Member States, but is now also systematically

---

[43] Paras. 59–60 and 63.

[44] In Opinion 1/75 the ECJ had clarified that CCP entails a mixture of internal and external measures *without one taking priority over the other* (emphasis added), [1975] ECR 1355, 1363. This is precisely the difference with implied powers where first internal action needs to be taken (Case 22/70 ERTA [1971] ECR 263) or in exceptional circumstances where this is necessary to fulfil an objective of the EC Treaty simultaneously internal and external measures (Opinion 1/76 [1977] ECR 741).

[45] Opinion 1/94, n. 40, paras. 29–34.

[46] Case C-281/01 *Commission* v. *Council* [2002] ECR I-12049. This case concerned trade and environmental protection rather than IP-related issues.

[47] On the role of the Trade Barriers Regulation in the IP enforcement strategy, see Section 15.2.5.

[48] Para. 103.   [49] Directive 2004/48/EC of 29 April 2004, OJ 2004 L 157/45.

used as a benchmark by the EC in IP clauses included in its bilateral agreements with third countries or regions.[50] The possibility, if not necessity, of maintaining a consistent approach to both internal (Member States) and external (third countries) IP enforcement is now an important tool which firmly rests in the hands of the EC.

15.3.2 Silence as to potential root causes

The IP enforcement strategy focuses clearly on enforcement standards of IP and protection of private interests of EC industry abroad but turns a deaf ear to the underlying reasons why States may be reluctant to fully enforce TRIPS. To a large extent, it plainly ignores the interference of the proposed strategy with public policy choices of (third) countries, whereas the latter is precisely the topic of concern and debate in the context of the WTO itself.[51] The main discussion in substance relating to TRIPS for the past few years has been whether respect for public policy choices could be achieved through a relaxation of the stringent flexibility conditions or whether the TRIPS Agreement itself should be renegotiated. The EC has played an important role in this discussion, taking an intermediate position between the US and the (least-)developing countries.

At least formally, the objective of the TRIPS Agreement is not to combat counterfeit and piracy at the source – and thus to secure export markets – but rather 'to contribute to the promotion of technological innovation and to the transfer and dissemination of technology, to the *mutual advantage* of producers and users of technological knowledge in a manner *conducive to social and economic welfare*, and *to a balance of rights and obligations*'.[52] The fulfilment of those objectives requires a complex approach, whereby attention is paid not only to the enforcement of private rights of IP holders but also to public policy choices. Yet whereas the middle- to long-term advantages of IP protection in terms of stimulating research and development and attracting technology transfer are readily emphasised (although not necessarily substantiated),[53] also in the IP

---

[50] On such TRIPS-plus clauses in the IP enforcement strategy, see also Section 15.2.2.

[51] See for instance C. Correa, 'Patent Law, TRIPS and R&D Incentives: A Southern Perspective', CMH Working Paper Series, Paper N° WG2:12,WHO, 2001.

[52] Article 7 TRIPS (emphasis added).

[53] The fact that the potential benefits of TRIPS in terms of improving long-term research and development results in the public interest are too readily taken for granted is underlined by

enforcement strategy, the downside is often ignored or minimised. The costs are not only economic but may also be social in nature. Temporary restraints on local competition will often lead to higher (monopoly) prices, as IP exclusivity typically renders scarce a product that would otherwise be freely available. As such, it is immediately apparent that imposing an obligation under TRIPS to grant patents on all products and in all fields, thus including pharmaceuticals, would have potential repercussions on public health policies of States.[54]

The need to find a balance between vital public interest relating inter alia to public health and private interests of IP holders is also acknowledged by the TRIPS Agreement. The latter, in substance, focuses exclusively on the worldwide regulation of IP rights and is not at all – nor is it the proper forum to be – concerned with the worldwide harmonisation of public health policies. Instead, it introduces so-called flexibility mechanisms or safeguard clauses that may be invoked in the public interest. Yet, those receive far less attention as, first, their use is not obligatory under TRIPS and, second, they need to be further elaborated upon by domestic law. The TRIPS Agreement introduces two important flexibility mechanisms, although not unconditional, in Article 8 TRIPS. Members are allowed to adopt 'measures necessary to protect public health and nutrition, and to promote the public interest in sectors of vital importance to their socio-economic and technological development' as well as 'appropriate measures ... to prevent the abuse of IPR by rights holders or the resort to practices which unreasonably restrain trade or adversely affect the international transfer of technology'. The public interest, however, only prevails in appearance as, in both cases, the condition is that any such a measure is consistent with the provisions of the TRIPS Agreement itself.[55]

---

several authors, among others Reichman who writes: 'A fundamental problem is that international trade negotiations have not self-consciously postulated the need to seek intellectual property norms and incentives that would best advance the incipient worldwide system of innovation as such. On the contrary, special interest lobbyists claiming to know what best serves that system have promoted normative solutions that maximize rents from existing innovation. These self-serving IP proposals are then exchanged for trade concessions in other areas that may or may not advance the long-term interests of the technology importing countries', see J. Reichman, 'Nurturing a Transnational system of Innovation', in Govaere and Ullrich (eds.), *Intellectual Property*, pp. 17–42.

[54] Article 27(1) TRIPS.

[55] Note the difference with the public health exception in Article XX(d) GATT, for instance, where the only condition is that it should not constitute an arbitrary discrimination or a disguised restriction on trade.

In other words, the public interest is conditioned by the need to respect to a maximum the private interests protected under the TRIPS Agreement.[56] This is the source of many problems. The outspoken preference given to protecting the interests of a few over the interests of the community at large is, not surprisingly, also one of the root causes for the reluctance to enforce TRIPS, adequately and unquestioningly. Instead, in particular (least-)developing countries would like to redress the balance in favour of the public interest through re-opening the discussion and amending TRIPS.[57]

The domestic policies that may be taken by any WTO member, including the EC, in accordance with TRIPS are to be found, in particular, in Article 6 TRIPS and Article 40 TRIPS. The first provision leaves it up to each country whether to introduce the principle of (international) exhaustion of IP rights, this is the IP trade liberalising principle in order to counter market segmentation.[58] The latter provision relates to the adoption and application of competition rules with respect to IPR, in particular to counter licensing practices or abusive behaviour having an adverse effect on trade and impeding the transfer and dissemination of technology.[59] The fact that the necessary flexibility is not unconditional is,

[56] Abbott points out that 'developed countries consistently evidence two principal objectives in WTO negotiations with developing countries. The first is to enhance their access to developing Member markets. The second is to prevent developing Members from exercising discretion in a way which would be considered unfavorable to the developed countries', see F. Abbott, 'Are the competition rules in the WTO TRIPS Agreement adequate?', 4 JIEL (2004), p. 697.

[57] As a consequence of the difficult discussions in that respect under TRIPS, the developing countries also increasingly put IP protection on the agenda of other international fora such as the WHO, the FAO and Human Rights Commissions. Helfer has made an interesting and detailed study in that respect, whereby it is argued that 'the expansion of intellectual property lawmaking into these diverse international fora is the result of a strategy of *regime shifting* by developing countries and NGOs that are dissatisfied with many provisions in TRIPs, or its omission of other issues and are actively seeking ways to recalibrate, revise, or supplement the treaty ... Developing countries and their allies are shifting negotiations to international regimes whose institutions, actors and subject matter mandates are closely aligned with these countries' interests', see L. Helfer, 'Regime Shifting: The TRIPS Agreement and New Dynamics of International Intellectual Property Lawmaking', 29 YJIL (2004), p. 6.

[58] For the EC, see Section 15.3.3.

[59] This possibility is deftly used in particular by the developed countries. In the EC, Articles 81-82 EC are applied to IP rights, see inter alia I. Govaere, *The Use and Abuse of Intellectual Property Rights in EC Law* (London: Sweet & Maxwell, 1996); I. Govaere, 'Het actuele spanningsveld tussen EG mededingingsregelen en intellectuele eigendomsrechten', in *Actualiteiten in het Europese Mededingingsrecht* (The Hague: Asser Press, 2006), pp. 57–72. For significant examples of the use of compulsory licences to restore competition in the US, EC and Canada, see F.M. Scherer and J. Watal, 'Post-TRIPS Options for Access to Patented Medicines in

first and foremost, illustrated by the restrictions imposed on domestic measures that may be taken in order to ensure that there is a true transfer of technology, and not just of technology-based products. The restrictive approach towards compulsory licensing (CL) for patents has encountered a great deal of opposition from mainly the (least-)developing countries. Article 27(1) TRIPS first of all imposes important restrictions as *to when* CL may be invoked. It would appear that the local working requirement for patents is now held to be fulfilled through importation of IP-based products by the IP holder and not only through local manufacturing, in spite of the stated objective to enhance technology transfer.[60] Article 31 TRIPS further lays down a rather detailed list of *under what conditions* CL may be imposed.[61] In particular condition (f), which stipulates that 'any such use shall be authorised *predominantly* for the supply of the domestic market of the Member authorising such use',[62] is considered problematic for (least-)developing countries as it – often wrongfully – presupposes a local capacity to manufacture technology-based products.

It should be recalled that the tension between private rights of IP holders, which the EC wants to enforce to the utmost, and the public policy choices in particular relating to public health were fully exposed in March 2001.[63] As many as 41 global pharmaceutical companies initiated legal action against South Africa, only to withdraw under insistent public pressure. South Africa had duly implemented Article 27(1) TRIPS and provided patent protection for pharmaceutical drugs among other things to treat HIV/AIDS. At the same time South Africa had invoked domestic

Developing Nations', 5 JIEL (2002), pp. 913–19, esp. at pp. 915–19. For a critical view of the impact of the TRIPS competition provisions, arguing that they 'might contribute to deepening rather than overcoming the technology dependence of developing countries', see H. Ullrich, 'Expansionist Intellectual Property Protection and Reductionist Competition rules: a TRIPS Perspective', 7 JIEL (2004), p. 401.

[60] Article 27(1) TRIPS stipulates that patent rights shall be enjoyable without discrimination as to whether products are imported or locally produced. The Mutually Agreed Solution in the dispute US–Brazil seems to confirm this interpretation with respect to the local working requirement, see WT/DS/199/4 of 19 July 2001.

[61] The conditions are, inter alia, that first a voluntary licence should be sought (except in case of national emergency, extreme urgency or public non-commercial use), limited scope and duration, non-exclusive and non-assignable character, and adequate remuneration for the IP holder.

[62] Emphasis added.

[63] For those events leading up to the TRIPS Amendment, including the negotiation of the contested TRIPS provision itself, see in particular T. Cottier, 'The DOHA Waiver and its effects on the nature of the TRIPS System and on Competition Law: The Impact of Human Rights', in Govacre and Ullrich (eds.), *Intellectual Property*, pp. 173–200.

law providing for the possibility to grant CL on grounds of public health, on the basis of Article 31 TRIPS but to the dismay of the IP holders concerned.[64] This case exposed to the full the impact of the trade objectives of TRIPS on other non-trade objectives of countries, especially relating to public health. It not only exposed the causal link between compliance with the strict obligations under Article 27(1) TRIPS and practical problems in terms of access to essential (and affordable) medicine. It acted as a public eye-opener and fuelled the reluctance of certain countries to fully implement and enforce TRIPS as it stands. Instead, the debate was launched as to what could be the appropriate remedies to redress the balance between private and public interests. Interestingly enough, for the first time it was openly acknowledged that the trade-off is not only short-term private interests of the IP holder against long-term public interests in terms of research and development (including development of new medicine) and technology transfer. The newly found understanding is that public interests, too, namely the need to make existing drugs available to those that need them, enter into the short-term equation.[65]

Identifying the problem is one thing, finding an appropriate response in the mutual interest appears to be less obvious.[66] The developing countries first of all point to the core problem and call for a renegotiation and modification of substantive TRIPS provisions relating to IPR. Developed countries such as the US and the EC are mainly concerned with safeguarding the acquired rights of the IP holders and maintain that TRIPS in essence offers sufficient flexibility, as it is, to take such public interests into account.[67] A second point of discord is the developing countries' claim

---

[64] There was some discussion as to whether the South African law fully complied with all the requirements of Article 31 TRIPS, see D. Matthews, 'WTO Decision on Implementation of Paragraph 6 of the DOHA Declaration on the TRIPS Agreement and Public Health: A Solution to the Access to Essential Medicines Problem?', 7 JIEL (2004), pp. 78–81.

[65] WTO Director General Mike Moore, interview in International Herald Tribune of 22 February 2001. Another short-term interest in the public interest is of course to render public instead of resorting to secrecy.

[66] On the difficult negotiations and different drafts leading up to the DOHA Declaration, see C. Otero Garcia-Castrillon, 'An approach to the WTO Ministerial Declaration on the TRIPS Agreement and Public Health', 5 JIEL (2002), pp. 212–19. At p. 213 she points out that: 'Essentially, developing countries aimed at a recognition of freedom to adopt measures on public health grounds, particularly on access to medicines, while developed countries instead pursued assurances that the rights and duties under the Agreement were not devalued.'

[67] This is still now the position taken by some authors, such as Thomas Cottier who was the chief negotiator for Switzerland during the Uruguay Round of the GATT. He points to the solution in the form of the flexibility mechanisms of Article 31(k), namely the possibility to grant

that TRIPS should not interfere with domestic public health policies in general. Whereas the developed countries interpret any scope left for flexibility much more narrowly. The EC takes only a slightly broader view than the US through holding that there should be a (restricted) flexibility for identified and limited public health issues but including all epidemics and not just pandemics. The turning point in the discussion came with the DOHA Declaration on the TRIPS Agreement and Public Health of 14 November 2001.[68] The latter follows closely the EC approach and stresses the possibility of using the flexibilities in TRIPS to protect public health, including for epidemics.[69] However, it leaves the contested IP provisions providing for exclusive rights on pharmaceutical products untouched.[70] Instead, the DOHA Declaration – rather paradoxically considering the forum – calls upon the adoption of measures in support of differential pricing of pharmaceutical products, namely charge what is fair in each market, reinforced by a targeted use of the flexibility mechanisms of Article 6 TRIPS.[71] The underlying idea is that developing countries would

compulsory licences for anti-competitive conduct, although in the end also he recognises that the TRIPS waiver was a 'a proper answer, at this stage', see T. Cottier, 'The DOHA Waiver and its effects on the nature of the TRIPS System and on Competition Law: The Impact of Human Rights', in Govaere and Ullrich (eds.), *Intellectual Property*.

[68] The DOHA Declaration on the TRIPS Agreement and Public Health, WT/MIN(01)/DEC/W/ 2, of 14 November 2001. For a detailed analysis, including of the different position papers, see D. Matthews, 'WTO Decision on Implementation of Paragraph 6 of the DOHA Declaration on the TRIPS Agreement and Public Health: A Solution to the Access to Essential Medicines Problem?', 7 JIEC (2004), pp. 78–81.

[69] The DOHA Declaration emphasises among others the following: 1. Teleological interpretation of TRIPS; 2. right to determine grounds upon which CL are granted; 3. rights to consider that public health crisis, incl. HIV/AIDS, tuberculosis and malaria and other epidemics represent a 'national emergency' or other circumstances of extreme urgency in the sense of Article 31 TRIPS (so that no voluntary licence needs to be sought first).

[70] Yet with a further extension of the deadline for patenting of pharmaceutical products in least-developed countries until 1 January 2016 (instead of January 2005). As mentioned before, on 29 November 2005 a further decision was taken to extend the deadline until 1 July 2013 for least-developed countries compliance with protection for trademarks, copyright, patents, and under IPR under the TRIPS Agreement, see Section 15.1.

[71] This solution was also advocated in the Joint Study by the WHO and the WTO Secretariat entitled 'WTO Agreements and Public Health' of 2002, see WTO News Press/310 of 20 August 2002. Such a policy consistent with the TRIPS Agreement was also advanced by well-known economists such as Scherer, in order to deal with the 'life and death consequences for the citizens of less well-developed nations' of TRIPS interpretation and implementation (p. 938), see F.M. Scherer and J. Watal, 'Post-TRIPS Options for Access to Patented Medicines in Developing Nations', 5 JIEL (2002), p. 934. They analyse in particular AIDS drug pricing by multinational pharmaceutical companies in the late 1990s to see whether they (spontaneously) exhibit patterns suggesting Ramsey pricing. The authors also put the

be better off introducing the principle of international exhaustion, so that lower priced drugs may readily enter their markets and thus help to provide medicine at affordable (low) cost. To the contrary, developed countries should refrain from introducing the principle of international exhaustion so as to allow IP holders to segment the higher priced markets.[72] In other words, in order to secure the same strict standards of IP protection worldwide it is argued, within the framework of the WTO of all places, to adopt differential pricing measures, diverging trading rules and a segmentation of the global market in pharmaceutical products.

The DOHA Declaration also identifies the major problem with the flexibility condition of Article 31(f) TRIPS which offers a solution in terms of CL only to those developing countries that have a sufficient production capacity. The breakthrough comes as late as 30 August 2003 when a temporary waiver of Article 31(f) TRIPS is finally agreed upon.[73] Countries are now allowed to import cheaper generic medicine made under CL if they are unable to manufacture the medicines themselves and respect certain procedural requirements, such as prior notification to the Council for TRIPS. Conditions are also imposed on the exporting countries, such as a limitation of quantities to fit the identified need, the clear identification of such products and specific labelling requirements, the payment of adequate remuneration to the IP holder and, importantly, the adoption of measures to prevent the re-export of the products manufactured under CL.[74] Developed countries such as the EC, the US and Japan, have declared that they will not use this exception as importers. There is also a differentiation discernible among developing countries, with for instance EC targeted countries such as China, Korea and Turkey[75] declaring only to use this possibility in case of national emergency or other circumstances of extreme urgency. Significantly, the temporary waiver has later been replaced by a formal amendment of Article 31(f) TRIPS by virtue of a General Council Decision of 6 December 2005, which should be ratified by at least two-thirds of the WTO members by 1 December 2007.[76] An Article 31bis

emphasis on the need to give a crucial role to generic drugs in future policy as well as drug donations to the poorest countries.

[72] On the EC implementation measures, see Section 15.3.3.

[73] WTO General Council Decision of 30 August 2003, Implementation of paragraph 6 of the DOHA Declaration on TRIPS and Public Health, WT/L/540 of 1 September 2003.

[74] For implementation in the EC, see Section 15.3.3.   [75] See Section 15.2.1.

[76] WTO General Council Decision of 6 December 2005, Amendment of the TRIPS Agreement, WT/L/641 of 8 December 2005. Only 5 out of 150 countries had already formally accepted the

TRIPS is thereby inserted, which mainly sets out the modalities already agreed upon in the temporary waiver with respect to the interpretation of Article 31(f), as well as a more technical Annex to the TRIPS Agreement which was originally also annexed to the temporary waiver decision.[77]

It cannot go unnoticed that the amendment of the TRIPS Agreement only represents a minimal fine-tuning of the conditions inherent in the flexibility mechanisms and does not even begin to meet the expectations of the developing countries to curtail the very scope of TRIPS in view of safeguarding public policy choices. To the contrary, it is now firmly anchored in TRIPS that the respect of public health policies in (mainly developing) countries at least in some cases becomes dependent on the willingness of other (including developed) countries to enact the necessary laws in order to prevent the re-exportation of sometimes life-saving drugs. The reluctance of certain developing countries to fully enforce IP rights becomes more understandable in the face of this blunt refusal of developed countries, including the EC, to tackle important root causes and to re-examine the most controversial IP standards that are being enforced. Such a refusal may perhaps be explained by the fear that renegotiating certain substantive TRIPS provisions would quickly lead to the whole TRIPS Agreement being called into question, especially bearing in mind the difficult negotiating history. The impression is nonetheless being created that the TRIPS Agreement is instrumental to a beggar-thy-neighbour policy in flagrant contradiction with the objectives set out in Article 7. The stated goal of the IP enforcement strategy firmly to take the direction of a future TRIPS-plus through the negotiation and enforcement of IP standards which even exceed current TRIPS obligations,[78] which then potentially also further reduces the scope left for flexibility, can only further fuel this controversy.[79]

TRIPS amendment on 25 January 2007, namely US, Switzerland, El Salvador, Korea and Norway, see the WTO website, available at: http://www.wto.org/english/tratop_e/trips_e/amendment_e.htm.

[77] For an analysis of the difference between the 2003 Waiver and the 2005 TRIPS Amendment, see C. Godt, 'The so-called *Waiver Compromise* of DOHA and Hong Kong; about Contested Concepts of the Nature of the International Intellectual Property System', in I. Govaere and H. Ullrich (eds.), n. 23, pp. 201–228.

[78] See Section 15.2.2 and 15.2.3.

[79] Also some American authors such as Jerome Reichman call for 'a moratorium on stronger international intellectual property standard-setting' as 'the developing countries need a breathing space in which to accommodate the social costs of the TRIPS Agreement (and posterior TRIPS-plus Agreements, if any)', see J. Reichman, 'Nurturing a Transnational system

15.3.3 The unwarranted effect on EC trade policy

It is interesting to recall the very *raison d'être* of TRIPS as set out in the preamble. It is stated, inter alia, that the aim is to reduce distortions and impediments to international trade as well as 'to ensure that measures and procedures to enforce intellectual property rights do not themselves become barriers to legitimate trade'. The practice learns that TRIPS is essentially squaring the circle. It is illustrated above that, in particular, the developed countries, not least the EC, have radically opted for the fullest possible enforcement of private IP rights by all WTO members, also in the face of public policy choices. But public policy choices cannot merely be ignored so that the burning question then becomes what strategy, if any, is adopted in this respect. On the one hand it is clear that the WTO, and in particular TRIPS, is definitely not the proper forum to harmonise such non-economic public policy interests. On the other hand, public policy choices are also not unconditionally left to the discretion of States but should themselves comply with TRIPS. As mentioned above, the solution found under TRIPS is the quite paradoxical plea for the adoption of a different approach to the issue of international exhaustion of IP rights under Article 6 TRIPS, for developed and developing countries, as well as the intro-duction of measures facilitating price-differentiation and market segmen-tation of certain IP-based products. Unilateral trade policy measures of developed countries, such as the EC, should thus be used or even newly introduced in order to allow for the adequate protection of public health in third countries. The EC IP enforcement strategy, targeting exclusively third countries, therefore goes hand-in-hand with a renewed EC trade policy in IP-based products. Or to put it differently, although the IP enforcement strategy is clearly aimed at eliminating as much as possible inter-brand competition at the source, in the end it also has a high potential for intra-brand and EC market access restrictions.

When assessing the potential impact on international trade flows it is crucial to bear in mind that, in spite of the enactment of an IP enforcement strategy by the EC, IP holders are never under an obligation to exercise their

of Innovation', in Govaere and Ullrich (eds.), *Intellecual Property*. Others, such as Dreier, point out that such a moratorium is not very realistic having regard precisely to the conclusion of FTAs, providing for a TRIPS-plus standard, by both the EC and the US, see T. Dreier, 'Shaping a Fair International IPR-Regime in a Globalized World', in Govaere and Ullrich (eds.), *Intellectual Property*, pp. 43–76.

exclusive rights. Just as trade laws facilitate but do not impose an obligation to also effectively engage in trade, IP laws are adopted essentially in
order to allow or facilitate the use of such rights by technology-based
industries. The EC Counterfeit and Piracy Regulation 1383/2003 goes a long
way in that respect and exceeds the obligations under TRIPS.[80] It provides
for a prominent role for the customs authorities in detecting and detain-
ing (essentially for three working days) goods suspected of counterfeit and
piracy, so as to make it possible for the IP holder to enforce his exclusive
rights quickly and effectively.[81] As the name suggests, the EC Counterfeit and Piracy Regulation only applies with respect to the crossing of the
external EC border (both importation and exportation) without the
consent of the IP holder of products manufactured without the consent of
the IP holder. Those conditions are cumulative.

The Counterfeit and Piracy Regulation does not apply to parallel
imports into the EC of products marketed with the consent but imported
without the consent of the IP holders. The possibility for the IP holder to
impose intra-brand trade restrictions is subject to the introduction, or
not, of the principle of international exhaustion of rights subsequent to
the flexibility mechanism of Article 6 TRIPS.[82] The principle of international exhaustion implies that an IP holder may no longer invoke IP
exclusivity in order to prohibit the importation of products brought on
the third-country market (under parallel protection[83]) with his consent. It
counters market segmentation and price differentiation practices based on
IP exclusivity. Conversely, in the absence of the principle of international
exhaustion, it is up to the IP holder in each case to authorise, or not, the
importation of such products. In other words, it is then the IP holder who
holds the 'master key' to potential market segmentation and who may

---

[80] Regulation 1383/2003 of 22 July 2003 concerning customs actions against goods suspected of
infringing certain intellectual property rights and the measures to be taken against goods
found to have infringed such rights (repealing and replacing the former Counterfeit
Regulation 3295/94), OJ 2003 L 196/7, is based exclusively on Article 133 EC.

[81] See in particular Articles 4 and 5.

[82] This is expressly made subject to respect of Most-Favoured-Nation and National Treatment
conditions.

[83] According to the ECJ the condition of parallel IP protection does not apply with respect to the
principle of Community exhaustion, see Case 187/80 *Merck I* [1981] ECR 2063, as reiterated in
Joined Cases C-267/95 and C-268/95, *Merck II* [1996] ECR I-6285. For a critical discussion of
those highly controversial *Merck* cases, see for instance Govaere, *The Use and Abuse*.

determine international trade patterns.[84] Whereas Article 6 TRIPS initially left this issue to be decided freely by each WTO member, subject to the respect of Most-Favoured-Nation (MFN) and National Treatment (NT) principles, it has now become an instrumental and differential tool in 'solving' the access to affordable medicine issue created by the straightforward enforcement of TRIPS, thus potentially affecting the EC.

As a rule, and in the absence of EC secondary legislation to that end, the ECJ has until now consistently refrained to extend the principle of Community or EEA regional exhaustion. To the contrary, it has plainly refused the application of the principle of international exhaustion of IP rights, at least with respect to trade marks.[85] As a logical consequence IP holders may, in principle, freely invoke their exclusive IP rights in order to isolate the EC market and to ask higher prices, but they are of course by no means obliged to do so. A correction mechanism may nonetheless be triggered through qualifying such a behaviour as an abusive practice under the competition rules, a possibility which is also allowed for under Article 40 TRIPS.[86] This will most likely be the case where the IP holder occupies a dominant position in the EC market and enforces significant price differences with respect to comparable markets.[87]

The EC approach thus appears to be fully in compliance with the expectations under TRIPS subsequent to the access to affordable medicine debate. TRIPS indeed calls upon the developed countries such as the EC not to introduce the principle of exhaustion of IP rights (contrary to the developing countries who in this logic should introduce the principle). The question is whether this alone is sufficient or whether the EC should take further measures. The DOHA Declaration on IP and public health clearly acknowledged the problem of the causal link between the enforcement of

---

[84] For more details see I. Govaere, 'The quest for a master key to control parallel imports', 4 *The Cambridge Yearbook of European Legal Studies* (2001), pp. 191–216.

[85] Case C 355/96 *Silhouette* [1998] ECR 1998 I-4799. For an analysis of this ruling of the ECJ and related cases, see the above mentioned article in the Cambridge Yearbook. It is unlikely that the ECJ would rule differently for other types of IP rights inter alia as it is especially international exhaustion of trademark rights that is on the agenda and topic of international debate.

[86] See Section 15.2.2.

[87] See Case T-198/98 *Micro Leader* [1998] ECR II-3989. For an analysis of this ruling of the Court of First Instance, whereby Article 82 EC was invoked to counter the potential negative effects for the EC market and on EC consumers of invoking copyright to justify differentiated pricing and an isolation of the EC market, see P. Demaret and I. Govaere, 'Parallel imports, free movement and competition rules: the European experience and perspective', in C. Cottier and P. Mavroidis, n. 3, pp. 147–75.

IP rights, inter alia by the EC, and the elimination of inter-brand (including generic medicine) competition at the source, so that products including essential drugs are rendered scarce and may be priced higher. But in the framework of TRIPS, no legal obligation is until now put on IP holders to provide the global market with essential medicine, let alone to do so at an affordable cost.

It is precisely in order to induce (EC) IP holders to take duly into account the public interests of third States that the EC has now domestically implemented the 'TRIPS paradox' in the form of two regulations. First, Council Regulation 953/2003 of 26 May 2003 to avoid trade diversion into the EU of certain key medicine was adopted.[88] This is the so-called 'Tiered Pricing Regulation' which is based exclusively on Article 133 EC. Second, Regulation 816/2006 on Compulsory licensing of patents relating to the manufacture of pharmaceutical products for export to countries with public health problems ('CL Export Regulation'), based on Articles 133 and 95 EC, was enacted recently.[89] Both Regulations have in common that they plainly prohibit (re)importation into the EC of identified pharmaceutical products which are manufactured and/or lower priced specifically to meet public health needs of clearly identified (least-)developing countries. Yet they also share an important weakness in that they cannot truly guarantee that the possibilities provided for by such a new legal framework will also be used by the pharmaceutical industry in practice.

The Tiered Pricing Regulation is meant to encourage the IP holders themselves to engage in differential pricing, namely to sell essential drugs cheaply in the poorest countries and at a higher price in the EC, whilst preventing tiered priced products from being (re)imported into the EC. This is different for the CL Export Regulation which is specifically limited to implement the temporary waiver under Article 37(f) TRIPS, now formally a TRIPS amendment. In the preamble of the CL Export Regulation it is unequivocally stated that '(g)iven the Community's active role in the adoption of the Decision, its commitment made to the WTO to fully contribute to the implementation of the Decision and its appeal to all WTO Members to ensure that the conditions are put in place which will allow the system set up by the Decision to operate efficiently, it is important for the Community to implement the Decision in its legal

---

[88] OJ 2003 L 135/5.   [89] OJ 2006 L 157/1.

order'.[90] The aim is thus only to allow for the exportation of drugs under a compulsory licence and produced in the EC, to eligible WTO countries with insufficient local manufacturing capacity, as well as to enact uniform rules to prevent the reimportation of such drugs. There is nonetheless a direct correlation between the two Regulations, to the extent that export under compulsory licences will only be allowed where the IP holder does not already meet the public health requirements himself through sufficiently providing the third market concerned with affordable medicine. Yet also here, there is no guarantee that demands for compulsory licences for exports of essential drugs will at all be made or that they will fully meet the needs of the countries concerned.

It is too early to assess the impact of the CL Export Regulation, but the first reports on the functioning of the Tiered Pricing Regulation are not very promising in that respect. In the first year, no products were registered under that system. In 2004 only one pharmaceutical company had registered nine products all relating to the same illness,[91] whereas in 2005 again no new products were registered.[92] This may point to the crucial weakness of a system that essentially relies on the willingness of industry to put public interests above its private interests. Another and probably additional reason may simply lie in the above-mentioned rejection of the principle of international exhaustion by the ECJ. As a consequence, IP holders may already freely engage in price differentiation. They may decide on a case-by-case basis whether they want to block the importation of lower-priced products into the EC, regardless of whether the products or countries are identified in a regulation and, importantly, without any need

---

[90] *Ibid.*, see preamble.

[91] See the *Annual Report (2003/2004) on the application of Council Regulation (EC) N° 953/2003 of 26 May 2003 to avoid trade diversion in to the European Union of certain key medicines*, SEC (2005) 896 of 23 June 2005. In 2004, only Glaxo Smith Kline had registered nine products for HIV/AIDS treatment, see also *Commission Regulation (EC) N° 1876/2004 of 28 October 2004 amending Annex 1 of Council Regulation (EC) N° 953/2003 of 26 May 2003 to avoid trade diversion in to the European Union of certain key medicines*, OJ 2004 L 326/22.

[92] See the *Annual Report (2004/2005) on the application of Council Regulation (EC) N° 953/2003 of 26 May 2003 to avoid trade diversion in to the European Union of certain key medicines*, SEC (2006) 1256 of 29 September 2006. In 2005, there was only a modification of the distinctive features of two products already registered in 2004, see also *Commission Regulation (EC) N° 1662/2005 of 11 October 2005 amending Annex 1 of Council Regulation (EC) N° 953/2003 of 26 May 2003 to avoid trade diversion in to the European Union of certain key medicines*, OJ 2005 L 267/19.

for prior registration or other cumbersome formalities.[93] The master key to parallel (international) trade thus remains firmly in the hands of IP holders in the EC. But this now implies that they also hold an important key in hand to achieve public health policies of third States, with or without making use of the Tiered Pricing Regulation.

The IP enforcement strategy and the uncompromising approach under TRIPS essentially puts the EC in a strange pivotal position. On the one hand, the EC has undertaken to force third countries to protect the interests of (EC) IP holders to the full, in spite of their public policy choices. On the other hand, and as an indispensable counterpart, the EC now has to convince (EC) IP holders also to pursue public policy interests of third States, and not just their own private interests. The most important leverage to try and achieve both is, not surprisingly, related almost exclusively to trade and market access.

15.4 Conclusion

The forcefulness and credibility of the EC IP enforcement strategy as a whole is to a large extent dependent on the success of the alternatives it offers to meet the root causes for the reluctance of third countries to enforce such exclusive rights. Hence, the importance of identifying such root causes and the solutions offered in the framework of TRIPS and the EC. In particular the precedent set by the access to essential medicine debate and which touches upon essential public policy choices is highly instructive. The EC has been successful in proposing an alternative approach in TRIPS and has subsequently enacted unilateral trade measures with a sole objective of protecting public health in third countries. This appears to be the counterpart – or trade-off – for third countries' enforcement of exclusive rights for EC IP holders, including on key pharmaceutical products.

It cannot hide the fact, however, that the price to pay for the full enforcement of IP rights worldwide is at least double, and hence a cause for concern. First and foremost, the pursuit of public (health) policies of (third) countries now more than ever before rests in the hands of the IP

---

[93] To the extent that those products come from developing countries that are not in a comparable position to the EC, it appears that also the earlier mentioned *Micro Leader* case approach under Article 82 EC would not prevent that here.

holders and their willingness to use the newly created incentives to engage in price differentiation in the public interest. It is not certain whether this solution will be sufficient to appease the apprehensions of certain countries, which may then easily translate in an overall poor IP enforcement record. It is also paradoxical, to say the least, that the EC and other developed countries in the framework of TRIPS do not hesitate to advocate the introduction of differentiating trade measures which segment the global market and isolate the domestic market, as an indispensable counterpart for effective and adequate enforcement of IP rights abroad. Yet with respect to such unwarranted and questionable effects of the pursued policy, the EC IP enforcement strategy firmly keeps the eyes wide shut.

EU environmental law and its green footprints in the world

KIRSTYN INGLIS

16.1 The Union's positive and negative green footprints

It is fair to say that the European Union (EU) has left both positive and negative footprints on Europe's environment and, necessarily by extension, on the entire world's environment.

The adjectives used by the scientific community[1] in relation to the degradation of the environment underline the urgency on a global scale and not only at EU level: population or demographic 'explosion' threatening mass migration and pressure on borders; 'catastrophic' events such as the summer floods in central Europe and the severe droughts in the Iberian Peninsula; 'dramatic' increase in global temperatures (from 0.7° Celsius over the last one hundred years to between 1.4° and 5.8° Celsius over the next hundred years); 'disastrous' effects of the deforestation in southern Europe; the 'devastation' wrought by hurricane Katrina. And in its report of 2 February 2007, the UN Intergovernmental Panel on Climate Change (UN IPCC) gives its best estimate of increases in global warming of between 1.8° Celsius and 4° Celsius and a rise of between 18cm and 58cm in sea levels, both by 2100. Sea levels can be expected to rise a further

This contribution was initiated in part within the framework of an IUAP project with the Universities of Liege, Ghent and Brussels (ULB) and was then further elaborated as part of the Post-doc Research Fellowship (FWO) at the European Institute, Ghent University.

[1] Although generally speaking these effects or results seem self-evident, see the International Labour Organisation Study, Donatella Giubilaro 'Migration from the Maghreb and migration pressures: current situation and future prospects', August 1997, available at: http://www.ilo.org/public/english/protection/migrant/download/imp/imp15e.pdf; see also EEAg Report, *The European environment - State and outlook* 2005 (Copenhagen: EEAg, 2005); see the research theme undertaken in the Community's sixth and seventh Research Framework Programmes, information available at: http://www.ec.europa.eu/research/environment/newsanddoc/article_3762_en.htm.

20cm if the recent melting of polar ice sheets continues.[2] Global warming is now beyond any doubt the result of human action. These increases are higher than previously thought – the 1995 Second Assessment Report of the IPCC predicted a lower temperature increase of 2° Celcius above pre-industrial levels and it was this figure that formed the baseline for Community measures designed to combat climate change that are considered further. All this will adversely affect human health in many ways, even introducing malaria to Europe, affect the food production and the capacity of the world to feed the growing population, cause demographic, economic and social dislocation in Europe and present enormous challenges for strategies to cope.[3] To quote James Lovelock, the Earth has 'caught a morbid fever that will last 100,000 years'.[4]

16.1.1 Economic development has resulted in environmental degradation

It is fair to say that the EU's positive footprints since its first action programme for the environment of the early 1970s, have not covered over its negative footprints. It should always be remembered that since the inception of the EU, the state of Europe's environment has only continued to deteriorate, despite the fact that it is undoubtedly leading in progressive environmental policy and law on the global stage. The EU's environmental initiatives so far have not compensated for the negative impact of 'unsustainable trends' in the EU's development[5] on Europe's and the world's environment in spite of snowballing evidence of the cost benefits of early action to preserve the environment and ensure the sustainable development of economic activity. Because the environment knows no borders, Europe's environment and the success of Community action is inextricably linked with the environment that lies beyond EU borders.

---

[2] See 'Climate Change 2007: The Physical Science Basis, UN Intergovernmental Panel on Climate Change', 2 February 2007, available at: http://www.ipcc.ch.

[3] See *The European Environment - State and Outlook* 2005, n. 1. As to the possible future situation the Union is still building exploratory scenarios for the purposes of contributing meaningfully to a well-structured framework for strategic policy-making that is broad enough in time and space, see in particular the speech given to Friends of the Earth by the EEAg's J. McGlade, *Visions of the future for Europe – Prelude to change – Five scenarios for 2030*, available at: http://www.eea.europa.eu.

[4] See J. Lovelock, *Revenge of the Gaia: Why the Earth is Fighting Back and How We Can Still Save Humanity* (London: Allen Lane, 2006).

[5] See EEAg, *The European Environment - State and Outlook 2005*, n. 1, p. 8.

16.1.2 The external dimension of Community environmental policy

At the same time, it must be said that today the EU defines its environment policy to take account of its own impact on and influences from the world environment. While the external dimension was recognised prior to the Fifth (1992–2000) and Sixth (2001–2010) Environment Action Programmes, there was a general lack of an external dimension to Community environment policy before then. The 1992 European Commission Communication *The State of the Environment in the European Community*[6] was a key document in taking up the flag of the UN Conference on Environment and Development of 1992. This document was a building block for the Fifth Environment Action Programme. In the context of the completion of the Internal Market, the emergence of the transition economies in Central and Eastern Europe, the imminent integration of the European Free Trade Association (EFTA) economies in the European Economic Area (EEA) and the General Agreement on Tariffs and Trade (GATT) negotiations that would later lead to the establishment of the World Trade Organisation (WTO), the Communication would set the policy ball rolling but was remarkable for its lack of coverage of the international dimension and its focus purely on the state of the environment in the Community.[7]

The Community's Sixth Environment Action Programme that was adopted in 2002[8] and programmes EC work between 2002 and 2012, came into its mid-term review in April 2007, which was overdue. The policy direction and tasks that the Member States and EU institutions have set themselves display the global ambitions of the Community environment policy. The integration of environmental concerns into all aspects of the EU's external relations is an objective of the Sixth Environment Action Programme. The programme identifies four major areas of action:

- *Tackling climate change*: to achieve the EU's target of reducing greenhouse gas emissions by 8 per cent by 2008 to 2012 and target more radical global emission cuts in the order of 20 to 40 per cent by 2020;

---

[6] See COM(92)23, vol. III.

[7] In the introduction to COM(92)23, mentioned previous note, p. 8.

[8] Decision 1600/2002 of the European Parliament and of the Council laying down the Sixth Community Environment Action Programme, OJ 2002 L 242/1; see Commission Communication on the Sixth Environment Action Programme of the European Community, *Environment 2010: Our future, our choice*, COM(2001)31; Mid-term Review, COM(2007)225.

- *Nature and biodiversity*: to avert the threats to the survival of many species and their habitats in Europe: completion of the Natura 2000 network, new sectoral biodiversity action plans, paying greater attention to protecting landscapes, new initiatives for protecting the marine environment, measures to prevent industrial and mining accidents and a thematic strategy for protecting soils;
- *Environment and health*: fundamental overhaul of the EU's risk-management system for chemicals, a strategy for reducing risks from pesticides, protection of water quality in the EU, noise abatement and a thematic strategy for air quality.
- *Sustainable use of natural resources and management of wastes*: increased recycling and waste prevention with the aid of an integrated product policy and measures targeting specific waste streams such as sludges and biodegradable waste.

The Sixth Environment Action Programme broke away from the approach of its predecessor, the Fifth Environment Action Programme – see below – and in all four cases, these areas for action hold external implications.

6.1.3 The Lisbon Agenda and the future of sustainable development

Therefore, another very important ingredient in raising the profile of environment and sustainable development issues in the EU's external relations, although with limited success,[9] has been the recognition of the importance of respect for the environment alongside economic growth by the Member States in the Lisbon Agenda, including external factors. Launched by the 2000 Lisbon European Council, the Lisbon Agenda aims to create 'the most dynamic and competitive knowledge-based economy in the world capable of sustainable economic growth with more and better jobs and greater social cohesion, and respect for the environment by 2010'. The sustainable development and respect for the environment axis of the Lisbon Agenda was only later introduced as the third pillar of the Lisbon Agenda by the 2001 Stockholm European Council and the (June) Gothenburg

---

[9] See the Report of the High Level Working Group Chaired by Wim Kok, under mandate from the March 2004 European Council, which found there to have been little progress in the first five years of the Lisbon Agenda.

Summit three months later, which adopted the guiding principles.[10] These guiding principles include various operational objectives and targets in a broad range of areas,[11] including taking advantage of 'synergies' between the Lisbon priority of growth and jobs on the one hand, and the priority of sustainable development on the other. Moreover, the European Council endorsed the approach that the external dimension of sustainable development (e.g. global resource use, international development concerns) be factored into internal policy-making and there is a commitment to integrate sustainable development considerations into all EU's external policies.

The basis for this future action under this axis of the Lisbon Agenda is the Sustainable Development Strategy (SDS), which is rooted in the Commission's *The 2005 Review of the Sustainable Development Strategy: initial stocktaking and future orientations*[12] and should also be read alongside the *2004 Environmental Policy Review*[13] and the *Communication on Climate Change Policy*.[14] The European Commission's first progress report on the Lisbon Agenda[15] added to the Lisbon priorities,[16] the need to develop a common energy policy in the face of the global energy challenge, which is inextricably connected with sustainable development and environment concerns. Thus, EU efforts under the Lisbon Agenda and the SDS will play a key role in the evolution of the EU's environment policy, including its climate change initiatives, in its external relations. An obvious hindrance to Community level actions in energy matters is the lack of an energy chapter in the EC Treaty and energy policy is still regarded largely as the preserve of the Member States.[17] The Lisbon Treaty will introduce a new Title on Energy – see Conclusions below.

[10] See Council Press Release 10117/06, 9 June 2006.

[11] Climate change and clean energy, sustainable transport, sustainable consumption and production, conservation and management of natural resources, public health, social inclusion and demography and migration, global poverty and sustainable development challenges, cross-cutting policies contributing to the knowledge society, financing and economic instruments, communication and mobilising actors and multiplying success, implementation and monitoring and follow-up.

[12] See COM(2005)37.   [13] See COM(2005)17, OJ 2004 C 98.

[14] See COM(2005)35 together with COM(2007)37.

[15] See Commission Communication to the Spring European Council, *Working together for Growth and Jobs; a new start for the Lisbon Strategy*, COM(2005)24.

[16] These can be summed up as more investment in education and research, more support for SMEs and higher employment rates.

[17] Energy is included as one of the objectives of the Community (Art. 3(1)(u)) and under the environment title of the EC Treaty (Art. 175(2)) and in the context of trans-European networks, Articles 154, 155, 156 and 158 EC. The Constitutional Treaty would have introduced a distinct

16.1.4 The impact of third countries on the success
of Community action

Significantly, it has to be said that others of the world community look set to out-do the EU in terms of their economic growth and do not have in place adequate environment policies to accompany their growth. Some are experiencing exponential economic growth with alarming implications for the world's environment in the absence of strong national environment policies, the example of China being a case in point. Others have refused, for whatever reason, to take responsibility for their polluting behaviours: take for example the refusal of both the United States of America and Australia[18] to participate in the Kyoto Protocol.[19] Equally, this global situation threatens the usefulness and purpose of the EU's relationships with its neighbours, increasing the pressures on its borders in terms of immigration, access to water resources and so forth. Taking the Kyoto example again, failure to curb CO_2 emissions holds ominous implications for the African continent - for it is, among others, Africa's environment that will bear the brunt of industrialised nations' inability to curb their climate pollution while Africa will not experience such development itself.[20]

chapter on energy (Art. I-14(2)(i)) defining energy as a shared competence; Sect. 10, Art. III-256, the aims for the Union's policy on energy are: to ensure the functioning of the energy market; to ensure security of energy supply in the Union and; to promote energy efficiency and energy saving, and the development of new and renewable forms of energy.

[18] See the speech of Clive Hamilton, Director of the Australia Institute, *Speech to an Open Forum on International Environmental Governance*, Organised by the European Union Delegation in Australia, Sydney on 24 November 2006. Australia ratified on 12 December 2007.

[19] The 1997 Kyoto Protocol is a protocol to the 1992 UN Convention on Climate Change. It covers emissions of cabon dioxide, methane, nitrous oxide, sulphur hexafluoride, hydrofluorocarbons and perfluorocarbons. The Convention was approved by Council Decision 94/69 of 15 December 1993, OJ 1993 L 33/11. The Kyoto Protocol shares the Convention's objective, principles and institutions, but significantly strengthens the Convention by committing Annex I Parties to individual, legally-binding targets to limit or reduce their greenhouse gas emissions. Only Parties to the Convention that have also become Parties to the Protocol will be bound by it, i.e. by ratifying, accepting, approving, or acceding to it. The Kyoto Protocol was approved by Council Decision 2002/358 concerning the approval, on behalf of the European Community, of the Kyoto Protocol to the United Nations Framework Convention on Climate Change and the joint fulfilment of commitments thereunder, will commit the Community and its Member States to reducing their aggregate anthropogenic emissions of greenhouse gases listed in Annex A to the Protocol by 8 per cent compared to 1990 levels in the period 2008 to 2012.

[20] See N. Stern, *Review on the Economics of Climate Change*, 30 October 2006 (Cambridge: Cambridge University Press, 2006).

Consequently, it is also fair to conclude that the behaviour of neighbouring and other third countries as they undergo economic growth will play a crucial role in the ultimate positive or negative impact of the EU's green footprints on the world environment. Within the borders of the EU, Europe's environment will fall prey to the polluting behaviour of third countries and policy will have to be devised to cope. It is easy to predict then, that the EU is obliged to incorporate environmental concerns and conditionality in its external relations if its efforts to combat climate change for Europe's environment are not to be dwarfed by external factors. Ultimately, what is at stake is the EU's own economic development. Sir Nicholas Stern's 2006 *Review of the Economics of Climate Change*,[21] commissioned by the UK's then Chancellor Gordon Brown, carries a 'simple and apocalyptic message: climate change is fundamentally altering the planet; the risks of inaction are high; and time is running out'.[22] For the economy this means that the effects of climate change could cost the world between 5 per cent and 20 per cent of GDP, not to mention the human and health costs.

16.1.5 A new and ambitious Union energy strategy with a considerable external reach

The EU is responding on the international stage. In the field of energy policy, for example, the EU is increasing its consumption of fossil fuels at a time when it is already dependent on third-country imports, much of which is sourced in trouble spots, and struggling to tackle climate change effectively. The European Commission's 2006 Green Paper *A European Strategy for Sustainable, Competitive and Secure Energy*[23] has led to the first ever review of Community energy policy. The Strategic European Energy Review (SEER) was launched on 10 January 2007 and paves the way for a central European energy objective for the EU. Part and parcel of the SEER, which was endorsed by the European Council on 8 and 9 March 2007, is an integrated approach to climate change.[24] The core objective of the overall strategy is to achieve a 20 per cent reduction in greenhouse gas

---

[21] See previous note.
[22] See 'Simple verdict after complex inquiry: time is running out', *Guardian*, 31 October 2006.
[23] See COM(2006)105.
[24] See COM(2006)105, p. 10. The Council published its conclusions on 2 May 2007.

emissions from energy consumption by 2020 compared to 1990. The
European Parliament is pushing for a reduction of 30 per cent by 2020.[25]
Energy Commissioner Andris Piebalgs, presenting SEER at the official press
conference in Brussels on 10 January 2007, declared: 'If we take the right
decisions now, Europe can lead the world to a new industrial revolution:
the development of a low-carbon economy.'

In the accompanying Press Release, the challenge is summarised neatly:

> In energy specific terms, meeting this overall greenhouse gas target will
> require the EU to reduce the amount of CO_2 from its energy use by at least
> 20%, and probably more, within the next 13 years. But this will help
> transform Europe into a highly efficient and low CO_2 energy economy, able
> to face with confidence future energy challenges. It will mean the EU taking
> global leadership in catalysing a new industrial revolution, benefiting the
> developed and developing world alike, while accelerating the change to low-
> emission economic growth and dramatically increasing the amount of local,
> low-emission energy produced and used.

Conceptually, the *Energy Efficiency Action Plan* of 19 October 2006[26]
and the Commission Communication *External Energy Relations – from
principles to actions* of 12 October 2006,[27] should be considered part and
parcel of the SEER. The EU aims to reduce its external dependence on
energy products. It is designed to influence neighbouring European and
Mediterranean countries as well as the world energy policy and markets.
Energy efficiency and the expansion of the low-carbon economy both
internal and externally, are cited as explicit aims in the EU's external
relations alongside the completion of the Internal Market in energy and
the creation of new interconnections (oil and gas pipelines) outside the
EU's borders. The intention is made clear: the EU should use all its weight
in future bilateral relations and agreements to reach these goals by
offering 'balanced, market based solutions'. The aim is also to play a
greater role in the design of international agreements, such as the Kyoto
Protocol,[28] and to further develop Community participation in relevant
international fora.

---

[25] See European Parliament Resolution adopted 14 February 2007, P6_TA(2007)0038, debated
on 31 January 2007.
[26] Available at: http://www.ec.europa.eu/energy/action_plan_energy_efficiency/index_en.htm.
[27] Available at: http://www.ec.europa.eu/comm/external_relations/energy/docs/com06_590_en.pdf.
[28] See Commission Communication, *External Energy Relations – from principles to actions*, n. 27.

In addition, the SEER foresees a Road Map and other initiatives to promote renewables, including biofuels for transport and to explore a possible role for nuclear energy. Overarching the entire plan will be various initiatives to encourage technological innovation, and a European Energy Strategic Technology Plan is being drawn up to this effect.

The review of the EU's fledgling Emissions Trading System (ETS), which created a new Community currency in CO_2 emissions, is also fundamental to this strategy. The *External Energy Relations* Communication[29] sees the extension of the ETS, as well as other environment measures, to global trading partners as a means of contributing to the energy mix and therefore also to security of energy supplies.[30] This same Communication sets out the EU approach for negotiating the new comprehensive framework agreement in the context of the post-Partnership and Cooperation Agreement with Russia. It highlights the EU's concern to encourage Russia's compliance with its Kyoto commitments but also the breadth of safety, security and environmental aspects of its energy *acquis*, especially for trade in electricity, alongside the implementation of competition rules. The SEER also reaches out to other neighbouring countries in the Balkans and around the Mediterranean, the Caspian and Black Seas and foresees the use of European Investment Bank (EIB) and other financing instruments in energy cooperation with these countries.

As is seen below, the success of the system in terms of reducing CO_2 emissions lies in the balance and the ETS review will have to be daring if the ETS is indeed to make a real contribution to bringing about this new industrial revolution and the low-carbon economy. It will have to be all the more daring in light of the UN IPCC report of 2 February 2007,[31] which was written by international experts and is generally accepted as the most comprehensive review of climate change science to date. It will underpin international negotiations on new emissions targets to succeed the Kyoto agreement, the first phase of which expires in 2012. World governments were given a draft last year and invited to comment. Given that the predictions are worse than thought previously,[32] the revision of the ETS will have to be far more than superficial if this system is to leave any truly positive green footprint.

---

[29] See n. 27.   [30] See contribution by P. Van Elsuwege in this volume.
[31] See n. 2.   [32] *Ibid.*

16.2 EU external relations and the environment: recent trends

A survey of recent trends in the EU's external relations from an environment standpoint merits a book in itself. Some of the recent developments are too new to be evaluated yet. For example, in the last years the EU has stepped up its efforts to promote environmental concerns in its development policy following the focus of development policy on sustainable development as one of the Millennium Development Goals (MDG) at the UN Millennium Summit in 2000. With the adoption by the December 2005 General Affairs and External Relations European Council of the EU strategy for Africa,[33] the EU embarks on the process of establishing its new environment conditionality in its relations with countries of the region. It enters a new phase in its influence on world developments in pursuit of sustainable development and protection of the environment. In December 2005, the European Parliament, the Member States and the Commission reached a development policy consensus[34] which reinforced the mainstreaming of environmental concerns into all types of development programmes and projects, and made environment and natural resources one of nine priority sectors for funding. While it is too early to assess the effectiveness of the mainstreaming of the environmental concerns in development policy, the Commission is updating the 2001 Environment Integration Strategy[35] in the meantime, as well as improving the effectiveness and efficiency of its procedures and cooperation instruments.[36]

Certain developments in the EU's environment law and external relations stand out. This Part makes a brief introduction to the seven Thematic

---

[33] See Commission Press Release IP/05/1260 of 12 December 2005.

[34] The consensus reached by the General Affairs and External Relations Council of 21 and 22 November 2005, in agreement with the Commission, on a 'Joint Statement by the Council and the representatives of the Governments of the Member States meeting within the Council, the European Parliament and the Commission on European Union Development Policy: "*The European Consensus on Development*"'.

[35] The 31 May 2004 European Development Council adopted the first integration strategy (Art. 6 EC) calling for the integration of environmental considerations through policy issues and programming and stressing the importance of mainstreaming environment issues into the six priority areas of EU development cooperation, see Conclusions *Strategy for the Integration of Environmental Considerations in Development Policy to Promote Sustainable Development*, available at: http://www.fern.org/pubs/eudocs/integr.pdf.

[36] Of particular interest in this context is the Special Report 6/2006 of the European Court of Auditors on the Environmental Aspects of the Commission's Development Cooperation, together with the Commission's replies, OJ 2006 C 235/1.

Strategies (see 16.2.1 below) that guide today's environment law and policy generally before turning to a few highly topical developments in Community environment law, namely:

- the fifth and sixth enlargements (see 16.2.2 below);
- the judgment of the European Court of Justice (ECJ) to annul a Community Decision and accompanying Community Regulation concerning the Rotterdam Convention and the export of dangerous chemicals outside the EU, ('the PIC cases'), (see 16.2.3 below);
- the adoption of the REACH Programme, the Community based system for chemicals which will impact heavily on the world trade in chemicals (see 16.2.4 below), and;
- the Union's Emissions Trading System (ETS), operational since January 2005, which is the first supranational Market Based Instrument (MBI) of its kind in the world and the cornerstone instrument in the EU's 'European Climate Change Programme' which can be thought of as the EU's action plan for reaching its Kyoto Protocol[37] targets (see 16.2.5 below).

These examples have been selected because they provide ground for exploring certain key themes in the external relations dimension of Community environment law and policy. This gives an insight into how external relations figure in the anticipated future evolution in Community environment law and policy generally speaking (the seven Thematic Strategies). The benefits and drawbacks of extending the entire environment *acquis* to 12 new countries as a result of the enlargement of the EU, are explored. This same approach can be seen in the preparations of Turkey and the Western Balkans. On another tack, the Luxembourg judiciary has played its role in defining the balance between the Community's external trade rules with its (and its individual Member States') environment agenda (the PIC cases). The REACH Programme, in force since 1 June 2007, aims to take precautionary action in respect of potential or unknown future risks in chemicals and to adapt long established practices accordingly. It promises considerable knock-on effects for third countries and their industries. Lastly, the Emissions Trading System is an example of a Market Based Instrument (MBI), MBIs being generally recognised as essential instruments for environment policy and sustainable development.

[37] See n. 19.

The external impact of Community environment law is obviously affected by policy-making internally within the Community itself. In the overall aim of improving governance at Community level – including better/simplification of the regulatory environment – the input of stake-holders worldwide (industry, administrative authorities, consumers and Non-Governmental Organisations (NGOs), etc.) into the policy process has become increasingly apparent in recent years, including the tendency of the European Commission to publish in full all position papers received as part of the consultation. The impact assessment of policy and legisla-tive proposals and the broad public consultation promises a policy and regulatory environment fit for purpose. As will be seen in the context of the REACH programme in the EU, for example, the impact on inter-national production and trade in chemicals is anticipated to be enormous.

The recent developments in Community environment policy and law treated in this contribution, show how the Community is adopting instruments which will hold far-reaching and global consequences for third countries and their businesses, without waiting for those countries to act or without even fully consulting them as to their interests.

Overall, the Community's work on the environment has been under-pinned by the work of the European Environment Agency (EEAg). Before its establishment, the Commission would work from the approaches traditionally adopted by the Organisation for Economic Cooperation and Development (OECD), which had its limitations. It was in 1994 that the EEAg began to operate and the decade of its efforts since have made an invaluable contribution to the policy development at Community level. It aims to establish a seamless environmental information system to assist the Community in its environment policy work, including the EU's efforts to integrate environmental aspects into economic policies and interna-tional activities. This information has also been significant because it has provided a valuable basis for the assessment of the true costs of envir-onment action and inaction at Community and international level. The EEAg compiled the State of the Environment Reports in 1995[38] and again in 1997,[39] and the improvement compared to their predecessor Commission reports is obvious. As will be seen in the context of the seven

---

[38] See EEAg Report 1/1995, *Europe's Environment: the Dobris Assessment* (Copenhagen: EEAg, 1995).

[39] See EEAg Report 1/1998, *Europe's Environment: the Second Assessment* (Copenhagen: EEAg, 1998).

thematic strategies, such information has proved valuable to policy-makers to properly assess the true costs of continuing with current behaviour patterns compared to less polluting behaviour, as well as the true costs of harnessing advances in technology for example, and revising policy and regulation accordingly. The true costs of products and processes and consumption can be pinpointed. For administrations beyond EU borders, it also provides useful comparative material and models for action.

16.2.1 The seven thematic strategies

Broadly speaking, the overall direction of Community environment policy forges ahead with the implementation of the seven thematic strategies.

The Sixth Environment Action Programme broke away from the approach of its predecessor, the Fifth Environment Action Programme, in that it did not propose new quantifiable targets and timetables for fulfilment of its objectives. The earlier approach had weakened the effectiveness of the overall programme in areas where targets had not been agreed or because it was not clear which stakeholder was responsible for fulfilment.[40] The approach taken was to forge ahead with what are known as Thematic Strategies, all seven of which were adopted between September 2005 and September 2006.

By mid-2005, Commissioner Dimas came under heavy fire from his fellow Commissioners when he presented the Strategy on Air Pollution, because some of his colleagues feared that new legislative action in areas such as air pollution could give rise to high costs for industry and undermine the EU's ambitions to become the most competitive knowledge economy by 2010 (the 'Lisbon Agenda'). He won the day, however, by emphasising the costs of inaction compared to the benefits of acting now.[41] The seven thematic strategies cover a 20-year period and address:

---

[40] See European Commission, 'Global Assessment: Europe's Environment – what directions for the future?', Commission Communication on the global assessment of the European Community Programme of Policy and Action in Relation to the Environment and Sustainable Development, *Towards sustainability*', European Communities 2000.

[41] He pointed out that there will be costs to take action but the 'costs of inaction' are much larger: the benefits of our new Strategy are at least six times higher than the costs. The level of ambition chosen for the strategy has been estimated to deliver at least € 42 billion per annum in health benefits. Attainment of these targets is estimated to cost approximately € 7.1 billion per annum (representing about 0.05 per cent of EU-25 GDP in 2020); see Council Conclusions, *Bulletin EU*, 3/2006, 1.21.12.

- air pollution;[42]
- the marine environment;[43]
- prevention and recycling of waste;[44]
- the sustainable use of resources;[45]
- the urban environment;[46]
- pesticides and;[47]
- soil protection.[48]

Legislative actions thereunder have now to pass through the EC legislative processes. All seven have an external relations component, which underlines the interdependence of the global community in terms of the effects of economic activity on the environment and recognised transfrontier nature of the environment. Thus, for example, the Thematic Strategy on Soil Protection includes international actions in order to reach its objectives in soil protection: in addition to the many other elements of the Thematic Strategy, the Commission is to ensure that the initiatives taken under the United Nations Convention to Combat Desertification and the United Nations Convention on Biological Diversity as well as under the Kyoto Protocol and the Alpine Convention, are 'mutually supportive, consistent and complementary' with the Community Thematic Strategy.[49]

---

[42] Commission Communication, *Thematic Strategy on Air Pollution*, COM(2005)446 of 21 September 2005, see also the unanimous Environment Council Decision of 9 March 2006 adopting Council Conclusions on the Thematic Strategy on Air Pollution, Council Press Release 7329/06.

[43] See Commission Communication, *Thematic Strategy on Protection and Conservation of the Marine Environment*, COM(2005)1290. A proposed Directive under this strategy is in the legislative pipeline; see proposal for a Directive of the European Parliament and of the Council establishing a framework for Community action in the field of Marine Environmental Policy, COM(2005)505.

[44] See Commission Communication, *Thematic Strategy on the Prevention and Recycling of Waste*, COM(2005)666, together with the accompanying proposal for a Directive of the European Parliament and of the Council on Waste, COM(2005)667. This eventual Directive will revise the Waste Framework Directive (as codified by Directive 2006/12) in order to set recycling standards and to include an obligation for EU Member States to develop national waste prevention programmes. It will also merge, streamline and clarify legislation, contributing to better regulation.

[45] See Commission Communication, *Thematic Strategy on the Sustainable Use of Natural Resources*, COM(2005)670.

[46] See Commission Communication, *Thematic Strategy on the Urban Environment*, COM(2006)718.

[47] See Commission Communication, *Thematic Strategy on the Sustainable Use of Pesticides*, COM (2006)327.

[48] See Commission Communication, *Thematic Strategy for Soil Protection*, COM(2006)231.

[49] See the *Thematic Strategy for Soil Protection*, previous note, p. 12.

16.2.2 The fifth and sixth enlargements

In terms of its external relations, the biggest geographical green footstep of the EU recently has been the EU's fifth enlargement on 1 May 2004 followed by its sixth on 1 January 2007. By enlarging to take in 12 new Member States, the EU has increased the diversity of its environment. In the first place, from early in the 1990s, the environment had been a major preoccupation of the EU in its relations with the fledgling democracies. The Central and East European Countries (CEECs) both suffered the disastrous legacy of unregulated industrial development of the Communist era but also benefited from vast tracts of untouched biodiversity and forest that are vital to the health of Europe's environment.

The PHARE technical assistance and funding and then the vast approximation exercise of the pre-accession preparations by the 12 new Member States, can be commended for the contribution to the evolution of environment policy and law as well as structural improvements in the environments of neighbouring countries. Of course, this was necessary in order to prepare these countries for the obligations of membership in terms of compliance with the *acquis*. The new Member States were obliged to transpose the *acquis* in its entirety into national law as well as to implement it and guarantee its enforcement before the date of their accession. Also, of course, it was necessary in order to help these countries limit the environmental costs of economic growth once fully fledged Member States.

However, at one and the same time it is important to emphasise that adopting and enforcing the environment *acquis* cannot and is not intended to substitute national environment policies and action, which contribute to the overall health of Europe's environment. Long before the pre-accession strategy was properly in place, the EEAg was already questioning the appropriateness of the *acquis* for the new Member States' environments.[50] Moreover, it is fair to say that there is plenty of room for the introduction of beneficial EC initiatives which have been obstructed by the Member States themselves, such as has been the case in respect of the Commission's proposed Directive on criminal penalties for breaches of environment law.

---

[50] See EEAg Report, *Europe's Environment: The Second Assessment* (Copenhagen: EEAg, 1998), pp. 7 *et seq.*

Under the fifth and sixth Accession Treaties[51] bringing in the 12 new Member States on 1 May 2004 and then again on 1 January 2007, there are a limited number of transitional arrangements giving the new Member States time within which to bring themselves fully into line with the environment chapter of the *acquis communautaire*. The transitional arrangements are not generally applicable, they do not give the new Member States any dispensation from the obligation to transpose the law concerned (only for the temporary non-application in given circumstances) and they are always limited in time and scope; there are no permanent derogations from a given law.

In the case of the environment *acquis*, the transitional arrangements contained in the relevant Accession Treaties are more designed to enable these countries to attract the necessary external financing for the structural investments required in order to meet the obligations of the environment *acquis*. For example, in some cases waste and water infrastructure has had to be built from scratch. While the situation of nuclear installations is not a matter for the environment *acquis* proper, there are obvious environment implications of such installations. These include the special funding and provisions concerning the upgrade or closure and dismantling of such installations which even go beyond what is required of the 15 Member States (being those that made up the EU prior to the enlargement of 1 May 2004).

These transitional arrangements have not allowed the new Member States to delay in adopting the relevant directives or regulations into national law. Nor do they allow the new Member States to escape from their obligations as Member States to comply with those same laws beyond the limits stipulated in the transitional arrangement. Thus the new Member States are obliged to put in place the necessary administrative and judicial capacity in order to so comply.

But it can be said that the EU's enlargements to take in the ten CEECs, as well as Malta and Cyprus, will carry positive environment footprints on neighbouring countries, which will in turn contribute to the EU's overall impact on the wider global environment. The benefits of the EU's last two

---

[51] See Accession Treaty of 16 April 2003 (with the Czech Republic, Estonia, Latvia, Lithuania, Hungary, Cyprus, Malta, Poland, Slovenia, Slovakia), OJ 2003 L 236/1, last amended by process verbal, OJ 2007 L 60/1 (referred to as 'the Fifth Accession Treaty') and Accession Treaty of 25 April 2005 (Bulgaria and Romania), OJ 2005 L 157/1 (referred to as 'the Sixth Accession Treaty').

enlargements are predicted to be enormous[52] purely in terms of the adoption of the *acquis* measures that they took on board in order to be able to accede to the EU. However, this does not detract from the over-riding caveat that economic development always impacts negatively on the environment. Moreover, it is too early to predict the behaviour of the new Member States in decision-making and in the future implementation and compliance with the environment *acquis*. The uncertainties high-lighted by the European Commission in its *Agenda 2000* document of 1997 remain. It is not clear whether the new Member States will resist raising standards at Community level in order to concentrate on meeting their transitional arrangements and other socio-economic priorities. It is too early to draw conclusions on the impact of enlargement on Community decision-making in environment protection and sustainable development initiatives at Community level in order to determine any positive or negative evolution in Community environment law.

16.2.3 The ECJ on the evolution of community environment law: the PIC cases

The ECJ has a strong influence on the balance that has to be struck between the Community's (external) trade policy and its environment policy. Two recent and interrelated cases stand out in this regard, Cases C-94/03 *Commission* v. *Council*[53] and C-178/03 *Commission* v. *European Parliament and Council*,[54] referred to here as the two PIC Judgments to reflect the Prior Informed Consent system set up under the Rotterdam Convention and subsequently enacted into Community law – see further. These cases not only point to a shift in the political importance attributed to environmental concerns in the EU's trade relations with third countries but threaten to increase tensions between trade and environment concerns in the imple-mentation of the Common Commercial Policy (CCP), traditionally a sacred cow of exclusive Community competences and the fiercely guarded preserve of the European Commission in its management. These cases open the door to unilateral actions by the Member States in their external relations

---

[52] See European Commission external service contract report, *The benefits of compliance with the environmental acquis for the candidate countries and their preparations for accession*, carried out by Ecotec Research and Consulting Limited, 2000.

[53] Case C-94/03 [2006] ECR I-1.   [54] Case C-178/03 [2006] ECR I-107.

to restrict trade in hazardous chemicals and pesticides, provided that those actions can be justified on environmental grounds, even if such actions would bring about trade or competition distortions between undertakings of the Member States in external markets.

In its two PIC decisions of 10 January 2006, the ECJ annulled two Community measures approving and giving effect to the Rotterdam Convention on the Prior Informed Consent Procedure for certain hazardous chemicals and pesticides in international trade ('the Rotterdam Convention'). These two actions centred on the legal bases for the measures, the first being the Council's Decision[55] concerning the approval of the Rotterdam Convention ('the Council Decision') and the second being the implementing Regulation of the European Parliament and the Council ('the 2003 PIC Regulation').[56]

The 2003 PIC Regulation, like its predecessor Regulation 2455/92 of 1992,[57] put in place a system of Prior Informed Consent. Basically, any EU country that exports hazardous chemicals and pesticides to another EU Member State or to a third country, has to send that other country certain information on those chemicals or pesticides and has also to obtain the consent of the importing country prior to export. The Rotterdam Convention was adopted in 1998 and built upon the earlier Community system but goes further in that it foresees certain circumstances where the Parties are able to take more stringently protective action in order to protect human health and the environment beyond that envisaged in the Convention. The new Regulation also aims to extend the 1967 and 1999 Directives on the classification, packaging and labelling of dangerous substances and preparations[58] to chemicals that are exported beyond the EU.

While the European Commission had proposed that the Council Decision and the 2003 PIC Regulation be based on the EC Treaty Article for the CCP, namely Article 133 EC, the European Parliament and the Member States in Council chose instead to proceed using the legal basis for environment measures, Article 175(1) EC which had been the (sole) legal basis for the previous system as set out in Council Regulation 2455/92, then Article 130s EC Treaty. In its proposals for the new instruments

---

[55] Decision 2003/106 of 19 December 2002 concerning the approval on behalf of the European Community of the Rotterdam Convention, OJ 2003 L 63/27.

[56] Regulation 304/2003 concerning the export and import of dangerous chemicals, OJ 2003 L 63/1.

[57] OJ 1992 L 251/13, as last amended by Regulation 2247/98, OJ 1998 L 282/12.

[58] The 1999 Directive amended Directive 67/548, OJ 1967 196/1. See also REACH, n. 61.

approving and implementing the Rotterdam Convention, the Commission did not see that the new aims and objectives brought these measures beyond their core, essential purpose of regulating the rules and procedures for the international trade of certain hazardous chemicals.

The ECJ neither agreed with the Commission on the one hand, nor with the Parliament and the Member States/Council on the other, and declared that both the 2003 Decision and the 2003 Regulation should have been based jointly on Article 133 and 175(1) EC. In the past the ECJ has dealt with various cases concerning the appropriate legal basis for Community measures in implementation of international commitments. The ECJ's decision that the measures should be based on both of these legal bases at first appears consistent with previous case law:[59] the ECJ took account of the evolution of the Rotterdam Convention in terms of its trade implications as well as its aim to give greater protection for human health and environment. It judged the two objectives to be equally important so that the classical approach (that the lead legal basis absorbs the other) does not apply. The ECJ concluded, at paragraph 51 in Case 94/13, that:

> Having regard to all the foregoing considerations, and as is also clear from the express terms of the eighth recital in the preamble to the Convention, according to which the commercial and environmental policies of the parties to the Convention should be mutually supportive with a view to achieving sustainable development, it must therefore be concluded that the Convention includes, both as regards the aims pursued and its contents, two indissociably linked components, neither of which can be regarded as secondary or indirect as compared with the other, one falling within the scope of the common commercial policy and the other within that of protection of human health and the environment.

This new situation holds certain other practical implications for environment law. In the longer term, however, this dual legal basis bodes of a new situation of increasing tension between the CCP and Member States' environmental standards in the context of the PIC system. Whereas the Commission enjoys a considerable competence in the implementation of

---

[59] For a comprehensive legal analysis of legal bases and the rationale of the Court when determining the appropriate legal basis, see M. Maresceau, 'Bilateral Agreements concluded by the European Community' *Collected Courses of the Academy of International Law*, 2006, vol. 309, pp. 149–202; see also S. Adam, 'Cour de Justice, 10 janvier 2006, Aff. C-94/03 and C-178/03', *Revue des Affaires Européennes* (2006), pp. 127–35.

the CCP, under the legal basis for environment policy the Member States are able to take their own stricter national standards (albeit subject to procedural requirements and other conditions, including of course that they must be justified and proportionate to the objective sought, and that they are not merely disguised restrictions on trade). This reasoning has not gone without criticism. In particular, the ECJ's reasoning has been criticised for being out of line with its previous reasoning in Opinion 2/00 on the Cartagena Protocol on biosafety.[60] It can also be criticised for damaging the EU's external face towards third countries in terms of its commitment to environment protection.

The room for trade disputes is clear, both at Community and international levels. The fact that REACH introduces a programme for the registration of chemicals and will take into account the health and environmental hazards of chemicals generally, ought in the longer term to help dilute future tensions between trade and health/environment interests in the context of the Community's PIC system. Once the REACH Regulation[61] comes into effect and the new European Chemicals Agency is up and running, it will manage the information that will be disclosed to the third countries under the replacement rules for the 2003 PIC system[62] in respect of chemicals information in its possession.[63]

16.2.4 REACH

Many industrial chemicals once thought to have been safe are now known to be capable of causing serious harm to human health and the

---

[60] For a critical analysis, see P. Koutrakos, 'Case C-94/03: Case C-178/03', 44 CMLRev. (2007), pp. 171/94. See also A. Dashwood, 'Opinion 2/00, Cartegena Protocol on Biosafety', 39 CMLRev. (2003), pp. 353–68.

[61] See Regulation 1907/2006, OJ 2006 L 396/1. REACH will work in conjunction with Council Directive 67/548 on the approximation of the laws, regulations and administrative provisions relating to the classification, packaging and labelling of dangerous substances, OJ 1967 196/1, as last amended by Commission Directive 2004/73, OJ 2004 L 152/1 as corrected in OJ 2004 L 216/3, as well as Directive 1999/45/EC concerning the approximation of the laws, regulations and administrative provisions of the Member States relating to the classification, packaging and labelling of dangerous preparations, OJ 1999 L 200/1, as last amended by Commission Directive 2006/8, OJ 2006 L 19/12.

[62] Or, alternatively, under Article 181a EC which is the legal basis for economic, financial and technical cooperation with third countries.

[63] See Regulation 1907/2006, Article 120 on cooperation with third countries and international organisations, n. 60, p. 218.

environment.[64] Some industrial chemicals have novel molecular compositions and structures that can make them hazardous to people and the environment. Some accumulate in living organisms and cause damage to the nervous system, to reproductive capacity and hormone systems, and also to the natural environment.[65]

The highly controversial and ambitious EC rules that will overhaul the regime for the registration, evaluation, authorisation and restrictions on the sale and use of chemicals, were adopted on 18 December 2006.[66] Known as 'the REACH programme', it proved to be the target of the biggest ever lobbying offensive[67] – on a par only with the services Directive – as much by third-country chemicals companies as by the EU chemicals industry.

There are some 3,000 chemicals currently on the Internal Market that have been registered under the relevant Internal Market rules. These are basically those chemicals that have come on to the Internal Market since 1981. But 99 per cent of all the chemicals on the Internal Market are not registered. Scientific evidence of chemical contamination of air, water, soil and the human environment has led the Community legislature to take action to preserve biodiversity and safeguard the health of workers' and citizens' health and safety. This is to be balanced with the goals of a competitive, innovative and job-creating European industry and the proper functioning of the Internal Market.

The REACH proposal aims to provide for the registration of all chemicals that have not so far been regulated by Community law, which will cost

---

[64] See EEAg, *Late lessons from early warnings: the precautionary principle 1896–2000*, Denmark, EEAg, 2001; see also the joint publication of the EEAg/United Nations Environment Programme, *Chemicals in the environment: low doses, high stakes*, Denmark, EEAg, 1998.

[65] See European Commission, *Extended Impact Assessment of the Economic, Social and Environmental impacts of the New Chemicals Policy Proposals*, SEC(2003) 1171/3, 29 October 2003.

[66] Regulation 1907/2006 of the European Parliament and of the Council of 18 December 2006 concerning the Registration, Evaluation, Authorisation and Restriction of Chemicals (REACH), establishing a European Chemicals Agency, amending Directive 1999/45 and repealing Council Regulation 793/93 and Commission Regulation 1488/94 as well as Council Directive 76/769 and Commission Directives 91/155, 93/67, 93/105 and 2000/21, OJ 2006 L 396/1-850. It is accompanied by Directive 2006/121 of the European Parliament and of the Council of 18 December 2006 amending Council Directive 67/548 on the approximation of laws, regulations and administrative provisions relating to the classification, packaging and labelling of dangerous substances in order to adapt it to Regulation 1907/2006 concerning the Registration, Evaluation, Authorisation and Restriction of Chemicals (REACH) and establishing a European Chemicals Agency, OJ 2006 L 396/850.

[67] See 'Bulldozing REACH: the industry offensive to crush EU chemicals regulation', *Corporate Europe Observatory*, March 2005, http://www.corporateeurope.org/lobbycracy/BulldozingREACH.html.

industry anything between € 4.3 (Commission estimates) and € 230 billion (industry estimates). It effectively transfers the burden of proof of the safety of a chemical from the Member States to industry. REACH is intended to rationalise the existing Community system and will involve replacing or amending over 40 laws that make up the EC chemicals *acquis*, in order to provide a single system for all chemical substances.

To illustrate the ambitiousness of REACH, it will require any company that manufactures or imports more than one tonne of a chemical substance per year to register the chemical in a central database. Failure to register will mean a chemical cannot be manufactured or imported into the Community. The European Chemicals Agency will be established and has considerably greater powers than was first envisaged in the original proposal. The manufacturer or importer will have to provide scientific data as a precondition to selling a chemical. Any data furnished should include information on the intrinsic properties and risks of each substance and the identified uses of the substance. Data submissions requirements would address what environmental groups have called 'a major failing of environmental policy' so far – that is to say, the inability of governments to require a chemicals manufacturer to provide basic data on the potential health and environmental hazards of the chemicals that they produce and sell.

The list goes on: the management of (potential) risks arising in relation to a chemical would involve obligations such as ventilation in the workplace or protective clothing in occupational settings; EU institutions will hold powers to introduce restrictions on any substance that poses an unacceptable risk, such as partial bans on the use of a product, or how the product can be used by consumers, or even total bans on that chemical.

Being a Regulation, REACH will not require transposition into national law. It takes effect on 1 June 2007, although the breadth of its provisions will only enter into force progressively over a ten year time frame. Thus, the European Chemicals Agency should become operational by June 2008, the pre-registration of phase-in substances is foreseen between June and November 2008, the registration deadline for substances in quantities of over 1,000 tonnes and certain carcinogens, mutagens and chemicals toxic to reproduction is set for December 2010, the registration deadline for substances in quantities of over 100 tonnes is set for June 2013 and the registration deadline for substances in quantities of over 1 tonne is set for June 2018. Guidance and IT tools for industry, whether with registration or as users of chemicals, are anticipated for the entry into force of the REACH Regulation in June 2007.

The US has responded in two ways throughout the remarkable, mammoth lobbying exercise that surrounded the progress of the proposal[68] to the ultimate Regulation. First, a draft bill 'Child, Worker and Consumer Safe Chemicals Act' was proposed following the report by the US Government Accountability Office (GAO). It came after a 2004 US Senate Report which detailed the tactics used by the Bush administration and the US chemicals industry to amend the EU's REACH programme and which was outwardly critical of it as a costly, burdensome and complex regulatory system. In this report the GAO recommended that the US Environment Protection Agency (US EPA) be given additional powers to assess chemical risks. The GAO justified its recommendation by highlighting the failures of the US 1976 Toxic Substances Control Act (TSCA) in protecting Americans from hazardous chemicals. In particular, the EPA has to prove that a chemical poses an 'unreasonable risk' before it can be restricted or banned. The GAO emphasised that the procedures under the TSCA are so daunting that only five toxic substances have been regulated by the US EPA since 1976.

Second, the US State Department has brought a complaint concerning (June 2005) the WTO compatibility[69] of the REACH proposal on the grounds that REACH will distort global markets. Their major concerns are that importers will bear the greater burden compared to EU manufacturers in part because REACH only provides the possibility for EU manufacturers to gain exemption from the registration of chemical substances. The argument is that the obligation to register chemical substances will in itself amount to a technical barrier to trade contrary to the Technical Barriers to Trade (TBT) Agreement. The *demarche* by the US State Department in 2003, was followed by notification under the TBT Agreement[70] and characterised REACH as an 'obstacle to trade' which will distort global markets. Japan also submitted documents to the WTO and the list of countries that are objecting to it is long, including China. But the Community maintains that REACH is fully TBT compatible.[71] The

---

[68] See COM(2003)644.

[69] See United States' Foreign Trade Association, *FTA position on REACH 2005*, available at: http://www.fta-eu.org/doc/unp/opinion/en/ftapositionreach2005en.pdf.

[70] File G/TBT/N/EEC/52

[71] REACH was notified to the WTO under file G/TBT/N/EEC/52add.3 on 22 January 2007.

main reason for this assertion is that REACH applies to EU and non-EU producers alike; most WTO members have national legislation that non-nationals have to comply with; as far as confidentiality is concerned, non-EU manufacturers can appoint an 'only representative';[72] the Commission is preparing guidance materials for all companies concerned, irrespective of nationality. Overall, the Community justifies REACH on the grounds that it is to ensure risks from substances of very high concern are properly controlled and that they are substituted if possible.

The Community's notification of REACH is still open for comments before the WTO at the moment of writing. REACH may well prove to be the next big battle at the WTO level. In the meantime, importers and third-country operators are directly implicated in REACH. Ultimately, chemicals that are produced and marketed in their own countries may be prevented from being placed on the market in the Community and subject to marketing and the full breadth of other requirements.

16.2.5 MBIs and external relations: the example of the emissions trading system

The ETS, touched on above in the context of the EU's energy initiatives and the Lisbon Agenda, is one of a number of Community level Market Based Instruments. Market Based Instruments (MBIs) are used for 'harnessing market forces' to environmental ends[73] and basically, to the environmental cost of processes and products into their overall costs, the logic being that without incorporating the environmental and human health costs into consumption patterns, the costs of processes and products are distorted. MBIs often complement or reinforce regulation and policy objectives in whatever form they take – taxes; fees and charges; subsidies; tradable permits; eco-labelling; financial mechanisms; and liability and compensation schemes – and for whichever purpose they are designed, whether to curb polluting behaviour for example or to encourage more conscientious consumption.[74]

---

[72] See Regulation 1907/2006, Article (6)(a).

[73] See Reports of the OECD for 1998, 1991 and 1998, available at: http://www.rff.org/Documents/RFF-DP-03-43.pdf.

[74] See the study commissioned by the European Commission, *The Use of Market Incentives to Preserve Biodiversity*, available at: http://www.ec.europa.eu/environment/enveco/studies2.htm. This study examines 204 examples of market-based instruments currently being used to

For the moment it has to be concluded that the ETS is of limited success in terms of positive impacts on the environment and human health.

The Community CO_2 Emissions Trading System (ETS) was launched in January 2005 with the entry into force of Directive 2003/87.[75] There were already examples of such schemes in operation in individual countries, the first being that of the UK in 2002.[76] It is the first EU-wide market based instrument of its kind in the world to have been adopted by a Regional Integration and which, while confined to the EU, has been unashamedly devised by the EU as a model for third countries and the creation of a global CO_2 emissions trading system. A variety of mechanisms that are being put to the test at EU level will, it is intended, act as peer examples to other industrialised countries, including the non-participants, such as the US. But, overall, the EC approach to reaching its commitments under the 1997 (UN) Kyoto Protocol is one that applies a proactive environmental model to third countries operating both within the EU territory and even those that are somehow coming into contact with the Internal Market.[77] Directive 2003/87 expressly provides for emissions trading by the EU Member States with other Parties to Kyoto and links the Community scheme to greenhouse gas emission trading schemes in third countries with the intention of increasing the cost-effectiveness of achieving the overall Community reductions targets under Kyoto. There is also the incentive to third country operators to participate in this new EU market for trading in CO_2 emissions, together with the incentives of installing more efficient technology.

The ETS is the cornerstone instrument in the EU's 'European Climate Change Programme' which can be thought of as the EU's action plan for reaching its Kyoto targets.[78] The Kyoto Protocol sets down binding limits

---

preserve biodiversity including: taxes, fees and charges; subsidies; tradable permits; eco-labelling; financial mechanisms; and liability and compensation schemes. Overall, the evidence is that well-designed and credibly implemented instruments that are tailored to local needs are able to deliver biodiversity objectives cost-efficiently. Many of the examples of market based instruments show that they work best not as a substitute to regulatory approaches, but complementary to them. Certainly, there seems to be wider scope for their application and a number of recommendations are made on how to use them most efficiently.

[75] OJ 2003 L 275/1 as last amended by Directive 2004/101. The consolidated is available at: http://www.eur-lex.europa.eu/LexUriServ/site/en/consleg/2003/L/02003L0087-20041113-en.pdf.

[76] The UK Greenhouse Gas Trading Scheme was established in 2002 pursuant to the UK Pollution Prevention and Control Act 1999, as amended.

[77] OJ 2002 C 75 E/33.   [78] See n. 24.

for the greenhouse gas emissions of each participating (industrialised) country (not US, Australia, Liechtenstein and Monaco). Through the ETS the EU has established a brand-new supranational market in emissions allowances with a value of € 4 billion, by creating a new currency for trading based on tonnes of CO_2. The EU openly declares this innovative market approach to tackling the problem of climate change to be a model for the development of a global market in emissions of greenhouse gases. The EU holds to this aspiration even in the face of the non-participation of the United States in the Kyoto system, a position that seems to be changing recently.[79]

The rationale and means of the ETS show innovative thinking and mark a new era in the interdependence of economic development and environment concerns at international level. The use of such an MBI marks a departure away from regulating polluting emissions and the behaviour of a company, for example. Basically, the Directive fixes the overall amount of emissions that any Member State is allowed to make and then allows them to trade any emissions that they do not use among each other. It is particularly innovative because for the first time, on the one hand, the Member States' governments set the environment goals in their own national plans – crucially important to these plans is the fact that they are established with the meaningful participation of corporate and civil society – while on the other hand, the Member States and the Commission must then stand back and allow business to decide how and where they will reduce the emissions in reaction to the market.

The Commission's role is to manage the system. In a recent judgment of the Court of First Instance, in Case T-178/05[80] brought by the UK against the Commission, the role and powers of the European Commission and the Member States have been clarified. It also emphasised the need for balance between the needs of the economy and economic development and employment. In particular, the CFI made clear that Member States, within certain limits, may exceed their national emissions allowances allocation. While the Commission manages the quotas, it is restricted from preventing Member States from exceeding their quotas where, after public consultation, errors have been found in the National Allocations Plans, for instance, or new information comes to light. But the Commission

---

[79] See 'The Greening of America' in *The Economist*, 27 January 2007, p. 9.
[80] CFI 23 November 2005 in Case T-178/05, *United Kingdom* v. *Commission* [2005] ECR II-4807.

may still assess the amendments to National Allocation Plans for their compatibility with the Directive. Future revisions to the system take this decision into account but nevertheless it is the Member States that must fix the threshold of national allowances before the trading period and they may not add to or subtract allocated allowances from the quantity determined for each operator or according to some pre-determined rule.[81] This approach is consistent with the Kyoto commitments, which, after all, are binding at international level. But this approach is not easy and the future is not certain: for example, already Slovakia has challenged the Commission's cap on its national emissions limit and argues that the EU has no competence to dictate how national quotas are calculated.[82]

The ETS certainly needs revision if the Kyoto commitments are to be reached.[83] The ETS covers almost 11,500 industrial installations, which combined account for between 46 per cent and 51 per cent of total greenhouse gas emissions in the 25 EU Member States. The problem with the ETS is that emissions have not fallen because companies were given too many permits generally speaking and also that, in general, the permits were given away rather than auctioned[84] – which is tantamount to rewarding the polluters with 'windfall profits'.[85] The problems with the National Allocation Plans[86] in the first phase, to end-2007, mean that a considerable number of the Member States were exceeding the emissions that they were actually allowed in line with their national Kyoto targets. Austria, Beligum, Denmark, Finland, Germany, Ireland, Italy, Luxembourg, the Netherlands, Portugal, Slovenia and Spain are not sufficiently on track to meeting their Kyoto targets. The task of the Commission to reach the Kyoto commitments is not made easier by challenges brought by the Member States, such as in the case of Slovakia above, in order to raise their national emission limits – Slovakia is seeking a 41.1 million tonne limit for CO_2 emissions

---

[81] See COM(2006)725.

[82] Challenge lodged with the CFI on 7 February 2007, see 'Slovakia sues Commission over emissions cap', available at: http://www.EurActiv.com.

[83] See *Greenhouse Gas Emissions: Trends and Projections in Europe 2006*, Technical Report 9/2006, (Copenhagen: EEAg, 2006).

[84] See *Application of the Emissions Trading Directive by EU Member States*, Technical Report 2/2006 (Copenhagen: EEAg, 2006), p. 30. Only four Member States (Denmark, Hungary, Ireland and Lithuania) intend to allocate allowances by means of auctioning while two others are still developing rules for auctioning.

[85] See *The Economist*, 27 January 2007, p. 9.

[86] See Commission Communication, *Further guidance on allocation plans for the 2008 to 2012 trading period of the EU emissions trading scheme*, COM(2005)703.

where the Commission has foreseen a cap on its emissions of 30.9 million tonnes.

The knock-on effect of all this is to discourage investment in alternatives rather than to promote clean energy products.

Finally, the long term legal certainty of the ETS is undermined by uncertainty as to the future of Kyoto after 2012 and how the US in particular will proceed. The long-term global playing field is not clear, which further undermines the investment in alternative technologies and energy sources or carbon capture technologies for example, all of which have a long term gestation period for research and development.[87]

Can the EU redeem this situation? The various options for improving the ETS are under preparation. The first review of the ETS is due by 30 June 2007 and will pave the way for legislative revision of the ETS in the second half of 2007, but this will not take effect until the third phase of the ETS, which begins in 2013. The extension of the ETS to include other activities, notably the chemicals, aluminium and transport sectors, has been proposed together with non-CO_2 greenhouse gases.[88]

In the meantime, the National Allocation Plans were to be submitted on 30 June 2006 for the second phase (the trading period 2008 to 2012). The Commission Decisions of 29 November 2007[89] aim to ensure consistent and correct application of the system and ultimately also to ensure that there is sufficient scarcity of allocations to make it feasible to reach the Kyoto reductions. These only address ten of the 25 Member States (Bulgaria and Romania were not Member States at the time) because the other Member States either had not submitted sufficient or adequate data for evaluation, or the data supplied was insufficient for the purposes of evaluation. Those countries that had not submitted plans at all were the subject of infringement proceedings, launched on 12 October 2006.

In parallel, a sector-based MBI is being put into place at EC level for the airline industry[90] because the progress of the EU Member States under the

---

[87] See EEAg Technical Reports 2 and 9 of 2006, ns. 84 and 85.

[88] See European Commission Directorate General for Environment/Ecofys, *Inclusion of additional activities and gases into the EU-emissions trading scheme: Report under the project 'review of the EU Emissions Trading Scheme'*, October 2006.

[89] See COM(2006)725.

[90] See Proposal for a Directive of the European Parliament and of the Council amending Directive 2003/87 so as to include aviation activities in the scheme for greenhouse gas emission allowance trading within the Community, COM(2006)818.

ETS towards their Kyoto targets, is under threat of being wiped out by the emissions increases as a result of the boom in short haul 'bucket shop' airlines and the tendency in tourist culture to take long haul flights. The proposal has only just entered (February 2007) the Community legislative decision-making process and is unlikely to be adopted before 2008. The European Commission proposes to fix the number of emission allowances for each airline in order to cap their greenhouse gas emissions on international flights. The proposal reads:

> The objective of this proposal is to provide a model for aviation emissions trading that can be a point of reference in the EU's contacts with key international partners and to promote the development of similar systems worldwide. The Commission also supports the objective of a global agreement aimed at effectively tackling aviation emissions at global level.

As the proposal reads today, as of 1 January 2012, this law will apply to all flights leaving EU airports regardless of their nationality. To limit the system to intra-EU flights, that take off and land in the EU, would not address even 40 per cent of the emissions of all flights departing from the EU. Aircraft operators will be responsible under the ETS and the greenhouse gases which will be 'capped' include emissions which are not even recognised by the International Civil Aviation Organisation (ICAO).

Consequently, the ETS has been conceived of as a platform for the extension of the ETS on the global stage, in order to stimulate international efforts to combat climate change. However, its shortcomings undermine its potential as a truly effective green instrument at global level. The ETS has been limited from the outset and certain inherent failings in its design have limited its positive impact on emissions reductions within the EU, which then translated to the global level. As already noted above, the success of the system in terms of reducing CO_2 emissions lies in the balance and the ETS review will have to be daring if the ETS is indeed to make a real contribution to bringing about this new industrial revolution and the development of a truly low-carbon economy.

16.3 Conclusions

Recent trends in the external dimension of EC environment law that have been identified in this contribution relate to the general environment policy, in the context of today's hot topics of the Lisbon Agenda and energy, the impact of enlargement and the contribution of the ECJ to the balance between environmental concerns and international trade. Two regulatory developments are also explored briefly (REACH and emissions trading). These examples stand out because, in addition to being innovative mechanisms, they will directly affect third-country legislatures and businesses. They illustrate the global ambitions of the EU on the world stage to take the lead in curbing the trends of environmental degradation that have already ensued economic development or that can now be predicted in third countries only now experiencing economic growth.

Generally speaking, there was a marked lack of an external dimension to Community environment policy and law before the landmark 1992 European Commission Communication *The State of the Environment in the European Community.*[91] The crucial importance of the external dimension of Community actions to protect and preserve human health and the environment was then reflected in the Fifth and then the Sixth Environment Action Programmes.[92] With the Sixth Environment Action Programme, in place for the years 2002 to 2012, the policy direction and the tasks that the Member States and EU institutions have set themselves, display the global ambitions of the Community environment policy of today. In particular, while the Sixth Environment Action Programme follows the Fifth, it has shifted from a legislative approach to a strategic approach using a whole range of instruments and measures to influence decisions made by business, consumers, policy planners and citizens. This is a departure from the previous approach of concentrating on certain pollutants or types of economic activity.

Seven Thematic Strategies work to tackle four major areas for action: climate change; nature and biodiversity; environment and health; sustainable use of natural resources and management of wastes. The Thematic Strategies address air pollution; the marine environment; prevention and recycling of waste; the sustainable use of resources; the urban environment; pesticides and; soil protection. All of them comprise an external relations component, which underlines the interdependence of the global community in terms of the effects of economic activity on the environment and recognised trans-frontier nature of the environment. Indeed, the integration of environmental concerns into all aspects of the EU's external relations is an objective of the Sixth Environment Action Programme. The

[91] See n. 1.   [92] See n. 8.

application of international agreements on the environment is strongly encouraged in all external relations now and the Sustainable Development Strategy will reflect these concerns. As for determining the green footprints left as a result of the Thematic Strategies, it is simply too early to tell as they have only been adopted between September 2005 and September 2006. It takes time for measures to pass through the Community legislative procedures.[93] This must be for future evaluation and review.

Turning now to the REACH programme, this instrument is a powerful Community instrument in terms of its ambitiousness. It is ambitious both at Community and international levels, in terms of its intended pioneering role as a model for third countries, notably the US, to regulate the classification, labelling, marketing and use of chemicals. Such action is experienced as unilateral Community actions, although the Community habitually opens proposals to consultation at conception phase, and takes into account the views of interested parties from outside the EU. Third-country operators played a core role in the massive lobbying and public relations exercise that surrounded REACH in the run-up to its adoption and the lessons learned will no doubt be transposed to future Community proposals in the environment field that have an external dimension. The extension of REACH to operators beyond the EU's borders is justified by the EU on the grounds that it is to ensure risks within the Community from substances of very high concern. A side effect of this purpose is that REACH also shapes third-country markets and the behaviour of third-country operators. It will be interesting to see the outcome of the anticipated WTO battle over REACH and whether it will provide any new international precedents in support of such environmentally motivated regulatory instruments.

Another crucial development in the EU's external relations has been the evolution of the Lisbon Agenda to include environmental concerns. The emergence of China and India as competitor economies has demanded a concerted response from the EU. Should they follow the same environmentally destructive path as the EU in its economic development, however, the positive green footprints of the EU at home and abroad would be threatened. The Lisbon Agenda was launched before the Sixth Environment

---

[93] Under the marine strategy, for example, the draft Directive establishing a framework for Community action in the field of marine environmental policy is only now at first reading in the European Parliament, see COM(2005)505.

Action Programme, and the sustainable development and respect for the environment axis of the Lisbon Agenda was only later introduced in 2001, while the need to develop a common energy policy in the face of the global energy challenge was only added in 2005. It is only as a result of mounting insecurity in the world energy market that the Member States have loosened the reins on their national energy sectors in order to seek security in joint action at EU level. The lack of an energy chapter in the EC Treaty does not help such efforts and energy policy is still largely guarded by the Member States. The European Commission's Green Paper *A European Strategy for Sustainable, Competitive and Secure Energy* launched on 10 January 2007, is the first ever review of Community energy policy. It directly links energy policy with an integrated approach to climate change, with the development of alternative energy sources and research and technological development. Supporting policy actions to programme strategic actions on energy also foresee environment conditionalities in external relations, especially with neighbouring countries both to the South and East, including Russia.[94]

Commissioner Piebalgs's vision of Europe leading the world to a new industrial revolution with the development of a low-carbon economy has certainly been taken up by the US in February 2007. Whether the EU will continue to lead global action will depend on the success of the Emissions Trading System in terms of meeting its Kyoto commitments. As it stands now, this contribution has looked at how the ETS is not capable of reducing emissions enough. Worse, the fact that polluters within the EU have reaped the financial benefits of their pollution paints a decidedly negative green footprint. And the efforts of third countries is, unavoidably, also a determining factor. The French Prime Minister Dominique de Villepin in November 2006, proposed a Community carbon tax on industrial products from countries that refuse to accede to the Kyoto Protocol. This suggestion, apart from being unworkable, is flawed because refusal to participate in or commit to Kyoto is not illegal and nor is it a subsidy under WTO rules.[95] Commissioner Mandelson emphasises the

---

[94] See *Energy Efficiency Action Plan*, n. 26, and *External Energy Relations – from principles to actions*, n. 27.

[95] Commissioner Mandelson, however, questioned how such a tax would be implemented, asking how the EU would choose which goods to target. For example, China has ratified the Kyoto Protocol but does not have any Kyoto targets because of its developing country status.

Community approach: dealing with climate change is an international challenge and requires international cooperation, and coercive policies will do more harm than good. The revision of the system that should take effect in 2008 becomes crucial if the Community is to meet its Kyoto commitments, if it is to secure its future energy supplies, and if it is to remain a leader in the world struggle to combat climate change.

Turning to the role of the ECJ in balancing environmental concerns with trade, in the PIC cases the ECJ decisively raised the profile and significance of Community and national environmental ambitions in the context of external trade. It required that Community measures giving effect to the Rotterdam Convention concerning the international trade in hazardous chemicals and pesticides outside of the EU, be based on both the legal bases for the Common Commercial Policy and the protection of the environment and human health. The ECJ thus shows itself ready to play its part in determining the balance of the Community's trade interests with the Member States' and Community environmental instruments. It is certainly a new development in the administration of the CCP and opens the door to future tensions between national/Community environmental standards and the CCP.

It is also worth mentioning the ECJ judgment of 13 September 2005 in Case C-176/03 *Commission* v. *Council* where the ECJ confirms the power of the Community to provide for adequate criminal penalties in order to give effect to Community environment law, including the implementing rules for the Rotterdam Convention. The ECJ annulled third-pillar measures[96] that were intended to do the job instead of a proposed Community Directive on the subject. Given the 'serious non-observance'[97] of Community environment law in the Member States, this judgment is welcome. It prevents the Member States from agreeing intergovernmental measures outwith the

---

The US has not ratified the Protocol, but states like California have ambitious climate change policies, Commissioner Mandelson's podcast of 18 December 2006.

[96] Council Framework Decision 2003/80/JHA on the protection of the environment through criminal law, OJ 2003 L 29/55; see ECJ case C-440/05 *Commission* v. *Council*, Judgment of 23 October 2007, nyr. On the Court as a protagonist in favour of environment protection, see F. Jacobs, 'The Role of the European Court of Justice in the Protection of the Environment', *Journal of European Environment Law* (2006), pp. 185–205 at 200–5.

[97] See Commission Staff Working Paper, *Establishment of an acquis on criminal sanctions against environmental offences*, SEC(2001)227, 7 February 2001; see, for example, also the Commission report on the matter, *Commission Staff Working Paper Fifth Annual Survey on the implementation and enforcement of Community environmental law 2003*, SEC(2004)1025, 27 July 2005, pp. 3 *et seq.*

Community pillar of the Treaties, which the Commission cannot enforce before the ECJ and which bypass the democratic input of the European Parliament in the Community legislative processes. However, ultimately the Member States must nevertheless agree among themselves and adopt a Community measure setting out minimum criminal penalties for serious breaches of Community environment laws – a first try at such a Directive[98] failed miserably in 2002 when the Member States failed to even reach a political compromise that could form the basis of a common position.[99] Thus, the reach of the ECJ's influence is restricted in that the Member States must now adopt a Community measure to institute criminal penalties.[100] Currently, therefore, there is neither a Community nor a third pillar measure in place providing for criminal penalties in respect of breaches of Community environment law.

A final important development is the entry into force on 28 June 2007 of Regulation 1367/2006[101] applying the 1998 UN Aarhus Convention.[102] It will give individuals access to information on all steps in the infringement proceedings taken by the European Commission against any Member State for breach of EC environment laws. In spite of the Article 9(3) Aarhus Convention provision for access to justice of public interest defenders, Regulation 1367/2006 only gives limited opportunities of administrative and judicial review by non-governmental organisations of acts of Union institutions and bodies. But the European Investment Bank will, for the first time, be open to such review.

---

[98] See Commission Proposal COM(2001)139, 13 March 2001 and *Bulletin EU*, 3/2001, 1.4.39. Taking account of revisions made to the proposals following the European Parliament's opinion, the Commission's Amended proposal, COM(2002)544.

[99] At Justice and Home Affairs Council meeting 2477 of 19 December 2002. The initiative of the Danish presidency was reverted to as an alternative; see the Initiative of Denmark with a view to adopting a Council Framework Decision on combating serious environmental crime, *Bulletin EU*, 1-2/2000, 1.4.8, OJ 2000 C 39/4.

[100] See Commission MEMO 'Questions and answers on the protection of the environment through criminal law' MEMO/07/50 of 9 February 2007.

[101] OJ 2006 L 264/13.

[102] The first pillar of the Convention on public access to information was implemented at Community level by Directive 2003/4/EC OJ 2003 L 41/26. The second pillar, on public participation in environmental procedures, was transposed by Directive 2002/35, OJ 2002 L 112/21. The third pillar provides for access to justice; Regulation 1367/2006 of the European Parliament and of the Council of 6 September 2006 on the application of the provisions of the Aarhus Convention on access to Information, Public Participation in Decision-making and access to justice in Environmental Matters to Community institutions and bodies, OJ 2006 L 264/13. See also the new Art. 11 TEU revised.

Since writing this contribution the Lisbon Treaty (TL) has emerged. From the point of view of access to justice in environmental matters, Article 263 of the consolidated version of the future Treaty on the Functioning of the European Union (TFEU) makes certain changes to Article 230, fourth paragraph EC,[103] apparently opening up access to individuals to challenge laws that are of direct concern to them, without having to show individual concern. A new paragraph will additionally specify the conditions and arrangements for actions brought by individuals against acts taken by bodies, offices or agencies set up by the institutions.[104] This would seem to try to fill the vacuum in legal protection and access to justice in environmental matters.[105] On closer reading, this is not so clear. Measures of general application (referred to as 'regulatory acts') must be shown to be of direct concern but not individual concern. However, the act in question must not entail 'implementing measures' in which case individual concern must be shown. This terminology confuses the true intent of these changes. It remains to be seen whether standing will actually be opened up as a result of the TL amendment and further input from the Court will no doubt be needed.[106]

The TL will also affect the broader spectrum of the environment *acquis* but only a few developments can be mentioned by way of conclusion. The Environment Title, Articles 174 to 176 EC, will become Article 191 to 193 TFEU. Climate change is expressly included as an objective for international action, although the Member States are already active on this

---

[103] Art. 263, fourth paragraph, TFEU will read, 'Any natural or legal person may, under the conditions laid down in the first and second paragraphs, institute proceedings against an act addressed to that person or which is of direct and individual concern to them, and against a regulatory act which is of direct concern to them and does not entail implementing measures.'

[104] Art. 263, fifth paragraph will read, 'Acts setting up bodies, offices and agencies of the Union may lay down specific conditions and arrangements concerning actions brought by natural or legal persons against acts of these bodies, offices or agencies intended to produce legal effects in relation to them.'

[105] See B. Dette, 'Access to justice in environmental matters: a fundamental democratic right', in M. Onida ed., *Europe and the environment: legal essays in honour of Ludwig Krämer* (Groningen: Europa Law Publishing, 2004), pp. 3–22 at pp. 7–10; see also Jans, Jan H., 'Did Baron von Munchhausen ever Visit Aarhus? Some Critical Remarks on the Proposal for a Regulation on the Application of the Provisions of the Aarhus Convention to EC Institutions and Bodies', in Richard Macrory, ed., *Reflections on 30 years of EU environment law: a high level of protection?* (Groningen: Europa Law Publishing, The Avosetta Series, 2005) Vol. 7, pp. 475–490.

[106] See René Barents, 'The Court of Justice and the Renewed European Treaties', A. Ott and E. Vos, eds., *50 years of European Integration: Foundations and Perspectives*, (The Hague: TMC Asser Press/CUP, 2008).

front. However, a new Title on Energy (Art. 194 TFEU) will, like the Titles on Environment and Transport, be an area of shared competence in terms of Article 4 TFEU. Alongside the Internal Market in energy and security of supply issues, Union energy policy will aim to promote: energy efficiency and energy saving and the development of new and renewable forms of energy, and interconnection of energy networks. The Member States retain the right to determine the conditions for exploiting their energy sources, as well as to choose between different energy sources and the general structure of their energy supply. As with the Environment Title, any fiscal measures under the Energy Title will require a unanimous Council vote, making the Commission's hopes of a CO_2 tax on energy products – as it proposed again in its 2008 Work Programme – as unlikely as ever.

New Titles on Tourism and on Civil Protection (Arts. 195 and 196 TFEU respectively) provide for supporting, coordinating and supplementary Union action in terms of Article 6 TFEU. To date, Community level actions have been cobbled together using Article 308 EC and 208 Euratom, requiring unanimity. These new legal bases will use the ordinary legislative procedure: co-decision of Parliament and Council acting by qualified majority.

Other novelties of the TL will improve governance aspects. Under Article 260(2) and (3) TFEU (Art. 228(2) EC today), if a Member State has not complied with a Court ruling against it for failing to meet its Treaty obligations to properly apply the *acquis*, the Commission will be able to skip the reasoned opinion stage and go straight to asking the Court to impose lump sum or penalty payments. Moreover, an entirely new provision allows the Commission to request a lump sum or penalty payment at the earlier Art. 226 EC procedure stage in cases of non-transposition of Directives into national law.

Finally, the new Article 16(8) TEU revised, will make public how the Member States vote in Council when adopting legislation. This should prove a useful yardstick for measuring whether the national governments stand by their green manifesto pledges. It will put the spotlight on those members that hold the majority back from pursuing a truly effective, common European 'green' front at home and abroad.

TABLE OF TREATY PROVISIONS

INDEX

In this Index entries do not refer to text in footnotes.

Printed in Great Britain
by Amazon

87033974R00290